THE BLACK HOOD OF THE KU KLUX KLAN

Jim Ruiz

The Black Hood of the Ku Klux Klan

by

Jim Ruiz

This book is dedicated to Douglas J. St. Romain.
A true and unflinching friend.

The liberties of a people are never more certainly in the path of destruction then when they trust themselves to the guidance of secret societies. Birds of the night are never birds of wisdom. . . . The fate of a republic is sealed when bats take the place of eagles. (Josiah Quincy)

TABLE OF CONTENTS

FOREWORD

How often have we heard it lamented that men should learn from the past in order that they not repeat the mistakes of their predecessors? Unfortunately, such sound counsel seems to perpetually fall on deaf ears. As evidenced by our love for war and violence, we seem to be afflicted with some mysterious strain of selective amnesia which causes us to be on a continuous voyage of discovery, never learning from our past ports of call.

For the most part, we are gregarious creatures who seek the company and approval of others. In order to satisfy this need to congregate, we join ourselves with various cultural, religious and social organizations including secret societies.

Like war and violence, secret organizations and secret societies can be traced back to some of the early vestiges of civilized man. Secret organizations and societies have existed in many forms throughout history. Groups such as the priests and builders of the ancient pyramids of pharaonic Egypt, the Essenes during the time of Christ, the Knights Templar, Freemasons, the Independent Order of Foresters, the Independent Order of Odd Fellows, the Ancient Order of Rechabites, the United Ancient Order of Druids, B'Nai B'Rith, the Mafia, Molly Maguires, Knights of Columbus, Knights of Pythias, the Knights of the White Camelia and the Ku Klux Klan, just to name a few. It is, however, only the composition and actions of the Ku Klux Klan in northeast Louisiana of the 1920s that shall be explored in this book.

Klan-like organizations are not new. The first organization with Klan characteristics appeared during the Middle Ages. There existed in Germany a secret organization known as the *Vehmgericht*, or secret tribunal. The precise origin of the *Vehmgericht* is unknown, although some have claimed that the system was authored by Charlemagne. Others contend that it was some dark vestige from the unwritten pages of prehistoric Germany. It is generally agreed, however, that the society made its appearance in Westphalia during the year 1180, from which location it dispersed rapidly over all of Germany.[1]

The emperor held the reins of the society. He was aided by those of nobility in his court, and under those nobles were persons of all classes. It was from this lower strata of society that was formed the "free courts," whose purpose it was to

---

[1] Henry P. Fry, *The Modern Ku Klux Klan.* (Boston: Small, Maynard & Co.,1922). p. iii

v

stand in judgment of persons charged with offenses against persons and property. Those with membership in the *Vehmgericht* were called *Wissende* or the initiated ones. They were also known as "free judges."

In order to gain entrance into this society and become one of the initiated, those applying must have been of good moral character, and they were to have two guarantors who were already "free judges." The rites of initiation were usually conducted in some secret location during which the candidate was obliged to deliver his most solemn oath to keep secret his membership in the brotherhood. A system of signs was used by the brotherhood to recognize one another. By their membership, they were obligated by profound vows never to disclose the context of a trial or sentence inflicted on a violator when found guilty.[2]

The *Vehmgericht* was quite mobile, and it could be convened quickly anywhere be it in an open pasture, private home or building, woodland, or grotto. As a rule, most meetings were closed to the public except for the accused. It was the customary procedure that a person charged with a violation be arrested and bound over until the secret tribunal could be marshaled. Should the accused elude capture, a written notice was nailed to his door accompanied by a small coin left as the calling card of the dread tribunal. Failure to appear or send an emissary was considered a denunciation of the holy *Vehmgericht* and prompted automatic condemnation, which, in nearly all cases, carried the sentence of death by hanging. The condemned stood no chance of reprieve or appeal, and his only hope of survival was to flee the country. For an outsider to be caught interloping carried the penalty of a swift and sure death.[3]

This perverted assembly survived and thrived until 1461 when the intended victims of its corrupt and twisted justice banded together to form an alliance to challenge its power and put an end to its clandestine tyranny. The organization continued to weaken, and in 1495 Maximilian I inaugurated a new criminal code, which substantially diminished the influence of these secret tribunals. Although *Vehmgericht* trials continued to be held into the early 1800s, their ability to instill fear or apply any significant influence had been removed by the end of the seventeenth century .[4]

---

[2] Ibid., iv
[3] Ibid., iv-v
[4] Ibid., v

Some 445 years later, like a Phoenix rising from the ashes of the holy *Vehmgericht*, on a cold Thanksgiving evening in 1915, standing on the windswept summit of Stone Mountain in Georgia, William J. Simmons, a World War I private self-promoted to colonel, sometimes preacher, sometimes teacher, sometimes organizer, and a small band of followers presided over the rebirth of the much-venerated Ku Klux Klan. Crowning himself Emperor for Life, Simmons almost single-handedly lead a large portion of the nation back into the barbarism of the *Vehmgericht* of medieval Germany as he installed the clandestine courts of the Ku Klux Klan.

In many ways, Simmons' "New Klan" was quite similar to the dreaded *Vehmgericht*, but it bore little resemblance to the original Klan. As with the *Vehmgericht*, the power of the Klan was reserved mostly for those influential members of the community who rarely took part in any of the dirty work. In the *Vehmgericht* as in the Klan, there existed the title of Emperor and "Wissende," or wizard. The Klan mimicked the *Vehmgericht* in other ways, such as having its own court try persons accused of crimes, conducting trials in absentia, forcing persons accused of wrongdoing to flee for their lives, binding its members through secret initiation rights, maintaining secret signs of identification, and making members promise never to reveal the secrets of the organization. The Klan was organized with the political goals of white supremacy, and it solemnly gave itself the name of the "Invisible Empire." For over a decade, Simmons held autocratic rule over his subjects, as he reined as Emperor for Life.[5]

---

[5]Ibid., vi

Acknowledgments

I would like to express my thanks to my wife Lynn who has endured the loneliness of years of separation as I pursued a Ph.D., my long-time partner Lt. Victor J. Manale III NOPD, Ret. for standing by me, Douglas J. St. Romain, Lt. Chris Maurice NOPD Ret. and Isabella Anderson who were there for me during the darkest hours of my life, Dr. Harry Hoffman of Minot State University for showing me the value of research, Superintendent Warren Woodfork NOPD, Ret. for having faith in me, Captain John Hughes NOPD, Ret. for his compassion and understanding, Stephanie Whitus-Goodner for her untiring editing, and Sherman, my dearest companion.

INTRODUCTION

I first became acquainted with the Ku Klux Klan while conducting research on David Duke for Carl Kalvelage's political science course during my undergraduate career at Minot State University in North Dakota. While gathering information for a paper, I became intrigued by a reference to a double homicide perpetrated by the Klan in Mer Rouge, Louisiana. Although the information was very sketchy at that time and limited to a few lines, the story was told of two white men who were critical of the Klan and had been accused of an assassination attempt on a Klan leader. I had no idea at that time that this seemingly inconsequential revelation would later occupy a major portion of my life.

While searching for a university from which to secure a master's degree in criminal justice, I received an offer of an assistantship from Northeast Louisiana University (NLU) in Monroe, which is very close to the towns of Bastrop and Mer Rouge. Because Minot State was operating on the quarter system, I arrived at NLU a few months early. Having time on my hands and remembering the paper on Klan activity in the area some 70 years earlier, I went to the microfilm section of the Percy Sandel Memorial Library on the campus of NLU just to pass some time. What I found was a day-by-day month-by-month chronicle of Klan activity not only in northeast Louisiana, but around the United States and Canada as well.

I was amazed to see that the *New York Times* had carried front page stories daily for nearly three months on the kidnappings and brutal murders of Watt Daniel and Thomas Richards, as did many other major newspapers. As I read the day-to-day accounts of what had occurred, I was amazed that an incident of this magnitude had passed all but unnoticed in history. This research is a compilation of newspaper accounts of *The New York Times*, the *Monroe New-Star*, *Times-Picayune*, just to name a few.

I visited the location of the kidnapping and attempted to reconstruct the events which followed. I visited Lake LaFourche where the bodies were dumped and later recovered after the bank of the bayou had been dynamited in an attempt to cover the bodies, as well as the now hidden grave sites of the victims on the banks of a tranquil bayou filled with cypress trees laded heavily with Spanish moss.

I shall attempt to sketch for the reader the climate of prejudice, fear and hatred which permeated northeast Louisiana then and which regrettably, to a great degree, still exists today. While so doing, I shall attempt to recreate the events of that terrible evening in August of 1922. All the information contained in these pages has been gleaned from newspaper articles, doctoral dissertations, master's theses, Governor John Parker's personal papers in the archives of the University of Southwestern Louisiana, and my own personal investigation and observations.

This story begins on a hot Louisiana summer's evening in August 1922 after a baseball game between the town teams of Monroe and Bastrop. While on their way home from the game, Watt Daniel and Thomas Richards along with three other men, all family or friends, were kidnapped by hooded Klansmen one mile east of the town of Bastrop on the road leading to Mer Rouge. After being paraded around Morehouse Parish in the rear of an open pickup truck, their hands tied behind them and blindfolded, these men were put to death in a fashion rivaling any medieval torture or Nazi death camp device ever conceived. Although the deaths of these two men did not lead to the immediate downfall of the Klan in northeast Louisiana, it was, nevertheless, the beginning of the end of the reign of Klan terror in northeast Louisiana. This incident became the shame of Louisiana, and riveted the attention of the United States and even Europe to this backwoods enclave, exposing for all to see the hideous acts of the Klan and their supporters.

Despite a protracted open hearing conducted by Louisiana's attorney general, a grand jury hearing during which identification was made of some of the perpetrators, the presence of four units of the Louisiana National Guard, as well as assistance from agents of the United States Department of Justice and the Louisiana State Police, no one was ever tried much less convicted for these heinous crimes.

Since an "open hearing" was conducted by the attorney general of the state of Louisiana in the Bastrop courthouse, I had expected to find a wealth of information in the weeks of testimony given in the case. I was quite surprised to learn that ALL of the transcripts from that open hearing had mysteriously disappeared. Clearly, this was another indication of the power the Klan exerted over the criminal justice system in Morehouse Parish.

The beginning of this book will be devoted to describing the origin of Morehouse Parish and the general social climate in northeast Louisiana and other portions of the so-called "Bible Belt," of which it is a part, during the early 1920s. As the reader will learn, the Klan had a stranglehold on power since its membership included the district attorney, the sheriff and his deputies, judges, and nearly everyone who was anyone in northeast Louisiana.

Some articles will be presented verbatim as they appeared in each respective publication. Particular attention should be paid to the manner in which these were written, because it is there, in the verbiage of these compositions, that the mood and feelings of the time are expressed. Also, to set the stage for the drama, the reader will also be served occasional descriptions of articles describing the day-to-day happenings in Louisiana, nationally and internationally, which will further communicate the mood and feeling of the populace during that period.

I had been living away from Louisiana for almost six years prior to my return in April of 1991. It had been a long drive from Minot, North Dakota where I had lived for five years immediately following my retirement from the New Orleans Police Department. I had attempted a small furniture repair and refinishing-antique business there for a few years. However, Minot was too small to support more than the half-dozen such shops already there, not to mention the dozen or so antique dealers who had long been established. Realizing that I would either be forced to expand and advertise the business or close it down and pursue another line of endeavor, I decided to shut the business down and enter Minot State University. While doing my bachelor's work, I decided that I wanted to teach criminal justice at the university level. I realized that in order to do that I had to, at least, obtain a master's degree. After receiving my undergraduate degree in criminal justice, I applied to a number of graduate schools. As fate would have it, I was accepted by the Criminal Justice Department at Northeast Louisiana University in Monroe, Louisiana.

My return to Louisiana on that April evening in 1991 was an event that I shall never forget. The sun was setting as my aging van, with an over loaded U-Haul trailer in tow, strained over the last few hills on U.S. 81 as it snaked its way through the tiny hamlets in Arkansas toward the Louisiana border.

The trees and tree limbs are trimmed further back from the roadway in Arkansas than they are in Louisiana. I noticed this after passing the sign that said "Welcome to Louisiana, The Dream State." Suddenly the trees and limbs were much closer to the roadway, and it was as though the branches of the pines were reaching out to me with a warm embrace saying "welcome home" to a prodigal son.

The soft evening breeze was blowing ever so gently through the Spanish moss in the oak trees, reminding me of the legend of Evangeline's hair. The entire scene appeared to be something out of Walt Disney's "Fantasia." Shafts of golden

3

sunlight occasionally broke through the trees, some giving the appearance of such strength that they could be walked upon. I began to muse of sugar plum fairies dancing on the petals of the sacred dogwood flowers that were just beginning to bloom. Driving a little farther a sign said "Morehouse Parish." Little did I know then that I was passing through the area and perhaps using the same road that had been traveled by the members of the Klan and its two victims en route to perhaps the most savage and brutal double homicide ever recorded in this nation.

CHAPTER ONE

A Historical Profile of Northeastern Louisiana

In order to understand those who populate the northeastern section of Louisiana, otherwise known as the North Delta Region, it is essential to gain knowledge of the background and heritage of the residents of the region, and with that in mind I give you the founder of the region, the Baron de Bastrop. Nering Bogel, alias Baron de Bastrop, was born in Paramaribo, Dutch Guiana in November 23, 1759.

After enlisting in the Dutch cavalry, he served at the Zutphen garrison and was discharged in 1782. He had been appointed as tax collector in the Dutch province of Friesland in 1782 but was forced to flee in 1793 when he was charged with embezzlement. While a fugitive, he assumed the title of the Baron de Bastrop. After coming to Louisiana in 1795, he asserted himself to be an escapee from the French Revolution and petitioned Governor Carondelet of Louisiana for authorization to found a settlement of expatriates along the Ouachita River. The land grant was finalized in June 21, 1796, and as was the custom in Louisiana, the name which appeared on the land title was given as the name of the town rather than the rightful surname. Thus, the seat of parish government was given the name "Bastrop," which it still bears today.[1]

According to the terms of the grant, the Baron was obliged to bring 500 families to the area but was only successful in persuading 99. Governor Carondelet withdrew support for the grant in 1797, and total governmental approval was withdrawn in 1800. In 1799, the Baron was able to sell the 144 league concession to Col. Abraham Morehouse in Kentucky.

A History of Morehouse Parish

The City of Bastrop

The Baron himself had a reputation of being a bit of a rogue. According to one account, he was described as "an American adventurer who succeeded by masquerading as a Dutch baron in duping the Baron de Carondelet." Another had chronicled him as "a French nobleman."[2]

---

[1] Conrad, Glenn. R. *A Dictionary of Louisiana biography.* (New Orleans: Louisiana Historical Assn, 1988), 598.

[2] Leeper, Claire. *Louisiana places.* (Baton Rouge, LA: Legacy Publishing Co., 1976).

In his last will and testament, the Baron described himself as "Felipe Eurique Neri, ancient Baron de Bastrop." According to this document, he asserted that his lands in Holland had been seized during the Revolution of 1795. Try as they may, historians have been unable to either authenticate or refute this assertion. In any event, after selling out to Morehouse, the Baron then took up residence in Texas. There he met Moses Austin, the father of Stephen Austin who would later play a major role in the liberation of Texas from the Mexican government. Although he became a man of influence, he died penniless. This is attested to by the following passage:

> The Baron de Bastrop died at Saltillo, Coahuila, at ten o'clock in the morning of February 23, 1827. The President of the Legislature named a committee to assist with the funeral; they were authorized to incur any necessary expense to insure the Baron a decent interment. On the following day, the committee reported back that the deceased did not have sufficient money to defray the expense, but that Antonio Padilla, in whose house the Baron had lived while in Saltillo, had advanced the funds and that he had been given a burial befitting his station in life. The chamber voted the reimbursement of Padilla."[3]

Following in the footsteps of the Baron de Bastrop, Abraham Morehouse, for whom the parish is named, proved also to have a tainted past. The assertion has been made that the "Father of Morehouse Parish was, in addition to being the parish's first permanent settler and chief colonist- a bigamist."[4] What's more, the claim was made that "for 47 years no man [in the Morehouse Parish area] was able to assert with any degree of confidence that his vine and fig tree were rooted in his own ground. Boys had grown to manhood, reared families, and died without knowing whether the acres on which they lived and labored all their lives would be passed on to their children, and to their children's children."[5]

Even the spelling of the name has come into question, due to evidence which has surfaced showing where Col. Abraham Morehouse had signed his name as "Morhouse." Originally a native of New York, Morehouse had married Abigail Young in 1790 in New York. This union produced two sons, Andrew Young and George Young. After deserting his family, he went to live in Kentucky where he encountered the Baron de Bastrop. The Baron was such a convincing salesman that Morehouse purchased the land from him sight unseen.

---

[3] Ibid., 23
[4] Ibid., 164

6

Upon his arrival at Fort Miro, Morehouse claimed to be a widower, never concealing the fact that his two sons were living back East. It was not long before Col. Morehouse began to court Eleanor Hook, whom he later married on September 9, 1799. Rumors began to circulate that Morehouse was not a widower as he had claimed, and in 1809 Andrew Young Morehouse appeared at Fort Miro. From Andrew Eleanor learned that Abigail Young Morehouse was alive and well in New York. Even after this revelation, Eleanor continued to live with Abraham and their five children until his death.[6]

The City of Mer Rouge

The town of Mer Rouge lays claim to being one of the first townships in northeastern Louisiana, its first settlers having arrived in the early 1800s from the New England states. Originally called Prairie Mer Rouge, the town is said to have derived its name from the red sumac (Rhus Glabra L) which thrives in the area. Legend has it that the arrival of the first French scouts coincided with the blooming of the red sedge, which gave them the impression of a sea of red flowers, or in French-Mer Rouge. Also, part of the legend is that the name may have been a corruption of the French term Maison Rouge, meaning "red house." This arises from the fact that the 1855 United States Surveyor General's map showed the area as the "Rejected Maison Rouge Claim."[7]

Such was the tainted beginnings of Morehouse Parish and the people who were later to inhabit it. As we shall see, the descendants of the Baron de Bastrop and Abraham Morehouse would commit such acts of infamy and depravity as to rivet the attention of the nation to this backwoods hamlet during the fall and winter of 1922-23.

The City of Spyker

Located on the southern city limits of Bastrop, the earliest record of Spyker [pronounced "speeker"] appears in *Northeast Louisiana: A Narrative History of the Ouachita River Valley and the Concordia Country*. It tells of the journey undertaken by Spyker and his family as they made their way to their plantation named "New Hope," located on the banks of Bayou Bartholomew near Bastrop. This same publication chronicled a raid by the Union Army on the plantation, one of the

---

[5] Ibid., 164
[6] Ibid., 164
[7] Ibid., 158

largest in the area, during the Civil War.[8] It will be from a carbon plant located on the site of this former plantation that some of the events in this story will occur.

The Plight of Blacks in Northeast Louisiana 1915-1920

The economic situation for blacks in Louisiana had improved somewhat since the ending of the Civil War. They had reaped some of the financial benefits of World War I, but racism was still as pervasive as ever. Whites felt particularly threatened after WWI because black soldiers experienced social acceptance for the first time in France. It was said that "French women ruined niggers," and this belief may have been responsible for an increase in lynchings.[9] In 1919 alone, 82 lynchings of blacks were reported nationwide.[10] The murders of Sampson Smith and George Bolden were prime examples of the accepted level of violence in northeast Louisiana toward blacks. Early in 1919, Smith was tried in Columbia, the center of Caldwell Parish, for the murder of a white man. To the surprise and dismay of all those gathered, an all-white jury returned a guilty verdict but failed to impose capital punishment. Within the courtroom, spectators seized Smith, in the presence of the court and its officers, and hauled him out and immediately hanged him. Curiously, the *Shreveport Journal*, while condemning the actions of the mob, stated that the verdict "was almost as bad" as the hanging.[11]

The case of Bolden, which occurred a year later, came to be known as the "Monroe Horror" because of the incredible brutality involved in the murder. Bolden, a carpenter by trade, lived and worked in Monroe, which is the seat of Ouachita Parish. Bolden had incurred the wrath of his local white competitors because of his lower prices.

In a scheme to eliminate Bolden, someone, more than likely one of his white competitors, wrote "an insulting note to a white woman," to which Bolden's name was signed. Any such act by a black man toward a white woman was considered a capital offense, and very little effort was made to prove or disprove allegations in such cases. Had someone bothered to review the allegation, they would have learned that Bolden could not write and that he endorsed all of his checks with an

---

[8]Daughters of the American Revolution. *Northeast Louisiana: A narrative history of the Ouachita River Valley and the Concordia Country*. [This was type by an individual and placed into the holdings of the Morehouse Parish Library.]

[9]Hair, William I. *The Kingfish and his realm*. (Baton Rouge: LSU Press, 1991), 33.

[10]Ibid., 34

8

"X."[12] This was learned in after-the-fact testimony by whites who had employed him. It was enough for the white lynch mob to know that a "nigger" had suggested sex to a white woman.

The mob caught Bolden, shot him numerous times and, thinking they had struck a blow for white womanhood, departed, believing Bolden to be dead. When Bolden's friends arrived on the scene, they found him still alive and took him to the "colored ward" of Monroe's St. Francis Sanitorium in Monroe. When the mob learned that he was not dead, it raced to St. Francis where it laid hold of another black man just emerging from surgery, thinking that he was Bolden. As mob members were taking him out, they realized they had the wrong man, and they dropped him to the ground. This second man died the next day due to shock.[13]

In an uncharacteristic display of compassion, the nurses hid Bolden. Realizing that they could not conceal him there for any period of time, the nurses advised his wife to spirit him out of town. Bolden was secreted on the next Shreveport-bound train in the baggage car, but not without this information being leaked to the populace. The train was barely eight miles outside Monroe when it was stopped by the mob.[14]

Resolved to finish the job that they had started, the members of the mob jerked him from the train and shot him innumerable times. This time they succeeded. As a result of this murder, the grand jury indicted only two of those in the mob. They were placed on $100 bonds, and that's as far as the case went.

Before giving undue credit to the nurses for aiding Bolden's attempted escape, notice should be taken of the letter to the editor sent by them to the *Monroe News-Star*. Apparently, they were not upset by the death of Bolden or the other black patient that the mob had killed. They said, "We think it is a disgrace to Monroe for a mob to come to the sanitorium to carry out their vengeance, and to scare the nurses and patients, when they could have easily have waited until the patient was carried home."[15] So much for the milk of human kindness.

Despite the horrible cruelty shown by whites to blacks, there was every so

---

[11] Ibid., 35.
[12] Ibid.
[13] Ibid.
[14] Ibid.
[15] Ibid., 36

often a glimmer of kindness and understanding displayed toward blacks. One such benefactor of blacks was J. C. Stovall. Stovall, the white owner of the black baseball team called the Monarchs of Monroe, operated a local drilling company. Because he was keenly aware that his company had attained the status that it had mainly through the labor of blacks, he had constructed a beautiful ball park with adjoining swimming pool and dance hall, exclusively for the use of blacks free of charge. The team went on to become a powerhouse in the late 1920s and 30s. Later when the black club was disbanded, the stadium was leased to an all-white team from Monroe, which was part of the old Cotton States League in the Class-D circuit.[16]

John Parker: Governor of Louisiana

The governor of the state of Louisiana at the time of the kidnappings and murders of Watt Daniel and Thomas Richards was John Parker. Because he was such a central figure in the events that will unfold in this book, a knowledge of him and his background will be helpful.

John Milliken Parker was born in Bethel Church near Port Gibson, Mississippi on March 16, 1863. Parker's maternal grandfather served as chancellor of the Mississippi Supreme Court and his paternal grandfather was a substantial landholder and slave owner in Mississippi. When John Jr. was nine years old, his father moved the family to New Orleans, where he prospered as a commission merchant, wholesale grocer and cotton broker.[17]

Young Parker learned his politics from his father, who was a member of the anti-Republican White League of the 1870s and the anti-machine reform movements of the 1880s. After attending school in Virginia and Poughkeepsie, New York, young Parker returned to the family plantation at Bethel Church before entering the employ of his father in the 1880s. He was elected to the post of president of the Cotton Exchange and the New Orleans Board of Trade in the 1890s.

Parker harbored a great dislike for the social life of high society in New Orleans, and only on one occasion did he relent and participate. This occasion was to reign as the king of Comus, one of the oldest and most prestigious carnival

---

[16]Peterson, Robert. *Only the ball was white*. 1970, 122

[17]Dousson, Joseph. *The Louisiana Governors: From Iberville to Edwards*. (Baton Rouge, LA: LSU Press, 1990).

crews.[18] Parker was also a member of both the Boston and Pickwick clubs of New Orleans. Membership in these organizations was then and is still now reserved to the manor-born blue-blooded aristocracy of New Orleans.[19]

Through the influence of Theodore Roosevelt, his friend and hunting partner, Parker organized the Progressive Party in the South on a "lilly-white basis."[20] Parker first ran for governor in 1916 and polled 38% of the vote. His defeat came largely at the hands of state Democrats, who claimed that the Progressive Party was a threat to white supremacy. It was not two months after his defeat in the governor's race that he was nominated for vice-president of the United States by the Progressive Party. After winning the governor's chair in 1920, Parker, who had been an open advocate of women's suffrage, opposed ratification of the 19th Amendment because he felt that, "It might establish precedents for black enfranchisement."[21] Clearly, Parker was no friend of women or blacks.

Parker was considered an inconsistent Democrat. Four years prior to his election as governor, he had run as a Progressive, and because of this his election was seen as a threat to white rule. To those in northeast Louisiana, Parker was believed to keep company with "nigger-loving" Republicans and a part of the rich aristocracy which paid no heed to the plight of the common man. James Aswell, a Congressman from the Eighth District, labeled Parker as tenuous on the issue of white supremacy and as "a boll weevil eating at the heart of Louisiana Democracy."[22]

Clearly, race was a false issue because during the Parker-Stubbs campaign as only .05%, or 725 persons of the entire registered electorate in Louisiana were black. Most political pollsters today have margins of error 10 times that amount.[23] Furthermore, neither Parker nor Colonel Stubbs seemed to be overly concerned with the welfare of blacks because neither one bothered to comment on the sharp increase in the number of blacks lynched, which totaled 82 for the year 1919.

---

[18]Ibid.

[19]Conrad, Glenn R. *A Dictionary of Louisiana Biography.* (New Orleans: Louisiana Historical Assn., 1988), 630.

[20]Dousson, 1990, 216.

[21]Ibid., 217

[22]Williamson, Fredrick W. *Northeast Louisiana: A narrative history of the Ouachita river valley & the Concordia country.* (Monroe, LA: The Historical Assn., 1959) 29.

[23]Ibid., 30.

CHAPTER TWO

Klan 101: An Introduction to the Ku Klux Klan

In order to understand the mind set of Southerners before the Civil War and the forces which propelled the rise of the Ku Klux Klan, it is necessary to look at the history of slavery and white supremacy. The idea of white supremacy was transported to the New World by Europeans and first took root with the enslavement of Native Americans. Although the Klan did not invent this concept, Athens, Georgia, Klan No. 2 coined the phrase "white supremacy." Not long afterwards, a lively slave trade emerged from Africa. At the time of the signing of the Declaration of Independence and the United States Constitution, bondage was as American as apple pie. Slaves were held in the North and South, but only the South was able to make slavery profitable.[24]

The concept of white supremacy was solidified from the pulpit, in the school classroom and in the newspapers. To question this idea was to risk being insulted, threatened, driven away or even killed. In short, the theory of white supremacy made the unquestioned assertion that what mattered was white skin. This premise pledged to the lowest of whites advantages that no black could ever hope for. In this way, the claim of white supremacy over blacks was easily maintained. This ideal was to be and still is the main draw for Klan membership.[25]

The Origin of The Ku Klux Klan

There has long persisted the popular misconception that the Klan had been conceived to protect the "Christian way of life," the purity of the white race, and to preserve the virginity of poor defenseless white women. Nothing could be further from the truth.

The Klan had its humble beginnings in the small market center of post-Civil War Pulaski, Tennessee, in December of 1865. Six Confederate officers and gentlemen all, Calvin Jones, Frank McCord, Richard Reed, John Kennedy, John Lester and James Crowe, returned to Pulaski only to find their way of life gone, the economy depressed and strangers in government. For the lack of something to occupy their time, these men decided to form a club to amuse themselves.[26]

---

[24]Katz, William L. *The Invisible Empire: The Ku Klux Klan impact on history.* (Seattle: Open Hand Publishing, Inc., 1987), 9.

[25]Ibid., 11.

[26]Wyn, Craig W. *The Fiery Cross; The Ku Klux Klan in America.* (New York: Simon and

In order to select a proper club name, a committee was selected. This committee was also charged with the responsibility of dreaming up some special club ceremonies. The first names to be chosen were "The Merry Six" and the "Pulaski Social Club," but these were considered unsatisfactory selections. Being gentlemen of education and good breeding, they were familiar with college fraternities, and they were particularly smitten by "Kuklos Adelphon."

They were aware that the Greek "Kuklos" meant a close circle of friends. As they played with the words, it became "Ku Klux" and they all agreed that "Ku Klux" would be the name. In order to give it further pizazz, they added the word "Klan." Because of the Scottish influence in that general area, the term "Klan" was a natural choice. In his memoirs, John Lester wrote of that time, "There was a weird potency in the very name Ku Klux Klan."[27] The strength of the name is still felt over 130 years later.

To accompany this mysterious name, they created elaborate rituals, signs ,and even a partial language of their own. So, for the lack of an Elks Club or YMCA in Pulaski, the Ku Klux Klan was formed.[28]

The Klan was officially incorporated in Pulaski, Tennessee on December 24, 1865. Erected on the side of one of the most revered buildings in Pulaski is a plaque which reads:

Ku Klux Klan
Organized In This,
The Law Office
Of
Judge Thomas M. Jones
December 24th, 1865

This plaque remains fixed to the same building today in Pulaski. However, the townspeople have chosen to turn the inscription toward the building so that the plaque is visible, but the inscription is not.

The Klan would meet in the evenings, at which time they would don disguises and masks, after which they would cavort through the countryside, making strange noises and attempting to scare whomever they could. They soon learned that the white population did not amuse them because they, the whites, did not scare easily.

Schuster, 1987), 29.

[27]Katz, 1987, 7.

[28]Lowe, David *Ku Klux Klan: The Invisible Empire.* (New York: W. W. Norton & Co., 1967), 9.

However, they quickly noticed that they created fear and dread within the black population. This reaction appeared to be a product of their superstitious beliefs, some of which were brought over by blacks to the United States from Cuba and other Caribbean islands.

Their favorite trick was to gallop up to a black home dressed in their white robes and pointed white hats and to demand water from the newly Freedmen. They were fond of telling the blacks that they were dead Confederate soldiers who had ridden around the world twice since suppertime and that they had not had a drink of water since the Battle of Shiloh.[29]

Almost invariably, the blacks would exhibit the fear and trembling that the pranksters sought. However, this exhibition of fear may have been more an act by blacks because they knew that fear was what these night riders were seeking. Later it was to be observed by S. F. Horn in his *First History of the Klan* that the situation was "rotten ripe" for the Klan to exercise their control over the blacks and their new-found Northern friends.[30]

Initially, violence was not a part of the Klan's plan. This, however, was soon to change. It was not long before these pranks became serious, and attacks on blacks by the Klan became the order of the day.[31]

The typical Klan member then was between the ages of 18 and 35, single and usually from the upper strata of society. Low whites were allowed to join, but the power of the organization was jealously controlled by those wealthy planters and businessmen who were the prime beneficiaries of this new terrorism. For many of those who joined, the Klan fulfilled deep psychological needs. It gave a sense of power for those who felt they lacked mastery of their lives, and the power of life and death over others. It also conferred upon its members the assertion of domination over all blacks.

---

[29] Wyn, 1987, 34.

[30] Home, Stanley F. *Invisible Empire: The Story of the Ku Klux Klan 1866-1871*. (Boston: 1939), 45.

[31] Chalmers, David M. *Hooded Americanism: The First Century of the Ku Klux Klan 1865-1965*. (Garden City, New York: Doubleday & Co., 1965), 9.

The Role of the Klan Costume

> It was a long gown with loose flowing sleeves, with a hood in which the apertures for the eyes, nose and mouth were trimmed with some red material. The hood has three horns, made of some common cotton stuff, in shape something like candy bags, stuffed and wrapped with red strings; the horns stand out on the front and sides of the hood.[32]

> It was thought to be a very pleasant and innocent amusement for the chivalry of the South to play upon the superstitious fears of the recently emancipated colored people. The Ku-Klux took heart from these cheerful echoes and extended their borders without delay.[33]

The early Klan outfits of 1868 consisted of a white mask to cover the face, with holes cut for eyes, nose and mouth; a tall cardboard hat made in such a way as to increase considerably the wearer's height; and a robe long enough to cover the entire body. Again in Lester's words, the costumes were to be colorful, "hideous and fantastic" and "mostly flashy."[34]

To keep from being recognized, Klan members would communicate by blowing children's whistles. In such garb, they attended fairs and other social gatherings, and soon other bored young men were applying for membership. Membership increased dramatically. All this occurred long before anyone thought of whipping or murder, but that would not be long in coming.

The First Act of Klan Violence

Shortly after Den No. 2 formed just across the state line in Athens, Georgia, the membership became outraged when white teachers opened a school and began to educate black children in the area. One of the members observed that the teachers were "treating their students like human beings." A white female teacher at this school was kidnapped in the dead of night, taken to an icy stream and tossed in much to the delight of the Klan members. This is the first recorded action taken by the Klan into the realm of lawlessness. Den No. 2 adopted the aim of "Maintaining White Supremacy." Soon the Dens that had formed in the other 11 Southern states adopted this philosophy.[35]

This perversion from the original aims of the Klan did not go unnoticed. Frank

---

[32]Mecklin, John M *The Ku Klux Klan: A Study of the American Mind.* (New York: Russell and Russell, Inc., 1924), 74.

[33]Tourgee, Albion W. *The Invisible Empire: A Concise Review of the Epoch.* Ridgewood, N. J.: Gregg Press, 1883), 13.

[34]Katz, 1987, 8.

[35]Ibid.

16

McCord, one of the original charter members and editor of the Pulaski *Citizen*, wrote, "The simple object of the original Ku Kluxes" had become "so perverted. Better the Ku Klux had never been heard of."[36]

Although the Klan had been founded in December of 1865, it was not until 1867 that it spread like a wildfire across the South. This occurred because the radicals in Congress had displaced state governments put in place by President Abraham Lincoln and Vice President Andrew Johnson. Lincoln's original plan called for the control of state government in the South to be passed back to the whites in each state, but only after they had made an outward acknowledgment that the Civil War was over.[37]

The Klan, Reconstruction and Southern Blunders

> The commander of each district was to have registered as voters all persons, without regard to race and color, who had not taken part in the war. As this law disfranchised all leading White men of the South and gave ballot to the negro, many of whom were only one generation removed from savagery, the result can be imagined.[38]

During the Reconstruction years of 1866-67, President Andrew Johnson and Congress were locked in legislative combat regarding how the seceded Southern states should be handled. Johnson, a Southerner, felt it sufficient that these states had repealed their laws of secession and that they had ratified the 13th Amendment. Congress, however, was not willing to acquiesce to these stipulations. It wanted additional security for the newly freed slaves.

Although the South had lost the Civil War, this did not mean that it had lost political control as well. Quite the contrary. The Southern gentry was firmly in political control, as the election of 1866 displayed. The entire Southern delegation sent to Washington as a result of this election consisted of former Confederate military and political officials. The Southern delegation consisted of 58 Confederate congressmen, nine Confederate generals and admirals, six Confederate cabinet members, and the vice president of the Confederacy, Alexander H. Stephens. Blacks were not allowed to vote in this election, nor for that matter were most

---

[36]Ibid.

[37]Chalmers, 1965, 10.

[38]Grob, Gerald N. *Papers read at the meeting of Grand Dragons Knights of the Ku Klux Klan.* (New York: Arno Press, 1977), 42.

whites.[39]

The political victory of these individuals, who played an integral part of the Civil War, invoked a precipitous response from the North. Congress declined to seat these delegates, and they were summarily sent packing back to the South. Believing that the South was still firmly in control of the ex-Confederates, Congress began to develop its own plan to reconstruct the South.[40]

Because of Southern rejection of the 14th Amendment, concern for blacks, and anxious about the political future of the Republican Party, President Johnson rejected the brand of reconstruction that the South had adopted. Johnson ordered that the former Confederacy be divided into separate districts, where he installed military rule.[41]

With the stroke of a pen, Southern Democrats were removed from government, their constitutions invalidated and their leaders disfranchised. Tennessee escaped this treatment because its governor, Parson William G. Brownlow, had been a Union sympathizer who suffered imprisonment and exile for his pro-Union stand. All of these conditions working in concert caused the Klan to change into a terrorist organization and to become a major force in the old Confederacy.[42]

The Role of the 14th Amendment

The 14th Amendment declared that all persons born or naturalized in the United States to be citizens of the United States and the state in which they resided. This not only gave the freedmen the right to vote, but it also caused reapportionment which meant that blacks would then be counted as one whole person instead of three-fifths of a person. This amendment also outlawed abridgment of citizenship rights or the deprivation of life, liberty or property without due process. By granting blacks full citizenship and the right to vote, whites in the South became terrified that these newly freedmen would gain control of the entire South.

Congress was prompted to take such drastic action because the influential Southerners who regained regional power after the Civil War did their best to suppress blacks by every means at their disposal. They denied the freedmen the

---

[39]Katz, 1987, 17.
[40]Ibid., 18.
[41]Chalmers, 1965, 11.
[42]Ibid.

right to vote and charged excessive fees for them to acquire and maintain property.

Post-Civil War Life on the Plantations

For those blacks who were so unfortunate as to have to remained on the plantations, they found that their lot, in many instances, had worsened. Having no resources to draw upon, they were completely at the mercy of the plantation owners. In order to work on the plantations, they were required to sign a contract during the first month of January, and they were bound by that contract for the entire year.[43]

They lived on the plantation as before, only now the owner had various deduction clauses built into the contracts that the freedmen, nearly all of whom could not read because it was illegal for slaves to read, would sign. Some of these deductions were for food and lodging; breakage of any equipment; including normal wear and inadvertent damage to anything on the plantation; fighting, discourtesy; vile language or disrespect to anyone in authority. Each violation was considered a separate infraction and would, therefore, be penalized separately.

The Black Codes

> No person of color shall pursue the art, trade, or business of an artisan, mechanic, shopkeeper or any other trade or employment (beside that of husbandry or that of a servant under contract labor), until he shall have obtained a license, which license shall be good for only one year.[44]

Probably the most vile legislation ever to be enacted in Louisiana was the "Black Codes." The codes stated that blacks were required to apply for a license to work in a trade. These licenses were only valid for one year and could cost anywhere from $10 to $100 to secure. No such requirements were made for whites.[45]

Also connected to these codes were the vagrant laws, which were also directed toward blacks. Blacks were forced to labor under contract, and those who would not comply were declared vagrants. As vagrants, they were eligible to be seized by the sheriff and their labor sold at auction to the highest bidder to pay the costs and the fine. When they traveled they were also required to have in their possession a certificate or pass for their "master" or "mistress"; otherwise they were likely to be declared as vagrant. Such outrageous abuse eventually prompted the Reconstruction

---

[43]Tourgee, 1883, 20.
[44]Ibid., 42.

19

Act.[46]

Those blacks that were able to achieve some measure of success were considered a threat by the white establishment and were almost always dealt with violently. Standard fare in dealing with blacks who were a threat or not "respectful" was threats, exile, flogging, mutilation, stabbing, shooting and hanging. The fear among whites was that the black population had become so numerous that it presented a serious threat to the white political base.

The Klan Turns Militant

> Under the rule of the carpetbagger and the scalawag the negro ran riot. Every indignity was offered the people of the South, and they were force to stand idle while their wives and daughters were openly insulted, without hope of redress. Then, when hope had almost fled and destruction seemed inevitable, the pure 'Anglo-Saxon blood' in the South rose in its might and the Ku Klux Klan was born.[47]

> The Ku Klux threatened the negroes on the lower plantation and they were afraid to stay. They never slept in their houses (they dug caves for themselves) while they were on the plantation.[48]

From this time on, the Klan was transformed from a purely social organization into a militant and violent terrorist movement which swept across the South with incredible speed. With the coming of age of these new radical state governments of 1867-68, the Klan sent out a call to all Klaverns to send delegates to a secret convention which was to be held in Nashville, Tennessee. At this convention, ex-Confederate General Nathan Bedford Forrest was elected First Imperial Wizard of the Ku Klux Klan, a position he was to hold until he ordered the Klan disbanded in 1869.[49]

Although the South had lost the Civil War, the North soon learned that winning a war did little to change the plight of blacks, or the thinking of the whites in the South. Surely, the blacks were free. But, free to do what? Lacking education and skills, many blacks found themselves back on the same plantations by their own choice because nothing else was available. Attempts, a few successful, were made to alleviate the suffering of the blacks. However, this took the form of

---

[45]Ibid.
[46]Ibid.
[47]Gorb, 1977, 42.
[48]Tourgee, 1883, 56.
[49]Chalmers, 1965, 132a.

welfare payments or social security. Whites were bitter because of the preferential treatment being shown blacks and for what they considered interference in the social order of the South.[50]

Although each state had a standing militia, these groups proved ineffective against the Klan and, in fact, usually promoted fear and anger from the white population and attacks from the Klan. A prime example of Klan violence would be the Klan-led riot in Meridian, Mississippi in 1871. On that occasion, certain black leaders were brought up on charges of disturbing the peace by making inflammatory speeches. As other blacks gathered in a show of support, someone, no one knows whether black or white, produced a gun and began firing. In short order, numerous dead and wounded blacks littered the ground with only one white being wounded. Blacks ran into the woods, leaving their leaders in the hands of the Klan. These black leaders were spirited from jail and summarily hanged.[51]

Those blacks who ran into the woods remained there and were not hunted down. This was not always the case because it became common practice during the mid-1870s to hunt down the blacks that had fled to the woods and to murder them. Without the direct protection of federal troops, the safest place for blacks was the woods during surges of Klan violence. Due to the high level of Klan activity in South Carolina, for example, the majority of blacks lived in the woods during the winter of 1870-71.[52]

White Southerners Declare War on Blacks

> Negroes and whites, but principally negroes, have been killed, whipped and imposed on in various ways. It has been very common for two years—so common that it would take a right sharp case now to attract much attention.[53]

Appearing once again on the Southern landscape were the slave patrols. These patrols consisted of poor whites armed by rich planters with the expressed purpose of frightening blacks into enduring their demeaning caste. It was also the duty of these patrollers to torment all whites who had endorsed the North during the war and those who had not been in favor of secession.[54]

---

[50]Ibid., 12.

[51]Ibid., 14.

[52]Ibid.

[53]Ibid., 47.

[54]Katz, 1987, 19.

By the year 1866, whites were waging an undeclared war on the newly freedmen all across the South, while receiving reassurance from influential circles. In the spring of 1866, whites rioted in Memphis, Tennessee, at which time 46 blacks were killed and another 80 wounded. Months later in New Orleans, the mayor spearheaded the police and a white mob that went on a murderous rampage during which 34 were killed and 200 more were wounded. Compounding these affronts to humanity was the outrageous positive reinforcement given to these acts by the press.[55]

The plan devised by the Klan during this period had defined its terrorist aims quite clearly. Low-class whites were not to be allowed to vote alongside blacks. Were this to happen, white supremacy would be toppled for all time. Because profit from the land was inexorably linked to cheap labor from blacks and low whites, it was of paramount importance that these two groups not be allowed to unite, even if it came to murder. Interference was not to be tolerated either from whites from the North or whites from the South who aided blacks. These were to be driven off, intimidated or murdered. Finally, the U.S. Government must be made to understand that to challenge the resolve and ardor of white supremacy would be an exercise in futility.[56]

Around 700,000 blacks and nearly as many whites registered in the South as first-time voters between 1865 and 1877. Many ex-slaves and poor whites were elected to state office and immediately began pushing for reform. The white Southern gentry of wealth and power responded to this threat by utilizing Klansmen as their "shock troops."[57]

The Beginning of the End of the First Klan Era

The year 1869 was not only the high-water mark for Klan success, but it also marked the beginning of the end for the early Klan, at least temporarily. The Klan was a force that had become uncontrollable. This had occurred because this secret society, composed of autonomous units who used wanton violence at will, was no longer responsive to the leadership of Forrest. The better and more educated citizens were turned off by the random violence, and the quality of the membership

---

[55]Katz, 1987, 20.

[56] bid, 25.

[57]Sher, Julian. *White Hoods: Canada's Ku Klux Klan.* (Vancouver, B. C.: New Star Books, 1983), 20.

was declining.

Because the Klan was no longer controllable, Forrest ordered that it be disbanded and that all records be burned. In the words of Alabama Klansman Ryland Rudolph, "the Klan had fallen into low and violent hands." Clearly, it has remained in these hands even to this day.[58]

Nearly all Klans followed this order. This happened because, in most states, great advances had been made in regaining pre-Civil War white domination. Also, those more clear thinking in leadership were probably not only willing but eager to disband the Klan because of the violence and lack of control. There were, however, those independent Klans who did not heed the order to disband.[59]

Klan Atrocities

> They beat him with long sticks, and wore out a long fishing pole on him. They had him down, and put a chain on his neck, and dragged him about a good deal. Joe said, "I ain't done anything, gentlemen: what are you abusing me for?" They said, "We will kill you, God damn you. You shall not live here." He said, "I have bought my land, and got my warrantee title for it: why should I be abused this way?" They said, "We will give you 10 days to leave, and then, God damn you, we will burn your house down over you, if you don't go."[60]

> General Hatch, then Assistant Commander of the Freedmen's Bureau, reported the following outrages to the Bureau in the State of Louisiana during the first nine months of 1868:-(Blacks) Killed, 297; wounded by gunshot, 50; maltreated, 142-Total, 489.[61]

> They shot a colored man by the name of Joe Kennedy what that he married this mulatto girl, and they (the Klan) did not intend that he should marry so white a woman as she was; and they beat her also for marrying so black a negro as he was.[62]

After having visited this vicious attack on Joe, these paragons of virtue and defenders of the Southern way of life whipped the rest of the family. All of the females were then stripped and raped before his eyes.[63]

Official records reveal that between 1892 and 1950 over 3,500 blacks were lynched by Klan members in the South. It is impossible to tell how many blacks

---

[58]Chalmers, 1965, 19.

[59]Ibid.

[60]Tourgee, 1883., 47.

[61]Ibid., 20.

[62]Ibid.

[63]Ibid., 47.

and whites were whipped, shot, lynched and burned to death by the Klan.[64]

During this time, the Klan had never departed from its depraved modus operandi. One particular victim was flogged, castrated and caked with tar. He then had his leg plunged into a boiling tar bucket." The man died nine days later.[65] A group of hooded Georgia Klansmen murdered a freed black slave in 1868 after he received 900 lashes with stirrups.[66] By the turn of the century, blacks were being denied the right to vote in every state in the South, and no blacks held office.[67] Clearly, the white population had regained total control of the South.

During one 12 month period during 1920-21, the *New York World* reported Klan involvement in four murders, one mutilation, an acid branding, 41 floggings, 27 persons being tarred and feathered, five kidnappings, 43 persons receiving ultimatums to leave town or some other threat, 14 towns discovering threatening Klan posters and 16 towns experiencing Klansmen parading through their streets carrying warning signs. Two common threads found in these occurrences were 1) the Klan claimed that particular laws, almost always those involving behavior or moral turpitude, had been violated, and 2) they were perpetrated by groups of masked men in the dead of night. [68]

The Second Coming of the Klan

> The Klux is the living dead, and it is the strength of weakness. (Edward Dixon, 1868).[69]

> The mask is a millstone about the Klan's neck which, unless discarded, will sooner or later drown the Klan in the sea of hate and suspicions which it has created.[70]

Although the Klan had ceased to function in the South, it received credit for the restoration of the South. Be it true or not, Southern youth were reared on rousing tales of their fathers, as righteous vigilantes, riding the countryside to protect the Southern way of life. Like other legends, the more they were told, the greater and more noble the exploits became. Over the years, these embers were fanned to such

---

[64]Sher, 1983, 19.
[65]Sher, 1983, 23.
[66]Ibid., 19.
[67]Ibid.
[68]Mecklin, 1924, 6-10.
[69]Wyn, 1987, 29.
[70]Mecklin, 1924, 81.

an extent that when the proper occasion arose, the Klan sprang back into existence.[71]

The stage for the revival of the Klan was set by Thomas Dixon, Jr. and David Ward Griffith. Dixon, who had studied with Woodrow Wilson, was a Johns Hopkins graduate, a sometimes preacher, legislator, lawyer, actor and lecturer. He wrote two books, entitled *The Leopard's Spots* and its sequel, *The Clansman: A Historical Romance of the Ku Klux Klan.*

Each of these books was a highly romanticized account of the exploits of the Klan and had very little to do with truth or reality. In these works, Dixon portrayed the North as the villain, blacks were savages, ladies and gentlemen of the South as paragons of virtue and the Klan as the champion of Southern values.[72]

Not long after he wrote his book, Dixon met a young Kentuckian named D. W. Griffith, a director in the new motion picture industry. Griffith undertook the task of translating *The Clansman* to the motion picture screen. The result was a film that broke new ground in the industry departing from the customary short subjects and slapstick comedy which, heretofore, had been the order of the day. Lasting nearly three hours, Griffith's *Birth of a Nation* received such acclaim that crowds stood in line to pay $2 to view the film.[73]

For a while, controversy threatened the life of the film until Dixon arranged a private showing for his old classmate, President Woodrow Wilson. After viewing the film, Wilson, a Southerner and one-time Klansman, stated, "It's like writing history with lighting, and my only regret is that it is all so terribly true." From Supreme Court Justice Edward White, Dixon received this response: "I was a member of the Klan, sir. Through many a dark night, I walked my sentinel's beat through the ugliest streets of New Orleans with a rifle on my shoulder."[74]

Whenever there is money to be made and people to exploit, there always seems to be someone to realize the potential and take advantage of it. One such person was William Joseph Simmons. This silver-tongued devil and jack-of-all-trades had a vision of what the Ku Klux Klan could be, and almost singled-handedly presided over the second coming of the Ku Klux Klan.

---

[71]Lowe, 1967, 12.

[72]Ibid., 14.

[73]Ibid.

[74]Ibid., 15.

The second coming of the Klan had its dramatic beginning when, on Thanksgiving night in 1915, Simmons and 16 men drove from Atlanta, Georgia, to nearby Stone Mountain. Climbing up a rock trail in the dark, they worked their way to the top and "braving the surging blasts of wild wintry mountain winds and . . . a temperature far below freezing," hastily constructed a rock altar upon which they laid an American flag, an open Bible, an unsheathed sword, and a canteen of water. There, under a blazing cross, these men took a sacred oath of allegiance to the Invisible Empires, Knights of the Ku Klux Klan. On July 1, 1916, on petition of Simmons and 11 others of his radical group, the Klan began in Fulton County, Georgia.[75]

Simmons' attempt to revive the Klan sputtered along for a few years until the summer of 1920 when Klan membership began a dramatic rise. Up until that time, there were only a few thousand members in and around Atlanta. What turned the trick was the hiring of Edward Young Clarke and Mrs. Elizabeth Tyler, both experienced advertisers and fund-raisers. Their method of marketing the Klan was quite successful because in just 16 months membership mushroomed to 100,000 nationwide. Because of their illicit business dealings, Clarke and Tyler were to run afoul of the law in 1922. Clarke was later indicted by a Georgia grand jury.[76]

Simmons, having been exposed to the oaths of other secret societies, devised one similar to others and one which would grant him unlimited power and unquestioned loyalty from Klan members. Officers of the Klan were required to swear the following:

> I _____ do freely and voluntarily promise, pledge and fully guarantee a lofty respect, wholehearted loyalty and unwavering devotion at all times and under all circumstances and conditions from this day and date forward to William Joseph Simmons as Imperial Wizard and Emperor of the Invisible Empire, Knights of the Ku Klux Klan. I shall work in all respects in perfect harmony with him and under his authority and directions.[77]

All other regular members were mandated to "render at all times loyal respect and steadfast support to the Imperial Authority of [The Ku Klux Klan]," and they also swore to "heartily heed all official mandates, decrees, edicts, rulings, and

---

[75]Rice, Arnold S. *The Ku Klux Klan in American politics.* (Washington, D. C.: Public Affairs Press, 1962), 1.

[76]Mecklin, 1924, 17-18.

[77]Fry, Henry P. *The Modern Ku Klux Klan.* (Boston: Small, Maynard and Co., 1922), 32.

instructions of the Imperial Wizard thereof."[78]

It would have been impossible for the local Klans to engage in their campaigns of violence and intimidation without the assistance of the local law enforcement officers and the courts. It was not at all uncommon for the members of an entire local criminal justice system to be Klansmen, from the officers making an arrest to the judge on the bench, and the Klan did not hesitate to brag about such enrollment. The Klan Newsletter dated May 20, 1921 proudly proclaimed the following:

> You may state in your weekly letter that in one city in Virginia we have the chief of police, the common-wealth attorney, the postmaster, the police court judge, members of the city council and managing editor of the leading paper and many other prominent business and professional men. This is Newport News.[79]

Another ruse operated cleverly by the Klan was its open display of willingness to assist local law enforcement. It realized that by infiltrating the ranks, it would be able to control the actions of that agency. The Klan Newsletter dated June 10, 1921, gave this example:

> We have just taken in the chief of police. When he learned he was to have our support in upholding the law he was certainly pleased, especially with our military organizations, which we offered him in case of trouble. He then informed us that the city is insufficiently protected and that we are sitting on a volcano regarding the negro question, that there is a great deal of unrest among them and that we might have a riot at any time. He welcomed us and the military company is to be trained and two hundred and sixty repeating rifles will be turned over to us in time of trouble. I asked how many of the three hundred present at the meeting would be willing to join the organization to assist the chief, and every one of them stood. The chief of police states that any man we select to head these two hundred and sixty Klansmen will be made by him assistant director of public safety in charge of the Klansmen."[80]

The Klan Under the Leadership of Simmons

> The present Klan is a memorial to the original organization, the story of whose valor has never been told, and the value of whose activities to the American nation have never been appreciated. The name of the old Klan has been taken by the new as a heritage. The regalia and insignia of the old have been adopted by the new. Beyond this point the connection and similarity between the two organizations do not exist.[81]

---

[78]Ibid., 68-70.

[79]Ibid., 59.

[80]Ibid., 59-60.

[81]Simmons, William J. *The Klan Unmasked* (Atlanta: William E. Thompson Publishing Co., 1924), 24-28.

The Klan organizational setup under Simmons went this way, directly under Simmons was the Imperial Kleagle, whose duty was to advertise and promote the Klan. The United States itself was carved up into eight sections called "Domains." Each Domain was made up of an uneven number of states under the control of a Grand Goblin. Each state was a "Realm" presided over by a King Kleagle. The state was then broken down into individually numbered "Klaverns," which were each under the control of an Exalted Cyclops.[82]

As a result of all this, the Klan was granted an unwarranted amount in credence and acceptance. This was the setting in which W. J. Simmons, a private self-promoted to "colonel," announced the rebirth of the Ku Klux Klan. On the heels of these books, the film, and the leadership of Colonel Simmons, the Klan rose like the proverbial Phoenix from the ashes of the still-recovering South.[83]

In addition to the books by Dixon and the film by Griffith, there were other factors which contributed significantly to the rebirth of the Klan. There had been a severe emotional let-down at the end of World War I, race riots in the North and South, mass migrations of blacks into the major urban centers of the North, fear of Bolshevism, the growing Catholic population, and a growing population of aliens and foreigners who were seen as subversive. These rapid changes made a number of people feel ill at ease.[84]

The Klan thrives in this type of atmosphere because it feeds on ignorance, fear, jingoism, nativism and conformity. Fredrick Lewis Allen rightly observed that the Klan afforded "a chance to dress up the village bigot and let him be a Knight of the Invisible Empire. The formula was perfect."[85] In the first 14 months after World War I, 70 blacks had been lynched and 14 had been burned alive.[86] The murders in Mer Rouge occurred on the heels of this period, and they made such a stir nationally that more than 133 articles concerning the case appeared in *The New York Times* alone.[87]

Oddly enough, many believed the victims of the Klan to be black. During the

---

[82]Ibid. 44-47.

[83]Lowe, 1967, 15.

[84]Ibid., 18.

[85]Ibid.

[86]Ibid., 62.

[87]Davis, Lenwood G. and Sims-Wood, Janet L. *The Ku Klux Klan: A bibliography.* (Westport, Conn.: Greenwood Press, 1984), 214-233.

second resurgence of the Klan, attacks on whites were much more commonplace than attacks on the blacks. The reasons can be found in the following passage:

> As a general thing, the negroes have behaved so well since the war that it is a common remark in Georgia that no race on earth, released from servitude under the circumstances they were, would have behaved so well. The behavior of the negroes during the war was remarkable. When almost the entire white male population old enough to bear arms was in the army, and large plantations were left to be managed by women and children, not a single insurrection had occurred, not a life had been taken: and that, too, when Federal armies were marching through the country with freedom, as was understood, upon their banners. Scarcely an outrage occurred. The negroes generally understood that if the South should be whipped their freedom would be the result.[88]

It was Simmons who enhanced the mystery of the Klan by adding new twists to the old Klan. He instituted a complex and confusing Klan version of pig Latin, rituals, titles, slogans and signals which further romanticized and mysticized the Klan. During that time, any pure "100% American" (a phrase that would come to permeate Klan literature and song), native-born, white Protestant American citizen over the age of 18 was eligible to join the Klan. It is interesting to note that of the $16 membership fee, $10 was an initiation fee, and the balance was to pay for the inexpensive white Klan robe.[89]

Under the direction of Simmons, the Klan found fertile ground in the North as well as the South. In less than 18 months, the Klan had increased by over 100,000 new acolytes and spread from Maine to Oregon. Applications for membership were pouring in at a rate of over 5,000 a day. Truly, the Klan seemed to be on a roll that was unstoppable.[90]

The roots of the Klan in the 1920s were located in the growing cities and the degenerating farms and villages. Growth in the large cities generated stress in city inhabitants and country folk as well. Many people joined the Klan for reasons completely different from those who started the organization. There were many who presumed the Klan to be a sincere patriotic group and were either unaware or unconcerned about the prejudice that lay at the heart of the organization. The Fair Employment Practices Commission has noted that there was a great deluge of blacks into northern regions of the United States until depressions or recessions

---

[88] Senator J. B. Gordon, Personal Papers. 1870, Vol. 6, 334.
[89] Lowe, 1967, 75.
[90] Lowe, 1967, 17.

made jobs scarce. It was then that the old hatred was revived.[91]

> Experts say the Negro exodus has slowed up. But 500 milling, sweating, pushing blacks belied the statement in a decisive fashion last night when they tried to concertedly shove their way past the gateman at Central Station to get on Illinois Central train No. 4 bound for Chicago.[92]

There were those who were attracted to the Klan because of its rhetoric by which it claimed to stand for better public schools, enhanced law enforcement and traditional marital standards which, they felt, were disintegrating. Then there were those who joined to safeguard Protestantism from the rising tide of Catholic and Jewish immigration.[93]

The federal government was aware of the threat embodied in the Ku Klux Klan. In fact, the 67th Congress's House Committee on Rules held hearings on the Ku Klux Klan from Tuesday, October 11 through Monday, October 17, 1921. The committee took testimony in an attempt to halt the growth of the Klan, but to no avail.[94]

From 1922-24, Klan membership displayed a substantial shift from the South to other sections of the nation. In the Southwest (Texas, Oklahoma, Arkansas, Louisiana, New Mexico and Arizona), the percentage of Klan membership fell from 61.0 to 25.6%. The South (all Southern states east of the Mississippi, Kentucky and West Virginia) displayed a similar decline from 22.2 to 16.1%. Corresponding increases were shown in the north central region (Indiana, Ohio and Illinois), from 6.4 to 40.2%. The Midwest, Far West and North Atlantic regions also recorded similar increases in membership.[95]

By 1924, the Klan had amassed a membership of an astounding 6 million members, and it was grossing over $75 million a year. This, however, was to be the high-water mark for the Klan because it was also in this year that Klan membership began to slide, due to the intense negative press given to the murders in Mer Rouge and its defeat at the Democratic presidential convention. Despite attempts to stop the decline in Klan membership, by the beginning of the Great Depression, the Klan had lost all political power, and it had ceased to function as an

---

[91]Sherwin, Mark *The extremists.* (New York: St. Martin's Press, 1963), 169.

[92]Ibid., 89.

[93]Jackson, 1967, ix.

[94]Fogelston, Robert M. and Rubenstein, Richard E. *Hearings on the Ku Klux Klan.* (Washington, D. C.: Government Printing Office, 1921), 8.

organized unit.[96]

The Klan's Claim of Biblical Proof of God-Sanctioned White Supremacy

The Klan has repeatedly pointed to the 11th chapter of Genesis in the Bible's Old Testament and the 12th chapter of Romans in the New Testament as clear proof that God had sanctioned the premise of white supremacy and the subjugation of the black race.[97] This assertion has been found to be totally without support.

The 11th chapter of Genesis tells the story of the construction of the Tower of Babel, after which it launches into a dissertation on the lineage of the descendants of Shem. From the Interpreter's Bible, Genesis 11: 8-9 states, "8. So the Lord scattered them abroad from thence upon the face of all the earth: and they left off to build the city. 9. Therefore is the name of it called Babel: because the Lord did there confound the language of all the earth: and from thence did the Lord scatter them abroad upon the face of all the earth."[98]

In the commentary on this chapter of Genesis, the interpreter comments on the claims of racial distinction by saying "this is only a childlike explanation of the physical differences in languages and in racial life." In checking the 12th chapter of Romans, absolutely nothing could be located that would even remotely refer to racial distinction or supremacy. In this chapter, the apostle Paul is exhorting the Romans to love one another.[99]

Klan Psychology

The Klan loves a good hater.[100]

In order to understand Klan psychology, it is necessary to recognize the origins of the ancestors of Klan members. A large percentage of original Southern stock was Scotch-Irish, which was largely Protestant. Although this group was originally Presbyterians, it had converted by then to mostly the Baptist or Methodist faiths. It brought with its Presbyterian ancestry an intense hatred for the Roman Catholic Church.[101]

---

[95]Ibid., 15.

[96]Lowe, 1967, 65.

[97]Grob, 1977, 129: Lowe, 1967, 70.

[98]Harmon, Nolan *The Interpreter's Bible: General & Old Testament Genesis-Exodus.* (New York: Abbington-Cokesbury Press, 1952), 562-569.

[99]Harmon, 1952, 580-599.

[100]Mecklin, 1924, 55.

[101]Ibid., 101.

The true strength of the Klan lies in the huge, but unthinking, middle class. Its unbending loyalty and unquestioning faithfulness to the values of the original Southern stock has kept the Klan alive. Klan leaders have exploited these characteristics by playing on its prejudices and inflexible loyalties. The Klan is also intensely suspicious of all things which are foreign.[102]

The Klan seeks to exert control over the community by use of intimidation through the ominous display of masked Klansmen. Fear of this large and unseen Invisible Empire that "sees all and knows all" is the main tool used to exert control.

The appeal of the Klan is, for some, almost irresistible. The Klan offers the traditional ideals of Americanism and at the same time affords its membership wonder and mystery in its secrecy to escape the hum drum routine of daily rural life. This type of inexpensive moral idealism clearly fulfills a requirement which business, social and civil life fail to meet.[103]

The appeal of the Klan to the small-town mind was quite potent. This was primarily due to the lack of education among the residents in such localities. Also in these rural pockets, family traditions and mind sets tended to be preserved and passed down from generation to generation with little or no change.

Our industrialized society also played a large part in this drama. For a large portion of the middle class, the stress and strain of social competition had made it realize its mediocrity. The Klan, on the other hand, offered a soothing balm and consolation to the sense of defeat by conferring upon an individual the title of Knight of the Invisible Empire for the tiny sum of only $16. He was labeled by his peers as "100% American." On the Klan literature, there was printed "an urgent call for men." This jingoism played to his manly pride and served as an ointment on the wounds of mediocrity and defeat. He was a member of a society that "sees all and knows all" with all of its mystic trappings.[104]

Demands of the Klan on its Membership

> The Klan draws it members chiefly from the descendants of the old American stock living in the villages and small towns of those sections of the country where this old stock has been least disturbed by immigration, on the one hand, and the disruptive effect if industrialism, on the other.[105]

---

[102] Ibid., 103.
[103] Ibid., 104.
[104] Ibid., 108.
[105] Ibid., 99.

Klan literature is filled with declarations and intolerant demands for "like-mindedness." The Klan member is not encouraged to engage in independent thought. Klan members are taught that things that appear to be alike are alike and those that appear different are different. Although this may seem like an oversimplification, simplicity is, in reality, the hallmark of the Klan. It is this doctrine that permits the Klan to point to black skin as inferior, and not "100% American." Yet, if a man meets all the physical requirements of the Klan, he is accepted without question. A superficial conformity is all that is required. In the final analysis, the Klan is held up to its members as the last bastion of goodness of the old American stock to stand against the tides of evil which are perverting American society.

That same sentiment was expressed in the motion picture "Mississippi Burning." In this film, one of the characters told a story about how his father had killed the mule of a black farmer out of jealousy. During the conversation, the father stated, "Son, if you're not better than a nigger, then who are you better than?" This is an obvious reference to white supremacy and an indication of the need to feel superior.

The Klan oath was designed to protect the Klan at the expense of the member's loyalty to the United States. An example of this can be found in Section IV of the Klan Oath where it states:

> I swear that I will keep secure to myself a secret of a Klansman when same is committed to me in the sacred bond of Klansmanship--the crime of violating this oath, treason against the United States of America, rape and malicious murder alone excepted.[106]

As will be shown later, the Klan oath demonstrably took precedence over any other oath or obligation.

The question naturally arises as to what type of person joins the Ku Klux Klan? Perhaps it could best be summed up in the words of one who joined over 70 years ago:

> I went into this one partly because I was a joiner and was curious to see what it was all about, but principally because I thought it was a fraternal order which was actually a revival of the original Ku Klux Klan. That old organization has always had a certain glamour for me as it has for every other Southerner. I knew nothing about the structure of the new Ku Klux Klan, took it on faith, and assumed that in its government and administration, it would function like any

---

[106]Fry, 1922, 68-70.

other of the standard fraternal orders.[107]

This statement may appear a bit naive, but when we analyze ourselves, we are a nation of joiners. During that period and up to the present time, fraternal organizations have flourished. Secret organizations have always possessed the ability to draw us for the drama, mystery and romance which tend to surround such organizations. I also was drawn into that same web when I became a Mason in the early 1970s. I learned what was necessary and was initiated. After attending meetings for a few months, I became bored with the childishness of the organization. It seemed as though this organization was little more than an excuse for "Boys Night Out," and to a large extent this is probably one of the main reasons for the success of most fraternal organizations. The other main reason would be that membership in such an organization confers a badge of distinction and honor on the member. For instance, had I stayed with the organization, sooner or later I would have become a Worshipful Master of the lodge, and who could resist the opportunity to be a Worshipful Master?

The Ku Klux Klan offered the same type of opportunity. For just $16 any white Anglo-Saxon Protestant could become a "Knight of the Ku Klux Klan" and a member of the all-seeing "Invisible Empire." With the blessing of the local criminal justice system, he could cavort about the countryside issuing dictates, performing kidnappings, beatings, tar-and-featherings at will and, last but not least, murder most foul. How could sitting on the front porch swing ever hope to compete with that?

The Klan on Catholicism

Aside from the Scotch-Irish carryover of its intense dislike for Catholics, the Klan is at odds with the Catholic Church because its members owe allegiance to the pope in Rome and not the United States. In the town of Mer Rouge, Louisiana, anti-Catholic sentiments were at a dangerous level during the Klan murder trials and political campaigns of the early 1920s. Lafayette, Louisiana, was another site of dangerous anti-Catholic sentiments.

The Klan on Secrecy

> No state of society of laws can render men so much alike, but that education, fortune and tastes will interpose some differences between them . . . They will, therefore, tend to evade the provisions of legislation, whatever they may be; and

---

[107]Ibid., 2-3.

34

> departing in some respect from the circle within which they were to be bound, they will set up, close by the great political community, small private circles, united together by the similitude of their conditions, habits and manners.(DeTocqueville)[108]

Secret societies exist in many sections of American society. Some of the commonly recognized secret societies are the Masons, Shriners, Knights of Columbus, Odd Fellows, Elks and the Loyal Order of Moose, just to name a few. Secret societies, whose priority has been chiefly social, have often developed to meet the shortcomings of customs and traditions in small towns.

The unenlightened were attracted to the Klan by the street parading, high-sounding titles, unusual costumes, hocus-pocus, the drama of secret rituals and the alliterative appeal of grotesque neologisms. The wall of secrecy encourages the existence of an enchanted land of mystery, imagination and exclusive friendships. Clearly, it was a land of make-believe which could offer its members a cheap and flashy substitute for life. All this notwithstanding, secrecy was its chief power. This secrecy was indispensable for carrying out the mission of such a militant organization. Without a doubt, the Klan was, and still is, a law unto itself.[109]

The Klan in Louisiana

> The mind of a bigot is like the pupil of the eye, the more light you pour on it, the more it will contract. (Oliver Wendell Holmes, Jr.)[110]

The Klan of the 20th century was quite different from the original movement of the Reconstruction Era. Where the target of the original Klan was blacks, the new Klan attacked what they considered the "foreign" and "immoral" components of society. Factors which aided the spread of the Klan during the post-World War I era were apprehension concerning change, a heavy alien immigration and general nonconformity. As an example of this expansion, Oregon and Indiana became two of the Klan's most heavily organized outposts. Nationwide, the Klan boasted a membership of three million strong during 1923. Also distinctive of the new Klan was an explosion of bigotry which far and away outdistanced its former paramilitary function. However, of those Klaverns which became notorious for violence, the Klan in Morehouse Parish was to stand head and shoulders above the

---

[108]Mecklin, 1924, 207
[109]Ibid., 229.
[110]Jackson, 1967, 25.

35

rest.[111]

The first locale in Louisiana to fall victim of the Klan was, strangely enough, the predominantly Catholic city of New Orleans. "Old Hickory Klan No. 1" was signed into existence during July of 1921 with a membership of about 500. As its leader or exalted cyclops Thomas DePaoli was chosen, despite the fact that he was a man of Italian descent and a member of the state legislature. But, the Klan held little allure in the Crescent City, and it began to disintegrate almost as soon as it was formed.[112]

However, as the bastion of Protestantism and conservativism in northern Louisiana, Shreveport soon became the center of state Klan activity, and it was "greeted with enthusiasm" by its citizens.[113] It was not long before throngs of both the elite and common folk were clamoring for entry into the "Invisible Empire."

The enthusiasm was fueled by endorsements from such pillars of the community as the Reverend M. E. Dodd of the First Baptist Church, Shreveport's largest. In his words, the Klan was "for nationality, race and religion . . . the deepest, highest and mightiest motives of man." The Reverend E. L. Thompson of the Central Christian Church was the exalted cyclops of the Shreveport Klan's 3,000 members, and Lee E. Thomas, the Klan candidate for mayor of Shreveport, was victorious over stiff resistance generated by Catholics, Jews, the famous Huey Long and Governor James Parker.[114] It was from Shreveport, the second largest city in the state, that the Klan spread throughout northern Louisiana, southern Arkansas, and east Texas during the early 1920s.

Typical methods used by the Klan to exert control over the population were boycotts and threats of violence. Outright harassment of Catholics and Jews was customary, but blacks usually went unmolested as a rule unless they were thought to be involved in bootlegging or some other violation of law. This new Klan was most active against whites who were considered as leading "irregular lives." "Irregular" was twisted by the individual Klans to suit whatever purpose they had in mind. Otherwise, when Klaverns met they did so "to socialize and reinforce their dogmas, enjoy fiery oratory, experience the thrill of frightening others, and cavort

---

[111]Hair, 1991, 26.
[112]Ibid.
[113]Ibid., 28.
[114]Ibid., 29.

36

in a perpetual Halloween."[115]

The Klan in Morehouse Parish

The Ku Klux Klan in northeast Louisiana became a terrorist organization after the creation of the new constitution during the Reconstruction period. The ability of the Klan to strike fear and dread in the hearts of blacks and carpetbaggers made the temptation to wield its power totally irresistible to the white population. On the occasions when Federal troops came to probe transgressions perpetrated by the Klan, all of the local whites would deny knowledge of any such occurrence. Furthermore, they would refute the assertion that the Klan even existed in this parish. One chronicler wrote, "So secret was its organization that in one household in Ouachita parish as mother, daughter, and a daughter-in-law were sewing Ku Klux robes for their husbands, each without the knowledge of the other." [This sentence is reproduced as written.][116]

The Union League Club of New York created the Union League, whose sole purpose was to organize the South into a unified Republican block vote. It was not uncommon for unscrupulous organizers to promise blacks all of the lands owned by whites, immediate social equality, not to mention all elected and political positions, all the while exhorting blacks to assassinate white men and put homes of whites to the torch. A common tactic for these organizers was to have blacks join Loyal League societies, which were structured as companies of armed militia.[117]

In Monroe, Louisiana, the Loyalty League endorsed Judge T. S. Crawford of Caldwell Parish and Franklin Sinclar, a black, for coroner. After Crawford's election, he prevailed on Governor Wormoth for protection. Wormoth, in turn, wrote to President Johnson requesting that troops be sent to protect Crawford since he refused to go to certain towns because he feared for his life. This fear became a reality in 1873 when Crawford and a traveling escort were bushwhacked while en route to Winnsboro, Louisiana. Crawford's head was entirely "blowed away and many bullets shot into his body. His head was collected in a handkerchief."[118] Sinclar did not fair much better, for he was slain while returning from a political speech in Bastrop. Not long after this incident, in the town of Oak Ridge a riot

---

[115]Ibid., 30.
[116]Williamson, 1959, 169.
[117]Ibid.
[118]Ibid., 170.

occurred in which 12 blacks and two whites were killed along with "the injury of other negroes, some being driven out of the country."[119] [It should be noted that when the word country was used during that era, it did not necessarily mean the United States. In this instance, it meant leaving the "area."] Forcing people, both black and white to leave the area under threat of losing their lives was another common tactic used by the Klan to maintain its iron-fisted control. These horribly savage acts were to carry forward to the 1920s.

Another example of white tyranny occurred on the Burns plantation near Waterproof, also located in northeast Louisiana. It was rumored that blacks were planning an uprising against whites. However, "having been tipped off, they [the whites] raised an armed force in Madison and Franklin [Parishes] who charged and dispersed the negroes and hanged their leaders."[120] In Grant Parish at about the same time, the infamous "Colfax Riot" occurred on Easter Sunday, April 13, 1873.

On that day, well over 150 blacks were massacred, shot in the back and bayoneted as they lay wounded on the ground. Later a great many blacks were executed summarily after they had surrendered. When these stories are read, the whites always appear as the underdogs, and the blacks are painted as the villains. Yet it is always the blacks who wind up with disproportionate casualties. The fear of a black uprising was always a good excuse for the white population in northeast Louisiana to engage in a spree of murder and lynchings of blacks. In August of 1868 in Rayville, which is located just a few miles from where the bodies of Daniel and Richards would be recovered, 15 such heroes kidnapped a deaf-and-dumb black man and cut of his ears.[121]

Because of the lawless element that had begun to permeate the Klan, its leaders decided to disband the organization. However, certain pockets refused to obey, and it was these that "degenerated into societies of the lowest type."[122] The Ku Klux Klan Act was passed in 1871, and a concerted effort was made to erase every remnant of the Klan. Not long afterwards, The White League reared its head and in time became the successor to the Klan. The White League became the vehicle by which southern whites regained political power.

---

[119]Ibid.
[120]Ibid.
[121]Ibid., 169.
[122]Ibid., 172.

The Klan had held power by way of fear and terror and being a secret society. In contrast, the strength of the White League was its open organization and proclamation of revolt. In the words of Will H. Strong of the Winn Parish League, "responsible men" would not allow their society to be pillaged by blacks inflamed by "the worst white men that ever imposed themselves upon any civilized country; that they were going to openly unite into one firm compact organization to protect lives, the honor and property of our people. We wish it understood that we have no war to make upon any class in our State in consequence of race, color or previous condition; but the hordes of thieves . . . and plunderers who have brought ruin . . . and insult on all alike, must and shall cease to rule over us; . . . all we ask is fair and honest dealing from officials, let their political proclivities be what they may."[123]

Long before the Klan appeared in Morehouse Parish, many of the local community's leading citizens formed the "Law and Order League." The purpose of the organization was to help elevate post-Civil War conditions, which the residents deemed intolerable. When the Klan arrived in Morehouse Parish, it was welcomed with open arms because the aims of the League and the Klan were identical.[124]

Standard procedure for the Klan was to first warn offender, giving him or her the opportunity to change his or her behavior or find a new place to live. If the offender failed to heed the warning, the Klan would take whatever action it deemed necessary, from kidnapping, flogging, tar and feathering to murder.

In Morehouse Parish, the Klan became a gang of violent thugs. Morehouse and Richland Parishes had long been the leaders in lynchings in Louisiana.[125] One of the most ghoulish acts of these vigilantes occurred in Morehouse Parish in 1881. A black had been accused of cattle rustling. He was tied up and stuffed inside a dead cow so that only his head was left protruding from the cow's stomach. This was done intentionally so that birds would pluck out his eyes. According to the *Morehouse Clarion*, "The tortures that the buzzards gave the thief," it mused, composed "COW-PITAL . . .punishment."[126]

Some 40 years later, "Captain" J. K. Skipwith opened a new chapter of Klan

---

[123]Ibid.
[124]Mecklin, 1924, 40.
[125]Williamson, 1959, 32.
[126]Ibid., 33.

violence and terror. Skipwith was nearing 80 years of age in 1921, and "Old Skip," as he was known to his friends, seemed to have difficulty distinguishing myth from reality. Skipwith had made it his personal quest to purge Morehouse Parish of those persons whom he considered "disorderly" and those whom he believed conducted "irregular lives." Included in this grouping were moonshiners, bootleggers, immoral women and white men, who in the eyes of Old Skip "associated with niggers."

The title "Captain" was self-conferred by Skipwith because he claimed that at one time he was a steamboat captain. Having moved to Morehouse Parish around 1920 as a cottonseed buyer, he was instrumental in organizing the local Klan since he claimed to have been a member of the original Klan.[127]

It is interesting to observe the manner in which the local press treated the Klan and its rationalization of its unlawful activities. During the summer months of July and August of 1922, Old Skip directed the Klan's activities, which included mercilessly beating a number of white men for a variety of offenses, sending women termed "undesirable" by train to Arkansas, and pressuring the local school board to dismiss the solitary Catholic teacher in its employ. Another Catholic, who owned the local icehouse, had the gaul to utter "scurrilous remarks" regarding the Klan. He was taken to the train depot with instructions to leave and not to come back.[128]

Blacks were seldom the target of Klan activity because as a rule they were terrified of the Klan. This worked to the advantage of the plantation owners in that blacks were "kept in line" with regard to behavior. Blacks were a vital element for the local economy as farm hands.

As in other parts of northern Louisiana, the reins of Klan leadership in Morehouse Parish were in the hands of the affluent politicians, including the pastor of Bastrop's First Baptist Church. However, the drones of the organization were mostly from the ranks of the poor and uneducated.[129] The Klan under Skipwith operated without interference from the local authorities for over a year. "There were numerous accounts of hooded mob activity with no record of any arrest or

---

[127]Ingram, Alton E. *The Twentieth Century Ku Klux Klan in Morehouse Parish, Louisiana.* (Masters Thesis: Baton Rouge, Louisiana: 1961), 27.

[128]Williamson, 36.

[129]Ibid., 35.

conviction prior to the intervention by the governor of Louisiana."[130]

Sentiments for the Klan still run deep in northeast Louisiana as evidenced by the strong support given to David Duke during the 1992 race for governor of Louisiana. Duke, the charismatic leader of the NAAWP (National Organization for the Advancement of White People) and former Grand Dragon of the Knights of the Ku Klux Klan, opposed the populist and controversial Edwin Edwards in a runoff election. Duke never had a chance from the outset. For Edwards, it was like dueling with an unarmed man. Although Edwards won the election handily, election results indicated that Duke was very popular in northeast Louisiana. He carried nearly all of the 13-parish region, which includes the parishes of Morehouse and Ouachita.

Contained below is an account of the coming of the Ku Klux Klan to Louisiana as told by Fredrick W. Williamson in his *Northeast Louisiana: A Narrative History of the Ouachita River Valley & the Concordia Country,* written in 1939.

> With the new Construction, the Ku Klux Klan came into being in this section. (Northeast Louisiana) In the beginning, the Klan had been a secret society organized just to frighten the negroes and carpetbaggers near Pulaski, Tennessee. Its methods had been so successful that when the Reconstruction period got under way, white men all over the south could not forbear using its power of mystery over the credulous negro race, and Klan dens were organized in all of the southern states. In Northeast Louisiana as well as elsewhere, it soon became a terrorist organization. It had to be. If its commands were not obeyed, destruction came surely and swiftly.[131]

> To combat the Klan, the Radicals and negroes had the union League, and it is quite probable that during the period of their rivalry for control, more inexcusable violence proceeded from the League than from the Klan.[132]

---

[130]Ingram, 1961, 28.
[131]Williamson, 168.
[132]Ibid.

41

CHAPTER THREE

Summer and Fall 1922

In the preceding two chapters, I have given a brief history of Morehouse Parish and the Ku Klux Klan. Through the actions of its previous residents, I have attempted to display the social setting of Morehouse Parish up to the summer of 1922. In order to further set the stage for events yet to come, I have poured extensively through *The New York Times*, *Times-Picayune* (New Orleans) and the *Monroe News-Star*. As a result of this research, I have assembled numerous articles containing the then current events. From these, I have extracted articles which tell what was in the news regionally, nationally and internationally.

These happenings will mainly be focused on the activity of the Ku Klux Klan in Morehouse Parish, the state of Louisiana, the United States, and even Canada. Also included will be masked mob violence, which may or may not have been Klan led, organizations associated with the Klan, violence concerning a nationwide coal strike at that time, activities of the Irish Republican Army in Northern Ireland, Howard Carter's opening of King Tut's tomb, the first helicopter flight and a great deal more.

FRIDAY JUNE 2, 1922
Band Concert to be Given Tonight[133]

Appearing on the front page, the headline for this article would have been cause for excitement and anticipation as The Knights of Pythias (KOP) Band was well known and respected in the area. Included in the selections to be presented were the works of Dvorak and Paderewski. However, it will be shown later that the KOP supported the local Klan in that it played the music for a Klan initiation on the night of September 4, 1992 in Forsythe Park in downtown Monroe, Louisiana, when about 100 candidates were initiated into the Ku Klux Klan.

The Knights of Pythias is a Masonic-styled organization founded by Justus H. Rathbone, a government clerk in Washington, D. C., and a member of the Red Men and a Freemason, on February 19, 1864. Similar to the Patriarchs Militant in the Independent Order of Odd Fellows and the Knights Templar of York Rite Freemasonry, the Knights of Pythias also had within its order a uniformed

---

[133]*Monroe News-Star*, 2 June 2 1922.

delegation.[134]

TUESDAY JUNE 6, 1992
Measure to End Ku Klux Here Withdrawn[135]

Legislation that would have prohibited the existence of the Ku Klux Klan as a secret organization was withdrawn Representative John Dymond in the Louisiana House of Representatives in Baton Rouge, Louisiana this day. He had originally introduced the bill at the request of Governor Parker, but when it came before the conference committee it was said to have been "overwhelmingly beaten." After addressing the House and withdrawing the bill "The house applauded." Clearly, the Klan had strong support in the Louisiana House of Representatives.

WEDNESDAY JUNE 7, 1922
Bastrop Marshall Dies in Local Sanitorium, Wound is Received Accidentally When "Gun" Falls[136]

City Marshal George G. Wise, of Bastrop, died as the result of an accidental discharge of his pistol when his pistol dropped from its holster to the pavement. This tragic event would go unnoticed were it not for the happenings to come in the Bastrop area. This will not be the last area peace officer to die from an "accidental discharge."

WEDNESDAY JUNE 14, 1922
Pastor is Given Money by the "Klan" [137]

Rev. Frank Tripp, pastor of the First Baptist Church of Monroe, Louisiana, was recognized by the local Klan for his "noble career in life, to which we desire to add our expression of highest esteem." Their "esteem" took the form of a gift of $55, courtesy of Morehouse Klan No. 34, Realm of Louisiana, Knights of the Ku Klux Klan. Klan members marched into the tabernacle where revival services were being held in full regalia, presented him the gift and then marched out. Accompanying the gift was a letter which read as follows:

---

[134]Schmidt, Alvin J. *The Greenwood encyclopedia of American institutions: Fraternal organizations.* (Greenwood Press: Westport, Conn: 1980), 183.

[135]*Monroe News-Star,* 6 June 1922.

[136]*Monroe News-Star,* 7 June 1922.

[137]*Monroe News-Star,* 14 June 1922.

Morehouse Klan No. 34
Realm of Louisiana
Knights of the Ku Klux Klan

Bastrop, La., June 10, 1922

Rev. Frank Tripp,
City,
Dear Sir:
We are handing you herewith $55, a small substantial recognition of your noble career in life which we desire to add our expression of highest esteem and admiration for you as a man, and one hundred per cent American, and an ardent defender and able exponent of the tenets of Christian religion, the very corner stone of our noble order.
May your efforts be long lasting and fruitful of good results. With expressions of highest esteem and affections, we are,

Sincerely yours,
MOREHOUSE KLAN NO. 34
Realm of Louisiana
Knights of the Ku Klux Klan.

As might be expected, Rev. Tripp will surface later as a defender of the Klan, particularly when the head of the Mer Rouge Klan, Dr. B. M. McKoin, is accused of the murders of Watt Daniel and Thomas Richards.

SATURDAY JUNE 17, 1922
Five Hundred Join Ku Klux[138]

From Springfield, Missouri came the report that by the light of a flaming cross, 3,000 members of the Ku Klux Klan, hooded and robed, initiated a group of 500 candidates "somewhere in Greene county" last night. Small articles concerning Klan initiations and Klan activities both locally and nationally were commonly found in the daily papers.

It was commonly believed that many Masons held dual membership in both their Masonic organization and the Ku Klux Klan. Yet from the Grand Master in Boston came a letter declaring that the Ku Klux Klan is an "unMasonic organization and utterly without Masonic support or sympathy." [139]

During this time, a nation-wide coal strike was in progress, and it had become very violent. An article spoke of the first coal to be mined at the Herrin, Illinois and how it was being shipped guarded by 60 men armed with machine guns. [140]

---

[138] *Monroe News-Star*, 17 June 1922.
[139] Ibid.
[140] *Monroe News-Star*, 16 June 1922.

WEDNESDAY JUNE 21, 1922
Says Klan Appeared in Answer to Needs[141]

From Bastrop, the Rev. Frank Tripp was back in the news as he told an audience of 1,500 people assembled at a revival here of his respect for the Ku Klux Klan. Contained below is the text of his sermon.

> The time has come when we need an organization calculated to uphold and enforce the law, and which is 100 per cent American, and whether I am a charter or an honorary member of the Ku Klux Klan I want you to know that I'm for you as you press forward in your campaigns for right.
>
> Lodges and fraternal organizations were founded only when the church failed to exercise her God-given privileges, and if the people of this southland had been properly treated in the enforcement of the law the Ku Klux Klan of the present day would never have been born. No more attention is being paid to Louisiana's Sunday laws than though they were on scraps of paper. We can have no patriotism without law enforcement. Law enforcement is the scaffold upon which patriotism must build all her perfect works. Laws are made to enforce, not to avoid. I know the good people are in the majority in our nation. If not, we would see bootleggers, horse thieves, black-leg gamblers, and immoral profligates running rampant. Our trouble is that the good people of the land lack backbone. Instead of being formed, as some would have us think, to run negroes out of the South, the Ku Klux Klan stands for the upholding of the law.
>
> We are traveling at an airplane pace on a wheel-barrow income. It is breakfast at the restaurant, canned goods for lunch, a card party in the afternoon, dinner at the club, a theater attraction, a cold biscuit for dad, no regard for the church or Bible, while the children are allowed to go to the devil.

It appears quite obvious that the Rev. Tripp, by his own words, was, at the very least, a member and staunch supporter of the Ku Klux Klan.

MONDAY JUNE 26, 1992
Borderline is Scene of Great Gathering, Men Parading There: Klansmen from Ouachita and Morehouse Parishes Traverse Ashley County [142]

It was reported that hundreds of Klansmen from Ouachita and Morehouse Parishes and Ashley County, Arkansas, descended upon Ashley County and distributed literature pertaining to the Klan. It was said that the Louisiana-Arkansas border had been the scene of considerable lawlessness during the preceding months and this was said to have been the leading reason for the parade.

When the townspeople learned of the parade of the Klansmen banners were displayed in front of various stores, "welcoming the vigilantes to that region."

---

[141]*Monroe News-Star,* 21 June 1922.

[142]*Monroe News-Star,* 26 June 1922.

Some of the establishments invited the Klansmen in for "cigars and cold drinks [that] were free for the asking." It was claimed that 4,000 Hamburg residents turned out to welcome the Klansmen.

The fact that more than 30 automobiles were said to have conveyed scores of Klansmen from Monroe to Ashley County will be significant in the forthcoming Klan-orchestrated deaths of Watt Daniel and Thomas Richards. The fact that Klansmen from other locales will travel to aid other Klansmen will be demonstrated to have occurred in the case of Daniel and Richard. A circular distributed by the Klansmen stated the following:

> We are traversing the domains of your magnificent county today to disseminate the pure and Holy teachings and principals of the Knights of the Ku Klux Klan in hopes of bringing to our assistance and support all one hundred per cent Americans residing in your midst. This order stands for law and order above all things and its members stand ready at all times to give prompt assistance to the legally constituted officers of the law in maintaining and upholding the same.

Again from Herrin, Illinois, came the news that Mine Superintendent C. K. McDowell of the Southern Illinois Coal company had been found guilty of the murders of the 20 union and non-union men.[143] This gives an indication of just how violent this strike had become as well as how little value was placed on human life.

FRIDAY JULY 7, 1922
Give Pastor of West Monroe Fat Purse: Monroe Klan, Knights of Ku Klux Klan, Give Rev. Evans Purse of Fifty Dollars

Another member of the clergy to play a, presented the Rev. J. L. Evans, pastor of the West Monroe Methodist Church, was next to be the beneficiary of Klan gratitude when he was presented with a purse containing 50 $1 bills. This time it was role Monroe Klan No. 4, Knights of the Ku Klux Klan, Realm of Louisiana doing the honors.

Just as it was with Rev. Tripp a few days previous, the purse was accompanied by a letter in which the Klansmen praised the pastor's efforts "to present to the people the pure doctrines of the Christian Religion, as found in God's Holy Word." This must have been quite a spectacle because it was reported that 10 Klansmen in white hoods and gowns filed into the church carrying a fiery cross, marched to where Evans stood, presented him the tokens of their esteem and

---

[143] Ibid.

without a word, marched out as silently as they had come in. The letter read as follows:

Monroe, La., July 6, 1922

Rev. J. L. Evans, Pastor
West Monroe Methodist Church,
West Monroe, Louisiana.
Dear Sir:

We, the members of Klan No. 4, Knights of the Ku Klux Klan, Realm of Louisiana, take this opportunity to present a small token of our regard for and faith in your splendid efforts to present to the people the pure doctrines of the Christian religion, as found in God's Holy Word.

We, the members of this great American organization, having at heart the best interest of our great country, and particularly of the people of the city of Monroe and West Monroe, do most earnestly believe in the Holy Bible as God's only revelation to man, and in His Son Jesus Christ; and we believe that the Holy Bible is the only expression of his revelation to men of the Son of God. We believe that this American government was founded on the teachings of this Holy Book.

We further believe that so long as the American people believe in and practice the teachings of this Book, this nation and government will be safe and prosperous; but when the people of this nation turn away from its teachings, this nation will soon go the way of those nations that forgot God, to utter oblivion and everlasting doom, as have nations that now fill the graveyards of history.

We hereby wish to say that we stand by and commend the earnest efforts of all preachers, of all evangelical Protestant dominations who faithfully preach these true doctrines of this Bible. Nay more, it is our sincere desire, as Klansmen, to practice these teachings in our own lives, and to commend them to all people in the world.

MONDAY JULY 17, 1922
Baton Rouge Klan now Ready for Warpath[144]

The Baton Rouge Ku Klux Klan announced that it was prepared to clean up Baton Rouge following the initiation of nearly 200 this past Saturday night. The ceremonies were said to have had between 400 and 500 Klansmen participating, including those who were initiated.

The only invited guests to the "naturalization" ceremony were two newspaper reporters who were said to have received their invitations in a sealed message delivered by a messenger. The following announcement was made to the reporters present by a Klansman following the ceremonies.

To bootleggers, moonshiners, gamblers, bookmakers, prostitutes, owners of houses being operated as common nuisances and consorts of negro women of East Baton Rouge parish, we issue this warning--'mend your ways or seek a

---

[144]*Monroe News-Star,* 17 July 1922.

more congenial environment for your nefarious and parasitical vocations. We have given you long enough. You have violated our laws, preyed upon and debauched our youth, disgraced our city and parish, and exhausted the patience and forfeited the respect of all decent law-abiding citizens. Cut it out or get out. The Klan speaks only once.

In another instance of Klan violence, it was reported this day that J. D. Whitten of Globe, Arizona had been arrested as a result of a Klan raid on the rooming house where Whitten and his wife were living. According to Mrs. Whitten, her husband was protecting himself from the Klansmen "who were bent on spiriting [him] away."

TUESDAY JULY 18, 1922

Four Young Men of Texas Flogged for Taking Strike Jobs[145]

From Fort Worth, Texas came a report that some non-union workers at the local Frisco shops, four men all under the age of 25, were seized by a band of approximately 100 men at 11 o'clock last night while at a local dance hall, taken six miles out on the Cleburne road and flogged, according to reports made to the police early this morning by the men. The men were stripped and lashed with leather straps after which they were warned to "head south and not return." Several shots were fired at the fleeing men, but none took effect. They arrived in the city at 2:10 o'clock this morning..[146]

MONDAY JULY 24, 1922

Negro is Lynched in Georgia after White Girl's Assault There[147]

A lynching was reported in Ellenton, Georgia this date as the bullet-riddled body of Will Anderson, a black man charged with having attempted an attack on a 15-year-old white girl near Ellenton Sunday, was found on the road near Reedy Creek Church. Anderson was allegedly captured by a posse of four men who were taking him to Moultrie with the supposed intent of placing him in jail. However, when they reached the town, the men left the automobile with Anderson in it to search for the sheriff. Not long afterwards, an unidentified man drove Ellenton to the outskirts of Moultrie. His body was found later on the roadside.

This type of incidents was not unusual when blacks were involved. Rather, it was common to read stories of similar incidents involving blacks, as well as black

[145]*Monroe News-Star*, 14 July 1922.
[146]*Monroe News-Star*, 18 July 1922.

prisoners being taking from police officers and hung on the spot.

TUESDAY JULY 25, 1922
Religious Argument at Bastrop Results in White Cap Affair[148]

The Klansmen of Morehouse Parish had a very effective and efficient way of settling disputes regarding religion. In one such dispute, eight hooded and masked members of the Ku Klux Klan took G. A. Griffin, the manager of the Consolidated Ice plant at Bastrop, forced him into an car, drove him to Collinston, where he was given a beating and warned to leave Bastrop. It was said that Griffin had been in Bastrop only two months at the time of this incident. Little wonder that he returned home to Cannon, Miss., following his experience.

Incidents involving kidnappings and beatings by the Klan, such as that which occurred to Griffin, were quite common in Morehouse Parish and rarely worthy of note. The frequency of such activities could well be why few people took note of the kidnappings of Watt Daniel and Thomas Richards by the Klan. It was also reported this day that Alexander Graham Bell had died.[149]

SATURDAY AUGUST 5, 1922
Dastardly Effort to Assassinate Dr. M'Koin, Mer Rouge: Former Mayor of Morehouse Town Has Been Active Against Lawlessness[150]

Such was the way a self-manufactured assassination attempt on the life of Dr. B. M. McKoin was reported by an obviously sympathetic press. According to the good doctor, he received a phone call at his office, where he was doing lab work late at night, by someone that he did not recognize. The unknown caller informed him that the condition of a black patient on the White plantation, whom he had visited early in the day, had worsened.

Upon his arrival at the plantation, he learned that no call had been made for him. He claimed not to suspect a sinister motive in the message and as he was returning to Mer Rouge, he was fired upon twice at close range with buckshot. The first shot was fired while he was approaching and the second after he had passed. He attributed his escape to the fact that he was driving fast and that he was leaning over the steering wheel of the car.

---

[147]*Monroe News-Star,* 24 July 1922.

[148]*Monroe News-Star,* 25 July 1922.

[149]*Monroe News-Star,* 2 August 1922.

[150]*Monroe News-Star,* 5 August 5 1922.

The article reported that Dr. McKoin, the former mayor of Mer Rouge, had been active in attempting to break up bootlegging and other law violations. He claimed to have recently received a threatening letter, warning him to leave town or he would be killed. According to this report, the "citizens are much wrought up over the affair and if the guilty person or persons is apprehended summary punishment will doubtless result." Of course, the article failed to mention that McKoin was the head of the Mer Rouge Ku Klux Klan.

Although this article was not front page news that day, the alleged assassination attempt would be the catalyst to set in motion a chain of events that would ultimately cost the lives of Watt Daniel and Thomas Richards in one of the most brutal and inhumane fashions ever recorded. Because of the refusal of the Morehouse Parish Klan-dominated authorities totake action on the disappearances of Daniel and Richards, Governor Parker would send in the Attorney General of the State of Louisiana, along with his staff, to conduct an investigation and prosecute those responsible for the kidnappings and deaths of Daniel and Richards. Governor Parker would also dispatch four companies of the Louisiana National Guard, under the command of Colonel Guerre, to quell the possibility of a civil war between the towns of Bastrop and Mer Rouge, to protect state and federal investigators and to protect and transport witnesses for the open hearing.

It is important that this assassination attempt be examined here in order for the reader to understand that this incident was the foundation upon which the kidnappings and later murders of Daniel and Richards was based. There are a number of inconsistencies in the incident that was alleged by McKoin. Some were addressed by investigators, and others were not.

Firmly addressed by agents of the Justice Department were the following: 1) the type of weapon used, 2) the trajectory of the pellets of buckshot, and 3) the findings of the first two in relation to the position Dr. McKoin claimed to be at the moment the assassination attempt occurred.

According McKoin's statement, the weapons used against him were shotguns, and that "the first shot was fired while he was approaching and the second after he passed." The only evidence to be discovered by federal agents was what appeared to be a shotgun blast that entered through the rear curtain. The trajectory of this blast passed through the rear seating area of the vehicle and passed directly over the driver's seating area with one of the pellets striking one of the spokes of the

51

steering wheel. If this trajectory were to be followed from the rear of the vehicle backwards, it would seem as though the person firing this shot had to have run into the middle of the road after the vehicle had passed, taken aim and fired at Dr. McKoin, who said "that he was driving very fast and leaning over the steering wheel of the car."

Miraculously, the first shotgun blast as McKoin was approaching assassin No. 1 missed his car completely, or McKoin's "leaning over the steering wheel. . .," and "the fact that he was driving fast . . ." caused Assassin No. 1's shot to pass through the driver's side window, through the front seating area and exit through the passenger side window without a single pellet striking McKoin or any portion of the vehicle.

Dr. McKoin said that he was "leaning over the steering wheel of the car." The usual meaning of this phrase is that the driver would have pulled his body very close to or on top of the steering wheel. Dr. McKoin did not say that he had laid down on the front seat. Had he claimed that, perhaps it could have happened as he claimed. However, the trajectory of the pellet which entered from the rear and struck the spoke on the steering wheel would have had no choice but to have passed through Dr. McKoin's body in order to do that.

Dr. McKoin claimed that he was working late at his office when he was called away "by a voice he did not recognize . . ." to a patient's home "only to learn that no call had been sent for him." It would seem reasonable that given these circumstances, and the fact that he had allegedly received letters threatening his life, that any reasonable person would deduce that he was being set up. Yet, he claimed that "not suspecting a sinister purpose of the message, he was returning to town" when the alleged assassination attempt took place. The good doctor must think we all just fell off the banana truck!

It will also be revealed later that the threatening letters sent to McKoin had been typed on his own typewriter and that he even admitted to typing them himself. I have jumped ahead a bit, and I have made revelations which do not surface until later to inform the reader that this incident, the incident that propelled Morehouse Parish into the forefront of daily national news for over a month, was started by this bogus assassination attempt. The author of the article printed in the *News-Star* also displayed a personal bias that is easily detectable, first in the headline, and then in the body of the article. The author was also a prophet as the statement was made "if the guilty person or persons is apprehended summary punishment will doubtless result." That is exactly what was to occur.

Not addressed in the investigation was 1) the questioning of the black family on the White plantation to ascertain whether McKoin had been visited there that day and whether he returned that same night, 2) the reason why Dr. McKoin was traveling with a bail of hay on his running board on the driver's side of his vehicle, 3) whether McKoin owned a shotgun, 4) was anyone at his office when he received that call from the White plantation, 5) would such a call necessarily have to come through the operator's switchboard for the town, and if so did the operator on duty that evening remember a call to Dr. McKoin.

In an unrelated event, the price of gasoline went down on this date from 22 to 20 cents per gallon. [151] Also reported in a small article was the annual encampment in Alexandria of 1,200 Louisiana National Guardsmen under the command of Colonel Louis F. Guerre. [152] Little did Colonel Guerre know at that time, but he would command the garrison of Louisiana National Guard troops to be sent to Morehouse Parish in the coming December to assist in the investigation of the murders of Watt Daniel and Thomas Richards.

MONDAY AUGUST 7, 1922
Klan Leaders on Trial for Raiding[153]

Klan activity continued to spread across the nation, and it seemed as though no community was immuned to its influence. In Los Angeles, California, 37 Knights of the Ku Klux Klan were brought up on charges stemming from a raid April 22 on the home and winery of Fidel and Mathias Elduayon at Inglewood. One alleged raider, Constable M. B. Mosher of Inglewood, was killed and his son and deputy, Walter Mosher and Leonard Ruegg, a deputy sheriff, were wounded. Young Mosher and Ruegg are among the defendants.

Mob of 20 Lynch Negroes[154]

The headline on this story was deceptive because no lynching took place. However, a detachment of 20 men assigned to the Durham North Carolina National Guard Machine Gun Company and another detachment of 15 members of the

---

[151] Ibid.
[152] Ibid.
[153] *Monroe News-Star*, 7 August 1992.
[154] Ibid.

53

Raleigh Service Company of the North Carolina National Guard, were assigned to guard three blacks following their arrest in connection with the shooting of E. F. Ketchen, of Miami, Fla., near Southern Pines. The troops were ordered by the adjutant general last night after Governor Morrison had authorized their use.

This action was taken because not long after the blacks had been brought to Durham by the sheriff of Moore County, 50 cars with over 100 men appeared outside the prison, and rumors spread that the mob had come here to lynch the blacks. As shall be demonstrated, use of local national guard units to preserve order had become a common event.

TUESDAY AUGUST 8, 1922
Democrats Choose Nominees in Big Arkansas Contest: Klux Klan Takes Major Part in Races[155]

From Little Rock, Arkansas came a report that in the race for state offices, the Ku Klux Klan became a prominent issue in the closing days of the campaign. In many counties, the endorsement of the Ku Klux Klan was openly given to some candidates, and in some cases entire Klan tickets were placed in the field.

In Little Rock as well as in other locations, an advertisement signed by the Ku Klux Klan appeared in which rewards were offered for evidence of "crooked work" at the polls. It should also be pointed out that anti-Klan forces replied to these advertisements by castigating the Klan as "unAmerican" and warning that the Klan was attempting to gain political control of the state.

FRIDAY AUGUST 11, 1922
Unity League Would Curb Activities of Ku Klux Klan in U.S. [156]

The danger represented by the Ku Klux Klan was acknowledged in Chicago, Illinois as a nation-wide effort to curb the activities of the Klan was announced with the formation of the American Unity League. Bishop Samuel Fallows, of the Reformed Episcopal Church, was named honorary chairman. Patrick H. O'Connell, a Chicago attorney, is chairman. Plans were being made for a weekly newspaper for distribution to national, state and municipal officials who may want to work toward outlawing the Klan.

Although the league claimed to be non-political, it planned to oppose candidates who were supported by some 27,000 Klansmen in Chicago.

---

[155]*Monroe News-Star*, 8 August 1922.

[156]*Monroe News-Star*, 11 August 1922.

Recognizing the threat of the Ku Klux Klan, former Governor Edward F. Dunne of Illinois sent a telegram to Bishop Fallows in which he said:

> The Ku Klux Klan is a menace to religious freedom, a source of danger to the state and its growing strength should be curbed through the united efforts of all true Americans, regardless of creed, race, or condition of life.

Rev. Tripp, friend of the Klan and pastor of the Baptist Church at Monroe, was once again a headline in the news. It appears as though the Reverend was quite upset that the swimming pool as co-ed, and he made a request that the city segregate the sexes at the pool during the Louisiana Baptist Encampment taking place in Monroe. His request was denied. The pool, declared the authorities, was public property, and the segregation of the sexes could only be done only by popular demand. Chalk one up for the Devil. [157]

MONDAY AUGUST 14, 1922
Dr. M'Koin Leaves Mer Rouge Because of Threat on Life: Former Mayor of Town Receives Threatening Letters After Attempt on Life[158]

With what appeared to be the full support and sympathy of the Mer Rouge community, it was reported that Dr. McKoin left in fear of his life. It was said that "Authorities and citizens are making every effort to apprehend the guilty person or persons, but have not succeeded. Dr. McKoin is at the present in New Orleans." Now, at first blush, this may seem to be an unimportant piece of news.

However, what appears to be unimportant now, will play a major role later on during the open hearing to be held in Bastrop concerning the tortured murders of Watt Daniel and Thomas Richards. Less than a week from the date of this report, Daniel and Richards would be kidnapped and murdered, and Dr. McKoin will be identified by witnesses as being on the scene of the kidnapping. He will use this news report as an alibi.

Also reported in today's news in and around Monroe was an incident of "tarring and feathering" that occurred to A. H. Lansdale, Jr., a drug clerk of West Monroe. He claimed that he was forced at gun point into a waiting car occupied by four men who said they were members of the Ku Klux Klan. He said they drove him into the swamps, stripped, tarred and feathered him, and later returned him to the main thoroughfare in the town and forced out in front of the Central Savings Bank. He said that the men who attacked him, while wearing no masks, were

---

[157]Ibid.

strangers to him. Lansdale stated that he had received repeated warnings to leave town which he refused to obey.

It was interesting to note that the Monroe New-Star reported that "No violence of any sort was resorted to during the process, other than the tar and feather treatment." Clearly, the paper was attempting to pound a square peg into a round hole by saying that kidnapping and tarring and feathering were not acts of violence.

Lansdale's description of the incident is important because many of the same characteristics that he described will later be mentioned either by victims of witnesses of Klan activity at the open hearings to come. For example, he said, "Upon entering one of the two cars--there were two Ford cars waiting bearing four or six men, I am not quite certain--a piece of cloth was draped about my eyes and I was unable to see where the men were driving me." Testimony will demonstrate that the Klan used the same method during later kidnappings, including those of Watt Daniel and Thomas Richards. He also noted that "The men--who were unmasked and strangers to me, asked if I had ever heard of the Ku Klux Klan, and when I replied I had, they declared that they were members of the Klan and that they were going to punish me." That these men were unmasked Klansmen was not uncommon for Klansmen from other states to assist local Klansmen. For example, we have seen how Klansmen from Monroe went into Arkansas to assist Klansmen there. [159]

It was clear that the original article was written with a positive slant toward the Klan. In the second paragraph, the article did say that "the attack, which occurred about 8 o'clock, was the culmination of repeated warnings received by Lansdale to leave town, and which he refused to comply with."

This information clearly did not come from Lansdale, because in the last line of the article he was quoted as saying, "I had not been warned of the occurrence. . . " The question arises then from whom did the author of this article receive the information? The only answer could be some direct or indirect Klan source. The author was careful not to mention the source of this information and presented it in such a fashion that the reader, the vast majority of whom would either be Klansmen or Klan sympathizers, would not question its origin.

---

[158]*Monroe News-Star,* 14 August 1922.
[159]Ibid.

The author's pro-Klan bias is also evident in the third paragraph in which he said "no violence of any sort was resorted to during the process, other than the tar and feather treatment." The author was attempting to put this incident on the same level as some schoolboy prank.

Make no mistake, this was an act of kidnapping of the first order. The victim was, through intimidation, forced into the car, blindfolded and taken to a remote location, where he was forced to completely undress. Hot tar was then applied to his body, and, before the tar cooled, the feathers had to be applied otherwise they would not stick. This was far from being a painless process, and eons away from a schoolboy prank.

Anyone familiar with the operation of a responsible publication is aware that authors must submit articles to their various editors for approval before they are allowed to be published. Since these articles and those of the future must have passed editorial muster, it can then safely be held that the *Monroe News-Star* presented Klan related news in a light favorable to the Klan for reasons known only to its editorial staff.

With regard to the manner in which the kidnapping was conducted, the Klan's cowardly custom of having at least 10 Klansmen to each victim was evident. All of the previous articles presented have shown clearly that whenever the Klan conducted a raid, it made certain that the victim had no other choice but to submit. Two days after this Klan kidnapping, the first Klan kidnapping of Thomas Richards, one of the men to be falsely accused of the bogus assassination attempt on Dr. McKoin, was to occur.

FRIDAY AUGUST 18, 1922
Richards Put Through Third Degree by Men in Masks at Bastrop[160]

This is one of the newspaper articles that must be presented in its original form in order for the reader is to savor the full flavor of pro-Klan sentiment in the local press as well as how little regard was given by the press and local law enforcement to the kidnapping of a citizen by armed vigilantes. Also be aware the article refers to Thomas Richards as "Sam Richards." So much for journalistic accuracy.

> Sam Richards, former citizen of Mer Rouge and lately a resident of Bastrop, was taken into the woods between Bastrop and Mer Rouge late Thursday night by a party of masked men in automobiles and questioned in regard to what he knew

---

[160]*Monroe News-Star*, 18 August 1922.

relative to recent attempt to assassinate Dr. B. M. McKoin, former mayor of
Mer Rouge and for a number of years a leading physician there.

Satisfied that Richards knew nothing about the attempt to kill the physician, the
party brought him back to Bastrop and released him near the edge of town.

Richards said he could not recognize any of the men under their masks. He said
no attempt was made to offer him any violence when it was found out he knew
nothing in regard to the recent attempt on Dr. McKoin's life.

Sheriff Carpenter, of Morehouse parish, said today he had secured no evidence in
regard to the attempt to assassinate McKoin and that there would probably be no
arrests.

McKoin has gone to New Orleans and has entered Tulane University for a post-
graduate course and at its completion will practice his profession in some other
town than Mer Rouge, having been advised by his friends to do this.

It is obvious that kidnapping continued to be presented in an acceptable manner
as the article concentrated on ferreting out those involved in the bogus attempted
murder of McKoin, and absolutely no attention was given to the kidnapping
offense. The soon-to-be-infamous Sheriff Carpenter's only remarks were
concerning Dr. McKoin. Clearly, he saw nothing wrong with the kidnapping of
Richards. As will be shown later, Sheriff Carpenter was pro-Klan and a Klansman
himself. Two of his deputies, one of whom would later be charged with the
kidnappings and murders of Daniel and Richards, were Klansmen.

It is interesting to note how the author attempted to protect the Klan by saying
that Richards said "no attempt was made to offer him any violence when it was
found out he knew nothing in regard to the recent attempt on Dr. McKoin's life."
When a person is kidnapped by masked persons, taken at night to an unknown
location in the woods and interrogated, violence has already been committed against
that person, and future violence is inferred. The reputation of the Klan preceded it,
and the threat of whippings, tar and feathers, or summary execution would be ever
present in an incident of this nature.

Most important in this article was the claim that Dr. McKoin had already
departed the area, and that he would be living in the New Orleans area where he
attended Tulane University for a postgraduate course in medicine. McKoin did not
attend Tulane, but rather Johns Hopkins in Baltimore. This article appeared five
days before Daniel and Richards were to be kidnapped and murdered and would be
pivotal in Dr. McKoin's alibi that he was not in Morehouse Parish when the
kidnappings and murders of Daniel and Richards occurred. Unfortunately, we may
never know the whereabouts of McKoin because he never testified, nor was he
obliged to present a defense since he was never brought to trial for either murder.

MONDAY AUGUST 21, 1922
Huge Ku Klux Klan Class is Initiated Under Fiery Cross: Spectacular and Picturesque Scene Presented in Chicago Initiation Saturday[161]

Beneath the red glare from a blazing cross what was said to be the nation's biggest class of new Ku Klux Klansmen--4,650 candidates--was initiated in a huge field just outside of Chicago late Saturday night.

Most assume that the activities of the Klan were mostly restricted to the deep South, but this is one myth that will soon be despelled. We have already seen that the Klan was active in on the West Coast of the United States. As this story unfolds, it will become quite apparent that the Klan had surged North and, as the above captioned article indicates, had taken hold in Chicago. Future articles will demonstrate that it had spread across the length and breadth of this nation, and that no community, be it large or small, was immuned to its influence.

This article also spoke in reverent tones of "the mystic rites" and how 25,000 people came to witness the ceremonies. The article claimed that 18 Klans in Chicago and 12 outside of Cook County were represented at the "naturalization."

Springfield, Missouri was also cited this day as a place where the local Ku Klux Klan had purchased a large tract of land, including the big Percy's Cave, which Klan officials said would be used for Klan ceremonials. The purchase price was $40,000. This seemed to upset some of the residents because Percy's Cave was a point of interest to sight-seers in the Ozarks.[162]

WEDNESDAY AUGUST 23, 1922
Ku Klux Statement by Fergerson Today on Late Incident: Shall We Be Ruled by Mob Law?" Asks Former Governor James Fergerson.[163]

Houston, Texas was the scene of a public demonstration of support for the Ku Klux Klan when James E. Fergerson, candidate for the Democratic nomination for United States Senator, was prevented for some few minutes from speaking by people in the audience.

The "demonstration" consisted of a sudden departure by a substantial portion of the audience when Fergerson began a verbal attack on the Ku Klux Klan. Fergerson's attack on the Klan drew jeers and cat-calls from Klan supporters in the audience. Mr. Fergerson further attacked the Klan and Earl. B. Mayfield, his

---

[161] *Monroe News-Star,* 21 August 1922.

[162] Ibid.

[163] *Monroe News-Star,* 23 August 1922.

opponent, whom he declared a member of the Klan in a speech at San Antonio.

Also on this date, U. S. Attorney General Daugherty sent a letter to Gov. Olcott of Oregon endorsing the governor's stand against the Klan in Salem. In his letter, Daugherty refereed to the Ku Klux Klan as "a distinct menace to decent government." The letter was a reply to a letter sent by Governor Olcott thanking the Daugherty for his cooperation in the prosecution of Klan outrages in Jackson County.[164]

From Chattanooga, Tennessee came the news that a temporary restraining order enjoining Lookout Klan No. 15, Knights of the Ku Klux Klan. This extraordinary action was taken in response to an application filed by Imperial Klan Headquarters in Atlanta. The bill of information charged that Lookout Klan violated its charter by failing to account for its finances and by passing a treasonable resolution, and as a consequence its charter was revoked.[165]

THURSDAY AUGUST 24, 1922
Monroe Loses Game with Bastrop Team[166]

Monroe lost the first game of the five game series with Bastrop yesterday on the latter's ground by a score of 5 to 1. Inability to deliver the necessary "punch in a pinch," coupled with some poor base running, probably cost Monroe the game.

This article is presented in a shorten form because it is not the game that was important, but rather the spectators and the Klan conspirators lurking about the fringes. Seated as spectators at this game were Watt Daniel, Thomas Richards, J. L. Daniel, C. C. "Tot" Davenport and W. C. Andrews. Unknown to these men, as they enjoyed the game and feasted on barbecue provided by those looking to pass a bond issue to improve the road between Bastrop and Mer Rouge, on that very road the Ku Klux Klan had already torn down the telephone lines between Bastrop and Mer Rouge to avoid any communication that would alert their victims. Just as they were to do in a raid on the Arkansas town of Smackover, upwards of two dozen black-hooded Klansmen armed with pistols and rifles lay in ambush for them.

---

[164]Ibid.
[165]Ibid.
[166]*Monroe News-Star*, 24 August 1922.

FRIDAY AUGUST 25, 1922

Night Riders in Morehouse Parish
M'Koin Case Believed to Have Caused New Mer Rouge Flare Up
Maskers in Cars Get Victims After Baseball Contest
Sheriff Fred Carpenter Reported Early Today Men Had Not Returned
Citizens were Going Home to Mer Rouge[167]

The above headline and sub-headlines were splashed across the front page of the *Monroe News-Star*. Contained below is the article as it appeared that day. From here on whenever there are headlines regarding Klan activity which will be explained in the text, the headlines will appear as above and the commentary below.

W. C. Andrews and J. L. Daniels, farmers, and "Tot" Davenport, a young man, returned to their Mer Rouge homes today after being taken into the woods, according to a long distance telephone report to the Monroe News-Star from Mer Rouge.

Watt Daniels and Samuel (Thomas) Richards, two other victims of the affair, were reported to be still "out" late this afternoon.

W. C. Andrews and J. L. Daniels, according to a report received by Sheriff Fred Carpenter, were whipped. He said he could not verify the report.

Sheriff Carpenter denied the report circulated at Monroe today that one of the baseball players had been whipped. "There is nothing to that report," he said. "Tot" Davenport was released soon after being kidnapped, the sheriff said.

W. C. Andrews, Tot Davenport, J. L. Daniels, Watt Daniels and a man known as Richards, all residing in Mer Rouge, were stopped by a band of masked men armed with revolvers, Winchester rifles and sawed-off shotguns, while returning from the good roads meeting at Bastrop late Thursday night and whipped at the roadside, according to a late report from Bastrop.

Richards and Wat(t) Daniels, two of the victims, have not returned to Mer Rouge, according to advices received in this city, while the others are reported to be in critical condition as a result of the beating administered.

Cumberland telephone officials in Monroe declared this morning that three telephone lines between Mer Rouge and Bastrop were cut some time during the night and that communication between these two points was impossible. Linemen were sent out this morning to repair the lines.

Monroe citizens returning from Bastrop, where they attended the meeting yesterday, report that they were stopped at the fork of the road three miles out of Bastrop and requested to detour by way of Collinston.

It is also reported that the car in which the band had ridden was ditched on the return trip and that patrols armed with guns were stationed along the road to stop cars from getting too close to the ditched automobile. No threats, however, were made against the occupants, all of whom complied with the request and either detoured or halted until given permission to proceed.

Five citizens of Morehouse parish who were taken to the woods by a party of twenty-five or thirty men wearing **black masks** [my emphasis] last night have disappeared, according to Sheriff Fred Carpenter, of Bastrop, early today. Sheriff

---

[167]Ibid.

Carpenter and deputies made a search for hours in different parts of the parish early today without success.

The names of the men taken out were Watt Daniels, L. J. Daniels, W. C. Andrews, Tot Davenport and a man named Richards. "I do not know that these names are accurate," said the sheriff. "I was told that these were the men who were victims of the **white cappers**. These men all live in Mer Rouge, or in that vicinity, and are in business or engaged in farming.

The victims of the raid were on their way in an automobile to Mer (Here there appears to be a section that the typesetter failed to enter. What follows is a guess as to what might have been in the missing area: "Rouge where they live. Earlier in the. .) day they attended a barbecue and baseball game between Bastrop and Monroe. The men are believed to have started late for their respective homes and almost immediately it is said cars began to take the Bastrop-Mer Rouge highway from every direction.

The victims are believed to have been marked men for several days, or perhaps weeks, and to have been watched all day Thursday at Bastrop and the signal that they were going on their way to their homes is believed to have been circulated almost immediately after they left Bastrop. The men were captured about midway between Bastrop and Mer Rouge.

McKoin Case Involved

The victims of the night riders are believed to have been connected with the attempt to assassinate Dr. B. M. McKoin, former Mer Rouge physician and mayor, who was forced to leave that town several weeks ago because of the attempt on his life. Sheriff Carpenter said it was assumed that the vigilantes had taken the point of view that their victims knew something of the McKoin case.

Feeling has been intense in Northern Louisiana because of the attempt on Dr. McKoin's life, not only in Mer Rouge, but also in other parts of Morehouse parish and in Ouachita parish as well. It has been reported that the case was being investigated by the Morehouse parish authorities and also by private citizens, and bands of citizens, and some time ago it was announced that an important clue had been obtained, which might lead to arrests.

A few nights ago, Sam Richard[s], a citizen of Morehouse parish, was taken to the woods by masked men and given a court trial to determine whether he had any connection with the case. The midnight jury brought in   verdict of "not guilty" and Richard[s] was taken to his home unmolested.

A better understanding of the sentiments of the general population and the news media may be gleaned by examining the manner in which this article was written. Although there are times when editorial policy will be opposed to the general feeling of the community it serves, for the most part it reflects community sentiment. Editorial policy does not simply apply to the editorial section of a publication. Rather, editorial policy is contained in a publication from cover to cover. Therefore, each article and even advertisements are subject to censure by those governing what is admissible and what is not. With this in mind, I would suggest that the reader again read the previous article, and I shall attempt to point out some of what appears to be leanings on the part of the publication.

First and foremost, the reporter does not name or refer to the Ku Klux Klan as being the perpetrators of this incident, although it was common knowledge that they were. The only reference to the Klan can be found in Sheriff Carpenter's statement when he referred to those involved as "white cappers." This, in itself, raises one of many questions concerning what Sheriff Carpenter knew and when he knew it. "White cappers" was a term used by some when making reference to the Klan. Reports up to this point have said that the kidnappings had been carried out "by a party of twenty-five or thirty men wearing black masks" How would Sheriff Carpenter have connected "men wearing black masks" to "white cappers" unless he knew that when the Klan went on raids they wore a black hood instead of their traditional white hood?

From the manner in which the article was written, it appeared as though Sheriff Carpenter had not spoken personally with any of the victims of the kidnappings or beatings. All of his information appeared to be hearsay. Was the appearance of armed vigilantes on a highway stopping all traffic, searching vehicles, terrorizing the public, kidnapping at gunpoint, administering beatings to those kidnapped to where the victims "are reported to be in critical condition," ripping down of telecommunications lines, and last but not least the continuing absence of two of the kidnap victims of such little concern to Sheriff Carpenter that he could not have at least spoken with the victims?

According to Sheriff Carpenter, he and his "deputies made a search for hours in different parts of the parish" but without success. It is difficult to believe that Sheriff Carpenter and his deputies made such an all out search, and yet uncovered nothing. How could it be possible for Carpenter to have conducted such a search without speaking to anyone who could shed light on the roadblock, kidnappings and murders? Could it be that the people of the parish knew that Carpenter himself was a Klansman? Surely he must have been aware that one of his deputies, Burnett, was a Klansman. A Klansman whom witnesses would directly identify as having participated in the roadblock and kidnapping on that fateful day. As this story unfolds, Sheriff Carpenter will prove himself to be a definite friend of the Klan and a staunch foe of the attorney general of the state of Louisiana sent by Governor Parker to investigate these crimes, and also of the Louisiana National Guard sent to keep order in the parish.

In the second paragraph, little importance seems to be placed on the absence of

Daniel and Richards as the reporter wrote "two other victims of the affair were reported to be still 'out' late this afternoon." Although it was blatantly obvious to all that this incident had been perpetrated by the Ku Klux Klan, no mention was made of it.

The fingerprints of the Ku Klux Klan were all over this incident. The first indicator of Klan involvement was the use of the black hood, which will later be identified as being used by the Klan on raids. Second, the Exalted Cyclops of the Morehouse Klan, Captain J. K. Skipwith, was observed at the scene of the kidnapping, speaking with black-hooded Klansmen. He appeared to be directing the operation. What is more, in an interview to come with a reporter from the *St. Louis Post Dispatch*, he will admit Klan involvement in the kidnappings and murders. Third, the telephone lines between Bastrop and Mer Rouge had been cut. This was the same tactic that will be used by the Klan when they invaded Smackover, Arkansas, in December. It will be further revealed that Captain Skipwith had made a visit to the telephone switchboard in Bastrop and that he ordered that all communication between Bastrop and Mer Rouge be interrupted during the time period that the Klan was to perpetrate the kidnappings. Fourth, a few of the vehicles on the side of the road near the roadblock had their license plates covered, another favorite tactic of the Klan.

Curiously, the correspondent reporting this incident did not pursue any of these lines of questioning with Sheriff Carpenter. It can only be wondered how the reporter, speaking of the armed black-hooded Klansmen at the roadblock, could have written "no threats, however, were made against the occupants, all of whom complied with the request and either detoured or halted until given permission to proceed." This reporter would have us believe that armed Klansmen searching vehicles did not terrorize those with whom they came in contact, and that all was calm, cool and orderly. Where did this information come from? The reporter, aside from the portion which is attributed to Sheriff Carpenter, keeps us in the dark as to where all of the other information originated.

Where did the information come from when the reporter declared that the "band of masked men armed with revolvers, Winchester rifles and sawed-off shotguns" intercepted the victims. More importantly, that the victims were supposed to have been "marked men for several days, or perhaps weeks, and to have been watched all day Thursday at Bastrop?" This is important because later testimony revealed that the victims had, indeed, been watched, and that Captain Skipwith, the exalted cyclops, was seen pointing them out near the courthouse square in Bastrop on the day of the kidnapping.

Again the reporter evaded calling these kidnappers Klansmen later in the article when they were referred to as "night riders." In this section the bogus assassination attempt on Dr. McKoin was presented to the reader in a more sympathetic fashion than the report of the kidnappings, beatings, and continued absence of two of the kidnap victims.

Although the correspondent made no attempt to communicate the feelings of the community concerning the kidnappings and beatings, s/he was quick to report that "feeling has been intense in Northern Louisiana because of the attempt on Dr. McKoin's life, not only in Mer Rouge, but also in other parts of Morehouse parish and in Ouachita parish as well." It appeared as though there was no sympathy for those who had been kidnapped and beaten. There also seems to exist a sense of justification for the actions of the Klan as the reporter continued: "It has been reported that the case was being investigated by the Morehouse parish authorities, and also by private citizens, and bands of citizens, and some time ago it was announced that an important clue had been obtained, which might lead to arrests." Just who these "private citizens, and bands of citizens" were was never explained. This may have been another feeble attempt by the reporter to get around saying "Klan." The "clue" also was never revealed. It is thought that the reporter might have been told about some of the threatening letters which Dr. McKoin claimed to have received, and which turned out to have been written on his own typewriter by his own hand in an attempt to gain sympathy.

Richards is again referred to as "Sam." Later reports will give his correct name, Thomas F. Richards. Take special note of how the first kidnapping of Richards is presented. The article said that Richards was "taken to the woods by masked men." What the reporter failed to say was that Richards was kidnapped from his place of employment, an auto repair garage in Bastrop. The reporter also forgot to mention that the black-hooded kidnappers, Klansmen, forced him to abandon his young daughter there. When Mrs. Richards arrived at the garage her daughter told her, "The Ku Klux got daddy." Out of the mouths of babes.

The reporter continued to dignify this felonious kidnapping by saying that Richards was "given a court trial" by a "midnight jury" which returned a verdict of "not guilty." The last few words of this sentence are possibly the best indicator of prejudice in the article as the reporter said "and Richard[s] was taken to his home unmolested."

Richards had been kidnapped by masked men from his place of employment, forced to abandon his young daughter on the scene, brought to some unknown location where he was tried by a "midnight jury," and yet this was not considered a crime much less a molestation, but perhaps a minor inconvenience. Richards, as will be later shown, was not "taken to his home" but rather was dumped off at the edge of town and forced to walk home. So much for journalistic accuracy!

After reading this article, it should be clear that little by way of unbiased journalism was to be forthcoming from the *Monroe News-Star* concerning this series of kidnappings, beatings and murders. For those who still remain skeptical, an article which will appear in the September 1, 1922 edition of the *Monroe News-Star* will once and for all demonstrate the honor and homage paid to the Ku Klux Klan by the editorial staff of the *New-Star*.

National Army's Troopers Capture Two More Towns: Irish Regulars in County Cork Are Beaten Back From Their Positions[168]

From Belfast, came the news that national army troops captured the towns of Kinsale and Dunnaway, the last two positions held by Irish irregulars in county Cork. Also from Dublin came the tragic news of the funeral of Michael Collins, the Free State commander. His flag-covered coffin was interred in Glasneve Cemetery.

SATURDAY AUGUST 26, 1922

Vigilantes' Victim asks Court Help
Watt Daniels and Sam Richards Fail to Come Back Home
Morehouse Parish Authorities Are Not Inclined to Believe Foul Play
"All is Quiet" Report of Morehouse Sheriff[169]

The wife of Thomas Richards traveled from Mer Rouge to Bastrop on this day "to interrogate Judge Fred M. Odom, District Attorney David I Garrett, and Sheriff Fred Carpenter" as to the continued absence of her husband, who had been kidnapped two days earlier. Just who these "authorities" were who did not believe that Daniel and Richards had been murdered was never really spelled out. Sheriff Carpenter, however, was quoted as saying that "all was quiet" in Morehouse Parish, and he confirmed that Daniel and Richards had not been seen.

---

[168]*Monroe News-Star*, 25 August 1922.
[169]

It is easy to understand how the general population would not be alarmed about the disappearance of these two men, considering the manner in which other citizens had been ordered to leave the parish under threat of violence or had been tarred and feathered and/or beaten. Since others before had departed abruptly, it could be assumed that these two men had left the area, but had not yet communicated with their families. The hope generated by this line of thinking was soon to evaporate as the days passed into weeks and months.

A somewhat mysterious and ominous line appeared in this article concerning the continued actions of the vigilantes in Bastrop. It read as follows:

"A report was received in Monroe this morning to the effect that 'fifty or sixty men were lined up on the courthouse square at Bastrop' and the more timid were inclined to believe that there might be additional raids."

Strangely enough, the next paragraph spoke of Sheriff Carpenter's claim that "all was quiet." With 50 to 60 men on the Bastrop courthouse lawn intimidating the citizens who feared further raids, Carpenter made the all quiet claim. Again, it appears that the Klan has Sheriff Carpenter in their back pocket.

Although the name "Ku Klux Klan" does not appear in this article, it is clear that the reporter was speaking of the same group. The term "raiding party" was used a number of times in this article. This was the same term to be used by witnesses and Klansmen alike in future testimony concerning Klan raids. It was also reported that one of the whipping victims, W. C. Andrews, had had his teeth kicked out when he and the 68-year-old J. L. Daniel had been kidnapped. This claim was to be proven false the following day.

Ford's Plant to Close on Sept. 16 Because of Shortage of Coal[170]

From Detroit, Michigan, Henry Ford, of the Ford Motor Co. announced, that its plants at Highland Park, Dearborn and River Rouge would close on September 16, because of a lack of coal. The closure of the three plants directly affected over 50,000 workers and indirectly hundreds of thousands throughout the country.

Locally, the Rev. Tripp was back in the news as it was reported that Rev. had been called to fill the vacancy at the Highland Baptist Church in Shreveport. Tripp refused to comment on the rumor.[171]

---

[170]*Monroe News-Star,* 26 August 1922.
[171]

MONDAY AUGUST 28, 1922

Daniels (sic) Puzzled by Failure of Watt to Return, Asks for Peace
Morehouse Parish Men Send No Word as to Whereabouts
Wife of One of Kidnappers' Victims Trying to Get Probe Started
Mrs. Richards Visits Mother in W. Monroe[172]

"I have not heard a word from my son, Watt, since he was kidnapped Thursday night," J. L. Daniel, father of Watt, told a reporter in the telephone interview this day. "I do not know what has become of him and I cannot say as to what was done with him. I have not heard from my son since the day we were captured and taken into the woods between Bastrop and Mer Rouge."

With regard to the reason behind the kidnappings and beatings, the elder Daniel said, "The first I knew was that we were blindfolded and I do not know what was done with my son and with Sam Richards, who was also taken out and is still missing." Daniel said that before and during his beating he was interrogated concerning the bogus assassination attempt on Dr. McKoin "and a few other things of unimportance." He said he told the black-hooded band that he knew nothing about the assassination attempt, but they would not believe him and beat him anyway.

Curiously, he said he had made no attempt to pursue the matter with legal authorities. This could be interpreted as a lack of interest. The more likely possibility was that Daniel was only too cognizant that the Klan held the criminal justice system in the palm of its hand and that his best course of action was to attempt to placate the Klan, at least until his son, Watt, returned.

"My husband is innocent of any crime," Mrs. Richards told reporters. "This was proved when he was taken out the first time. The men found out that he was innocent and after they had questioned him they brought him back and turned him loose. My husband talked to me about this affair and said he could not understand why he was taken out. I thought that the affair had ended when he was taken out the first time."

Mrs. Richards told of a conference she had had with Judge Odom and Sheriff Carpenter concerning her husband's kidnapping. It was reported that they told her "that they were as much mystified as she as to the affair. They said that the affair was being investigated from many different angles." As the story unfolds, it will

---

[172]Ibid.

68

become clear that both men were privy to much more information than they would admit.

In later statements, the term "investigated from many different angles" was a favorite used by Klan members. Other phrases often used by the Klan to describe other Klansmen was to refer to them as "leading citizens." This phrase will also surface from time to time in an effort to justify and consecrate Klan activities.

Wichita Falls is Scene of Violence, Restaurant Burned[173]
Attempt Is Also Made to Destroy Church Building Belonging to Blacks
Negro Porter Held in Case Involving Girl[174]

Wichita Falls, Texas was the scene of civil unrest as a crowd of 500 to 600 people surrounded the combination city hall and jail at Electra late last evening where John Love, 25, a black porter, was being held in connection with an attack on a white girl. He was under the protection of 15 deputies. After Love's arrest, a black restaurant was burned, and it was reported that firemen working to extinguish the flames were told by the crowd to let it burn. A garage owned by a black family was also burned to the ground. An attempt was also made to burn a black Baptist church, but the fire department was able to extinguish the blaze. The attempt to burn the church was during the services and the building was packed. It was said that as the sparks began to fly the members of the mob outside yelled "down with blacks." The congregation escaped through the windows and door and none were seriously injured.

The white woman who was allegedly attacked could not be found, nor was there any evidence that she had been attacked. Mob action of this sort was common place during this era, and many more cases of incidents such as this will be reported.

Also in this day's news was a report from Dublin, Ireland telling of guerrilla warfare by Irish irregulars "the criminal element posing as part of the republican army." The report went on to say that "Many telephone and telegraph wires have been cut. In remote country districts there are but few soldiers and armed bands are robbing, looting and committing other excesses."

---

[173]*Monroe News-Star*, 28 August 1922.
[174]Ibid.

TUESDAY AUGUST 29, 1922
Missing Men From Mer Rouge Not in Territory
Investigation by Sheriff Grant and Deputy Roper Refutes Report
Officers Succeed in Quieting False Report[175]

Because of the flurry of rumors circulating in both Morehouse and Ouachita Parishes, Sheriff Grant and Deputy Roper searched the entire premises of the St. Francis Sanatorium at Monroe. Rumor had it that Watt Daniel and Thomas Richards were either being treated there for injuries, or were hiding out there. "The missing men are not in Monroe," said Sheriff Grant after his inspection of the facility.

Sheriff Carpenter was reported to be in Mer Rouge this date, but not to investigate the kidnappings and beatings of J. L. Daniel and W. C. Andrews or the continued absence of Watt Daniel and Thomas Richards. The paragraph in the article read as follows:

> Sheriff Fred Carpenter, of Bastrop, and a number of other leading citizens of the Morehouse parish seat went to Mer Rouge yesterday to investigate a report that Mer Rouge citizens were arming to make a raid on Bastrop, according to telephone messages received from Mer Rouge today. Sheriff Carpenter and the citizen's committee was informed the report was false in every particular: that Mer Rouge people had not been buying shells and arms for a raid. The committee is reported to have held a conference with leading citizens of Mer Rouge and they were given assurances the best of feelings prevails.

Nothing could have been further from the truth!

Later testimony will reveal that the first armed camp was composed of Klan members meeting at the Thomas store in Bastrop on the night of the kidnappings. Testimony will show that weapons were kept at the ready and that the exalted cyclops, Captain Skipwith, was present on and off the entire evening at the Thomas store. When word of this reached Mer Rouge along with the open threats of Captain Skipwith to bring an overwhelming Klan force into Mer Rouge to "clean up" the town, is it little wonder that the citizens of Mer Rouge did, in fact, arm themselves in preparation for an attack from the Bastrop Klan. Truth be known, tension was at an all-time high between the residents of Bastrop and Mer Rouge. It was far from the "best of all worlds" as described in *Candide*. It was a powder keg ready to explode!

From Jackson, California came a report of a cave-in at the Argonaut mine.

---

[175]Ibid.

Despite desperate attempts to rescue those trapped 3,000 feet below, it was feared that hundreds of men had died. Canary birds were lowered into the mine to test the quality of air. Most of the birds returned to the surface dead.

WEDNESDAY AUGUST 30, 1922

West Monroe Citizens Protest Against Acts Not Within the Law[176]

The first vestiges of an anti-Klan organization made itself known this date in West Monroe when about 100 citizens of W. Monroe gathered to protest against "recent lawless acts perpetrated by "night riders," the Klan by another name. The thrust of the meeting was to form a permanent organization of W. Monroe citizens to combat lawlessness and to force local law enforcement officers to enforce the statutes and arrest these violators.

G. B. Haynes, one of W. Monroe's most notable citizens, volunteered to temporarily head the organization in the absence of Mayor C. C. Bell. Mr. Elliot Wall, a drug store owner, took responsibility for calling the meeting. He said that he felt compelled to do so because of the recent occurrences by masked night riders about whom it was impossible to speak with impunity. He also told the audience that he had been warned personally on quite a few occasions to "keep your mouth shut." Suppression of free speech was also a common tactic employed by the Klan, and such warnings as to "keep your mouth shut" will trip from the lips of the exalted cyclops of Morehouse Klan No. 34, Captain J. K. Skipwith himself.

Wall also spoke up concerning the beating, kidnapping, and tar and feathering of one of his employees a few weeks prior. "The young man in question," said Wall, "was one of our finest youngsters and had given very little cause for offense during his residence among us. There were many men more guilty than he was in W. Monroe who have not been taken out and made victims of "parties." The situation is a serious one, and will inevitably lead to revolution if not suppressed. If possible, let bygones be bygones, but no more "night riding," declared Wall.

Following Wall, W. Monroe Councilman E. Smith delivered a scathing attack on the law enforcement officers of the W. Monroe area, which would not only include the local police department but also the Ouachita Parish Sheriff's Department, in which parish W. Monroe is located. Smith said quite bluntly that the police were not doing their job. "Nothing has been done to suppress the night

---

[176]Ibid.

71

riding," said Smith. "There are at present two powers which contend for supremacy in the community. The lawful constituted authorities and night riders. Either enforce the law or give the reins of government over to the latter and let us desist from paying further taxes."

"For their own protection," Smith continued, "young men of this community are arming themselves with .44 pistols. The first thing they do before leaving the house is to equip themselves for fear they might be set upon and whipped. This must be stopped. Either the officers do their duty or they get out. We must let night riders and all who advocate such rule know that in West Monroe it will not be tolerated. We must get behind the authorities, make them do their duty and help them in every way possible."

Before the meeting ended, this group of citizens collected donations in order to pay for an ad for the next meeting to be held on the following Friday at 8 p.m. Unfortunately, this was the last ever heard of this brave group of people. If there were further meetings, the *News-Star* was careful not to report them. This article proved that there were conscientious citizens in the area and that not all were either Klan members or sympathizers. Unfortunately, as in most cases such as this, these citizens remained silent or were afraid of the repercussions of speaking out.

Despite the publicity being generated by the disappearance of Daniel and Richards, not to mention the creation of the afore mentioned anti-Klan organization, Monroe Klan No. 4 Realm of Louisiana, Knights of the Ku Klux Klan, did not change its plans to hold a mass initiation ceremony in a park smack in the middle of downtown Monroe. That was demonstrated quite plainly in the article that appeared in the next day's edition of the *Monroe News-Star*.

Negro Hung by Mob[177]

In Shreveport, Louisiana, Tom Rivers, a black man and the alleged confessed assailant of a young white woman of Shreveport was taken from two officers by a band of about 25 men. This occurred while he was being transferred to the Bossier Parish Jail at Benton, La. the previous evening. The report said, "It is believed, however, that the body will be found hanging from a tree limb in the vicinity of Brownlee, where the mob overpowered the officers and near which neighborhood some years ago three negroes were lynched from the same tree." This prediction

---

[177]*Monroe News-Star,* 30 August 1922.

72

would later be proven true as an article the following day reported that he was found "swinging from a tree limb."[178]

In general, mob violence was the order of the day. From Birmingham, Alabama, came the report that sheriff's deputies were attempting to locate Hampton Martin, a black man, who had disappeared a week ago. His disappearance occurred only hours after he reported that he had been taken to the woods and flogged by masked men. In a similar incident, deputies were trying to run down the tormentors of George Gill, a truck farmer, who was in a hospital as a result of a whipping he received the previous evening.[179]

A great sigh of relief could be heard across the Monroe area as it was announced the Rev. Tripp would not be accepting the call to fill the pulpit of the Highland Baptist Church, in Shreveport, Louisiana. Commenting on his refusal to accept a higher paying position, the article stated, "In this day of extreme selfishness it is unusual to find a man willing to sacrifice personal advancement for a cause he knows to be right.[180] It is obvious that he was a deeply loved and highly respected member of the community.

From Senatobia, Mississippi came the account of how the entire congregation of a black church was arrested this day in an effort to learn the identify of parties who murdered Andrew Johnson, church treasurer. Three hundred dollars of church funds were missing. When he was found, Johnson's pockets had been turned inside out.[181] No follow up article could be located to this story.

FRIDAY SEPTEMBER 1, 1922

Monroe Klan Plans Big Ceremony for Next Monday Night
More Than 500 Novitiates to Be Initiated Into Unusual Organization
Public Ceremonial to be at Forsythe Park[182]

A representative of the Monroe News-Star is reliably informed that Monroe Klan No. 4 Realm of Louisiana, Knights of the Ku Klux Klan, will stage an open air initiation of members at Forsythe park at 8 o'clock Monday night.

The public is cordially invited to witness this novel exhibition from the grand stand at the park which will be prepared for their accommodation. A brass band will dispense suitable music during the performance.

The grandstand will be securely guarded by Knights of the Ku Klux Klan in full uniform, assisted by policemen from the city force, assuring perfect order and

---

178 Ibid.

179 Ibid.

180 Ibid.

181 Ibid.

182 *Monroe News-Star,* 1 September 1922.

73

good feeling during the ceremony.

All visitors are warned not to attempt to pass the ropes or guards in front of the grandstand, as no outsider will be permitted to pass beyond this line.

The ceremony promises to establish a red letter day in the history of Labor Day in Monroe, as there will be a class of approximately 500 men naturalized into the invisible empire on this occasion. Monroe Klan now numbers among its members nearly 1000 citizens, according to the Klan.

Monroe Klan has contributed $100 to striking shopmen. The letter accompanying the donation follows:

August 31, 1922.

Mr. C. N. Story,
General Chairman
Federated Shop Crafts
Monroe, La.

As a small token of our regard for the laboring men of Monroe and to emphasize our approval of the orderly and sensible manner in which they have handled their difficulties with the railroad companies, we present to you herewith our check for one hundred dollars, to be used by you, or by your board, for the relief of families, which may be in distress among the striking shopmen of Monroe, Louisiana.

May the God of justice guide and direct you and your brethren in your every effort for a settlement of your troubles and may the success which you deserve crown your efforts in the end, and may that end be near.

Yours for justice tempered with mercy in all things human,

MONROE KLAN NO. 4
Realm of Louisiana, Knights of the Ku Klux Klan.
By order of the Exalted Cyclops.

Can you imagine the excitement created by this news? Bear in mind that, for the most part, people during this time were left to their own devices for entertainment. There were some movie houses, and broadcast radio was in existence, but it was still in its infancy during this period. People, especially in northeast Louisiana where boredom was the order of the day, jumped at the chance to witness this once-in-a-lifetime event. Read carefully the preceding article, and you may notice a distinct bias in the author.

The preceding article also quotes a letter and a donation given by Monroe Klan No. 4 to the striking rail workers. This had been a long and bloody strike. Many had been killed on both sides, many injured, and the rail companies had suffered untold losses in trestles, track, rail cars, and equipment, which had been sabotaged by the strikers. As you have seen by previous articles concerning the strike, it was an issue which touched the lives of everyone because during that period nearly all goods were shipped either by rail or by ship.

The day after the initiation, September 5, 1922, the *Monroe News-Star* again treated the Klan initiation with great homage and respect.

TUESDAY SEPTEMBER 5, 1922

Large Numbers in Allegiance to New Invisible Empire
Spectacular Ceremonial Is Conducted in Orderly and Peaceful Manner
Initiation ends with Song of the South, Home[183]

Under a flaming red cross, while from 3,000 to 5,000 people watched, Monroe Klan No. 4, Realm of Louisiana Knights of the Ku Klux Klan, last night at Forsythe Park inducted into the mysteries of that organization about one hundred noviitiates from various parts of Northeast Louisiana.

Hundreds of people began to come in automobiles and by train early, crowding rural highways and thoroughfares.

Prior to nightfall and sometime before the ceremonies began they were assembled at the baseball grandstand at Forsythe Park and in cars around the building, eager for the opportunity to witness one of the most weird and picturesque ceremonies ever given in this part of the state.

The crowd which witnessed the ceremony was enthusiastic but orderly. Klansmen in uniforms kept spectators back from the field where the initiation was staged.

Shortly after 9 o'clock a bugle sounded in the distance, the ritual then began. In a wide open field, in a semi-circle, stretching for a mile, more or less, Klansmen began to gather in their hoods and white robes, marching along the race track that stretches over that section of the park.

Although possibly 100 Klansmen were on the field, when the signal was sounded for the ceremony to begin and two Knights in uniform rode down the stretch, hooded figures sprung up as if by magic from the wooded section to the rear.

"Onward Christian Soldiers" was played by the **Knights of Pythias** [my emphasis] band during the ceremony.

Spectators Thrilled

Scoffers and those who may believe in the tenets of the Ku Klux Klan were alike thrilled by the ceremony. At times they cheered: on other occasions, when there was a particularly effective or solemn part of the ceremony, there was silence throughout the vast throng.

No effort was made at any time to interfere with the ceremonial, nor was there apparently any desire to get beyond the ropes, which held back the spectators from the vast natural amphitheater.

Right in the middle of the ceremonial, as if part of that weird initiation, flames shot high in the sky from the city to the south. An alarm of fire was sounded and through the audience it was whispered that "Monroe was on fire."

Later spectators were reassured that the fire in the city was not part of the ceremony, but was incidental.

Klansmen at this stage of the ceremony began to gather around the fiery cross and there, with the novitiates on their knees, the most impressive part of the ritual was carried out. Klansmen far back from the audience sang "My Country

---

[183] *Monroe News-Star,* 5 September 1922.

'Tis of Thee" and when the patriotic hymn began thousands of spectators rose to their feet and cheered.

The Klan ceremonial was brought to a close when the Knights of Pythias band played "Dixie," which brought repeated cheers from the spectators, the song of the south being followed by "Home Sweet Home."

One hundred and twenty-two candidates were admitted to the order at last night's ceremonial, according to official announcement of Monroe Klan No. 4.

Spokesmen for the Klan were not able to state as to how many Klansmen took part in the exercise. They said a large number of their members were in the audience. They said they believed they had close to 500 Klansmen at the initiation exercise, many of their numbers being in groups a considerable distance from the field where the exercises were staged, hence not visible to the spectators.

A number of persons in the grandstand counted as high as 298 Klansmen in uniforms.

Circulars were distributed at the initiation, giving the objects, aims and purposes of the organization, as follows:

"To unite Native-born White Christian men who owe no allegiance to any foreign government, nation, ruler, person, or people, who attain to the standard of good morals and sound minds, in a common brotherhood for the purpose of cultivating and promoting real patriotism toward our civil government; to practice an honorable clannishness toward earth other; to shield the sanctity of the home and the chastity of womanhood; and to forever maintain white supremacy.

"If you believe in these principles, we are entitled to your support and cooperation, if you do not, we shall not expect it. We are growing faster than any organization has ever grown, and increasing in numbers at the rate of Ten Thousand per week."

The reverent manner in which the reporter composed this article clearly speaks volumes as to the author's sentiments concerning the Klan. Again, bear in mind that this article had to have been approved by the editorial staff of the paper. Therefore, the solemn and dignified fashion in which the Klan was handled by this author was sanctioned by those managing the paper.

This preferential and loving treatment also demonstrates quite clearly how near and dear to the hearts of many in northeast Louisiana the Klan was. The ideas and tenets of the Klan still burn bright in the hearts of many in northeast Louisiana nearly three-quarters of a century later. This was made empirical by election results from northeast Louisiana of the 1992 Louisiana gubernatorial election, which pitted David Duke, long-time standard bearer for the Ku Klux Klan and founder of the National Association for the Advancement of White People (NAAWP), against Edwin Edwards, who had been tainted by scandal and two trials in federal court, from both of which he emerged victorious. Almost as a solid block, nearly all of the parishes in northeast Louisiana voted overwhelmingly for Duke. Ouachita and

Morehouse Parishes, the two parishes that became the focus of the nation, were counted in Duke's corner and by a large majority.

It was also reported this day by the Associated Press that delegates to the Texas State Democratic Convention were preparing to introduce resolutions to denounce the Klan and its tenets. This concern was generated when Earle B. Mayfield, an alleged Klan candidate and member of the Texas Railroad Commission, received the nomination for United States Senator over James E. Fergerson, a former governor of Texas. Unlike the vast majority of the politicians in the state of Louisiana who turned a blind eye to the Klan, the political community in most other states began to recognize the danger incarnate in the Klan.

In what must have been one more in a series of embarrassments for the Ku Klux Klan, Dorsey J. Dunlap, a member of the last House of Delegates, and an admitted member of the Ku Klux Klan and a candidate for Congress in the Fifth Maryland District on a "bone dry" platform, was arrested for driving under the influence. Dunlap claimed that the charges were a "frame up."

Young Woman Dies of Overstudy[184]

From Syracuse, New York, came the story of the 23-year-old daughter of Professor and Mrs. Joseph Park, Helen, would had "died at the family home in Oswego today from overstudy." She was attending Wells College at the time of her death.

FRIDAY SEPTEMBER 8, 1922
M'Koin to Testify at Investigations Into Recent Events
Morehouse Jury Said to Have Failed to Secure Evidence On Kidnapping[185]

The last witness to testify before the grand jury convened in the Bastrop courthouse concerning the reign of terror in Morehouse Parish at the hands of the Ku Klux Klan was Dr. B. M. McKoin. Interestingly enough, the *Monroe New-Star* felt the alleged assassination attempt on McKoin to be more important than the kidnapping of five Mer Rouge men and the continued disappearance of two of those who were kidnapped by Klansmen. The manner in which the article was written seemed to focus more attention on the alleged assassination attempt than the other happenings.

---

[184]*The New York Times*, 5 September 1922.
[185]Ibid.

Bastrop District Attorney David I Garrett, of Monroe, summed up the lack of action of the grand jury, which was under his direction, with the following statement:

"We have found out absolutely nothing in regard to the mysterious kidnapping of five Mer Rouge citizens by a band of masked men in Morehouse parish as a result of the investigation of the Morehouse parish grand jury," declared Garrett.

"The kidnapping of the five and the disappearance of the two men, Watt Daniel and Thomas Richards, is as great a mystery as ever and will probably never be solved. My opinion at the present time is that these two men were killed and their bodies thrown into some bayou."

In short, District Attorney Garret threw up his hands and gave up on the case. The last line of his statement bears close scrutiny. It appears as though Garret had a great deal more information concerning the whereabouts of Daniel and Richards because their horribly mutilated bodies would be found floating in Bayou LaFourche three months later. Was this just a good guess, or did Garrett already know the location of the bodies? In light of the fact that there are only two or three bayous in Morehouse Parish, and given the myriad of possibilities of disposal of dead bodies, it seems more than just coincidental that he would make such a statement.

As for the all-seeing eyes of the grand jury, the general public has little knowledge of just how grand juries operate and how they are often manipulated by unscrupulous self-serving district attorney-politicians. The district attorney guides the grand jury in whichever direction s/he so wishes, by either including or excluding evidence or witnesses concerning a certain matter. As will be revealed later, certain witnesses were not called before the grand jury.

Furthermore, it is the responsibility of the district attorney to make certain that the grand jury is composed of unbiased members of the community. An Associated Press dispatch this date from Bastrop reported today that John McIllwain, a Mer Rouge resident, had refused to testify before the grand jury. In the grand jury room, McIllwain said that one of the members of the grand jury had been a member of the black-hooded Klan which had kidnapped the five Mer citizens, including the two missing men, Daniel and Richards, that August evening on the Bastrop-Mer Rouge road. Garrett and other members of the grand jury refused comment on McIllwain's statement. Regarding witness statements, District Attorney Garrett said:

"J. L. Daniel, 'Tot' Davenport and W. C. Andrews, three of the five men who were kidnapped and who returned to their homes at Mer Rouge alive following the mysterious kidnapping affair, testified before the grand jury," Garret said. "They gave considerable evidence, but nothing that would aid officers of Morehouse parish and the district court to solve the murder or kidnapping mystery. So far as the session of the grand jury is concerned, the incident is closed. I do not believe that the mystery will ever be solved."

Once again, Garrett appears to give indications that he knew more concerning the disposition of Daniel and Richards. He referred to Daniel, Davenport and Andrews as those who "returned to their homes at Mer Rouge **alive** [my emphasis]." Why would he, a seasoned barrister and district attorney, use such a word if he did not already have an indication that Daniel and Richards were dead? In his next sentence, he declared that "the **murder** [my emphasis] and kidnapping mystery" would never be solved. Again, he seemed to have knowledge that Daniel and Richards had been murdered. These statements appear to indicate that District Attorney Garrett was well aware that Daniel and Richards had been murdered and that he knew that the bodies had been thrown into a nearby body of water. Yet, he made the statement, "the incident is closed." An unsolved murder case is never closed. There is no statute of limitations on murder.

All things taken into consideration, it seems to appear as though District Attorney Garrett knows a great deal more than he is willing to say. It also appears as though he is very anxious to dispose of this case for reasons known only so himself. As will be shown later, it appears as though District Attorney Garrett intentionally maneuvered the grand jury to protect the Klan and that he knowingly refused to allow willing witnesses to testify before it. In all likelihood, Garrett may have been himself a Klansman.

Negro Killed by Mob[186]

Beaumont, Texas, was the scene of mob murder of O. J. Johnson, a black man, charged with the murder of a turpentine camp foreman near Hemphill. The report said that Johnson "was taken from the jail at Newton at 1 o'clock this morning by a mob, strung to a tree limb and his body riddled with bullets.

---

[186]Ibid.

In San Antonio, Texas, democrats refused to take a stand on the issue of the Ku Klux Klan. As a result, an anti-Ku Klux Klan political party was to be organized in Texas. While a desperate effort was made by anti-Klan democrats to have passed a resolution condemning the Klan and its activities, the convention refused to either condemn or commend the Klan. The fight on the Klan question occurred when a move was made to bring to the floor a minority report openly denouncing the Klan. An uproar followed, culminating in the convention tabling the minority report by a vote of 691 to 135. Chief among the planks in the adopted platform of the democratic party was recommendation establishing the democratic party is a "white man's party."[187]

In Chicago, the first issue of the weekly paper called "Tolerance," published by the American Unity League, opposed to the Ku Klux Klan, appeared,[188] and over Mahasset Bay, near Port Washington, L. I., Glenn H. Curtiss, pioneer in American aeronautics, unexpectedly made a sustained flight lasting nine seconds while his aquatic gliding plane was being towed by a speed boat back to the hangar. The glider had a wingspread of 28 feet, a length over all of 24 feet, and a height of 7 feet. Its weight empty was 140 pounds.[189]

SATURDAY SEPTEMBER 9, 1922

Morehouse Jury is Unable to Secure Kidnapping Clues
Report to Judge Fred M. Odom in District Court as to Its Findings[190]
Ku Klux Klan Held Responsible and Citizens Urged to Assist in Fathoming Crime by Parker
Chief Executive Directs Full Power of Attorney General For Morehouse Probe[191]

The Morehouse Parish grand jury officially reported to Judge Fred. M. Odom that they were unable to locate any evidence concerning the atrocities committed by the Ku Klux Klan in that parish, including the case involving Watt Daniel and Thomas Richards. Again the article seemed written to garner support and sympathy for Dr. McKoin as a number of paragraphs chronicled his alleged assassination attempt.

---

187 *Monroe News-Star*, 7 September 1922.

188 *Monroe News-Star*, 8 September 1922.

189 *The New York Times*, 6 September 1922.

190 Ibid.

191 Ibid.

Meanwhile, Governor Parker received the following letter from the wife of the missing and presumed dead Thomas Richards:

> I am left entirely without a home, no relatives, or money for my two children or myself. I have two little girls to raise and was absolutely dependent upon my husband's daily labor for support. And just because he was not scared by the klan they have done this, and they are now trying to make out it was not the klan, but it was the klan, as otherwise they would have been willing and ready to help me find my husband. I believe he is dead because I know he would have written if he is alive, and I am nearly crazy with suspense and pray to God for help. Won't you do what you can?

Mrs. Richards' letter prompted Governor Parker to direct the following letter to Attorney General Coco:

> When mob violence and the 'invisible klan' attempt to rise superior to the laws of our state, every power at our command should be exercised to stamp out such violence and have peace, law and order prevail.
>
> You are hereby requested to make vigorous and through investigation of the outrages committed in Morehouse parish. Take prompt steps for a thorough investigation, early indictment and vigorous prosecution of those responsible. The full power of the state, civil and military, will be at your command.
>
> The issue is clearly drawn. Neither mob violence nor the Ku Klux Klan shall run this state. The law must and shall prevail and your vigorous prompt assistance is relied on.

Governor Parker also issued the following proclamation:

> Whereas, in violation of the law, masked men have forcibly taken reputable citizens from their homes, flogged and punished them and,
>
> Whereas, T. F. Richards and Watt Daniel, two of these citizens have disappeared, and it has been impossible to find them,
>
> Now, therefore, I, John M. Parker. governor of the State of Louisiana, do hereby issue this, my proclamation, offering a reward of $500 for the arrest and conviction of those responsible for this gross violation of the law and appeal to good citizens in the parish of Morehouse to lend me a helping hand in securing the prompt arrest and conviction of those guilty of such outrages.

Unfortunately, very little help would be forthcoming from the 'good citizens' in Morehouse Parish.

Move is Made to Oust Floggers and Such by Gov. Jelk's Committee[192]

Texas was not the only site of anti-Klan sentiment. It was also stirring in Birmingham, Alabama, as former Governor Wm. D. Jelks headed a committee of 25 citizens who appeared before Commissioner of Safety Cloe and offered their services to aid in a campaign to apprehend floggers and others responsible for lawlessness in the community. Jelks said that it was long past time "to give the

---

[192]Ibid.

floggers a 'dose of their own medicine.

> It has come to pass that to beat a man up, to take him away from his family and flog him unto death and even murder a man, is a mere pastime, free from danger. We understand the mob spirit running through the community. We understand your limitations, your small police force. At the same time we are impressed that a larger force would probably not greatly mend matters. Any force you could get would be too small, and hence, we appear, representing some thousands of good citizens from every walk of life, to make the fight with you. The men associated in the movement will undertake to help you find the criminals; but, more that that, they will furnish every protection to witnesses to the end that the murderers, beaters and floggers get a swift trial and justice.
>
> We offer you our moral support, some finances and physical force to the end that we can write across the gates of Birmingham a line like this: "Status shall be respected."

The Royal Confectionery in Monroe announced the special for the day as Tutty Frutti Ice Cream, Pineapple Sherbet and Sultana roll for 50 cents per quart.[193]

MONDAY SEPTEMBER 11, 1922

Rev. Tripp Breaks Down in Grayson's Revival on Sunday
Popular Pastor is Removed to St. Francis Sanitarium in This City[194]

While conducting revival services at Grayson, Louisiana, Rev. Frank Tripp, suffered a nervous breakdown and was transported to Monroe by ambulance. John S. Raymond, assistant pastor, said that the breakdown had been brought about by the strain under which Tripp been working. Fear not, he will return in plenty of time to vouch for the character of one of the murders of Daniel and Richards, Dr. B. M. McKoin.

TUESDAY SEPTEMBER 12, 1922

Mrs. Richards Claims to have Additional Evidence[195]

> Mrs. Thomas Richards, wife of one of the victims of the Mer Rouge kidnapping, states that she has written Governor Parker to determine as to whether it is advisable for her to take action against the Morehouse Ku Klux Klan to force the klan to give her information as to the present whereabouts of her husband, if he is still alive, or information that would disclose the cause and manner of his death.
>
> Mrs. Richards declared that she was anxious to testify at the session of the Morehouse parish grand jury, but was not permitted to offer evidence.
>
> "I could have helped to have cleared up the mystery surrounding the kidnapping of the five Mer Rouge men and the disappearance of my husband and of Watt Daniel," she said. "The fact of the matter is that I have evidence which I believe would lead to the identification of the first band that took my husband to the

[193]Ibid.

[194]*Monroe News-Star*, 11 September 1922.

[195]*Monroe News-Star*, 12 September 1922.

woods and I am ready and willing to offer it."

That there may be a resumption of the investigation into the Morehouse parish kidnapping is the belief of most people throughout this region. The Morehouse parish grand jury will remain in session for six months and is subject to the call of David I Garrett, district attorney, who states he is willing to go into the case more thoroughly, if there is additional evidence to be secured.

Mrs. Richards stated that she would like to get the opportunity to testify before the parish grand jury. "I offered to testify last week," she said, "but I was not permitted to do so. I would be glad to go before the jury and tell the jurors what my husband told me when he was first kidnapped. I have something that I want to say to the jury. I have evidence that ought to be in their hands. I do not understand why they did not permit me to testify last week, because what I know, what I was told by my husband, would go a long way toward clearing up the mystery."

In Baton Rouge, Attorney General A. V. Coco met with Governor Parker regarding the state's judicial investigation of the Mer Rouge outrages and the Klan kidnappings of Watt Daniel and Thomas Richards. Parker had received additional letters giving confirmation that the Klan was responsible for the kidnappings.[196]

In a demonstration of Klan boldness, from Jasper, Alabama, came a report that State Senator M. L. Leith, Circuit Judge T. L. Sowell, Circuit Solicitor J. M. Rennington and 13 other leading citizens of the county were warned in a letter and signed "Ku Klux Klan" to "shut up your big talk, otherwise you will carry marks to your grave." The letter was sent to derail and investigation into the flogging of a woman and two men the previous week. The text of the entire letter read:

> This is service on you as well as those listed below that we will not tolerate any more of your big talk of what you are going to do to the Klan. We care nothing about what your name is, station in life, or your title. This is a farewell warning, otherwise you will carry the marks to your grave that your folks will always be able to distinguish you from other people. Shut up is the word. Don't think that our number is not sufficient to handle all of you as we can call in aid from adjoining counties as well as other states[197]

THURSDAY SEPTEMBER 14, 1922

Mer Rouge Mayor Makes Public His Anonymous Letters
Dade's Life Not Threatened by Letters from Monroe and Rayville[198]

At a news conference today, Robert L. Dade, mayor of Mer Rouge, made available to reporters the contents of the two threatening letters which he had recently received. Mayor Dade denied that his life had been threatened. "I have not

---

[196]Ibid.
[197]Ibid.

been ordered out of town in any of the anonymous letters received," said the mayor, "but the letters are threatening in their nature."

The first letter displayed by Mayor Dade was typewritten and post marked September 7 from Rayville, and it was as follows:

> The mayor and good citizens of Mer Rouge:
> You are wallowing in a cesspool of corruption and lawlessness has become a menace to the parish and community. You are shielding within your gates men who live in open concubinage with negroes and who make whiskey and sell it. These men have formulated plots to assassinate good citizens in the night time and who are deluging good, law-abiding citizens of your parish with written and oral threats against their lives.
> The condition must be rectified, or we will swoop down upon your town, and wipe out the organization responsible for these conditions and who are pleased to call themselves Anti-Ku Klux Klan. We know everyone of the men who formulated and attempted to execute the plot to assassinate Dr. McKoin. Two of them have passed into obscurity and the balance will soon follow unless they read between the lines and leave while the leaving is good.
> [signed] Regulators.

The second letter was dated September 11, and was postmarked on that date by the Monroe post office. This letter was also typewritten in red and executed on yellow paper. The letter was similar to the previous letter, and it is believed that not all of the letter was printed. What was printed follows:

> honorable mayor, Mr. R. L. Dade:
> We will give you ample time to clean up and will, if you fail to do so, bring one thousand men to Mer Rouge and do the job right. The names of the men who sat at the round table and planned and submitted the planning to assassinate Dr. McKoin are known to us. We have had able men to get all data up. So now we know all that was said and done and will attend to them in due time.

There was no indication of signature on the letter.

Concerning other rumors, the mayor said, "The report that I have received any other communications or that the contents were other than I have given is untrue. There are the only two letters I have. The statement that I was ordered out of town of course does me injustice and these are the facts. We are all doing what we can to overcome the difficulties arising out of the recent Morehouse parish affair."

Questions arise as to, who was the author of these letters, and, if we accept that the Klan was responsible for these letters, did the Klan have the wherewithal to back up the threats? With regard to the first question, it will be shown later that the typewritten threatening letter which had been received by Dr. McKoin had been

---

[198]*Monroe News-Star*, 14 September 1922.

written on Dr. McKoin's own machine by none other than Dr. McKoin himself. It is entirely possible that Dr. McKoin was the author of these letters also. Bear in mind that Dr. McKoin had left Mer Rouge and was residing in Monroe at that time. Clearly, Dr. McKoin was a diabolical conscienceless man bent on forcing his will on all around him.

As to whether the threat to clean up the town by the Klan was an idle boast, it will be shown through news reports that on November 28, 1922, over 250 Klansmen attacked the area residents of Smackover, Arkansas, in an attempt to "clean up" that town. This vigilante purge left one man dead, many wounded and property burned to the ground. With such evidence, the answer to the second question is an unqualified yes.

Flogging was not a punishment restricted to men as this dispatch from Ft. Worth, Texas indicates. According to the report, Ms. I. C. Tatum, of Stop Six, Dallas, was decoyed from her home and given 100 lashes with a cat-o-nine-tails by four masked women. The whipping was allegedly given by a "committee of four" of the "Ladies 'Invisible Eye.' " The beating was administered for alleged ruining of her daughter Naomi Tatum, 14.[199]

FRIDAY SEPTEMBER 15, 1922
Branded by Masked Men
White-Robed Mob Punishes Pennsylvania Laborer for Abuse of Mother[200]

From Chambersburg, Pennsylvania, came an account of Klan related violence. William Hollingsworth, a laborer of Waynesboro, was "taken out" and mistreated by masked men robed in white like the Ku Klux Klan and had the letter "K" branded on each cheek and his forehead. There was no clue to the identity of the 15 to 20 men Hollingsworth said attacked him.

His attackers told him that he was branded because he had treated his mother cruelly. His hair had been cut in a grotesque manner and one side of his mustache was cut off. When he denied he had cruelly treated his mother he was beaten with sticks. A rope was tied about his neck and his attackers talked of hanging him. The white-robed mob left him in the field and he found his way home.

---

[199]Ibid.
[200]*The New York Times,* 15 September 1922.

SATURDAY SEPTEMBER 16, 1922
Alexandria Ku Klux May Parade of Ku Kluxers Want To[201]

In Alexandria, Louisiana, the local Ku Klux Klan was given permission to hold a parade. A proposed city ordinance, which would have prevented masked or Klan parades, was defeated in a city election by a majority of 341 votes. The vote was 1,184 against the ordinance, 843 for. The total of 2,027 votes out of a possible 2,100 qualified was a record vote for Alexandria.

Rev. Tripp is Back on Streets, Preaches at Church on Sunday[202]

The residents of the Monroe area rejoiced in the news that Rev. Frank Tripp would resume his pulpit Sunday. Praise the Lord!

Dispatches from Paris told of a storm of controversy that had resulted from the showing of D. W. Griffith's "Orphans of the Storm."[203] Griffith had just a few years earlier produced and directed the three-hour silent epic drama "Birth of a Nation" which played a major role in the second resurgence of the Klan because of the strong emotions it evoked from theatergoers.

MONDAY SEPTEMBER 18, 1922
Judge Odom in his Charge Asks Probe of Growing Unrest
Ouachita Grand Jury is Organized Today[204]

A strict enforcement of the law, particularly at this time, was the underlying sentiment contained in Judge Odom's charge to the Ouachita Grand Jury, which was empaneled Monday morning for the coming term.

While not mentioning the outrages at Mer Rouge, which have stirred the entire community, Judge Odom by expressly pointing out the state of unrest which is manifested in the community, urged the members of the grand jury to bring all delinquents to justice, and irrespective of favoritism to return indictments in those cases where evidence warrants.

"We must enforce out laws. Strict adherence to the statutes is the only solution to our troubles and the only way to bring peace to the community," said Odom.

"The state is supreme and the grand jury as its servant must assist it in every manner by bringing in true bills where there is evidence of guilt."

The judge called attention to the censure leveled against the courts and officers in authority, admitting that the courts and officials were not doing all that might be done to enforce the law, but at once pointed out the duty of each citizen in the community to act in the event of a law violation.

"It is your duty not only to bring in indictments, but to report all violations. Each citizen in the community should consider himself bound to bring violators

---

[201] *Monroe News-Star,* 16 September 1922.

[202] Ibid.

[203] *The New York Times,* 16 September 1922.

[204] *Monroe News-Star,* 18 September 1922.

to justice thus materially assisting the courts and officials to perform their duty."

Examination of later events during and after the open hearings conducted on the kidnappings and murders of Watt Daniel and Thomas Richards will cause questions to arise as to where the loyalty of Judge Odom lay.

Mer Rouge Affair Remains Unsolved, No Clues Obtained
Missing Men, Dead or Alive, Were Probably Taken Into Arkansas[205]
Ku Klux Klan is Viewed as Big Issue in Louisiana Politics[206]

It was reported today that search parties had been unsuccessful in their attempts to learn the whereabouts of Watt Daniel and Thomas Richards. The reason they were unsuccessful was probably because they had been "sent out by those directing the processes of the law in Morehouse." The assertion was made that W. C. Andrews and J. L. Daniel, father of Watt, had been "released not far from the Louisiana-Arkansas border," and because of this it "leads investigators to believe that Watt Daniel and Richards, either dead or alive, were taken into Arkansas."

This sounds good until you check out the facts on a map. Collinston, the location where W. C. Andrews and J. L. Daniel were released, is located nine miles southwest of Mer Rouge and eight miles southeast of Bastrop. Bastrop and Mer Rouge are located seven miles east and west of each other, respectively. Even without a map, it is clear that a triangle is formed between the three towns and that Collinston is located on the southern tip of that triangle. This means that the *Monroe New-Star* story is totally misleading because Collinston is located 25 miles from the Louisiana-Arkansas border, and it would be necessary to pass through either Mer Rouge or Bastrop to get there.

There were three pieces of conventional wisdom circulating in Morehouse Parish at that time concerning the fate of Daniel and Richards. The first was that they were both being held prisoners in Ashley County, Arkansas, which is the county that directly borders Morehouse Parish. The second rumor was that Daniel had been murdered and Richards was being held captive along the same border. The last was that both men had been murdered and that they had been buried somewhere in Arkansas. The last paragraph of this article contained the following unattributed claim:

---

[205] *Monroe News-Star*, 18 September 1922.
[206] Ibid.

> Arkansas cars were also seen in the crowd that took the men out, according to relatives of the missing citizens who say they believe that a majority of the members of the band which kidnapped them were not residents of Morehouse parish.

This would have been entirely possible, as it was common practice for neighboring Klans to cross state borders to assist other Klans.

On the political front, is was revealed today that L. E. Thomas, who was nominated for mayor of Shreveport, Louisiana, in last Tuesday's election primary, shall be the a candidate for the next governors race and that he was slated to receive the full endorsement of the Ku Klux Klan.

Political observers in Shreveport remarked that the Klan had been an open issue in the primary, and that the Klan had lined up solidly behind Thomas. Thomas, who was the bank examiner for the state of Louisiana, was to step down from that post when he became mayor of Shreveport. Also out of Shreveport came the report that Joseph Dixon, an avowed Klansman, had won the primary nomination for commissioner of finance. He too received the full backing of the Klan.

It was said that Caddo Parish, of which the city of Shreveport is a part, was a stronghold for the Klan in Louisiana. Informed sources claimed that there were as many as 4,500 Klansmen in the parish. The Klan was not, however, without an adversary.

The then chairman of the public service commission and soon to be nationally famous Louisiana governor, Huey Long, was said to be " 'at outs' with the Ku Klux Klan and will fight candidates backed by that organization in the next state campaign." The unnamed author of the article summed up the Klan's involvement in Louisiana politics this way:

> Victories of the Klan in Shreveport and Alexandria elections in the opinion of politicians who were here this week, will precipitate the opening of the state campaign much earlier than was expected. In spite of efforts in certain quarters to prevent it, political wiseacres believe that the Ku Klux Klan will be one of the big issues in the next state contest.

Out of Alexandria, Louisiana, came the account of Nathan Richardson, a black man, who was shot four times when he was apprehended in LaSalle Parish by a white posse. He was charged with the assault of an aged LaSalle Parish farmer who was also his landlord. In order to avoid the lynch mob that was gathering, Sheriff J. B. Peyton, of Jena, moved Richardson to another jail in the early hours of the morning. He was charged with having assaulted S. R. Crooks, a LaSalle farmer.

'Sea Monsters' Attack Newfoundland Boats
Scare Fishermen From Grounds--Expedition to Capture Them is Planned[208]

From St. John's, N. F., came the report of sea monsters 40 to 60 feet long attacking boats fishing in British Harbor and Trinity Bay. A large school of these "monsters," for which no detailed description was received, appeared off the coast and were still thought to be in the bay. The appearance of the school was reported to the Department of Marine and Fisheries by the telegraph operator at British Harbor.

TUESDAY SEPTEMBER 19, 1922
Dr. M'Koin Will go to Johns Hopkins to Study for Six Months[209]

Differences among residents of Mer Rouge growing out of the kidnapping of five citizens nearly four weeks ago and the disappearance of Watt Daniel and T. F. Richards have been reconciled to a great extent, it is reported. "People are now more willing to let bygones be bygones," said Dr. B. M. McKoin.
Dr. McKoin said he would not return to Mer Rouge to practice his profession, but that he would leave within a few days to become a student at Johns Hopkins university at Baltimore. On his return to Monroe within six months, he will take up the practice of his profession here.

After all that has been written concerning the kidnappings and the then possible murders of Watt Daniel and Thomas Richards, it seems incredible that the foregoing article could have been printed in any responsible publication. This article further serves to indict the *Monroe New-Star* and gives a clear indication as to its editorial policy concerning the outrages involving the Ku Klux Klan. It can only be wondered just how many persons in the employ of the *New-Star* were members of the Klan.

---

[207] Ibid.
[208] *The New York Times*, 18 September 1922.
[209] Ibid.

Klan Gives Ouachita Pastor Purse of $10: Letter Commends Him[210]
Rev. J. W. Saterfiel,
Peniel Baptist Church,
Ouachita Parish, La.

Dear Sir:
Please accept this small offering as an evidence of our desire to express to you our sincere approval of the work you are doing and assure you that we wish to co-operate with you in every way we possibly can.
The foundation on which our order is built is made up of the Bible, the Cross and the American flag, and from these three, we draw all that we pretend to believe and endeavor to exemplify. From the Bible, we learn of the way the Master trod, and in our own weak unworthy way we try to follow in His footsteps to the cross, where we learn of sacrifice and service, and from the flag we draw the inspiration to endeavor each day to practice those principles which we call American.
May God bless you sir, and the church you are serving, and grant that you may be an instrument in His hands to help to bring about the things that we strive for each day, and make this old world a better place in which to live and more worthy to be called "the footstool of God."

Sincerely yours, (ITSUB)
Monroe Klan No. 4
Realm of Louisiana
Invisible Empire
Knights of the Ku Klux Klan.
(By the Exalted Cyclop.)

This foregoing letter with $10 was presented to the pastor of the Peniel Baptist Church on the night of Sept. 14 by 15 masked men bearing the American flag and the burning cross, whose visit and offering was said to have been appreciated by the pastor.

A report from Frederick City, Maryland this date told of open opposition to the formation of the Ku Klux Klan when 20 shots were fired at members of the Frederick Klan during a ceremony at which a number of candidates were inducted. One of the bullets shattered the windshield of a Klansman's automobile. A member of the Klan returned the fire until the attacking party retreated.[211]

WEDNESDAY SEPTEMBER 20, 1922
Ku Klux Commend Work of Girard Minister

Rev. Dan C. Barr, pastor in charge of the Methodist church at Girard, Richland parish [Louisiana], is in receipt of the following self-explanatory letter:

---

[210]*Monroe News-Star*, 19 September 1922.
[211]Ibid.

The tenets of the Christian religion being the foundation of our faith, we are therefore interested in the well being and welfare of our Protestant churches, and as a token of our appreciation and in recognition of your service in the uplifting of man and the upbuilding of God's Holy Kingdom, we take this method and opportunity of extending the greetings and felicitations of Richland Klan No. 6, Knights of the Ku Klux Klan, Realm of Louisiana.

In our creed we reverentially acknowledge the All Wise Creator, His supremacy and goodness and admonish obedience to his commands.

The government of the United States, its constitution and laws; the union of states and the constitutional laws thereof, we uphold and defend. Pure Americanism being one of our sublime principles, we shall be valiant in the defense of American ideals and institutions.

The distinction between races of mankind, as decreed by the Creator, impels us to avow the faithful maintenance of white supremacy, and any compromise thereof shall be opposed by us in any and all things.

We appreciate the real value of a practical, fraternal relationship among men of kindred thought, purpose and ideals and the infinite benefits accruable therefrom, and shall faithfully devote ourselves to the practice of an honorable clannishness, so that the life and living of each may be a constant blessing to others.

We abhor and purpose to suppress all manner of vice and immorality by the most adequate and efficient legal means at our command.

We propose to promptly and properly meet every behest of duty "without fear and without reproach."

"Non Silba Seb Anthar."

Please accept the enclosed contribution as a token of our appreciation, love and esteem, and may you be spared many more years in the performance of that noble service you are rendering for the glory of God and the good of His Kingdom.

> Very respectfully
> RICHLAND KLAN NO. 6
> Knights of the Ku Klux Klan
> Realm of Louisiana.[212]

Rev. Barr will appear later to give a brazen endorsement of the Ku Klux Klan. The reader is reminded that many Southern Protestant ministers wore two different sets of ceremonial robes: One for the church and the other for the Klan.

Also appearing in the news this date was a call to free Armenia. The American Committee for Armenian Independence circulated a memorial to be presented to the State Department urging the powers to create an independent Armenia.[213] This article is another that seems as though it could have stepped off the front page of any present-day newspaper.

---

[212]*Monroe News-Star,* 20 September 1922.

[213]*The New York Times,* 20 September 1922.

91

FRIDAY SEPTEMBER 22, 1922
Henry Ford Plant's Resume Work Today
His Son Arranges With Operators to Obtain an Adequate Supply of Coal Affects 70,000 in Detroit[214]

From Detroit, came the news that Henry Ford's plants reopened at the same rate of operation as when they closed down. This meant work to 70,000 in Detroit at once and later to thousands around the country. Edsel Ford, Henry's son, sent the order from Cincinnati. About 4,000 tons daily were required to run the plant.

A dispatch from Paris announced that Sadi Lecointe, a French flyer, broke the standing world's speed record at Etampes with a speed of more than 341 kilometers an hour (213.08 miles).[215]

SUNDAY SEPTEMBER 24, 1922
Revolt over Klan Gaining in Texas
Many Democrats Support Independent Candidate for Senator Against Mayfield[216]

It was announced in Washington, D.C. that the revolt of Texas Democrats against the Ku Klux Klan and its candidate for the Senate, Earl B. Mayfield, was gaining impetus. Mayfield had been the nominee of the Democratic Party, but his endorsement by the Ku Klux Klan angered many Democrats. As a result, a convention was held in Dallas and an independent Democratic candidate, George E. B. Peddy of Houston, was selected to oppose Mayfield for Senator.

MONDAY SEPTEMBER 25, 1922
Klan Opposition Must Force Issue[217]

Conventional wisdom in Louisiana political circles declared today that the Klan will be obliged to place itself in a position to be attacked in order to become an issue in the upcoming governor's race. It was suggested that this could be accomplished by the Klan secretly selecting a candidate sympathetic to, but not a member of, the Klan. In this fashion, word could be passed through the Klan grapevine in order to align support for that candidate. This would also afford the candidate the opportunity of truthfully denying membership in the Klan when asked. By proceeding this way, Klan opposition would be forced to attack the organization

---

[214]*The New York Times,* 22 September 1922.

[215]Ibid.

[216]*The New York Times,* 24 September 1922.

[217]*Monroe News-Star,* 25 September 1922.

and not the candidate.

Allegedly, this tactic had been successful in the recent governor's race in Georgia, in which Clifford Walker, who had been supported by the Klan, was nominated over incumbent Governor Thomas W. Hardwick, who ran on an anti-Klan platform. Although there seemed to have been much talk concerning the formation of a state-wide anti-Klan organization in Louisiana, it would never materialize.

Klan Demands Dry Raids[218]

In Pittsburgh, Pa. it was reported that Pittsburgh Klan No. 1 informed Federal Prohibition Agent Hawker that he must raid a North Side saloon named by the Klan, and that he should follow the same procedure with the saloons that will be named by the organization. Clearly, the Klan was starting to flex its muscles.

TUESDAY SEPTEMBER 26, 1922

Communists Shown at Work in Klan
Papers Decoded Contain Program for Action in Unions and Ku Klux Organization[219]

Papers seized at a meeting of Communists at St. Joseph, Michigan near Bridgman detailed minutely plans to work within the American Federation of Labor and the Ku Klux Klan. This information was learned after coded papers taken in the raid were deciphered.

Push Lusitania Claims[220]

A meeting of the Lusitania Claimants' Committee, and claimants and counsel representing claims arising out of the sinking of the Lusitania, was to be held in the office of Hunt, Hill & Betts, Room 3111, Equitable Building, 120 Broadway. George Whitefield Betts, Jr. announced that the purpose of the meeting was to "consider the course to be pursued with reference to the bill in Congress for the formation of a claims commission and the payment of claims out of the German Alien Property Fund, and with reference to the joint claims commission arranged for by the Executive Department of the Government."

---

[218]*The New York Times,* 25 September 1922.
[219]*The New York Times,* 26 September 1922.
[220]Ibid.

WEDNESDAY SEPTEMBER 27, 1922

Monroe Klan Will Provide Books for Ouachita Children[221]

Monroe Klan No. 4, Realm of Louisiana, Invisible Empire, Knights of the Ku Klux Klan, at its last regular meeting, according to information given out by the Klan, adopted a resolution whereby free school books will be supplied to the children of Ouachita parish who want to attend the free public school and have been unable to do so on account of the financial condition of parents preventing the purchase of school books. The resolution states that the Knights of the Ku Klux Klan are vitally interested in the free public school system and have been advised that hundreds of children are unable to attend the Ouachita schools because they have no school books and their parents are unable, because of financial reasons, to provide them. The resolution, which was unanimously adopted, provides that the school books may be obtained at a Monroe drugstore. The resolution follows:

Monroe, La., Sept. 26, 1922

At a regular meeting of Monroe Klan No. 4, Realm of Louisiana the following resolution was adopted whereby free school books will be supplied to the children of Ouachita parish, who want to attend the free public schools and have been unable to do so on account of the financial condition of parents preventing the purchase of school books.

Whereas, the Knights if the Ku Klux Klan are vitally interested in the free public school system, whereby it has been made possible for all children, rich and poor alike, regardless of religious belief, to receive a suitable education in strict accord with American principles, and,

Whereas, it has come to our knowledge that some of the children of Ouachita parish are unable to attend school on account of the inability of their parents to provide suitable school books.

Be It Therefore Resolved: That suitable arrangements be made for all children of Ouachita parish, who are unable to provide otherwise and that the treasurer of this klan be authorized to pay any and all bills for this purpose.

Be It Further Resolved: That a copy of this resolution be provided the News-Star Publishing Company in order that anyone knowing of a child, who is in the need of school books, can provide the name and address in order that they can be supplied free of charge by Collens Pharmacy or the New South Drug Store.

Be It Further Resolved: That a copy of this resolution be supplied the superintendent of education of the City of Monroe and the parish of Ouachita and that they be assured that Monroe Klan No. 4 will at all times make necessary provisions to assist the needy children in order to make it possible for them to attend the free public schools.

MONROE KLAN NO. 4
Realm of Louisiana
Invisible Empire
Knights of the Ku Klux Klan
By order of the Exalted Cyclops.

What better way to legitimize the Klan than to offer to buy school books for

---

[221]*Monroe News-Star,* 27 September 1922.

needy families? Although the resolution said "all children," the question goes unanswered as to whether it truly meant all children, regardless of race.

THURSDAY SEPTEMBER 28, 1992

Monroe Citizens Take in Ku Klux Klan's Big Rayville Initiation

It was estimated that more than 200 Monroe citizens were guests and spectators at the initiation of the Ku Klux Klan held at Rayville. Elaborate arrangements were completed by the Rayville Klan for the reception of visitors and candidates and the fair grounds which was converted into an amphitheater. There Rayville residents and spectators, from Vicksburg, Shreveport and Monroe strained to see and hear to mystic ceremonies.

A large barbecue feast was given by the local Klan to the hundreds of visitors and Klansmen and merry-making was said to have continued well into the night. Monroe residents returning from Rayville praised the welcome given them and spoke highly of the Klan which had provided such elaborate entertainment. [222]

Negro Lynched[223]

The report of the lynching of another black man appeared this date from Sandersville, Georgia. Jim Johnson had been taken from officers and lynched while en route to Wrightsville to stand trial. Johnson had been charged with attacking a white woman.

From Los Angeles, California came a report of continued Klan growth as William. S. Coburn filed an application for a charter for the National Ku Klux Klan, Inc. Coburn was believed to be the "grand goblin" of the Pacific Domain, comprising six western states in the Ku Klux Klan, with headquarters in Los Angeles. Coburn was one of 37 alleged members of the Ku Klux Klan indicted on five counts each by the Los Angeles County grand jury, in connection with a raid on the Elduayen home in Englewood last April. The trial resulted in acquittal of 35, including Coburn.[224]

SATURDAY SEPTEMBER 30, 1922

Women Klan Members Reveal Family Life

Those Who Would Join Ladies of the Invisible Empire Must Answer Many Questions[225]

---

[222] Ibid.

[223] *Monroe News-Star,* 28 September 1922.

[224] Ibid.

[225] *The New York Times,* 30 September 1922.

95

Insight as to the role of women in the Klan was reported this date from Baltimore, Maryland. In a questionnaire sent to Baltimore women seeking to join the Ladies of the Invisible Empire contained questions concerning many aspects of the private life of the applicant and her family. The application appeared as follows:

> I, the undersigned, a true and loyal citizen of the United States of America, being a white woman of sound mind and a believer in the tenants of the Christian religion and the principles of 'pure Americanism,' do most respectfully apply for affiliation in the Ladies of the Invisible Empire.
>
> I guarantee on my honor to conform strictly to all rules and requirements regulating my initiation and the continuance of my membership, and at all times a strict and loyal obedience to your constitution and laws of the order. If I prove untrue to my obligations, I will willingly accept as my portion whatever penalty your authority may impose.
>
> The sum of $10 must accompany this application as a voluntary contribution.

Contained below are the questions that the applicant was required to answer.

> Are you serious and unselfish in seeking membership in this organization?
> Are you past 18 years of age? Married? Single? Widowed? Divorced?
> Have you any children?
> What is your religious faith? Catholic, Jew, Protestant or Mohammedan?
> With what secret organization is your husband, father, son or brother affiliated?
> What is the religious faith of your husband?
> Of what church are you now a member?
> Can you keep a secret? Will you do so?
> What are your political affiliations?
> Are you a registered voter?
> Do you owe allegiance to any foreign nation, government, institution, people or ruler?
> Do you esteem the United States of America, its flag and government, and will you ever be loyal in supporting same?
> Can you always be depended on?

Having answered all of the questions, the applicant was required subscribe to the following:

> I most solemnly assert and affirm that each question above is truthfully answered by me, and in my own handwriting, and below is my signature."

MONDAY OCTOBER 1, 1922

Candidate Charges 'Ku Klux' Threat
Edward S. Brogan Makes Public Letter Purporting to Be on Society's Stationary[226]

From New York came a report that Shannon Brogan, a defeated candidate for Judge of General Sessions in the recent Democratic primary. Brogan said that he

---

[226]*The New York Times*, 1 October 1922.

had received a letter from the Ku Klux Klan of New York threatening that if he did not withdraw the Klan would force him out, even if it had to commit its first overt act in this city. The letter was typed on the general stationary of the "Imperial Palace, Invisible Empire, Knights of the Ku Klux Klan," Atlanta, and sub-dated with the typewriter "Klan No. 51, New York, Sept. 19, 1922." It was signed Knights of the Ku Klux Klan, Klan No. 21. The letter read:

> Edward S. Brogan,
> Columbus Circle,
> New York City.
> Sir:
> Your persecution of the Ku Klux Klan has reached its limit. We have stood silently by while you maligned us through your campaign. Now it must cease. You have been posing as a man unprejudiced by religious prejudices while you always been a low kneeler to the Pope in Rome. It is to him you owe your allegiance not to your people or your flag. Now your duplicity must end. Immediately upon receiving this communication you will withdraw from the present campaign and leave the way clear for a real man. This will be your sole warning unless you immediately drop from the race we shall force you to do so even though it be our first public act in New York.
> Beware, you have been warned.
> > KNIGHTS OF THE KU KLUX KLAN,
> > KLAN NO. 21.

FRIDAY OCTOBER 5, 1922

Clarke Quits Post as Head of Ku Klux
Imperial Wizard Pro Tem. Will Turn Over the Order to Col. Simmons on Nov. 10[227]

From Atlanta came the surprising news that Edward Young Clarke, Imperial Wizard pro-tem. of the Knights of the Ku Klux Klan and virtual dictator of the order for several years, announced his resignation the Klan hierarchy. Simmons was to resume his post as active head of the organization he founded.

Clarke claimed he had been the victim of cruel persecution, and he denied making a fortune from his association with the Klan. This will later prove to be a lie, and that both Clarke and his lover, Mrs. Elizabeth Tyler, had made huge sums of money from the revenue received from the sale of cheap Klan costumes and money paid for dues. In fact, Clarke was indicted by a Federal Grand Jury the following day on mail fraud charges.[228]

---

[227] *The New York Times,* 5 October 1922.
[228] *The New York Times,* 6 October 1922.

MONDAY OCTOBER 9, 1922

Giants Take Series Without a Defeat: Win Last Game, 5-3
Each Club's Share, $41,218, Barely Will Meet Expenses--Ruth Bats .118 for the Series[229]

No world championship flag will fly in the new Yankee Stadium next spring. The giants attended to that ambition yesterday, and the world's series of 1922 in now baseball history. The Giants won, 5 to 3, by a tremendous rally in the eighth inning, in which they scored three runs. They are still champions of the universe, and a better team of champions never won the highest honor of the game.

What Babe Ruth Did at Bat In Final Game of the Series

First inning--One out, one on base. Ruth up. Bunted first pitched ball and advanced Dugan to second base.

Fourth Inning--None out, none on base. Ruth up. Strike one. Strike two. Ball one. Strike three.

Sixth Inning--One out, none on base. Ruth up. Ball one. Strike one. Hit to Nehf and was retired at first base.

Eighth Inning-One out, one on base. Ruth up. Hit first pitched ball to Kelly and was retired.

It was announced this date in Mineola, Long Island that Lillian Gatlin, the first woman to cross the continent by airplane, had landed at the United States Mail Service Station at Curtiss Field. She completed the flight from San Francisco in the flying time of 27 hours and 11 minutes.[230]

TUESDAY OCTOBER 17, 1922

Kansas Mayor Lashed After Assailing Klan
15 Men Whip Theodore Schierlman of Liberty and Warn Him of a Worse Fate[231]

A report from Coffeeville, Kansas contained the news that Theodore F. Schierlman, mayor of Liberty, had been called out of his office late Saturday night, taken into the country by 15 men in three cars, and "lashed with blacksnake whips." In a statement, Schierlman described his ordeal as follows:

"The three cars drove out in the country about four miles," said the statement. "The men tied his hands to a post, tore his upper clothing off and laid about thirty stripes on his bare back.

"They told him 'We are unknown to you. You have never seen us. Your neighbors have had us do this to you. You are one of those fellows that has denounced the Klan.'

"After about twenty stripes had been laid on, he said: 'Men, if this is 100 per cent American, I don't like it.' One of the men said, 'You don't, eh?' and they gave him ten more stripes, saying 'Maybe you will like it better.'

---

[229]*The New York Times,* 9 October 1922.
[230]Ibid.
[231]*The New York Times,* 17 October 1922.

"In the whipping two men did it, one on each side, alternating. They took him back about two miles and turned him out, saying, 'Now, keep your mouth shut. If you don't we will have to do this again and the next time we will use tar and feathers.' "

WEDNESDAY OCTOBER 18, 1922
Navy for Defense, Says Trotsky[232]

In an address before the Union of Young Communists in Moscow, War Minister Trotsky ridiculed some sections of the foreign press who claimed that Russia was becoming militaristic and imperialistic because of the rebuilding of its navy. Quite the contrary was true, claimed Trotsky, as the fleet was being rebuilt for home defense only.

MONDAY OCTOBER 23, 1922
Ku Klux Klansmen Invade a Church
Seven Members, All Masked, Interrupt Baptist Service at Patterson Pastor Reads Their Plea[233]

A dispatch from Patterson, New Jersey told how worshipers at the First Baptist Church were startled when the Ku Klux Klan appeared at the church door. During a sermon delivered by Rev. Frank McDonald pastor of the church, seven men dressed in the costume and emblem of the Ku Klux Klan entered the church, one of carrying the American flag. Rather than paraphrase this article and thereby lose the flavor of the time, the article will be presented as is.

> The flag-bearer stationed himself at the back of the church, while the other Klansmen proceeded down the center aisle. One of them advanced to the altar of the church, where he knelt apparently in prayer.
> He rose and handed a letter to Mr. McDonald. On the envelope was a written request that the letter be read to the congregation. Mr. McDonald read the letter. It contained a platform of the Ku Klux Klan, specifying as its object "pure womanhood, the advancement of patriotism, the furtherance of charities and cooperation with churches." At the conclusion of the reading the seven Klansmen filed out of the church.
> Mr. McDonald before continuing his sermon commented on the visit. He said he favored the sentiment expressed in the letter and had no objection to the appearance of the Klansmen. The letter was signed, Mr. McDonald said, "Kligrap, Patterson Provisional Klan No. 15, Realm of New Jersey." Between two and three hundred persons were at the church service.

It would not be long before the Rev. McDonald would be called to task for the appearance of the Klan in his church, as well as his apparent ringing endorsement of Klan principles and ideals.

---

[232]*The New York Times,* 18 October 1922.

FRIDAY OCTOBER 27, 1922
Nearing Secret of Atom

English Scientist Tells Gain in Being Able to Measure Crystal Unit[234]

It was announced in London on this day that mankind was one step closer to the discovery of the secret of the atom. In a lecture on the significance of crystal structure, Sir William Bragg said, "By means of X-rays, we have now found a method of measuring the crystal unit. Once this crystal unit is fixed, we ought to be able to say what are the reactions of the atoms in it and so be able to understand the atomic forces which are the bases of all material structure." How ignorant we were of the nightmare that we were creating.

MONDAY, OCTOBER 30, 1922
Allen to Drive Klan From Kansas

Governor Orders Attorney General to Move Against Ku Klux Officials. Publicly Brands Order as Breeder of Chaos and Hatred--Shocked at Whipping of Mayor[235]

In response to the whipping of the Mayor of Liberty at the hands of the Ku Klux Klan, reports from Coffeyville said that Governor Henry J. Allen asserted that he had instructed Attorney General Richard J. Hopkins to expel from Kansas every official of the Ku Klux Klan. While the Governor was denouncing the Klan as a secret order, operating without obeying the law by first seeking a charter as other fraternal and social organizations had done, about 50 men left the theater. He said:

> We confront in Klans an astonishing development of prejudice, racial and religious. It is seeking to establish the un-American idea that we can improve the conditions of the State by turning over the reigns of government to a masked organization which arrogates to itself the right to regulate the individual.
>
> It has taken the old Ku Klux Klan from its grave. It has set up the incredible philosophy that we require religious instruction from masked men whose characters and capacities are concealed by disguises.
>
> In the South and in the Far West it has committed many crimes upon the individual and only recently has invaded this State, which built strongly upon respect for law and order, and has given us the shocking exhibition, at Liberty, Kansas, of taking the Mayor of the town by violence, carrying him to a secluded place and whipping him because he refused to allow this masked society to hold a meeting in his hall.
>
> It has introduced into Kansas the greatest curse that can come to any civilized

---

[233]*The New York Times*, 23 October 1922.

[234]*The New York Times,* 27 October 1922.

[235]*The New York Times*, 30 October 1922.

people--the curse that arises out of the unrestrained passions of men governed by religious intolerance and racial hatred. It brings chaos and hatred and menace to every law-abiding citizen who may fall victim of the private quarrels and animosities of men who hide their identities behind a mask. If we deliberately allow this organization to take the law into its own hands, then we breakdown all the safeguards of society.

I am here to tell your quite frankly tonight that I have directed the Attorney General to bring an action against the officials of the Klan to expel them from this State.

In Boston Professor Albert Rushnell Hart of Harvard, a writer on American history, today attacked the Ku Klux Klan in an address at St. Paul's Cathedral. He said that Southerners had "revived a corpse" which should have been forever buried years ago.

TUESDAY OCTOBER 31, 1922

Masked Kidnappers Routed in Oklahoma
Two Men Killed When Four Try to Seize Head of Anti-Klan Organization[236]

Klan activity was reported in Henrietta, Oklahoma as Tom Bogus, of Spelter City, died of wounds received in a gun battle with four men wearing black masks. Bogus, who was President of an anti-Ku Klux Klan organization called the "True Blue Americans," was said to have opened fire only after the masked men attempted to kidnap him and force him into a waiting car. One of the black-masked men was killed and two others were wounded in the exchange on the streets of Spelter City.

THURSDAY NOVEMBER 2, 1922

Warns Klan in Maine.[237]

No community was safe from the influence of the Klan as was demonstrated by the report emanating this day from Augusta, Maine. There Governor Percival P. Baxter, concerned about reports that branches of the Ku Klux Klan had been established in Maine, characterized the organization as "an insult and an affront to American citizens." He said that law-abiding citizens who believed in fair and open play would stand firmly against it, adding:

It seeks to array class against class, sect against sect, religion against religion. Such an organization must not, and never will, get a foothold in this State. Secrecy is dangerous, and those who practice it seek to escape legal and personal responsibility for their actions. I believe Maine people prefer the light of day to deeds of darkness, and they will never allow any secret order to take the law into its own hands, for our courts have the respect of all good citizens

---

[236] *The New York Times*, 31 October 1922.
[237] *The New York Times*, 2 November 1922.

In Chicago, a report that A. E. Olson, President of the Washington Park National Bank, was a member of the Ku Klux Klan caused him to announce his resignation. He said that he signed an application card of the Klan two years ago in the belief that it was a fraternal organization.[238]

THURSDAY NOVEMBER 16, 1922
Arkansas Citizen Shot From Ambush[239]

Murder at the hands of the Ku Klux Klan was reported this day in Hot Springs, Arkansas. Jeff Howell, of Buckville, was shot and killed, and Earnest Wheatly, of Hot Springs, and John Newkirk, of Jessieville, were wounded when they were ambushed after a community meeting at the Jessieville public school. A number of Klansmen entered the school house during the meeting but took no part. It was believed that these Klansmen were responsible to initiating the violence.

The previous evening, Klansmen wearing robes and masks marched into a church at Lonsdale during a meeting and handed one of the speakers, Rev. J. Ellsworth Coombs, of Hot Springs, a note declaring that the Klan was determined to stop bootlegging.

---

[238]Ibid.

[239]*Monroe News-Star,* 16 November 1922.

CHAPTER FOUR

THE SEARCH AND DISCOVERY OF THE BODIES OF WATT DANIEL AND THOMAS RICHARDS

MONDAY, NOVEMBER 20, 1992

Louisiana Governor Comes to Washington to see What can be Done With the Ku Klux: Mentions Disappearance of Several Men[240]
Harding Refused to Help Parker Fight Klan[241]
Louisiana Chief Executive not in Washington to Bring About Federal Intervention in State[242]
Attorney General and States Executive ask Harding to Curb K.K.K. in Interstate Operations[243]
Governor Parker's Mission in Capital is one of Mystery[244]

Not only did the headlines of the *Times-Picayune* announce the trip of Governor Parker to Washington to consult with President Harding concerning the Ku Klux Klan, but the above headline also appeared in *The New York Times*. As to the allegation that he was seeking a federal takeover of the state because of the power of the Ku Klux Klan, Parker said:

"The report that we are asking the federal Government to take over the Government of Louisiana because we are unable to cope with the influences of the Ku Klux Klan is, of course, out of the question. We are certainly able to manage our own affairs down that way."

When asked by reporters, if the situation was under control in Louisiana why he was making the trip to Washington, Parker said that plans were being made to deal with the Klan and that Attorney General Coco was scheduled to speak with United States Attorney General Daugherty "for advice as to the powers of the State to deal with persons threatening it." Parker added:

"I cannot say with whom we shall confer. I am not going to ask for federal troops. Neither am I going to ask the federal courts to handle any situation. The government of Louisiana is able to care for itself. I believe the other side broadcast that report that I am going to Washington to ask the Government there to take over

---

[240]*The New York Times*, 20 November 1922.
[241]*Monroe News-Star*, 20 November 1922
[242]Ibid.
[243]Ibid.
[244]Ibid.

our State Government," Parker claimed. Although he did not say it directly, those in attendance felt he was making reference to the Ku Klux Klan.

It was common knowledge that Governor Parker and President Harding were close personal friends. It was also reported that Parker and Harding had been exchanging correspondence concerning the Ku Klux situation for quite some time, so it would be difficult to estimate just what understandings existed between Harding and Parker on the matter. Later, however, it will become evident that federal operatives had been in Louisiana investigating the disappearance of Daniel and Richards long before this trip to Washington.

Governor Parker was also scheduled to meet with William J. Burns, the chief of the Justice Department, who already had men working undercover in Morehouse Parish investigating the disappearance of Daniel and Richards. Governor Parker, as will be demonstrated later, could not count on the cooperation of local authorities to properly execute the duties of their office, if it conflicted with the dictates of the Klan. Other towns in which the Klan was alleged to be strong were Alexandria, Shreveport, Monroe and Ruston. Ruston is a neighboring town 30 miles west of Monroe.

From the November 18 issue of the *Washington Post* came an article which kindled the interest of the nation in the goings-on of the Klan in Louisiana, and brought a storm of protests from elected officials from around the state of Louisiana. The article, which is lengthy, appears below in its entirety:

Invisible Power of Ku Klux is Said to Rule Louisiana in Washington Paper's Story of Appeal to Harding [245]

The Washington Post's Baton Rouge dispatch today to the effect that Louisiana is under the rule of the Ku Klux Klan and that Governor John M. Parker, accompanied by the Attorney General of the state, is on his way to Washington to ask President Harding to take over the administration of law in Louisiana, as the State Government is unable to function, was sent by George Rothwell Brown, a staff correspondent of the Post.

The text of Mr. Brown's dispatch is copyrighted, but is sent to *THE NEW YORK TIMES* with the permission of the Post. It reads:

The Ku Klux Klan has reached out boldly for civil powers over officers of law and justice over an immense territory and has virtually reduced the sovereign State of Louisiana to the vassalage of the invisible empire.

The machinery of State government has almost ceased to function as the unseen power of the mysterious secret society exerts its force on the offices of State and

---

[245] *The New York Times*, 20 November 1922.

local authorities and in the very courts of law.

Governor John M. Parker has gone to Washington to lay the whole situation before President Harding, to inform the federal authorities that State law has virtually come to a stop in Louisiana in the face of the mysterious power of the klan, and to ask the United States Government to take over the administration of the law in Louisiana or in certain specified portions of the State.

The Governor's conference with the President on Monday will disclose to the country one of the most amazing and humiliating catastrophes in the whole history of American government. Not since reconstruction times, at least, has any Governor of a State laid bare to the nation the fact that a secret power in that State has usurped the functions of government and brought the administration of laws to a stop.

The governor of Louisiana today is virtually helpless in the face of the power of the most gigantic secret organization which has ever reared its head in America.

Not only has it become impossible for the State Authorities to cope with the unseen power of the new Ku Klux Klan, reared upon the ashes of that institution born of a highly emotionalized chivalry which saved white supremacy throughout the South in the "carpet bag" days which followed the Civil War, but it is almost impossible to detect the presence of the vast invisible empire which apparently covers Louisiana and has extended its way to adjacent States, where there is reason to believe conditions almost as bad as those in this State now prevail. Certain counties in Texas are reported through confidential "grapevine" channels to be in the grip of the invisible empire, which has reared itself above the constitutional law of the State and dictates the administration of justice behind an impenetrable veil of mystery and intimidation.

Governor Parker will appeal to the federal Government to go into the State of Louisiana and take over the administration of government in the face of the complete paralysis of the local government, under an impelling constitutional mandate, which will leave the Federal Government no alternative but to act with promptness and vigor if the facts to be disclosed at the Washington conference on Monday justify that drastic course.

That these facts will lead to the protection of the State Government in Louisiana by the Federal Authorities is a widely entertained option here in Louisiana, where the condition which the Governor will lay bare are as yet merely the subject of whispered confidences among trusted friends.

The power of the "invisible empire" has settled like a shadow upon the State, and men scarcely dare to breathe what little they know of the inner secrets of the great secret society whose unuttered orders are silently and mysteriously carried out by invisible agencies which are superior to the constituted and elected law officers of the Commonwealth.

There is among men in this part of the South whispered speculation as to what course of action the Federal Government will pursue. The state of affairs to be disclosed by Governor Parker is so out of the whole ordinary experience of Americans as to be fairly stupefying. The very courts of jurisdiction are paralyzed.

Governor Parker will disclose that the State authorities have now become powerless to cope with the situation. His administration cannot move hand nor foot to enforce the laws, the administration of which in certain parts of the State has passed into the keeping of a secret government superior to the State, which sets the State itself at defiance.

No only has the invisible empire usurped the functions of government, but at every turn are disclosed evidences that in many instances the sworn officials of the State are themselves members of the Ku Klux Klan.

The powers of the Federal Government which Governor Parker will seek to invoke are embodied in Section 4 of Article IV of the Constitution of the United States, which reads as follows:

"The United States shall guarantee to every State in this Union a republican form of government, and shall protect each of them against invasion, and on application of the Legislature, or of the Executive--when the Legislature cannot be convened--against domestic violence."

The extent of "domestic violence" in Louisiana under the State-wide sway of the invisible empire of the Ku Klux Klan may be disclosed in the confidential communication to be made by Governor Parker and by the Attorney General of the State, who has accompanied him to Washington. It has been reported that there have been a great many murders and other acts which, without a full possession of the facts, would be classified as outrages against citizens.

It is a significant fact, however, and this must be borne in mind, that there is every evidence that the Klan enjoys the support and confidence of thousands of the best and most law-abiding citizens in the State. The very scope which the secret society has attained bears testimony to this fact.

It is claimed on behalf of the Klan that it stands for the maintenance of law and order and of Anglo-Saxon supremacy, that its actions setting at naught the law itself have been dictated by the highest feelings of patriotism; that it has punished the law breaker and the violator of the sanctity of the home; that it has driven from the community the worthless and degenerate elements. Thus the system has its defenders, and has been able to extend its sway with substantial absolutism as to choke off and stifle the machinery of the law which stands in the way of the exercise of will.

The mystery which envelops the whole institution of invisible government constitutes one of its most baffling characteristics. Nobody knows who belongs to the Klan, nobody knows when or where it will strike. Its aspects, as a super-government taking the administration of the law out of the constitutionally constituted officials of the law and administering justice according to its own conception of what constitutes civil and social justice, render it peculiarly terrifying to the lawless and those who have fallen within whatever limits of ban may have been imposed by the secret objects of the society.

A man is seated in his office, and a stranger enters and asks for a confidential conference. A few minutes later that man is at the railroad office buying a ticket. "Where to?' asks the agent.

"It makes no difference, any place," is the answer. The man vanishes. The community knows him no more. There is whispered discussion, and then the subject is dropped. The same thing happens again and again. Men mysteriously drop out of their accustomed haunts. Neighborhoods are suddenly relieved of the occasional individual long regarded with suspicion. A man who has been living with a low-caste woman in violation of the moral code, bringing scandal to a community, suddenly decides to leave. Nobody knows why. He simply leaves and is heard of no more.

From other States have gone to Washington reports of similar conditions in other communities. Evidence has been presented that the Klan has permeated the whole fabric of official life, that its members are themselves the officials charged with the enforcement of the law, and the law is administered not according to the law of the State, but according to the law of the invisible power lodged in what is known in popular parlance as the Ku Klux Klan. Nobody really knows whether in fact this is the true name of the society.

In Louisiana conditions are said to be worse in Morehouse Parish, in the norther part of the State.

Governor Parker denied that his trip to Washington was to secure federal troops to bring Louisiana under control. The governor did, however, say that, prior to going to the White House to confer with President Harding, he and Attorney General Coco did visit with William J. Burns, chief of the bureau of investigation of the department of justice. The purpose of that meeting, Parker claimed, was to give Burns information concerning the influence exerted by the Klan. Parker also said he spoke with Burns about the Daniel/Richards case, and the belief that Klansmen from Mississippi and Arkansas were involved in the incident.[246]

Four Irish Rebels are Killed by Mine[247]

From Dublin came the news that four men were killed and three severely injured last evening in a terrific explosion in the village of Inchichore, in the suburbs of Dublin. The men were preparing an ambush for the national troops who pass through the village on their way to the Curragh Camp and the Baldounel airdome when the mine they were planting exploded.

Fired on White-Robed Men[248]

Again from Hot Springs, Arkansas, came a report of Klan violence. This time, however, it would be the citizenry rising up against the Klan. Travis Conros, a deputy sheriff, Al Baldwin and Tom Talley, were indicted for murder in connection with the slaying of Jeff Howell. Howell was a member of a white-robed group of men who were fired on as they were leaving a law enforcement meeting in Marble Township near Hot Springs.

The three indicted men admitted firing on the Klansmen with the intention of frightening them out of that part of the country, where illicit whiskey trade is reported to flourish. The attack on the band at the Marble township meeting was followed by a series of raids by officers an citizens' posses not only in that township but in and near Hot Springs where more than a 12 moonshine stills were destroyed and 140 men arrested.

---

[246]*Monroe News-Star*, 20 November 1922

[247]*The New York Times*, 20 November 1922.

[248]Ibid.

Out of New York City came a report of Klan activity in the Calvary Baptist Church. The Rev. Dr. John Roach Straton, pastor of Calvary Baptist Church, repudiated the charge that his church had become a "Ku Klux nest." The pastor resented the assertions that church machinery had been used to spread Klan propaganda. However, in a telegram to the Rev. Oscar Haywood, later to be recognized as an organizer and chaplain of the Ku Klux Klan, Straton said:

> It is true that I am interested and actively engaged in the work of propagating the Ku Klux Klan in New York City. In it I am just as zealous as I was in the work of endowing Calvary Baptist Church four years ago. The Ku Klux Klan will be a loyal ally of every Protestant church, every patriotic society, every home in New York city. In those sections where the Protestant churches have died it will spring up and live. It is the most dauntless organization known to men.[249]

TUESDAY NOVEMBER 21, 1922

Louisiana to Fight the Klan Without Federal Aid Now[250]

After meeting with President Harding, U. S. Attorney General Daugherty, and William J. Burns, chief of the Bureau of Investigation of the Justice Department (soon to be renamed the Federal Bureau of Investigation), Governor Parker and Louisiana Attorney General Coco emerged from the White House with a statement for the press.

First Parker blasted the articles that had appeared in the *Washington Post* and *The New York Times* which claimed that the government of the state of Louisiana was firmly in the hands of the Ku Klux Klan. Second, he said that the trip to see President Harding was not to request federal troops be sent into Louisiana.

"We will be able to rid Louisiana of this vicious development the more quickly, " said Parker, "if we can have the help of other States and the Federal Government. We can deal effectively with our own situation if it can be cut off from the support and encouragement it is receiving from the outside.

"The responsible Government of the State is determined that regardless of cost or consequences, a most through investigation will be made of the outrages reported to have been committed by the Ku Klux Klan in Louisiana. Certain outrages have been committed, certain horrifying crimes have been recorded, and it is vital that responsibility shall be fixed and offenders punished, not because of any organized association but in spite of it. The laws of the State and nation must be

---

[249]Ibid.
[250]Ibid.

upheld under any and all circumstances."

Not long after Parker made his statement, the U. S. attorney general made the following statement on behalf of President Harding:

"It appears that the State of Louisiana will be fully able to take care of the situation. There is nothing at this time for the Federal government to do except give assurance to State authorities that whenever Federal interests are involved the Federal authorities are ready to extend full co-operation."

While Governor Parker was conferring with President Harding, he protested the appointment of Walter Cohen, a black man, as collector of customs at New Orleans. Governor Parker was seeking the aid of Senators Ransdell and Broussard in blocking the nomination of Cohen when it came before the Senate for a vote. Parker, obviously, was no friend of blacks.

Governor Parker was not the only elected official in Louisiana to protest the article which appeared in both the *Washington Post* and *The New York Times*. From nearly every elected official in Louisiana came a flood of angry telegrams repudiating the claims made in the article. In researching these claims and counter claims, it can be safely said that the influence of the Ku Klux Klan was strong in the state from just south of Alexandria to the Arkansas state line. Incidentally, this is the same area of Louisiana that David Duke, long time klan leader and founder of the National Association for the Advancement of White People, carried during his race for the governor's office against Edwin Edwards. The Klan was never able to get a firm hold in the southern part of Louisiana because of the cosmopolitan live-and-let-live atmosphere that prevailed then and still does to this day.

Klan Carries Gold to Pastor in Church [251]

The Klan continued to visit churches in New York, the latest report emanating from Peekskill. While delivering his sermon last evening, Rev. G. C. Winters, pastor of the First Baptist Church, and his congregation were startled when four Ku Klux Klan members in full regalia walked up the aisle and handed the pastor a package. The pastor just managed to say, "Thank you." Then went on with his sermon after the Klansmen departed.

Upon opening the package, it was found to contain five $20 gold pieces wrapped in silk paper accompanied with a letter to the pastor which read as follows:

---

[251] Ibid.

The Rev. G. C. Winters, pastor of the Baptist Church greetings:

The unseen eye has seen and observed your good work for the service of Christ in Peekskill. The Knights of the Ku Klux Klan stand to a man to endorse the Christian efforts of men like you, who preach the true light of humanity. Our Christian ideals are synonymous to the teachings of the true Christian church--to wit we magnify the Bible as a basis of our constitution, the foundation of our Government, the source of our laws, the sheet anchor of our liberties, the most practical guide of right living and the source of all true wisdom. We teach the worship of God, for we have in mind the divine command, 'Thou shalt worship the Lord thy God.'

We honor the Christ as the Klansman's only criterion of character. And we seek at His hands that cleansing from sin and impurity which only he can give.

We believe that the highest expression of life is in the service and sacrifice for that which is right, that selfishness can have no place in a true Klansman's life and character, but that he must be moved by unselfish motives, such as characterized Our Lord the Christ and moved Him to the highest service and one supreme sacrifice for that which was right.

In the name of Our Savior, please accept this token as an appreciation of your splendid service in out community and to be used as you deem necessary in your Christian ministry.

Yours in the sacred unfailing bond,

KNIGHTS OF THE KU KLUX KLAN.

We were here yesterday, we are here today, we will be here forever."

Klan Warning at Harvard[252]

Hubert K. Clay of Colorado Springs, Colorado and a student at Harvard University at Cambridge, Massachusetts, reported to police that he had received a warning from the Ku Klux Klan to leave Harvard at once or suffer the consequences. The note was composed of different words clipped from newspaper advertisements and it read: "You have been too indiscreet. Remain in Cambridge at your own peril."

A dispatch from Dublin, Ireland this day told of the concern of the fate of Erskine Childers who had been condemned to died this day in Joy Prison. No word had been given whether or not the execution had been carried out. Eight others were said to also be awaiting execution.

From London, England also came the new that J. P. Morgan had suddenly taken ill. No other information was available.[253]

From Atlanta, Georgia , F. L. Savage, Chief of Staff at the headquarters of the Ku Klux Klan, denied that the Klan was "in politics in Louisiana or elsewhere." He made this statement regarding the visit of Governor Parker of Louisiana to

---

[252]Ibid.

110

President Harding today.[254]

WEDNESDAY NOVEMBER 22, 1922

Louisiana is Not Under Domination of Ku Klux Klan: Condemns Governor's Action[255]

Declaring a point of personal privilege, Representative Aswell, Democrat from Louisiana, attacked the article carried in the *Washington Post* yesterday claiming that the Ku Klux Klan was in control of Louisiana.

"The scurrilous story which erroneously reflects on the state of Louisiana is false," said Aswell. "The whole thing to any fair-minded man reveals two facts. First, that the *Post* story is entirely false, and second, to the humiliation and regret of our people, that the governor of Louisiana, with his insatiable thirst for publicity, is responsible for the great injury done to our state.

What's it About? Is Men's Query as Lady Maskers Start March[256]

A dispatch from Atlanta, Georgia this day told of masked women, estimated at fully 300, parading in Atlanta's streets for the first time last evening. The women taking part in the parade said they were members of the Dixie Women's League, a "patriotic society." They were arrayed in white costumes with flowing sleeves trimmed in red and blue. The masks completely covered their faces and were similar to those worn by the Ku Klux Klan. They also wore V-shaped hats with red tassels. The parade was led by mounted policemen and a band. The members, grouped in pairs, each carried a small American flag. Newsboys dubbed them "women Ku Kluxes."

THURSDAY NOVEMBER 23, 1922

To "Tear Mask of Klan," Asserts Governor on Return to Louisiana: Denies Political Moves[257]

Returning to New Orleans, Governor Parker declared his intention to "tear the mask off the Ku Klux Klan." Speaking to reporters, he told of his trip to Washington.

"My mission to Washington was two-fold; to prevent the appointment of a negro to a federal office and to take up the matter of the securing of information

---

[253] Ibid.

[254] Ibid.

[255] Ibid.

[256] *The Monroe News-Star,* 22 November 1922.

[257] Ibid.

111

against lawbreakers who belong outside the state from coming into the state and endeavoring to constitute themselves judge, jury and prosecutor," said Parker in an obvious reference to the Mer Rouge incident.

"I had absolutely no idea of calling on the federal government for troops to put down disturbances. I was never so surprised in all my life as when I saw that alleged interview in the paper. To the best of my knowledge, I never saw the correspondent, and I certainly never gave out any such interview."

"What are my present intentions? To do what I have been doing all along. I am opposed to any kind of secret organization who keeps its members masked. I have dedicated myself to tearing these masks off this organization. I mean the Ku Klux Klan. The strength of this organization is largely outside the state. It is to prevent these masked men from other states coming into Louisiana that prompted my visit to Washington. The state government can deal with the members within the state."

Enter John Rogers

Just a few days prior to the sending of the troops into Morehouse Parish, the *St. Louis Post Dispatch* sent correspondent John Rogers to cover the goings-on in northeast Louisiana. Rogers intercepted Governor Parker on the train between New Orleans and Baton Rouge. At first Parker was reluctant to speak with the reporter, but as the interview progressed, he became more relaxed.

Parker told Rogers that he had information that Daniel and Richards had been murdered and that their bodies had been "thrown into a lake." Parker admitted that he had only hearsay evidence and lacked sufficient information or hard evidence to go on.[258]

Confiding in the reporter, Parker gave Rogers the names of a number of people in the Mer Rouge area that he felt were principled individuals for Rogers to contact with instructions to forward whatever information he would glean to his office. Rogers agreed, and he left that night for Mer Rouge.

Rogers wrote of his arrival in Mer Rouge in this fashion:

"The town that day was like any one of innumerable southern country towns, with its quiet, unostentatious life, and I observed no sign of unusual activity. A few drowsy negroes were basking in the sun; a few white men leaning against things, and some muddy automobiles parked in disorder on the main street. That was

---

[258]Rogers, John. *The murders of Mer Rouge.* (Security Publishing Co.: St. Louis, 1923), 11-12.

all."[259]

One of the first places visited by Rogers in his search for information was the town barber shop, and much to his surprise he found the barber to not only be Mayor Robert Dade of Mer Rouge, but also one of the very people that Governor Parker had directed him to see. Telling Dade of his cooperation with Governor Parker, Rogers was directed to the billiard parlor connected to the shop and to the three men playing. Mayor Dade told Rogers that these three could supply the information that he was seeking. The mayor introduced Rogers to one of the players, Earl Andrews, his brother-in-law.

Andrews was quick to say that there was "a big story in Morehouse Parish for anyone with courage to go out and get it." He was also just as quick to say that he would not accompany Rogers on his fact-finding mission. Andrews did, however, take him about town where he introduced him to J. L. Daniel, the father of Watt, and W. C. Andrews, Earl Andrews' brother, and C. C. "Tot" Davenport. These three men were the ones who had been kidnapped along with Watt Daniel and Thomas Richards on August 24, 1922. The elder Daniel and Davenport had been whipped that evening, despite the fact that these were some of the oldest, respected and well-to-do families in the Mer Rouge area.[260]

Rogers had barely been in town a few hours when he received a phone call in one of the stores. "You have no business in Morehouse Parish, so get out, and be quick about it," he was told by some unknown caller. When he contacted the operator as to the origin of the call, she told him that it had come from Bastrop. Clearly, the Klan network was at work and was aware of his presence and mission in Mer Rouge.[261]

Rogers learned that the man who was running Morehouse Parish was none other than Captain J. K. Skipwith, Exalted Cyclops of Morehouse Klan No. 34. When he told of his intention to interview Captain Skipwith, nearly everyone recoiled in horror.

"Brother," Rogers was warned, "don't do it. Keep off that Bastrop road. This Captain is boasting of things, and you cannot tell what might happen."[262]

---

[259]Ibid., p. 12.
[260]Ibid., p. 12-13.
[261]Ibid., p. 13.
[262]Ibid., p. 14.

Rogers, accompanied by Louis Felton, the only man in Mer Rouge with the nerve to take Rogers to see Skipwith, first proceeded to Bastrop where Rogers first met Sheriff Fred Carpenter, who he identified as "a klansman."[263]

Sheriff Carpenter refused to talk about the disappearance of Daniel and Richards, and in a surprise move, directed Rogers to seek out Captain Skipwith on the farm of his son, Oliver, in Vaughn, Louisiana, some 15 miles from Bastrop.

Contained below is the account of Rogers' encounter with Captain Skipwith:

"Oliver Skipwith, a man about 30 years of age, answered our hail and drove the dogs away. He said his father was walking in a nearby wood, and called him with a resounding 'yoo-hoo-oo.'

"A bareheaded man with silvery hair, erect and with steady gait, presently emerged from the wood at our left, and when he was within a few yards of us I advanced to meet him, wishing to avoid strained formalities. He extended his left hand in greeting and placed the other hand in his coat pocket. I gave him my right hand, which he grasped with his left, but, for the moment I kept an eye on the hand in the pocket. He was clean shaven, had pale blue eyes that fixed on with an emotionless stare; a firm jaw, and thin lips that turned sharply down at the corners.

" 'Who are you, and what do you want from me?' he calmly demanded.

" 'A St. Louis reporter, come to see you concerning the disappearance of Daniel and Richard(s)?' I answered adding: 'I have been to Governor Parker, and to Mer Rouge, and I would like to have your version of the abduction.'

" 'Well, what of it; what are you going to do about it?" he exclaimed, a note of annoyance in his tone.'

" 'Publish your version of it, if you wish it,' I replied.

" 'So, you are just a reporter, eh?' he remarked, half reflectively. 'I assumed you were one of those fake detectives who have been snooping around here.' "[264]

Skipwith mentioned that he was in need of a ride back to Bastrop where he could produce documentation as to the guilt of Daniel and Richards, and he asked Rogers if they would be returning to Bastrop shortly. Realizing the opportunity to have Skipwith at close quarters for the duration of the ride, Rogers was quick to offer a lift.

---

263 Ibid., p. 15.
264 Ibid., p. 16.

During the ride, Skipwith spent most of his energies maligning Governor Parker. " 'That Governor,' said Skipwith contemptuously, '"has boasted that he would unmask the Klan in Louisiana, but he isn't going to do anything. He's just windjamming.' "[265]

All during the ride, Rogers was attempting to steer the conversation to the disappearance of Daniel and Richards, but Skipwith continued to avoid answering. Finally, Rogers pressed Skipwith to answer, saying that securing an answer to the disappearance of Daniel and Richards was the purpose of his being in the state.

" 'It is enough for the world that you say that I, Captain J. K. Skipwith, Exalted Cyclops of Morehouse Klan No. 34, Knights of the Ku Klux Klan,' said the Captain, 'officially announced that Daniel and Richard(s) were spirited away by friends of Dr. B. M. McKoin, captain of our Klan at Mer Rouge, who they attempted to assassinate, and that they will never return.' "

" 'Captain,' I remarked, 'I have heard a lot of gossip today, and I want to ask if you know that of your own knowledge?'

" 'I have said it, ' he exclaimed, 'and that is final.' "[266]

Incredible as it seems, from the mouth of the exalted cyclops himself, Captain J. K. Skipwith, came the claim that it was, in fact, the Ku Klux Klan that had kidnapped Daniel and Richards. That being established by the Klan leader himself, coupled with the fact that Daniel and Richards were last seen in the company of their kidnappers on the road to Lake LaFourche late on the night of the kidnapping and that those vehicles were seen returning from Lake LaFourche minus the two kidnap victims places the blame for the murders of Daniel and Richards squarely on the heads of the members of Morehouse Klan No. 34, Knights of the Ku Klux Klan!

When they arrived back in Bastrop, Captain Skipwith left them at a restaurant eating while he went to retrieve the documents he claimed would prove the guilt of Daniel and Richards. When he returned, he displayed to Rogers the following letters. The profanity was deleted by Rogers.

---

[265]Ibid., p. 19.
[266]Ibid.

August 10, 1922.
(mailed on a train)
Cap. Skip. what do you think now? got your No. Your bully has hike. You see now how long he last with us. We don't fear your mask or bluf, so take this for what it is worth. We entend to get more next time. We mean business and you don't know us. Just leting you know we are not afraid.
                              (signed) Not your friend.[267]

August 15, 1922.
(mailed at Monroe, La.)
Oh you dam old white head --------, you Ku Klux ------, you need not think by running off to Monroe you will escape for we are waiting for you.
(signed)   Anti C. C.

" 'Now,' exclaimed the Captain, 'could anything be more convincing of the guilt of those outlaws?'

" 'Did Daniel or Richards write those letters?' I inquired.

" 'Who but those scoundrels would have stooped to such a low-life act?' he countered. 'I have no evidence except the rotten characters of those people,' said Skipwith.

" 'About Daniel and Richards,' I said, 'have you any evidence of any kind or from any source that you which would justify their being put to death?'

" 'Yes,' he exclaimed. 'They associated with niggers and attempted to assassinate a splendid gentleman, the captain of our Klan at Mer Rouge, Dr. McKoin. Why doesn't that Governor of ours investigate that?' "

In the end, Skipwith, a Mason stricken from the rolls for failure to pay his dues, admitted that he had no solid evidence to link Daniel and Richards to the bogus assassination attempt on Dr. McKoin, but he said he was "morally certain that Daniel or Richard [s] or one of their gang" was responsible.[268]

Before continuing the coverage of the contact with Captain Skipwith, it is important to recap what was revealed so far. From Skipwith's own admissions we know:

1) That the Klan was responsible for and had authored the plan to kidnap J. L. Daniel, Watt Daniel, Thomas F. Richards, C. C. "Tot" Davenport and W. C. Andrews,
2) That the evidence against Daniel and Richards, or anyone else for that matter, was nonexistent and existed only in the twisted mind of a hateful old man,
3) That the Klan was responsible for and party to the beatings administered to J. L. Daniel and W. C. Andrews,

---

[267]Ibid., p. 20.
[268]Ibid., p. 20-21.

4) That future testimony will show that descriptions of vehicles, kidnappers and the two blindfolded captives seen at various locations in Morehouse Parish on the night of the kidnapping were also seen headed toward the Eason Ferry at Lake LaFourche late in the evening by a motorist who had broken down on the road,

5) That these same described vehicles and occupants would be seen returning from the direction of Lake LaFourche a short while later minus the two blindfolded kidnap victims,

6) That the soon-to-be-recovered and horribly mutilated bodies of Watt Daniel and Thomas Richards would be pulled from the waters of Lake LaFourche at the foot of the Eason Ferry and finally,

7) That Dr. B. M. McKoin was the captain of the Mer Rouge Klan. A claim and a title that he will consistently deny.

There is another aspect of these letters which bears mentioning now. It will be later revealed that Dr. McKoin typed on his own typewriter and sent to himself threatening letters prior to those letters which appear above sent to Skipwith. Although it is impossible to determine now, one can only wonder if when Dr. McKoin left Mer Rouge did he do so by train, and on what day did he depart? Unlike today, travel by train was quite common during that time.

The second issue is Dr. McKoin's stay with his family in Monroe. Clearly, he could have easily been in Monroe during the time that this letter was sent. The third and final issue is the manner in which the letters were written. They seem to have been executed with intentional ignorance. In some places, it seems as though it was written by a person of limited grammatical skill. Yet, there are places that do not jibe with the rest.

For instance, in the first letter, we have the phrase, "take this for what it is worth." This one phrase seems out of place in this letter because of its grammatical correctness. In the second letter, the phrase "you need not think by running off to Monroe you will escape for we are waiting for you." This, too, seems out of place. Given what we already know and what will be learned about Dr. McKoin, I believe it is quite likely that he authored these documents the same as he originated those threatening letters that he sent to himself.

Captain Skipwith continued to argue his contention that Daniel, Richards or "one of their gang" had attempted to kill Dr. McKoin. During the discussion, Skipwith admitted to Rogers that he was the Klan leader of many night raids on the residences that the Klan believed was making or selling moonshine whiskey, cattle-dipping vat wreckers and men keeping company with black women, all of which he claimed was accomplished without a search warrant. Skipwith also boasted of having been responsible for forcing "undesirable women" to leave the parish. One of these women was a young school teacher whose only transgression was being Catholic.[269]

Feeling he had made his point, Skipwith decided to end the encounter by asking Rogers if he was to see Governor Parker in the near future. Rogers said that he would, and Skipwith gave Rogers the following message to carry to Parker:

"You have imparted the revelation to me that you are going to unmask the Ku Klux Klan and break it up in the State of Louisiana. Therefore, I desire to impart to you the revelation that every klansman of every state is perfectly familiar with the braying of a jackass."[270]

Continuing on his boisterous roll of bravado, Skipwith also gave a message to Rogers to deliver to the residents of Mer Rouge. According to Skipwith, they were to "behave themselves and stop discussing Daniel and Richard(s)." If they did not, Skipwith said that he would "come over some night and get a few more." He said that he was especially unhappy with Hugo Davenport, J. L. McElwain and Mr. Whipple, all businessmen from Mer Rouge. He said he was particularly upset with Whipple because he had taken in the penniless wife and two children of Thomas Richards, the soon-to-be-discovered murder victim of Skipwith and his Klan.[271] So much for the milk of human kindness.

After Rogers and Captain Skipwith parted company, Skipwith displayed one last expression of irrational behavior. When Rogers returned to Mer Rouge, he was informed by an unnamed merchant that Captain Skipwith had just phoned him and told him not to believe anything Rogers might say because he was "only another of governor Parker's liars."[272] As the expression goes in Louisiana, it is quite possible that Captain Skipwith allowed his alligator mouth to overload his mosquito ass, but only realized his faux pas after the incident occurred. The phone call was an obvious attempt at damage control.

A few days later, Rogers had another conversation with Sheriff Carpenter concerning the abductions and disappearances of Watt Daniel and Thomas Richards. It is unknown as to which date this occurred, and since the information will not break the sequence of events, it is presented here.

---

[269]Ibid., p. 23.
[270]Ibid.
[271]Ibid.
[272]Ibid.

Rogers wrote that he learned that the grand jury which allegedly investigated the abductions of Watt Daniel, Thomas Richards, J. L. Daniel, W. C. Andrews and C. C. "Tot" Davenport had returned no indictments or even any recommendations concerning the kidnappings, beatings and the continued absence of Watt Daniel and Richards. Rogers remarked that this came as no surprise as it was commonly known that nine of the 12 men seated on the grand jury were Klansmen.[273] Armed with that information, Rogers paid another call on Sheriff Carpenter while in the company of C. C. "Tot" Davenport.

Sheriff Carpenter admitted that he was aware of the kidnappings, but that he had not initiated an investigation because "he had feared trouble."

"What kind of trouble?" Rogers inquired.

"Well," he explained, "I saw Richard(s) when he was taken from the garage, (in Bastrop) before he and Daniel were taken, and would have rescued him at that time, but feared for my life."

"Who did you fear?"

"The masked men."

"Who are they?"

"I don't know, and I don't know what they might do. It didn't turn out seriously anyhow, as Richard(s) was only given a talking to."

"About Daniel and Richard(s)," Rogers persisted. "I understand you knew of that abduction and did nothing."

"I was in town when that happened," he explained, "and went as far as the edge of town, but saw nothing. I did not think that that would turn out seriously either."

"The people in Mer Rouge think it has turned out seriously," Rogers suggested.

"I am afraid it has," he said, "but I don't see that anything can be done now."

"Is it too late to begin an investigation now?" Rogers inquired.

"I understand the Governor has started one," he said, "and it is now in his hands."[274]

Not unlike many law enforcement officers in the South during this period, it

---

[273]Ibid., p. 21.
[274]Ibid., P. 28-29.

would appear that Sheriff Carpenter had sold his soul, honor and responsibilities of his office to the Ku Klux Klan for a total of $16, the price of membership in the Ku Klux Klan. To say that Sheriff Carpenter was not aware of who had kidnapped and murdered Daniel and Richards would be ludicrous. As a Klan member, he most probably had knowledge of the plans to kidnap and murder Daniel and Richards and intentionally stayed in town so as not to be involved in the crimes. By the same token, we have only his word that he was, in fact, in town at that time. Could it be possible that Sheriff Carpenter did participate in the kidnappings and murders of Daniel and Richards? If so, it could easily explain his reluctance and resistance to investigate these blatant offenses. Whatever the case, Sheriff Carpenter's failure to act in such a case displays the stranglehold that the Ku Klux Klan had on the elected officials of Morehouse Parish.

When Rogers returned from Bastrop to Mer Rouge, he met clandestinely with an unknown black man who had information for him. He told Rogers that a black man who operated the Eason Ferry across Lake LaFourche had told him that the bodies of Daniel and Richards "had been thrown off the ferry there and drowned."[275]

Taking the only road to get to the Eason Ferry, located four miles south of Oak Ridge, which is some 14 miles southeast of Mer Rouge, Rogers traveled the same road used by the kidnappers when they drove Daniel and Richards to their place of execution on the evening of August 24, 1922.

Rogers located the black ferryman, who told him that he had received a personal visit from masked Klansmen. They told him a couple of days before the kidnappings and murders not to be around the ferry on the night of August 24th. He not only complied, but gave up the job altogether. He told Rogers that on the morning of the 25th of August two iron wheels, which had been at the foot of the ferry for some time, were missing. It was believed that the bodies of Daniel and Richards had been fastened to the wheels and thrown into the lake. There appears to be a conflict with regard to the exact date. However, since this interview took place between three to four months after the incident, being off by one day seems of little consequence.

Armed with this information, Rogers left Morehouse Parish and returned to

---

[275]Ibid., p. 30.

Baton Rouge to the office of Governor Parker. He told Parker that he believed that Daniel and Richards had been murdered by the Klan and that the bodies had been thrown into Lake LaFourche.

Governor Parker attempted to enlist the aid of a professional diver from New Orleans, but had no success. Hearing this, Rogers told Parker that he knew of two divers in St. Louis and that he would attempt to secure the services of one of them when he returned to St. Louis the following day. Rogers did secure a diver who was recommended to him by the Eagle Boat Store Company in St. Louis. The diver accepted the job, but attempted to back out when he heard that he would be operating in a hostile Klan environment. However, he decided to keep the job when he learned that Watt Daniel had fought in World War I. "Well," said the diver, "here's a chance for me to do something for one of the boys who fought for me. I'll go." His only stipulation was that Rogers remain by his air hose while he was underwater. This same diver was to be later accused by the Klan of having been part of a plot to frame the Klan by bringing two bodies with him to plant in Lake LaFourche.[276]

Strange as it may seem, Rogers was never called to testify about his interview with Skipwith, nor anything else of which he may have had knowledge. This seems very strange, especially in light of the fact that much of what he did was with the full knowledge and cooperation of Governor Parker.

Denies Membership in the Klan[277]

From Topeka, Kansas, it was reported that the attorney general of that state had filed an "ouster suit" against the Ku Klux Klan. Summons were served on seven residents of the state who were named as defendants in the suit. It was reported that Klan officials claimed the ouster suit classified the Klan as a business organization when it was a "benevolent association." One of the defendants in the suit Noble T. McCall issued a statement denying his membership in the Klan.

From Chicago came the news that a 41 pound Illinois turkey, fattened on chocolate and other delicacies, was to be a Thanksgiving gift to President and Mrs. Harding. The turkey was the gift of the Harding Girls Club at Morris and Company packers. The club sent its first turkey to President Harding when he was visiting in

---

[276]Ibid., p. 31.
[277]Ibid.

the Canal Zone. Last year's bird made the trip to Washington in an airplane, garbed in a sweater, an aviator's helmet and goggles.[278]

SATURDAY NOVEMBER 25, 1922

Morehouse Quiet and Peacable as can be, Says Sheriff[279]

This was a slow news day in Morehouse Parish. The only utterance of note came from Fred Carpenter, sheriff of Morehouse Parish in a telegram to Riley J. Wilson, fifth-district congressman, declaring that all is quiet in Morehouse Parish. His telegram follows:

> Bastrop, La. Nov. 24, 1922.
> Riley J. Wilson, M. C.
> Washington, D. C.
> The statement that lawlessness and terror exists in Morehouse parish is absolutely untrue and without foundation. The only disturbance occurring in this parish recently was caused by two fake detectives who pretended to represent Attorney General Daugherty. Since their sudden departure, for reasons best known to themselves, matters have resumed their normal condition of peace and quiet. As sheriff of this parish, I resent with all the emphasis at my command the unjust and unwarranted assertion of Gov. Parker that ends of justice have been retarded or thwarted by me in my official capacity, and pronounce the same to be absolutely false. The parish of Morehouse is more quiet, peaceable and law abiding than for many years past.
> J. F. CARPENTER,
> Sheriff of Morehouse Parish, La.

Having read all that has occurred in Morehouse Parish in the two months preceding this telegram, it would seem the last thing the conditions in Morehouse Parish could be called was that of "peace and quiet." What is more, testimony that will be given in an open hearing to commence shortly after the discovery of the bodies will tell of almost nightly Klan raids, beatings, kidnappings and deportations. Sheriff Carpenter was either covering for the Klan, or he was the dumbest man that ever lived!

Klan Chief Denies Capital Initiation[280]

Meanwhile in Atlanta, Georgia, Fred L. Savage, chief of the Ku Klux Klan investigating staff, was busy denying knowledge of Klan initiation ceremonies had been performed in Washington, D.C. in one of the chambers of the war and navy building. He said, "If such an initiation took place, it was the work of the

---

[278]*The Monroe News-Star*, 23 November 1922.
[279]Ibid.
[280]*Monroe News-Star*, 25 November 1922.

Washington Klan and we have not heard a word from that branch of our order on the subject." Col. W. J. Simmons, imperial wizard of the Klan, could not be reached for comment.

Los Angeles, California was the origin of a report that Charlie Chaplin, and Pola Negri, Polish screen tragedienne, were planning marriage. Chaplin told newspapermen any announcement "must come from her." "I cannot say 'yes,' " he declared. "And if I said 'no,' think of the position it would put her in."[281]

At Franklin Field, Philadelphia, more than 50,000 persons saw the Army and Navy return to their old battle-ground on Franklin Field this day to struggle for victory in their annual football game. The final score was Navy 7; Army 3.[282]

MONDAY NOVEMBER 27, 1922

To Probe Morehouse Crime in Open Session
Coco Promises Quick Move in Crime Mystery[283]

While in New Orleans, Louisiana Attorney General A. V. Coco promised to hold opening hearings to ferret out the perpetrators of the outrages in Morehouse Parish. The attorney general said the procedure would be discussed at a conference with Governor Parker. It was seldom that "open hearings" were used in criminal cases. The process was authorized by the state's constitution in that should all means fail, the attorney general may seek an order through the district court and hold open hearings summoning witnesses as may be desired. It was a process to secure evidence. State officials have pointed out that great difficulty had been encountered obtaining evidence in Morehouse Parish.

Klansmen Renew Mer Rouge Terror
Residents Appeal Against Reprisals Following the Start of a Federal Inquiry[284]

In Baton Rouge this day was received a plea for help from the residents of Mer Rouge. Signed by W. B. Stuckey, attorney; W. F. Campbell, the town marshal; A. C. Whipple, garage proprietor, and C. A. Brunson, the letter rebuked those who criticized the article in the *Washington Post*, and begged the author of the article to come to Mer Rouge to see the situation for himself first hand. The letter read as follows:

---

[281] Ibid.

[282] Ibid.

[283] Ibid.

[284] *The New York Times*, 27 November 1922.

We do not know the conditions all over the State, but we, as citizens of Mer Rouge, know that our parish, Morehouse, is being dominated by the Invisible Empire. Several of our citizens have been threatened if they even voice criticism of the Klan for kidnapping five of our citizens, beating and whipping two of them and making off with two others, whom we believe now have been foully murdered.

The Klan dominates Morehouse Parish. The administrative machinery of the local Government is so broken down that it is practically impossible either to indict or convict members of the Klan for their violations of law.

For weeks Mer Rouge has been prepared, rifles and revolvers at hand, for the threatened invasion of our village by the Klan force. Telephones have been cut and we feared invasion. We appeal for protection, appeal to the State and Federal Government. This is in no sense a reflection on Governor Parker, from whom we expect and believe we will get aid and protection.

Now that the *Washington Post* and Mr. Brown are under fire, we invite Mr. Brown to come to Morehouse parish and take evidence to show not only that all he said in his first article in reference to the conditions in Louisiana is true as far as Morehouse Parish is concerned, but to show that conditions are even worse.

Those who wrote the letter further contended that an attack had been planned against one of the government agents by the Klan. They said it was the agent's sudden departure from town that afternoon that saved his life. Contained, almost matter-of-factly, in this article was a piece of information which will surface again as the reader progresses. It was stated as follows:

"It is known that the Federal agents have what they believe is positive information that the bodies of the two missing men are in Lake LaFourche, near Oak Ridge, and that the bodies were dropped into the lake bound to two iron wheels picked up from the shore."

What makes these few sentences so important will be the decision of the Justice Department agents to search Lake Cooper first instead of Lake LaFourche. Since they knew that the bodies were in the lake, and they knew they were bound to the iron wheels, it can only be surmised that they knew that these wheels were at the Eason Ferry landing when they disappeared. That being the case, then it would be logical to conclude that the bodies would be close to the ferry landing. That line of reasoning accepted, there can be no reason why a guard should not have been placed at the ferry landing in order to prevent the removal of the bodies.

Their extreme negligence in this matter could easily have caused the bodies to have been removed by the perpetrators. As it was, the perpetrators did make an attempt to destroy the evidence by detonating a large quantity of dynamite on the shoreline with the intent of covering the bodies with the earth tossed up by the explosion. Fortunately, their efforts failed.

Pastor Says Klan Plans World Drive
First Step in Movement Will Be Made Soon in Canada, Declares Dr. Haywood[285]

Meanwhile in New York, the Rev. Oscar Haywood, national lecturer of the Klan, revealed the intention of a world-wide Klan movement. He remarked that during the past four weeks, while he was lecturing in Pennsylvania, 500 applications for membership from Canada and the British Isles were received at Klan headquarters in Atlanta. He said that he felt that this was a clear indication that the Klan had universal appeal. Haywood said that the Klan was not a Southern organization. "Its field is the world, and its pulpit is the ages," he declared.

"It is not a political organization," Haywood said referring to the Klan. "It is a racial movement, but not in any sense to oppose, oppress, abuse or ridicule any other race. The Ku Klux Klan is moving for the solidarity of the Protestant Gentile white race not only in the United States but throughout the world."

"Then you think the establishment of an international Ku Klux Klan is likely?" he was asked by a reporter present.

"There isn't any doubt of it," Haywood declared.

With regard to his comment about the Klan being closely identified with Protestantism, he said, "The Methodists and Baptists are closer to the people than the Episcopalians." Concerning clergy membership in the Klan, Haywood said that Methodist and Baptist clergymen were the dominant groups. "In Pennsylvania, where I have been working, I should say that the majority of the ministers in the Klan were Presbyterians. In the South the number of Methodist and Baptist ministers in the Klan is about equal."

Dr. Haywood said a special membership drive would soon be under way in New York City, which will be under the direction of Major E. D. Smith of Buffalo, King Kleagle of the Realm of New York in the Invisible Empire. Smith was then working the area of Middletown, N.Y., where it was said that he had recruited over 100 members with the help of the Rev. Sam Campbell, another national lecturer, whom the Rev. Haywood said was helping him "sow the seed" of the Klan in the New York area. Haywood also mentioned that a Rev. Dr. Newton was also

---

[285]Ibid.

involved in the membership drives here, and that he was in Connecticut where a number of Klans were in the process of forming.

During the interview, Rev. Haywood also explained the Klan's position on the refusal of membership to women. He said that women could not be expected to do the "work" of a Klan member. Exactly what the "work" was that he referred to was not asked, but it can safely be assumed that he was making reference to the raids, beatings and lynchings so closely related to the Klan. "It isn't because women can't keep a secret," said Haywood. "We know they can. It was Adam, not Eve, who did the talking. We will never admit women because they cannot do some of the work we have to do. We will probably form an auxiliary women's organization."

Rev. Haywood also expressed the Klan position on a number of other topics, which could easily be considered a political platform. He said the Klan was violently opposed to birth control, "On the topic of birth control, we are bitterly opposed to it for the reason that, while every other race in the world is growing, there is a tendency to diminish the white race." He said that they were in favor of the 18th Amendment, commonly known as the Volstead Act.

Rev. Haywood said that the Klan was opposed to lynching, but in his next breath, the Rev. Haywood contradicted the Klan's position on lynching by saying that the Klan would oppose as ineffective the Dyer Anti-Lynching bill, which had been expected to surface during the next Congressional session. "We are opposed to lynching," Haywood said. "We wouldn't countenance it at all, and would stand between the negro, and a lynching. I believe the Klan will finally stop lynching in the South and throughout the country."

What the Rev. Haywood meant by his last sentence is difficult to understand. Taken as is, it would appear as though he is saying that the Klan would sometime in the future stop lynching people. Or, it might be interpreted as meaning the Klan would be the force to stop lynchings. The reader should decide which meaning Haywood was attempting to convey.[286]

In St. Louis, Missouri, considerable damage was caused by an earth quake of moderate intensity in Eastern Missouri, Southern Illinois, Western Indiana and Northwestern Kentucky last evening. According to reports, the tremors shook buildings and homes, toppled chimneys from their residences. broke windows,

---

[286]*The New York Times*, 27 November 1922.

knocked chinaware from shelves and frightened residents in the parts of the four states, the reports said. Evansville, Indiana, Mattoon, East St. Louis, as well as Benton, Clinton and El Dorado, Illinois, and points in the northwestern part of Kentucky reported feeling the quake about 9:30 p.m. Attendants at the seismographic observatory in St. Louis University said that the tremors were centered southeast of St. Louis and lasted 10 minutes.[287]

TUESDAY NOVEMBER 28, 1922

Klan Challenge to Gov. Parker at Capital Considered Lightly
Governor's Mansion Grounds Sprinkled with Ku Klux Klan Hand Bills[288]

In an act of blatant defiance, Baton Rouge Klan No. 3, Knights of the Ku Klux Klan, posted bills all around the governor's mansion announcing the public "naturalization" ceremonies [rites of initiation] to be held on Greenwell Spring Road at 8:30 p.m. Thanksgiving night. At this same time Baton Rouge was playing host to around 2,000 teachers attending the State Teachers' Association meeting and the upcoming Thanksgiving Day football game between Louisiana State University and Tulane. The posters were attached to small sticks and arranged in rows over the mansion grounds appearing to be so many tombstones. Printed on the handbills was the following:

> Baton Rouge Klan number three, Realm of Louisiana Invisible Empire of the Knights of the Ku Klux Klan, announces public naturalization of candidates Thanksgiving night 8:30 p.m. on Greenwell Springs Road.
> The public is cordially invited. Parking space will be provided in the main grounds. Traffic will be handled by competent persons. Visitors are requested not to arrive before 8:30 o'clock, this to avoid congestion of traffic.

Coincidentally, the Klan ceremonies were scheduled to begin at the same time the governor was scheduled to address the State Teachers' Association.

Smackover Hooded Men Drive Out Denizens of Oil "Jungle
More than 250 men Wearing Masks and Some in White Robes in Party[289]

Smackover, Arkansas was the scene of an invasion as 250 robed Ku Klux Klansmen. Marching in military formation, they visited several small towns and oil camps in the Smackover oil field section the previous evening and warned proprietors and habitues of alleged disorderly places to depart. It was said that no violence had been done. Ouachita City, Laneytown, Patagonia and some of the

---

[287] *Monroe News-Star*, 27 November 1922.
[288] *Monroe News-Star*, 28 November 1922.
[289] Ibid.

smaller oil camps were visited by the band

This Klan action followed the shooting of Cotton Persons of Camden, a driller, allegedly by a black man. His body had been found in front of a black business in Laneytown, a bullet in his chest. According Sheriff Eber at Camden, all roads leading from the Smackover field were "dotted with fleeing negroes."[290]

Although this Klan action occurred in Arkansas, it does have significance to the kidnappings and murders of Watt Daniel and Thomas Richards. First, it has already been established that Klansmen travel freely across state lines to assist one another, and, in fact, this was a point raised by Governor Parker to President Harding when Parker asked Harding for assistance in keeping the Klan from crossing state borders, Second, this type of Klan-helping-Klan will surface in the upcoming open hearings when Morehouse Klansmen are questioned about their activities in this regard.

A rich silver strike was reported this day from Tombstone, Arizona. A six-inch vein of rich ore had been found a few feet beneath the surface of the main street in Tombstone during regular street repairs.

THURSDAY NOVEMBER 30, 1922

Vigilantes Thoroughly Clean Smackover Areas of Undesirables and Thousands are Departing

Net Results Given Show One Dead and Others 'Feathered'[291]

For the first time since the free-for-all encounter between a band of 200 white-robed vigilantes and a party of alleged high-jackers and gamblers along Smackover Creek in Ouachita County, Arkansas, Tuesday midnight, telephone communication with the new oil field town of Smackover was restored this morning.

People on the Smackover end of the line, however, were far from being communicative. The only information given out was that Smackover was quiet "and always had been."

They admitted that the town was invaded by several hundred "white-robers" Tuesday night and that gamblers and barrel-house denizens and owners were "told to go" and that practically all places had been closed.

A battle was fought at Smackover Creek, two miles north of Smackover, it was stated, and one man was killed.

A dispatch received at Monroe from reliable sources at El Dorado this morning stated that so far as El Dorado could ascertain the net results of the fight Tuesday night on Smackover was the death of one man, feathering of another and a "few wounded."

"We have not been able to get any definite information out of Smackover," it was stated by Floyd Miller, circulation manager of the El Dorado Tribune,

---

[290]*Monroe News-Star*, 28 November 1922.

[291]*Monroe News-Star*, 30 November 1922.

"because all wires were cut at Smackover when the battle started. Everybody who ought to know something about the affair is reticent.

"Information received at El Dorado this morning is that a man known as "Airplane Slim" Saunders was tarred and feathered by vigilantes Tuesday night before the battle. He was captured at a road-house by white-robed figures.

"The man who was killed in the battle on Smackover Creek has not been identified. At El Dorado he is called 'Don Few-clothes,' this being, of course, his nickname. The man was shot at a road-house. I was told he was a gambler.

"The vigilantes gave him a .45 calibre revolver as he had no weapon just before the battle began. The body was brought to the El Dorado undertaking establishment and an effort will be made to identify it.

"Smackover is reported quiet this morning, but there is much muttering going on and a renewal of trouble is expected."

Smackover is only about 80 miles from Bastrop. It would have been quite easy for Klansmen from Morehouse Parish to have traveled to Smackover to participate in the attack on the citizenry. It is equally possible that Dr. B. M. McKoin himself could have been at the forefront of the battle. He has already admitted to participating in civilian law enforcement action in Arkansas. This type of lawlessness would seem to have been right up his alley.

From Waynesboro, Mississippi this day, came a report of the shooting and attempted kidnapping of Albert Evans at the hands of five masked men who came to his home near Boyce the previous night. According to Evans, the men called him from his home shortly after 10 p.m. and ordered him to accompany them. After going a short distance, he jerked himself away. As he did, one of the party fired two shots striking him in the chest.

According to the sheriff, Evans had been under indictment for several years on a charge of "kidnapping." It was alleged that he had left notes in the yards of a number of blacks near Boyce warning all them not to work for R. R. Prescott, a well-known farmer near Boyce. It was said that there was animosity between the two men for some time.[292]

FRIDAY DECEMBER 1, 1922

Coco Promises Arrests in Mer Rouge Crimes
Holds Conference With Parker as to Morehouse Crime[293]

Attorney General Coco met with Governor Parker concerning the disappearance of Watt Daniel and T. F. Richards. After the conference, Coco said that a course of action had been decided upon and that open hearings would take

---

[292]Ibid.

129

place in Morehouse Parish, probably in January, to determine those responsible.

He said that although the state had the right to hold this open hearing investigation, the order for it must come from the local district judge. This judge would be none other than Judge Odom.

In Baton Rouge this evening, Governor Parker addressed the Louisiana Teachers Association last evening and told the gathering that they must be steadfast against any secret organizations attempting to gain control of the public schools.

> We should never have politics in our schools, as long as we are a free people. It would be absolutely unthinkable to permit the Masons, the Knights of Columbus or any other secret organization to dictate how our public schools systems should be conducted. It would be equally unthinkable that a band of masked men, masquerading in hoods and night shirts, should be permitted to control our public schools.
> We have no place in our system of government for such an organization. We have no nobility of any kind in this country except an emperor elected for life by a certain Klan with headquarters in Atlanta. The emperor of the Klan is a huge joke and is looked upon as such.

Needless to say, such terms of endearment did little to soothe the ruffled feathers of Klansmen. As a matter of fact, while Governor Parker was addressing the teachers, Baton Rouge Klan No. 3, Knights of the Ku Klux Klan was conducting an initiation of about 400 aspiring Klansmen into the mysteries of that order about six miles outside of the city limits of Baton Rouge.

Surrounded by about 800 robed and hooded Klansmen and with an estimated crowd of about 10,000 curious onlookers, they heard an unknown Klansman revile Governor Parker, bolshevism and the immigrants flocking to the shore of the United States. The speaker said that the Klan would tolerate the Jew as long as he does not undermine American institutions; blacks as long as they stayed in their place and did not try to ascend to the level of the white man; and Catholics were not objected to except for the Knights of Columbus who were accused of "carrying on bitter warfare" against the Klan.

From Alexandria, Louisiana came a challenge to Governor Parker as well as an endorsement of the Klan. Both were issued by Rev. Leon I. McCain, of the Methodist Church, of Woodworth, Louisiana. This challenge was issued by Rev. McCain on Thanksgiving Day. At the same time, circulars were distributed announcing that Rev. McCain would deliver an address at Woodworth that evening

---

[293]*Monroe News-Star*, 1 December 1922.

on "Why the Marvelous Growth of the Ku Klux Klan.[294]

Haynesville Mayor Asked to Resign his Office by Ku Klux[295]

John W. Norton, mayor of Haynesville, Louisiana, was told to resign in a letter purporting to have come from the Ku Klux Klan. The letter alleged that the police force was shielding bootleggers and law breakers and attacked the town marshal as a "law breaker of the worst type." Norton declared that he was going to retain his office and go ahead "attending to his business as before."

The letter was written on paper stamped with the name of Klan No. 63, Knights of the Ku Klux Klan, realm of Louisiana, and was headed Homer, La., but postmarked in Haynesville. The letter also threatened the police force with action in federal court unless it resigned.

Both the Haynesville and Homer Klans denied any knowledge of the letter. Many residents at Haynesville thought it the work of political enemies of the present administration. A portion of the letter read as follows:

> After waiting and looking forward to the time that you as a Christian man with the administration of this city in your hands would take steps to stamp out lawlessness in your city, our patience as citizens is worn threadbare. We will state a few facts that are in our hands at this time. The marshal is a lawbreaker of the worst type.

Initiate 1,000 in Klan
Government Agents Are Near Scene of Louisiana Ceremonies[296]

The Ku Klux Klan announced in New Orleans their plan to initiate 1,000 members on the Greenwell Springs Road located six miles from Baton Rouge that evening. In New Orleans a small class was initiated across the Mississippi River. Police placed a strong guard near the scene of the initiation to stop any outbreak, and said they would stop the proceedings the moment anything out of line occurred. Federal agents were said to have been near the Klan meetings in both Baton Rouge and New Orleans.

From Atlanta, Georgia came the report that the "Klonvocation" of the Ku Klux Klan had closed with instruction in the Kloranic and scientific divisions of Exalted Cyclops, Grand Dragons and King Kleagles. The resolution repudiating affiliation

---

[294] *Monroe News-Star*, 1 December 1922.
[295] Ibid.
[296] *The New York Times*, 1 December 1922.

with woman's auxiliaries had been referred to a special committee.[297]

In a dispatch from Laurel, Delaware, the Rev. Mr. Bennett, a Methodist minister, denounced the Ku Klux Klan without naming it in a union Thanksgiving sermon this day. His sermon caused quite a sensation because the Klan was said to be strong in Laurel.[298]

From Moscow came a report that the Third Internationale had adopted a resolution declaring that inasmuch as America was the center of the black culture of the world, it is there that the Communist campaign to bring freedom to blacks of all countries should be concentrated. "The Communists will use all their power and influences with trade unions," it said, "to admit negroes as members, and if necessary the Internationales will undertake a special campaign to achieve this aim. If these efforts fail, the Internationales will organize special negro unions to further their cause."[299]

It was announced this day at the annual convention of the National Cloak, Suit, and Skirt Manufacturer's Association in Cleveland, Ohio that longer skirts and shorter jackets will be in vogue for the Spring of 1923.[300]

MONDAY DECEMBER 4, 1922
Ku Klux Klan Must Go, Says Dr. Straton
Pastor of Calvary, However, Wins Applause by Praising Their Ideals[301]

The Klan was in the news again in New York. It was reported that the Rev. John Roach Straton, pastor of Calvary Baptist Church, preached a sermon condemning the methods but not the motives of the Ku Klux Klan He further declares that there was no room for the man in the mask in America, or any secret society either Protestant, Catholic, Jewish or black. At least 2,000 person heard the sermon and at least half were unable to gain entrance to the church. Dr. Straton announced that he would preach the following Sunday on "How to Fight the Negroes, Foreigners, Catholics and Jews in the More Excellent Way."

---

[297] Ibid.
[298] Ibid.
[299] *The New York Times*, 2 December 1922.
[300] *The New York Times*, 3 December 1922.
[301] Ibid.

TUESDAY DECEMBER 5, 1922
Two Grand Juries to Sift Activities of Ku Klux Here
Haywood Ready to Appear[302]

From New York came a report of an investigation of the activities of the Ku Klux Klan in New York County by two grand juries now sitting was directed yesterday by Judge Francis X. Mancuso of the Court of General Sessions. Judge Mancuso, speaking from the bench, declared that the invasion of New York City by the Klan was aimed not only at blacks, Jews and Catholics, but at all who did not accept the Klan's principles. He directed the members of the two grand juries to conduct a thorough investigation and to return indictments of the evidence should warrant such action.

The Rev. Dr. Oscar Haywood, national lecturer of the Klan, said he would be very glad to go before the grand jury and explain the principles of the organization if he should be called. Asked if he would reveal any of the Klan's secrets, he replied: "I would die rather than reveal any of the secrets of the order, but I will answer any questions that I consider proper."

In Chicago, report of a special aldermanic investigation of the infiltration of the Ku Klux Klan among municipal employees was made public by Alderman Robert J. Mulcahy. Also Chief Justice Michael L. McKinley of the criminal court barred members of the Klan from serving on the December grand jury. The committee was to investigate of a report that a city fire station was used recently as a lodge hall by the Klan.[303]

Meanwhile in Kansas City, Rev. Roger O. Fife, evangelist, bitterly assailed the crusade of Governor Allen of Kansas against the Ku Klux Klan. In an address before more than 800 persons in the Temple Christian Church, Fife said, "You fight the devil with fire, and it would be absurd to ask the Klan to do effective work in the open. Oh, how Allen does love that pillowslip joke of his." Fife also thrashed Mayor Hylan of New York for his attack on the Klan. The church was too small to hold those seeking to hear the address.[304]

While Rev. Fife was attacking Gov. Allen in Kansas City, Gov. Allen was in Madison, Wisconsin where he announced that the "problem in government created

---

[302] Ibid.

[303] Ibid.

[304] Ibid.

by the rise of the Ku Klux Klan throughout the country" would be placed before the state governors at their annual conference at White Sulphur Springs, West Virginia between December 14th to 16th.[305]

From the office of the United States Attorney General Daugherty in Washington, D.C., came the opinion that illegal acts attributed to the Ku Klux Klan fall within the police powers of the states, and that the federal government had no jurisdiction over such matters. This opinion was issued in response to an inquiry made by Senator Walsh of Massachusetts.[306]

WEDNESDAY DECEMBER 6, 1922
Police Give Banton List of 800 in Klan[307]

Reports from New York City indicated that Mayor Hylan issued instructions to Police Commissioner Enright to run the Klan out of the city. Also that all the evidence concerning Klan activity was turned over to the district attorney. According to Acting District Attorney Ferdinand Pecora, the most important material received from the police department was a list of approximately 800 Klansmen and their addresses. Most of these were residents of New York City, but many lived in New Jersey and in up-state cities such as Poughkeepsie, Schenectady, Yonkers, Buffalo and Syracuse.

Blame Church Fires on Klan in Canada
Old Presbytery at Oka Destroyed--Simmons Wires Montreal, Denying Responsibility[308]

Dispatches from Oka, Quebec told the tragic story of how priceless historical records of the early days of New France were destroyed in a fire that swept the home of the Order of the Gentlemen of St. Sulpice. These priceless records had been removed to this village in 1821 for preservation. Property damage was estimated at nearly $100,000. A denial that the Ku Klux Klan was in any way responsible for the series of fires at Catholic institutions across Canada was contained in a telegram received by the authorities this day from William J. Simmons, Imperial Wizard of the Ku Klux Klan.

Mayor Martin claimed that he had received numerous communications signed "K.K.K." claiming responsibility for the Montreal University fire a few weeks

---

[305]Ibid.

[306]Ibid.

[307]*The New York Times*, 6 December 1922.

previous, and that "K.K.K." threats to burn other Catholic institutions also had been received. The burning of the Sulpician Fathers historic seminary and church at Oka was the fifth fire in Catholic institutions in the Dominion in two weeks.

Klan activity was reported this day in Atlantic City, New Jersey when James A. Lightfoot, a black attorney, received a note written on Klan stationary that staid, "Segregation is right." Lightfoot had been one of the chief opponents of the move by the Board of Education to segregate black school children. There have been frequent reports that Klansmen in their white regalia have been seen in various parts of the city. [309]

In Youngstown, Ohio, the local board of education considered a request by the Youngstown branch of the Ku Klux Klan that representatives of the Klan, the Knights of Columbus and B'nai 'Brith have a conference to work out a design of religious instruction in the public schools. The board decided to consider the proposal, but took no definite action.[310]

Dispatches from the Luxor, Egypt correspondent of *The London Times* broke the news that Lord Carnarvon and Howard Carter had discovered the tomb of the Pharaoh Tutankhamen. Of the find, Carter said, "Our impressions, gathered from our initial investigation, are that the chambers opened are really ante-chambers to the King's mausoleum, and from the seals on the doorway still unopened there is every indication we shall find Pharaoh Tutankhamen.[311]

THURSDAY DECEMBER 7, 1922
Louisiana's Governor Carries War on Klan into Gotham, Asks Insurance Convention "To Aid" [312]

From New York City came a report that Governor Parker of Louisiana asked the National Convention of Insurance Commissioners to use their influence "in aiding red-blooded Americans to wage war on the Ku Klux Klan. If you will join in this great patriotic duty," the governor continued, " you will put out of business all the 'isms' that threaten the stability of the state and national government."

"What must we think," he said, "of grown-up men who go parading about the country in their nighties trying to take the law into their own hands?" He called the

---

[308] Ibid.
[309] Ibid.
[310] Ibid.
[311] Ibid.

Klan a "growing menace," and compared its growth to that of the Fascisti in Italy.

Judicial Candidate Got Ku Klux Threat[313]

The first tangible evidence to show the members of the Ku Klux Klan have made threats against any one in New York City was received by Acting District Attorney Pecora. It was a copy of a letter sent to Edward S. Brogan, former Assistant District Attorney, while he was a candidate for the office of Judge of General Session. A copy of the text of the letter was as follows:

> "The Most Sublime Lineage in All History, Commemorating and Perpetuating as it does The Most Dauntless Organization Known to Man.
> IMPERIAL PALACE
> KNIGHTS OF THE KU KLUX KLAN
> Incorporated.
> ATLANTA, GEORGIA.
> Department of Propaganda
> Office of
> IMPERIAL KLEAGLE.
> KLAN NO. 51 NEW YORK.
> September 19, 1922.
>
> Edward S. Brogan,
> Columbus Circle,
> New York City,
>
> Sir:
> Your persecutions of the Ku Klux Klan has reached its limit. We have stood silently by while you maligned us through one campaign. Now it must cease.
> You have been posing as a man unprejudiced by religious prejudices while you have always been a low kneeler to the pope in Rome. It is to him you owe allegiance not to your own people or your flag. Now your duplicity must end.
> Immediately upon receipt of this communication you will withdraw from the present campaign and leave the way clear for a real man.
> This will be our sole warning unless you immediately drop from the race. We shall force you to do so even though it be our first public act in New York.
> Beware, you have been warned.
> KNIGHTS OF THE KU KLUX KLAN, KLAN 21.

A dispatch from Washington, D.C. carried the news that an investigation of Ku Klux Klan activities by a House Committee was proposed in a resolution introduced by Representative Ryan of New York. The resolution also called for an examination of the financial condition of the organization, "in order that just and proper returns be filed with the collectors of the internal revenue." The resolution called the Klan "unAmerican," and asserted it had expended "large sums for the

---

[312]Ibid.

building of palaces" and had issued "propaganda of religious bigotry and racial hatred."[314]

Correspondents in New York City reported that Chief Sheet Lightning startled 250 persons who attended the 87th dinner of the St. Nicholas Society of New York in the Biltmore Hotel, when garbed in a feathered headdress and beaded costume of the Iroquois tribe, he presented a bearskin to the toastmaster and demanded the return of Manhattan or a barrel of rum.[315]

FRIDAY DECEMBER 8, 1922
Wizard is Defiant of Foes of Ku Klux
New Official Attacks Catholics and Jews in a Speech at Dallas[316]

At an address of supporters of the Ku Klux Klan in Waco, Texas, newly elected Imperial Wizard, H. W. Evans of Dallas told his audience that every resource that will make stronger and perpetuate the principles of the Knights of the Ku Klux Klan will be brought to bear to combat the attacks made against the order.

He claimed that the Jewish race was allied with the Catholics assaulting the Klan "because the Jew in America sees in the rise and extension of Klanishness an arrest placed on his activities in money getting." With regard to the position held by the Klan that Jews and Catholics have aligned with blacks in their attacks on the Klan, he said, "When in the '60s the negro was enfranchised, it was at once the greatest crime ever committed against his race and against our race."

A bulletin from New York City announced that Grady K. Rutledge, secretary of the American Unity League, had arrived from Chicago to start a campaign against the Ku Klux Klan in New York City. Rutledge said that the League intended to start its fight against the Klan here by publishing the names of New York City Klansmen in the League's weekly newspaper, "Tolerance." He said that this method had been successful in Chicago, where the publication of names resulted in the reduction of Klan members from 55,000 to about 10,000.[317]

---

[313] Ibid.
[314] Ibid.
[315] Ibid.
[316] Ibid.
[317] *The New York Times*, 8 December 1922.

Negro Burned at Stake
Mob Seizes Suspect in Teacher Murder from Sheriff[318]

Perry, Fla., Dec. 8.--Charlie Wright, negro, accused of the murder of Miss Ruby
Hendry, young school teacher, was taken from the sheriff and burned at the stake
at the scene of the crime early tonight by a mob estimated at several thousand
men.

SATURDAY DECEMBER 9, 1922

Secret Klan Inquiry by Chicago Aldermen
Committee Decides That Oath of Order is 'Violative of the Constitution'[319]

A communiqué from Chicago said that the special aldermanic committee on the
Ku Klux Klan had decided that the obligations taken by Klansmen is "violative of
the Constitution" on the ground that the oath contravenes guarantees of racial
equality and religious freedom. At the close of the executive session, Chairman
Mulcahy announced that an open session of the committee would be held next
Wednesday, at which a witness, then out of the city, would testify to the use of a
Chicago fire station for Klan initiations.

From New York City came the news that Rev. Dr. Oscar Haywood, national
lecturer of the Ku Klux Klan, met with Acting District Attorney Ferdinand Pecora.
Although he was head of Klan propaganda in New York City, Haywood told
Pecora that work for the Klan was not his chief activity, and that his principle
business was to organize an American Protestant Church. "So far as I know, there
is no Klan recruiting campaign going on in New York City. There may be one, but
I don't know it. The Klan is watching certain groups in this country. One of the
bodies of the Christian Church has predicted a bloody revolution in the United
States in 1925, and we are watching that."[320]

Also from New York came the announcement that the Motion Picture
Commission voted to disregard the complaint of the National Association for the
Advancement of Colored People against the picture, "The Birth of a Nation." In an
opinion filed at the hearing, one member said that the "film pictured the negro in an
unfavorable light, and that the showing of the picture tended to stir up racial
prejudice."[321] This silent motion picture had depicted the Ku Klux Klan in a very

---

[318]*Times-Picayune*, 8 December 1922.

[319]Ibid.

[320]*The New York Times*, 9 December 1922.

[321]Ibid.

favorable light, and it has been credited by many as being responsible for the second resurgence of the Klan.

MONDAY DECEMBER 11, 1922
Masked Klansman in Brooklyn Pulpit Defies Police Ban
Clothed in Full Regalia, He Defends "Invisible Empire" in Crowded Church[322]

As incredible as it seemed and in defiance of Mayor Hylan's order to Police Commissioner Enright to run the Klan out of New York City, a Klansman in full costume appeared in the pulpit of the Washington Avenue Baptist Church, located at Gates and Washington Avenues in Brooklyn. Although it had been reported that a hooded Klansman had recently given a speech in a church at West Sayville, Long Island, this was thought to be the first time a Klansman had mounted a pulpit in New York City. This was a planned appearance as the Rev. Dr. Robert McCaul, the pastor of the Washington Avenue Baptist Church, paid for the following advertisement to appear in a Brooklyn newspaper:

> The Washington Avenue Baptist Church, Gates and Washington Avenues, Brooklyn. The Rev. Dr. Robert McCaul will preach on the Ku Klux Klan Sunday evening. A speaker in mask and costume will be present to tell about this mysterious organization. The speaker will give the possibilities, purposes and perils of the Ku Klux Klan.

That Sunday evening, instead of the usual crowd of 200, the church was jammed with over 1,000 all anxious to listen to the visiting Klansman. After the hymn, church announcements, and the collection, the church doors swung wide to reveal the Klansman in full regalia. Dramatically, he walked slowly to the Chancel. He was described as wearing "the regulation Klan regalia, a sheet-like garment covering his body and a white hood, pyramidical in shape with slits for eyeholes covering his head."

After shaking hands with Pastor McCaul, the Klansman climbed into the pulpit, stared silently at his audience, and withdrew a prepared statement from his robe. He began reading a rather glorified history of the Klan.

> The Ku Klux Klan of today was called into being to see that law and order reigns throughout the country. Among the purposes of the organization is to see that the trade of the country is not controlled by Jews, and that the educational institutions of the country are not controlled by Catholicism. It is also the purpose of the Ku Klux Klan to revive chivalry of the people and to combat those who would tear down our institutions.
> We are opposed to the bootlegger, and we are organized to maintain this

---

[322]*The New York Times*, 11 December 1922.

supremacy of the white race and to keep Protestantism in the ascendancy.

After delivering his speech, the Klansman stepped back and sat down. The Rev. Dr. McCaul then stepped into the pulpit, and told the congregation that he was in harmony with the principles of the Ku Klux Klan. "The Klan's program harmonizes with that of civilization. Every man with a feeling of righteousness should be behind that program. I do not believe in the methods of the Ku Klux Klan. I believe we should convert opponents rather than kill them."

From the pulpit of the Calvary Baptist Church, the Rev. Dr. John Straton, pastor, came the statement that the Ku Klux Klan in the South and West was mostly dominated by 'lame duck' preachers who could not make it good in the ministry. Straton pointed out that William J. Simmons, Klan founder and newly deposed leader, and William J. Mahoney, the "Imperial Klokard," along with numerous other national officers were clergymen. They play out in the ministry, and then instead of selling insurance, or peddling churns, as they did in former times, they devote their time and talents to 'saving the country' by organizing men into secret, disguised societies and dressing them up in nightgowns and dunce caps."

Back in Louisiana, charges of misuse of Klan funds had been admitted by the former secretary of the New Orleans branch of the Klan, V. K. Parmalee. Because of the dissatisfaction concerning the manner in which the Klan was being operated, the Grand Kligrapp (secretary) of the Louisiana Klans in Shreveport, H. K. Ramsey, sent N. C. Williamson, the state senator from East Carroll Parish [about 20 miles east of Mer Rouge], to Atlanta to investigate.

When he returned from Atlanta, Williamson claimed to have made a thorough and exhaustive investigation into the financial affairs and operations of the Klan. He claimed to have done so in the scope of two days. In essence, this report is nothing but a whitewash, and a bombastic yet unsophisticated attempt to vindicate the Klan.[323] Although he claimed to have made an exhaustive investigation for the "two days" that he was in Atlanta, it would have been impossible for him to have done all that he had claimed in a competent and serious manner. Clearly, Kligrapp Ramsey chose wisely when he selected this windy, double-talking politician to go to Atlanta to clear the Klan.

---

[323] *Times Picayune*, 11 December 1922.

Clique Rule in Klan Ranks Prompts Members to Quit[324]

From Atlanta came the news that dissatisfaction over the management of the Ku Klux Klan, the installation of W. J. Simmons as "emperor" for life and charges of misuse of Klan funds had caused many members in Louisiana and Mississippi to quit.

Doctors ask Ban on Poor Whiskey
They Want Their Prescriptions Filled With Bottled-in Bond Liquor Only[325]

A bulletin from Washington, D. C. proclaimed that representatives of the American Medical Association and bonded distillers had conferred with Secretary of the Treasury Mellon this day seeking better enforcement of prohibition by relaxation of the ban which Prohibition Commissioner Haynes placed on medicinal liquor.

TUESDAY DECEMBER 12, 1922
Young Negro Lynched by Big Mob in Texas
Man Accused of Attacking Girl Is Taken From Sheriff, Tied to Tree and Shot Dead[326]

Mob violence was reported in Streetman, Texas as George Gay, a black man, was arrested in connection with an alleged attack on a young white woman. Feelings ran high in the community following the alleged attack and local and county officers decided the only chance for the Gay's safety was to move him to Fairfield. When the sheriff's party removed the Gay from the jail, approximately 250 automobiles were in the line. At this point, it would have seemed obvious to anyone that there would be trouble on the road.

Sure enough, at a point where the highway crossed a creek, the sheriff's party was overtaken by the mob and Gay was seized. The officers were held under a armed guard while Gay was chained to the tree and his body riddled with bullets. Approximately 1,000 persons witnessed the lynching. The evidence against Gay was declared by officers to be circumstantial, the young woman having failed to identify him as her assailant. This situation, as well as the many like this one that have preceded it and those that will follow, seems to suggest strongly that either those in law enforcement were dumb as a stump, or there actions were intentional knowing full well that the arrestee would be taken from them and murdered.

---

[324]*Times-Picayune*, 11 December 1922.

[325]Ibid.

[326]*The New York Times*, 12 December 1922.

Klan Letters Sent to Grand Jurors
Every Alderman Also Receives Message Defending Ku Klux Activities

Every member of the two December Grand Juries which were instructed recently by Judge Francis X. Mancuso to investigate the activities of the Ku Klux Klan in New York City received a letter defending the Klan. A similar letter was received by each member of the Board of Aldermen, which recently voted to support Mayor Hylan's attempt to keep the Klan out of New York City. The letter to the Grand Jurors, headed "Keep America Protestant," was as follows:

> Mayor Hylan's order to 'hunt down' the Klansmen and 'treat them as you would Reds and bomb throwers,' is proof that Roman Catholic hierarchy believes itself now strong enough to institute the diabolical system of inquisition in America. Rome has overlooked the fact that there are seventy-nine million or more Protestants in the United States and that once they are thoroughly awake to the Papal conspiracy they will rise in a body and drive every alien Papist from our shores. Abraham Lincoln prophesied this event sixty years ago in these words:
> "I see a dark cloud on the horizon, and that dark cloud is coming from Rome. It will rise and increase, till its flanks will be torn by a flash of lightning, followed by a fearful peal of thunder. Then a cyclone such as the world has never seen will pass over this country, spreading ruin and desolation from North to South. After it is over, there will be long days of peace and prosperity for popery, with its Jesuits and merciless Inquisition, will be forever swept away from out country."
> Christian Protestant Americans are the latter-day Children of Israel. In this crisis, as of old, their God goeth before them "by day in a pillar of cloud to lead them the way, and by night in a pillar of fire to give them light."
> Who shall stay his hand?
> P.S.--Patriotic organizations are invited to reprint and broadcast.

Klan Gift to Evangelist[327]

The Rev. William Senior of Midvale, New Jersey was the latest member of the clergy to be paid homage by the Ku Klux Klan. While delivering a sermon at the Methodist Episcopal Church at Midvale, five masked Klansmen bestowed a $50 contribution to a fund being raised because of the recent death of his wife.

Just as the congregation finished singing a hymn, the doors of the church opened suddenly and the masked Klansmen entered single file. They proceeded up the middle aisle and all bowed to Rev. Senior. The leader gave Senior and envelope, and the five Klansmen then filed out in silence. The letter contained 10 five-dollar bills and the following letter:

---

[327] Ibid.

Dec. 10, 1922.

Reverend Sir:--Having heard of your misfortune in the loss of your noble wife and baby's mother, we hasten to express our sincere sympathy, and condole with you in this your sad hour of bereavement. 'Time heals all sorrow.' Fortunately for us it is true. 'God moves in a mysterious way,' but it is not for us to question, although we sometimes long for 'the touch of a vanished hand and the sound of a voice that is still.' As a token of high esteem for yourself and the good cause for which you are laboring, we beg of you to accept this donation from

THE KNIGHTS OF THE KU KLUX KLAN.
Provisional Klan 16 of This Immediate Vicinity.

WEDNESDAY DECEMBER 13, 1922

Klansmen Initiate 75 more in Newark
Lincoln's Son Denies Ku Klux Charge that Father Warned of "Storm From Rome"[328]

The Ku Klux Klan continued to expand in New Jersey as a report was issued that a Klan of the Knights of the Invisible Empire had received its charter from the Imperial Wizard of the Ku Klux Klan at a meeting at 17 West Park Street in Newark. The meeting initiated about 50 to 75 new members and heard "a message of world-wide importance" from the Imperial Cyclops of the Klan, who returned recently from the Imperial Klonvokation in Atlanta.

According to a Klansman in attendance, it was George Washington Klan No. 3, of the Realm of New Jersey, that received its charter. This Klansman declared that this particular Klan was only one of 40 in Newark and vicinity, and that it had a membership of 1,500 and 400 more waiting to join.

In response to a letter sent to grand jurors in New York City, Robert Todd Lincoln of Washington, D. C., son of Abraham Lincoln, denied allegations by the Ku Klux Klan that his father had made any anti-Catholic utterances.

A dispatch from Rome this day told of a victory of the constitutional parties in the municipal elections in Milan. The resignation of practically all the Socialist Municipal Councils was forced by the Fascisti during the recent violent upheaval.[329]

Women's Clan Hits Snag in California
Incorporation Papers Sent Back to Bring Them Within Law[330]

Reports from Sacramento, California indicated that incorporation papers of the "Ladies of the Cu Clux Clan of California," were returned by the secretary of state

---

[328]*The New York Times*, 13 December 1922.

[329]Ibid.

[330]*Times-Picayune,* 13 December 1922.

for amendment to bring them within California law. According to the secretary of state, the corporation cannot do business in the state under the articles submitted which stated that the term of the organization shall be perpetual. California law limited the existence of corporations to 50 years. Another objection was that the corporation was formed with trustees and incorporators, of whom a majority are nonresidents of California.

THURSDAY DECEMBER 14, 1922
Violence Will Kill Ku Klux, Says Allen
Those Who Gave It Birth Will Strangle It if Lawlessness Continues[331]

Speaking from the Conference of Governors at White Springs, West Virginia, Gov. Henry Allen of Kansas predicted that the Ku Klux Klan will die in time because of the lawlessness which its mysterious rites and disguises lead. Allen said that the Klan was losing ground in the South because its original leaders have left it since the lawless element obtained control.

> It amused us at first, then we became interested in it because of the superb salesmanship responsible for its growth. It was the A.P.A. (American Protective Association) plus antipathy to negroes, plus antipathy to Jews, rolled in the American flag and sold for $10 a throw, of which the organizer gets $4 and the profiteers at Atlanta get the rest.
> The chief hobgoblins, or whatever they are, have got a lot of money out of it. In addition to the original profit, they sell a cheap cotton robe and hood, which would not cost more than $2.35, for six. If they have acquired the membership of 9,000,000 that they claim, then these people who have exploited the Klan have cleaned up several millions of dollars.

A dispatch from Paris reported that a police court judge decided that a husband had the right to strike his wife. The decision was based on an article of the Civil Code regarding the principle of marital authority in relation to public order and family organization. The woman accused her husband of knocking her down, but a witness declared that he struck her, then pushed her down, after she had responded violently to a reprimand. The Magistrate declared that under the circumstances the husband was acting within "the right of correction" bestowed upon him by the code. [332]

---

[331]Ibid.
[332]Ibid.

144

FRIDAY DECEMBER 15, 1922
Negroes Taken From Jail
"Both Got What They Had Coming," an Unsigned Note Says[333]

Two black men were reported missing this day from the jail at Pilot Point, Texas. They had been detained on a charge of horse theft. An unsigned note found on the door of a local newspaper office read: "Both negroes got what they had coming. Let this be a warning to all negro loafers. Negroes get a job or leave town." Two black men disappeared from the Pilot Point jail in a similar manner several months prior and nothing had been heard from them. The jail was unguarded at night.[334]

From Washington, D.C. came the news that Hell's Half-Acre had been officially designated to be in Wyoming, and that it would be given to Natrona County for park purposes.

SATURDAY DECEMBER 16, 1922
Protestant Body Denounces Klan[335]

Meeting in New Orleans, the Federal Council of the Churches of Christ in America (Protestant) in their bulletin, printed an anti-Klan article entitled "Ku Klux Klan Disowned by the Churches." Because so often the Klan has been associated by the general public with the Protestant faith, this organization banded together to combat the evils of the Klan. Contained below is a portion of the article:

> The mistaken impression that the Ku Klux Klan deserves and is receiving the support of the Protestant churches has led the Federal Council of the Churches to make its position clear and unmistakable. The administrative committee of the Federal Council of Churches of Christ in America records its strong conviction that the recent rise of organizations whose members are masked, oathbound and unknown, and whose activities have the effect of arousing religious prejudice and racial antipathies is fraught with grave consequences to the church and society at large.
>
> Any organization whose activities tend to set class against class or race against race is consistent neither with the ideals of the churches nor with true patriotism, however vigorous or sincere may be its profession of religion and Americanism. The administrative committee of the Federal Council of Churches is opposed to any movement which overrides the processes of law and order, and which tends to complicate and make more difficult the work of cooperation between the various political, racial and religious groups in the Republic.
>
> No such movements have the right to speak the name of Protestantism, and the

---

[333] Ibid.

[334] Ibid.

[335] *Times-Picayune*, 16 December 1922.

churches are urged to exert every influence, to check their speed.

The reader should bear in mind that this originated in New Orleans, which is located in southeastern Louisiana. As mentioned before, the Klan did not do well in New Orleans, nor did it get a foothold in nearly all of southern Louisiana. The strength of the Klan has traditionally been the northern parishes of Louisiana, and this is where we find churches and the Klan in bed with one another.

SUNDAY DECEMBER 17, 1922
Denies Masons Join Klan[336]

Speaking in New Brunswick, New Jersey, Governor-elect George S. Silzer denied a statement attributed to a Brooklyn organizer of the Ku Klux Klan that 70% of Klansmen were Masons. In an address before 500 Masons at the laying of the cornerstone of the Masonic Temple in Highland Park, Silzer declared that Masons were not the type of men to hide their faces behind masks, and he urged all Masonic members to repudiate the charge to the grand lodge next year in Trenton.

MONDAY DECEMBER 18, 1922
Parish in Arms Against Spread of Ku Klux Klan
Aroused Citizens Pledge Time and Money for Drastic Campaign[337]

Reports from Jena, Louisiana, which is located about 50 miles South/Southwest of Mer Rouge, indicated that the Ku Klux Klan had been attacked bitterly at a hastily called session yesterday of the La Salle Parish Law and Order League and the Jena Citizens League. An editorial printed Sunday in *The Times-Picayune* that assailed the Klan was approved in resolutions which included a determination to wage war on the Klan and to prevent its taking root in that parish. As I have indicted before, southern areas of Louisiana were not fertile grounds for the hatred and violence of the Klan.

Lord Carnarvon Describes Contents of Chamber of Tutankhamun[338]

Dispatches reaching *The Daily Mail* in London from the Earl of Carnarvon continued to describe his discoveries in the Valley of the Kings in Egypt. He claimed that the examination of the first chamber had convinced them that they had discovered the tomb of King Tutankhamun.

---

[336]*The New York Times*, 17 December 1922.

[337]*Times Picayune*, 18 December 1922.

[338]*The New York Times*, 18 December 1922.

Deciphering Key to Ancient Maya Writings[339]

While the excavation of King Tut's tomb was underway in Egypt, archeologists in Charlottesville, Virginia, were retrieving the almost forgotten Maya language. With the aid of a nearly illiterate full-blooded Quiche Indian from the highlands of Guatemala, Dr. William Gates of Charlottesville saved a language which heretofore never had been thoroughly studied.

TUESDAY DECEMBER 19, 1922
Ku Klux Klansmen March into Church
Hooded Band of Ten Give Kearny [N. J.] Pastor Letter, Which He Reads From Pulpit[340]

On Sunday evening, reports from Kearny, New Jersey, indicated that 10 Klansmen, in full regalia, paid a visit to the Grace Methodist Episcopal Church, thereby disclosing the presence of an organized Klan in that town. The Klansmen entered the church by the main door while the congregation was singing "Onward, Christian Soldiers." They walked to the pulpit and presented a letter to the pastor, the Rev. Fredrick L. Rounds.

At the end of the hymn, the Klansmen left the church and rode away in an car. After his sermon Mr. Rounds read the following letter:

> Rev. Fredrick L. Rounds, Pastor,
> Grace M. E. Church, Kearny, N. J.:
> Dear Sir: With a sincere desire to assist in all things, we, the members of the Kearny Provisional Klan, Realm of New Jersey, Invisible Empire, Ku Klux Klan, offer this slight donation to your building fund, and ask that it be received as a gift from the klansmen, who in their humble way try to follow the teachings of Jesus Christ.
> The K. K. K. is ever ready to assist in a worthy cause, without regard to race, creed, or color. You will find us at all times ready and willing to answer any call of charity that may be brought to our attention.
> We have been attacked by the enemies of pure Americanism, and our only reply has been, 'God forgive them, for the know not what they do.'
> To you, sir, and your congregation we extend our greetings and pledge anew our faith in Him who gave His life that we might be saved. As klansmen we are pledged to the Bible, our country and the flag, and to protect the chastity of pure womanhood. Can men be banded together in a more noble cause? While our enemies and near enemies are attacking our great organization from all angles, we are standing four-square, picking our men by the thousands, men of dependability and character, who accept Christ as their Savior. In due time, when

---

[339]*The New York Times*, 18 December 1922.
[340]Ibid.

147

the storm of vile abuse has passed over as a dark cloud, the sunshine will appear and the whole world will know the truth.
(Signed)
THE KNIGHTS OF THE K. K. K."

The letterhead bore the name of the "Kearny Provisional Klan," but it did not contain the names of any of its officers. It is interesting to note that the Klan never seemed to be interested in "pure manhood."

Southern Judge Asks Grand Jury to Combat Klan
"Beast Is Loosened Under Protection of Mask," He Declares[341]

The Ku Klux Klan was the recipient of sharp criticism this day from U. S. District Court Judge William H. Barrett in Albany, Georgia. In a charge to a federal grand jury, he tendered these suggestions for combating the Klan.

> With the earnestness and zeal of a Georgia citizen, one who loves his state and his country, I implore you to cooperate in combatting what is unquestionably a menace, and if we are to treat it wisely we should treat it now, in its incipiency, and that is the Ku Klux Klan.
> I am told that the constitution of this organization is worded in such a way that no patriotic citizen can quvil at it, but my information is that the real motives that lead to joining are usually one of four.
> One that perhaps had considerable force at its initiation was on anti-negro sentiment, founded upon the proposition that by reason of unusual treatment accorded some negro soldiers abroad there might be an effort on their part to create an unhappy situation here. Another is an anti-Catholic sentiment, which would seek if not to punish, at least to greatly subdue all those who believe in that religion. Another was an anti-Jewish sentiment. Another, and perhaps the most general, was in arrogating to themselves a super knowledge and virtue, by which they would determine what things were wrong, and what they could correct wholly independent of government, courts and law.
> I ask you, gentlemen, eye to eye and face to face to ask any member of the klan, if perchance he has a young daughter, if he is willing to so carry on his life and his activities that her virtue and her protection shall depend, not upon courts, not upon law, but upon the passions of men. Ask him, if he has a young son, if he is willing for him to grow up in a country that knows no law. Ask him, if he knows he is right, why mask? The cure of wrong is light and you may count upon it when a man feels he must act with a hidden countenance and in secret, in the depths of his heart he doubts his rightness.
> I ask him, if a mask cannot just as well hide a negro's face as a white face, a Catholic face as a Protestant's, a Jew's as well as a Gentile's. Ask him if he does not realize that by this practice, however worthy he may think for the moment, he is turning loose the beast which will overrun all good government, all law, all justice, all love of man, and bring our country to desolation and despair.

---

[341] Ibid.

148

War Veteran Defies Klan[342]

In Peru, Indiana, Colonel Hiram L. Bearas, retired, internationally known as "Hiking Hiram," the fighting marine, backed his automobile into a parade of the Ku Klux Klan last Saturday night. The colonel's car was immediately surrounded by the Klansmen who opened the door and assaulted the veteran.

Picking up a wrench, the marine commander climbed to the running board of his car and shouted: "Come on you Kluxers, one and all: I'll take on the lot of you." Cooler heads prevented a further clash.

WEDNESDAY DECEMBER 20, 1922

Louisiana Troops are Sent to Guard Hearings on Kidnappings of 5 Citizens by Hooded Men[343]
Monroe Militia Fails to Arrive, Bastrop Reports[344]
Ku Klux Head Holds Klan Innocent of Louisiana Crimes[345]

Attempting to avoid fanfare, Governor Parker dispatched Company G of the Louisiana National Guard in Monroe to Mer Rouge. This was the first overt action taken by Parker which was a clear signal that the attorney general's office was prepared to initiate a full on-scene investigation into the kidnapping and disappearance of Watt Daniel and Thomas Richards. Company G consisted of 63 enlisted men and three officers commanded by Captain W. W. Cooper. They were said to have drawn rations for about a month.

Captain Cooper had arrived back in Monroe on that same morning after a trip to Baton Rouge, where he had personally received his instructions from Governor Parker and Attorney General Coco. He refused to speak with the reporters present as to the happenings in Baton Rouge or the operations that were to unfold.

As rumors flew wildly around Bastrop and Mer Rouge, Robert Dade, the Mayor of Mer Rouge and-soon-to-be major player in the unfolding drama, said that he had received an order from Governor Parker to prepare a location for the troops to camp. It was rumored that the troops were 1) going first to Bastrop, 2) stranded on the road between Monroe and Bastrop because the truck carrying them had broken down, and 3) that the rumor was a hoax. Dade told reporters that he had no first-hand information as to the whereabouts of the troops. "I am beginning to

---

[342]*Times Picayune*, 19 December 1922.

[343]*The New York Times*, 20 December 1922

[344]*Times-Picayune*, 20 December 1922.

[345]Ibid.

believe that all this talk about the company coming to Mer Rouge is a hoax," was the way Dade described it.

Fred Carpenter, the Sheriff of Morehouse Parish, played his usual role of a lost ball in high weeds, as he professed to know nothing about the troops. "They have not reached Bastrop," said Carpenter. "I heard it reported that fifteen or twenty of them arrived in Bastrop early tonight and then departed. Another report was that the army trucks had broken down between Monroe and Bastrop. I am without any information as to the troops at all. In my opinion there is nobody in Morehouse Parish that knows a single thing about this troop movement, which is as mysterious as the Mer Rouge kidnapping. I have an idea that the company will make its way to Mer Rouge."

That Sheriff Carpenter was left out of the loop is no surprise. As a law enforcement officer, he had shown himself to be totally ineffective, and as it will be shown later, his status as an officer in the Morehouse Klan made him unsuitable for the investigation which was about to commence.

Also left out of the loop was David I. Garrett, the local district attorney. "I know nothing officially of this move," Garrett said. "I have been informed by the sheriff and others in Morehouse parish that all is quiet there."

Clearly, Garrett was not included in the plans because he, like Sheriff Carpenter, had also shown himself to be ineffective, with possible Klan leanings, after his inability to uncover anything of substance in his investigation into the kidnappings and disappearance of Daniel and Richards.

Meanwhile in Washington, D. C., Dr. Hiram W. Evans, a dentist from Dallas, Texas and the new Imperial Wizard of the Ku Klux Klan, was steadfastly denying the Klan in Louisiana had anything to do with the kidnappings and disappearances of Watt Daniel and Thomas Richards. He made the statement that he was "willing to stipulate that the life or death of the Klan should stand upon the 1922 record of criminality in either Louisiana, or any of the other fifteen other states in which the Klan's organization is largest."

Little did Dr. Evans know that those hollow words spoken in defiance would actually be the exact measure by which the Klan would be judged by the general public. In fact, the criminality of the Klan was exactly what caused both the membership and the citizenry to abandon the Klan.

A report from Laurel, Mississippi announced that 50 memberships in the Laurel Library Association for poor boys and girls unable to pay for library privileges would be provided with $50 donated by the local Ku Klux Klan.[346] This is but another of many examples of how the Klan attempted to buy respectability.

THURSDAY DECEMBER 21, 1922

Diver to Assist State in Search for Missing Men[347]
Troops Seek Bodies in Louisiana Lakes
Mer Rouge Citizens Believe the Two Missing Victims of Hooded Men Were Drowned[348]

It was revealed on this date that the state had contracted a professional diver to explore the bottom of Lake LaFourche for the bodies of Watt Daniel and Thomas Richards. No information was released then or later to indicate why search efforts were to be concentrated at Lake LaFourche, except that some unnamed state official told reporters that two old iron wheels, which had been on the bank of the lake near the ferry landing had disappeared on the night of the kidnappings. It was believed that the bodies of Daniel and Richards had been attached each to a wheel and submerged in the lake. Obviously, someone had given this information to them. To think that they had arbitrarily picked Lake LaFourche as a starting point would not be logical. There are a number of small rivers and lakes that dot the region, any one of which could have been used for the purpose of disposing of the bodies.

Captain Cooper of Company G, whose men had arrived that morning in Mer Rouge and were camped in a vacant lot next to the electrical plant, was to provide security for these operations. It was said that the troops were well equipped in that they had four machine guns and about 8000 rounds of ammunition. The diver arrived this same date and was given quarters with the men of Company G.

Theories concerning the motive(s) behind the kidnappings were still matters of speculation. Some said it grew from a 25 year dispute as to whether Bastrop or Mer Rouge should be the seat of parish government. Others said it was an alleged assassination attempt on Dr. McKoin, head of the Klan in Mer Rouge. It was also rumored that Klansmen from Arkansas and Mississippi were employed in the kidnappings, it being customary to bring in Klansmen from other areas to do such dirty work.

---

[346]*Times Picayune*, 20 December 1922.
[347]Ibid.

It was reported in *The New York Times* that the location of the bodies had been ascertained and that four detectives of the Justice Department were on location. Strangely enough, this report seemed to indicate that the bodies were in Lake Cooper. Guardsmen were to drag the lake and provide cover for the diver who was enroute to help in the recovery.

An article from Atlanta, Georgia told of how the Ku Klux Klan was shaping a plan for aggressive participation in the 1924 national political campaigns. In an effort to appear moderate, Klan leaders had passed the word throughout the country to "soft pedal" any Klan opposition or criticism of the Catholic faith. Instead, Klan strategy was to spotlight a "white supremacy" program which they hoped would gain thousands of voters. The Klan planned to support congressional and senatorial candidates in 1924, but would probably wait until 1928 before placing avowed Klan candidates in the field for president.[349]

FRIDAY DECEMBER 22, 1922

Soldiers Explore Cooper Lake in Search of Two Missing Men[350]
Governor Issues Summary Order for Sheriff to Meet Captain[351]

Federal and state investigators, Louisiana National Guardsmen, and about 20 or more civilian volunteers from Mer Rouge dragged Cooper Lake for the bodies of Watt Daniel and Thomas Richards. Located about seven miles northeast of Mer Rouge, Cooper Lake is relatively shallow and much of the work was done by men wading in the lake using rakes and grappling hooks. The diver was not prepared to begin work as he had not yet completed checking his equipment.

The lake is about 20 to 300 yards in width and about a half-mile long. It was decided to begin the search there because it had been said that the masked band had been seen in the area on the night of the August 24th kidnappings. It was also thought that the Klansmen were looking for a body of water deep enough to hide their monstrous crimes. The work there proved fruitless. Work was scheduled to begin the following day at Lakes Boeuff and LaFourche and because of the depth of these lakes, the services of the diver would be needed.

---

[348]The New York Times, 21 December 1922
[349]Times-Picayune, 21 December 1922.
[350]*Times-Picayune*, 22 December 1922.
[351]Ibid.

Two attempts were made to secure the help of a couple of black men to aid in the search of the lake. The caravan of agents and soldiers first stopped at the cabin of a black man known only as "Jim." He gave all the appearances of a man willing to help as he went back into the cabin to retrieve his gear. Seeing the soldiers with their rifles and the agents with their guns, "Jim" quickly figured out that this was not a place he wanted to be because "an aged mammy reported that Jim had suspected a Ku Klux enterprise of some mysterious nature and had 'done flew into de woods for a few weeks.' "[352]

The second black was brought to the lake from a plantation close by. He was known by people in the area as having been familiar with the lake bottom as he would fetch ducks for hunters. Referred to as "Sambo," he too was no fool and soon figured out what was going on.

"Gentlemen," said Sambo as he donned his rubber boots, "I believes I'se becoming seriously ill."

Although Rogers and the others attempted to reassure him that he had nothing to worry about, this did not allay his fears. When Rogers and the others refused to tell "Sambo" what they were looking for, he became even more suspicious.

"Well gentlemen," said Sambo, "is you all Christians?"

The party said that they were.

"Then, please let me go home," he begged. "I'se too weak to wade, and when I gets my feet wet I gets spasms."

They attempted to calm him by saying that his boots would protect him from the spasms, but it was clear that he wanted no part of the operation.

"But the boots might spring a leak," he pleaded. He began to cry while continuing to ask to be relieved of the job. They excused "Sambo," and he immediately fled into the woods not even taking time to don his shoes.

"The Ku Klux have got the negroes down here scared stiff," remarked one of the natives. "As the klan grows the negro loses faith in the white man. He used to look to us for protection in time of distress, but now depends only upon his sprinting powers."[353]

Speaking of Lake Cooper, Rogers said that it "was no lake at all" and called it "The Dismal Swamp." He said that their party first traveled through a "negro

---

[352]Rogers, 1922, 37.

graveyard" and then down a near vertical drop and passed through a thick forest in order to reach the lake.

Work was scheduled to begin the following day at Lakes Boeuff and LaFourche. Because of the depth of these lakes, the services of the professional diver from St. Louis would be necessary. In the between time, the *Times-Picayune* reported that Captain Cooper had stationed groups of men at each of the lakes in the area to keep the bodies of Daniel and Richards from being exhumed from the watery graves and removed to another location. This line was in the *Times-Picayune*, "Guards were put out to prevent anyone from placing dynamite in the lakes in an attempt to destroy the bodies."

Either the *Times-Picayune* was in error when it reported that Captain Cooper had stationed the men at Lake LaFourche, or they were never sent there, because it was through the use of a large cache of dynamite that the murderers of Daniel and Richards were to later attempt to cover over their bodies in Lake LaFourche. Also, it was obvious that the information had leaked out that there would be an attempt to dynamite the lake, otherwise why would it have appeared so specifically in the press?

Even though confidence was high with federal and state investigators that they would find the bodies of Daniel and Richards, "they did not expect to find anything more than skeletons and shreds of clothing." They held this belief because they thought "that the fish undoubtedly have devoured the flesh, leaving nothing but bones and scraps of clothing." People reading such a report must have envisioned the waters of Louisiana to be filled with meat-eating fish capable of stripping a human to the bone.

It was revealed that plans had already been made to convene an "open hearing" if and when the bodies were found, and arrangements had already been made with Judge Odom to preside over the hearing. The authority to hold such a hearing was covered by legislation which had been passed on a few years prior. Under this law, the state would have the power to subpoena witnesses and force them to testify. Said testimony would then form the foundation for prosecution. Although this seems highly unconstitutional in that such a law would flagrantly violate the 5th Amendment concerning the right to remain silent and avoid self-incrimination, be

---

[353] Ibid.

aware that these tenets did not truly exist until *Escibedo v. Illinois* and *Miranda v. Arizona* some 30 to 40 years later. This law also gave the power to the attorney general to increase his prosecutorial staff, which he had already done.

Both the state and federal governments were interested in prosecuting these cases, but for different reasons. The state was interested in the kidnapping and probable murder charges that were to evolve once the bodies were discovered. The federals, however, were probing violations of the Volstead Act regarding moonshining and bootlegging. Charges of interference with interstate commerce were also under investigations with regard to the cutting of the telephone and telegraph lines between Mer Rouge and Bastrop on the afternoon of August 24, 1922. These wires were the property of the Cumberland Telephone and Telegraph Company, and it was believed that they had been cut in order to prevent communications between Mer Rouge and Bastrop concerning Klan actions on that date. It was said that the identity of the person(s) responsible for the cutting of the lines was known.

"Mer Rouge welcomed the coming of the soldiers who are protecting the diver and assisting in the search for the bodies of F. W. Daniel and T. F. Richards. The town has been an armed camp for more than four months. The majority of the citizens here are opposed to the Ku Klux Klan and have been empathetic in their denunciation of methods attributed to the klan." It seems difficult to believe that such a condition could have existed. It sounds barbaric, or at the very least, medieval. In less than two years time, the hate, mistrust, and reprehensible spirit that the Klan naturally fostered engendered a true "Tale of Two Cities." It was further described this way:

> The situation caused the anti-klansmen of Mer Rouge to organize and arm themselves for self-protection. For weeks a large number of citizens of the town have kept magazine rifles and shotguns loaded and ready for instant use in their places of business and in their residences. Each of these citizens slept at night with a loaded rifle or shotgun at the head of their beds.
> During the day loaded guns were kept in the stores, offices and shops. A signal of four shots was agreed upon as a call to arms. These firearms were in evidence throughout the town today in the different places of business, but the citizens felt that they would not be called upon to use them now that the soldiers were here.

Unlike the citizens of Mer Rouge who were happy at the arrival of the National Guardsmen, the residents of Bastrop, the stronghold of the Klan, did deeply resent their presence as they did Governor Parker, the man who had ordered them there.

155

The populations of the towns of Mer Rouge and Bastrop mushroomed overnight as newspaper corespondents from across the nation and abroad began arriving to cover the situation which was unfolding by the hour. Because of the flood of correspondents, Western Union was forced to increase dranatically the compliment of dispatch agents in Monroe, Bastrop and Mer Rouge in order to manage the volume of telegraph traffic in and out of the area.

A conference was scheduled by Captain W. W. Cooper and representatives of the federal and state governments with regard to coordination and management of the investigation to which an invitation was sent to Sheriff Carpenter. The sheriff refused to attend and arrogantly sent word "that he would take the matter under consideration."

Weary of playing games with the sheriff, Captain Cooper sent the following telegram to Governor Parker:

> Mer Rouge, Dec. 21, 1922.
> Honorable John M. Parker, governor
> State of Louisiana,
> Baton Rouge
> Sheriff Fred Carpenter of Morehouse parish has refused point blank to come to Mer Rouge at my request for a conference. He stated that he will come here only to serve legal papers.
> (Signed) "Captain Cooper.

From Governor Parker came this dispatch to Sheriff Carpenter:

> Baton Rouge, La., Dec. 21, 1922.
> Honorable J. Fred Carpenter, Sheriff
> Bastrop, La.
> As chief executive of this state and in compliance with Section 14 of Article 5 of the constitution, I hereby direct and instruct you to immediately go to Mer Rouge in your parish and consult with Captain Cooper, in charge of the troops who has instructions to give ample protection to those who by my orders are now making an investigation of the reported outrages which took place on Aug. 24.
> Acknowledge receipt of this telegram immediately and advise action you will take in the matter.
> (Signed) John M. Parker

To Captain Cooper, Governor Parker sent this telegram:

> Baton Rouge, La., Dec 21, 1922.
> Captain W. W. Cooper
> Mer Rouge, La.
> Have wired Sheriff J. F. Carpenter of Morehouse parish to immediately get in communication with you and to go to Mer Rouge and co-operate in assuring ample protection to those now making an investigation as to the disappearance

156

and beating of Daniel, Richards and others on August 24.

Report to me fully by wire as soon as he advises you in the matter.

(Signed) John M. Parker.

Governor

SATURDAY DECEMBER 23, 1922

Explosion Reveals Wire-Bound Bodies of Supposed Ku Klux Victims in Lake: Louisiana Governor Sends More Troops

While They Drag Lake Cooper Explosion Occurs at Lake LaFourche, 20 Miles Away[354]

More Troops Rushed to Trouble Zone as Conflict Threatens After Finding Victims of Masked Band[355]

Soldiers Fire 150 Shots at Band of Waders in Lake Cooper[356]

A series of events occurred in the area overnight which culminated in the discovery of the bodies of Daniel and Richards. They began at about midnight when the detachment of guardsmen left to guard Lake Cooper observed what appeared to be persons with lamps wading in the shallow part of the lake. The militia men opened fire on these persons, and it was estimated that about 150 rounds were fired. During the action, the officer in charge of the troops at Lake Cooper sent two runners eight miles to Mer Rouge to advise Captain Cooper of the encounter and to request reinforcements. Captain Cooper immediately commandeered a number of automobiles and used them to transport 35 of his troops to Lake Cooper. Upon their arrival, they secured the area, but were unable to find any evidence of the waders. About one hour later, residents of the Lake LaFourche area experienced a loud explosion which they reported shook their homes.

John Rogers, the reporter for the *St. Louis-Dispatch*, was a witness to the incident and recorded it this way:

> All were sound asleep when, about 1 a. m., there came a violent pounding on the power house door. Farland, Captain Cooper, all sprang to their feet. The door was flung open and there stood one of the soldiers who had been left to guard Lake Cooper, pale and panting.
>
> They dragged him inside and demanded to know the cause of the alarm. He had run six miles from Lake Cooper, and some moments elapsed before he could speak.
>
> 'Sir,' he exclaimed, saluting Captain Cooper, 'The Ku Klux have us surrounded at the lake and are firing into our men.'
>
> He knew no details; that was all.

---

[354]*Times-Picayune*, 23 December 1922.

[355]Ibid.

[356]Ibid.

The decision was immediate. Every man seized rifle or pistol and lunged through the door to the automobiles. Word was quickly sent to a few others among the citizens who had wanted to be counted on in case of emergency, and a wild drive to the lake was begun.

There were only a few cars and a handful of men. How many were the klansmen? The soldier did not know. He had been dispatched for reinforcements at the first alarm.

When yet a mile from the lake the faint report of rifle firing was heard, and it continued and grew louder as the little band proceeded. Upon reaching the graveyard the cars were stopped and all scrambled out. Captain Cooper led the way, single file through the impenetrable dark of the dense wood. It was a moonless night and a light was out of the question in the circumstances.

At the crest of the mound, from which the steep descent to the bottoms began, Captain Cooper halted the party, and, with automatic pistol in one hand, took his whistle in the other and sounded a shrill blast to apprise his lieutenant of the presence of reinforcements.

The sputtering of the soldier's automatic rifles was now quite distinct and probably prevented the whistle being heard. Captain Cooper sounded another blast, and a faint 'who's there' came from the lieutenant.

'This is your captain with reinforcements,' Captain Cooper called back.

'Advance, Captain, and be recognized,' came the distant challenge out of the night.

'This is your Captain, I tell you,' the Captain exclaimed. 'Don't you dare turn those machine guns over this way!'

'Yes,' shouted the lieutenant, 'come ahead.'

Firing ceased, and with this assurance that the machine guns would not be aimed the wrong way, there was a rush down the hill by the rescuers.

'Well, here we are,' exclaimed Captain Cooper; 'what's up, lieutenant?'

'We don't know, sir,' the lieutenant stammered.

'Then, what in the hell 's all the shooting about?' demanded the Captain.

The lieutenant was apologetic. He did not know precisely the why of all the shooting, but he knew that he was nearly out of ammunition.

Something mysterious had come to pass, and he took no chances. He did know that, sometime after midnight, the sentinel aroused the camp with information that lights were flashing in the lake, and when the intruders were challenged, there was a scurrying away along the opposite bank.

Not knowing what might be under way, the soldiers put their automatic rifles into action and dispatched a courier for aid. They argued that they did not know but that an attempt was being made by enemies to remove the bodies.

Huddleston [One of the federal agents], fondling his Winchester, was sorely disappointed that it was only a false alarm, but Captain Cooper remarked that he was glad it was a mistake. He knew that more than one man in the party, to say nothing of his own men, had had just about enough of threats and would have welcomed a little action.

The incident at the time was attributed to nervousness either of the sentinel or the lieutenant, but that was a mistake. The soldiers had been disturbed by design, as the events of the day will show, and their promptness in getting into action was justifiable. Indeed, they might have brought down by a chance shot that

158

Captain Cooper secured his troops, and returned to Mer Rouge.

The midnight hour of December 24, 1922, was ushered in with the roar of dynamite on the west bank of Lake LaFourche near the foot of the Eason ferry some 16 miles south east of Mer Rouge. As dawn broke that day, J. C. Nettles, a wholesale fisherman and owner of the Eason ferry, came to the lake to check his lines. It was then that he discovered what remained of the bodies of Watt Daniel and Thomas Richards floating "face down" in the water. That term, face down, was found to be incorrect as those investigating the crime soon learned that neither Daniel nor Richards had a face. As they were to pull the bodies out of the water, they were to discover that the bodies lacked heads, hands and feet. Were this not horrible enough, the autopsies which were later performed were to reveal mind-boggling atrocities which appear to have no equal in recorded history.

At about 7:00 a.m. that same morning, the phone rang in the power house. "This is Miss _____ [The original author deleted the name], at Oak Ridge," said an excited female voice. "Those bodies are up this morning. The ferryman at Lake LaFourche said the lake was dynamited about 2 a.m., and that he found the bodies floating at daybreak."[358]

On his way out of town, Rogers told Agent Farland and Captain Cooper of the information he received. As Rogers was driving through Main Street in Mer Rouge, he was hailed down by J. L. Daniel. In the excitement of the moment, he told the elder Daniel of the news and he begged to accompany Rogers to the lake. Rogers consented, and upon arriving at the lake was met by James Nettles, the owner of the Eason ferry.

"There they are," said Nettles as Rogers and the elder Daniel started toward the lake. Rogers was later to admit that he was sorry that he had agreed to bring Daniel when he heard the elder Daniel cry "Oh-h-h, Watt, Watt, my dear boy!"

Rogers described the scene this way:

> The head, hands and feet appeared to be off, and the arms and legs were bound with rusted wire, indicating by this means they had been fastened to weights. On both bodies were shreds of trousers, but no other garments.[359]

The news was quickly broadcast and the countryside soon came trooping to the

[357]Rogers, 1922, 40-43.

[358]Ibid., 44.

[359]Ibid., 45.

scene. Among the early arrivals were Sheriff Carpenter and about a score of klansmen from Bastrop and vicinity.[360]

Rogers made no comment on how he was aware of the identity of the klansmen. Rogers took this opportunity to interview Sheriff Carpenter while on the scene. The interview follows:

"What do you think of it now, Sheriff?' I inquired.
"This is terrible--horrible," he answered.
"I have heard it said," Rogers remarked, having in mind the statements of Captain Skipwith, "that Daniel was an outlaw--what do you know of him?"
"He was a good boy," said the Sheriff. "He worked hard for my election, and I never knew of his being in trouble."
"Did you know him as an associate of negroes?"
"Certainly not. I tell you, he was a good boy."
"Was he so much as rowdy at times?"
"No."
"Do you know anything of Richard(s)?"
"He was alright. I never had any trouble with or on account of him."
"Have you any idea why these men were put to death?"
"None whatsoever. There could be no reason for so horrible a crime."

The irony of this situation was that J. L. Daniel and Watt Daniel were two of the men who had signed Sheriff Carpenter's $20,000 bond as sheriff and tax receiver of Morehouse Parish.[361] Carpenter's incompetence and/or misappropriation of funds were to later cost him his job a sheriff the following year.

At first blush, all that appeared to remain of the bodies was the torso, as they floated in the midst of thousands of dead fish. It was thought at that time that the force of the explosion had caused the dismemberment of the bodies. Metal wires were also noticed to be wound around the bodies in what later would be called a basket fashion.

Agent Farland along with fellow investigators J. D. Rooney, J. P. Huddleston and W. F. Arkens, who were assisting the diver load his equipment in Mer Rouge, proceeded immediately to the Lake LaFourche site. These agents had been in Morehouse Parish investigating Klan activities and the disappearance of Daniel and Richards. They were sent in by William Burns, the director of the Bureau of Investigation of the Justice Department to aid the state after the governor visited with President Harding and requested federal assistance in dealing with the Klan in Louisiana.

---

[360]Ibid.

160

The diver had been called to the scene to search for the missing parts of the bodies and the metal wheels, with which, it was presumed the bodies had been secured. However, because of the large excavation made by the dynamite, the diver was unsuccessful in locating any further evidence from the bottom of Lake LaFourche. The explosion itself was of such magnitude that a new ferry landing had to be constructed before the ferry could again haul traffic. The ferry itself was found damaged and in mid-stream upon their arrival, dispite the fact that the ferry was located a considerable distance from the location of the blast.

Upon receiving word of the discovery of the bodies, Captain Cooper immediately moved his troops from Lake Cooper to Lake LaFourche. A perimeter was set up on both sides of the lake, which is the dividing line between Morehouse and Richland Parishes. Also by this time, hundreds of sightseers had gathered to watch the goings-on, and the troops were deployed to control the onlookers.

There is a question that arises from this incident which was never addressed in any of the publications reporting it. If, as had been previously reported, the state and federal authorities had reliable information that the bodies had been sunk in a lake in the area, and that Lake LaFourche was considered next to be searched after Lake Cooper, and having already searched Lake Cooper on the day prior to the explosion and discovered nothing, would it not be logical to dispatch troops to guard Lake LaFourche, the lake to be searched next rather than maintain a guard on the lake which had just been searched? According to the *Times-Picayune*, this was supposed to have been done. Evidently, it had not.

One of the last to arrive at the Lake LaFourche scene was Sheriff Fred Carpenter. This was his first official visit to the area since the arrival of the National Guard troops. Although he said that he had come to offer his assistance, it was commonly known that he had refused to meet with Captain Cooper and that he had received a telegram from Governor Parker ordering him to meet with Captain Cooper. Carpenter told reporters that he was certain the "conditions in the parish had been exaggerated." He was also to have said "there is no danger of molestation of the agents of Governor Parker or the federal men and that they could carry on their work without the protection of the militia." How Sheriff Carpenter could make such a statement, in view of the latest happenings, only serves to show his total

361 Ibid., 46-47.

lack of concern for his oath of office and for those whom he was sworn to protect. His statement is also indicative of how the icy tentacles of the Ku Klux Klan pervaded his office and his actions, and how he was more interested to shielding his fellow murderous Klansmen whom he had also sworn an oath to protect. An oath, which we will see, superseded the oath of allegiance to the United States of America. Carpenter's comments to these reporters also seem to run contrary to those taken down by John Rogers of the *St. Louis Post-Dispatch*.

Two metal caskets were brought to the scene at Lake LaFourche, and the two bodies were loaded into them, placed in a National Guard truck and transported to the lower floor of the Masonic Hall in Mer Rouge under heavy guard.

J. L. Daniel was also on the scene of Lake LaFourche, but made no attempt at that time to identify the bodies. He offered a reward of $5,000 for the arrest and conviction of those involved in the kidnapping and death of his son and Richards. He also told reporters that afternoon that he had recognized license plates from Richland Parish and Arkansas on the scene of the August 24th kidnappings. He would later refute this from the witness stand.

Mrs. Anna Garrison of West Monroe, Thomas Richards' mother, traveled to Mer Rouge to identify the body of her son. She told reporters that she felt she would be able to identify her son by the clothing that he wore. Mrs. Richards was reported to be in destitute condition. Having been an orphan herself, she suddenly found herself without a husband, and her children, two girls ages 3 and 6, found themselves to be without a father. J. L. Daniel told her that she could live in a house he owned rent free for three months, and he also helped her financially. And, as mentioned before, she was also being helped by Whipple.

One evening, after Mrs. Richards and her children were finished having supper at a friend's home in Mer Rouge, the adults were in the living room listening to music when the 6-year-old asked for a pencil and paper and went into the kitchen. When Mrs. Richards went in to check on her, she asked the child what she was doing. With tears running down her cheeks, she told her mother, "I am writing a letter to the Ku Klux Klan to please let my papa come home."

Richards was known to carry his children with him to work, and this was the same child who had witnessed the first kidnapping of her father by black-hooded Klansmen from the auto garage where he was working in Bastrop while he was still living in Mer Rouge. This kidnapping occurred just as he finished work and was going to his car to drive home to Mer Rouge. This was when the black-hooded mob grabbed him, leaving his crying child on the scene, threw him into the rear of a car and took him into the woods, where he was questioned, threatened and told to leave the area. During this time, some anti-Klansmen of Bastrop who had observed the kidnapping cared for the child until Richards was returned. Clearly, even the child knew who was responsible for these dastardly crimes.

Hearing of these events, Governor Parker phoned Colonel Guerre, the commander of New Orleans based Company D, 158 Infantry, a machine gun outfit, and issued orders to mobilize immediately and proceed with all haste to Bastrop. The Washington Armory located at 724 St. Charles Avenue had been bustling with activity all afternoon. At about 6 p.m., two trucks were backed into the armory as four machine guns and 12 boxes of ammunition were loaded, each box containing 1,000 rounds.

Shortly thereafter, the troops, under the command of Colonel Guerre and his officer corps, which included Captain Oscar Schneideau, commander of Company D; Lieutenant Terry of the same company; and Lieutenant M. Sternberg of the Intelligence Corps, were trucked to the Texas and Pacific train station about a half mile away. At 7:30 p.m., under sealed orders, they left on the first leg of their trip which was to take them to Alexandria. After opening the orders, they found that there had been a change, and they would be switching to a special car at Gouldsboro, a town that no longer appears on the map.

Correspondents traveling with the troops described the feeling of the troops in this fashion:

> The militiamen were in happy spirits as they departed, and when the train reached Gouldsboro and they were ordered out, there was a wild scamper for bags and sandwiches.
> Before the train left from Gouldsboro, the militiamen, safely installed in the special car, were singing "Where Do We Go from Here."

Company D was said to be composed mostly of young business and professional men from around the New Orleans area. The short notice drew many of them from the jobs, and although they were not notified officially about where they were going, it was understood among them that they were headed for Morehouse Parish. "Back for Christmas?" one the soldiers parroted a correspondents question. "We don't know. This is our own little Christmas party," one said.

The mobilization of Company D was seen as meaningful because it was known that it contained the best marksmen in the Louisiana National Guard. Company D had also been the recipient of the silver cup which is awarded each year to the best drilling unit at the yearly National Guard encampment.

While en route to Bastrop with the troops, Attorney General Coco called a news conference at which he announced:

> We are going to Mer Rouge to make a personal investigation relative to the finding of the two bodies there. We will investigate all available facts in regard to the Mer Rouge outrages, and the autopsy on the bodies will be made by Dr. Duval and Dr. Lanford.
>
> We mean to make every possible effort to determine the manner in which those two lake victims came to their deaths, and I am confident that public sentiment will be with us. In fact, I believe that the people as a whole are thoroughly in sympathy with us in our desire to ferret out the facts of the crime and to bring the guilty persons to justice.
>
> This crime has been a blot on the record of the state and there are many good citizens, members of the Ku Klux Klan among them, who not only agree with us in this position, but who, I am sure, will assist the prosecution in every way. I have never thought that the klan as a whole would condone an offense of this kind, much less be an instrument to it, and I am counting on the support of klan members in the approaching investigation.

While the attorney general's staff and the men of Company D, 158th Infantry were making their way to Bastrop from New Orleans, Company A in Alexandria, commanded by Captain Petrie, was mobilizing after having received marching orders from the adjutant general's office earlier in the day. At about 6 p.m. Captain Petrie, along with his officers, Lieutenants E. D. Phillips and Grove Stafford, was entraining at Alexandria headed for Mer Rouge. It was not made clear how or where Companies A and D were to link up.

There emerged this day three distinct versions of the alleged attack on Dr. B. M. McKoin. The first was the one most commonly told, that he had received a call to go to the cabin of some blacks outside of town because of an illness. The call, it was said, was false, and the two men whom he observed on the side of the road on his way out of town were the same two who fired on him as he passed them again on his way back into Mer Rouge. Those who observed the direction and flight of the bullets commented at the time that they could not understand why he could not have been struck by the bullets as they passed from back to front directly through the steering wheel area.

The second version was that the attempted assassination was in fact true in that it was the work of family members or agents of the family of the late Dr. Thomm, whom Dr. McKoin had killed a few years earlier.

The third version was that Dr. McKoin had faked the assassination attempt and that he himself had fired the shots into his vehicle. This version would seem to be supported by the evidence stated by witnesses who claimed that the path of the bullets would surely have struck the driver had he been seated behind the steering wheel. Many citizens of Mer Rouge felt that Dr. McKoin wanted to get out of both Mer Rouge and the Ku Klux Klan, and that this would have been a face-saving way of doing both.

Naturally, his fellow Klansmen believed Dr. McKoin's story, and, not long afterwards, both Daniel and Richards were taken out into the woods separately by black-hooded Klansmen and questioned and threatened as to the alleged attempt on McKoin's life. After they were released, it was said that Daniel and Richards told friends that they had recognized the voices of some of the Klansmen that had taken them out, and that they named these Klansmen. One of those named was Captain Skipwith, the exalted cyclops of Morehouse Klan No. 34. Both Daniel and Richards told the Klansmen that they could prove their whereabouts on the night of the alleged assassination attempt and that they were playing cards with about seven others at the home of J. L. Daniel.

Richards was also alleged to have gone to some unspecified Klansman in Mer Rouge after he had been taken out and quizzed him on the alleged assassination attempt. This Klansman was supposed to have been the one who implicated him in the alleged plot. He told this Klansman that if any further accusations were made against him that he would hold this Klansman personally responsible.

The following night the Klan held a meeting in the woods near Mer Rouge. Watt Daniel told his friends later that he followed Klansmen to that meeting and that he hid in the woods during the meeting. He told his friends that he recognized many of those present and that he heard what they were planning. He said that he stepped on a stick which cracked and attracted the attention of the Klansmen. Although he hid himself, the Klansmen located him, and at gun point forced him to join their meeting. Boldly, Daniel said that he had intentionally hid himself with the intent of exposing the Klan and their plot.

Needless to say, this drew a heated exchange. Daniel told his friends that he was permitted to leave with the warning to "keep his mouth shut or take the consequences." Daniel did not heed the warning and continued to talk of the Klan, speaking specifically of the encounter in the woods and naming those who were present. Again, he identified Captain Skipwith as having been there and as being the leader of the Klan.

It was thought that the alleged assassination attempt coupled with the voice identification of Klansmen by both Daniel and Richards, the bold move by Richards to confront his accuser and the confrontation Watt Daniel had with the Klan in the woods may well have been the actions which sealed their fate and set the wheels of the Klan in motion.

One citizen, who asked Rogers that his name not be used described the kidnapping scene of August 24th, saying, "that no event in the wildest days of the Wild West ever equaled the performance." He went on to describe the kidnapping scene as follows:

> A few days after Richards and Daniel were taken out by masked men, a mass meeting was held at Bastrop in the interest of good roads. We have a movement there to issue $1,000,000 of bonds for building roads in the parish.
>
> To attract the people a barbecue and baseball game were advertised. People from all over Morehouse parish went to Bastrop. There were at least 4,000 people in attendance. Among those who went to Bastrop were T. F. Richards, F. W. Daniel, J. L. Daniel (father of F. W.Daniel), W. C. Andrews and C. C. (Tot) Davenport, all of Mer Rouge.
>
> After the close of the mass meeting, barbecue and baseball game, the people began leaving for their homes. The roads leading from Bastrop were literally lined with automobiles, buggies and wagons.
>
> Suddenly a band of men wearing the hooded masks of the Ku Klux Klan appeared on the Bastrop-Mer Rouge road. An automobile was placed directly across the road blocking traffic. Within a few minutes the road was blocked for a mile and a half, as the autos and vehicles came to a halt.
>
> With traffic blocked, the masked men began searching the automobiles and vehicles. Armed with shotguns, Winchester rifles and revolvers, the hooded men went from auto to auto, shoving their guns in the faces of occupants.
>
> A wild panic followed. Women screamed and several of them fainted, while some became hysterical. The masked men continued their search of the cars in spite of the panic and uproar along the highway. The scene beggared description. No event in the days of the Wild West ever equalled the performance. Some of the women became so ill that their relatives had to send for doctors after they reached home. One woman, who was in a delicate condition, came near dying. She was critically ill for several days afterward.
>
> Finally the masked men seized T. F. Richards, F. W. Daniel, J. L. Daniel, W. C. Andrews and C. C. (Tot) Davenport and disappeared with them, going in the direction of Collinston.

I afterward learned that they whipped W. C. Andrews and J. L. Daniel, father of F. W. Daniel and took them to the outskirts of Collinston, where they were released. C. C. (Tot) Davenport was not whipped but was released at Collinston after being mistreated, along with the elder Daniel and Andrews.

The masked band disappeared from Collinston with T. F. Richards and R. W. Daniel and I have not learned of anything further as to what happened to them. There is a well-grounded belief, however, that they were killed, their bodies weighted with iron and thrown into a lake near Oak Ridge. A quantity of iron near the roadside at the lake was missing the next morning after Richards and Daniel disappeared.

All of the members of the hooded band were in automobiles, some with Louisiana and some with Arkansas license plates, but everybody was so excited that it appears nobody took down or remembers the numbers. When the masked party left the Bastrop-Mer Rouge Highway they had the two Daniels, Richards, Andrews and Davenport in a trailer that was hitched to an automobile. The five men were tied in what is known as hog-fashion, their legs being bound together with ropes and their hands tied behind them.

I was in one of the automobiles that was held up and saw much of what happened, but I was too excited to take down the license plate numbers of the masked party. The trailer containing the five men who were seized passed within a few feet of my car. The five men were all blindfolded, with hooded men guarding them with guns.

The performance of the masked band and the kidnapping of Richards and Daniel created great excitement in the parish as well as adjoining parishes. I observed that those who were known or suspected of being klansmen, upheld the work of the hooded men, while many citizens who were not members of the klan condemned the whole affair.

Feeling at Bastrop and Mer Rouge ran high. At Bastrop, where the klan was strong, the predominant sympathy was with the hooded band. At Mer Rouge, where there were many citizens opposed to the klan, the highway gunplay performance and the kidnapping were condemned.

A few nights after the kidnapping a report was circulated at Mer Rouge that the Bastrop klansmen would appear that night and attempt to punish the citizens of Mer Rouge who opposed the klan. The same night a report got out in Bastrop that Mer Rouge citizens would attack Bastrop klansmen.

The result was that a crowd of men assembled on the courthouse square at Bastrop armed with guns, while another crowd gathered in the white way at Mer Rouge similarly armed.

Bastrop and Mer Rouge are about eight miles apart. Both sides waited for each to attack the other, but no attack was made. However, the situation was tense and Morehouse parish was threatened with civil war. Everyone realized that something should be done to prevent a clash of the armed forces.

The next day cool heads got together and arranged for a peace parlay. Leaders of both sides appeared and an armistice was agreed upon. Since that time no open clash has occurred but the feeling between the factions in the parish is still very bitter.

The normal routine of the small hamlet of Mer Rouge must have been in total upheaval. The presence of federal and state investigators, the National Guard on main street, the attorney general's staff, and the numerous reporters and independent news men must have created a carnival atmosphere. The *Times-Picayune* described the press coverage this way:

"Every press association in the country except one has a special representative here and there are a half dozen reporters from individual papers. A corps of telegraph operators were sent here today to handle the press stories. Hotels and rooming houses are jammed."

Qualified tax payers and electors of Morehouse Parish in the two designated road districts voted overwhelmingly this day in favor of the bond issue of $1,150,000 for building 150 miles of highway.[362] This was the same roads bond issue that was placed before the people on the day of the August 24th kidnapping of Watt Daniel and Thomas Richards, and the same day of the baseball game and the barbecue.

The American Civil Liberties Union rose to the defense of the Ku Klux Klan this day when they lodged a protest with President Harding against Mayor Hylan of New York suggestion that the President order the Post Office Department to suppress Colonel Mayfield's Weekly, a pro-Ku Klux Klan paper published in Texas. A letter by Harry F. Ward, Chairman of the Union said:

> We beg to enter our protest against any such course of action as the Mayor of New York requests, in the firm conviction that any attempt to use the agencies of Government to interfere with the right of a free press does more harm than good. It is contrary to American traditions and principles. If it is sanctioned with reference to propaganda of the Ku Klux Klan, it might be applied with equal logic to other organizations and movements. Who shall sit in judgment upon what movements and opinions should be suppressed and what allowed access to the mails?[363]

Governor Ritchie Bars Use by Organization "Under Mask."

From Baltimore, Maryland came the news that Governor Ritchie had declined to allow the Ku Klux Klan to use the Fifth Regiment Armory for a lecture. In a letter to Dr. J. H. Hawkins, Governor Ritchie said that the Adjutant General himself felt "that permission to use the State armory should not be given to any organization whose agenda is conducted 'under mask.'" The Klan wanted to use the armory for a lecture by William J. Simmons of Atlanta, emperor of the Klan.[364]

---

[362] *Monroe News-Star*, 23 December, 1922.
[363] Ibid.
[364] Ibid.

168

SUNDAY DECEMBER 24, 1922
First Arrests Made in Supposed Klan Mer Rouge Murders
T. J. Burnett, Former Deputy Sheriff, in Bastrop Jail, Guarded by Machine Guns[365]
Morehouse Citizens Wonder Who Will be Next[366]
Klan Membership Denial Permitted[367]

Jeff Burnett, a former deputy of Morehouse Sheriff Fred Carpenter and one of the accused slayers of Watt Daniel and Thomas F. Richards, was arrested today. The arrest took place at the Southern Carbon plant in Spyker, two miles south of Bastrop, where Burnett was then employed. This action was not an independent action by Sheriff Carpenter, but done only after he was given an affidavit signed by Attorney General Coco charging him with murder. Burnett, who was married and had two children, was said to have very influential friends in the parish.

Interestingly enough, Burnett asked Sheriff Carpenter if he could go home first and change his clothes. Sheriff Carpenter granted this request, telling him to report to the machine-gun covered jail when he finished. Another shining example of Sheriff Carpenter's interest in this case.

Attorney General Coco arrived in Bastrop on the morning train, accompanied by T. Semmes Walmsley and two additional companies of the 156th Infantry of New Orleans, Colonel Louis F. Guerre commanding. A petition signed by Attorney General Coco, Assistant Attorney General T. Semmes Walmsley, District Attorney David I. Garret, St. Claire Adams, special attorney for the prosecution, and Judge Fred M. Odom of the Sixth Judicial District court ordered a public hearing into the kidnappings and murders of Watt Daniel and Thomas F. Richards. Said hearing was to begin on January 5, 1923 in the Bastrop courthouse under the protective eye of the state militia.

In a surprise move, Captain Skipwith, exalted cyclops of the Morehouse Parish Ku Klux Klan, also met with the attorney general and T. Semmes Walmsley. Skipwith introduced himself as the leader of the Morehouse Parish Klan, which he said numbered about 500. He said that the Klan was not involved in what had happened to Daniel or Richards, and he promised to assist in the investigation. This was a bold in-your-face move by Skipwith, and it displayed just

---

[365]Ibid.
[366]Ibid.
[367]Ibid.

how much control he and the Klan believed they possessed in the area.

The bodies of Daniel and Richards were turned over to the families in the afternoon of this day, the autopsies having been completed. This article having been written on Saturday, it reported that the funeral would be held on the next day, Sunday, in the afternoon. The two side-by-side graves had already been prepared on the Daniel plantation. The ground floor of the Masonic hall in Mer Rouge, which served as a make-shift morgue, had a large American flag draped across the plate glass window. When the bodies were moved from the Masonic hall, they were placed in metal caskets draped with American flags.

Unexpectedly, the attorney for Burnett applied to Judge Odom for a preliminary hearing. It was believed at that time that such a hearing might prematurely force the state to expose what information it possessed against Burnett. Under Louisiana law, anyone charged with a capital crime can demand a preliminary hearing.

Attorney General Coco was notified of the application after he had left Bastrop that evening enroute to his home in Avoylles Parish to pass Christmas day with his family. After contacting Judge Odom, it was agreed that no decision on the preliminary hearing would be made until the following week.

The Ku Klux Klan had always presented itself as a reputable organization priding itself on its theme of "100 % Americanism" and for telling the truth. This, however, was reported not to be the case today. It was learned that when Klansmen were initiated, they were told that they could deny membership. Such denial would, in effect, be a resignation from the Klan. However, they would be allowed to reinstate themselves at the earliest possible opportunity. One ex-member of the Klan said that when he was initiated he was told that his membership must be kept secret.

Strangely enough, the manner in which the question was asked had much to do with the manner of the reply. Members were told that they must deny being "members of the Ku Klux Klan," "Ku Kluxers," "Kluxers" or "Klansmen." They were, however, obliged to tell the truth if they were asked if they were "citizens of the Invisible Empire." A novel way of circumventing the truth.

Federal agents were said to have been working under cover in the parish for the last three months, but the arrival of troops in Mer Rouge clearly had the small town turned on its ear. Citizens flocked to the lot next to the power plant where the soldiers were pitching the camp to watch the goings-on. In the crowd were women, children, and a few Klansmen.

One particular citizen in the group, known to all as a Klansman, paced the sidewalk as he watched the soldiers. His pacing attracted the attention of one young school girl. "What's the matter mister?" the little girl asked.

"I am nervous," said he. "I can't understand why I feel that way."

The little girl paused, looked at the soldiers as they stacked their rifles with bayonets fixed, and prepared one machine gun, and then turned to the Klansman.

"Mister," said the little girl, "you ain't the only Ku Kluxer in Mer Rouge who is nervous."

Secret Service Explodes Mayor's Claim of Attempted Assassination[368]

The Secret Service released the results of their investigation of the claim by Dr. B. M. McKoin that an attempt had been made to assassinate him. It was the opinion of the agents of the U. S. Department of Justice that the former mayor had fired the bullets into his automobile at the time he claimed an attempt was made to assassinate him. This finding confirmed the same belief held by a large number of citizens of Mer Rouge. After making a critical examination of McKoin's automobile, which he sold when he left Mer Rouge, they found that two loads of buckshot were fired through the curtain from the rear of the car. Most of the pellets passed directly over the steering wheel and one of them even shattered a spoke in the wheel.

The investigators placed one of their men in the automobile and photographed him in the car. The picture showed that if a man had been sitting at the wheel both loads of buckshot would have entered his body and he would have been killed or, at the very least, wounded. The Secret Service agents said that McKoin could not have escaped death or injury from the bullets. Citizens who believed that McKoin fired the bullets himself declared that they had information that he had contemplated leaving Mer Rouge and quitting the Ku Klux Klan. His motive, these citizens asserted, was to have an excuse for leaving here and getting out of the Klan.

Klansmen Banish Catholic Ice Man at Mer Rouge

Despite the presence of federal state and local law enforcement officers not to mention four companies of guardsmen, reports from Mer Rouge chronicled another lawless act by members of the Ku Klux Klan in Morehouse Parish. Investigators learned a group of Klansmen some weeks ago threatened a man named Griffin,

---

[368]Ibid.

manager of an ice factory at Bastrop, and ordered him to leave the parish and not return. Griffin's sole offense was that he was a member of the Catholic Church and had denounced the Klan. He left when ordered to do so and his whereabouts were unknown.[369]

Mer Rouge Citizens are Fully Armed: Back-Fire of Auto Causes General Display of Artillery

Since the kidnappings of Watt Daniel and Thomas Richards, arms of all kinds, ranging from Winchester rifles to shotguns, six-shooters and pocket derringers, were being carried openly by many of the citizens of Morehouse Parish. Neighbor had been arrayed against neighbor, and in many cases brother against brother and fathers and sons against each other. Few citizens ventured out of their homes at night without being heavily armed.

An illustration of the tense situation in the parish was seen when suddenly, an automobile down the street back-fired. Instantly, men reached for their guns and began craning their necks, looking in the direction of the noise. "Aw, tain't nothin' but an automobile," yelled a man near the place where the "Lizzie" had backfired.[370]

From Alexandria, Louisiana, came a report of an open letter addressed to Governor Parker and to the newspapers of the state charging Governor Parker with responsibility for "the major portion of any animosity that exists between the people of this state." The author of the letter was Judge Al Hundley of the Alexandria City Court. "You are subjecting the state of Louisiana to a great humiliation. You have without warrant or reason ordered troops to the peaceful town or Mer Rouge."[371]

Disturbing news of thievery by the murderers of Watt Daniel and Thomas Richards was announced in Mer Rouge this day. It was known that when Daniel was kidnapped and murdered by a masked mob of men, he had a diamond stud pinned to his necktie, a diamond ring on one of his fingers and $80 in cash in his pockets. The diamond stud, ring and cash were not found on the body when it was taken from Lake LaFourche.[372] The reader should bear in mind that the autopsy of the two bodies will show that the hands and feet of both victims had been cut or mashed off. That no ring was found would be expected since there were no hands

---

[369]*Times Picayune*, 24 December 1922.
[370]Ibid.
[371]Ibid.
[372]Ibid.

attached to the body. Also, it was quite possible that the diamond pin could have easily have dislodged when the bodies were horribly mashed and mangled.

MONDAY DECEMBER 25, 1922

Hooded Murders of Mer Rouge Men Known to Agents
List of Names is in Attorney General's Hands and Arrests Are Expected Tomorrow[373]
Two Victims of Hooded Mob Subjected to Indescribable Butchery[374]
Dramatic Funeral for Pair Held on Daniel Plantation[375]

Following the revelation that the heads, hands and feet were missing from the bodies when they were recovered, much speculation arose as to how this had occurred. It was the opinion of Drs. Duvall and Lanford that the explosion did not cause these conditions. The attorney general's office maintained that they concurred with the autopsy report. They also said they believed that the bodies were subjected to some special torture device, which caused the members to be severed.

Still other members of the community had a different opinion. They held that the dismemberment of the bodies was done intentionally before they lowered them into the murky depths of Lake LaFourche. They clung to this belief because they said the intent was to make the bodies totally unidentifiable should they be recovered and an autopsy performed.

Federal investigators were also looking into the allegations that Watt Daniel and Thomas Richards were bootleggers. They determined that Watt Daniel did, in fact, operate a small still on his property, and to this fact he even made a public admission to Klan members on the evening he followed them alone after his first kidnapping. He told them that he had stopped making corn whiskey before they kidnapped him. As for Richards, they could find no evidence whatsoever to indicate that he had ever been involved in bootlegging. Then the question remained as to why the Klan would sight in on Richards.

That question may have been solved when investigators learned of a run-in that Richards had had with the exalted cyclops of the Morehouse Parish Klan, Captain J. K. Skipwith. Several months prior to the kidnappings and murders, Richards was working in an automotive repair shop in Bastrop. Around that time, Captain Skipwith, aside from being the exalted cyclops of the Morehouse Parish Klan, was

---

[373]Ibid.

[374]*Times Picayune*, 25 December 1922.

[375]Ibid.

also chairman of some other secret fraternal organization which was never named. In his capacity as chairman of that unknown organization, he was seeking a place to hold a large banquet; however, no hall in Bastrop could handle the crowd.

Skipwith prevailed on the owner of the repair shop where Richards worked to allow him to hold the banquet there, it being ascertained that the front portion of the garage would be big enough to hold all of those expected to attend. Early on the day of the banquet, Richards went to Skipwith and explained that his work area was in the rear of the garage and asked Skipwith to leave just enough room for him to get the vehicles that he was working on out at the end of the day. Skipwith said that he would.

When the work day was about to end, Richards attempted to move the autos out of his area, and he discovered that the tables had been set in his path, and there was no way for him to move the vehicles. Richards went to Skipwith to complain, and it was said that Skipwith cursed him. This turned into a heated argument, and only because of the intervention of those present was a fistic encounter avoided. This incident created deep resentment between the two, which some feel may have been reason enough for the egotistical Skipwith to seek revenge.

Not long after that encounter came the bogus assassination attempt on the life of Dr. McKoin. This was followed by Richards being kidnapped from his place of employment and the forced abandoning of his child. Richards maintained his innocence, saying that he had been playing cards at the home of J. L. Daniel on that night and that Watt Daniel was also present. He was told to stop talking about the Klan, or he would pay the consequences.

Having been released after his interrogation in the woods, Richards told his wife and others that he recognized the voice of Skipwith and others who were in the black-hooded mob that kidnapped him. It was alleged that he was questioned and threatened again the next day by "the mob." This was the first and only time that a second sequential encounter with "the mob" was mentioned.

Richards, as did Watt Daniel, continued to be an outspoken opponent of the Klan. The incident in the garage, his confrontation with the Mer Rouge Klansman, his continued outspokenness against the Klan and his refusal to stop talking about the Klan may well have been the ingredients which led to his murder.

Watt Daniel, however, went a step further. A few days later, he learned of a klan meeting which was to take place in the woods not far from Mer Rouge. He went there, and hid in the woods during which time he saw those who attended the meeting and recognized them. He made a noise and was discovered by the Klansmen, who immediately surrounded him with their weapons trained on him.

Daniel told them that he had come to the meeting with the intent of confronting and identifying those who had kidnapped him. Boldly he got up into Skipwith's face and said:

> I came here to see for myself exactly who you are. You can shoot me if you wish, but I want to tell you that I have a couple of guns myself, and if you start shooting I will get some of you before the fight is ended.
>
> I know you. You and your crowd have accused me of making whiskey on my farm. It is quite true that I have had a still on my place, but I have sold it, and I quit the business.
>
> You fellows claim you are after bootleggers. I tell you the son of your leader [That would be Oliver Skipwith, the son of Captain Skipwith.] here is the principal bootlegger in this parish. I know because I let him have whiskey. I know further that your leader here owes $80 for whiskey obtained from his bootlegging son.
>
> I propose to expose your whole damned crowd and tell the people your names and what kind of hypocrites you are. I am not afraid of your whole damned bunch.

Although Daniel was allowed to leave unharmed, it was believed that his defiance, threats to expose the identities of the Klan members and continued denunciation of the Klan placed him in the same category as Richards, which was that they were a real and present danger to the Klan, and as such they must be killed. One unnamed citizen of Mer Rouge put it this way:

> Daniel could not be silenced. Fearing exposure, Klansmen put him to death. I think this explains the motive for killing him. He was absolutely fearless, and could not be silenced by threats.

Again and again, it appears that merely speaking negatively of the Klan was enough to bring down the Klan's wrath. One such incident was recorded by a *Times-Picayune* reporter as he interviewed an unnamed Mer Rouge citizen.

> A few days after Governor Parker offered the reward for the kidnappers of Daniel and Richards and instructed Attorney General Coco to prosecute the case, I was seated in a moving picture show. A woman I know quite well came in and took a seat by my side.
>
> During the show, this woman asked me what I thought about the kidnapping of Daniel and Richards and the beating of the elder Daniel and Andrews.
>
> I replied that it was my belief that if Governor Parker and Attorney General Coco would order the arrest of the two leaders of the Ku Klux Klan in Morehouse parish, whom I named, they would get the two guilty parties, who were the ring leaders of the mob.
>
> The next day a klansman from Bastrop came to my place of business, called me

aside, and repeated to me what I had said to the woman and delivered a message to me from one of the men whose name I had mentioned that I must shut up and quit talking about the kidnapping case under the penalty of meeting the same fate that befell Daniel and Richards.

I replied that I had the right to express my opinion, based on what I considered good evidence and that I did not propose to be bulldozed, browbeaten or intimidated by any leaders of the Ku Klux Klan or anybody else.

Since then I have kept a loaded rifle and shotgun in my place of business during the day and by the side of my bed at night. Can you or any one else blame me? I think not.

After the autopsies had been performed, "the bodies were prepared for burial and removed in sealed caskets to the Gibson home, relatives by marriage of Mrs. Bessie Daniel Gibson of Memphis, Tenn., cousin and childhood companion of Watt Daniel." Next day, Christmas Eve, all that remained of the two unfortunate men was laid to rest in a little private cemetery on the Daniel estate, on the banks of Bayou Bonn Idee.[376] It should be said here that this is but one of the ways that Bayou Bonn Idee will be spelled.

The funeral and burial of Daniel and Richards was also reported on this day, although it had occurred on Sunday, a day earlier. The wording of the article is important in that it is not only descriptive of the event, but also of the social environment at that time.

The funeral ceremony took place on the Daniel Family burial plot on the plantation home seven miles from Mer Rouge, a place being made for Richard's grave near that of his fellow victim of the mob.

While soldiers with loaded rifles and side arms glistening in the bright sunlight passed through the throng at the grave, the Reverend E. W. Hayward, Pastor of Grace Episcopal Church at Monroe, consigned the bodies to the dust which had been denied them as a resting place for exactly four months after the murders.

The funeral was one of the strangest and most dramatic in the history of the South. The caskets of the two men were placed on trucks at Mer Rouge, a United States flag was thrown over them and while soldiers stood at attention the cortege started the long journey to the burial place. Fully 200 conveyances were in the procession. They ranged the gamut of the big touring cars, flivvers and buggies and mule-drawn spring wagons.

When the funeral ground was finally reached by the cortege it was found that an enormous crowd of country folk had gathered there to await it. Young Daniel was a great favorite with the negroes on his father's plantation and they had made a special request, which was granted, that they be permitted to attend.

The graves were only a few feet apart, both of them shaded by large live oaks whose foliage is almost completely hidden by the Spanish moss which droops from every branch. The caskets were taken out and placed beside the graves and the pastor took his position to read the rites of the faith. An old negress who had

---

[376]Rogers, 1922, 49.

suckled Watt Daniel and mothered him from the time of his birth broke the stillness with a cry of pain that perhaps was as deep as that of the father and brother of Daniel who were nearby, dry-eyed but steeling themselves to prevent a breakdown, or the mother, the widow and two daughters of Richards who were almost already prostrated by the suffering they have undergone and were ill-fortified for the strain of the service.

While Dr. Hayward read the ritual, Leota Richards, 7 years old, and her sister Zorra, aged 3, only children of Richards, stood with tears streaming down their sorrow-pinched faces. It was little Leota who a few days ago wrote a letter to the Ku Klux or at least asked her sister to do so, begging the Ku Klux to "send daddy home for Christmas."

Upon the afternoon air bathed in the gold of Southern sun that filtered through the trees fell the song of the choir. It was 'Lamb of Calvary.' Softly, they sang it. Men turned their heads. Women wept openly. Little children fretted. Into the grave enclosure a dog slowly walked. 'That's Watt Daniel's dog,' said a spectator. 'He seems to know.'

The grief of the aged parents and the wife of Richards was great. At times the sobbing of the wife was heard above the words of the minister. On the stone surface of the grave adjoining the newly-made bed of Richards sat the father of the dead man. In his eyes were tears, in his hand a small American flag over and over he repeated: 'They killed my boy, they killed my boy.'

It was a scene that brought tears to the eyes of many, the open graves, the plain casket, the one flag-draped but both covered with flowers, the bereaved wife and aged mother and the grieving old man seated on the nearby grave, about them all the people of the countryside, bareheaded, silent, sympathetic.

Daniel's body was placed in the grave first and rested on cross bars until the funeral ceremony was read. The body of Richards was lowered into the grave first. Both bodies enclosed in grey metallic caskets were taken to the cemetery on the same truck. The same pallbearers served for both and included several ex-service men. The funeral procession with more than 100 cars in line left the home of Harry L. Gibson, where they were taken yesterday from the morgue after the autopsy had been completed. Although scheduled to leave for the cemetery at 12:30 p.m., it was after 3 o'clock when the procession left. The cortege reached the cemetery about 4 o'clock.

The final words of the minister ended, a hymn was sung by selected voices and the body of Watt Daniel was lowered into the grave. The squad of soldiers under Lieutenant Randolph H. Percy stood at attention. A salute of three guns was fired, then the clear tones of the bugle came as the sun was reddening in the west at the close of the wonderfully perfect day.

Taps sounded the end of one of the most dramatic scenes ever witnessed in Louisiana. For more than a minute, the vast crowd stood motionless, few with dry eyes, as they scarcely realized that the final chapter in the tragic lives of two prominent young men of the community had ended. It marked, too, the beginning of a new chapter that will be written around the causes and perpetrators of one of the most brutal murders in the history of Louisiana.

The little family burying ground on the Daniel place where many members of the family rest is located on a wooded hill on the banks of the Bonne Idee, a bayou that has its origin in Arkansas and means, good idea. Through the center of the little enclosed section that contains the members of the Daniel family is a row of graves containing the mother, stepmother and five brothers and sisters of

177

Watt. His body lies between those of his brother, James Sisson Daniel, and sister, Mrs. Susie Batavia Dade, wife of R. L. Dade, mayor of Mer Rouge.

There was talk in Mer Rouge as to why the minister from Monroe had come all that distance to bury Daniel and Richards when there were numerous ministers in the area. Most thought that the vast majority of them were Klansmen also, and as such would have placed themselves in jeopardy performing the service. Previous evidence has indicated that many Protestant ministers in the northern section of Louisiana were members of the Klan, and how, on numerous occasions, Klansmen had paid visits to churches in session, paraded up the aisle, read a proclamation of the virtues of that particular minister and presented him with a financial gift.

At the same time as the funeral was taking place, friends of Jeff Burnett were busily trying to secure his release. With the help of his fellow Klansmen and other "well-to-do people," they were able to raise $300,000 for his bail. However, Sheriff Carpenter knew that the offense for which Burnett was arrested was not a bondable offense and he was unable to accommodate his friend and fellow Klansman.

In the meantime, Burnett had become quite a celebrity and to some a hero. He could be seen daily behind the bars of his window merrily chatting with friends and laughing about his imprisonment.

> "I am wholly innocent of anything wrong," said Burnett. "There ain't nothin' for me to fear."
> "Guess there wasn't anyone more surprised than I was when the sheriff drove up to the carbon plant, at Spyker, where I work and told me to come along with him.
> " 'For what, I asked the sheriff.
> " 'You are wanted in connection with the killing of Daniel and Richards and you will have to go with me.'
> " 'I'm innocent of that charge.' said Burnett.
> " 'I can't help that,' the sheriff told me."

Police Mutiny Due to Klan Activity
Fourteen Members of New Britain Force Refuse to Obey an Order From the Chief[377]

A bulletin from Hartford, Connecticut described what amounted to a strike in the police department of New Britain. The controversy surfaced over the recent activity of the Ku Klux Klan, and, although the city was being patrolled and

---

[377] *The New York Times*, 25 December 1922.

property protected, there was a virtual mutiny.

The situation was brought about on Friday when 14 members of the night shift disobeyed an order from Chief W. C. Hart to attend their weekly physical drill. They did so because they claimed that their instructor was reported to have attended a meeting of the Ku Klux Klan the previous evening. Mayor Anglo M. Paomessa, a Catholic whom Klansmen were fighting, said the patrolmen had failed in their duty in not taking up the matter with Chief Hart.

> If the report is true that Joseph Hergstrom, the instructor of the Y.M.C.A, who drills the police, is affiliated with the Klan, I am free to say that I sympathize with the patrolmen, although I think they should have brought their complaint before the Chief and should have waited for him to investigate the matter.

Hergstrom denied that he attended a Klan meeting, and Clarance H. Barnes, General Secretary of the Y.M.C.A., issued a statement backing Hergstrom's denial. A special meeting of the Police Commission had been called at which time Chief Hart was to submit his report on the matter.

> While my sympathy may be with the policemen, that is not in the question to be considered, rather, it is one of flagrant violation of the rules of the department and the order of a superior. If this matter is let go unpunished, we might just as well throw up our hands.

Reports of men believed to be members of the Ku Klux Klan made Christmas gifts of money and food to churches and private families in Montclair, Kearny and Belleville, N. J. Three men in an automobile, with the curtains drawn, delivered baskets of food at the homes of Addison Bitters, 3 Sheridan Avenue, and Edward Purtz, 5 Sheridan Avenue, both in Kearny. They left notes wishing the recipients a Merry Christmas and Happy New Year, and signed it, "Invisible Empire, Kearny Provisional Klan."

Last evening six Klansmen paid a visit to the Silver Lake Baptist Church in Belleville. They marched into the church in formation. Three men walked in front, the middle one carrying an American flag, and the men at his side held torches. Behind the middle one walked a man with a letter in his hand, and behind him two guards. The six Klansmen marched up the aisle until they reached the altar. There they handed the envelope to the pastor, the Rev. Benedicte Pasculent. After a short interruption of the services the intruders left. The envelope contained two $5 bills and a Christmas Greeting signed, "Invisible Empire, Ku Klux Klan." A similar incident happened at the Italian Presbyterian Church in Montclair where Rev. J. J.

Reave was pastor. Six men handed him an envelope, but he declined to tell what it contained.[378]

TUESDAY DECEMBER 26, 1922

Prisoner Held for Mer Rouge Murders Denies He's In Klan
But Relatives, Story Goes, Will Identify Burnett as One of Hooded Band[379]
Trial of Morehouse Murder Suspect May be Transferred From Bastrop to New Orleans[380]
Lawyers Turn Down $25,000 Defense Fee[381]
Dr. M'Koin Coming Home, His Wife Says[382]
Murder Attempt of Ku Klux Klan Foiled by Agents[383]
Man Who Carried Water to Hooded Mob to Tell All[384]
Prisoner Said to Have Two Homicides on His Record[385]

Word reached the press on this date that the trials of those charged in the murders of Daniel and Richards may be moved from Bastrop to New Orleans. The change of venue was said to be sought because the prevailing pro-Klan sentiments of so many citizens in Morehouse Parish could well prejudice the jury. When contacted at his home in Marksville, Attorney General Coco denied that such a move was being contemplated. Coco had previously made the statement that he was determined that the trial would take place in Bastrop and that he felt confident that he would be able to get a conviction there, despite the pro-Klan feelings of the citizens.

An unnamed Monroe, Louisiana law firm, it was announced, turned down the $25,000 the state had indicated it would pay to have the two defendants represented. Percy Sandel, a former district attorney for Ouachita Parish and the same man for whom the Percy Sandel Memorial Library on the campus of Northeast Louisiana University was named, was to be one of the lead attornies in the defense of the two Klansmen identified as having taken part in the kidnapping and murders of Watt Daniel and Thomas Richards, Dr. B. M. M'Koin and Morehouse Parish Deputy Sheriff Jeff Burnett.

---

[378] Ibid.
[379] *The New York Times*, 26 December 1922.
[380] Ibid.
[381] Ibid.
[382] Ibid.
[383] Ibid.
[384] Ibid.
[385] Ibid.

It was learned that the Justice Department agents had obtained an eyewitness to the kidnappings of Daniel and Richards at the roadblock on the Bastrop-Mer Rouge Road on August 24th. This witness was identified as Berry Whetstone, an Oak Ridge farmer.

Allegedly, Whetsone was walking home on the Bastrop-Mer Rouge road. As he reached the roadblock, he said one of the black-hooded Klansmen called him by name, and told him to stop. Whetstone said he was told to go over the hill to a nearby ranch and bring back a pail of water for the Klansmen. In order to be certain that Whetstone would return, the Klansmen told him to leave his jacket.

After returning with the water, one of the Klansmen offered him 50 cents which he declined. Whetstone said he attempted to leave, but the Klansmen would not allow him to do so. They were afraid that he might warn those approaching the roadblock and cause them to miss their prey. He was told to sit on a log close by until the operation was over.

As he sat there, he observed the Klansmen come to the pail for a drink, and he saw them lift their hood in order to do so. It was there under those circumstances that he told federal agents that he positively recognized Jeff Burnett as Burnett lifted his hood to get a drink of water. While he was detained, he said he also witnessed the black-hooded Klansmen seize Watt Daniel, J. L. Daniel, Thomas Richards, W. C. Andrews, and C. C. "Tot" Davenport.

Whetstone also informed agents that Burnett had allegedly murdered two blacks a few years prior. The circumstances surrounding this allegation were never explained nor was there any further mention of this incident in any of the publications.

Fearing for his life, agents moved Whetstone to a place of safety. It was said that Klansmen employed detectives to find Whetstone, and, in fact, they trailed him to New Orleans, but there they lost track of him. It was rumored that he was somewhere in Mississippi and that he would return when needed to testify.

While federal agents were conducting their investigation into the kidnapping and murders of Daniel and Richards, they learned of a plot by Klansmen to kill two of them. During the first few weeks that federal agents were in Morehouse Parish, Klansmen were following them to every location. At that time, the Klansmen did not know that aside from those agents working in the open there were others who were under cover. It was through these operatives that the plot was discovered.

Fearing what these agents might uncover, the Klansmen continued following the agents but were unable to obtain any information on what they were discovering. The chief agent was carrying a large portfolio, which they were anxious to get their hands on because they were convinced that it contained evidence against them. Unable to obtain any information, the Klansmen decided to kidnap the agents, take the portfolio, and "give them the same klan dose that was given to Daniel and Richards."

Having been alerted to the intentions of the Klansmen, the agents decided to send them on a wild-goose chase. The two agents made overt their plans to travel to Monroe on a certain train. The Klansmen took the bait. The Klansmen made plans to intercept the train at Collinston, "a hot bed of klanism, about eight miles south of Mer Rouge." Considered "the most accessible place in Morehouse parish," Collinston was the junction of two lines of the Missouri Pacific Railroad and a number of highways. Messages were sent to Klan "terrors" (enforcers) by telephone of the Klan plan. The Klan also dispatched runners in automobiles to make certain that they would have enough manpower to handle the job when the train rolled into Collinston.

Needless to say, the agents took another route, and when the Klansmen did stop the train in Collinston, they were surprised not to find the agents. It was precisely this type of anarchy which many felt afforded Governor Parker the reason to dispatch the state militia into Morehouse Parish to protect the federal and state investigators, not to mention the prospective witnesses.

Jeff Burnett again made another denial that he had anything to do with the kidnapping or murder of Daniel and Richards. Speaking from his jail cell, he said, "I am innocent and will prove it when the time comes. I don't know why I have been singled out when I know nothing of the murders with which I am charged."

A correspondent asked Burnett, "Are you a member of the Ku Klux Klan?" At the same time he was asked the question, the reporter made a hand gesture which Klan members may make in public without revealing their identity. The nature of the gesture was not stated. However, one of the common gestures made by Klansmen is to slide the thumb and pinky finger of the right hand inside the waistband of the trousers leaving the index, middle, and third fingers exposed. Together against the trousers with the fingertips pointed downward, the three exposed fingers indicated K. K. K.

"I am not a member of the klan and have never been. I know nothing of them except what I have heard," declared Burnett.

"Do you think the klan is responsible for the deaths of Daniel and Richards?" he was asked.

"I don't think so, but as I have told you before, I know very little about the klan. However, I believe the klan has been wrongfully accused of many things," he said. "On the night of August 24, when Richards and Daniel were killed, I was nowhere in the vicinity in which they were kidnapped. I am an employee of the Southern Carbon Company at Spyker. On that night I was working as engineer and did not hear of the deaths of the two until a day or two later."

This statement should have sent a shock wave throughout the press, not to mention the investigators and the attorney general's staff. However, it went totally unnoticed by everyone. Notice where he said "when Daniel and Richards were killed." The fact that they were dead had not yet been established a day or two after the original kidnappings. Some thought they were being held somewhere. Others thought that they had been run out of the state, as the Klan had done so many times before. It had not been determined that they had, in fact, been murdered on the same night of the kidnapping.

Burnett repeats his knowledge of the deaths again when he said, "and I did not hear of the deaths of the two until a day or two later." How could he have known a day or two after the kidnappings that Daniel and Richards were already dead unless he had some first-hand knowledge?

Burnett did go on to say that he did attend the baseball game in Bastrop on August 24th with a friend, William Bird, a farmer. Burnett was described as a slightly built man of 40 years. Those soldiers guarding him said he was "a silent, surly, suspicious man, not inclined to talk but sitting in his cell for hours reading the newspaper stories of the crimes and subsequent developments."

Burnett was not starved for company as he was said to have received approximately 50 visitors on this date alone. This must have put a severe strain on the jail which was described as "a small brick structure with four rooms divided into as many cells with a door and window commanding a view of the street and the Missouri Pacific station."

The citizens of Bastrop, whose pro-Klan leanings were well known, resented the fact that Burnett was in jail being guarded by the soldiers. Most claimed that the incarceration was unnecessary because of Burnett's good reputation and the fact that he was the nephew of Madison Flood, a prominent local barrister. It was also learned that David I Garret, the district attorney for Morehouse Parish, was also the son-in-law of Mr. Flood. Imagine that! This is the same Garret who, already named as a probable Klansman, failed to present any evidence to the first grand jury assembled to investigate the disappearance of Daniel and Richards, thereby insuring that no indictment came forward.

Meanwhile, as the search for Dr. McKoin continued, his wife made the announcement that her husband was in Baltimore, Maryland, attending Johns Hopkins University and that he was not in custody. She also told reporters that he had told her that he would be returning voluntarily to give testimony.

"I have heard from my husband regularly since he left here last August," said Mrs. McKoin. "He left Mer Rouge openly and told everyone where he was going and has since written to many of his close friends there. It was not cowardice that forced him to leave the town after threatening letters had been sent to him but considerations for his family. He planned to practice medicine in Monroe after completing a special course at Johns Hopkins. I wired him today to come back. He practiced medicine in Mer Rouge for nine years and never had an enemy until he became mayor and began to stop the lawlessness." Evidently, Mrs. McKoin did not see the killing of Dr. Thomm by her husband as a major problem.

Christmas was also celebrated by Mrs. Garretson, Thomas Richards' mother and his wife and children, who were staying with Mrs. Garretson in Monroe. Mrs. Richards was supposed to return to Mer Rouge where she would have been employed in Whipple's garage where her husband had worked. "There is only one satisfaction that we have," said Mrs. Garretson, "and that is the knowledge that my boy was not guilty of the crime they accused him of. It is our only comfort in this dark hour. Tom was a good boy and never could have done the things they said he did."

Members of the Justice Department also played host to a Christmas dinner. A. E. Farland, agent in charge, officiated at the occasion, which was attended by Colonel Louis F. Guerre, Commander of the 156th Infantry; Major Enoch S. Fulton of the medical corps; Captain W. W. Cooper and Lieutenant Walter L. Hayden of G Company; J. D. Rooney and W. F. Arkens, Justice Department agents; J. L. Daniel, father of one of the murder victims; J. G. Ewing of Baton

Rouge, and virtually all of the newspapermen in town. It was described by saying, "While the setting was somewhat crude the dinner that was served would have graced the tables of any of the finer New Orleans Cafes."

Expert Marksman Thrills Spectators

Federal agents gave a public display of marksmanship this day in an obvious attempt to send a message to those who would think to do them harm. In Mer Rouge, one of the Secret Service agents tied a thread to a cartridge, hung it from a tree limb, stepped off 25 paces, took aim with his pistol and cut the thread with the bullet as he fired. "Gosh," said a citizen who witnessed the performance, "I wouldn't like for that fellow to shoot at me with a gun, even if I was five miles away."[386]

As early as this decade, the clods of World War II were seen by some gathering on the horizon. U.S. Navy Admiral Ide warned that Japan was proceeding with preparations for naval reorganization. He added that as long as America did not alter her progress Japan would have a ship ratio of six to America's ten. Questioned as to whether there was danger that the Japanese Navy would outclass the American Navy, the Admiral replied that Japan's navy was superior in the speed of ships and the accommodations of dock yards.[387]

"Rest? I can't rest--if I did I would die." These were reported to be the words of the "Divine Sarah," Ms. Sara Bernhardt, who was reported to be gravely ill in Paris. Ms. Bernhardt's doctors said one hopeful sign was that she had taken an interest in food.[388]

WEDNESDAY DECEMBER 27, 1922

Arrest of Dr. M'Koin, Reputed Klan Head, As Mer Rouge Slayer
Physician Who Accused Murdered Men of Seeking His Life Held in Baltimore[389][390]
Lake LaFourche Dynamiters are Known to State[391]
State and Nation Join in Effort to Clear up Parish[392]

From Baltimore came word that Dr. McKoin had been arrested at the Johns

---

[386] Ibid.

[387] *The New York Times*, 26 December 1922.

[388] Ibid.

[389] *The New York Times*, 27 December 1922.

[390] *Times-Picayune*, 27 December 1922.

[391] Ibid.

[392] Ibid.

Hopkins University-Brady Institute. This, despite the fact that officials of Johns Hopkins denied that Dr. McKoin was there, and in fact they said that mail received for him there had been returned. The circumstances surrounding his arrest were truly bizarre. It appears that a police officer was injured on the waterfront in Baltimore and was taken to Johns Hopkins for treatment of his injuries. Days later when the hospital report reached headquarters, Dr. McKoin's name appeared on the report as the attending physician.

Not only had Dr. McKoin been attending Johns Hopkins, as he and his wife said he was, but he was also working in the medical facility treating patients. Why the officials at Johns Hopkins chose to lie about his presence there was neither questioned nor revealed.

Reporters were the first to reach Dr. McKoin. He spoke with them freely. He said that he was not a fugitive and that he had made no attempt to conceal his whereabouts. He said that he had arrived in Baltimore about October 1st, after leaving Mer Rouge due to the alleged attempted assassination.

McKoin told reporters that he was not a member of the Ku Klux Klan. The reader is reminded here that it was permissible for Klansmen to deny publicly that they were members of the Klan and that it would not be considered a lie. They would, however, have a much more difficult time denying that they were a member of the "Invisible Empire," a question that was not asked of him. It also bears mentioning again that Captain Skipwith had said twice before that McKoin was the Captain of the Mer Rouge Klan, a claim that would be repeated later by McKoin and others who were there when McKoin was initiated into the Klan.

All along claiming that he was not a member of the Klan, McKoin had nothing but high praise for the work that the Klan was doing. He said, "the members do much to hold down bootlegging and immorality while I was mayor of Mer Rouge." He also said that lawlessness was not considered unusual in Mer Rouge.

"Just before I left Mer Rouge," McKoin said, "a boy of a good family was shot in the back. What did the sheriff or governor do? The case was dismissed after a jury filled with bootleggers and the vicious element declared the alleged murderer innocent.

"Now, however, when a bootlegger (referring to Daniel) and someone else (Richards) is killed, the governor joins in the investigation. This affair, in my opinion, will decide whether the decent and good element of the town will control.

"All I know," he said, speaking of Daniel and Richards, "is that both men were on the bad side-the side of bootleggers, gunmen and men who associated with negro women."

Since the news of the murders of Daniel and Richards was common talk around the nation, and as a physician, McKoin was aware of the manner in which they were murdered, it is inconceivable that a man who took the Hippocratic Oath would be so unfeeling. Obviously, moonshining and keeping company with black women were offenses worthy of murder most foul in the eyes of the good doctor. His rhetoric was also very much like any other Klan official in that regard.

In Monroe, Dr. McKoin's mother told reporters of her son's innocence. "My son knows nothing in regard to the Morehouse affair. He was willing to return to Monroe, but he is an unwilling witness, as he knows nothing."

"We have been greatly humiliated," said the wife of Dr. McKoin, "by the reports that my husband has fled to Europe or that he intended to leave the United States. Nothing could be further from the truth. He has been a student at Johns Hopkins University and has been working day and night that he might prepare himself for his duties and work as a physician."

Although Dr. McKoin said that he was not a member of the Klan, this was not the information coming out of Mer Rouge. According to some local residents, McKoin became associated with the Klan in 1921, when he joined with other members of the Mer Rouge community. These former Klansmen, whose identities were not revealed, said that his tenure as mayor "was one of turmoil and strife from the time he joined the klan to the date of his departure from here."

These same Klansmen said that McKoin was appointed Captain of the Mer Rouge Klan by Captain Skipwith, the exalted cyclops of the Morehouse Parish Klan. They also told of several Klan raids in which McKoin actively joined. Captain Skipwith also attested to this fact. One in particular was the raid on the home of Miss Addie May Hamilton, a teenager who lived with her parents. The Klan alleged that she was leading an immoral life. What the nature of the immorality was has never been ascertained.

Allegedly, McKoin, along with other Klansmen, went to the Hamilton home on a night when they knew that the husband and brother would be away. Wearing black hoods over their faces, the band led by McKoin forced their way into the house and forced Miss Hamilton to accompany them to the train station immediately. Despite the pleas of her mother, whom McKoin struck and threatened to kill, she was taken away with only the clothes on her back.

Miss Hamilton said that she recognized Dr. McKoin because he was their family doctor and that she was present at the McKoin home on a regular basis as she took piano lessons from Mrs. McKoin. She said that McKoin, along with "Pink" Kirpatrick, brought her to the train station, gave her just enough money to get her to Little Rock, where she had relatives, and threatened her life if she returned.

Although it was leaked that the identities of those who dynamited Lake LaFourche were known, that was to prove to be little more than loose talk. It would also have been, perhaps, part of the "fishing expedition" that the investigators were conducting. Mr. Walmsley, assistant attorney general, told reporters, "Much will result from the open hearings next week and much of the state's course will be determined by it." By leaking statements such as the identities of the dynamiters being known and the like, perhaps the investigators hoped that it would cause information to develop or surface. Clearly, the attorney general's office was looking to the open hearing to provide substantial evidence for the state, according to Mr. Walmsely's statement.

Rumors were also flying about that more troops were on the way to Morehouse Parish. Commenting on that rumor, Mr. Walmsley said, "Our office knows nothing of orders for additional troops and does not consider them particularly necessary at this time." Attorney General Coco was still at his Marksville home, passing the remainder of the Christmas holidays with his family.

In the event that more state troops were required, there would be more than ample manpower to meet the need. From New Orleans would come the First Battalion of the 141st Field Artillery and the hospital company consisting of Batteries A, B, and C and the Headquarters Company. Also available throughout the state would be 156th regiment of infantry and a squadron of cavalry. Companies of infantry available for duty were Company A, Alexandria; Company D, New Orleans; Company B, Crowley; Company C, Opelousas; Company E, New Iberia; Company F, Breaux Bridge; Company H, Shreveport; Company I, Morgan City; Company K, Lake Charles; Company L, Ruston, Company M, Lafayette; Headquarters Company, Baton Rouge; Supply Company, Monroe and Howitzer Company, Forest.

As for the soldiers, they felt no threat from the inhabitants of the area. "These people," said some, "are like folks at home. They are not going to harm anyone." Yet, the report continued, "but the machine guns of the troops are still mounted at the jail and at the camp and are ready for instant use."

Further allegations of violations of federal laws surfaced this day when it was learned that the "Post Office Department" had dispatched agents as early as September 1922 to investigate charges of mail tampering by the Ku Klux Klan. This investigation was said to have begun "because of complaints that the mails in North Louisiana, where the Ku Klux Klan has a large membership, were being tampered with. Charges were made by responsible citizens that important letters containing information about Morehouse Parish conditions did not reach their destinations."

Morehouse Klan No. 34 Realm of Louisiana, Knights of the Ku Klux Klan took the offensive this day to these allegations and issued the following press release:

> Everything possible is being done by the klan that would be of assistance to the state and other authorities. On Christmas Day the Ku Klux and citizens of Morehouse parish gave the soldier boys at Bastrop a big barbecue and turkey dinner and a dance Christmas night at the Village Club.
> Captain J. K. Skipwith, exalted cyclops of Morehouse parish Klan No. 34, Realm of Louisiana, tendered to the attorney general the assistance and cooperation of 500 klansmen to be used in any capacity deemed necessary and assured him that it was the wish of the entire citizenship of the Morehouse klan that no stone be left unturned in ferreting out and bringing to justice the guilty parties connected in the case of the alleged kidnapping of Daniel and Richards.
> Although it is rumored that the bodies of Daniel and Richards have been found, there is, however, no positive evidence that this is true. Two objects were reported to have been floating near the banks of Lake LaFourche and it was presumed that these bodies were those of the missing men.
> Dr. O. M. Patterson, coroner of Morehouse parish, was summoned to the scene, but upon his arrival, he was not permitted to hold a coroner's inquest, being told and informed by a man who stated that he was a government representative that an inquest could not be held until after the arrival of Attorney General Coco, at which time it would be concluded at Mer Rouge. Immediately on his arrival Attorney General Coco was interviewed by coroner Patterson as to the necessity of holding a coroner's inquest over the bodies that were supposed to have been found in Lake LaFourche but was informed by the attorney general that such would not be necessary.

The arrogance and tone of this communiqué speaks volumes for the true feeling of the Klan. Clearly, they were trying to discredit the identification of the bodies of Daniel and Richards. Klansmen were also upset that their friend, and

189

perhaps fellow Klansman, Dr. Patterson, was not allowed to have access to the bodies. With Patterson performing the autopsies, he could possibly either lose some evidence that would point to their identities or claim that the bodies were unidentifiable. This way the state's case would have reached a dead end.

Some of the residents were also asking why the professional diver had not moved more quickly to Lake LaFourche to search for the bodies of Daniel and Richards. The diver arrived in Mer Rouge from St. Louis on December 20th. His equipment was shipped from Boston, the location of his last job. His equipment arrived on December 21st. At that time, he performed the necessary checks to assure it was operating safely. Following that, plans were made for him to proceed to Lake LaFourche on the following day to perform a search. Undoubtedly, the all-seeing eyes and ears of the Klan learned of the plans and detonated the dynamite in an attempt to foil the government's plans.

After the explosion and discovery of the bodies, the diver did perform a search of the lake bottom. The diver found that the explosion had torn a hole 60 feet in length and 25 feet wide in the lake bank. He also found that the blast caused a massive quantity of mud to slide down the bank into the deep section. This mud slide would have been more than sufficient to cover over any of the body parts or other evidence that may have been present.

Although Jeff Burnett received few visitors this day, life in the Bastrop jail was anything but dull. It was reported that "three insane negro women are quartered in one section of the parish jail where Burnett is confined. One of them constantly berates the klan, cursing it and asserting that 'all them white klansmen will be killed. Passing pedestrians and motorists stop and listen a moment, then pass on. In some instances there is a visible tightening of facial lines, a grim smile or a low murmur. Others merely pass on."

The roads in and around Bastrop-Mer Rouge are the scene of constant traffic. Speaking of the road where Daniel and Richards were kidnapped, the report said, "It was on this long, winding dirt trail, that Daniel and Richards were kidnapped. The exact spot where they were taken from their car is pointed out to visitors. On both sides of the woods, dark, forbidding giant pine, cedar and oak trees loom." Thanks to the logging industry, those trees are long gone, only to be replaced by the generic pine that can be seen planted by the millions over the area.

190

"Occupants of the cars on the roads," it continued, "wave to one another. It is the custom of the country, a friendly greeting to friend and stranger. Some of them are more than casual greetings. To the uninitiated it is a friendly wave; to others it is a secret sign-a greeting of the Ku Klux Klan."

It was learned that an important conference was to be held the next day, Thursday, December 28, 1922, in New Orleans. Governor Parker, Attorney General Coco, St. Clair Adams, special prosecutor for the attorney general's office, and E. A. Farland, agent in charge, were all scheduled to be present at this meeting. This was to be a strategy session to determine how the attorney general's staff would proceed with the case. This meeting may have been the beginning of the end for St. Clair Adams' association with the attorney general in this case. It is very likely that Adams disagreed with Coco on the matter of not seeking a change of venue. Although this is speculation, there did arise an issue between Coco and Adams that caused Adams to sever his association with the case.

With regard to the Louisiana law concerning the change of venue at that time, Section 1021 of the Revised Statutes amended by Act No. 95 of 1876 read as follows:

> Whenever it shall be established in any criminal prosecution by legal and sufficient evidence that a fair and impartial trial cannot be had in the parish where the case is pending, the judge of any court having jurisdiction of the case may, upon the application of the attorney general or district attorney, for a change of venue, grant such application. Provided, that said case be transferred to any parish or judicial district adjoining the one in which the case is pending.

The last sentence in this statute may well have been why Attorney General Coco decided not to seek a change of venue and to take his chances with a Morehouse jury. As read, it requires that the case be transferred "to any parish or judicial district adjoining the one in which the case is pending." Such being the case, even if the court did grant a change of venue, the trial would have to have been held in an adjoining parish in northern Louisiana. Because the Klan had a stranglehold of all of northern Louisiana, the outcome would have been a done-deal for the Klan.

A total of four murders have been attributed to the Klan along the Arkansas-Louisiana border from May 1922, through November 1922, the most prominent being Daniel and Richards. The third victim was at Wilmot, Arkansas, when E. L. Gills, a local farmer, was shot to death and his body burned by Klansmen outside his home.

The Smackover Invasion, an event when hundreds of Klansmen from Louisiana, Arkansas and Mississippi descended on Smackover, Arkansas to "clean out undesirables" in the town, was the fourth murder attributed to the Klan. It was there that J. G. Woods, a 25-year-old from Mississippi, was shot to death as he attempted to defend his property from "several hundred masked and white 'sheeted' men who marched into the new oil fields of south Arkansas to clean out undesirables. One man was flogged and a gambling house, a two-story frame structure, torn down. An exodus of more than 2000 people from this region resulted. Officials made no effort to learn the identity of the mob, so far as is known." In all likelihood, no effort was made because, as was the case in Morehouse Parish, all of the officials were either Klansmen or Klan sympathizers.

The New York Times reported that the arrest of Dr. McKoin took place at the Brady Institute, Johns Hopkins Hospital, where he had been taking a post graduate course in urology. McKoin said that he was not a fugitive from justice, and that he had traveled to Baltimore on October 1st, to take the course under Dr. Hugh Young.

> I am practically ruined financially. Physician friends of mine are providing the money to enable me to study here. My friends advised me to leave because my work required me to go into rural communities at nights. Shot at once from ambush and just missed, I was told that I could not protect myself from such attacks.
> The trouble, as far as I am concerned, began six years ago when I was elected Mayor of the town for a period of two years. I did not want the position but the best people of Mer Rouge wanted me to run. They elected me and I did my best to stop the association of white men with negro women, gambling and other evils. Mer Rouge is a town of between 750 and 1,000 people. It is surrounded by a prosperous farming community. You know how things are in a small town when change is attempted. One-half is with those who are in. The other half is against them.
> When I had finished my first two years I received a letter telling me not to run again. After such a threat of course, I had to run. I was elected. I finished my second term in 1920. Since then there have been some disorders at various times. Last Summer some of the men who were opposed to me used to come out in front of my house and fire off their guns and shout. It frightened my wife and children and I asked that it be stopped, but it wasn't stopped.

Dr. McKoin then retold his version of the alleged attempt on his life. Added to this, he claimed that he received a letter telling him that "they would get me next time."

"It was then," he said, "after my friends had told me that I could not practice medicine, make calls and protect myself from such night attacks as that, that I got out. I received this letter on Friday and I left Mer Rouge on Tuesday. That was last August. While I know nothing about the death of Richards and Daniels [sic], the attack of the mob on these men and on J. L. Daniels, W. C. Andrews and C. C. Davenport occurred after I left. I do know the men."

At first blush, Dr. McKoin's version sounds believable-almost. He claimed that he did not want the position of mayor. Yet, he ran for a second term, despite receiving a threatening letter. The alleged attempt was made on his life at the beginning of August 1922, two years **after** he left office. Yet he did not leave Mer Rouge until he received a threatening letter, and he departed immediately upon its receipt. Why didn't the first letter cause him not to run for office for a second term, when the second letter frightened him into leaving immediately?

Dr. McKoin said that he left in August, but he would not give a date. Whereas it is possible for Dr. McKoin to have left in August, it must be remembered that his parents lived in Monroe, just a short distance away. In fact, that was where his wife was staying when he was arrested in Baltimore. Had he wanted to participate in the murders of Daniel and Richards, it would have been easy for him to do so even if he were staying with his parents in Monroe.

"Were you identified with any church?" McKoin was asked.
"Yes; I was a deacon in the Baptist Church."
"Were the church people with you when you were Mayor?"
"Yes, generally."
"Was the Ku Klux Klan active in the neighborhood?"
"Well, they used to parade around a great deal with their robes and their masks on, but I never knew of anything like this that they did."
"Are you a member of the Ku Klux Klan?"

It was here that the good doctor ended the interview, as he refused to answer the last question.

A dispatch from Luxor, Egypt announced the discovery of a gigantic obelisk at Assuan on the Nile, south of Thebes. Obviously, this was not as important as the discovery of Tutankhamun's tomb but still of great interest. The obelisk, which was still attached to its granite bed, was 133 feet long, 14 feet wide at the base and tapered to eight feet at the small end. It was estimated that the weight, had the obelisk been extracted, would have been 1,168 tons, which was triple that of the largest obelisk--that of Queen Hatshepsut at Karnak in Upper Egypt.[393]

A bulletin from Cambridge, Massachusetts announced that the scientific world was convinced of the truth of the theory of evolution. This pronouncement was strongly affirmed this day in a formal statement issued by the Council of the American Association for the Advancement of Science.[394]

THURSDAY DECEMBER 28, 1922

Say U.S. Attorney Tried to Save Klan in Federal Inquiry
Assert He Threatened Federal Agents With Arrest and Kept the Ku Klux Posted[395]
Parker and Coco Confer on Mer Rouge Case[396]
Warrant is Issued for M'Koin to Foil Attempts to Obtain Freedom with Habeas Corpus[397]
Former Mayor Will Fight Extradition "To The Last Ditch"[398]
Ku Klux Jurors Enact Farce in Bastrop Inquiry[399]
Klan Ranks Thin Out at Bastrop After Murders[400]

Attorney General Coco was asked to comment on the fact that the citizens of Morehouse Parish are walking the streets visibly displaying firearms. Incredibly, he said that the presence of firearms was the best "guarantee of peace" for the parish. He went on to say:

"If a man is prepared to fight no one is going to provoke him. And I understand that practically every man of the parish is armed." This statement makes absolutely no sense whatsoever. If these were his true feelings, then why did he send the state militia into Morehouse Parish to begin with? I would also venture to say that the state militia forces would have disagreed with this position. The parish was on the verge of all out civil war, and the attorney general is telling everyone to arm themselves.

Attorney General Coco also made known his decision to seek convictions in Morehouse Parish and that he did not intend to seek a change of venue. He expressed the belief that the citizenry was firmly behind the state and that he did not feel that a change of venue would be necessary. This decision also flies in the face

---

[393]*The New York Times*, 27 December 1922.
[394]Ibid.
[395]*The New York Times*, 28 December 1922.
[396]*Times-Picayune*, 28 December 1922.
[397]Ibid.
[398]Ibid.
[399]Ibid.

of logic.

Clearly, the grand jury that had met previously on the Daniel and Richards matter did nothing, and it was known that Klansmen filled the jury. Knowing that Morehouse Parish was a hot bed of Klan activity and pro-Klan sentiment was high there, not to seek a change of venue appears to be an act of overconfidence, arrogance, or ignorance of what the true state of affairs was in the parish. Shortly after he made this decision known, St. Clair Adams, special prosecutor, removed himself from this case. As previously stated, it is believed that Adams did not believe that a conviction could be won in Morehouse Parish. Attorney General Coco continued speaking to the press:

> We intend to arrest a number of men, but it is my desire that these men shall be given a fair trial in court, and not tried in the newspapers, therefore I am not willing to express any convictions at this time.
> I believe-in fact, I am confident-that public sentiment is thoroughly with us in this investigation, and unless conditions change, the men will be tried in Mer Rouge. The people there seem to want justice done in this manner. They have assured me of their support, and I believe they will do all in their power to help in this investigation.
> The murders in Mer Rouge were among the most atrocious in history, and Mer Rouge and all that section are eager that the perpetrators of the crimes shall be properly punished.

Further evidence of the planning of the kidnapping, including the involvement of Dr. McKoin, was learned this day. It was said that three officers of the Klan were leaders of the mob, and that the plan to do away with Daniel and Richards was split into three separate and distinct portions with a Klan leader assigned to each.

One of the Klan leaders was in charge, and he supervised and directed the operation. The second served as a spotter for the rest, identifying Watt Daniel, J. L. Daniel, Thomas Richards, W. C. Andrews, and C. C. (Tot) Davenport at the roadblock set up about a mile outside of Bastrop on the Bastrop-Mer Rouge road. There they were taken from their vehicles at gunpoint, blindfolded, hog-tied, placed in the rear of a truck or trailer, and whisked away. The third Klan leader was in charge of the torture and murder scene. He was said to have supervised and even participated in the beatings of J. L. Daniel and W. C. Andrews and in the torture and murders of Watt Daniel and Thomas Richards.

Dr. McKoin was said to have been the leader of the third group, and it was this mob that performed the surgical operation that the *Times-Picayune* said "cannot be

---

[400] Ibid.

described in print." This is an obvious reference to the castration of Watt Daniel. The good doctor was also said to have joyfully kicked W. C. Andrews in the face and sides as he was being beaten by other black-hooded Klansmen.

Dr. McKoin was no longer willing to return to Louisiana to testify at the open hearings and had vowed to fight extradition "to the last ditch." Having been arrested at Johns Hopkins Hospital where he had been shielded by hospital officials, Dr. McKoin was now residing the Baltimore city jail. Having been arrested by only a verbal request, McKoin was seeking release on a writ of Habeas Corpus. It was said that Klansmen in Morehouse Parish were assisting him in this effort, mainly because they did not want him to return for fear of what might come out at the open hearing or a later trial.

Attorney General Coco and Governor Parker hastily issued an arrest warrant. Special Morehouse Parish Deputy Laurie Calhoun, a Klan officer listed on Morehouse Klan No. 34's application form, and Captain Glynn of the New Orleans Police Department were dispatched to Baltimore to bring Dr. McKoin back to Louisiana by Sheriff Carpenter after he received the warrant from Attorney General Coco. In the meantime, Governor Parker sent Governor Albert Ritchie of Maryland a telegram which stated that the detention of Dr. McKoin was "of vital importance to the state and nation; that, he was not indicted, but charged with the murder on an affidavit." Governor Ritchie was asked if he would honor the extradition paper from the state of Louisiana. He took the wise position of refusing to comment until such time as he received and reviewed the extradition papers.

Fellow Klansmen in Morehouse Parish were busily trying to free Dr. McKoin, and in that regard the Central Savings and Trust Company in Mer Rouge sent a telegram which offered "to deposit any amount of money in a Baltimore bank in an effort to obtain the release of Dr. McKoin." Strange that this offer should come from the town in which Attorney General Coco was so cocked sure would easily convict Dr. McKoin.

Others in the medical profession were also doing what they could to help McKoin. In that number were the American College of Surgeons and Dr. Hugh Young, the head of the Brady Institute of the Johns Hopkins Medical School, with whom it was reported that Dr. McKoin had been associated, and who had undoubtedly shielded McKoin since his arrival on October 1, 1922. Dr. Young released the following telegram received by him from the Central Savings and Trust

196

Company in Mer Rouge:

> The Central Savings and Trust Company of Mer Rouge will indemnify you in any amount you might incur as a result of the arrest of Dr. McKoin. The bank will deposit in any bank in Baltimore sufficient funds to cover any bonds that you might pledge for Dr. McKoin.

When he made his appearance in police court in the morning, Dr. McKoin told reporters, "At one time, I was willing to go back and tell all that I could about the conditions at Mer Rouge, but now I will fight extradition to the last ditch."

When asked about whether he was a member of the Klan, Dr. McKoin again denied that he was a member. He also offered that he had not been asked to join either. He did, however, say, "In fairness to them, however, I must say they have done much good work in the matter of ridding Mer Rouge of undesirables. I don't mean to say that they have driven people out of town. On the contrary, they have by the use of common sense, talk and tact, made good men of individuals who would have undoubtedly landed in jail sooner or later." When asked to describe specific cases, Dr. McKoin replied, "I know of dozens of them, but I do not care to talk about the activities of the klan at this time."

These two statements seem to support the idea that McKoin was indeed a Klansman rather than indicate that he was not. The first statement cannot be considered anything but a defense of the Klan and an obvious knowledge of how the Klan did operate, or at least how he claimed it operated. Furthermore, how would he know of "dozens" of cases in which the Klan took action without having personal knowledge from participation? Me thinks he doth protest too much!

Intervening for his client, Robert B. Carman, McKoin's attorney in Baltimore defended his client by saying, "Dr. McKoin did not flee from Louisiana after the trouble at Mer Rouge. He remained there for many weeks after the death of the two men. He was with his father, thirty miles from Mer Rouge from August till October when he came to Baltimore at the request of Dr. Young, who offered to permit him to be associated with him at the Johns Hopkins Hospital." Once again, there appears to be evidence of Dr. Young knowing that McKoin was there when he was being sought, not to mention the fact that McKoin was in the Bastrop/Mer Rouge area and could have easily taken part in the Daniel/Richards kidnappings and murders. This time the evidence comes from the mouth of McKoin's own attorney.

It was reported that Dr. McKoin was busily attempting to fabricate his alibi with his father in Monroe. It was written this way:

197

It was said Dr. McKoin telegraphed his father at Monroe, La., an alibi, explaining in detail his actions on August 24, the day Thomas Richards and Watt Daniel are supposed to have been kidnapped and murdered. It was also said the telegram contained the names of many witnesses who would corroborate the story of Dr. McKoin should he be brought to trial. The telegram to his father said Dr. McKoin was in Monroe about forty miles from Mer Rouge, conferring with persons as regards office rental in the Ouachita National Bank building. Later, it was said, he called on a patient.

This was to be the exact same alibi that Dr. McKoin would give publicly when asked after he was returned to Morehouse Parish.

Prominent citizens of Morehouse Parish labeled the original grand jury hearing into the Daniel-Richards kidnappings and murders as "farcical." It was said that "nine out of the twelve members of the grand jury are commonly known in this parish as klansmen." When the jurors were summoned in special session by District Judge F. M. Odom to investigate the kidnapping and beatings, only six or eight witnesses were examined, and these were asked perfunctory questions. No real attempt to go to the bottom of the outrages and indict the guilty parties was made.

One witness, who was before the grand jury, was asked if he knew any members of the mob. To this the witness replied that he was of the opinion that the klansmen members of the grand jury could throw as much if not more light on the kidnapping of Daniel and Richards that he could, and he thought the jurors had better begin by placing some of their own members in the witness chair.
The witness said the grand jury dropped him like a hot potato and he was not asked any more questions about the case. The witness said he refused to be sworn when he entered the grand jury room because he proposed to afterward talk about what happened in the room.

This was the same grand jury that was under the direction of District Attorney Garrett.

This being the case, it is doubly difficult to understand why Attorney General Coco would not have applied for a change of venue. Clearly he must have realized that he would probably get another grand jury filled with Klansmen, or at the very least Klan sympathizers. Furthermore, Judge Odom had been the person to call the special session, and he was aware of the actions in the grand jury room and probably a whole lot more. How Odom could have been deemed acceptable by Attorney General Coco defies logic. This could have been another sticking point between Coco and St. Clair Adams, which caused Adams to withdraw from the prosecution team.

Word was circulating that Klansmen were resigning at a rate of 25 a day. This rumor was quickly denied by the exalted cyclops of Morehouse Parish Klan No.

34, Captain J. K. Skipwith. Skipwith also denied that Jeff Burnett had told reporters on the previous day that he was not a member of the Ku Klux Klan. "It's a lie, " said Skipwith, "and I'm going to hunt up and kick the man that wrote it." The reporter who made the assertion stood by his story. Furthermore, he said that Burnett's denial was made in the presence of two state militiamen.

Skipwith also said that he and other Klan members had received letters of a threatening nature from someone or group calling itself "anti- C. C. C." These life-threatening letters, claimed Skipwith, were also received by Dr. McKoin. These letters, said Skipwith, allegedly told that the "anti- C. C. C." was an organization opposed to the Klan.

Agents for the Department of Justice were said to have investigated this claim. These type-written letters were found to have been written on Dr. McKoin's own typewriter. When asked about this, Dr. McKoin verified the fact that his typewriter had been used, but offered the excuse that his office was always open, and anyone could have written the letters.

For the first time, Harold Teegerstrom, the name of the timekeeper at the Southern Carbon Plant where Burnett was employed, was quoted today as having said that Burnett was at the plant working on the night of August 24, 1922, the night that Daniel and Richards were kidnapped and murdered. His name was misspelled in the report. Instead of Teegerstrom, it was spelled "Peeyerstrom." Teegerstrom was to become a major player in this drama, for just a few days after this report appeared in the paper, Teegerstrom mysteriously disappeared after being interviewed by government agents.

Jeff Burnett appeared in good spirits today as he joked with his guards. "I'll be out before you know it," said Jeff Burnett. This he said in reply to the statement of one of his guards that "the first hundred years are the hardest."

The city of Bastrop continued to bulge at the seams as more newspaper correspondents arrived in town. The Campbell Hotel was said to be filled to capacity, and there was not a room to be had in the town. The surrounding communities also reported that they too were experiencing high rates of occupancy at their rooming houses and hotels.

It was revealed in *The New York Times* today that P. W. Mecom, federal district attorney for the Western District of Louisiana, would be called to Washington to answer to allegations made by "responsible citizens of Morehouse

Parish" that he did intentionally interfere with the investigation of federal agents sent by the Justice Department to investigate Klan activity. Contained in the allegations were charges that he threatened the agents with arrest if they did not stop their investigation. Most serious of all was the allegation that Mecom had told Klan leaders in Shreveport, Mer Rouge and other neighboring towns that federal agents were investigating without his authority and that without that authority, they were not empowered to conduct a legal investigation. Mecom was also said to have told the federal operatives that if they did not cease their investigation, he would have them arrested. Federal agents ignored his threats, because they were working under direct orders from Washington.

Because of the alleged misconduct of Mecom, Klansmen felt they were within their rights to plot against these agents, and that they did. These actions by Mecom may have been responsible for a plan to kidnap the agents by the hooded fraternity. This plot called for the Klansmen to seize whatever evidence the agents possessed and have them meet the same fate as Daniel and Richards. This was supposed to occur when a train carrying the agents was to pass through Collinston, some eight miles from Mer Rouge.

Morehouse Horror Rivals Dime Novel[401]

It was reported from Mer Rouge this day that one of the investigators of the kidnappings and murders of Watt Daniel and Thomas Richards predicted this day that the open hearing before District Judge F. M. Odom, scheduled to begin in Bastrop on January 5, would be followed by sensational developments. He said the full details of this plot and the savagery of the mob would startle and shock the whole country.

"No dime novel was ever written that has more thrills in it than this case will reveal when it goes on trial. There are many law-abiding citizens in the klan and I predict that they will not lose any time in getting out when the facts are laid bare in all of their horrible nakedness." This prediction was to become a reality for the Klan.

Recognition of Gov. Parker's fight against the outrages of the Klan was recognized this day in a *New York World* editorial under the caption, "Brave John Parker:"

---

[401] Ibid.

Governor Parker of Louisiana has performed a brave service to the American people in refusing to let the Mer Rouge murders be forgotten. He had every temptation to allow the kidnapping and murders of last August by masked and white-robed men to remain an insoluble mystery.

Instead he faced out the Invisible Empire and moved the wheels of American justice against the perpetrators of mob vengeance. The majesty of the law stands higher in Louisiana today because of John Parker's courage. In Louisiana today, because an unterrified man is in office, the American system of government prevails. A secret criminal conspiracy against the state has been caught in the grip of the law.

The Mer Rouge murders are the logical outcome of the attempt to set up an invisible empire. John Parker's pursuit of these crimes is the logical outcome of the determination to maintain the visible republic."[402]

Mer Rouge Editor Defends Morehouse in Recent Editorial

The editor of the *Mer Rouge Democrat*, W. A. Riley, was indignant because of the "free advertising" that Mer Rouge was receiving. In an editorial, Riley said:

The town is full of reporters from the city dailies and they are surely putting Mer Rouge on the may to the best of their ability. But the free advertising we are getting is not the kind that is likely to prove to our advantage.

People at a distance reading some of the articles published in the daily papers would naturally conclude that we are a gang of outlaws and cut-throats. There is not now and never has been any necessity for any military efforts to keep the peace. There isn't a more peaceful and law-abiding community in the state than this.[403]

From Washington, D.C. came a report that a tiny splinter of wood said to have been a part of the cross on which Jesus Christ was crucified was presented to President Harding this day by Archbishop Panteleimon Neapolis, in Palestine. The splinter was imbedded in soft wax and enclosed in a gold box set with diamonds. The president was also made a Knight of the Order of the Holy Sepulcher by the archbishop.[404]

---

[402] Ibid.

[403] Ibid.

[404] *Times-Picayune*, 28 December 1922.

FRIDAY DECEMBER 29, 1922

Reported 45 Linked to Mer Rouge Crime by Two Confessions

Bastrop Deputy Starts With Extradition Papers-Bodies of Slain Men Show Torture[405406]

Scathing Reply Hits Professor's Plea for M'Koin[407]

Dr. Hugh Hampton Young, head of a Johns Hopkins Hospital clinic where Dr. B. M. McKoin was arrested, sent the following telegram to Attorney General Coco:

> Baltimore, Md.
> Attorney General Coco:
> I am sure McKoin is innocent. A positive and complete alibi is furnished by doctors and businessmen who were with him in Monroe afternoon and evening of the crime. I beg you to investigate this at Monroe before taking him from his important work with me at Johns Hopkins Hospital. You are about to do an irreparable injury to an innocent man.
> DR. HUGH H. YOUNG.

To Governor Parker, Dr. Young fired off this message:

> Well known physicians and businessmen of Monroe furnish positive alibi for McKoin. Will you not investigate this before forcing him to return to Louisiana? I am absolutely sure he is innocent and you will do a great wrong in taking him from his position with me at Johns Hopkins. Investigate and then act. This is a reasonable request. The medical profession of the United States will hold you responsible.

Attorney General Coco wasted no time replying to Dr. Young. His telegram to Dr. Young speaks for itself and was as follows:

> Dr. Hugh Hampton Young.
> Baltimore, Md.
> Your telegram in regard to Dr. McKoin received. It is presumptuous of you to wire me concerning a matter of which you evidently have no information. The evidence against Dr. McKoin justifies affidavit against him and his extradition should be granted. No law-abiding citizen with knowledge of the evidence in the state's possession would aid Dr. McKoin in evading justice.
> A. V. COCO, Attorney General.

Although there appeared to be more than a mere employer/employee or teacher/student relationship between Dr. McKoin and Dr. Young, we are left to speculate as to why a person who held such a lofty position with Johns Hopkins would have 1) lied to authorities when they were first attempting to locate Dr. McKoin, and 2) why he would have jeopardized his position and the reputation of

---

[405]*The New York Times*, 29 December 1922.
[406]Ibid.

Johns Hopkins to shield someone he did not know. Or, perhaps he did know McKoin only too well.

Dr. McKoin appealed to Judge John C. Ross of the federal circuit court of appeals in Baltimore for a writ of Habeas Corpus seeking release from jail. He had already lost his first round when he was turned down the previous day by a Baltimore city court. The opinion of the circuit judges was not long in coming. From Chief Justice James P. Porter came this decision:

"We find that the charge is of such serious character that we believe the traverser should be held until the authorities of Louisiana have an opportunity to present the proper papers. The traverser is remanded to the police without prejudice." This meant that Dr. McKoin would be forced to remain in jail, at least until the extradition hearing was held.

The employee of a local funeral parlor in Monroe described for reporters his perception of the remains of the bodies of Daniel and Richards. P. S. Mulhern, who at the time was an assistant undertaker at the Peters Undertaking Company in Monroe, said that he had helped in the preparation of the bodies of Daniel and Richards for burial. Mulhern, whose descendants now operate one of the most prestigious funeral services in northern Louisiana, had kept silent because of the investigation, but now he felt he could speak because the information concerning the bodies had become common knowledge.

"The heads of both men were missing when I dragged the bodies out of the lake with a sheet used as a seine," said Mulhern. As he was preparing them for burial, he said he observed that all the bones in the bodies had been broken, that the hands and feet were missing and that the bodies appeared to have been "hacked." He said the compound fractures, which were numerous in the arms, legs and hips, were "apparently the result of beating with clubs."

"Both bodies showed the results of terrible mauling. Examination of the ribs and back showed also that the spinal cords of both trunks were badly bruised." He also contended that the body of Daniel appeared to have been "more maliciously mutilated" than that of Richards. He also made reference to the castration of Daniel by saying that "there were conditions of the body that could not be described."

From Atlanta, Georgia, came a press release by Edward Young Clarke, the

---

[407] *Times-Picayune*, 29 December 1922.

imperial giant of the Ku Klux Klan. He said that the Klan was in the process of revising its membership criteria. The revisions mentioned were 1) the admission of all Caucasian races, 2) the admission of persons of the Catholic faith and 3) the start of a membership drive in Europe.

He also made the bizarre statement that another masked and robed organization was operating in northern Louisiana. He issued the following statement, regarding the investigation in progress in Mer Rouge:

> Let me say that we have found after careful investigation that the klan is not responsible for the murders that were supposed to have been committed in Mer Rouge, La. It is just one of several other crimes that have been charged to us by our enemies. I understand from good authority that there is another masked organization in existence in that section of the country. Their gowns are similar to ours. The commander of the organization is a Civil War veteran whose name I cannot recall.
>
> As far as the Mer Rouge affair is concerned we are willing to co-operate with the authorities in ferreting out the case and bringing the guilty ones to justice. We are willing to assist Governor Parker in any way possible despite his unjust attacks upon us.
>
> All these unjust attacks by our enemies are only making us stronger every day. It is solidifying the klan. Our influx of new members was about 3,800 a week when the New York Herald launched its attack on us over a year ago. Now new members are coming in at the rate of 18,000 a week. Out total strength in the country today is 980,000 and we expect to double that by next year.
>
> In Louisiana the attacks of Governor Parker have boosted the membership of the klan to 40,000 in that state and since the unfounded charges made against us by Governor Allen of Kansas our new membership record has increased in Kansas from 800 a week to 3,000 a week.

Let's take a look at what Mr. Clarke had to say. A "careful investigation" to the Klan usually meant little more than a conversation, most of the time second-hand with other Klansmen, concerning an incident. What's more, those that he spoke with were probably the same ones that were involved in the incident.

To say that "another masked organization" was in existence in northeast Louisiana during that time was undoubtedly another facet of their careful investigation, because the Civil War veteran to whom he referred was none other than Captain J. K. Skipwith, exalted cyclops of Morehouse Klan No. 34. The claims of cooperation by the Klan were never anything more than lip service. As a matter of fact, it did everything it could to hinder and impede the investigation. It was reported today that two Klan officials were in Bastrop to investigate the Daniel-Richards incident. If this was true, then Mr Clarke was giving a conclusion of innocence in the middle of the Klan's own investigation. Business as usual for the

Klan.

Now comes a little truth sprinkled in with the other lies. His claims of an over all surge in membership during that general time period may have been true. The Klan was spreading very rapidly across the land, but it had very little to do with the general population's love of Klan principles. Rather, it was more the love and fascination we have with secret organizations, such as the Masons, Loyal Order of Forresters, Knights of Pythias, Knights of Columbus, Loyal Order of Moose, Woodsmen, etc.

Those now joining the Klan were to learn that this second vestige of the Klan was an organization built on a foundation of hate, ignorance and brutality. Just as in 1869 when the first Ku Klux Klan was ordered disbanded only four years after its beginning by the Imperial Wizard, the highly respected Civil War veteran Colonel Nathan Bedford Forrest, because it had fallen into low and violent hands, this second coming of the Klan was also to be short lived. It appeared that once the average person realized what the Klan was and what type of base creature was attracted to such an organization, his length of membership was usually short-lived.

His statement about membership booming in Louisiana may have been true, although it is believed that most of the memberships came long before the Mer Rouge incident. Documents show that Louisiana had a total of 50,000 members in the Klan from 1915 to 1944, so it would have been possible for Louisiana to have had 40,000 at that time. This total includes all males and females initiated into the Klan between 1915 and 1944. The figures are personal estimates, which are based to some degree on the claims of William Joseph Simmons, Edward Young Clarke, Hiram Wesley Evans, and Robert L. Duffus, the estimates of the *New York World, Washington Post, The New York Times*, The *Imperial Night-Hawk*, the evaluations of Charles Alexander, Emerson Loucks, and David Chalmers, and the report of the imperial kligrapp at the 1924 Klonvocation.

Special Morehouse Deputy Sheriff Laurie Calhoun and Captain Glynn of the New Orleans Police Department left Bastrop this date en route to Baltimore with the extradition documents for Dr. McKoin. They were expected to arrive in Baltimore within the next day or two.

Meanwhile, rumors were flying about Bastrop that two Klansmen had confessed to their parts in the kidnappings and murders of Daniel and Richards. In all likelihood, some of these rumors were started by those federal and state investigators with the intent of attempting to find the weakest links in the chain of those involved. It was reported that the Justice Department agents "do not believe it possible for the crowd that murdered the two men to hold together and are confident some will weaken under the pressure and with the hope they will be shown clemency." Once again, they underestimated the hold that the Klan had over its members. As will be displayed in upcoming testimony given by Klan members at the open hearing, the oath to the Klan superseded their oath of allegiance to the United States.

Life for the soldiers continued to be boring. In the morning, Captain Cooper and the members of Company G. 156th Infantry did an hour of close quarter drilling in the vacant lot across from their camp, which impressed all those who gathered to watch. Although the weather was clear and cold, the previous days of rain had made most of the roads impassable.

Amid all of the turmoil surrounding Dr. McKoin, the good doctor appeared to maintain an air of calm. His conduct was reported this way:

> The accused slept like a child on his cot in a cell in the police station last night. It was not until late in the morning that he awoke and had his breakfast sent from a tiny restaurant across the street. He ate this meal as he has all others with zest and apparently had no trouble on his mind. He was confident in the end everything would come out all right.
> In appearance Dr. McKoin is a typical country doctor. He is short and fat with a perpetual grin, keen eyes and a ruddy complexion indicating much outdoor life. He admits killing a rival doctor but points out that the jury accepted his view that he acted in self defense.

McKoin said that he had been one of the organizers of the Ark-La Law Enforcement League, but denied that either it or he had anything to do with the Ku Klux Klan. He said that the league had been formed to fight cattle rustling and the theft of hogs. He claimed to be a deacon in the Baptist Church, which one was not specified. It is, however, believed that it was the Baptist Church in Bastrop, where Reverend Leon W. Sloan was pastor.

On behalf of the Minister's Alliance and the church people of the town, this same Reverend Sloan issued a statement concerning the unfair publicity Mer Rouge was receiving. He told the press that "there was never a more peaceable, quiet, and law-abiding community to be found in the United States, and whatever the outcome of the deplorable affair which culminated in the attempt to assassinate one of our finest citizens and the doing away of two others, there can be no doubt that

Morehouse's reputation has been unjustly injured."

When the reverend's statement is analyzed, it is obvious that he is much more concerned with the faked assassination attempt on McKoin's life and all of the negative press Morehouse Parish was receiving. He also shows his allegiance to McKoin and the Klan when he casually dismissed the kidnapping and murder of Daniel and Richards as "the doing away with of two others." Such was, and to some extent still is, the character of religious leadership in northeast Louisiana. Even today vestiges of this pulpit ignorance still exist in this area.

An example of racism from the pulpit in Monroe occurred when I was doing my Masters work at Northeast Louisiana University in Monroe in 1991-92. I received information from a close friend that a certain "Brother Bob" in one of the more prominent Baptist churches in the area made the statement from the pulpit one Sunday, "There's a nigger in the wood pile somewhere." Relatives of my informant had attended the service when this was said and they returned home commenting on how inappropriate it was for such a statement to be make in church.

During that same time period, a female coach at Neville High School, one of the largest in the Monroe area, told her players, many of whom were black, during a game that they were playing "like a bunch of niggers." Clearly, these statements are indicative of residual racial prejudice and hatred that I observed to be common in that area.

McKoin made the statement that he was a Shriner, which also meant that he was a Mason, Masonry being a prerequisite to enter the Shriners. He also claimed that he belonged to several other unnamed fraternal organizations.

Multiple membership in these "secret" organizations was quite common. During that period, it provided a source of amusement and belonging for the male population. These organizations all had in common secret rituals, oaths of allegiance in which some pledged death rather than reveal its secrets, peculiar names for their leaders, stations within the organization, and, last but not least, a place to go to escape the boredom of rural life. The Ku Klux Klan was so easily accepted because it not only ascribed to all of the aforementioned criteria, but also because it allowed even the most lowly of the white population to experience a sense of power as a Knight of the Invisible Empire.

Reporters continued to press McKoin with regard to his knowledge of the kidnappings and murders. He responded to their questions by saying:

I know nothing about the kidnapping. I wasn't even in Mer Rouge at the time. But I had been fired on in attempts to murder me before that and it was because I owed to my wife and children to protect my life that I came here to take a post-graduate course. I had planned to go back there and aid in the fight on the lawless element. But now they have accused me of a dastardly crime and my fighting blood is up. I won't be forced and I will fight extradition to the very last ditch.

I knew Richards. That is, I knew him just as one knows any man who does odd mechanical jobs for him. After I left I heard he had been associated with the lawless element. But I didn't know it when I used to meet and josh with him in the streets.

He (Parker) seems strong on helping communities purge themselves of outlawry but he was not in evidence when I was trying to clean up my own little city.

SATURDAY DECEMBER 30, 1922

Klansmen Make Vain Effort to Enroll Odom as Member[408]
M'Koin May Face Murder Charge for Killing Thomm[409]

Intent on defending Dr. McKoin and getting in the last word, Dr. Hugh Young of Johns Hopkins fired off another telegram to Attorney General Coco. He said, "If you consider it presumptuous to give information affirming the innocence of Dr. McKoin given by six prominent physicians and two bank presidents of Louisiana, I thank God that I live in Maryland where our state executives welcome all information bearing on a case." Attorney General Coco wisely chose to ignore Dr. Young's telegram. Dr. Young was not heard from again.

In an effort at damage control, it seems Judge Fred Odom was attempting to distance himself from the Klan and install himself as a paragon of virtue who had not only resisted but attempted to fight the Klan. The story, which emanated from an unnamed source, claimed that Odom had agreed to join the Klan originally, but only if the Klan were to adhere to the law. Allegedly when he was told that there were certain areas which the Klan felt were outside of the reach of the law, Odom, as the story went, declined to join.

Not long afterward, the source claimed that a person was kidnapped from the courthouse square in Bastrop and whipped by Klansmen. Allegedly, Odom made an attempt to implicate the Klan in this matter and later in the Daniel and Richards murders, but was unable to secure indictments from the grand jury. However, the actions of Judge Odom just prior to the opening of the open hearing and during the open hearing would later suggest his allegiance to the Klan through a

---

[408] Ibid.
[409] Ibid.

preponderance of evidence.

Dr. McKoin granted another interview, this time from a nearby hospital where he had been taken after contracting a cold in his jail cell. He fed the fires of paranoia concerning his return to Bastrop to stand trial for the murders of Daniel and Richards when he said, "the sight of me will be the signal for the beginning of the greatest slaughter of human life this country has ever known. I would not live long enough to smell the smoke." The good doctor did, however, concede that "the respectable and law-abiding element would battle to the last man to save him." This respectable and law-abiding element seemed to be composed of other Klansmen and Protestant church leaders. What a strange combination.

From Dr. McKoin's rather checkered past also arose another good reason for him to avoid returning to Louisiana, and that was renewed interest in the killing of Dr. K. P. Thomm by Dr. McKoin in August of 1916 at Gallion, Louisiana. It was reported today that a close personal friend of Dr. Thomm was in Morehouse Parish reopening the investigation into the death of Dr. Thomm. He told reporters that he had located witnesses who were willing to testify that "McKoin shot Dr. Thomm twice in the back while Thomm was standing in his shirt sleeves talking to a man on the street at Gallion." The unnamed investigator also claimed that the witnesses had told him "that professional jealousy was the cause of the tragedy." Little by little the dark side of Dr. McKoin continued to be revealed. As time progressed and testimony was given at the open hearing, the twisted personality of Dr. McKoin would be revealed.

It would appear that murder by mayors in Louisiana was not limited to Dr. McKoin. In the *Times-Picayune* for this date appeared a story about Mayor G. C. Payne of Marion, Louisiana being released from jail after being cleared of murdering a local merchant, Marion being a community located about 20 miles west of Bastrop. Allegedly, the mayor fired in self-defense.

From Mer Rouge came accusation from three unnamed Klansmen and one former Klansmen that McKoin was lying when he claimed to have never been a member of the Ku Klux Klan. In an interview, these men claimed that McKoin was not only a member of the Klan, but he was the Captain of the Klan in Mer Rouge. From one of the Klansmen came the assertion that he had been present the night McKoin was initiated into the Klan, and that he had helped placed the hood over the head of McKoin as he took the klan oath. He also said that he had gone to McKoin and from him received membership applications for aspiring Klan members. He said:

> He may deny he is a member of the klan in Baltimore but when he gets back here he will never say that. If I am convinced that the Ku Klux Klan was implicated in the outrage as an organization, I will resign my membership in the order, repudiate my oath and tell everything I know about the order. I went out on two raids which Dr. McKoin headed. The first one, I think was justified. The other caused me to look at the klan in a highly different manner and my wife has begged me almost on bended knees to resign from the organization. I have not resigned. I am merely waiting to see whether the klan was behind the killing of Daniel and Richards. My wife insists that the order is such that a God-fearing man cannot afford to belong to it I am waiting anxiously to see whether her intuition is right.
>
> They say those two men who were killed were of a lawless type. This much is true, at least, they have never been guilty of taking a human life. Had I known that Dr. McKoin had ever killed a man, I would not have asked him to join the organization (the klan). In my estimation judged on Dr. McKoin's record and what I saw of his action in the two raids, Dr. McKoin is not one bit better that the two who were murdered.
>
> In taking the stand I have I am doing so knowing full well what my actions mean. I know that practically every man in Bastrop is a klansman. If I resigned, as I certainly will if I am convinced that the blood is on the hands of the klan, it may mean I will have to take my family and move to another locality. It is not for the klan to pass judgment and mete out punishment.
>
> If the klan is not implicated by the public hearing and the trial I shall retain my membership in the order but, before God, I state that I will never again go out on a raid.

The other Klansmen who were present verified the assertions made by their fellow Klansman concerning Dr. McKoin.

As happens in most cases of this nature, certain officials involved in the investigation will give information to reporters. Sometimes this is done as a favor to the press. Other times, it is done to see what certain suspects involved in the investigation will do once the information is made public. Whatever the case, investigators made the claim today that they knew of the origin as well as the assignments of the Klansmen at the roadblock on the Bastrop-Mer Rouge highway on August 24. They claimed that the Klansmen had been summoned from five surrounding parishes in Louisiana and two counties in Arkansas. It was standard practice among Klans to provide "terrors," the term used to describe members of Klan raiding parties. By operating in this manner, alibis could be established for local Klansmen. It is uncertain to what extent this tactic was used in the case of Daniel and Richards because it will be established later that certain local Klansmen were identified at the roadblock.

They said that the highest Klan official in the area, probably Captain Skipwith, had organized the action to be taken against Daniel and Richards and that two other high Klan officials, probably McKoin and Jeff Burnett, lead the mob and directed their actions. Later testimony will place Captain Skipwith at both the baseball game in Bastrop where he was alleged to have pointed out Daniel and Richards, and at the roadblock on the Bastrop-Mer Rouge highway. Jeff Burnett will also be identified by a witness as having been part of the black-hooded band at the roadblock. It will also be revealed by investigators that the Klan had two masks: a white one used mostly for public demonstrations, initiations and public ceremonies, and a black one used while on raids.

It was announced by state officials of the Louisiana Klan that they were going to make their own investigation into the deaths of Daniel and Richards. They held a press conference during which they released the following statement:

> "Columns have been printed and statement after statement has been issued by state authorities, all tending to fasten on the klan the blame for the Mer Rouge murders. Leaders of the klan know differently. I myself only recently returned from Morehouse parish where I discussed the outrage with many folks who know their community well: I know the klan is not to blame." This, the unnamed klan spokesman said before they launched their investigation. Seems as though they had already made up their minds before the investigation had begun. By our investigations now," the klansman continued, "we hope to uncover the facts that will enable us to convince the entire public of what we already know and believe."
>
> "Will the investigators work in the open, or will they work under cover?" the klansman was asked.
>
> "Our investigators will be made of picked men under cover. The results of these investigations, however, will be given to the newspapers," he replied. "We will depend on this method of getting our side before the public."
>
> "We have no idea of setting up any defense at public hearings for anyone and reports that the klan is interested in obtaining brilliant attorneys for the defense of those arrested are not true," said the klansman in response to questions concerning the defense of McKoin and Burnett. "We are interested in clearing the klan of any connection in the public mind with these outrages."
>
> "Suppose your investigation should develop that the klan in Morehouse parish had something to do with the outrages?" reporters asked.
>
> "In that case," he replied, "the charter would be withdrawn. If any individual klansman were found to be connected with the outrages, he would be outlawed. But I am confident out investigation will show nothing of the sort."

The last line of this statement seems to suggest that the findings of this investigation had already been made, even before it began. Obviously, this is another vain attempt to cleanse the Klan's blood-soaked hands.

With regard to the assertion by the press that local Klansmen have confessed to their involvement in the Daniel-Richards murders, Captain Skipwith said it was "a damnable lie conjured up by despicable imaginative enemies of the klan," and that the stories connecting the Klan with the Daniel-Richards murders were "a pack of lies." Angered by stories in the press, Skipwith said, "you are having your day now, but the day of retaliation will come. The press of Louisiana is trying to wreck Morehouse parish and disrupt the state. Only one side of the story has ever seen print." When asked by the press to give the other side of the story, Skipwith replied, "When I do issue a statement it will be one worth reading."

In an announcement from Atlanta, Georgia, Imperial Giant Edward Young Clarke of the Ku Klux Klan said he was contemplating a trip to Europe. He declared that he is in communication with officials of the Fascisti in Italy with a view to joining forces with them abroad, as this organization stands for what is termed the ideals backed by the Klan. He exhibited a letter from Premier Mussolini lauding the work of the Ku Klux Klan in America.

Clark said that under the proposed internationalization of the Klan, members of all Caucasian races would be admitted to membership. This would mean that Catholics would be eligible for membership. Heretofore, Catholics have not only been debarred but it has been understood generally that the klan was hostile to adherents of the Catholic faith. With regard to the Klan's relationship with blacks, Clark said:

> I would also have it understood that we are not warring against the negro. We have no grudge against the black man. But the negro must keep his place, for he is not the white man's equal either socially or politically. All good negro citizens know that this is practically the unwritten law in a white man's country. We are in favor of the good negro and want him to stay here.[410]

An item from Washington, D.C. this day gave an indication that the Ku Klux Klan had become a national political hot potato. Rep. Gallivan, Democrat, Massachusetts, declared that Democrats who go before the party caucus as candidate for speaker of the House in the new Congress will be called upon to say where they stand on the question of the Ku Klux Klan.[411]

---

[410]*Times-Picayune*, 30 December 1922.
[411]Ibid.

SUNDAY DECEMBER 31, 1922

Say Case is Perfect in Mer Rouge Crime

Louisiana Prosecutors Spur Assembling of Evidence for Hearing on Jan. 5[412]
Attorney General has List of Men Who Will be Arrested[413]
Brother of Man Shot by M'Koin Demands Justice[414]

Agents for the Justice Department revealed that they possessed the names of some of the men whom they believed were involved in the kidnappings and murders of Daniel and Richards. However, they refused to reveal the identities to the members of the press.

J. L. Daniel, Watt's father, told the press today that the report in a Shreveport paper that the Mer Rouge State Bank had offered to bond Dr. McKoin out of a Baltimore jail was false. Speaking as one of the directors of that bank, he said that the story had brought a storm of angry protests from depositors in the Mer Rouge bank. He said that the offer had been made, but it had come from a bank in Monroe.

Additional light was shed on the 1916 killing of Dr. Thomm by Dr. McKoin today. Mr. H. H. Thomm of Bessemer, Alabama, told reporters that he had received information concerning the scenario leading up to his brother's murder. He said McKoin and a banker named Wimberly went to Gallion [located in northeast], Louisiana, where his brother was located, and that they met his brother on the streets. He said there was bad blood between his brother and McKoin and that when they met on the street Wimberly engaged his brother in a fight or tussle. It was during this tussle that McKoin shot his brother twice in the back, he alleged. Mr. Thomm stated the first shot penetrated his brother's heart, causing his death. According to Mr. Thomm, Dr. McKoin never stood trial for this shooting. Mr. Thomm asserted Wimberly owned half of Mer Rouge and controlled the rest of it. He charged that it was through Wimberly's efforts that McKoin was freed without trial other than a farcical examination.

It was revealed today that the Louisiana-Arkansas Law Enforcement League, of which Dr. McKoin had admitted being the director, was organized at Wilmot, Arkansas, and it is said that its membership had been composed exclusively of Klansmen. When asked about the contradictions, Dr. McKoin told reporters, "The

---

[412]*The New York Times*, 31 December 1922.
[413]*Times-Picayune*, 31 December 1922.

principles of this organization are kindred to those of the klansmen and I am proud of its achievements in the vicinity of Mer Rouge. We did wonderful work in ridding the community of undesirables during my tenure in office as mayor." A rose by any other name is still a rose. Once again, the good doctor demonstrated his proclivity to tell half-truths.

In Baltimore, the local Ku Klux Klan, headed by general counsel Albert Ecke, was aiding McKoin in whatever way they possibly could. However, Dr. J. G. Hawkins, imperial representative of the Ku Klux Klan for Maryland and Delaware, said that McKoin was not a member of the Klan. Allegedly, his information came from Klan headquarters in Atlanta.

It was announced that Judge W. C. Barnett of the city of Shreveport and legal adviser of the Caddo parish police jury had been retained to represent Jeff Burnett and Dr. McKoin. With regard to his acceptance of the case, Judge Barnett had this to say to reporters:

> Undue excitement has been created by newspaper stories, many of them without substantiation and foundation. The town of Bastrop is entirely quiet and the town and community seems to be made up of exceptionally high class citizens.
> Yes, I have been retained by friends of Burnett and Dr. McKoin, the parties under arrest, to defend them. I have no statement to make as to the merits of the case for I do not try my cases in the newspapers but in the court

As promised by Captain Skipwith, he called a press conference this day in Bastrop to make a statement concerning the Daniel-Richards case. His statement follows:

> The Morehouse Chapter of the Ku Klux Klan had nothing to do with the murder of Watt Daniel and Thomas F. Richards and we will welcome an investigation. The klan is innocent of any wrong doing. The klan stands for law and order, for the tenets of the Christian religion, for the protection of pure women, for closer relationship between pure Americans and for everything that is of benefit to the community and country. As long as the klan exists, and it is a permanent institution in America, absurd charges will be made against it fostered by enemies of the organization. Klansmen are not mere puppets of higher officials but are guided by their God and their conscience.
> They call the klan murderers and law breakers, terming it a 'masked mob' bent on destroying the laws of the land and the taking of human lives. But they do not speak of the good work of the organization, yet there are many among us who are fully cognizant of all that the klan has done for the community.

As he stood on the steps of the Bastrop courthouse surrounded by Klansmen, his voice became shrill as his emotions took over. In a final defense of the Klan, he

---

[414]Ibid.

214

said, "Ask the good women of this parish about the klan." As he ended his presentation, he was greeted by applause and nods of approval from those gathered.

The New York Times reported that Attorney General Coco said this evening, "We are whipping the evidence, which we believe to constitute practically a perfect case, into shape, and have made reservations to go to Bastrop Wednesday night." One cannot help but wonder if this air of overconfidence concerning not only the evidence in the case but also the fact that he was adamant in his refusal to ask for a change of venue could have been key elements in the failure to obtain indictments on anyone concerning the kidnapping and murders of Daniel and Richards.

Word was also on the street that threats had been received by the attorney general, his staff, and Governor Parker, and this was the reason that he and his staff members had traveled with state militiamen on their way to Morehouse Parish. "Neither myself, nor any of my assistants or Mr. Adams, the special prosecutor, have received any such communications, and I do not believe the Governor has," said Coco, "I have never gone out armed or been guarded in my life," he said, concerning the trip with the troops. "It merely happened that the New Orleans and Alexandria troops were going to Bastrop at the same time my assistants and myself made the trip last week. The troops were not a bodyguard for us."

Friends close to Coco said that this was not the first time that he has taken on hooded organizations. A similar incident such as this occurred in Avoylles Parish when he was a young district judge some 30 years prior. It happened when a mob of about 50 hooded men, known as "white caps," attempted to storm a jail and lynch two prisoners held inside. When the mob approached the jail, the then Judge Coco was said to have been standing in the door of the jail with two revolvers in hand. He had drawn a line in the sand 20 feet from the doorway, and he told the mob that he would kill whomever crossed that line. No one did.

The *Times-Picayune* in New Orleans ran a letter to the editor which told how a black woman had died because her friends and relatives were afraid to venture into the dark due to their fear of the Ku Klux Klan. The letter from Thomas H. Hewes, a planter from Oscar in Pointe Coupee Parish read:

To the Editor of The Times-Picayune:
The record: died, Elizabeth Harrison Tousaint; race, colored; married; age 38; cause of death, internal hemorrhage; September 16, 1922.
The facts: A child had been born. The mother in good shape but complications were feared by an attending physician. The patient and relatives were warned an instructed to call the physician at the first indication of need.
At 11 p.m. the necessity for medical help was apparent, but the Ku Klux had recently had one of their parades in a nearby vicinity, Livonia, and it seemed to those of the watchers who could have gone for the doctor, that their cabin was the safest place. They fooled her. All night long the patient felt herself weakening and wondering why the doctor did not come as he said he would.
When daylight came the messenger started and the doctor came as soon as possible. Life and consciousness still there but it was too late. The Ku Klux had gotten another victim.
I am wondering if they are proud of their work and of their brand of 100 per cent Americanism.

THOMAS H. HEWES[415]

From Houston, Texas it was announced this day that Judge Murray B. Jones, avowed Ku Klux Klan candidate for mayor, conceded victory to his opponent, Mayor Oscar F. Holcombe. Holcombe had a lead of approximately 1100 votes, with but five city boxes missing.[416]

There was shocking new from Chicago. A robber held up Mrs. Katherine Donovan, head bookkeeper of the Palmer House, famous old hostelry of World's Fair days. The robber escaped with $10,000.[417]

SUNDAY DECEMBER 31, 1922

Kidnap a Witness Against Man Held as Ku Klux Slayer

Band in Auto Seizes Co-worker With Burnett, Following Visit of Federal Agents[418]

It was reported today that Harold L. Teegerstrom, a timekeeper at the Southern Carbon Plant at Spyker and principal witness against Jeff Burnett, was kidnapped last Friday night, December 29, 1922, and his location and condition was unknown. Although the kidnapping had occurred on Friday, it was not until today, Sunday, December 31, that Secret Service agents learned of the abduction. Teegerstrom had been scheduled to testify at the open hearing on the coming Friday, January 5, concerning the whereabouts of Jeff Burnett on the evening of August 24, 1922, the date that Daniel and Richards were kidnapped and murdered

---

[415]*Times-Picayune*, 31 December 1922.

[416]Ibid.

[417]Ibid.

[418]*The New York Times*, 1 January 1923.

216

by black-hooded Klansmen.

Teegerstrom had been aroused from his sleep at the carbon plant, located about four miles south of Bastrop. Only a few hours earlier, Secret Service agents had interviewed Teegerstrom as to his knowledge of the whereabouts of Jeff Burnett on the night of August 24. It was said that the Secret Service agents who interviewed Teegerstrom learned from him that Burnett *was not* working at the plant on the evening of August 24. [The term Secret Service agents is a direct quote. Whether this was journalistic garnish is not known. The term does appear again in a number of places in the dispatches from Bastrop.] Furthermore, the agents were in receipt of a report which alleged that the time sheet records for that particular day had been destroyed, or at the very least altered.

It had been rumored around the area that the records at the carbon plant did not support Burnett's alibi. It's silly when you think of it. Surely, if Burnett were going to use work as an alibi, he should have at least been sure that the most important person to substantiate that alibi would do so. But then, the actions committed by these men of low morals and limited intellect have not demonstrated a modicum of common sense in their previous actions, so why should they be any different at this juncture?

The Klansmen who abducted Teegerstrom arrived at about midnight. They arrived in about six cars containing a total of 16 men. Two of the car's license plates were said to have been covered with cloth, and the other two had been taken off. This was a common tactic used by the Klan to avoid identification while on a raid.

News of the kidnapping of young Teegerstrom spread like wildfire among the citizens of Mer Rouge. These same citizens who had at first resented the presence of the uniformed soldiers in their town were now very much in their favor. There were some who thought that Governor Parker should go even further and declare martial law in the area. Clearly, this had been a blatant attempt to impede and intimidate Teegerstrom and any other prospective witness from testifying at the open hearing. As will later be in evidence, there were many who either were too terrified or intimidated by the actions of the Klan to testify.

The kidnapping of Teegerstrom, along with the happenings for the past few months, caused severe personnel shortages, especially among the ranks of the black employees "among whom rumors have inspired fear of an outbreak as the result of the tense situation. Many of the workmen lived five or six miles from town, and they say they are afraid to go to and from work."[419] One can hardly blame the black population for such fears. Although this was the 1920's, the black population was, in northeast Louisiana especially, only a half-step away from slavery, and in many respects they were looked upon as sub-human, their lives having little value. Is it any wonder they decided to stay out of harm's way?

Information continued to be received concerning the manner in which the kidnappings of Daniel and Richards and the later events had been divided up by the Klan. Klansmen had split themselves up into two groups after the kidnapping of the original five on the Bastrop-Mer Rouge road. These two groups were called the "death squad" and the "whipping squad." It was the "death squad" which took Daniel and Richard into custody, inflicted the horrendous tortures on their persons, which eventually was the cause of their deaths, and later dumped their bodies into Lake LaFourche. The job of the "whipping squad" was to beat J. L. Daniel and W. C. Andrews. The whipping was said to have been done near Lake Boueff, which is located a few miles to the south and west of Collinston.

Because of the negative publicity that the town of Bastrop was receiving nationwide, Mayor Goodwin of Bastrop, trying to put the best face he could on a horrible situation, released this statement:

> The community of which I am Mayor wishes to correct the false impression the public has obtained of our home country because of the outrage last August, which I together with the people of Bastrop most vigorously condemn. We hope the culprits will be brought to justice not by way of extenuation, but in justice to our people. One such unfortunate incident should not bring a blanket indictment of lawlessness upon us. We are not a gun-toting, wild savage people. We are law-abiding, like the rest of the people of the United States. Other communities throughout the country have had similar tragedies in their midst but have not been condemned as a unit. Some of the press reports, we know, have been exaggerated, but we welcome all correspondents and only hope they will stay to record the final result as well as the steps that led to the situation.

Somehow, the statements of Mayor Goodwin seem to fly in the face of the kidnappings and murders, dynamite explosions, young Teegerstrom's abduction, and the arming of two towns both anticipating an attack by residents of the other. After reading the mayor's statement, it can only be wondered into what dark orifice he had his head plugged?

---

[419]Ibid.

Attorney General's Family Takes Name from Coconut-Proud Of It[420]

In an unrelated event, it was learned on this date that Coco is not the real name of the Attorney General. He made this revelation in casual conversation with reporters. Responding to a question as to the strangeness of his last name, He said, "It's a nickname. Coco, speaking ancestrally, is not my name at all. My name legally, of course, is Coco, but my paternal grandfather was Dominick Baldonido, an Italian."

He explained that his grandfather would go to the waterfront and gather coconuts to sell. He soon became identified with the product he was selling, and because people were not able to so easily remember Baldonido, nor could they spell it, his grandfather changed the last name to Coco. It seems strange to know that the Attorney General of the State of Louisiana, the man responsible for the prosecution of this heinous crime, went by an alias.

57 Lynchings in Year of 1922: Texas Leads with 18[421]

In a press release made by the Tuskegee Normal and Industrial Institute in Tuskegee, Alabama, it was established that Texas led the nation in the number of lynchings during 1922. Coming in second was Georgia, and Mississippi was third.

A total of 57 people were lynched during 1922 and of that 57, 51 were Black and six white. The press release indicated that this was seven less than in 1921. Thirteen of those lynched were taken from jails, and 17 from officers of the law outside of jails. We have seen how the mechanics of how that works.

The 10 states where lynchings occurred and number in each state were: Texas, 18; Georgia, 11; Mississippi, 9; Florida, 5; Arkansas, 5; Louisiana 3; Alabama, 2; Tennessee, 2; Oklahoma, 1, and South Carolina, 1. There were 58 instances where officers of the law prevented lynchings. Fourteen of those incidents were in Northern States, and 44 in Southern States.

---

[420]*Times-Picayune*, 31 December 1922.
[421]*The New York Times*, 31 December 1922.

Kidnapping of Spyker Resident is Investigated by Federal Operatives and Morehouse Sheriff[422]
M'Koin in Monroe on Night of Murders, Asserts Friends[423]

While a quiet and happy New Year may have been the order of the day for the f First Family of the United States, such was not the case for those residents of Morehouse Parish, nor was it peaceful for Dr. B. M. McKoin, who was still sitting in the Baltimore, Maryland jail fighting extradition to Louisiana on charges that he participated in the murders of Watt Daniel and Thomas Richards. Governor Ritchie of Maryland had decided overnight that there should be a public hearing on the question of whether Dr. McKoin should be extradited back to Louisiana. He reached this decision after conferring with Special Deputy Calhoun of Morehouse Parish and Chief Detective Glynn of New Orleans, both of whom had transported the extradition request signed by both Governor Parker and Attorney General Coco.

In telegrams to local authorities, Governor Parker asked that a hold be placed on Dr. McKoin stating that his confinement was "vital to both state and nation." This notwithstanding, several telegrams were received by Governor Ritchie from many prominent citizens of Monroe, attesting to McKoin's assertion that he was 40 miles from the scene of the kidnappings on the date and time in question. Telegrams were also reviewed by McKoin himself, in which were offers of "financial assistance in his fight for freedom and others testifying to the good character of the accused." Although the names of the authors of these communiqués were not released, there is little doubt that these same people were also members and/or sympathizers of the Klan. McKoin's mysterious health had improved, and the bronchitis, which he had been suffering from for two days, had all but disappeared.

Meanwhile, the search for 20-year-old Harold Teegerstrom continued with no new leads. Sheriff Carpenter, in his usual devil-may-care fashion, left on this date to investigate the reported disappearance of young Teegerstrom from the Southern Carbon Plant in Spyker, Louisiana. Spyker is on the very city limits of Bastrop. Under the circumstances, the sheriff's actions and his statement that it was his opinion only that "he was not certain that Teegerstrom had been kidnapped, but that he was reported to have disappeared," certainly seems to suggest that he knew

---

[422]Ibid.
[423]Ibid.

much more than he was saying. The sheriff seemed to have taken this position because he claimed to have made a trip to Spyker the day before "but obtained no information other than Teegerstrom had been called from his room about 11 p.m. Friday by unknown persons and that he did not return."

According to the sheriff, the roommate stated that Teegerstrom had been awakened by a knock at the door, but that he [the roommate] paid no attention to it and went back to sleep. Typically, Sheriff Carpenter maintained his usual ignorance of facts by revealing that he was unaware if Teegerstrom was privy to knowledge concerning the identity of the persons responsible for the kidnapping of Daniel and Richards. This seems quite ludicrous since it was well known that persons unknown had whisked Teegerstrom away in the dead of night, and that Teegerstrom, being the timekeeper, would have firsthand knowledge as to whether Burnett was working or not. Also, it was quite possible for Teegerstrom to have knowledge of the missing dynamite that had been used in an attempt to cover over the bodies of Daniel and Richards in Lake LaFourche, since it was thought to have come from the dynamite shack at the Southern Carbon Plant.

According to Sheriff Carpenter, Teegerstrom said publicly that his former Deputy Sheriff "Jeff" Burnett, who was already in jail in Bastrop in connection with the kidnappings and murders of Daniel and Richards, was at the Southern Carbon Plant in Spyker on August 24, 1922. This was the alleged date that the kidnappings and murders took place.

Victor Teegerstrom, the father of Harold and former manager of the Monroe Gas Company, journeyed to Bastrop, where he conferred with Sheriff Carpenter as to the efforts being made to locate his son. Carpenter told him that he believed that "young Teegerstrom was probably in the hands of his 'friends' who wanted him only as a witness in the Morehouse parish kidnapping case." Although some of these statements seem incredible coming from what is supposed to be responsible authority, the reader must place these utterances into the time period and social context of that time. The coldness and arrogance of such statements only serve to demonstrate the stranglehold of terror and control that the Klan maintained in northeastern Louisiana, particularly through the offices of their elected officials.

S. T. Bennett, the Superintendent of the Southern Carbon Plant at Spyker, felt that there was little doubt that Teegerstrom had disappeared. Bennett returned to Spyker from a business trip to West Virginia on the same Friday night that

Teegerstrom disappeared. Bennett said that he had begun his own investigation of the matter because he wanted "to determine where he has gone and by whom he was taken. I do not know that he has been harmed, and I cannot say that he has not." Evidently, Sheriff Carpenter had better information than Bennett because it was Carpenter's contention that Teegerstrom was being held by "friends," a curious choice of words. Later, testimony in the open hearing will reveal that Bennett was also a Klansman.

Interesting enough, Jeff Burnett, foreman at the Southern Carbon Plant and the first to be arrested in the case of the kidnappings and murders, told reporters that he could prove his innocence by the timekeeper's records at the Southern Carbon plant in Spyker. Burnett made this statement from his jail cell in Bastrop on Friday, the same day that he was arrested, and, coincidentally the same day that Teegerstrom, the very man who could confirm or deny this assertion, was taken away, in all likelihood, by the same principals who kidnapped and murdered Daniel and Richards. Sheriff Carpenter was said to be wondering if the two might be connected. I mean, go figure!

Dean Ashcraft was the roommate of Harold Teegerstrom and was present in the room the night Teegerstrom disappeared. According to Ashcraft, it was "about 11 o'clock Friday night-or maybe it was about midnight-I was roused from sleep by Harold getting up and going to the door of the room in which we both slept together: fact is, I turned over and went to sleep. When I awoke this morning, I found he was gone, and he has not returned and I believe he was kidnapped." Ashcraft's statement seems believable until the last sentence. Why would he say that he believed that he was kidnapped? Obviously, there is something that propelled him in that direction. More than likely it was information that he possessed, but was afraid to disclose, because he feared for his own safety.

And then there is the story of Henry Jones, a sawmill employee who resided near Bastrop. He told Sheriff Carpenter that Teegerstrom showed up at his residence on Sunday, December 31. Teegerstrom allegedly requested $40 from Jones explaining that he needed it to "leave the community." Jones told the sheriff that he advanced Teegerstrom the money.

Finally, Sheriff Carpenter admitted that "Teegerstrom was called from his sleeping quarters at the plant at midnight Friday night and was whisked away in the darkness by the men who occupied six automobiles whose license plates had been either covered or removed." Word travels fast in the backwoods of northeastern Louisiana, for it had only been a few hours prior that federal investigators had questioned young Teegerstrom with regard to his knowledge of Burnett's claim to have been present at the plant on the night of the kidnappings and murders. It was clear that Teegerstrom could play a vital role in the state's case, which was due to begin on January 5, just a few days hence.

State and federal investigators had not only interviewed Teegerstrom. They were also busy obtaining statements regarding the ravages of the Klan which had continued unabated for years. Furthermore, representatives of the attorney general's office, it was said, "would not only reveal evidence as applying to the kidnapping and killing of Daniel and Richards, but would result in a rigid investigation of other alleged crimes laid at the door of masked bands, not only in Morehouse Parish but also in other Louisiana Parishes." Unfortunately, this would never come to pass.[424]

According to the *Times-Picayune*, the attorney general's office stated that it intended to use only that amount of evidence it believed necessary to obtain indictments on those Klansmen it believes participated in the kidnappings and murders of Daniel and Richards. This practice was not unusual and is often employed today. It was also announced that the format of the open hearing would be along the lines of a grand jury hearing. The state would be the only one posing questions to the witnesses. Although defense attorneys would be present in the courtroom, they would be unable to pose questions, nor be permitted to mount a defense for their clients.[425]

Meanwhile in Mer Rouge, the editor of *The Mer Rouge Democrat* had been speaking out against the Klan, and on this date he took the opportunity to clarify a misunderstanding concerning a previous article that had appeared in the *Democrat*. In an editorial, he wrote:

> In this article, we had no intention of expressing any sympathy with the Ku Klux, but was intended to express our concern for the good name and reputation of Mer Rouge and Morehouse parish which was being injured by articles being published in the daily papers that would be read by people at a distance who did not understand the conditions.
> We have repeatedly stated-not editorially, but in private conversations-that we did not believe that any man or set of men had any right to take the law into their own hands under any circumstances. The Constitution provides that everyone is

---

[424]Ibid.

[425]*Times-Picayune*, 2 January 1923.

entitled to a fair and impartial trial. Therefore, when they surreptitiously take anyone and administer punishment, they are violating the law and cannot be 100 percent Americans.

As to Governor Parker and the Ku Klux, he could not, consistently with his oath of office, take any other stand than he has in regard to that organization. If the reports that have been given out are true, the murder of Watt Daniel and T. F. Richards was one of the most cruel and fiendish that we have ever read or heard of being perpetrated in a civilized community, and it will be the desire of every good citizen that the guilty parties may speedily be brought to justice.

If there was no other way to obtain this result than the one taken, then we say go to it, and we hope the efforts may be successful in bringing the murderers to justice.[426]

Needless to say, most of the newspapers located in northern Louisiana came out strongly against Governor Parker when he first decided to intervene in the situation in Morehouse Parish. However, as time went on, their attitude changed, and they became supportive. One example was in Richland Parish in the *Richland Beacon*. Always known to have been a staunch supporter of the Ku Klux Klan, this publication made a complete turnaround in its editorial entitled, "Where We Stand." The editorial continued:

We deny the right of any man or any number of men of any organization, or any church, or any state, to put a padlock on our lips, to make the tongue a convict. If we are correctly informed, the Ku Klux Klan is not in full sympathy with this sentiment; hence our opposition to those principles, or rather practices, for which we understand they stand.

We do not wish to do anyone an injury, but we condemn the Morehouse parish crime and we will not excuse the criminal acts of alleged members hiding behind the mask and the cloak of the order.

For the sake of your state-for the sake of her reputation throughout the world-for your own sakes, citizens all-and those of your children and the children yet to be-say to the world that Louisiana shares in the spirit of this enlightened age--that Louisiana is not a survivor of the Dark Ages-and that Louisiana still believes in law and order and the preservation of constituted authority and will probe to its very depth this diabolical murder.[427]

The business community was beginning to take notice of the possible implications of these heinous crimes, and the probable financial impact they may have on the community. There were those who believed that the community would surely suffer from all of the bad press emanating from northeast Louisiana. There were others, however, who took a different view. One unnamed businessman in an interview with a *Times-Picayune* correspondent put it this way:

---

[426]Ibid.
[427]Ibid.

While it is humiliating to me to know that we have such conditions in Morehouse parish, I believe the present investigation and the free advertising we are getting all over the country will bring good in the end. It will help to clear the atmosphere and create more respect for law and better local government.

Publicity will be 75 percent of the value of this investigation, for it will teach the people of Morehouse a lesson that they will never forget. They will be taught that if they wish to escape unenviable notoriety and appearing on the front pages of newspapers with sensational articles and the pictures and trimmings that go with them, they must have a peaceful and law-abiding parish and quit furnishing crime news that places them in the limelight.

Plainly and bluntly stated, the people of Morehouse parish cannot escape their responsibility for the present conditions. They have not stood for law enforcement in the past as they should have done. I guess I should be censured along with the balance. All of us should have been more active and should have compelled obedience to law even if it had become necessary to impeach some public officials for neglect of duty.

Mer Rouge has suffered more than any other town in the parish but I believe we have turned the corner and better conditions will prevail hereafter.

This town has been persecuted by members of the Ku Klux Klan in Morehouse parish because a majority of our citizens are opposed to the Klan. Two of our citizens were murdered, others kidnapped and several whipped by Klan mobs.

While all this lawlessness was going on here we appealed for protection. No response came from the parish officers nor from businessmen of Bastrop and Monroe who now complain about publicity of crime conditions in Morehouse parish hurting their business. If these same men who are complaining had devoted as much time toward upholding the law and order and in compelling parish officials to do their duty under penalty of impeachment as they now are doing in complaining we would have had, in my opinion, different conditions in Morehouse.

A sample of how Mer Rouge has been treated can be shown by relating what happened at a peace conference held in the director's room of a bank at Monroe. Committees were named by citizens of Mer Rouge who were anti-klan and by citizens of Bastrop who were pro-klan to meet with a committee of Monroe citizens.

This conference was held after the kidnapping and murder of Daniel and Richards at a time when the parish was threatened with civil war. J. K. Skipwith, exalted cyclops of the klan of Morehouse, and Dr. B. M. McKoin, captain of the klan at Mer Rouge, appeared at the conference and demanded as a condition precedent to peace that Hugo Davenport, A. C. Whipple, City Marshal W. F. Campbell and Thomas Milner must leave Mer Rouge and never to return.

This insolent demand on the part of Skipwith and McKoin shocked the members of our committee but they kept their temper. They were seeking peace. Long arguments followed. Finally, Skipwith and McKoin said they would permit Davenport, Whipple Campbell and Milner to remain here provided 'they would shut up their mouths and quit talking against the klan.'

The conference ended at that point, when Skipwith and McKoin revealed their motive for seeking to force the four men to leave, which was that Davenport, Whipple, Campbell and Milner were anti-klan and persisted in talking against it. Davenport, Whipple and Campbell defied the klan and continued to denounce it, but Milner left.

Hugo Davenport is one of the leading merchants of Mer Rouge. He served in the

225

state Legislature and has been prominent in parish affairs. He is a grandson of Josiah Davenport, who with Abraham Morehouse, were the first settlers of the parish.

A. C. Whipple is in the automobile business, operating a sales house and a garage. W. F. Campbell is town marshal and stands well with the people.

Other citizens were also threatened from time to time. This forced us to arm ourselves for our own protection. For we could not get any help from the outside until the state and federal governments became interested.

We have given the government authorities our hearty support in their investigations, but this cannot be said of the members of the Ku Klux Klan in Morehouse parish. With the exception of some of our citizens who quit the klan not a Morehouse parish klansman aided the federal and state authorities prior to the coming of the militia, according to my information, and I am sure it is correct.[428]

Morehouse Parish Klan Holds Session[429]

A bulletin from Bastrop this evening indicated that the Ku Klux Klan was meeting at some undisclosed location in Morehouse Parish" tonight for the purpose of discussing the latest developments in the Mer Rouge murder probe. According to the report, Captain Skipwith could not be found and known Klansmen refused to comment. It was said around the town that the meeting was being held in or near Monroe.

Also from Bastrop came the news that the complement of federal agents in Morehouse Parish was heavily reinforced that evening by additional government men. It was said that the government had its best agents on the case.[430]

Skipwith Grants Interview While in Amiable Mood[431]

Captain J. K. Skipwith was truly enjoying the attention that he was receiving. On this afternoon, he lolled in a chair in an office of the parish courthouse in Bastrop. Near him, listening to each word that fell from his aged lips were three newspapermen, one from New York, another from Beaumont, Texas, and the third from the *Times-Picayune*. It was a bright warm day, and the leader of the Morehouse Klan was in amiable frame of mine. Addressing the correspondents, he granted them a long-awaited interview. He began by saying, "I am the exalted cyclops of the Morehouse Klan of the Invisible Empire, Knights of the Ku Klux Klan." He paused to let the significance of his words penetrate the minds of the interviewers. His interviewers properly impressed, the "Cap'n" continued.

---

[428]Ibid.
[429]Ibid.
[430]Ibid.

226

Boys, long before you were born, way back in 71 (1871), in the state of Tennessee, an organization similar to the Ku Klux Klan of today was in existence. It was known as the Forrest Klan, named after the famous Confederate general of that name. The Forrest Klan had its day, performed noble work and passed out. The government made it impossible for it to exist.

Again the "cap'n" paused. Perhaps he was living over those days again, those days of the carpetbagger and the up-hill struggle of the South to adjust itself. His pause gave interviewers ample time to study the "Cap'n." More than three score years and ten have rolled over the thin white hair on the captain's head and upon which rested a new pearl gray hat. From beneath his dark overcoat peeped a somber gray scarf. His trousers were grey checked and gray silk socks were visible.

The keynote of the apparel of the "Captain" was gray. The passing years have left their mark on his lined face but his complexion is ruddy and his eyes, pale blue, seemed to look through one.

The "Cap'n" was asked by the *Times-Picayune* reporter to pose for a picture. Something he had heretofore refused to do.

"What paper do you represent, young man?" he queried. He was told. For a moment the "Cap'n" scrutinized the reporter, the queried:
"Ain't the Saturday Evening Post published in Kansas City or is it St. Louis"
"It's published in Philadelphia, sir"
"Well, who was that man they sent down here to interview me?" The "Cap'n" was told that it was a reporter from the St. Louis Post Dispatch.
"Well, anyway," he said, "he quoted me wrong. He said that I called Governor Parker a dumb jackass."
"Did you call the governor that, Cap'n?" he was asked.
"No, sir, not yet," he replied. The words were accompanied by a smile and the blue eyes twinkled. "And you want a picture of me, eh?" asked the 'Cap'n.'
"I have refused to pose so far, but some durn fool on a Shreveport paper drew a pen picture of me and made me look like a cut throat. If you will do me justice you can have the picture. I wish, however, that you would take the libelous pen picture and publish it with the one you are going to take and above the good picture. Right here is the real "Cap'n" Skipwith. Come on, let's get it over with."

The "Cap'n" posed with his new hat on and with his new hat off. When the photographing was over he resumed his story.

"After the Forrest Klan went out of existence, conditions became intolerable. A few years later a second klan sprang into existence, known as the Bull Dozers. The Bull Dozers done a powerful lot of good, I tell you. Those were the days of reconstruction in the South and the organization was needed. The Ku Klux Klan today is the Bull Dozers of yesteryear."
"Are the principles the same?" he was asked.

---

[431] Ibid.

"No, not exactly, but in many ways they are," he replied.

"How long has the Morehouse chapter been in existence?" was the next query.

"Oh, 'bout a year or so, I think."

"Have you been the exalted cyclops since its inception?"

"Yep," laconically replied the "Cap'n".

"Is it an appointive office?" he was asked.

"Nope, I was elected."

"Do you use your judgement concerning klan affairs and activities or do you receive orders from national officers?"

The "Cap'n" paused, gazed reflectively at the ceiling and said; "Rather not answer that question right now."

"Has the klan met in Morehouse parish recently?" was the next question.

"I reckon not, and I guess I oughta know. I'm the exalted cyclops," he replied.

"Reports say," pursued the interview, "that many klansmen have resigned since the finding of the bodies of Richards and Daniel. How about it?"

The twinkle in the blue eyes disappeared. The "Cap'n" was defending the klan.

"All a damned lie, every bit of it. There has not been a single resignation in Bastrop."

"How about Mer Rouge?" he was asked.

"About six resignations there," was the answer.

"Do you think the klan will be exonerated of the charge of being responsible for the murders last August?" he was asked next.

The reply was vigorous. Again he was rising in defense of the klan.

"Know damn well it will be. The klan had nothing to do with their deaths."

"But you won't deny that klansmen were present," interpolated the questioner.

The Cap'n" reflected and replied:

"Maybe so, but the klan was not officially represented."

The "Cap'n" ended the interview by declaring that he was affiliated with the Klan because it stood for law and order and was an organization concerned with the good of the community.

TUESDAY JANUARY 2, 1923

National Guard Units Holding Down Kidnapping Situation for State are Increased to Four[432]

More Secret Service Agents Ordered into War Zone to Aid on "Final Round-Up in Morehouse"[433]

"Watchful Waiting" Police in Morehouse as Date Nears for Open Hearing of Crime Charge[434]

M'Koin Conference on Whether Local Man Will Return[435]
Parker Will Act to Bring Back M'Koin at Once[436]

A cavalry unit of the Louisiana National Guard stationed at Jennings,

---

[432]Ibid.

[433]Ibid.

[434]Ibid.

[435]Ibid.

[436]Times-Picayune, 3 January 1923.

Louisiana, received orders to proceed to Morehouse Parish. This troop movement brought the total unit number of Louisiana National Guard in Morehouse Parish to four. The troop consisted of three officers, along with 40 enlisted men and their mounts. Although no official reason was given for this unit's movement, it was believed that they were to reinforce the troops already stationed in Morehouse Parish and that they would probably be used in making arrests.

Meanwhile, the search for Harold Teegerstrom continued. Sheriff Carpenter claimed that he had information that Teegerstrom was en route to Pittsburgh, Pennsylvania, and that Teegerstrom was in hiding "for some unknown reason." The sheriff seemed to possess selective information, not to mention selective amnesia, with regard to Teegerstrom. At no time did Carpenter ever reveal the source of his information, and to say that Teegerstrom was hiding "for some unknown reason" flies in the face of the facts that he had been kidnapped.

One can only wonder as to just how those involved in the investigation of the kidnapping defined the term. This is exemplified by the following statement: "The only part of his disappearance that has, apparently, been cleared up is that he was not actually "kidnapped," but it is believed that he was taken in charge by a number of persons last Friday night, questioned as to his knowledge of certain witnesses in the Morehouse Parish kidnapping and probably advised to leave the state."[437]

Clearly, it appears that it was acceptable practice in northeastern Louisiana to take a person away and question him. This qualifies as kidnapping. Furthermore, Teegerstrom obviously had information that would be detrimental to Burnett, at least, and perhaps other Klan members as well. Otherwise, he would not have been "advised to leave the state." This falls under witness intimidation and interference with an investigation. Yet, this is the same group that claims to hold sacred the Constitution and professes to be 100 % American.

The press, in particular the *Monroe News-Star*, went further to make light of the kidnapping and intimidation by reporting "Teegerstrom's movements *after he was called out* are a matter of doubt. The general belief, however, is that the men made no effort to detain the young man, but probably took him into the woods or to some unknown destination, and there they satisfied themselves on several points

---

[437] Ibid.

which they wanted Teegerstrom for."[438] This raises the question of how a person can be taken somewhere they did not wish to go, endure questioning by a large group of men whose only purpose could only be to terrify and intimidate, and these actions not be considered wrong. Clearly, this is vigilantism of the first order.

Other reports were filtering in from undisclosed sources concerning the whereabouts and condition of young Teegerstrom. According to one, Teegerstrom had taken refuge in the home of a friend in Morehouse Parish and that the men who had initially kidnapped him from his room at the Southern Carbon Plant in Spyker had turned him over to this friend, and "that he was not held against his will." Emphasis was continually placed on the fact that Teegerstrom was a willing participant in his own kidnapping and interrogation. This contention flies in the face of logic.

Clarence Teegerstrom, the brother of Harold, also felt that his brother had been abducted. "My brother was kidnapped despite reports to the contrary. But he broke away from his capture and hid out." Clarence would not say where or how he obtained this information, but he did go on to say that he felt that his brother was no longer in Louisiana. The elder Teegerstrom also reiterated his belief that his son was no longer in Louisiana. In fact, he "refused to give out any information, but said he was not worried because of his son's absence." Clearly, it appears as though he had received some reliable information that reassured him of his son's safety. These statements appear to have coincided with the information that had been gleaned by the eight secret service men who had been investigating the Teegerstrom disappearance. They appeared to have developed information which led them to believe that Teegerstrom had, in fact, left the state.[439]

The *Times-Picayune* reported that Victor Teegerstrom said he had heard from his 19-year-old son Harold, and that he had made his escape from those men who had kidnapped him from the bunkhouse that evening. Teegerstrom made this statement to the press.

> I know that Harold was taken out by a number of men, because he sent word to me to that effect. He was in the bunkhouse with Dean Ashcraft, his roommate, last Friday night and was summoned to the door by a knock. This man took him out to where there was a group of men and they whisked him away in automobiles with only part of his clothing on.

---

[438] Ibid.

[439] *Monroe News-Star*, 2 January 1923.

He slipped away from them after he had been browbeaten and bull-dozed [A term used often by Slipwith], scantily clad and nearly froze by the cold, and he spent all night in an old shack. The next morning he secured a pair of shoes from a countryman and got his breakfast at a farmhouse. He continued hiding all day and slept at the farm house Saturday night and on Sunday he got in touch with Henry Jones, sawmill man of Morehouse Parish, an old friend, and was made comfortable.

He borrowed $40 from Mr. Jones and then told Mr. Jones to take his watch and keys to me to prove to me that he had been seen.

He left some time Sunday, and I have since not been able to locate him. I do not know that he has gone to Pennsylvania, but I do not feel that he can be found in this State. We came from Erie, Pa., a number of years ago and Harold has been in the gas fields for about six years and I have been here four years.

I am not saying who did this, but I am going to find out and I am going to make them explain why they did it.

According to rumors, young Teegerstrom had left the state and was probably in Pennsylvania. Conventional wisdom around town was that fear and intimidation was at the core of his hasty departure, and who could blame him?[440]

According to the *Monroe News-Star*, Dean Ashcraft, the roommate of Teegerstrom, did more than just roll over and go back to sleep on the night he was kidnapped. He told the *News-Star*, "there were several automobiles filled with men." It is obvious that he would have had to have gotten out of bed to 1) have seen there were automobiles, and 2) to have knowledge that the cars were full of men.

The long awaited autopsy report being prepared by Drs. George W. Duval and John A. Lanford, both of New Orleans, was to be turned over to Attorney General Coco soon. This announcement coincided with the arrival of more Secret Service men who, it was believed, would be taking part in mass arrests in Morehouse Parish.

With regard to the making of wholesale arrests, officers assigned to the National Guard did not believe that this was going to occur any time soon. They did not want to do this "because those in charge of the Morehouse situation do not want the 'opposition' to organize their forces unnecessarily. The plan is to jump into the hearing with a few defendants and to order the arrests of various persons alleged to be connected with the Morehouse kidnapping as evidence in the trial develops and warrants."[441] These statements seem to point to a reluctance to force a confrontation

[440]*Times-Picayune*, 3 January 1923.
[441]Ibid.

with the Klan. Furthermore, it displays good judgment, especially in the light of what had occurred to young Teegerstrom when it became known that he possessed information vital to the prosecution of these crimes.

Meanwhile, it was rumored among friends and relatives of Dr. McKoin that a deal was being hammered out between Attorney General Coco, Governor Ritchie and Robert R. Carman, a former United States District Attorney and counsel for Dr. McKoin. It appears as though numerous telegrams were sent to Dr. McKoin from many relatives and friends, including his father, E. M. McKoin, all exhorting him to return to Louisiana voluntarily. This confidence appeared to come from the impressive list of defense witnesses that were being lined up, including Travis Oliver, President of the Central Savings Bank & Trust Co., Dr. Vaughn, a local practitioner and friend, and "many other prominent business and professional men."[442]

In Baton Rouge, the *Times-Picayune* reported that Governor Parker was still wrestling with Governor Ritchie of Maryland over the extradition of Dr. McKoin. Because Governor Ritchie refused to honor the extradition papers sent by Attorney General Coco, Governor Parker announced that he would submit the question to the U.S. Department of Justice with regard to the proper procedure to extradite McKoin.[443]

Commenting on the extradition papers, the *Monroe News-Star* reported that Mr. Carman, McKoin's attorney in the extradition fight, said, "The papers contain affidavits made only upon information and belief and not actual knowledge. Therefore they would not stand the test of the courts." In the meantime, Governor Parker received the following telegram from Governor Ritchie:

> After examining the requisition papers in the McKoin case I do not think they are sufficient for the reason that the affidavits are made on information and belief and not by anyone who has any personal knowledge of the alleged crimes.
> Both the law and practice are clear in requiring this. If the case comes to trial before me, my decision will accordingly be not to grant the requisition at this time, but I will hold McKoin for a reasonable length of time in order to give the Louisiana authorities the opportunity to submit a competent affidavit.
> Dr. McKoin, while insisting on his extradition rights, nevertheless advises me through his counsel he is quite willing to return to Louisiana voluntarily, but he cannot do so until he is release by the court. He would like your deputy officers to accompany him back to Louisiana, and will you authorize your deputy

---

[442]*Monroe News-Star*, 2 January 1923.

[443]*Times-Picayune*, 3 January 1923.

officers to accompany him there?

The communiqué did not reach Parker's office in time for him to have a meeting with Attorney General Coco on the matter and was not addressed until the following morning. It was also reported that McKoin had been restricted to bed rest because of a case of bronchitis. This phantom illness was to have a miraculous recovery when the deal was finally resolved which allowed McKoin to return to Louisiana voluntarily. It seems quite a coincidence that Jeff Burnett in the Bastrop jail was also suffering respiratory problems. Perhaps Burnett and McKoin were experiencing a sympathetic response to one another.

The commander of all military forces involved in the Morehouse Parish action, Colonel L. A. Toombs, the adjutant general, refused to divulge any plans concerning his troops. It was the belief at that time, however, that he had in his possession an order declaring martial law in Morehouse Parish. It was also rumored that all National Guard units throughout the State were on emergency standby and were to be ready to respond quickly should the need arise in Morehouse Parish.

It was announced today by Captain Cooper of Company G, 156th Infantry that an advertising campaign will commence immediately for new recruits with an eye to bringing the unit up to wartime strength. At that time, he reported only 65 men in his unit. A recruiting station had been opened in Monroe, and a reproduction of a copy of an ad which appeared in the *Monroe News-Star* is shown below.

MEN WANTED
---for---
NATIONAL GUARD
Enlist in Company "G,"
156th Infantry
Recruits will be sent to
camp at Mer Rouge, La.
Apply at Armory Tonight
7 to 8:30 o'clock[444]

Meanwhile, Judge Odom had notified all parties that the preliminary hearing for Jeff Burnett would be held tomorrow, January 3. Special effort was being made to have the preliminary hearing as close to the beginning of the open hearing because it was said they had "no desire to stir up the people unnecessarily."

---

[444]*Monroe News-Star*, 2 January 1923.

Burnett's attorneys were listed as follows: Judge W. C. Barnett of Caddo Parish; Attorneys Percy Sandel, Newton and Newton of Monroe, and W. P. Todd of Bastrop.

Needless to say, this presented a formidable array of legal minds for the defense. As previously mentioned, one of these attorneys, Percy Sandel, was thought of so highly by the citizens of northeast Louisiana and the administration of Northeast Louisiana University that the library on its campus was later named in his honor.

Upon hearing the news of the possible declaration of martial law in Bastrop, the citizenry was whipped into a froth. Although the weather was deplorable, people were in the streets talking even as the Jennings Cavalry was removing their gear and mounts from the train. On the steps of the courthouse, Captain Skipwith was speaking to a gathering of admirers. "If he (the governor) does declare martial law in a town as peaceful and quiet as Bastrop, he's a bigger fool than I thought. Look at them people out there," Skipwith said angrily, "do they look bloodthirsty? Do they look like law-breakers?" Skipwith, despite his age, struck an intimidating figure, and those journalists gathered around seemed afraid to question him.

"There is not a more peaceful town in the parish," insisted Skipwith. "Nor in the state for that matter. Show me a town of like size in the United States that's more peaceful." Skipwith took advantage of the moment as a local attorney, John Shell, a rather demure man, entered the courthouse.

Shifting into a playful mood, Skipwith asked the journalists present, "Do you think that John will send any light artillery?" The reference to 'John' meant Governor John Parker. Answering his own question, Skipwith went on, "Well, if it gets as bad down here as one New Orleans afternoon paper paints it, the governor ought to send a few pieces of artillery, an armored tank or two and at least three bombing planes, eh?"

While he was joking with the press, attorney Shell had exited the courthouse, and he had joined the group gathered around Skipwith. Speaking to Shell, Skipwith said, "Had my 'pitcher' taken yesterday, Mr. Shell. Yep, I want people to see what I really look like. One paper up in Shreveport published a 'pitcher' taken from some rogues gallery and called it from me. I'm gonna fool'em though so I let this here *Times-Democrat* man have one. Used to read the old *Times-Democrat* before this reporter was born."[445]

It was reported this date from Fitchburg, Massachusetts, the site of the national convention of The Young People's Socialist League, that it had adopted resolutions condemning the Ku Klux Klan, opposing military training and all forms of censorship and amnesty for political prisoners.[446]

WEDNESDAY JANUARY 3, 1923

Jennings Calvary goes into Mer Rouge Camp at Early Dawn and Men "Ready for Eventualities"[447]

Next Move Will be by State Governor in Case of M'Koin[448]

Soldiers of the Rainbow Division Join Louisiana National Guard in Morehouse as Day Dawns[449]

State's Legal Advisers Reach Bastrop Ready to Start Moves for Arrest of Parish Citizens[450]

Morehouse People Treat Soldiers of State Splendidly[451]

Missing Witness in Mob Murders Outwits Captors[452]

Martial Law Threat Seen as Calvary Men Arrive in Mer Rouge[453]

Negotiations continued between Governor Ritchie, Governor Parker and Mr. Carman, counsel for Dr. B. M. McKoin. Obviously because of the reassurance that he has received from family and friends in Louisiana, Dr. McKoin was prepared to return to Louisiana of his own accord. However, the charge for which Dr. McKoin had originally been arrested in Baltimore, the murders of Watt Daniel and Thomas Richards, must be dismissed. Maryland State's Attorney Leach recommended to Attorney General Coco by telegram that he should convince Governor Parker to authorize Dr. McKoin's release because of McKoin's willingness to return to Louisiana with Special Deputy Calhoun of Morehouse Parish and Chief Detective Glynn of the New Orleans Police Department.

There also seemed to be an unconfirmed report that a move was underway to charge Dr. McKoin with the murder of Dr. K. P. Thomm at Gallion, near Mer Rouge, in 1916. It was alleged that Dr. McKoin had been cleared of any wrong

---

[445] Ibid.
[446] Ibid.
[447] *Monroe News-Star*, 3 January 1923.
[448] Ibid.
[449] Ibid.
[450] Ibid.
[451] Ibid.
[452] *Times-Picayune*, 3 January 1923.
[453] Ibid.

doing in that affair, but such was not the contention of Dr. Thomm's widow, Mrs. Virginia Edna Thomm, who was then residing in Jackson, Mississippi.

Mrs. Thomm, who had been living in Jackson since shortly after the death of her husband, was making ends meet for her and her 12-year-old daughter by making peanut candy. According to Mrs. Thomm, on August 12, 1916, at about 11 o'clock in the day, Dr. K. P. Thomm, of Gallion and Dr. McKoin met in front of a store. The shooting occurred and her husband, mortally wounded, was brought to her home where he died less than an hour later. She asked her husband how it happened. She said he told her, "I told him how dirty he was, and he shot me while I wasn't looking-he shot me while I wasn't looking." Dr. McKoin had not been charged nor tried for the murder of Dr. Thomm.

The introduction of this information places Dr. McKoin in a completely different light. Although it is quite important whether Dr. McKoin did or did not shoot Dr. Thomm "while he wasn't looking," what we learn here is that Dr. McKoin is capable of killing. And, if it took place as stated in Dr. Thomm's dying declaration, Dr. McKoin was guilty of a most foul and cowardly murder. Little doubt his position as a doctor, mayor of Mer Rouge and a captain of the Ku Klux Klan insulated him from any possibility that he would have to pay for his dastardly crime. It, therefore, stands to reason that his compatriots would come to his aid once again with his involvement in the Daniel/Richards kidnappings and murders.

The Jennings Cavalry arrived at Collinston in Morehouse Parish around midnight, and there they camped until dawn. By breakfast time, the overcast sky had given way to a light rain. This did little to daunt the spirits of this unit for it had been the famous Rainbow Division in the Great War. They were, however, on the frontier of a totally different type of military activity than they had heretofore experienced. Since the original orders for the Jennings unit had been countermanded, and they were to report to Mer Rouge instead of Bastrop, it gave rise to the speculation that the first arrests would be made in Mer Rouge. It was believed that the cavalry unit would be used to make arrests while Company "G" of the Louisiana National Guard from Monroe would be utilized to maintain the peace in that area of Morehouse Parish.

The northeast region of Louisiana had received an unusual amount of rain, making the roads nearly impassable. Travel by automobile was all but impossible due to the road conditions, making travel by horseback the only reasonable mode of transportation. It would, therefore, become the job of the cavalry units to transport witnesses to court in Bastrop as well as to make arrests. The arrests were not only being anticipated in Morehouse Parish, but also in Richland, Ouachita, and East and West Carroll Parishes.

Again it was circulated that Adjutant General Toombs was on the verge of issuing an order invoking martial law in Morehouse Parish. This report could not be confirmed by neither Governor Parker nor Attorney General Coco.

The preliminary hearing for Jeff Burnett on charges of kidnapping and murder of Daniel and Richards was postponed until after the open hearing which was scheduled to begin on Friday, January 5, 1923.[454]

Mob Lynches Negro[455]

A communiqué from Hattiesburg, Mississippi told the all too familiar story of a black man being lynched. Ben Webster was taken from an eastbound passenger train on the Alabama and Vicksburg Railroad at Lawrence, Mississippi by a band of about 25 men. His body was found the next morning hanging from a bridge about two miles from Waynesboro, and a distance of 25 miles from Lawrence. The men who took Webster from Deputy Sheriff Holston of Waynesboro, had their faces covered. Webster was said to have killed a road contractor named Alford at Waynesboro last November, and had been carried to Jackson for safe-keeping. He was being taken back to Waynesboro for trial.

Race Trouble Expected[456]

An article from Sapulpa, Oklahoma told of precautions being taken against possible race trouble over the slaying of a police officer, and the wounding of four others by a group of black men. The city spent a quiet night after a day of tension yesterday. More than 60 officers and deputized citizens, heavily armed, formed a cordon around the black district during the night and prevented the races from mixing. Negroes employed outside their quarters were permitted to go to their jobs under the protection of armed guards. They were escorted back before night fall with orders to remain at home.

---

[454]*Times-Picayune*, 3 January 1923.

[455]*Monroe News-Star*, 4 January 1923.

[456]*Monroe News-Star*, 4 January 1923.

Negro Restaurant Blown Up[457]

In Watertown, Tennessee a black-owned restaurant a few feet off the public square, and a center of black gatherings was blown up last night. The blowing up of the restaurant followed the shooting of Deputy Sheriff John Coffee Oakley by Clayton Winton, a black man and son of George Winton, whom Oakley and City Marshall Will Luck were seeking to arrest.

From Memphis, Tennessee came the strange story of a manhunt for a black man who was alleged to have assaulted a white woman and then threw her into the Mississippi River. She claimed, according to police, that she was seized by the black man soon after she alighted from a streetcar early the previous afternoon, dragged to a clump of bushes and held a prisoner for more than eight hours.[458] And if you believe that story, I've got a bridge across the Mississippi River I'd like to sell to you.

Luxor, Egypt was the site of tragedy for those following the news of the marvelous treasures coming from the tomb of Tutankhamen. Work on the project had been suspended due to the death of Howard Carter's faithful native headman. Some delay was also caused by the necessity of examining the contents of an ebony box covered with gilded plaster. The examination revealed the fact that the linen on top was Tutankhamen's underwear. It probably fit loosely, else he was hugely built. These garments are the first evidence found of Pharaonic underwear.[459]

---

[457]Ibid.
[458]Ibid.
[459]*The New York Times*, 4 January 1923.

THURSDAY JANUARY 4, 1923

Opelousas Infantry Going to Morehouse[460]

Louisiana's Military Commander in Morehouse Armed with Order to Involve Martial Law There[461]
Attorney General and Party in Morehouse Ready for Hearing on Kidnapping Cases at Bastrop[462]
M'Koin Begins Journey Toward Louisiana on Own Initiative: Will Return to Monroe Friday[463]
St. Clair Adams Quits Mer Rouge Murder Inquiry: Special State Prosecutor Disagrees with Coco on Eve of Hearing[464]

The weather forecast gave frost warnings for the interior of the state and predicted warmer temperatures for Friday, the day the open hearing was to begin. As dawn broke on the 4th of January, Morehouse Parish was buzzing with anticipation as to what would be the next move taken by Attorney General Coco or Col. L. A. Toombs, the adjutant general of the Louisiana National Guard. Although Toombs declared, "I am here as the ranking military representative of the governor to take such action under his direction as the situation at any time may warrant" he went on to say, "As conditions present themselves they will be met adequately. Thus far no action has been taken which would place the parish under control of the military and any reports to the contrary are incorrect." When Toombs was asked if a proclamation of martial law had been prepared and its implementation awaiting proper provocation, he refused to comment.[465]

While Attorney General Coco was en route by train from a meeting in New Orleans with Governor Parker, St. Clair Adams, a well-known New Orleans lawyer who had been appointed as a special prosecutor some weeks prior to assist the attorney general at the upcoming public hearing, made the surprise announcement that he was withdrawing from the case. It was reported that there were specific differences of opinion between he and Attorney General Coco as to how to proceed with the case. Whether this premise was true or not may never be known. It would not be difficult to imagine the pressures and subtle intimidations that could have been present in Morehouse Parish at that time. Further, Adams's

---

[460] Ibid.

[461] Ibid.

[462] Ibid.

[463] Ibid.

[464] *Times-Picayune*, 4 January 1923.

[465] *Monroe News-Star*, 4 January 1923.

reputation and standing could easily have been placed in jeopardy simply by his association in such a case.

When Attorney General Coco arrived in Bastrop from New Orleans, having already learned of the withdrawal of St. Clair Adams, he announced the appointment of Howard Warren, a Louisiana State Senator from Shreveport, as his special assistant. Mr. Warren would join the already assembled State prosecution team of Coco, Walmsley, Guion and Sompayrac.

The Opelousas Infantry Company of the Louisiana National Guard was placed on alert, and orders were dispatched as to rations and transportation to Morehouse Parish. Company Commander Captain Edgar A. Andrepont announced that directives had been received and that his company should be prepared "to move at a moment's notice." The movement of this company of infantry into Morehouse Parish would bring the total number of Louisiana National Guard units to five. A meeting was expected later that date, after the arrival of Attorney General Coco, that included Assistant Attorneys General Paul A. Sompayrac, T. Semmes Walmsley, George Seth Guion and Judge Fred M. Odom. The purpose of this meeting is to lay the groundwork for procedures for the beginning of the open hearing, which was scheduled to begin on Friday, January 5. It was anticipated that scores of witnesses would be called, and the general belief was that it would take two or three weeks to conduct the open hearing.

Meanwhile, Dr. McKoin had been released from the Baltimore jail and was en route to Louisiana in the company of Special Deputy Calhoun and Chief Detective Glynn of the New Orleans Police Department. McKoin's release had been negotiated after a flurry of telegrams between Governors Ritchie of Maryland and Parker of Louisiana.[466]

The *Times-Picayune* reported that the rhubarb between Governors Parker and Ritchie had been settled when Parker agreed to drop all extradition proceedings against McKoin in light of McKoin's willingness to return to Louisiana on his own recognizance. Governor Parker sent a telegram to Ritchie saying, "Attorney general advises if McKoin will return to Louisiana with state representatives, that will be satisfactory."[467] Parker agreed to this with the proviso that McKoin would be traveling in company with, but not in the custody of, Morehouse Parish Sheriff's

---

[466]Ibid.

Deputy Laurie Calhoun and Chief Detective James P. Glynn of the New Orleans Police Department.

The *Monroe News-Star* reported that McKoin had expressed a personal desire to return to Louisiana and stand trial. His decision to return was obviously influenced by the assurances he had received from friends and family that there would be more than ample "pillars of the community" and "persons of integrity" to supply him with suitable alibis and character references at the trial.

Much of the anxiety generated in the citizenry during this period was the persistent rumor that a declaration of martial law was eminent. Although the threat was almost ever-present, it was never declared, nor is it known for certain that the written declaration ever existed.

The power to declare marital law was found under *Section 14* of *Article 5* of the constitution of the state of Louisiana. In this section, it outlined clearly that the governor, "shall take care that the laws be faithfully executed." *Section 2 of Article 17* governs the use of the state militia and the governor's unlimited power to use the militia in the enforcement of the law. This section stated, "The governor shall be commander and chief of and shall have the power to call the militia into active service for the preservation of law and order, to repel invasion and suppress insurrection."[468]

The Claiborne Act of 1912 strengthened the power of the governor, and it read, " whenever any portion of the military forces of this state is employed in aid of the civil authority, the governor, if in his judgement the maintenance of law and order will thereby be promoted, may, by proclamation, declare the parish or city in which troops are serving, or in any specific portion thereof, to be in a state of insurrection."[469]

Section 77 of the Claiborne Act dictated that the regulations of the United States Army and that the Articles of War were to be used in governing the operations of the militia and the actions of the citizenry in the affected area. It read as follows:

> That whenever any portion of the militia shall be on duty under and pursuant to the order of the governor or shall be on duty or ordered to assemble for duty in time of war, insurrection, invasion, public danger, or to aid the civil authorities

---

467 *Times-Picayune*, 4 January 1923.
468 *Monroe News-Star*, 4 January 1923.
469 Ibid.

on account of any breach of peace, tumult, riot, resistance of process of the state or immanent danger thereof, or for any other case the articles of war governing the Army of the United States, as far as such regulations are consistent with this section and the regulations issued thereunder, shall be in force and regarded as a part of this section until said forces are relieved of such duty.[470]

Had martial law been declared, it was known that some or all of the following conditions would take effect:

1) Governor Parker would be the person to make such a declaration, and as the highest ranking military officer on the scene, Adjutant General Toombs would have become the military governor of whatever area the governor so decided.

2) The regular courts would be temporarily disbanded, and a military tribunal would be substituted in its place, and Roland Howell, assistant city attorney of New Orleans and judge advocate of the Louisiana militia, would have been the head of this tribunal.

3) Under the conditions of marital law, General Toombs would have absolute power over the declared area.

4) Law enforcement would be carried out by the military, the local authorities having their powers temporarily taken from them.

5) "Every citizen, man and woman, will have to disarm or be subject to arrest. The sale of firearms or ammunition will be strictly prohibited. Any person found in possession of a firearm, whether these arms are concealed or exposed, will be arrested and imprisoned under martial law."[471]

6) Citizens would not be allowed to assemble in small or large groups, except for the purpose of holding religious services.

7) All movie theaters and places of public assembly would be closed, and public processions of any sort would be prohibited.

Adding to the anxiety were the hours of drilling performed in the streets by the National Guard units. With two units in Mer Rouge and two in Bastrop, it was clear that General Toombs wanted the presence of his men felt, and what better way to demonstrate to the citizenry that his men were more than capable of dealing with any crisis should martial law be declared than by this public display of readiness.

Although it went unsaid, the effect on business in the area would be devastating, depending upon the length of time and the degree of severity in which the declaration of martial law would be enforced. With these conditions hanging over their heads, it is easy to understand why the residents of the area were not at all comfortable with the idea of martial law.

Having received the reports from Drs. Lanford and Duvall, the pathologists who performed the autopsies on the bodies of Daniel and Richards, Attorney General Coco was quoted as saying, "The reports are encouraging because they

---

[470]Ibid.

bear out the statements that tortures were inflicted upon the two men before they were put to death. The reports clearly strengthen our case against the persons we will accuse of the deaths, in a material way. I cannot discuss the details of the report, but they are gruesome to say the least."[472] Obviously, Coco was playing his cards close to his vest.

Attorney General Coco arrived in Bastrop this date and was questioned by reporters as to the reasons behind the withdrawal of St. Clair Adams from his team of prosecutors. Coco declined to comment on the matter. There was, however, no lack of speculation on the street of Bastrop. One known Klansman was quoted by a *Times Picayune* correspondent as saying:

> St. Clair Adams is a thoroughly capable man and knows when he has a good case. Seemingly the differences he had with the attorney general were over managership of the prosecution. The real cause, I believe, was for the reason that Mr. Adams, a farseeing man, realized that the case against the accused is a weak one; that there is little chance of their being found guilty on such evidence and that the best thing to do would be withdraw, rather than be aligned with a side that has no chance to convict innocent men.[473]

Jeff Burnett was approached with the same question prior to his transfer to the hospital in Shreveport. He was reported to have appeared indifferent and remarked, "Makes no difference to me who prosecutes. I don't care a damn. I know that I am innocent of the charge and I will prove it in court."

"Captain Skipwith, exalted cyclops of the klan, says he don't believe you ever denied begin a klansman," the same correspondent asked of Burnett. "Are you one?"

"No, I'm not," Burnett replied arrogantly.

"Harold Teegerstrom, the missing timekeeper of the Southern Carbon Company, who said you were working there on the night of August 24, is reported to have told Secret Service men a story that conflicts with his first statement concerning you," Burnett was told. The arrogance disappeared from Burnett, and the look of fear came upon his face. Moving close to the bars of his cell, he asked the reporter:

"What was his second story? He lies if he says I didn't work on that night."

---

[471] Ibid.

[472] *Times-Picayune*, 3 January 1923.

[473] *Times-Picayune*, 5 January 1923.

Burnett said he was not aware that the secret service had gotten a story from Teegerstrom that conflicted with his version. He expressed the opinion that such talk was perpetrated by "someone seeking to injure his case in the courts."[474]

J. L. Daniel, the father of the murdered Watt Daniel, was seen on this date in Bastrop watching the militia men cleaning their machine guns. He had turned his vehicle over to the state and federal agents to use and he was on foot. "I won't die satisfied until my son's murderers have felt the hand of justice," he said as he banged his cane on the ground and tears rolled down his cheeks.

Mrs. Richards, the wife of the murdered T. F. Richards, also spoke to the press on this date. "I don't know what I'll do-I don't know," she said, "but I won't stay here-I can't. I have good friends here but the other things that happened stand out too much."

A correspondent for the *Times-Picayune* captured the atmosphere of the town the day before the open hearing was to begin this way: "There is not much talk among these people-yet there is little in their minds save the hearing and its possible culmination. They do not know what will happen, but the spirit of fear hovers over this town."[475]

Body of Negro Who was Taken Out is Found Early Today[476]

A news bulletin from Shreveport, Louisiana told of finding the body of Leslie Leggett, a black man, known as "Yellow Lester," who had been kidnapped the previous evening by five unidentified white men. This action was believed prompted by complaints that the Leggett had been associating with white women. His body was found this morning in the woods in the southern part of the city in a neighborhood sparsely settled. He had been shot to death. His body was reported lying on the ground and "not swinging from a tree limb." There was no clue reported as to the identity of his abductors and slayers.

---

[474]Ibid.
[475]Ibid.
[476]*Monroe News-Star*, 4 January 1923.

CHAPTER FIVE

THE OPEN HEARING

FRIDAY, JANUARY 5, 1923

Judge Warns Klan, Orders Gun Hunt at Murder Hearing

Crowd at Bastrop Court House are Searched for Weapons-Troops to Protect Witnesses[477] [478]

Louisiana Begins Probe into Kidnapping Cases Backed by Complete Power of Military Forces[479]

Martial Law in Abeyance Until Emergency Calls[480]

Next Move Here in M'Koin Cases Under Cloak of Mystery[481]

Bodies of Morehouse Mob's Victims Identified Beyond all Question at Bastrop Hearing[482]

Conditions Operate Against Successful Meeting at any Place[483]

"Bastrop, parish seat, was quiet but with an air of suppressed excitement. A detachment of cavalry is stationed across the roadway from the parish courthouse; a machine gun unit is on guard at the courthouse, and another machine gun detachment is guarding the parish prison; and a company of infantry is encamped within a stone's throw of the court building. At Mer Rouge, headquarters of a detail of department of justice investigators, where there has been assembled evidence which is expected to result in sensational disclosures and wholesale arrests, another infantry company and calvary detachment are on duty."[484] Such was the description of the atmosphere and state of readiness of the military units on station in Morehouse Parish this date.

In a surprise move, Judge Odom issued an order transferring Jeff Burnett from the Bastrop jail to the North Louisiana Sanatorium at Shreveport. The order was given on his lawyer's petition, which stated that Burnett's life was in jeopardy if he did not receive proper medical care. It was alleged that Burnett was suffering an acute attack of pleurisy. This move is highly suspect because this is the very date

---

[477]The New York Times, 6 January 1923.

[478]Monroe News-Star, 5 January 1923.

[479]Ibid.

[480]Ibid.

[481]Ibid.

[482]Times-Picayune, 6 January 1923.

[483]Ibid.

that the open hearings were scheduled to begin. It seems as though the idea was not only to make Burnett unavailable to appear to the open hearing, but also to remove him physically to the other end of the state. Surely, Judge Odom was aware that there was ample medical care a short distance away in Monroe. This order by Judge Odom brings his motives and sentiments into question. Counsel for Dr. McKoin also arrived in Bastrop on this date. Attorneys Thomas C. Newton and Percy Sandel of Monroe will be representing Dr. McKoin, and they were said to be closely guarding information regarding charges against Dr. McKoin.

On this date, the open hearing began amid extraordinary precautions by Judge Odom, who had given Sheriff Carpenter instructions that all spectators who entered the courtroom were to be searched for weapons. To this end, Sheriff Carpenter deputized 11 unknown individuals. More than likely some or all of these deputies were Klan members or, at the very least, sympathizers. There was obvious friction between those members of the Justice Department and Sheriff Carpenter. This was in evidence as he had given his special deputies instructions that the agents of the Justice Department would not be allowed to carry their firearms into the courtroom. This action prompted a meeting between Judge Fred M. Odom; Assistant Attorney General, T. Semmes Walmsley; A. E. Farland, chief of the detailed Department of Justice agents stationed in Morehouse Parish; and Fred L. Carpenter, Sheriff of Morehouse Parish. As a result of this meeting, it was decided that the agents of the Justice Department would be allowed to carry their firearms while in the courtroom.

According to *The New York Times*, the bell in the dome of the courthouse rang 10 times to signify 10 a.m. as it had done so many days before. This, however, was to be a day like no other, for it marked the beginning of the open hearing The opening session found 600 people crammed into the courtroom as Judge Odom entered at 10 a.m. to convene the open hearing. The very first action of Judge Odom was to call Sheriff Carpenter, a member of the Klan, to the bench and give these orders:

> You are to see that perfect order is maintained in this courtroom. I want all those who desire to attend these hearings and all those who may be installed as witnesses to know that I am not going to permit any interference with the orders and process of this court. There must be no disorder in or about the Court House and there must be no tampering with the witnesses. I want the witnesses to feel free to come here and testify, and that in doing so they will be afforded every

[484]Monroe News-Star, 5 January 1923.

protection that the State of Louisiana can throw about them.

If it should come to me at any time during this hearing, through information I think is reliable, that any person or groups of persons have attempted or are attempting to frighten, intimidate or in any manner interfere with any witness either before or after he has testified, I am going to have the parties implicated arrested and incarcerated at once. Every right-thinking, law-abiding citizen of the parish wants to see the slayers of Watt Daniel and Thomas F. Richards brought to justice. This hearing could have been carried on with all safety, I think without the presence of the State Militia. However, these troops are here and in order that the people may be assured I will state that they are subject to the orders of the Court and I shall not hesitate to call them in to protect citizens or to aid the Sheriff in the discharge of his duties if any emergency should arise.[485]

After this rather windy and pompous statement, Judge Odom ordered a recess until 2 p.m. "to give any of the spectators who might have weapons in their pockets a chance to take them home, Judge Odom announcing that any body discovered carrying concealed weapons, either here or in Mer Rouge, would be immediately put in jail until the hearing was over."[486] Such an order would seem outrageous today. However, this only serves to demonstrate the volatility of the situation in Morehouse Parish and the mentality of those attending the hearing. It also may demonstrate a leaning toward the Klan by Judge Odom, because most of those in attendance in the courtroom were Klansmen, and as we will see later in given testimony, Odom himself was present at some of the "peace conferences" which were held between the leaders of the Klan and certain members of the Bastrop/Mer Rouge communities. This, in itself, would seem to have been more than enough justification for Judge Odom to remove himself from this case. Just who Judge Odom represented at these conferences was never openly stated. However, as one of the chief representatives of law and order in the area, he consistently refused to use his power and influence to stop the actions of the Klan.

Prior to the opening of the afternoon session of the open hearing, "deputy sheriffs stood at each entrance to the room and 'fanned' every man and woman for weapons." As the court prepared to convene, it seemed as though there was a gigantic play about to unfold, and all of the participants began to take their places. Attorney General Coco and his assistants T. Semmes Walmsley, Seth Guion and Paul A Sompayrac stood huddled with those witnesses they planned first to call. Drs. Charles Duvall and John A. Landford; A. E. Farland, Chief of the Justice

---

[485]The New York Times, 6 January 1923.
[486]Ibid.

247

Department agents; J. L. Daniel, Watt Daniel's father; and John C. Nettles, the wholesale fisherman who was first to reach the location of the dynamite explosion which caused the bodies of Watt Daniel and Thomas Richards to come to the surface, were all gathered around.

The *Times-Picayune* noted that "By 1:30 o'clock every one of the 600 seats was taken; the three galleries were filled; and crowds thronged the doorways. Only those who could find seats were allowed in the courthouse."[487]

Continuing to describe the courtroom scene, *The New York Times* observed that Jeff Burnett with his attorneys, Judge W. C. Barnett of Shreveport, Percy Sandel and W. H. Todd were seated on one side of the courtroom. Todd, who suffered from a hearing loss, needed the assistance of an amplifier which had been placed on Judge Odom's desk with the wire running to where Todd was seated. Seated behind Burnett were a host of supporters and well-wishers. With all of the major players in place, the drama which was to rivet the attention of the nation on Morehouse Parish began as Judge Odom entered the courtroom and called the afternoon session to order.

Like any good field general, Coco coordinated the case while his assistants did the floor work. The state began its presentation by calling its first witness, John C. Nettles. Assistant Attorney General Walmsley began the questioning of Nettles, the fisherman who found the headless bodies of Daniel and Richards floating by the bank of Lake LaFourche.

Nettles described himself as a wholesale fisherman living near Lake LaFourche. He said that he had heard the explosion in the lake the night before, and went as usual to the lake to check his lines at first light. As he approached the ferry landing, he said he observed what later turned out to be the bodies of Watt Daniel and Thomas Richards floating in the water near the bank. Nettles said that he found a "bunch of keys," which he said had been turned over to him by an unnamed black man, and a hacksaw at the location of the dynamite explosion, which had ripped away a portion of the shoreline of the lake in an attempt to cover over the bodies of Daniel and Richards. Nettles also said that he had learned from another fisherman that the chains which had been used to secure a small boat had been severed, both on the morning before the explosion and on the morning of the explosion. Nettles

---

[487]*Times-Picayune*, 6 January 1923.

said he turned this evidence over to Captain Cooper of the State Militia.[488]

Contradicting *The New York Times*, the *Times-Picayune* claimed that Attorney General Coco himself called Nettles, and that Coco began the questioning. The *Picayune* wrote that Nettles was a 62-year-old resident of Oak Ridge, and that he was a wholesale fisherman who plied his trade in Lake LaFourche.

"I looked down, and there I saw Watt Daniel's body floating in the lake. I looked a little further and saw the other body, about fifteen feet out." This was the response given to Coco when he was asked how he first encountered the bodies in Lake LaFourche. Nettles told of finding scores of dead fish floating on the surface of the lake, and how they encircled the bodies of the dead men. He also described the recovery operations, how the bodies were loaded into boxes and carried away.

As Assistant Attorney General Guion took over the questioning, Nettles told of turning over to Captain Cooper a hacksaw. Whether Nettles had been the one to discover the hacksaw was not clear. He claimed that a chain which had been used to secure the boat to a tree had been sawed in two sometime during the night prior to the evening of the explosion. This would suggest that the boat would have been free to be used on the night before and the evening of the kidnappings and murders. Since the boat appeared to have been moored on the north side of the lake very near to the ferry landing where the explosion occurred, it seems to indicate that some planning had gone into the use of the boat and the location of the ferry landing, and that it was not just random chance that found the Klansmen and the murder victims on the shores of Lake LaFourche on the night of August 24, 1922.

Nettles also said a set of keys had also been found on the side of the lake near the ferry landing on the very night that the chain had been cut the second time, and near the same spot as the hacksaw was recovered. The discovery of these keys was laid to an unnamed black man. Not one black person would testify in this case.

Mr. Guion asked Nettles why he had gone to Lake LaFourche on the day that he discovered the bodies.

"To look after my fishing lines."

Were they baited?"

"Yes, sir."

"What with?"

---

[488]*The New York Times*, 6 January 1923.

"That's what we charge money for." This response brought chuckles from the spectators.

For some unknown reason, Mr. Guion continued to insist that Nettles reveal what bait he was using, and Nettles continued to resist. Finally, after a conference with the attorney general and his staff, it was decided that it would be stipulated that Nettles used a "certain bait" and that the bait was saturated with "some kind of oil." Following that stipulation, the witness was dismissed.

According to the *Times-Picayune*, the next witness called was James Ellington, the black ferryman who operated the ferry at Lake LaFourche. Here is the only instance when a witness was called that was not present. Whether this was the black man who found the keys and turned them over to Nettles is not certain, but it would logically follow. What is not logical is not locating the witness and placing him on the stand. Surely, as the ferryman, he could well have had valuable information, but alas, we shall never know. This witness was not present, and Captain Cooper was called.

Captain W. W. Cooper, Commander of Company G, 186th Infantry of Monroe, responding to Mr. Guion's question, said that he and his men had been stationed in Mer Rouge since December 19, 1922. With regard to the discovery and recovery of the bodies of Daniel and Richards, Cooper said that he received word that the bodies had been found on December 22 at about 7 a.m. by Chief Farland.

Taking over the questioning, Mr. Coco asked, "What did you see there?"

"I saw what I took to be two human bodies. I kept guard until they were removed from the water late in the afternoon by an undertaker and turned over to federal agents. I brought two coffins, got a truck and an undertaker and took them to Mer Rouge and guarded them until you arrived the next day."

"What disposition did you make of them?"

"I placed them in a building at Mer Rouge until your arrival."

"After the autopsy, what disposition did you make?"

"I turned both bodies over to Mr. J. L. Daniel."

Cooper told of inspecting the chain that had secured the boat to a tree near the ferry landing at Lake LaFourche, and that it appeared that the chain had been cut with a hacksaw. Even after recalling Nettles to the stand, Cooper was unable to identify Nettles as the person who had given him the keys and the hacksaw. Cooper was excused, and Attorney General Coco then called Assistant Attorney General

Walmsley to the stand.

In response to questions from Coco, Walmsely said that he arrived in Mer Rouge on December 23, the day following the discovery of the bodies of Daniel and Richards. He said that he proceeded to the Masonic Hall in Mer Rouge, where the bodies had been placed and were under guard of Captain Cooper's men.

"I was present during the autopsy."

"Were there any objects of identification?"

"There were." From his pocket, Walmsley produced a small cloth sack. From it, he withdrew a wristwatch which had the name "J. L. Daniel, Mer Rouge" engraved upon the back. "It was found on one of the bodies," declared Walmsley.

Also from the sack he took out a black necktie, *The New York Times* claimed it was a bow tie, bearing the initials "F.W.D." embroidered on it and a mutilated $5 bill. As those in the courtroom strained to see the objects, Walmsely said that the hands of the watch pointed to 10 o'clock. However, "The hands have since crumbled away," he explained. "The watch was found badly damaged when we found it. It looked as though it had been crushed. Part of the works were sticking out of the case," he said. This would be consistent with testimony given by future witnesses as to the approximate time the motorcade was seen at various locations throughout Morehouse Parish.

Walmsley said that Watt Daniel's trousers were in tatters and that his shirt had been ripped open at the neck. He also spoke of the wire that had been used to bind the hands of Daniel. "There were four strands of wire around his arms." This wire had been used to secure the bodies to what was believed to be metal wheels which had been located near the ferry landing for years. This theory was held because the wheels were not present the day after the kidnappings on the Bastrop-Mer Rouge Road. They, too, were never recovered.[489]

Having personally visited the location, I can say that all vestiges of the original ferry which operated there have disappeared. Within the past few years, a new concrete bridge was completed, crossing Lake LaFourche at the spot where the road ended at the ferry landing. Judging from the photos of the bodies in the lake, it does appear to be consistent with their being on the north shore of the lake very near the ferry landing. It is also plain to see in the photo the section of earth that had been

---

[489]*Times-Picayune*, 6 January 1923.

lifted by the explosion at the north shore ferry landing. It was on the north shore of the lake that the motorcade of black-hooded Klansmen was headed with Daniel and Richards bound and blindfolded.

The New York Times stated that after Walmsley, J. L. Daniel, the father of Watt Daniel and one of those kidnapped by the masked Klan members on the evening of August 24, 1922, was called to the stand. The elder Daniel identified certain articles of clothing taken from one of the bodies as belonging to his son, Watt. Further, the elder Daniel identified a wristwatch found on one of the bodies as the one that he had originally bought for himself, but had given to his son Watt as a gift when he entered the army. Other witnesses also identified bits of clothing taken from the bodies as having been the property of Daniel and Richards and others gave testimony as to the surfacing of the bodies after the explosion which destroyed the ferry landing.

A. E. Farland, chief of the Justice Department agents, was next called to testify. He said that he had traced some strips of clothing taken from one of the bodies as having belonged to Richards. Farland said that he traced the material to the clothing store of John McIlwain in Mer Rouge. Judge Odom interrupted the proceedings at this point and ordered that all school children be removed from the chambers. No reason was listed for this move. It could be assumed that he did not want them to be exposed to the horrors of the evidence. In a brief appearance on the stand, McIlwain said that he had ordered a suit made of similar material for Richards from a firm in Cincinnati. A sales receipt for the suit was produced by the prosecution, and presented. The New York Times claimed that McIlwain was the last witness to testify this day.[490] However, the Times-Picayune reported testimony from other witnesses following McIlwain this day.

The Times-Picayune reported that after McIlwain, the state called Lieutenant Randolph H. Perry of Company G, Monroe. During his brief testimony he told how he and his men had guarded the bodies of Daniel and Richards at the Masonic Hall in Mer Rouge.

After Perry was excused, Dr. O. M. Patterson, the Morehouse Parish coroner who was refused access to the bodies and denied by the state militia from performing an autopsy or inquest in the cases of Daniel and Richards, was called to

---

[490]The New York Times, 6 January 1923.

the stand. No content was listed of his testimony. The *Times-Picayune* tersely stated, "His testimony was brief and of formal character," whatever that meant. After Patterson, Coco said that he would next put the pathologists on the stand who conducted the autopsies and that he expected their testimony to be lengthy. Coco suggested that the proceedings end for the day. Judge Odom recessed for the day, giving orders that the hearing will reconvene on the next day, Saturday, at 9:30 a.m.

The *Picayune* also reported that some portions of the bodies of Daniel and Richards, which had been taken to New Orleans by Drs. Duvall and Lanford, arrived this date in Bastrop under the guard of New Orleans Police Detectives George Reyer and Reuben Victory. The container in their possession, which was alleged to contain evidence of bone and clothing from Daniel and Richards, was placed under heavy guard, and those charged with its safety were given orders to "shoot to kill" anyone who tried to tamper with it.[491] The focus was now in the upcoming testimony of state pathologists Drs. Duvall and Lanford as to the findings of their examinations of the remains of Daniel and Richards.

As would be expected, the notoriety of the hearing brought throngs of the curious to Bastrop, turning it into a Mardi Gras-type atmosphere. Cars were jammed all around the courthouse which still sits in a square in the middle of Bastrop. People walked around the courthouse speaking with friends and neighbors, all discussing the latest rumors. Across the street from the courthouse, enterprising businessmen had set up concessions, and were selling sandwiches, hot dogs and drinks to the crowd.

It was announced that evening by the attorney general's office that Harold Teegerstrom, the kidnapped timekeeper of the Southern Carbon Plant on whom Jeff Burnett was relying to substantiate his alibi, had been found and would be available to testify for the state. This euphoria that the state was experiencing at this time was to later become a grave disappointment when Teegerstrom could not be relocated.

To be presented at this juncture are two news accounts of the arrival of Dr. McKoin at Monroe, the first from the *Times-Picayune* and the second from the *Monroe News-Star*. When read closely, significant differences in perceptions can be detected.

---

[491]*Times-Picayune*, January 1923.

The *Times-Picayune* reported on the return of Dr. McKoin. His train arrived in Monroe at about 2 p.m. amid the cheers of approximately 50 men who were standing on the train station platform, a fanfare befitting a returning war hero. When McKoin stepped off the train, his physical appearance was described as "wearing a light suit, well-pressed, immaculate linen, and his hair plastered and his nails manicured to perfection, looked like a fashion plate . . . The doctor acted as if he hadn't a care in the world.

"Conspicuous among his sartorial ornaments was a Shrine pin in the lapel of his coat, a Masonic charm on his watch chain, and a finger-ring bearing the emblem of the thirty-second degree of Masonry."

When asked about his journey, Dr. McKoin responded, "Fine, I've never felt better nor had less."

When asked about his plans, McKoin said, "I have no plans. I'm going home. That's all I know." He refused to answer any questions on the upcoming open hearing. He did, however, say that he had been treated "splendidly" in Baltimore while fighting extradition back to Louisiana. He indicated that he intended to return to Johns Hopkins when the proceedings in Bastrop were over. He continued on to Bastrop where he arrived at about 3:20 p.m. to again be greeted by a host of well-wishers. [492]

The *Monroe News-Star* reported that at the station to greet McKoin's return were his father, B. M. McKoin, Mr. Keller, a brother-in-law, the notorious Rev. Frank Tripp, Dr. J. Q. Graves and Sheriff Carpenter. The station itself was "thronged with a mob of curious spectators anxious to catch a glimpse of Mer Rouge's former mayor who has been so much in the limelight of late." Mrs. McKoin was not at the station, but had stayed at home because of illness. McKoin avoided the crowd by going "through the negro waiting room to a closed Ford coupe." He then proceeded to his home at 101 Pine St. where Mrs. McKoin and his four children were waiting for him. Strangely enough, however, Deputy Sheriff Calhoun and Chief Detective Glynn were seen exiting the train from a different coach than the one from which Dr. McKoin alighted.

That same evening, McKoin was summoned to appear at the Bastrop courthouse where he was charged with the kidnappings and murders of Watt Daniel

---

[492]Ibid.

and Thomas Richards. At the insistence of Attorney General A. V. Coco, McKoin was made to post a $5,000 bond. Dr. B. E. Barham, a friend of McKoin and practicing physician of Oak Ridge in Morehouse Parish, signed McKoin's bond.

Friends and relatives of Dr. McKoin seemed quite confident that he will be exonerated from the charges. Dr. Byron Vaughn of Monroe was considered to be "the star witness for the defense," a defense that would never be called or necessary. According to Dr. Vaughn, he was in the company of Dr. McKoin on the night of August 24, 1922. He alleged that between 8 and 10 p.m., he and Dr. McKoin traveled to Swartz to transport Mrs. Luther Burnay to the sanatorium at Monroe for treatment. He said that Dr. McKoin then proceeded home to 101 Pine Street where he stayed until the next day.[493]

The New York Times approached the bond posting in Sheriff Carpenter's Office a bit differently. It reported that McKoin avoided the crowd at the station, and went straight to Sheriff Carpenter's office where he was greeted by a host of other friends. McKoin's entourage, including Sheriff Carpenter, Deputy Calhoun, and Captain Glynn of New Orleans, then proceeded to the hotel where the attorney general and his staff were staying. After a short conference with Mr. Coco, it was announced by the attorney general's staff that the state would not argue against bond for McKoin. The group then went to the courthouse where a bond of $5,000 was set by Judge Odom. The bond was immediately made by McKoin's friends and supporters. McKoin told reporters that he had no knowledge of the crimes of which he was accused. As he proceeded away, the crowd in the street gave him a hero's welcome.[494]

The *Times-Picayune* said that the Morehouse Klan was discovering that Klan members from the surrounding towns and parishes were busy putting distance between themselves and the members of the Morehouse Klan. It was said that the Morehouse Klan was "hard put" to find a place to hold their nightly meetings. They were afraid to meet in Bastrop because of the presence of the government agents and the state militia. Efforts had been underway in a door-to-door fashion to engender support for the Morehouse Klan as members called on residents of surrounding towns and parishes in an attempt to gather support. They met a rather cool reception from their fellow Klansmen. Offers of financial assistance were

---

[493]Monroe *News-Star*, 5 January 1923.

made with the proviso that such assistance would not implicate the other Klans.

"Let Morehouse handle her own case. Morehouse was responsible. Why get others into it," was the response from the surrounding Klans. At first blush, it seems as though the other Klans just didn't want to get involved. However, a close examination of the quotation reveals the sentence, "Morehouse was responsible." Here we have a statement attributed to Klansmen accusing the Morehouse Klan of the kidnappings and murders of Daniel and Richards.[495]

What follows below is a close as possible reproduction of a document that appeared on page 4 of the Friday, January 5, 1923 edition of the New Orleans *Times-Picayune*. The document was a Klan charter form. The print in regular type is that of the form. The print in **bold** is that which was filled in. It appeared under the following headline:

---

[494]The New York Times, 6 January 1923.

[495]Times-Picayune, 6 January 1923.

BASTROP KLAN OFFICERS REVEALED
KLEAGLE'S KLAN REPORT

This report MUST be made immediately after the institution of a Klan and sent to the Imperial Kleagle, by him approved and sent to the Imperial Palace without delay.

To the Imperial Wizard, Knights of the Ku Klux Klan:

I have this day instituted a provisional Klan at __Bastrop.__

County of ____Morehouse,__ State of _____ __La.__

with _____ __57__ , Charter____ __Members__

Name of Klan_____ __Morehouse   1st, & 3rd Tuesday.__

OFFICERS APPOINTED

Title   Name   Address

Ex'd C. __Capt. J. K. Skipwith Sr. Bastrop, La__
(Head of Klavern)

Kaliff __W. T. Smith__
(Vice President of Klavern)

Klokard __O. G. Skipwith__
(Lecturer)

Kludd __T. M. Milliken__
(Chaplain)

Kligrapp__John T. Hood__
(Secretary)

Klabee __J. F. Carpenter__
(Treasurer)

Kladd __T. M. McCreight__
(An official)

Klarogo __A. B. Calhoun__
(An official)

Klexter__J. D. Higgenbotham__
(An official)

Klokan __J. M. Jones__
(An official)   __A. B. Conger__
                             __Winsor Pipes__

Night-Hawk   __Geo. T. Madison__
(Chief investigator)

__Dues 6.00 per year, Quarterly in advance__
                Signed:
                            __R. H. Moodie__
                            K. O. I. E.
            Date__Oct. 6th, 1921,__ 192

Approved:

_____

                Imperial Kleagle(Organizer)

_____

M. B. - Be sure to write name and address plainly.
(Klan term equivalents from *Ku Klux Klan:The Invisible Empire* by David Lowe, 1967, NY., W. W. Norton & Co.)

257

The preceding is a photographic copy of the report of the kleagle who instituted the Ku Klux Klan at Bastrop showing a list of the officers of the Morehouse Klan. Below is a list of the charter members of the Ku Klux Klan at Bastrop:

John F. Watson	W. L. Pugh	B. U. Hood
George C. Madison	J. F. Carpenter	J. B. Rowlinson
T. H. McCreight	G. M. Patton	L. F. Leavel
J. N. Jones	O. G. Skipwith	A. B. Calhoun
W. M. Taylor	A. T. Turpin	J. K. Skipwith, Jr.
E. V. Loftin	John T. Hood	W. Pipes
J. H. Michie	J. F. Harp	F. L. Billington
J. W. Montgomery	W. L. Guildge	W. M. Pickett
E. L. Hetsler	H. T. Peede	Ernest Baker
J. K. Skipwith, Sr.	S. D. Graves	W. E. Conger
C. F. Shear	H. W. Davis	F. L. Higgenbotham
Francis Brown	J. D. Higgenbotham	J. Nelson Jones
T. R. Stevenson	J. T. Scogin	J. J. Norsworthy
R. E. Barham	G C. Harp	T. B. Pratt, Jr.
T. E. Barham	R. L. Thomas	W. E. Turpin
W. E. Aden	L. L. Morris	J. C. Freeland
A. B. Conger	T. H. Milliken	W. H. Gray
T. B. Pratt	R. L. Credille	W. T. Smith
D. N. Harper	S. R. Morris	J. R. Freeman, Jr.[496]

The article that was printed directly below this form verified that the name that appeared next to the title *Klabee* was, in fact, Sheriff Carpenter of Morehouse Parish. The reader is advised to become familiar with the names that appear on this list. Some of them should already be familiar. A number of the others will be introduced as the open hearing unfolds.

An interesting side bar was noticed on the bottom portion of the front page of *The New York Times* for the date Jan. 6. It read as follows: "MOST EXCITING MOTION PICTURE ever witnessed" is D. W. Griffith's "One Exciting Night."[497] This was but a small filler on the bottom of the page, of no particular importance unless you recognize the name, D. W. Griffith. This is the same Griffith that directed "The Birth of a Nation," the three-hour silent screenplay which glorified the Ku Klux Klan, and, it has been said, was largely responsible for the rebirth of the Klan under the tutelage of Col. Simmons. In all likelihood, it was not intentionally placed on the column next to the Ku Klux Klan story coming out of Bastrop, but it is quite a coincidence.

---

[496]Times-Picayune, 5 January 1923.

[497]The New York Times, 6 January 1923.

As the sun set on the first day of the open hearing, Bastrop could only be described as an armed camp. It was described by the *Monroe News-Star* this way: "Bastrop is guarded by three National Guard units, one machine gun company being stationed opposite the courthouse and another at the parish jail, while a company of infantry surrounds the Court House."[498]

Race War Started in Florida: Armed Men Guard 2 Towns[499]

Firing at Rosewood, two miles from here [Sumner, Florida], where more than a score of negroes were barricaded all night in a house with hundreds of armed men besieging them, ceased shortly before dawn, and had not been resumed at 8 o'clock this morning. The intermittent firing throughout the night could be heard distinctly here.

At that hour the known casualties were two white men dead and three wounded. What the negro casualties were could not be determined. It was regarded as certain, however, that the besieged blacks had suffered from the hail of bullets which penetrated the walls, windows and doors of the structure.

Since Monday, this section of Florida has been stirred as the result of an alleged criminal attack upon a young white woman at Sumner. Three negroes are alleged to have taken part in the attack. Monday night one negro was shot to death when he is said to have admitted to a mob that he had transported one of the negroes wanted several miles in a wagon.

Late last night a report reached Sumner that the negroes wanted were at Rosewood. A party of citizens went to Rosewood to investigate. In one house, it is said, they found about 25 negroes heavily armed.

Andrews and Wilkerson started to enter the house and citizens said they were shot dead without warning. Three other whites were wounded in the first skirmish.

The articles above and below describe the same incident. The above article was in the *Monroe News-Star* and the one below in *The New York Times*. If you read them both closely, you will notice some interesting differences.

Kill Six in Florida: Burn Negro Houses
Search for Escaped Negro Convict Leads to Race Riot, in Which Two White Men Die[500]

[Rosewood, Florida] Armed posses of white men, numbering between 200 and 300, were searching tonight for Jesse Hunter, escaped negro convict, who, in addition to an alleged attack on a white girl, has been the incidental cause of the killing of two white men and four negroes and the wounding of four other white men. The deaths and wounding resulted from a race riot fomented here last night by a search of the negro quarters for the wanted man.

Following the clash between the races the negro section was set on fire and nearly destroyed, six houses and a negro church being burned. All negroes have fled Rosewood and are believed to be hiding in the woods for protection.

---

[498] Ibid.
[499] *Monroe News-Star*, 5 January 1923.
[500] *The New York Times*, 6 January 1923.

C. P. Wilkinson, a merchant of Sumner, and Henry Andrews, superintendent of the Cummer Lumber Company, at Otter Creek, were killed when they advanced on a negro house last night to see Sylvester Carrier, negro, who was believed to know the whereabouts of Hunter. Their companions then rained bullets on the house, the negroes returning their fire. The number of negroes in the house was estimated at twenty-five.

Before dawn the white men's ammunition was exhausted and the negroes escaped before the supply could be replenished. A search of the house revealed that Sylvester Carrier and his mother, Sarah Carrier, had been shot to death. Lesty Gordon, negro woman, was shot to death as she was leaving her burning dwelling, it was reported. This afternoon the body of Mingo Williams, negro, was found on a road about twenty miles from Rosewood. He had been shot through the jaw.

The community had been aroused since an attack on a young white woman at Sumner on Monday. Hunter, who escaped from a road gang in Levy County, was accused in connection with the crime, which was said to have resulted in Carrier saying his act was an example of what the negroes could do without interference.

The white men went to Carrier's home last night to see if Hunter was there and to warn Carrier against further talk of that kind. Hunter was serving a prison term for carrying concealed weapons. It was believed he was in the house at the time of the clash.

Sheriff Wars on Klan: California Official Warns Deputies, Citing Mer Rouge Horror[501]

A sheriff in Woodland, California issued a warning against the activities of the Ku Klux Klan. Sheriff Monroe returned recently from Louisiana and declared he saw a sign on a tree near Mer Rouge in regard to the murders there, which read: "Unless prosecution is dropped the moss of Mer Rouge will be covered in red." Such a challenge constituted a menace against the law and cannot remain "unanswered," Sheriff Monroe's proclamation said.

Another dispatch from Luxor, Egypt told of the renewed excavation of the tomb of King Tutankhamun. Perfumes which still retain their scent after more than 3,000 years were found in four alabaster vases removed from the outer chamber of the tomb. It was thought that the perfumes were intended for anointing the king's body.[502]

Twelfth Night Ball is Ruled by Ye Merrie Lord[503]

An article from New Orleans told the news which heralded the end of the Christmas Season and the beginning of the Mardi Gras festivities by Ye Merrie

---

[501]Ibid.
[502]Ibid.

Lord in the city "that care forgot." He made his first appearance in the midst of a fantastic, merry crowd of revelers at the Twelfth Night Ball in the Athenaeum.

That which follows will cover all of the material and testimony presented during the open hearing. Normally, a court transcript would be available for any type of open court proceeding, and the open hearing at Bastrop should have been no exception. However, this was not to be the case.

It appears that the entire transcript of this open hearing is missing from the court records of the Morehouse Parish Clerk of Court's records. Ordinarily, this would be the end of any such quest. However, much to my surprise I discovered that *The New York Times*, *Monroe News-Star* and the *Times-Picayune* carried their own versions of the open hearing testimony. I used the term "versions" because the testimony should have been verbatim and little or no difference should be delectable between the versions. This was not the case.

There exists considerable differences between the versions of the testimony recorded in *The New York Times* and the *Monroe News-Star,* in particular. Although the gist of the testimony may be similar in most cases, the wording is rarely the same. What is more, there are sections of testimony that appear to be missing from the *Monroe News-Star* that are contained in *The New York Times*, and there are a number of witnesses whose testimony appears in *The New York Times*, but fails to appear in the *Monroe News-Star.*

Not knowing which of the versions of the testimony is correct, I will point out those versions witness by witness when necessary in order that the reader may compare and arrive at their own conclusion as to which of the versions is more nearly correct. Indeed, it would have been much easier to have simply recorded one version of the testimony, but this would not have been balanced. I apologize for some sections that will appear redundant, but there will be others which will validate my including both in the text.

---

[503] Ibid.

SATURDAY JANUARY 6, 1923
EXPERTS TESTIFY MER ROUGE MEN TORTURED[504]
Dr. M'Koin Secures Bond, Physician of Oak Ridge is Surety[505]
Specially Constructed Device for Inflicting Punishment is used, Assert N.O. Physicians[506]
Tendons and Ligaments About Stumps of Legs and Forearms Indicated They Had Been Pulled From Their Attachments, Report[507]
Dynamite Explosion Not Cause of Condition in Which Bodies Were Found, Witness Testifies[508]

The second day of testimony began with the calling of Drs. Charles W. Duvall and John A. Lanford, the pathologists who had performed the autopsies on Watt Daniel and Thomas Richards after their bodies surfaced in Lake LaFourche. Entered into evidence was their entire report. Because many of the injuries sustained by both Daniel and Richards were almost identical, the entire report will not be entered here, but is included in its entirety at the end of this chapter. Contained below are certain portions of the autopsy on the body identified as Watt Daniel .

The preliminary portion of the autopsy described the general condition of the body at the time the procedures were performed. Descriptions included various parts of clothing and a wristwatch with a crushed crystal, the hands of the watch indicating 10 o'clock. The report in the case of Daniel goes on to say:

> The tendons and ligaments about the bodies at stumps of the legs and forearms are ragged and uneven as though they had been torn or pulled from their attachments. The bones of the body, particularly those of the extremities (legs and arms), are found fractured. These fractures are compound and comminuted. The striking features of the long bones are their character, similarity and symmetry. The humerus of both arms, the radius and ulna of both arms, the femur of both thighs and the tibia and fibula of both legs are fractured in three different places. These fractures regularly occur at the upper, middle and lower portions, respectively, in each instance. As a rule they are equidistant and approximately three and one-half inches apart. The character of the fracture indicates that they were produced by crushing force on one in which the force is applied simultaneously from more than one direction. This explains the great number of small bits and fragments of bone, varying in size and shape, which are found at the fractures.
> Most of the ribs, together with the right clavicle and breast plate, are fractured and dislocated. The first eight ribs on the right side present fractures regularly at the angles posteriorly while the first six ribs of this side present in addition

---

[504]*Monroe News-Star*, 6 January 1923.
[505]Ibid.
[506]Ibid.
[507]*Times-Picayune*, 6 January 1923.
[508]Ibid.

fractures anteriorly and near their costal adjunction. On the left side the first seven ribs are broken from their costal junction and the seventh rib in addition is fractured at its posterior angle. The breast plate shows that the manubrium is dislocated from its costal attachment and its union with its middle portion. These fractures posteriorly are of the greenstick variety while these anteriorly are complete. The appearance and location of these fractures to the bones of the thoracic cage would indicate that the force was supplied simultaneously upon the front and back of the torso.

The vertebral column and the pelvic girdle are found intact showing neither fracture or dislocation.

The greater portion of the skull is missing, there being present only parts of the occipital and a piece of the sphenoid. These were sufficient to recognize the topography of the base of the skull, as they contained the foramen magnum and its connection with the bones of the neck, which later were in their proper relations and unbroken.

The scalp and underlying tissues are present for several inches beyond the margin of the basal skull bones, forming loose overlying flaps. The posterior skin flap is covered with short light brown hair. No brain tissue is noted.

The gross anatomical findings in this case, namely lacerations, amputations and hemorrhages of certain soft tissue in association with multiple comminuted fractures of the bony structures, permit the conclusion that some of these injuries was the primary, and the others, the contributing cause of death. The character of the injuries to the soft tissue and their proximity to the injuries of the bones indicated that the lesions to the soft parts and to the bones were dependent upon the other and produced simultaneously. The striking symmetry of the bone fractures and their relationship to the injuries surrounding soft tissues suggest that the body was subjected to some specially constructed device designed for inflicting punishment.

The first witness to be called to the stand on this, the second day of testimony, was Dr. Charles W. Duvall, one of the pathologists who performed the autopsy on Watt Daniel. It was the aforementioned finding that he read into the court record. As the courtroom breathed a collective sigh, Attorney General Coco began questioning Dr. Duvall.[509]

The New York Times reported that during the preliminary questioning Dr. Duvall said he was a professor of pathology at Tulane University and had been so employed for the past 13 years, six years in the same position at Louisiana State University, and that he had obtained his medical degree from the University of Pennsylvania. In reply to a question as to the number of autopsies he had performed, he responded, "I have made more than 6,000 autopsies or post mortem examinations."[510]

---

[509]*Monroe News-Star*, 6 January 1923.
[510]*The New York Times*, 7 January 1923.

Dr. Duvall plainly said he was certain that Watt Daniel and Thomas Richards were subjected to some "mechanical device" prior to the final act of murder. Further, he said that the mechanism had to have been one that would have conformed to a human body. He made this claim because of the manner in which it had pressed down at specific points. It was his contention that the kidnappers had inflicted a leisurely yet ghastly death to the victims. He claimed he did not know how long the victims had been tortured prior to their deaths.

Dr. Duvall was asked whether the dynamite blast could have caused those types of injuries. He, and later Dr. Lanford, unequivocally denied the premise that the explosion which had caused the bodies to surface could have dismembered them. Furthermore, he said that the absence of the heads, hands, feet and sex organs of one of the men was due to "atrocities for which medico-legal history. . . held no parallel."

Continuing his testimony, Dr. Duvall told of cutting the heavy gauge wires which had formed a "crude basket' around the bodies of the murdered men:

> I would say that the hands and feet had been chopped or mashed off. The bones at these extremities were jagged and protruding. In the body we found striking injuries, especially to the long bones in the arms and legs. Each of the twelve bones of the arms and legs was broken in three places. At the lower, middle and upper parts.
> We found that the thighs had the same sort of fractures at the upper, middle and lower parts. These breaks were always three in number and were equidistant from one another. The breaks were very striking because of the marked similarity. There is very good evidence these bones were fractured before death. We found also that the bones of the chest were fractured in a peculiar manner. The chest plate was fractured and crushed in and from the character of the fractures we deduced that the force that caused them came from more than one direction, that one or more forces were exerted from opposite directions.

Dr. Duvall commented little on the internal organs only to say that they were recognized, and they appeared to be uninjured. The sexual organs of Daniel were missing and the evidence indicated that a sharp implement had been used in the act of separation from the body.

"Was the cutting done before or after death?"

"It is our opinion that the organs were removed before death. The alterations found could not have been done after death. There was evidence that much blood had flown."

With regard to the injuries to the head, he commented: "We found it to be merely loose skin and a few bones. The brains were gone. The head had been crushed by forces coming from more than one direction, in our opinion. The nature of the damage to the head suggested that it had been crushed and not struck, and that in all probability some type of crushing device had been employed."

"Were these injuries inflicted simultaneously or at different times?"

"That would depend on whether the men were tortured."

"Tortured! What is your opinion of that?"

"I believe the men were most inhumanly tortured."

In his description of the body of Thomas Richards, Dr. Duvall told the court that the head had been crushed and that the hands and feet were missing. The body was nude and it was bound with the same type of wire in the basket shape as was the body of Daniel. Decomposition was more pronounced in the body of Richards than that of Daniel and there had been evidence of a severe loss of blood.

"We found the fractures in the bones of Richards almost identical to those of Daniel. The breaks were three in number and were also the same distance apart. Richards' spine, however, was not dislocated or broken. In Richards' chest bones, the injuries were the same as those of Daniel. The ribs, instead of being fractured, were separated from the breast plate. The bone injuries of both men were produced by the same method."

"What kind of device was used, in your opinion? Do you think the arms were outstretched at their sides and the devise applied to break the bones?"

"That may have been true. The injuries were crushing and I am inclined to believe that such a device may have been used. In injuries of that sort, death is not produced by loss of blood or hemorrhage, but it may be produced by shock."

The actual bones of Daniel were then brought forth and exhibited on a white section of cardboard. Dr. Duvall pointed out the fracture sites in both femurs. The knee bones were then brought out in a box and exhibited. The bones of Richards were also brought out attached to a white cardboard. Dr. Duvall pointed out to the court the location and character of the three fracture sites in the leg and arm bones.

"Could dynamite have had the effects you have described in these two bodies?"

"No, dynamite could not have brought out the regularity in the fractures. Dynamite would also have affected sections of the body that have escaped injury. Dynamite, according to all conditions, did not cause these injuries."[511]

---

[511]Ibid.

The account of Dr. Duvall's testimony in *The Monroe News-Star's* was no where near the same wording as that that appeared in *The New York Times*. Again the reader is reminded that, because of a lack of a court record of the testimony, it is impossible to say which of these versions is true or most correct. Although much of Dr. Duvall's testimony told the same story, there were a few instances that were more descriptive in the *Monroe New-Star*. For example, in his testimony about the fractures to the large bones he said: "Another thing, the breaks in the big bones of the two bodies-24 in all-were almost equidistant." Also, when Duvall was asked if the dynamite explosion would have caused the breakage of the bones in the two bodies, he said, "It would have torn the bodies to pieces." Dr. Duvall was dismissed. As the morning session ended, it was announced that Dr. John A. Lanford would be called to testify during the afternoon session.[512]

The New York Times reported that the afternoon session began with the calling of Dr. Lanford to the stand. When asked by Senator Warren, the special prosecutor, Dr. Lanford said that he had performed about 600 autopsies. His testimony buttressed, in almost every way, the testimony given by Dr. Duvall in the morning session. Dr. Lanford said that the wounds of the muscles and the state of the remaining blood suggested that the torture had been imposed shortly before death.

"Do you think it was possible to have inflicted these tortures without a specifically constructed device for inflicting human torture and suffering?" asked Seth Guion, assistant attorney general.

"I do not. I cannot conceive of this thing having been done by anything other than an instrument specially constructed."

Called next to testify was W. C. Andrews, a lifetime resident of Mer Rouge and a farmer who lived less than a mile from the town. Andrews was one of the five men kidnapped on the evening of August 24.

During preliminary questioning by Attorney General Coco, Andrews told of attending the baseball game and barbecue held in Bastrop on August 24 in the company of J. T. Norseworthy and their subsequent encounter with the black-hooded Klansmen while returning to Mer Rouge on that same evening.

"About a mile from Bastrop, we were held up. A bunch of men with black

---

[512]*Monroe News-Star,* January 6, 1923.

hoods on looked to me like fifteen or twenty, rushed up. One held a gun to me and told me to get out of the car. They blindfolded me and tied my hands and walked me about fifty feet."

"Did you recognize any of them?"

"No. They led me over beside J. L. Daniel. They had him too. 'We want some others too,' I heard them say. 'Is that you?' he [J. L. Daniel] said to me. I told him it was. Then Watt Daniel was brought over. He sat down and they pulled him to his feet."

" 'Wait a minute, Buddy, don't be so fast,' Watt said. They took me away. I asked them what they were going to do with me, but they would not answer. We all walked down the road and they put me in a car. We came back to Bastrop."

"How do you know where you were going if you were blindfolded?"

"I could smell the odor of the pulp mill. We drove quite a ways. The car stopped and they asked me what I knew about the attempted assassination of Dr. McKoin. I told them I didn't know anything about it, and told them that I was out of town that night. Then they pulled off my trousers and threw me down on the ground. Then they whipped me."

With regard to the odor mentioned by Andrews, in January 1994 state and federal warnings were in place on the Ouachita River, which coincidentally are the sites of these foul smelling pulp mills. Present-day residents of the area are much more concerned with short-term gains than they are the ravages that these compaines pump into the rivers and belch into the air that they breathe daily. Eventually, they will pay dearly for the day is not long off when the manufacture of paper and wood products will drop dramatically because of the advent of petroleum technology, and the lack of the need for paper products. When this happens, the economy will bottom out, and the artificial forests filled with the same species of pine tree planted two paces from one another will stand as a monument to their greed and lack of vision.[513]

"The next thing I remembered, they were beating old man Daniel. I could hear him yelling. Then they came back to me. They told me that if I didn't tell them about the shooting at Dr. McKoin they were going to hang me. I replied I did not have anything to tell, and they put me back in the car. They asked me if I had

---

[513]*Baton Rouge Morning Advocate*, 3 January 1994.

recognized any one of the party and I said I hadn't."

"'It's mighty good for you that you did not,' they said. 'Now go on back home,' they said."

Andrews said they took the blindfold from his eyes, and he was told, "Walk down the road and don't look back."

"How many men did you see?"

"I am not sure, about fifteen or twenty, I should say. Their faces were covered: black covering over their faces."

Andrews' next question was to the presence of any vehicles on the side of the road when they were originally stopped. He replied that he had seen only an "automobile truck." He was then asked if he was aware of the identity of any of his kidnappers.

"I don't know who the men were, but I believe they were members of the Ku Klux Klan. I don't accuse the Klan as a whole, but I believe that the mob was composed of Klansmen."

"Has anyone, other than an intimate friend or members of your family, asked you whether you knew who was in the mob?"

"Well, everyone has asked me."

"Did any one that you suspected of being in the mob ask you?"

"Yes."

After the beating and during the ride back, Andrews said that he was in a touring car with J. L. Daniel. He said that he knew Daniel by his voice and that Daniel continued to ask for water from his captors, who refused to honor his request. During this ride, Andrews admitted that he believed that he was being taken to where he was to be killed. After describing how he had been unable to get out of his bed for two days, Andrews said about the beating, "They must have given me about forty lashes." He said that he had not had any problems with Dr. McKoin and that he, Andrews, was a member of the Klan.

Following Andrews on the stand was J. L. Daniel, the father of the murdered war veteran, Watt Daniel. During preliminary questioning, he told of how he and his son had traveled to Bastrop for the festivities and to take care of personal business while there.

"That was the last time I saw Watt alive. I went home at noon and came back to Bastrop with 'Dad' Patterson to see the evening ball game. Coming back after the game my car was the first to be held up. I saw the touring car in the road ahead, and Patterson said, 'Somebody is in trouble up there.' I stopped the car. After we stopped men sprang up on either side of our car."

"How many were there in the crowd?"

"About twenty, maybe twenty-five. They wore black hoods. One man pointed at me and said, 'Here's one we want.' He put a gun on me, a .45, I think. They told me to get out of my car. I got out and they blindfolded me with a red bandanna handkerchief. I was led by the men about twenty-five feet beyond the road and told to sit down. A little while later, they brought Andrews and sat him down near me. I recognized him by his voice.

"My granddaughter, 15 years old, I knew was in the car behind us when we started, and I heard my granddaughters voice saying, 'Poor Watt, poor Watt.' We sat quiet for a time, and then Andrews and I were led off and loaded into a car. Andrews was the only man I know had been caught until I was released at Collinston."

"What happened after they put you and Andrews in the car?"

"We were driven back toward Bastrop for about an hour. Then they took us out of the car and we were led to a spot in the pine woods about thirty yards from the road. They told us we knew who had tried to assassinate Dr. McKoin and that if we didn't tell they would kill us."

"How many were talking to you?"

"About three. I told them I didn't know who tried to assassinate McKoin. After that they took my pants down and whipped me with a leather strap. After they got through with me they helped me up and started on Andrews. They whipped Andrews more than they whipped me. They beat him severely.

"Andrews and I were put back in the car after we were whipped and driven to Collinston. There they took off the blindfolds and untied our wrists and we were told to go home. We were put out just behind the depot at Collinston. The man who put us out at Collinston still wore his mask."

Daniel could describe his kidnapper only as a male about six feet in height, and he had no clue as to the identity of his assailants. Senator Warren continued the questioning of Daniel by asking him about the alleged assassination attempt on Dr. McKoin.

"I told Watt I was going to McKoin and talk to him about the shooting. A few days before Watt and a couple of the young men ran into a bunch of hooded men who held up some boys. Watt came home and told me about it. That was before the shooting I thought it was my duty, being a fellow Mason, to go to Dr. McKoin and talk over the matter. He told me he was not a Klansman."

The correspondent for *The New York Times* here commented on the courtroom behavior of Dr. McKoin this way: "Dr. McKoin, sitting in the gallery, seemed to find a great deal of humor in Daniel's testimony. He laughed uproariously when Daniel repeated their conversation." This behavior occurred in Judge Odom's courtroom while the court was in session. The question arises as to why such disrespectful conduct would have been allowed to occur without admonition from Judge Odom? Was this another indication of just where Judge Odom's loyalties lay? J. L. Daniel continued his testimony.

"A little while after that, Watt came to me and told me he'd been held up. Dr. McKoin, Laurie Calhoun and another man were in the party." The reader should bear in mind that Laurie Calhoun was the deputy sent to Baltimore by Sheriff Carpenter to extradite Dr. McKoin. Dr. McKoin must have been truly relieved to see the face of a fellow Klansman in Baltimore. Little wonder why McKoin displayed such arrogant behavior.

"That was the first time Watt was held up. He was then searched and a box of cartridges was taken from him."

At this point in the proceedings, Judge Odom declared the court to be adjourned and that it would remain so until Tuesday, Monday being a holiday. Following the adjournment, Attorney General Coco was asked his impression of the day's events. He told reporters that he was pleased with the way the case was progressing. "We'll get the men who wore the black masks."

Reporters also pressed Dr. Duvall for more information concerning the torture device that had been used on Daniel and Richards. "It was some kind of press that gave force from each side," Duvall said. "It could not have been flat on the order of a letter press, as some of the old torture instruments of the barbaric ages were. The peculiar manner in which the bones were broken with almost mathematical precision showed that."

Dr. Duvall said that the device could have been about the size of a man, but in the shape of a box. Inside of the box, it may have had projections or teeth which protruded out from two sides, these teeth coming in contact with the injured portions of the victim's body. "The evident torture of these two men is beyond believing. There is nothing in technical torture to compare with it."[514]

Traitor to Klan Gave Parker List, Declares Cyclops: "Absolutely Correct," Says Captain Skipwith on Reading T-P[515]

"The list is absolutely correct." This admission was made by Captain J. K. Skipwith, Sr. exalted cyclops of the Morehouse Parish Ku Klux Klan in response to the appearance of a full list of Klan members that appeared in *The Times-Picayune*. "A damned traitor to the klan gave out that list. You can quote me as saying that," Captain Skipwith declared. "A damned traitor-that's what he is. I know him; he took the list to the governor, and it was given out."

Shreveport Women Form Chapter----Aims Similar to Klan's[516]

"The Ladies of the Invisible Empire," was printed on the back of a pamphlet proclaiming the formation of a women's chapter of the Ku Klux Klan in Shreveport, Louisiana. It claimed to have 150 members, and the organization stated that it hopes to initiate a class of 1,000 members in Shreveport in February. Membership in the organization is limited to Protestant women of American birth.

Rosewood Quiet as Usual After Clash Over Race Question[517]

The news from Rosewood, Florida and the surrounding territory was that all was quiet following the racial clash in which two white men and four blacks were killed. The black population of Rosewood was in hiding in the woods or had left that section of the county.

SUNDAY JANUARY 7, 1923

Victims Tortured Brutally Before Death Ended Agony, State's Pathologists Prove[518]
Burnett, Hooded Murder Suspect, Sent to Hospital[519]

Although the news of Jeff Burnett being sent to a Shreveport hospital had been reported in both the *Monroe News-Star* and *The New York Times*, neither carried the information that was contained in today's issue of the *Time-Picayune*.

---

[514] *The New York Times*, 7 January 1923.
[515] *Times-Picayune*, 7 January 1923.
[516] *The New York Times*, 7 January 1923.
[517] *Monroe News-Star*, 6 January 1923.
[518] Ibid.
[519] Ibid.

The *Monroe News-Star* claimed that the Morehouse Parish coroner had examined Burnett and recommended treatment. It did not mention that Dr. Duvall, one of the physicians that had performed the autopsies on Daniel and Richards, had examined Burnett and found him in good health. This information was, however, contained in *The New York Times*.

Now comes the *Times Picayune* with a different spin on the same incident. The following is an excerpt from their article concerning the same occurrence.:

> He [Burnett] is seriously ill with pneumonia and has been rushed to a Shreveport hospital, where heroic measures will be taken to try to save his life. The utmost secrecy has been thrown about the case. Burnett, who is used to a life in the open, contracted a severe cold in his cell. This morning Major Trepagnier, a medical officer of the militia who examined him, found that he was suffering from a serious case of pneumonia and arrangements were made to rush him to the hospital.

With this rendition of Burnett's alleged illness, it has now been told three different ways. Again this illustrates how confused and tangled the "truth" appears to be.

The *Monroe News-Star* did not print a Sunday edition during this time period, and *The New York Times* and the *Times-Picayune*, for the most part, carried the testimony of Drs. Duvall and Lanford regarding the pathological reports on the bodies of Watt Daniel and Thomas Richards. I have moved nearly all of the testimony concerning these reports on to Saturday, January 6, 1923. Because this was a down day for the court and no new information was coming out of Bastrop, I will take this opportunity to list, in its entirety, the pathologists report as it appeared in the *Times-Picayune* on this date.

> Autopsies held in Mer Rouge on December 22, 1922, and performed conjointly by Drs. Charles W. Duvall and John A. Lanford, authorized by the attorney general of the state of Louisiana and witnessed by the following persons: Judge A. V. Coco, Semmes Walmsley, the official undertaker, Mr. Mulhern and his assistants, Mr. Fontana, assistant to the pathologist and several guardsmen.
> Case No. 1-F. Watt Daniel is removed from the burial box by the undertaker to an improvised table for the purpose of conducting the post-mortem examination. The body is completely wrapped in a dripping wet sheet and a woolen blanket, which coverings are removed by the prosecutors immediately preceding the autopsy. The odor of embalming fluid is pronounced.
> Inspection-The body is that of a well-developed and nourished white man without head, feet and hands. It is partially clothed with the remains of a soft collared white shirt and blue serge (woolen) trousers and underwear of white cotton material. About the hips and arranged like a diaper is a suspension basket made of four heavy galvanized wires. The wires composing the basket are angulated in front. There is a black leather belt with a plain sterling silver buckle holding the trousers in their natural position around the waist. About the neck in the correct

position is a black colored neckwear tied in the form of a bow. On the neck band of the shirt, posteriorly, are red embroidered letters-"F. W. D."-which are handsewed to the collar band.

On removing the belt from the usual straps on the trousers it is found that the latters are closed and intact around the waist, hips and upper part of the thighs. The trousers are removed by cutting with scissors and the several pockets examined. In the watch pocket is found a wristwatch, with leather strap attached to one side. The crystal is crushed and the hands indicate 10 o'clock. On the back side of the watch is engraved "J. L. Daniel, Mer Rouge, La." There also is found in the watch pocket a flattened pad of United States paper money, the outer bill showing a five-dollar denomination. The two ordinary side pockets of the trousers are empty. The left hip pocket contains an unmarked white handkerchief. The trousers have no right hip pocket. There are no special markings on the white underwear.

It is noted that some of the bones of the extremities, particularly the upper, are protruding, through the fragments of the clothes and the flesh.

The flesh, including the skin, while in an advanced state of decomposition, is intact and the nature and relation of component parts are readily differentiated. In general the skin covering the body does not peel off in layers and is more or less dry and encrusted. Their latter condition in part is the result of dehydrating substance previously used by the undertaker. This substance resembles sawdust, which has been impregnated with chemicals and deodorants. On scraping off this material, the skin is of a leathery consistence, showing a condition of adipocere and is firmly attached to the underlying structures.

On removing the clothes there is noted an entire absence of all the external genitals. Closer inspection shows that these organs were removed with some sharp cutting instrument, as evidenced by the relatively smooth remaining skin edges of the area and the inner sides of the thighs and perineum.

The skeletal muscles and tendons throughout the body are in comparatively good condition and in consequence readily recognized. Their consistency is flabby but not friable. It is noteworthy that the muscles and other soft tissues are entirely free from microscopic evidence of gas, and not filled with fluid except in deeper parts, particularly those of the thighs, buttocks and shoulders; however, in these situations, it is only moderately in excess. One of the striking features is the paleness of the muscles, indicating scarcity of the blood within the vessels, except in certain areas adjacent to bone injuries and where direct traumatism has occurred. These areas are noticeable in the soft tissues of the arms, forearms, thighs, legs, chest wall and back. Particularly in the latter there is evidence of extensive hemorrhage beneath the skin and involving the subcutaneous tissues and underlying muscles, extending as high as the seventh cervical vertebrae and as low as the tenth dorsal. The blood extravasations are chiefly on the right side of the vertebral column. In all these areas the muscles and soft tissues are of a dark greenish color in contrast to the pale pinkish brown color of the exsanguinated muscles and the reddish-brown color of normal muscles.

The tendons and ligaments about the stumps of the legs and forearms are ragged and uneven as though they had been torn or pulled from their attachments.

The viscera of the thoracic and abdominal cavities are in a marked state of decomposition and decay. Only the liver, heart, stomach, intestines and bladder are entirely recognizable. The stomach and intestines are completely collapsed and contain no gas.

The bones of the body, particularly those of the extremities (legs and arms), are found fractured. These fractures are compound and comminuted. The striking features of the fractures of the long bones are their character, similarity and symmetry. The humerus of both arms, the radius and ulna of both arms, the femur of both thighs, and the tibia and fibula of both legs are fractured in three different places. These fractures regularly occur at the upper, middle and lower portions, respectively, in each instance. As a rule they are equidistant and approximately three and one-half inches apart. The character of the fractures indicates that they were produced by a crushing force or one in which the force was applied simultaneously from more than one direction. This explains the great number of small bits and fragments of bone, varying in size and shape, which are found at the fracture sites.

The thorax-Most of the ribs, together with the right clavicle and breast plate (sternum), are fractured and dislocated. The first eight ribs on the right side present fractures regularly at the angles posteriorly while the first six ribs on this side present in addition fractures anteriorly and near their costal junction and the seventh rib in addition is fractured at its posterior angle. The breast plate shows that the manubrium is dislocated from its costal attachments and its union with its middle portion. These fractures posteriorly are of the greenstick variety (partially broken and partially bent) while those anteriorly are complete. The appearance and location of these fractures to the bones of the thoracic cage would indicate that the force was applied simultaneously upon the front and back of the torso.

The vertebral column and the pelvic girdle are found intact and show neither fracture nor dislocation.

Head-the greater portion of the skull is missing, there being present only parts of the occipital bone and a piece of the sphenoid. These were sufficient to recognize the topography of the base of the skull, as they contained the foramen magnum and its connection with the bones of the neck, which latter were in their proper relations and unbroke.

The scalp and underlying tissues are present for several inches beyond the margin of the basal skull bones, forming loose overlying flaps. The posterior skin flap is covered with short light brown hair. No brain tissue is noted.

Pertinent comments: the gross anatomical findings in this case, namely lacerations, amputations and hemorrhages of certain of the soft tissues in association with multiple comminuted fractures of the bony structures permit of the conclusion that some one or more of these injuries was the primary and the others the contributory cause of death.

The character of the injuries to the soft tissues and their proximity to the injuries of the bones indicate that the lesions to the soft parts and to the bones were dependent one upon the other and produced simultaneously.

The striking symmetry and character of the bone fractures and their relationship to the injuries of the surrounding soft tissues suggest that the body was subjected to some specially constructed device, designed for inflicting punishment.

CHARLES W. DUVALL, M.D. "Pathologist.

JOHN A. LANFORD, M.D. "Pathologist."[520]

Case No. 2-Thomas Fletcher Richards is removed from the burial box by the undertaker to the improvised table for the purpose of conducting this post-

---

[520]Ibid.

mortem examination. The body is completely wrapped in a dripping wet white sheet and woolen blanket, which coverings were removed by prosecutors immediately preceding the autopsy. The odor of embalming fluid is pronounced.

Inspection-The body is that of a well developed and fairly well-nourished white man without head, feet and hands. It is entirely nude, there being no clothes of any description found upon the body. There are two heavy galvanized wires circumferentially arranged about the hips and forming angulations anteriorly. The wires show very little rusting.

On inspection it is noted that fragments of the long bones are protruding from the stumps of the right forearm and right leg, namely, radius and tibia respectively. It is further noted that the upper fragment of the right femur has pierced the soft tissue and skin of the thigh. The scapulae are protruding through the overlying skin and the middle portion of the shaft of the right humerus is missing.

The skin with the exception of that about the stumps of the extremities, the head and parts where compound fractures occur is in a fairly good state of preservation. In general, it is rough, fairly dry, encrusted and shows no tendency to peel off. The dryness of the skin is in part due to deodorants used by the undertaker. Upon closer inspection of the skin and especially after the incision there is noted considerable adipocere and it is attached properly to the underlying tissue. The external genitalia are present and intact.

The muscles over the body are in an advanced state of decomposition, however, they are without difficulty recognized. Their consistency is soft, fluidy and friable, tearing quite readily on retraction. It is noteworthy that the muscles and other soft tissues are free from macroscopic evidence of gas. The color of the muscular tissues is pale pink, indicating ante-mortem drainage of the blood with the exception of those areas about the bone fractures and those where traumatism has occurred. Here the muscles of these areas are distinctly of a blue-black color which is indicative of altered extravasated blood. These discolored muscle areas are most in evidence along the vertebrae column posteriorly.

The ligaments and tendons are still intact with the exception of those about the stumps of forearms and legs where they are ragged and uneven. This appearance suggests that the tendons had been mashed or torn from their attachments.

The internal organs of the various body cavities are in a marked state of decay. The liver, heart, stomach and intestines are in place and easily recognized. The heart, in particular, has its various structures intact and presents a flattened shape the absence of blood in the chambers of the heart tend to show that the organ was emptied just prior to or shortly after death, which is to be expected from the lacerations and presumable amputations of the several distal portions of extremities. The liver is found in the normal position and appears shriveled to about one-third its natural size. The intestines are also in their normal position as far as their attachments are concerned and are found in a collapsed condition and well down against the spinal column. There is no evidence of gas in these or any of the other soft structures of these regions.

Bones-Many of these structures, especially those of the extremities, are found fractured. The fractures are compound and comminuted and present the striking features of similar bilateral location and symmetry.

The femur of both thighs and the humerus of both arms are similarly fractured in three different places. These fractures are fairly regular at the upper, middle and lower portions of each bone. With respect to the bones of the right forearm, only an upper fragment of the radius and ulna are found. These articulate properly with one another and the humerus. The distal portions of these fragments are ragged and irregularly broken. The bones of the left forearm present comminuted fractures at the upper and lower portions; the ulna is fractured completely at its upper end and the radius if fractured completely at its lower end.

This particular difference in the character of injuries to these bones is explained by the fact that the larger end of the radius is at the lower end, while the smaller ends of these bones are in the reverse position. Furthermore, the radius articulates with the ulna at the wrist, while the ulna articulates with humerus and the radius at the elbow.

Only small fragments of the right tibia and fibula are round. These fragments are of the upper portion and articulate properly at the knee joint. The tibia fragment contains the patella and its ligamentous attachment. The broken end is jagged and presents numerous lineal fractures that extend upward and into the articulating surface. Only a small portion of the upper side of the tibia and fibula are present. These fragments are in proper position with respect to the knee joint. The fragmented ends of these two bones present very similar appearance to those of the right leg.

Thorax-The breast plate is for the most part separated from its costal attachments, the right fifth, sixth, seventh, and eighth ribs in this situation are dislocated while the left second, third, forth, fifth, sixth and seventh ribs are likewise separated from the costal attachments and these cartilages are also separated from the junction with the sternum. There are no breaks to other parts of the ribs which are in proper articulation with the vertebrae. The explanation of this separation of the component parts at the anterior portion of the thoracic cage without any breaks to its osseous is found in the fact of the elasticity and flexibleness of the bones as compared with the weaker cartilaginous attachments. Presumably from the fact presented the force producing the injury was applied anteriorly and posteriorly to the thorax at one and the same time, the anterior force pressing and crushing the cage.

Of the shoulder girdle, the clavicles are in position and unbroken. The right scapula shows circular fractures three to four centimeters in diameter, in both the upper fossae. The left is unbroken. The spinous process of the sixth and ninth dorsal vertebrae are broken at their junction with the body of the vertebrae, but nowhere else is the spinal column found fractured or dislocated. The same is true for the bones forming the pelvic girdle.

Head-The greater portion of the skull, the scalp and underlying tissues and all of the brain are missing. Parts of the occipital, spenoid and temporal bones that form the base of the skull are present and while presenting numerous fragments are still in position, at least to the extent that it is easy to recognize the middle and posterior skull fossae. The portion of the occipital bone which contains the foreamen magnum is intact and articulating with the first two bones of the neck viz: Atlas and axis.

Pertinent comments: The gross anatomical findings in this case namely lacerations, amputations and hemorrhages of certain of the soft tissues in association with multiple comminuted fractures of the bony structures permit of the conclusion that some one or more of these injuries was the primary, and the others, the contributing cause of death.

The character of the injuries to the soft tissue and their proximity to the injuries of the bones indicate that the lesions to the soft part and to the bones were dependent one upon the other and produced simultaneously.The striking symmetry and character of the bone fractures and the irrelationship to the injuries

of the surrounding soft tissues suggest that the body was subjected to some specially constructed device, designed for inflicting punishment.
CHARLES W. DUVALL, M.D. Pathologist.
JOHN A. LANFORD, M.D. Pathologist."[521]

Klan Suit Dropped: Tarred Kansas Mayor Cannot Obtain Names of Members[522]

It was announced that a suit seeking $80,000 in damages against the Coffeyville Ku Klux Klan filed by Ex-Mayor Schierman of Liberty would be withdrawn. Schierman was tarred and feathered last fall. However, another suit pending against the city of Liberty for $20,000 under Kansas mob law in connection with the tarring would not be withdrawn. The reason given for dropping the Klan suit was the difficulty involved in obtaining names of Klansmen here.

MONDAY JANUARY 8, 1923

Warrants to be Issued Before End of Week in Morehouse Round-Up of Masked Band Violators[523]
Baptist Pastors in Resolution as Case of Dr. M'Koin[524]
Captain Cooper and Men in Monroe[525]
Probers Take Measurements at Lake LaFourche Where Victims Bodies Were Taken Out Dec. 18[526]

Seth Guion, assistant attorney general, speaking to *The New York Times* said that one of the chief concerns of the attorney general's office was the device that was used to torture Watt Daniel and Thomas Richards slowly to death. It was insinuated by Mr. Guion that officials have some knowledge of the manner in which it was constructed, and that their office has been attempting to locate the person or persons who had constructed the device and where it had been hidden. Mr. Guion said he believed that two 18-inch boards with teeth spaced 18 inches apart were used. The two boards on hinges would have allowed the bodies of the two men to be sandwiched in between. Mr. Guion further suggested that force could have been applied to the feet first in an attempt to extract knowledge, and when the victim(s) did not comply enough pressure was exerted to mash and eventually sever the feet of the victims. He believed that the kidnappers stood at the heads of the victims and demanded information of the attempted assassination of

---

[521] Ibid.

[522] *Times-Picayune*, 7 January 1923.

[523] *The New York Times*, 8 January 1923.

[524] *Monroe News-Star*, 8 January 1923.

[525] Ibid.

[526] Ibid.

Dr. McKoin.

Mr. Guion said that Drs. Charles W. Duvall and John A. Lanford, Assistant Attorney General Semmes Walmsley, and four Justice Department agents returned to the spot in Lake LaFourche today where the bodies had originally been discovered. The purpose of the visit was to attempt to locate further evidence such as body parts, or bits of clothing. They took soundings of the section that had been dynamited and used grappling hooks in an attempt to locate this evidence, but to no avail.

Officials believed the torture machine had been constructed near Bastrop. A small hut was found close to the original scene of the August 24 kidnappings in an area of old field pine. Mr. Guion believed that the device had been constructed there from the pine timbers on hand, transported to Lake LaFourche and later sunk in the lake.

"It was one of the most diabolical devices known to history," said Mr. Guion. "The old time methods of torture were tame in comparison to the machine these men used. In Nero's time victims were drawn and quartered. That was exceedingly mild compared to this, for the victims died quickly. In this case, they were apparently slowly crushed to death."

The assertion that a device was specially constructed with the specific purpose of torturing the victims seems a bit melodramatic and illogical as Mr. Guion expounded his theory. Rather than some specially constructed device hewn in a secret wooded location, transported to the lake and later sunk, I believe that the kidnappers used materials already on the scene, if in fact the murders were committed by the shore of Lake LaFourche. One consideration that seems to have been overlooked is the possibility of a normal piece of machinery being used for the torture. Since some of the witnesses mention the smell of the wood processing plant in their testimony, I think it quite possible that the device used to mash wood into pulp could be another possibility.

Sometimes one of the best ways to hide an article is to put it in plain sight. I have vivid recollections of an episode of Alfred Hitchcock in which a wife killed her husband with a frozen leg of lamb and then roasted it and fed it to the detectives investigating the case.

We do know that it appeared as though both Daniel and Richards were alive and had not been mutilated prior to their arrival at Lake LaFourche. This we can deduce from the upcoming testimony of the traveling salesman who saw the two victims when the two vehicles carrying them and the masked group passed him and his family while they were awaiting replacement parts for their broken-down vehicle. What occurred must have happened between that point and Lake LaFourche, which has been calculated to be about three-quarters of a mile from the point where the two vehicles carrying the victims passed the salesman.

The old ferry was rather crude and it utilized a pull rope to traverse the waterway. What has not been considered are the ramps that must have been used to give vehicles access to the ferry. It would seem quite possible that the ferry would have had boards thick enough to support the weight of a vehicle, and it would also be quite logical for these boards to have studs or teeth in order to allow vehicles traction as they climbed aboard.

If the victims could have been placed between these boards and a vehicle driven upon these boards, sufficient pressure would have been exerted to have caused these injuries without the use of some specially devised torture machine. Undoubtedly, much blood would have been let at the point of the torture, and evidence such as blood, hair, flesh, bone, brain matter, not to mention the hands feet and sexual organs of one of the victims, would have remained. Most of this could have been disposed of in the lake and either displaced by weather conditions, currents, animals, or covered over by the dynamite explosion, which displaced a large section of earth at the shoreline of the ferry landing. Taking into consideration the nearly four months which had gone by prior to the commencement of an investigation and the bodies recovered, it is easy to see how such evidence could have been lost.

Mr. Guion reviewed the testimony given on the previous day by saying that the autopsy had indicated that the removal of Daniel's sex organs had been performed by a person skilled in surgical procedures. The implication was that Dr. McKoin had performed this operation. The alleged attempt on McKoin's life was the pretext for the kidnappings and murders, and it logically follows that McKoin would have participated in this just as he had done so many times in past Klan raids.

Sergeant Dalton's Weekly, a Ku Klux Klan newspaper published in Winnfield, Louisiana, arrived in Bastrop on this same day. As expected, the headlines condemned the attorney general and others close to the investigation. Attorney General Coco was attacked and his alleged Masonic record, professing to have been lifted directly from the records of the Grand Lodge, printed. The article alleged that Coco had been initiated, passed and raised in the Masonic Order. In 1901 he had been Worshipful Master and in 1906 he was demoted. The article read:

> It is not generally known that he is a Catholic, but before Rome again received him to her bosom he was required to go into the Catholic Church and denounce and renounce Masonry and beg that the ban of excommunication be lifted.
> Is his record such that he can investigate and prosecute Masons and Protestants of Morehouse Parish and State of Louisiana? Shall he decide the use of sword and bayonet and machine guns in a Protestant country and talk of horrors of the Inquisition?[527]

The paper also attacked Governor Parker and came to the defense of Dr. McKoin and his sterling attempts to enforce Klan morals on the town of Mer Rouge.

> But what we are trying to bring out in this article for the edification of all, including old Adolph Coco and John M. Parker, is that when a man's home and his children and his neighbors are outraged and trampled under foot, so to speak, and insulted day after day, and assassination is attempted on the very champion of right, law and order and the constituted authorities are helpless, something else is liable to happen. And it will happen just the same after the Mer Rouge affair is forgotten.[528]

Another article in *Sergeant Dalton's Weekly* attacked the pope and Catholicism in America saying the pope was in control of American politics. Another article, written under the name of J. A. Boyett, viciously attacked Governor Parker:

> Due to your [the governor's] recent actions in the Mer Rouge affair, it is quite evident that you have become an ally of Romanism, bootlegging and negro concubinage. Why did you not go to the rescue of Dr. McKoin when this same bunch of lawbreakers sought to murder him? He was of unquestionable character, and was trying to suppress lawlessness in his home town of Mer Rouge.[529]

The lead column in *Dalton's* sought to legitimize the kidnappings and murders of Watt Daniel and Thomas Richards. Of the black-hooded band who perpetrated these hideous acts, it said "They did the best they knew how to do."[530] Judging from the pathologists' reports on the remains of Daniel and Richards, this statement would seem indisputable. The article continued:

> It was either surrender to the cutthroats and lawless element or take strenuous steps to clean house. Richards was first captured and taken out and questioned a few nights before [the] kidnapping[s]. Then the five men were captured and taken

---

[527]*The New York Times*, 8 January 1923.
[528]Ibid.
[529]Ibid.
[530]Ibid.

out and dealt with. The men who handled them were evidently masked and acted secretly. Just as was the would-be assassin who attempted to murder Dr. McKoin. They were attending to a serious matter in the name of law and order, and in the name of Christianity, and the sanctity of the home, and they used the same methods, fed the crooks of the same spoon that they were guilty of using in their treatment of law-abiding people, treated them rough.

As to the members of the Vigilance Committee being members of the Klan, that is just a pack of bunk, hatched up by the enemies of the Klan. No proof has been offered that any of them were Klansmen, and if such should be forthcoming, it would be no more significant than if it were shown that some of them were members of the Baptist or Methodist church. One thing is sure, the Klan did not officially order the kidnapping.[531]

This article speaks volumes concerning Klan sentiments with regard to the kidnappings and murders in Mer Rouge, not to mention the general arrogant and defiant nature of those leading the Klan.

Appearing in the *Monroe News-Star* were expressions of support for Dr. B. M. McKoin from family, friends and local religious leaders who threw their unqualified support to Dr. McKoin. To this end, the Twin Cities Ministerial Association, which was made up of those pastors from the Protestant churches of Monroe and West Monroe adopted resolutions on Monday, January 8, praising Dr. McKoin. Their resolution read as follows:

Be it resolved, by the Twin Cities Ministerial Association, composed of the pastors of the Protestant Churches of Monroe and West Monroe, in session assembled this 8th day of January 1923, that we concur in the sentiments expressed in the resolutions adopted by the First Baptist Church on Sunday night, January 7th, expressing their confidence and faith in the character and integrity of Dr. B. M. McKoin.

J. L. EVANS, President   JOHN S. RAYMOND, Secretary"[532]

These resolutions echoed the resolution adopted Sunday, January 7, 1923, which was offered to the First Baptist Church of Monroe by its pastor, the Rev. Frank Tripp. This is the same Rev. Tripp, who you will remember, blasted the city council for allowing men and women in the swimming pool at the same time. This is also the same Rev. Tripp to whom the Ku Klux Klan paid a personal visit while he was conducting services and paraded up the aisle in full regalia presenting him with a letter of compliment and a generous financial donation. Before offering the resolution, the Rev. Tripp said, "I have known Bunnie McKoin for more than two

---

[531] Ibid.
[532] *Monroe News-Star,* 8 January 1923.

years and have been very closely associated with him. I have no better friend in this country. I love him as I love few men, and I want the world to know that my faith and confidence in him as a Christian gentleman has never failed."[533]

Rev. Tripp's resolution reads as follows:

> Whereas Dr. B. M. McKoin, a faithful member of this church and in good standing has been accused of being implicated in the mysterious kidnapping and murder of two Morehouse parish citizens, and
>
> Whereas, There seems to be among those making the accusation a well-organized machinery that is making every effort to persecute, harass and otherwise humiliate the said Dr. McKoin, and
>
> Whereas, The exaggerated reports now being circulated throughout the country are calculated to bring reproach upon his character, to destroy his usefulness as a Christian gentleman, and to wreck his career as a physician, and
>
> Whereas, It has brought sorrow to his heart, and untold suffering and humiliation to his excellent and consecrated wife and children, and
>
> Whereas, We regard his influence as a Christian gentleman in the city of Mer Rouge to have been a benediction to the entire community, therefore, be it
>
> Resolved, That this church, representing a membership of more that one thousand, cause to be published throughout the land and country that our faith and confidence in Dr. McKoin as a faithful, loyal and consecrated Christian has never faltered or failed; be it further
>
> Resolved, That we call upon the people everywhere to refrain from passing judgement upon such a Christian man until he is at least given an opportunity to prove his innocence, and be it
>
> Resolved, That we pledge anew our prayers and sympathy to Dr. McKoin and his family, and say to them that this church and pastor will be with them until the shadows pass.[534]

These resolutions bear examination, especially that of the Rev. Tripp, who was the prime mover in this case. The Rev. Tripp, as it has already been documented, is thought highly of by the local Ku Klux Klan, of which Dr. B. M. McKoin was the Captain of the Mer Rouge Klavern. If the Rev. Tripp was as close to Dr. McKoin as he claimed, he could not help but know that McKoin was the Captain of the Mer Rouge Klan. Because not only Rev. Tripp but also the Twin Cities Ministerial Association closed ranks behind Dr. McKoin, this speaks volumes as to the accepted norms, values and the definition of what they believed "a faithful, loyal, and consecrated Christian [who] has never faltered or failed" would be.

As also has been demonstrated in the past by the minister in Shreveport, it was quite common during this period in northeast Louisiana history for leaders and pastors of the Protestant faith to hold membership or office in the Ku Klux Klan. It

---

[533]Ibid.
[534]Ibid.

282

is, therefore, quite possible that the Rev. Tripp was also a member of the Ku Klux Klan. In his rush to defend Dr. McKoin, Rev. Tripp seems to have overlooked the fact that the "two citizens," as he referred to them, were horribly tortured and murdered.

It is quite clear that there exists not even the slightest trace of sympathy or compassion for the dead or the widow and orphans left behind. At the very least, these Christian organizations should have been doing all they could to ease the pain and suffering of Richards' widow and children. Alas, Tripp and these other good Christians were more interested in the "humiliation" of this "Christian gentleman," Dr. McKoin, than in the grief and agony of the families and friends of the murder victims.

Because of the relative calm that had prevailed, two of the units of the Louisiana National Guard on duty in Morehouse Parish were given orders to leave Bastrop. For Infantry Company A, whose home was Alexandria, that meant that their two week stay in Morehouse Parish had come to an end. Infantry Company G, stationed in Monroe, had already received orders the previous day to return home. Still on duty were the machine gun company from New Orleans which was guarding the courthouse and the parish jail, and the Jennings cavalry detachment which had been divided into two groups. One group had replaced the Monroe infantry unit in Mer Rouge; and the other camped opposite the courthouse in Bastrop.

Scheduled to testify the following day was J. L. Daniel, the father of Watt, who had been on the stand when the hearing adjourned Saturday. During this testimony he said that his son, Watt, had told him that in the early part of August he had been taken into the woods and questioned by black-hooded men. Watt identified these men to his father as J. K. Skipwith, the Exalted Cyclops of the Morehouse Parish Ku Klux Klan; Dr. B. M. McKoin and Laurie Calhoun, a Morehouse Parish deputy sheriff. However, both J. L. Daniel and W. C. Andrews admitted under oath that they were unable to identify any of the hooded men who took part in their abduction and the later kidnapping and murder of Watt Daniel and Thomas Richards.

When Deputy Calhoun was asked to comment on Daniel's statement, he replied, "Any statement I may make will be from the witness stand if I am called upon to testify." Interestingly enough, Sheriff Fred Carpenter had used Deputy

Calhoun to serve the arrest warrant for murder on Jeff Burnett, the former deputy sheriff who was arrested in Spyker [pronounced "speeker"]. Sheriff Carpenter also sent him along with Chief of Detectives Glynn of New Orleans to bring Dr. McKoin back from Baltimore. It is becoming increasingly clear that Sheriff Carpenter had a significant role in stonewalling this case and did all in his power to control every aspect of the actions taken.

Also on the witness list to be called after the elder Daniel were Sidney White and "Nip" Echol, both of whom were in the vehicle with J. L. Daniel when they were forced to stop on the road by the hooded men. Others on the list to testify included Zoo Higgenbotham, one the first to arrive at Lake LaFourche and discover the bodies after the explosion, and J. T. Norseworthy, C. C. (Tot) Davenport and Dr. Willey, all of these having been in vehicles which were stopped by the black-hooded band at the roadblock. Others on the prospective witness list were E. W. Andrews, the brother of W. C. Andrews, whose previous testimony on Saturday described the beating he received at the hands of the hooded men in an attempt to force information from him relative to an alleged attack made on Dr. B. M. McKoin. Also on the list were M. F. Holloway, a man named Davis and Mrs. Thelma Dade, the daughter of the then mayor of Mer Rouge.

The New York Times told the story of Addie May Hamilton, a 19-year-old, life-long Mer Rouge resident, who, because of immoral conduct which was never defined either by the Klan nor in the court during her testimony, was kidnapped by six black-hooded Klansmen in the dead of night from her home, taken to the train station, given enough money to get her to Little Rock and told never come back. Her testimony will appear later in this book. She and her mother were observed by a reporter from *The New York Times* driving their car not far from Mer Rouge.

After following their car into Mer Rouge, the reporter approached the car, and Mrs. Hamilton became quite upset when asked about the kidnapping of Addie May.

"Don't make us talk about it," said Mrs. Hamilton. "We think about it often as it is. We are afraid-we do not know when they will come back. Why, for six months, whenever any one would pass our house and call out 'Hello!' my heart would leap to my mouth. The doctors tell me I have a leaking heart valve now. They say I am a sick woman. That all came from this experience to Addie May. I was never sick a day in my life before that."

The reporter asked Addie May if any of the men who kidnapped her that night were from Mer Rouge.

"Two of them did. One of them was Dr. McKoin and the second was 'Pink' Parkerson. [This is the only time the name Parkerson appears. It is believed that the name should have been "Pink" Kirkpatrick.]

"I can identify them positively. I don't know who the other four were, but Dr. McKoin--I recognized him, and I know he was the man who drove me away." Speaking to her mother she said, "Why should I not talk; they've already done to me as much as they could, and I don't fear anything further they can do. The first man was Dr. McKoin and the second was 'Pink' Parkerson."

"I guess they'll be coming around to kill us now," said Mrs. Hamilton in exasperation. "I guess we've talked too much, but I don't care. I believe in law and order, and if we all help by telling what we know maybe we can have it now."

Wishing to break off the interview, Addie May started the car as she said, "I'll be getting back to Little Rock in a couple of weeks, I guess."

Asked if she wanted to stay in Mer Rouge, Addie May responded, "No. I hate it here-I hate it! That terrible experience!"

Chiming in, Mrs. Hamilton added, "I wish we all could move away. But I suppose we must stay here."[535]

Jeff Burnett was moved today from the jail at Bastrop to the Shreveport Hospital. Dr. O. M. Patterson, the parish coroner, told Judge Odom that he had examined Burnett and found him to be suffering from a case of pneumonia and that it would be necessary for him to seek treatment in Shreveport. As one might guess, Dr. Patterson was also known to be a Klansman, and the two deputy sheriffs sent by Sheriff Carpenter to guard Burnett were also Klansmen.[536]

Dr. Duvall, one of the two physicians who performed the autopsies on Daniel and Richards, and a professor of medicine at Tulane University in New Orleans, examined Burnett and reported to the court that Burnett was faking his sickness.

"It looks like a ruse to get Burnett out of jail," said Dr. Duvall. "I examined him Friday and Saturday and found nothing wrong with him, neither in his appearance nor in his manner on either occasion."[537]

---

[535]*The New York Times*, 8 January 1923.
[536]Ibid.
[537]Ibid.

Despite Dr. Duvall's opinion, Judge Odom ordered Burnett transported across the state to a hospital in Shreveport. The question naturally arises, "Why should he move Burnett to a hospital in Shreveport when there was a fully operating hospital in Monroe just down the road from Bastrop?" A likely answer would be that Shreveport is over 100 miles away from Bastrop, and at that time being that distance away was like moving Burnett to another planet.

Klan "Wrecking Crew" Aimed at Politicians[538]

An article from Hartford, Connecticut told of a sinister threat being hatched by the hobgoblins in white. It was learned at a meeting held in a private home in Berlin that a new feature had been added to the Klan, the "Wrecking Crew." The aim of this Klan group was to jail politicians, preferably Catholics and Jews who dare to interfere with the Klan.

TUESDAY JANUARY 9, 1923

Ex-Klansman Links Mer Rouge Murders With Ku Klux Band[539]
Daniels (sic) Declares He Appealed to M'Koin as Mason to Prevent What He Believed Klan Action[540]
Invisible Government Held Full Sway Sending All Undesirables to Border, Asserts Norseworthy[541]
Men Flogged at Klan's Order[542]

Just as it is quite ordinary today for Klan members to hold dual membership in both the Klan and neo-Nazi organizations such as the Aryan Nation and The Order, it was quite common in the 1920s for Klan members to hold dual membership as Masons and/or Knights of Pythias. Having held a membership in a Scottish Rite Blue Lodge, I am familiar with Masonry. One of the major tenets is that should another Mason be in need of assistance, a brother Mason is obliged to render him assistance. It is, therefore, easy to understand why the elder Daniel attempted to utilize the commonality of Masonry between him and Dr. McKoin as a way of helping his son.

The open hearing began on January 9 with the recalling of J. L. Daniel. Attorney General Coco began the questioning by asking if the elder Daniel had spoken with Dr. B. M. McKoin relative to the safety of his son prior to the

538 Ibid.
539 *The New York Times*, 9 January 1923.
540 *Monroe News-Star*, 9 January 1923.
541 Ibid.
542 Ibid.

kidnappings during August. Daniel said that he went to Dr. McKoin and "appealed to him as a Mason" to stay any Klan actions planned against his son.

"Dr. McKoin told me that he would do all he could, but that he was not a Klansman. Following this talk, I received notices written on a typewriter to 'change up.' They were unsigned and written on yellow paper." As we have seen all along, this type of clandestine cowardice was the typical calling card of the Klan. It seems appropriate that such a notice was executed on "yellow paper!"

Continuing his questioning, Mr. Coco asked, "Now did anything else occur that led you to believe the Klan was active in your community?"

"Yes, prior to an attempt on Dr. McKoin's life, there was an effort to kidnap Addie May Hamilton."

"Where were you the night that Dr. McKoin's car was shot into?"

"I was home."

"Where was Watt?"

"He was at my house."

"Where was Tom Richards?"

"He was there also, we were all playing cards, poker."

"Was it an open poker game, it being openly understood that the boys could always find a game at your house at night?"

"That's right, most of the time."

"You are sure that you did not leave your house that night?"

"Yes, on that night, we played almost all night."

"When did you first hear that you were suspected of shooting at Dr. McKoin?"

"Not until I was held up on the Bastrop road."

"Did you make any inquiry or try to ferret out who shot at McKoin?"

"No, I always had a hard time managing my own business without meddling into others affairs."

"Anything said about Dr. McKoin during the game?"

"Not that I remember."

"What took place during the conversation between you and Dr. McKoin?"

"Well, I knew McKoin was a reformer and he should know about the notes, we talked a long time."

"That was before he was shot at?"

"About two or three weeks."

"Since the disappearance of your son, have you ever received any anonymous letters?"

"Not directly, but Joe Davenport told me that he had received word over the phone that Campbell, Whipple and his two bodyguards would have to get away from there or Campbell would be killed. Campbell and Whipple are citizens of Mer Rouge."

"Who did Davenport say told him?"

"Captain Skipwith."

"When did Davenport tell you that?"

"It was after the kidnapping, after I had told my friends I believed my son had been murdered."

Moving to the topic of the actual kidnapping itself, Mr. Coco asked, "How about the kidnapping, where did they take you-what direction?"

"We were on the Bastrop-Monroe Road."

It could easily be asked here how the elder Daniel could have known that he was, in fact, on the Bastrop-Monroe road. When a road has been traveled numerous times, there are certain ways that a person familiar with the road would realize it was being traveled upon, even blindfolded as was the elder Daniel. Certain turns, bumps in the road, specific sounds or smells can be clear indicators as to location and direction of travel. One unmistakable smell that would have alerted Daniel that he was on the road from Bastrop to Monroe would have been the putrid stench of the wood and pulp processing plant located on that particular road. Even today, travelers on that road are treated to that ghastly gagging aroma. In sum, if the abductors of the elder Daniel had taken this road, the smell of the plant would have been an unmistakable indicator of direction.

"During the period you were being held, did you hear your son Watt speak?"

"I did not."

"You did not recognize anyone?"

"No, if I did I would have gone to the man and faced him."[543]

Next called to the stand was Dr. F. J. Willey of Mer Rouge. Dr. Willey was asked by Mr. Coco if he had been the attending physician to W. C. Andrews on the night of August 24, 1922, and he acknowledged that he was. Mr Coco then

---

[543] Ibid.

requested that the Mer Rouge physician describe the Andrews' injuries.

"He looked like he had been severely whipped," Willey said. "I asked no questions. Andrews had several bruises on his back, but there were no lacerations."[544] In order to treat any type of injury or illness, it had always and still is basic to ask how an injury occurred in order to institute proper treatment. Obviously, Dr. Willey either knew prior to the treating of Andrews how it had occurred, or he had treated many similar injuries and knew the mechanics through past experience. Andrews had been one of the original group of five that had been kidnapped while returning from the baseball game at Bastrop.

Placed on the stand following Dr. Willey was Mr. M. F. Holloway, a fisherman who was one of the first to arrive at Lake LaFourche on the morning the bodies of Daniel and Richards bobbed to the surface. Attorney General Coco asked Holloway to describe the scene:

"Both bodies were floating face down. Both bodies reminded me of two old rag dolls, which had been chewed up, and thrown out there. There was some galvanized telephone wires around both bodies. I took a stick and examined one of the bodies. This was Daniel. I found a piece of skull hanging on a thread, it looked like. I went home and brought my wife back to see the bodies. She didn't see them because they had the place all roped off."[545]

The open hearing continued with the calling of J. T. Norseworthy to the witness stand. Mr. Coco began the questioning by asking him to recount the events of the day of the fateful kidnapping on August 24, 1922.

"We, Andrews, the Daniels and Richards attended a baseball game at Bastrop and on our return trip to Mer Rouge, we were stopped by four or five masked men wearing hoods. One nearest me had a rifle. I asked him what he wanted. 'We want him,' the man said, indicating W. C. Andrews. They took Andrews out and told me to drive on. I drove for about 200 yards and stopped. Two more masked men came up and held me up. I noticed several cars in the woods. Then I saw armed men all around me."

"I walked up to one car to see if I could get the number of the machine. It had a sack wrapped around the tag. I came back to the road and I saw men, women and children in about fifty cars held up. One of the ladies, Mrs. Hopkins, shouted,

---

[544]Ibid.

'What in the name of God have I done' when one of the hooded men shoved a gun at her. Pretty soon they let the cars go by. The women were frantic, some I understood, became sick. We drove back to the fork of the roads and waited for Andrews, believing they were just questioning him and would soon turn him loose. Several cars came up and told us the hooded men had carried him toward Monroe. I returned to Bastrop."[546] Judge Odom called a recess, with court scheduled to resume at 2 p.m.

The open hearing resumed as Attorney General Coco called J. T. Norseworthy to the stand once again. Coco began the questioning by asking Norseworthy what color of masks were used by the Klan, and if there were any special uses for these masks.

"When the Klan went out on raiding trips they wore the black masks, but when they met in the lodge rooms they wore white ones."

"Who was the leader of the Klan, the grand cyclops, or whatever they called him?"

"Captain Skipwith, we called him the president."

"He was the king of this community of this parish. His word was final, was it not?"

"Yes, Sir."

"What was the result of all this raiding? Wasn't the parish being controlled by a super government?"

"It caused all kinds of trouble. The people were all torn up. It wasn't what we called invisible government, but it sure was a change in government. As a matter of fact Captain Skipwith told that if the grand jury which was in session failed to bring about indictments [concerning the bogus attempted assassination of Dr. McKoin] we would, meaning the Klan. After I got out of the Klan, they sent me with a bunch of men to the Arkansas line. I had orders to flog these men and tell them to cross the line and stay across."

"They did not know that you had quit them?"

"I reckon not."

Attorney General Coco then turned his attention to the inner workings of the Klan. Coco asked Norseworthy what was his position in the Klan and that of Dr.

---

[545] Ibid.

B. M. McKoin. Norseworthy claimed that he had had the rank of captain conferred upon him by Skipwith and that "Dr. McKoin was likewise honored."

"Why did you quit the Klan, was it because they wore black masks?"

"Yes sir, but I did not like any part of it."

"How about the committees?"

"You mean the vigilantes?"

"Yes."

"Oh! They went around the country and scouted up stuff and reported to us what was going on."

"Wasn't men ordered to leave their homes, wasn't others told to clean up their household?"

"Yes, sir."

"Wasn't these orders executed by direction of the president, Captain Skipwith?"

"Yes, sir."

"Wasn't all this caused by parish officials not enforcing the law?"

"Yes, sir."

"As a matter of fact, the sheriff and other officials of this parish are members of the Klan?"

"Yes, sir."

"The members of the grand jury then in session were members, were they not?"

"Yes, sir."

"Do you know anything about the kidnapping of Addie May Hamilton?"

"I do. She was taken from her home, taken to Mer Rouge and put on a train to Little Rock and told not to come back."

"Tell us about it."

"Well, I don't know except W. P. Kirkpatrick, a Klansman, told me that he gave her money to take the trip. Dr. McKoin, said Kirkpatrick, was also with him. He (Kirkpatrick) told me that she did not have any money, so I just run my hand down in my pocket and gave it to her."

"Who were the men you were ordered to whip?"

---

[546]Ibid.

"A white man by the name of Jeff Wall, a negro by the name of Jurden Bailey, and another one by the name of King."

"What were your orders?"

"To take them to the Arkansas line, flog them within an inch of their lives and send them across the line never to return."

"Were these orders carried out by you?"

"No, sir."

The attorney general took this opportunity to withdraw a black cloth hood which had been rolled in newspaper on the table of the prosecution.

"Is this the regalia of the klan?"

"Yes, sir. Them is the eyes and this to breathe."

"Who did the vigilante committee make their report to?"

"To the captain-Captain Skipwith."

"What action was then taken?"

"Whatever he saw fit."

"Have these conditions gotten to the point of terrorism and chaos?"

"It has."

"Had such prevailed before the advent of the Klan?"

"It certainly had not. On one occasion, a woman came up to me and asked me to escort her home, she was afraid, because of the Klan's activities."

"How do you know Dr. McKoin, Higgenbotham and others you mentioned this morning participated in the banishment of Addie May Hamilton?"

"Mr. Kirkpatrick told me."

"Was she banished forever?"

"To return, she would have to get permission from Captain Skipwith; however, this was just common talk."

"Do you remember a meeting of [the] vigilance committee to consider the deportation of certain citizens of Mer Rouge?"

"Yes, sir."

"Some of these present were not Klansmen. We'll speak of them as not Klansmen, but not anti-Klansmen."

"You see, about that time, they were guarding the Bastrop courthouse because some threats had been made about Mer Rouge staging a raid on Bastrop. I was named a delegate to a meeting to arrange a sort of armistice get-together to bring about peace in the parish. We were to meet in a bank.

"When I reached Bastrop I met Bunny McKoin and the captain [Skipwith] coming out of the bank. They spoke to me as he and the doctor got in an automobile. They called me over to the machine. I told them that I had heard that an effort would be made to kill my brother, five men being sent to his farm.

"Captain Skipwith said everything was all right. I left the parish to go to El Paso. When I returned they had accused me and my brother of having plotted to kill Bunny McKoin. My brother went to Captain Skipwith, who told him everything was all right. It was just a false alarm."

"You were thinking about quitting the parish?"

"Yes. I did not like the way things were going."

"You were willing to go to Mexico even?"

"Yes, but after I went to El Paso and looked around, I decided I'd rather fight the Ku Klux Klan than Mexicans, so I stayed. Hugo Davenport, Walter Campbell, town marshal of Mer Rouge, A. C. Whipple and Tom Miller [Milner], were those named to be deported."

"A matter of fact, wasn't it said that they had two, and four more were to go?"

"That's what Captain Skipwith said."[547]

"Captain Skipwith told me that the Klan had already gotten two of the six marked men, Daniel and Richards, and would get the other four."[548] This condemning line of testimony from J. T. Norseworthy was recorded in *The New York Times*, but strangely missing from the *Monroe News-Star*. It is because of glaring inconsistencies such as this and what appear to be portions of testimony excluded, either intentionally or unintentionally, that I feel that it is vital to present variations of testimony appearing in *The New York Times*, *Times-Picayune* and *Monroe News-Star*.

Such was one of the high points in the giving of testimony on this date by J. T. Norseworthy, a former Klansman and Mer Rouge resident. Because of the testimony of this 300-pound wealthy planter, it was widely thought that the arrest of Captain Skipwith was eminent. He was believed to be under constant surveillance by government agents.

---

[547] Ibid.

[548] *The New York Times*, 9 January 1923.

The testimony given by Norseworthy seemed particularly brave, especially in light of the revelation that his assassination was being sought by the Klan. He not only told of the actions of Skipwith, but also others such as one of Sheriff Carpenter's deputies, Laurie Calhoun, Dr. McKoin and others. Interestingly enough, his testimony coincided with the widespread Klan prediction that anyone charged with regard to Daniel and Richards, either directly for the crime or for some other acts uncovered by the testimony, had no chance of being found guilty. This prediction was to not only become a reality, but the failure of the grand jury to return any indictments after the weight of the testimony given only serves to verify that the Klan did, indeed, control every aspect of life in Morehouse Parish.

Norseworthy painted a picture of the Klan as an organization, whose laws superseded those of the United States:

"I joined them about a year or so ago. I attended two meetings and I did not like it. I asked them to remove my name from their books. I went to Dr. McKoin and told him I did not like it. I saw things I didn't think were right. The black hood is used for a certain purpose, but the white hood is used most of the time. The black mask is known as the raiding mask. The white mask is used to set forth the ideas of the order, and they use the black mask for raiding purposes."

Perhaps one of the most dramatic differences between the versions of recorded testimony is that of Norseworthy. Because the version of the *Monroe News-Star* differs so greatly from that of the *New York Times*, the *Times* version will now be presented in its entirely. Hereafter, only the differences in versions of reported testimony will be noted.

Norseworthy told of his attending the festivities in Bastrop on August 24 with W. C. Andrews, and how he and Andrews were held up on their return to Mer Rouge. The traffic was stopped, but he could see a Ford truck on the side of the road. He and Andrews were under the impression that a traffic accident had taken place because of the large number of people on the side of the road.

"We were stopped by four or five men. They gathered on either side, one armed with a Winchester, and I asked what they wanted. 'We want that man,' they said, meaning Andrews. We all got out. They took Andrews. Then they made me drive on. Further away, I was stopped again and told to get out, which I did. I saw two or three cars there and other cars in the woods."

"How many men were in the crowd?"

"Well, they were shoving guns around and I scattered, but I don't think there were more than a dozen."

After Norseworthy told how he was given the rank of an officer in the Klan by Captain Skipwith, Mr Coco asked if he was ever asked to do things which he felt were wrong.

"Yes, I was ordered to help whip several men, take them to the Arkansas line and order them not to return." Norseworthy also told of how Klan committees would submit reports of investigations to Captain Skipwith.

"Doesn't it look as if a super-government has been established? Have the legal authorities been superseded by this order?"

"Yes sir, that's true. I've been told that the District Attorney and two-thirds of the grand jury are Klansmen and that no convictions against the Klan can be obtained."

"When you were appointed captain of your order in Mer Rouge weren't you given orders you refused to obey? Weren't you ordered to take people to the Arkansas line and give them a flogging?"

"Yes, and I refused to do it."

"About taking people to the Arkansas line and whipping them, what were your instructions as to these men?"

"Take them and whip them within an inch of their lives, and take them to the line and tell them never to return."

Norseworthy identified the three men as J. C. Walls, white, and Jordan Bailey and "Sunny" King, blacks, of Bayou Bonne Idee. It was on the banks of this same scenic cypress filled swamp waterway that the bodies of Watt Daniel and Thomas Richards were buried side by side.

From a brown paper wrapping, the attorney general unfolded a long garment topped with a black mask with eyeholes cut in it, and Norseworthy identified it as the raider garb worn by Klansmen. The cap was shown to fit loosely over the head.

"Give us an idea of the general operations of the Klan-they claim to be for law and order. In what way did they undertake to enforce the law? Were offenses reported by them to the officials or to the Sheriff?"

"No, they reported to Captain Skipwith."

"What action was then taken?"

"Whatever Captain Skipwith saw fit; they did whatever he ordered."

"He issued orders?"

"Yes."

"Have these conditions in the parish given rise to a condition of chaos and terrorism that previously did not exist?"

"Yes, sir."

When asked to relate his knowledge concerning the circumstances surrounding the kidnapping of Addie May Hamilton, he told the court that 'Pink' Kirkpatrick, a stablekeeper from Mer Rouge, had advised that he had been a member of the party, who, under the leadership of Dr. McKoin and also in the company of Tom Higgenbotham, Klansmen all, had taken her from her home despite the pleading of her mother, whom Dr. McKoin later knocked to the floor. He said that Kirkpatrick had given her the money to catch the train to Little Rock.

As to the other four Mer Rouge men who were, in Klan lingo, to be "got," Norseworthy identified them as Hugo Davenport, a planter and merchant from Mer Rouge; Walter Campbell, the Mer Rouge city marshal; Tom Milner, a former employee of the Interstate Cooperage Company of Mer Rouge; and A. C. Whipple. None of these men were ever kidnapped.

"Fear the Klan-hell no. There's not enough men in Bastrop to make me fear. Skulkers, [they are] yellow skulkers that haven't nerve enough to come out in the open and fight."

"I fear them?' he asked as he struck hammer-like fist against his massive chest, his entire 300-pound frame jolting in laughter. "Here's one they haven't got buffaloed. They kidnapped me the night they got Watt and Tom Richards, but they let me go. They knew better than to try anything with me."[549]

The *Monroe News-Star* reported that the next witness called to testify was C.C. (Tot) Davenport, one of those kidnapped with Daniel and Richards on the night of August 24, 1922. Davenport testified that he had served in the Great War and that he was then employed as an automobile salesman. He went on to say that he had attended the celebration at Bastrop with W. C. Andrews and T. F. Richards.

Continuing on, Davenport said, "On our return to Mer Rouge we were held up by masked men. I was told to 'get out, damn you, get out.'"

"We were blindfolded and thrown into a car. They drove away. Soon we

---

[549]Ibid.

stopped and I heard licks, I recognized Watt Daniel's voice. We were blindfolded, but my hands were not tied. I did not make any effort to take off the blindfold. I did not believe it would be healthy. They whipped 'Old Man' J. L. Daniel. During the whipping, Watt Daniel shouted: 'It's a hell of a note to whip an innocent man.' We were taken to Collinston and released. My instructions were to go on and not look back. Next time I saw Richards and Watt Daniel they were in the truck. Before they let me go, one of the hooded men said to me: 'One of these men may come back, but the other is going out of the country.' I had no idea who the hooded men were and know no reason why I was kidnapped. The general talk was that I was taken by mistake."

"About how many masked men were in the woods?"

"About eighteen or twenty."

"When and where did you know they had Daniel ?"

"When they put him in the truck with me and Richards."[550]

The New York Times recorded that C. C. "Tot" Davenport testified that he last saw Watt Daniel on the night of August 24, at about 9:30 p.m. in the rear of a truck. "We was blindfolded," explained Davenport. "Richards was there too."

"Have you made any effort to ascertain who those men were?" Coco asked.

"I wouldn't know how to go about it," asserted the witness.

Davenport admitted that he made no attempt to secure the license numbers of the vehicles used in the kidnappings, and made no attempt to obtain the identities of the kidnappers.[551]

While on her way to the stand to testify, Thelma Dade, niece of Watt Daniel, ran the gauntlet of numerous cameras. In her testimony, she related that as she was leaving Bastrop toward Mer Rouge on August 24, her car was stopped by black-hooded men. She said that she saw them blindfold Watt Daniel. As she reached the spot, he was out of his car near the side of the road. She said she observed a total of about 15 or 20 black-hooded men, and that three of these men had seized hold of Watt Daniel.

"Did you make any outcry?"

"I just called 'Watt! Watt! Watt!' "

---

[550]*Monroe News-Star*, 9 January 1923.

[551]*The New York Times*, 9 January 1923.

"Were any of the hooded men armed?"

"They were all armed."[552]

W. C. Andrews told of his return trip to Mer Rouge from Bastrop on August 24, and how he was also stopped by the band of black-hooded men. He said he observed Watt Daniel, "Tot" Davenport and Thomas Richards blindfolded and sitting in the back of a truck on the side of the road.

"Are you a member of the Klan?" Mr. Coco asked.

"I was a member, but not a charter member. I went to three or four meetings and then quit. I didn't like their methods."

"How do they enforce their laws?"

"I don't know. They get an order and just enforce it. Orders came from Captain Skipwith."

"Do you know anything about the deportation of Addie May Hamilton?"

"I was one ordered to get her out of town."

"Who gave you that order?"

"Dr. McKoin. I refused and I was not the only one who refused."

Sidney White, a resident of Oak Ridge and a passenger in the vehicle from which Watt Daniel was kidnapped, testified that "five men armed with guns walked up to our car and said, 'This is the man we want,' indicating Watt Daniel. Daniel got out and they took him away." After the kidnapping, White returned to Bastrop and went to a dance. He never tried to find out what became of Daniel. He did not recognize anybody who held up the car.

"When you saw the hooded men, what did Watt Daniel say?" asked Assistant Attorney General Seth Guion.

"He said he thought they wanted him."

White was a very uncooperative witness, and the state's attorneys had a difficult time extracting his testimony. However, suddenly there was unveiled a riveting facet of the case. Through White's reluctant testimony, it came to light that Daniel and Richards were tortured and murdered on the same night of the kidnapping. This was revealed when Mr. Guion asked White if he was familiar with Marshal Mott of Oak Ridge. Oak Ridge is a small township not far from Lake LaFourche. White verified that he did, and Mr. Guion asked:

---

[552]Ibid.

"Did not Marshal Mott tell you that on the night of August 24, two cars headed for Lake LaFourche were seen in the vicinity of Oak Ridge, one of them being a Ford?" White said that Mott had told him this approximately a week after the kidnappings.

"Isn't it a fact that Mott told you that a traveling man and his wife, motoring near Oak Ridge, had had a breakdown, and while their machine was being repaired they saw an automobile and a Ford truck passing, and the wife of the traveling man said she saw two bodies, covered with white cloth lying in the Ford truck?"

"Mott told me the story."

"Didn't you, late the same night, see a motor car and Ford truck coming out of Oak Ridge as you were going home?"

"I did."

"Didn't it arouse your suspicion?"

"No."

"When you heard Mott's story of the report made by the wife of traveling man, did you report it to the authorities?"

"No."

"You were Watt Daniel's friend?"

"Yes."

"Did you make any attempts to assist the authorities?"

"No."[553]

J. L. Daniel, the father of the murdered Watt Daniel, testified that his son told him how he and W. C. Andrews had been held up by a group of black-hooded men prior to his murder. He told the elder Daniel that he had recognized as being part of the black-hooded group, Dr. McKoin, Deputy Sheriff Calhoun [Calhoun had been sent by Sheriff Carpenter to Baltimore with Captain of Detectives Glynn of the New Orleans Police Department, to bring Dr. McKoin back.] and Captain Skipwith. Watt told him that the group had taken away their firearms. He testified that on the night of the alleged attempt to assassinate Dr. McKoin, Watt Daniel, Thomas Richards and others were playing poker at the Daniel home and had been present there at the time of the alleged assassination attempt. The elder Daniel told of receiving information that Captain Skipwith was going to "get him."

---

[553] Ibid.

"Joe Davenport told me that he got a message over the phone that Captain Skipwith was going to get me, if he had to kill me himself," said Daniel. This conversation was said to have occurred after the kidnapping and murder of his son. He also told the court of having received threatening notices in the mail.[554]

Following the day's testimony, Attorney General Coco called a news conference during which he discussed the Jekyll and Hyde nature of the Ku Klux Klan:

"The testimony offered today, while only a small part of the mass of evidence which we intend to offer, revealed in a positive way that Klan leaders were involved in a most active manner in the strife which led up to the shocking tortures and murders of two Mer Rouge citizens. The positive testimony offered by the former Klansmen as to the two-sided feature of the Klan movement-the white-hooded and virtuous side and the black-hooded and raiding and murderous side-leaves no doubt as to the dual nature of the 'invisible empire.'

> The Klan, not only in Morehouse, but in Louisiana and the nation at large, will have to seriously consider the narratives that were unfolded at today's session in the open hearing. The Klan is on trial and the Klan will have to answer. I dare say, also, that Captain Skipwith, the Exalted Cyclops in Morehouse, realizes that the State has in its hands considerable evidence bearing on his activities in Morehouse, and if Dr. B. M. McKoin was in the courtroom he doubtless felt that his toes were being stepped on at regular intervals.

Dr. McKoin, who has been seen at every session of the open hearings, was asked on this date as to his impression of the proceedings of the open hearings thus far. He replied by saying that "[I] haven't lost my appetite yet," with a cocky smile.[555]

Cavalry Detachment is Stationed at Home of Addie May Hamilton Today[556]

Acting on an anonymous telephone message that an attempt might be made to kidnap Addie May Hamilton, a prospective witness in the investigation into the depredations of the Ku Klux Klan in Morehouse Parish, several men stood guard at the Hamilton home near Mer Rouge and later two soldiers were assigned to guard duty there.

---

[554]Ibid.
[555]Ibid.
[556]*Monroe News-Star*, 9 January 1923.

WEDNESDAY JANUARY 10, 1923

Witnesses Identify 7 More Klansmen of Kidnapping Band[557]
Quiet and Rest in Burnett Case Now Physician's Order[558]
Washington First to Take Hand for Mob Investigation[559]
Evidence Revealed at Bastrop Hearing Only a Small Effort[560]
Hooded Men on Highway to Mer Rouge Seized Watt Daniels (sic) on Leaving Bastrop, States Youth[561]
Addie Mae Hamilton, Known as Daughter of Klan, Declares on Witness Stand She was Deported From State by Ku Klux Organization[562]

Prior to the commencement of the open hearing, Attorney General Coco recapped the gist of the testimony given the previous day by witnesses to reporters from the *Monroe News-Star*. Mr. Coco declared that the information tendered by the witnesses "revealed in a positive way that Klan leaders were involved in a most active manner in the strife which led up to the shocking torture and murders of two Mer Rouge citizens." Coco referred to what he termed the "dual nature" of the Klan, although he did not elucidate on the meaning of that term.

In a related event, it was reported that Jeff Burnett, the former Morehouse Parish sheriff's deputy arrested for murder, was still confined at a sanatorium in Shreveport, Louisiana. Although he was originally diagnosed as having pleurisy, generally his condition was not thought to be serious. Interestingly enough, his doctors have "warned him against conversing at length with anyone." This gives rise to speculation that the doctors were cooperating with the Klan in their attempts to keep Burnett from having to testify at the open hearing. It was also innocently reported in the same communiqué that G. A. Lee, a Morehouse deputy sheriff sent to Shreveport to guard Burnett, said that he had seen the group that had abducted Daniel and Richards. What a conicidence!

Lee said, "They passed my house about dusk that afternoon. There were about ten men in a truck wearing black masks. I saw them only at a glance, but my wife said she saw some of the men thought to be the men abducted with handkerchiefs

---

[557] *The New York Times*, 11 January 1923.

[558] *Monroe News-Star*, 10 January 1923.

[559] Ibid.

[560] Ibid.

[561] Ibid.

[562] Ibid.

over their faces."[563] There is reason to believe that neither the attorney general's staff nor any of the government agents were aware of this witness. There does exist, however, substantial doubt whether Sheriff Fred Carpenter of Morehouse Parish could make this same claim. It is quite probable that Sheriff Carpenter was well aware of Deputy Lee's value as a witness, and by sending him to Shreveport as a guard for Burnett, he killed two birds with one stone by removing both Burnett and Lee from the grasp of the open hearing.

Next to be called to testify was Addie May Hamilton. After giving her age as 17, Assistant Attorney General George Seth Guion asked Ms. Hamilton, "How do you know the Klan sent you to Little Rock?"

"Because Dr. McKoin and 'Pink' Kirkpatrick and about six others came to my mother's house about 10:30 o'clock at night and told me they were going to send me away."

"Do you know positively that it was Dr. McKoin and Kirkpatrick?"

"Yes, sir. I recognized Dr. McKoin, who was masked, but he was the only one doing the talking. They came to the house and pulled their guns and told my mother that 'Addie May will have to leave town tonight.' My mother asked them what for. 'Because Addie May has been leading an immoral life.' " This response was attributed to the person Ms. Hamilton identified as Dr. McKoin.

"My mother said, 'Why don't you send others away?' " The subject identified as Dr. McKoin responded, " 'We are going to.' "

"My mother got down on her knees and pleaded, but they made me leave. They told us that if anybody shoved their heads out of the door they would 'blow 'em off.' They made me leave without a hat."

"Dr. McKoin struck my mother when she made a final plea for me to be allowed to remain. My mother attempted to shove them out of the room. She begged them to let her go to the depot. They refused. They put me in an automobile and Dr. McKoin gave me $7 for my fare to Little Rock. He told me if I did not catch the train I would be tarred and feathered the next day." Ms. Hamilton paused occasionally to wipe the tears from her face.

"What did he do that for?"

"I don't know."

---

[563]Ibid.

"Where was your father?"

"About 10 miles away in the country."

"You had no baggage?"

"No."

"How much was the fare to Little Rock?"

"$6.55."

"Did you have any other money?"

"Yes, sir."

"When was this?"

"It was January, 1922."

"When did you return to Mer Rouge?"

"Last May."

"When you were sent away, were you told that you could not return?"

"Yes, sir."

"Didn't they tell you they would tar and feather you if you returned?"

"Yes, sir."

"Why did you return?"

"Mr. Hugh Clark and W. E. Hopkins said they could fix it up with the Ku Klux. I got a letter from them telling me everything was all right to come back. I came back. Mr. Clark and Mr. Hopkins were friends of my family and they interceded at the request of my sister."

"When you returned, how long did you stay?"

"About two weeks. I was scared every day. I returned to Little Rock and came back home in August. I went back and returned again in December."

"Are you positive that it was Kirkpatrick with the hood on?"

"Yes, sir. I recognized him under his hood and asked him why they were going to send me away. He gave me no reply."

"Did they threaten your mother?"

"They told her they would tar and feather her if I did not go."

"Who said they would shoot anybody's head off if they looked out?"

"Dr. McKoin."

"What size car was it?"

"A roadster. Dr. McKoin drove the car. Mr. Kirkpatrick sat on the door."

"Wasn't much room?"

303

"No."

"Did they give you a lecture?"

"No, sir: they told me to take the train to Little Rock."

"Are Mr. Clark and Hopkins Klansmen?"

"I believe Mr. Clark is. I don't know about Mr. Hopkins."

"How long had your parents lived in Mer Rouge when you were ordered away?"

"Thirteen years."

"Where is Fred Clemmons who was at your house the night the hooded men came for you?"

"I understand he is in New Orleans."

"Who was your family physician?"

"Dr. Doddy, Dr. McKoin also. Mrs. McKoin was my music teacher."

"What time did Fred Clemmons come to your house?"

"About 5:30 in the afternoon."

"You said Mrs. McKoin was your music teacher. How long had you been taking music lessons?"

"About one year."

"You were going to Sunday school?"

"Yes, sir."

"Where?"

"Mer Rouge."[564]

The New York Times recorded the testimony of Addie May Hamilton differently. There were a number of places where the testimony was "similar," but rarely was it exact. For example, the following was the *Times* account of the testimony of the kidnapping event by Ms. Hamilton:

"I heard them coming up to the house. It was about 10:30 on the night of Jan. 22, 1922. My mother went to the door and slammed it shut. But they got in a side door. Dr. McKoin said to my mother, 'Addie Mae has to leave Mer Rouge tonight. She has been leading an immoral life.' My mother asked him why he didn't get the people he knew who were immoral. My mother didn't want to let me go. She got down on her knees and pleaded and Dr. McKoin said they would tar and feather my

---

[564]Ibid.

mother if she objected. I offered to go with them, and as they took me away Dr. McKoin shouted that anyone who stuck their head out of the door would be shot. Dr. McKoin said my things would be sent to me, and that I wouldn't be hurt."

One very important portion of Ms. Hamilton's testimony concerning the clothing worn by the kidnappers was recorded in the *Times*, but not recorded at all in the *News-Star*.

"What kind of robes did these men wear?"

"Black."

"Black hoods and robes?"

"Yes."

Also not part of Ms. Hamilton's testimony in the *News-Star* was the reason why the rest of her family was not present when the Klan raided her home and kidnapped her.

Ms. Hamilton, now under the questioning of Attorney General Coco, testified that she took music lessons from Mrs. McKoin, the wife of the doctor, and that she was quite familiar with Dr. McKoin's voice and found it easily recognizable in the band of black-hooded men who transported her to the train station.

"How was it that your father and brothers were not home that night?"

"They were camping in the woods."[565]

The *Monroe News-Star* observed that after testifying for about a half an hour, Ms. Hamilton was excused, and Mr. W. C. Andrews, one of the men kidnapped and beaten on August 24, 1922, was recalled to the stand. Mr. Andrews testified that he and Watt Daniel had encountered a group of robed Klansmen at the town of Stampley, which is located three miles north of Mer Rouge. Mr. Guion continued questioning by asking, "How were they dressed?"

"Dressed in white, all hoods reaching to their feet."

"Where did they go?"

"They went out the Stampley road."

"Where did you go?"

"We followed them."

"Were you going to school?"

"I quit school in the eighth grade."

---

[565]*The New York Times*, 11 January 1923.

"Didn't Dr. McKoin tell you that night you couldn't come back to Mer Rouge without the permission of the Klan?"

"No, sir, he told me I never could come back."

"Are you positive it was Dr. McKoin?"

"Yes, sir. I know his voice. I knew him by his walk, and his height and weight."

"Why?"

"I had business with them."

"What for?"

"I had received a note. I found it in my automobile. It said I was running up and down the road and disturbing the peace at all hours of the night. It was signed by the vigilance committee."

"When were you advised that the Klan would let you come back?"

"I got a letter from Mr. Hopkins in May, telling me everything had been fixed."

"So you followed them to talk to them about the note?"

"Yes, sir."

"Did Watt Daniel and Harry Neelis who accompanied you have business with the Klan?"

"Not that I know of."

"Where did you overtake them?"

"They stopped at a negro house. We stopped one hundred yards away, some were out of their cars. It was a moonlight night and we could see them plainly. Some of them went into the negro house. When they came out they come down to where we were and surrounded our car. They told us to hold up our hands. They searched us and took Watt's gun. They accused Watt of making whiskey. He said that he had not made whiskey since November when he received a warning. They searched my car, took my pistol, but later returned it. They didn't return Watt's. We went on to the town. A few minutes later the Klansmen came through. One of the automobiles stopped and a man shouted, 'Here, Watt, is your pistol.' Watt went out to the automobile and got the gun."

"What did you do about the note?"

"I showed it to them when they held us up. They said they did not know anything about it."

"Who were these Klansmen?"

"I recognized two."

"Who were they?"

"Captain Skipwith and Lawry Calhoun," Lawry Calhoun is the same as Laurie Calhoun who was identified earlier as a special deputy sheriff of Sheriff Fred Carpenter of Morehouse Parish.

"Are you positive about them?"

"Yes, sir. I knew their voices well."

"They questioned Daniel at length about whiskey?"

"Yes, sir."

"Do you think you recognized others?"

"Yes, sir. Bob Dade and Dr. McKoin. Bob Dade said the next day he wasn't at my car, but was up the road."

"Did Watt recognize any?"

"He told me he believed it was J. D. Higgenbotham who returned his pistol to him."

"You thought you recognized Dr. McKoin?"

"Yes, by his walk as he came down the road toward the car."

"Were you ever asked to join the Klan?"

"Yes. Tom Milligan asked me to join. He said that some man was coming to Bastrop to lecture and organize. I told him from the accounts I had read in the papers about the Klan activities in Texas I did not care to join." The name Tom Milligan appears on the application for Klan membership.

"How long after this did you learn about men being flogged in the parish?"

"About three or four months."

"Well, you, Watt and others were whipped the night of August 24. How long before this time were shots said to have been fired at Dr. McKoin?"

"I believe it was about the first of August."

"Where were you the night Dr. McKoin was shot at?"

"I was up in the country to 'Bill' Barnes. I was trying to buy a horse."

"Did you complete the trade?"

"No. Barnes was not at home."

"Where did you go?"

"To J. L. Daniel's to play poker."

"Did you get into a game?"

"No, it had broken up."

"When did you next see the Klan?"

"They came to Mer Rouge and went into a negro restaurant."

"Where were you when they took Richards into the woods and accused him of shooting at Dr. McKoin?"

"I was in Mer Rouge."

"Did you talk to Richards?"

"Yes, sir. He came to Mer Rouge and told me all about it. He told me that they were going to get Watt and me and asked did he recognize any of them. He said that he did not."

"Then you did have some warning that you were going to be picked up by the Klan?"

"Yes, sir. After Richards told me about the woods, I wanted them to get me because I wanted to clear myself."[566]

Once again, *The New York Times* testimony of W. C. Andrews was different than that of the *News-Star*. With regard to the cabin of a black farmer, Andrews gave the following:

"What happened then?"

"We stopped and watched them. They came out of the house and surrounded the car."

"Then what happened?"

"About twelve of them surrounded our car and ordered us out. They took Watt Daniel's gun and mine. They accused Watt of making whiskey and Watt said he had not made any since being warned in November. I pulled out the note I had received and they laughed and denied writing it. They kept Watt's gun but returned mine. Later in Mer Rouge a man yelled, 'Hey, Watt, is this your pistol?' It was and Watt got it back. The man who gave it to him was in a car."

"Did you recognize any of the men who surrounded the car?"

"Two of them."

"Who were they?"

"Captain Skipwith and Laurie Calhoun."

---

[566]*Monroe News-Star*, 10 January 1923.

"How did you know?"

"I recognized their voices as they talked to Watt. I thought I recognized Bob Dade and Dr. McKoin."

As has been observed before, not only were the versions of testimony different, but another key section of testimony was missing from the *News-Star*. Andrews spoke of how he had encountered Thomas Richards on a later date, and how he, Richards, had been kidnapped from his place of business in Bastrop and taken into the woods and questioned about the alleged attempt on McKoin. He said Richards also said that Klan members had told Richards that they were going to "get" Watt Daniel and Andrews [himself].

"He didn't tell me that he did, but I've heard that he told others that he knew some of the men."[567] Clearly, this was an important statement, despite the fact that it was hearsay. We are left to wonder why it was not included in the *News-Star*.

The *Monroe News-Star* stated that Judge Odom called a recess at noon and scheduled the hearing to reconvene at 1:30 p.m. The afternoon session began with the summoning of Mrs. W. E. Hopkins, a resident of Mer Rouge. Mrs. Hopkins was asked by Assistant Attorney General Guion to relate to the court the circumstances under which she and others were held up along the Bastrop-Mer Rouge Road on August 24, 1922 by a group of masked men. Mrs. Hopkins began by relating how, after being stopped, one of the masked group threatened her son, who was driving the vehicle, with a pistol.

"I said, 'Mr. Ku Klux we haven't done anything' and then I saw a twinkle in his eyes, through the eye slits of his black hood. We were held at the point of a gun for about five minutes and then told to drive on. We were again held up by a second hooded man. We were told to proceed. I looked back and saw one or two of the hooded men running back and forth between two places."

"You have no personal knowledge of any other holdups?"

"No."

"Do you know of any activities of the Klan?"

"I don't know whether it was the Klan, but masked men took one or two negroes off my husband's place. They accused them of having whiskey."

"Do you know anything about warning notes being circulated?"

---

[567]*The New York Times*, 11 January 1923.

"Yes, I paid no attention to them until Watt Daniel and T. F. Richards had permanently disappeared." Mrs. Hopkins claimed that she did not know if it was the Ku Klux Klan that she had encountered that day. If that is so, then why did she address them as "Mr. Ku Klux?" It would appear that she did, at that time, believe that they were members of the Ku Klux Klan.[568]

The New York Times version of the testimony of Mrs. W. E. Hopkins appears much more detailed, but basically the same. It did reinforce the reference to those who held her up on the road as being members of the Klan as she stated:

"Our car halted and a masked man sprang into view and pointed a gun at my son. I cried out, 'Mr. Ku Klux, we haven't done anything.' "

Mrs. Hopkins was followed by Mrs. Thomas F. Richards, the widow of one of the slain men. Dressed in a black dress with a long black veil, she took her seat on the witness stand. Speaking in a calm and steady voice, she began her testimony before the court.

"When was the last time you saw your husband?" asked Attorney General Coco.

"The morning he went away to the ball game. I was at our home in Mer Rouge."

"Where do you live now?"

"With friends in West Monroe. I have no other place to go."

"Was your husband in good spirits when he left?"

"Yes. He was always in good spirits."

"Did he have any fear of impending danger?"

"Not that I know of."

"You knew he was going to Bastrop?"

"Well, he wasn't sure himself."

"Did your husband figure in a prior kidnapping?"

"Yes, on July 18 [1922]."

"When did you hear of the first kidnapping?"

"My husband was working in the garage in Bastrop, and I went over and left our four-year-old baby with my husband while I went to the dressmaker's. After I got back from the dressmaker's, I went to the garage and got my baby, which was

---

[568]*Monroe News-Star*, 10 January 1923.

there alone. I took the baby and started home. Although the baby told me that the 'Ku Klux got papa,' myself and a woman friend and the baby started for Mer Rouge, but the baby kept repeating that the 'Ku Klux got daddy,' and told me that the men who got him wore black masks. We then decided to go back to Bastrop and ask about it. The people at the garage told us they knew nothing and we started back again to Mer Rouge."

"How many children do you have?"

"Two, a boy and a girl."

"What did you do when you reached your home?"

"I told some people that my husband had been kidnapped. Later I went to town and waited for him. He finally came and after we got home he told me about it. He was laughing and joking about it on the way home. When we got there he told me they had kidnapped him and blindfolded him and questioned him about shooting at Dr. McKoin. They threatened to hang him and finally he said, 'All right, go ahead.' They walked him into the woods and asked him if he recognized anyone. He recognized Skipwith. Later, they told him they believed his story was true and they then drove him back to town. He said before they brought him back they removed their masks."

"What Skipwith do you refer to?"

"My husband called him Captain, but I don't. I call him 'Mr. Skipwith' when I condescended to speak to him," Her eyes swept the courtroom looking for Skipwith. She told the court that she had been married for 12 years and that she was 31 years of age.

"Has your married life been happy?"

"It certainly has."

"Did you ever report this kidnapping?"

"No."

"And your husband seemed satisfied?"

"Yes, my husband thought the matter was ended. They had turned him loose and told him they were satisfied he knew nothing about the shooting of McKoin's car. He thought that was the end of it."

"What kind of suit was your husband wearing when he left you on August 24?"

311

He wore brown trousers and a yellow pengee shirt. He had on no coat. He bought it from McIlwain."

"Do you know anything that would throw light on the kidnapping of your husband on August 24 [1922]?"

"No."

"Had he ever received letters of warning of any kind?"

"No, but it was remarked after the first kidnapping in a picture theater in Mer Rouge that my husband 'needn't act so smart,' that 'they would get him.' Mrs Hugh Clark made that statement, I was told by several. Mrs. Clark said that when they 'got Mr. Richards again he wouldn't get off so light.' That remark was made the same week he was killed."

"Was your husband a member of the Klan?"

"No."

"Was he asked to join?"

"He had been asked to join but he refused."

"How are you maintaining your home?"

"I don't know."

"There is a report that you were unhappy when you were married."

"I deny it. He never mistreated me and we were contented."[569]

The *Monroe News-Star* also gave its version of the testimony of Mrs. T. F. Richards. It was basically the same, but her narrative of the first kidnapping event is worth reporting.

"How old is your baby?"

"She is now four years old."

"Did you ask for your husband?"

"No."

"How did she know about the Ku Klux?"

"She had heard me talking and reading about them at home. We left for our home in Mer Rouge, but the baby kept talking about the Ku Klux. 'Oh Mama, they came with them black masks on and got Daddy,' the baby would keep on saying. I became so worked up that I returned to Bastrop and hunted for my husband. I was later joined by my husband who said he had been taken out in the woods and held

[569]*The New York Times*, 11 January 1923.

for two hours."

"Did your husband tell you about being kidnapped?"

"No, except he said that they came and got him out of the garage, blindfolded him, and tied his hands. They took him out on the Monroe road. They asked him about the shooting at Dr. McKoin. He told them he knew nothing about it. They told him they were going to hang him. He told me that they walked him about the woods. He said he thought they were looking for a place to hang him. He told me that they then said they were satisfied with what he said. He then said they unmasked. They asked him if he recognized any of them. He said he told them he recognized Captain Skipwith, but none of the others."[570]

For some unknown reason, the following testimony of Mrs. Hugh Clark was found in *The New York Times*, but not in the *Monroe News-Star*. Mrs. Clark was called to the stand and verified making the remark that "Richards needn't be so smart. They got him once and they'll get him again." "If I did make it," said Mrs. Clark, "I meant nothing. I was like the rest of the women-talking and not knowing what I was saying."[571] Ms. Clark's testimony may seem insignificant in both content and inclusion. However, when it is considered in the totality of circumstance surrounding this open hearing, her innocent denial of importance of her statement and its inclusion into the testimony given is serious.

The New York Times reported the testimony of Harry Neelis, manager of a Bastrop auto repair shop. He testified that he was present in the shop when his employee, Thomas Richards, was kidnapped by the Klan on the first occasion. He said that he reported the incident to Sheriff Carpenter, whom he located on the steps of the courthouse some time later. He further testified he was told by Sheriff Carpenter that "it would be best not to talk about these things if you want to get along here."

Neelis related to the court how a state of stark terror existed between the towns of Bastrop and Mer Rouge for a number of months, and how the citizens of Bastrop lived in constant fear of an attack on their town by the residents of Mer Rouge, and how the same state of fear existed in Mer Rouge as the residents there awaited for what they felt was an imminent attack from Klansmen of Bastrop.

---

[570] *Monroe News-Star*, 10 January 1923.
[571] *The New York Times*, 11 January 1923.

Neelis said that he and a black helper were riding in his truck on August 18 on the outskirts of the city of Bastrop when they were held up by seven black-hooded men. He expressed the belief that they were waiting for Richards. They permitted him to continue on his journey, but later he was held up by three unmasked men, whom he identified as Jeff Burnett, Dr. B. M. McKoin and a Mr. Rogers. He said that they took him and his helper back to the location where they had been originally held up by the seven black-hooded men. Once reaching that location, he and his helper were told to return to Bastrop. As they were leaving, Neelis said he observed Burnett and Rogers don the black hoods and join the others.

"Tell us what occurred." instructed Mr. Coco.

"I was to go to Monroe that day and I told Richards to stay in the shop while I went to Mer Rouge to catch the train for Monroe. I got into a truck with a negro to go to Mer Rouge, and about a mile out we were stopped by hooded men on the Mer Rouge-Bastrop road."

"How many men were there?"

"There were seven."

"What color were their hoods?"

"Blue, I thought; they might have been black."

"Were they armed?"

"They had pistols and shotguns."

"What did they say?"

"Told us to get on to Mer Rouge and say nothing."

"Were you held up again?"

"Yes, further on by two men who were not masked."

"Who were they?"

"Jeff Burnett and Mr. Rogers."

"Do you know Rogers's first name?"

"No."

"What did they say?"

"Told us to go back the way we came."

"What did you do?"

"Our truck wasn't working well, so we got in the car with them and went back to the first place we were held up."

"Did Burnett and Rogers stay with you?"

314

"Yes."

"How did you get back to Bastrop?"

"I was supposed to walk, but I got into a car with Mr. Graves and Mrs. Harris."

"What became of your truck?"

"We left it there and went back with Burnett and Rogers. I asked enough questions to learn that they were after Richards. At first I thought they were highwaymen but later on the road I met a car and told the driver to call the sheriff. When we were stopped I asked the men if they were the Ku Klux band. I understood they were after Richards. I asked them to give Richards a chance and they intimated they would. I was sure they had the truck spotted and thought Richards would be in it. When I got back to Bastrop I saw Richards and told him about it and informed him that the Klan was after him. I suggested that we go to the sheriff's office for protection. A car driven by Fred Higgenbotham came out to where we were being detained on the road and after a conversation with Burnett and Rogers I was released. When Higgenbotham got there Burnett and Rogers put on their masks. I then went to Bastrop. I saw Fred in town later and I asked, 'Fred, who is doing all of this?' I was mad at the way they were trying to treat Richards. I warned him that no harm had better come to him. Later the masked men came to the garage and got him."

"Have you ever heard of any other disturbances here?"

"Yes, sir."

"Was the community quiet and peaceful?"

"After the kidnapping of the five boys the town was up in arms. Then there was talk of a clash between Mer Rouge and Bastrop."

"Did you report Richards's kidnapping?"

"No, I didn't know whom to report it to."

"Why didn't you report it?"

"I was told by a citizen to say nothing about the Klan if I wanted to get along in Bastrop."

"Did Richards ever talk to you about the kidnapping?"

"Yes, I asked him how the Klan treated him and he told me a few things about it. He said he was threatened with hanging and accused of shooting at Dr. McKoin. The leader, he said, declared that he believed Richards' story and they brought him

315

back. He was asked if he recognized any of the men and he told me he recognized six voices."

"Did he tell you who they were?"

"Yes, but I don't remember."

Not satisfied with that response, Mr. Guion pushed the witness to answer the question. After much prodding, he told the court that Richards had identified Dr. McKoin, Captain Skipwith, "Jim" Tisdale, and A. B. Campbell. Further questioning revealed that he and Campbell were close friends. Senator Warren continued the questioning by asking if all of the men that had held him up on the road were armed.

"They were all armed."

Neelis told Warren that he had asked Rogers whose car he was driving, and Rogers told him that he did not know. Neelis said that he was aware of the owner as a man who had sat in the courtroom on the previous day.

"Was this man's name Hill?"

"I believe so." Neelis went on to say that Hill resided in Spyker and that he was employed at the Southern Carbon Plant.

"You talk to Fred Higgenbotham afterwards?"

"I asked him at the shop to tell me who was responsible and what they intended to do. The first thing I did was to get Richards and tell him that the Ku Klux Klan were after him and for us to go over to the Sheriff's office where he might have protection. Richards had his little girl with him and he suggested that we wait until his wife came back. About that time the automobile came up to the garage. I went to them and told them to leave Richards alone. They went into the garage and led Richards out to an automobile. I was mad and warned them again to let Richards alone. About that time Rogers pointed a long shotgun at me and told me to step aside. They left with Richards."

"What were the conditions in Bastrop at that time? Wasn't the Klan very active?"

"Yes, the Klan was active and the courthouse was being guarded by citizens. They said the people of Mer Rouge were coming over to attack them. They did not ask me to take part in guarding the courthouse."

"What did Higgenbotham say to your questions?"

"He said, 'I can't tell you. I am awfully sorry. I had nothing to do with it. I was simply the transfer man ordered to make the [The last word of this sentence is unreadable.] .' "

"Did you ask Higgenbotham if it was Skipwith's work?"

"Yes, but he didn't talk. He mentioned nobody's name."

"How did you come to suggest Skipwith's name?"

"Well, everyone said he was the leader."

Neelis then told of seeing Captain Skipwith in the Klan regalia along with a group of men dressin Klan regalia on Gallion Road on evening. He said that he and others had followed several cars containing Klansmen and saw them enter a house on the road. When they emerged, he said they surrounded their car and demanded to know who the occupants were. Neelis said that he recognized Captain Skipwith, Laurie Calhoun, Dr. McKoin, J. D. Higgenbotham, 'Pink' Kirkpatrick, Bob Dade "and another Calhoun and one of the Hart boys" as having been part of the raiding party that night.

When questioned as to his whereabouts on the night of the bogus assassination on Dr. McKoin, he said that he was visiting the home of H. H. Clark. When asked if he knew the whereabouts of Thomas Richards on the same night, Neelis said that Richards was working for him in the shop at that time. He said that 'Tot' Davenport was also there, but he was not sure about Watt Daniel.

"Has anyone talked to you about the testimony you would give?"

Neelis said that he had had conversations, but he could not remember with whom. Not satisfied with this response, Warren pressed the witness until he admitted that he had spoken with 'Tot' Davenport, Bob Whipple and a number of others.

"Has anyone asked you if you could identify any of the masked men you've seen? Who has suggested it would be better for you not to identify anybody in these masked proceedings?"

"That wouldn't be fair; if possible, I'd rather not answer."

"You know who it was suggested by-name them."

"I think the men who have talked to me have done it for my own good."

"I know, but we want to know."

"Well, Allen Turpin, President and manager of the Turpin Motor Company and Bastrop Supply Company. He just told me to take a neutral stand. He was my employer and was advising me. [If you will refer to the original application form submitted to Klan headquarters to form Morehouse Klan No. 34, you will observe that the name "A. T. Turpin" appears on the list of names applying for membership. If this is, in fact, the same person, it would be easy to understand why the *News-Star* would have opted not to print the damaging testimony of this witness. Undoubtedly, he would have had a lot of clout, not to mention the amount of advertising dollars they might lose.]

"You are getting out of this parish because of the conditions here?"

"Yes, that's the reason."

"Were you ever asked to join the Klan?"

"I'm not eligible. I'm a Catholic."

In further testimony, Neelis said that Sheriff Carpenter witnessed the kidnapping of Richards from the garage from the very steps of the Bastrop courthouse. Sitting only three feet from the witness, the sheriff gave no acknowledgment of the witness's claim. Following his appearance, Neelis went immediately to the train station and left Bastrop, headed for New Orleans.

Relative to the climate of fear that existed in Morehouse Parish during the reign of the Klan, a *New York Times* reporter occasioned to speak with one of the residents. With the promise of anonymity, the source said that he was a member of the Klan, but only because he was afraid to quit. He also was of the opinion that convictions were impossible for the murders of Daniel and Richards because of the undisputed rule of the Klan. In his words:

> I am a businessman and a great deal of my business is with men known to be Klansmen. I believe Governor Parker is right, but I am afraid he cannot obtain a conviction in this parish. Klansmen will not convict Klansmen, in my opinion. I am one myself and I know the oath of the organization. There are more men like myself in town, men who would gladly quit the Klan, but if the Klan wins the fight and we resign, it would not be healthy for us around here.[572]

Klan Not Guilty of Morehouse Crime, Says K.K.K. Imperial Chief[573]

From Atlanta, Georgia came a statement from Dr. H. W. Evans, imperial wizard of the Ku Klux Klan. He supported the denials of the Klan officials in Louisiana of any connection with the Morehouse Parish kidnappings and murders of Watt Daniel and Thomas Richards. Dr. Evans expressed confidence that the Klan

---

[572]*The New York Times,* 11 January 1923.
[573]*Monroe News-Star,* 10 January 1923.

will be vindicated both "legally and in the minds of all fair-minded men."

THURSDAY JANUARY 11, 1923
Witness Was Told Mer Rouge Victims 'Knew Too Much'[574]
Hooded Band Member recognized Only Exalted Cyclops While Participating in Organization[575]
Women Called to Testify in Large Numbers in Klan Probe to Corroborate Leading Testimony[576]
Judge Odom Issues Order as to Effort to Shoot Andrews[577]
Ku Klux Klan Met in Court House at Bastrop, Asserts Fred Higgenbotham[578]

The New York Times reported that the state continued its attack on the Klan and in particular Captain Skipwith today with the testimony of William Norseworthy. He said that he heard Captain Skipwith say in effect that Daniel and Richards would not have been killed "if the boys had not been so smart." "We intended to give them a trial in the country for shooting at Dr. McKoin, but they got so smart and had so much to say at the ball game and over at Jim Norseworthy's barbecue at the Bonn Idee that the boys decided that they knew too much."[579]

Needless to say, this testimony created quite a stir in and around the courthouse, much the same as did the testimony of his brother Jim. Heretofore, Captain Skipwith was quite visible in and around the courthouse, moving confidently among his fellow Klansmen in an attempt to keep their confidence level high. After William Norseworthy's testimony, Skipwith was conspicuous by his absence from his usual hangouts. The level of anticipation increased when the news circulated that Skipwith was looking to have a powwow with Attorney General Coco allegedly to give an official accounting of the Morehouse Klan.

It was through the testimony of Norseworthy and later of J. L. Davenport that the state continued to paint the picture of how the Ku Klux Klan in Morehouse Parish had obtained a stranglehold on the community turning brother against brother, neighbor against neighbor. What had previously been a sleepy backwater enclave, where peace and good will reigned, had now become a hotbed of suspicion and hate, each being afraid to trust the other.

---

[574]*The New York Times*, 12 January 1923.
[575]*Monroe News-Star*, 11 January 1923.
[576]Ibid.
[577]Ibid.
[578]Ibid.

The testimony of J. L. Davenport revealed that numerous attempts had been made to make peace between the Klan and the civilian population. In his testimony, Davenport described Captain Skipwith as the seat of power in Morehouse Parish and as being the one on whom pleas for peace were registered. In an interesting side bar, Davenport told how the Mer Rouge delegation enlisted the aid of Judge Fred Odom, the very person sitting in control of the open hearing, to sue for peace. However, Judge Odom declined to become involved, telling the committee that "he was powerless to do anything."

With regard to Klan loyalty and influence, the testimony of Kelly Harp spoke for itself. Being one of the first witnesses of the day, Harp freely admitted his membership in the Klan and that he had been part of the mob who had held up Daniel, Andrews and Neelis on the Gallion Road. His loyalty to the Klan was displayed when he was asked to name other members of the Klan. To this, he refused. "I took an oath to keep the secrets of the Klan," said Harp, "and I owe it to my oath not to reveal the names." Harp was reminded by the attorney general's staff that he had just taken an oath before the court, and he was asked which oath did he consider more sacred. "I took an oath not to reveal the secrets of the Klan," he said, "and I won't break it."[580] It was clear to everyone in the courtroom that the Klan oath took precedence.

The *Monroe News-Star* called this day as "Ladies Day" at the open hearing in Bastrop. It was so labeled because the state announced today that it intended to summon at least eight women to give testimony. At the same time, the state announced the rather ambitious intent of having a total of 20 witnesses to testify today. Those scheduled to be called were Mr. and Mrs. Hugo Clark, Mrs. Hamilton, the mother of Addie May Hamilton, W. E. Hopkins, John Davenport, Mr. and Mrs. J. C. Nettles, Mrs. Inabet, Mrs. Lewis, Mrs. Groves, Mrs. Morris, Mrs. McIlwain, Fred Higgenbotham, George Sims, Conrad McDuffie, John Barham, Kelly Harp, R. L. Dade, Joe Davenport and W. R. Norseworthy. Many of those scheduled to be called were the result of the testimony given the previous day by Mrs. T. F. Richards, the widow of one of the victims.

The morning session of the open hearing began with the calling of Fred Higgenbotham. Higgenbotham was a courier for the Klan at the time of the deaths

---

[579]*The New York Times*, 12 January 1923.

of Richards and Daniel. During preliminary testimony, Higgenbotham told Special Assistant Attorney General Howard Warren that, at the time of the deaths of Richards and Daniel, he was the owner of a cafe and a taxi driver. On the surface, this appears to be a rather strange combination of occupations.

"Do you remember an occasion on or about the 17th of August when it was said T. F. Richards was taken by a band of hooded men from a garage in Bastrop?"

"Yes. I was on my way to Mer Rouge."

"Did you go to Mer Rouge?"

"No, I was held up by masked men right outside of town."

(It should be noted here that the witness is not speaking of the incident which occurred on August 17th which had been asked originally by Mr. Warren, but rather of the second kidnapping which occurred on August 24th on the Bastrop-Mer Rouge Road.)

"Were they armed?"

"Yes, pistols and shotguns. I was frightened and paid no attention to the number of guns."

"Where did they take you?"

"Out in the woods."

"Did you see anyone who was unmasked?"

"Yes. Harry Neelis."

"Who else did you see?"

"I don't know, the rest of them were masked. Neelis was away from them."

"What did they do with you?"

"They detained me for a little while and told me to go back to Bastrop."

"How were they dressed?"

"They had on black hoods."

"Are you a member of the Ku Klux Klan?"

"I am-a charter member of the Ku Klux Klan."

"Who are the officers?"

"I don't know any in particular."

"Do you mean to tell me that you don't know any of them?"

"Well, I know a few."

580Ibid.

321

"Name them."

"Captain Skipwith."

"He is the cyclop or the sheik of the Klan?"

"Something like that, I believe."

"You have attended Klan meetings?"

"Yes."

"Have you ever heard them discuss the conduct of the people of this parish?"

"No."

"Where do they hold their meetings?"

"Several places-I attended one in the courthouse."

"As I understand it, you have no recollection of what was discussed at any of these meetings?"

"I have not."

"Your mind is perfectly blank on these things?"

"Yes, blank."

"You don't know anything at all about any of the Klan affairs?"

"No."

Seeing that this line of questioning was leading nowhere, Mr. Warren returned to the topic of the kidnappings.

"What did you do when you returned from the place where the black hooded-men held you?"

"I went to my restaurant."

"Did you see Harry Neelis?"

"I did."

"What did he say?"

"He asked me what I was doing out there. I told him I had been held up."

"Did you see the black hoods seize Richards?"

"Yes."

"Why didn't you help him out?"

"I don't know; there were plenty of other people around who didn't help him out."

"Who did you see standing around?"

"I don't remember."

"Can't you name some of them?"

"I didn't pay any attention to them."

"Were you afraid?"

"I was not."

"You did not recognize any of the masked men in the automobile?"

"No."

"Did you see Captain Skipwith?"

"Not that I know of."

"When Neelis came to see you, he didn't ask you why they had taken Richards out?"

"He did not."

"Didn't he ask you why you had been taken out by Captain Skipwith?"

"He did not."

"Where were you night before last?"

"Home."

"Where were you before then?"

"Uptown. I went to my home about 9:15 o'clock."

"Did you get a telephone call when you was home?"

"Yes, about 10:30 o'clock. I told my mother to tell whoever called to call the boy who drives for me."

"Did he get the call?"

"I understand he did."

"Did you receive any more calls?"

"No, at least I did not hear the phone."

"Where were you on August 24?"

"I was in Bastrop."

"Did you on that day see any masked men passing through town?"

"I did not."

"What happened that night?"

"Someone told me while I was working in the cafe that five men were taken out and whipped."

"Did you attend a meeting of the Klan that night?"

"No."

"Where was the last meeting of the Klan that you attended?"

"In the courthouse."

"Who was there?"

"I don't remember."

"You don't know anybody?"

"Well, Captain Skipwith."

"He wasn't holding the meeting by himself, was he?"

"No."

"Who else was there?"

"I don't remember."

"What happened at the meeting?"

"I don't remember."

"You are a man of average intelligence?"

"I guess so."

"How did you join the Klan?"

"Just joined."

"Who invited you?"

"Nobody."

"How did you know there was a Klan?"

"A strange fellow told me about it."

"You attended the initial meeting?"

"Yes."

"Who was there?"

"I don't remember."

"You don't know anybody else?"

"I don't remember."

"You are well acquainted here-you know practically all the town?"

"I do."

"Where were you yesterday?"

"I was here in the courtroom."

"How long did you remain in the courtroom?"

"I left when Neelis was on the stand."

"Where did you go?"

"I carried a strange drummer to Mer Rouge."

"Where else did you go?"

"I carried Mrs. Andrew Burnett, her daughter and a stranger to Spyker."

"Who paid for the trip?"

"The stranger."

"How about the drummer, did you ever see him before?"

"Don't believe I have."

"Did you see him in the courtroom yesterday?"

"I did not."

"Did you and him discuss about the happenings on August 24, the day Daniel and Richards was kidnapped on?"

"The only thing he asked me was 'Is this the road Richards was kidnapped on?' "

"You are well acquainted with the parish roads, are you not?"

"I am."

"How do you get to Guy Boyd's place?"

Higgenbotham described the roads which would lead from the courthouse to the Boyd residence.

"How do you get to Lake LaFourche?" Mr. Warren asked a bit more intently as he descried the route to the lake.

"What was the condition of that road on August 24th?"

"I don't know."

"What was the weather conditions?"

"It was dry."

"Did you know T. F. Richards and Watt Daniel?"

"I did. I spoke with him, but [I] did not run with him."

"You know that they have been missing since August 24th?"

"Yes."

"Do you approve of what happened to Daniel and Richards?"

The witness looked down and moved his head from side to side, indicating that he did not. Because he did not respond verbally, the court stenographer asked him to do so. Higgenbotham then said, "No."

"Is the man, the stranger you took to Spyker, in the courtroom now?"

"I don't see him."

"Stand up and look around," Mr. Warren said as he turned his back to the witness and looked out into the spectator section.

The witness again responded by saying, "I do not see him."

325

"What relation are you to J. D. Higgenbotham?"

"A brother."

"Are you related to Joe Higgenbotham?"

"No," said the witness.

"Do you know Jeff Burnett?"

"Know him when I see him."

"You know Horace Rogers?"

"Yes, he lives at Spyker."

"Did you see either of these two men in Bastrop when you returned from being held up on August 18?"

"I did not."

"Did you see anybody in the masked party that resembled Burnett and Rogers?"

"No.:

"Did you see the sheriff on your return to Bastrop that afternoon?"

"I don't think so-I believe not."

"Did you report being held up to any officer?"

"No."

"Wasn't it unusual to be treated like that-you had not done anything that warranted such?"

"I don't think I had."

"Then why didn't you say something to the officers that you, a peaceable citizen, had been held up by highwaymen on the edge of town?"

"I thought probably Mr. Neelis would report it. There was no need to make a dive at it."

"Did Neelis come to Bastrop ahead of you?"

"No. I left him with the masked men."

"Have you heard of such things before? It was entirely new to you being held up on a public road?"

"It was."

"Yet, you did not think it was important to report to officers knowing Neelis was still behind held by a band of masked highwaymen?"

"I didn't think it was important,"

"Do you know that there had been a grand jury investigation about holdups on the Bastrop road? Why didn't you report it?"

"They didn't do me no harm."

"Don't you know you went out there voluntarily to consult with those masked men?"

"I did not."

"Now, didn't you go out there for the purpose of talking with those men?"

"I did not. I was on my way to Mer Rouge and was held up."

"Now on the night of August 24th you said you went home when you closed up your business?"

"I did."

"Did you stay there?"

"I did."

"Didn't you see Sidney White at the dance and tell him three of the five kidnapped that afternoon had been whipped and released, but you did not know where the others were?"

"I did not see Sidney White."[581]

"Now you say you are a charter member of the Morehouse Ku Klux Klan. Please tell me some of the good things the Klan has done since its organization?"

"Have run several bootleggers out."

"Negroes or white?"

"Both."

"Where did you run them to?"

"I don't know."

"Do you know of any flogging?"

"I only heard they kidnapped five men."

"The Klan wants to clean up the bad elements?"

"Yes."

"On the occasion you were held up when they had Neelis in their possession, why did you return to Bastrop?"

"They told me to."

"As an American, isn't it true that you knew where Richards was and you went to the masked band and told them he was still in Bastrop?"

---

[581] *Monroe News-Star*, 11 January 1923.

"I did not."

"They followed you?"

"Yes."

"And went to the garage and seized Richards?"

"Yes."

"Right in open daylight, business going on, people on the street and a band of hooded men dash to a garage and seize a man. Didn't that create a commotion?"

"The people were excited all right."

"You say the Klan ran the bootleggers out of the parish?"

"I did."

"Why didn't they bring those bootleggers to court?"

"I don't know."

"They had established a higher government, had they not?"

"I don't know."

"You remembered the conversation between yourself and Neelis?"

"I do."

"But you don't know anything that had transpired in the Klan lodge room?"

"I do not."

"What oath is superior-the one you took an hour or so ago or the Klan oath?"

"The oath I am under now."

"You said you were a good Klansman-wasn't your duty to report the masked holdups to officers?"

"I guess so."

"Didn't you tell them Neelis was not Richards and to let him go?"

"I did not."

"In what room in the courthouse did you attend [the] meeting of the K.K.K.?"

"In this one."[582]

The testimony of Higgenbotham was a clear indication of how the Klan had usurped the power of the local government and had supplanted it with that of the "Invisible Empire." Higgenbotham also indicated that the Klan was of a higher authority by his not reporting the actions of the masked men on the Bastrop-Mer Rouge road.

---

[582]Ibid.

According to *The New York Times*, the afternoon session began with Attorney General Coco recalling W. C. Andrews to the stand. He was asked about the newspaper reports that an attempt had been made on his life. Andrews told of finding an indentation in the driver's side door of his vehicle which he said "evidently had been made by a bullet."

Andrews claimed that he had not noticed the indentation and that it had been called to his attention by a Mer Rouge barber shop employee. Andrews said that he had no knowledge of being fired upon while in his vehicle, and that he had not received any threats since he had given his testimony. Andrews confirmed that Farland had detailed one agent to accompany him in his travels.

E. A. Farland testified that he had assigned an agent to investigate the matter of the indentation, and that he had expressed the opinion that "the indentation had been made by a bullet of large caliber." Farland said he reported the matter to Mr. Coco whom, he said, did not think any further action was necessary.

Entering the questioning, Judge Odom asked Farland who was his supervisor in this matter. Farland explained that he was under the direction of Mr. Coco.

"Who sent you here?"

"I don't care to answer that question. I came from Washington."

Judge Odom then interrupted the proceedings and spoke directly to the journalists, warning them against any publication that might result in causing witnesses to fear to testify. This admonishment of the press was an obvious attempt to downplay the attempt made on Andrews' life and could also be considered an attempt to gag and filter information sent out from Morehouse Parish. This was another indicator of the leanings of Judge Odom toward the Klan. His words generated "hand clapping and applause from the spectators' benches and the galleries" which were packed with Klansmen.

Judge Odom would not have been the first to use the bench to protect the Klan. At a private screening of the silent movie entitled "The Birth of a Nation," for President Harding at the White House, Justice Black of the Supreme Court boasted how he, as a member of the Old Hickory Klan in New Orleans, walked foot patrol with his rifle.[583]

---

[583] *The New York Times*, 12 January 1923.

The *Monroe News-Star* reported that Kelly Harp was next to testify. In preliminary questioning, Harp admitted to having been a member of the Klan, but that he had quit. He also admitted to being part of the band who participated in the holdup of Daniel, Andrews and Neelis on the Gallion road near Stampley.

"You were with the party?" asked Mr. Guion.

"Yes."

"Who else was there?"

"I don't believe I should be obligated to tell that. I was a Klansman then under oath."

"You heard Mr. Dade testify?"

"Yes."

"Was his testimony correct?"

"I am not in a position to say, because what he said happened was when I was a member of the Klan and under oath to that order."

"Did they favor whipping the boys?"

"The majority of them were."

"Why didn't they whip them?"

"Dade and myself and others did not favor it."

"Was Captain Skipwith there?"

"I positively refuse to answer."

"Is George Sims a Klansman?"

"Yes."

"Is Mr. Andrews a Klansman?"

"Yes."

"Who named you on a committee to run Miss Addie May Hamilton out of the country?"

"I can't say."

"Why do you refuse?"

"I don't want to do it."

"What next occurred?"

"The job was pulled that night."

"What did the party who asked you to ask the woman to leave the country say when you refused to join them?"

"He said he would take the matter up with the proper authorities of the Klan."

"On the Stampley Road, how were you dressed?"

"I wore a black mask."

Mayor Dade had testified that he was the only Klan member on the Stampley raid to wear a black hood. Clearly, he was mistaken as Harp's admission indicates.

"Who furnished you with this regalia?"

"Members of the Klan."

"You were a member of the Klan at that time as were the others?"

"Yes, sir."

"You take an obligation as Klansmen not to reveal anything?"

"Yes sir. I know I did."

"Why did you quit the Klan?"

"Because I don't believe in the mask. It leads to disorders. The Klan's constitution is all right, but its operations are all wrong."[584]

The New York Times' version of Harps' testimony is unusual in that it contained only a portion of what was reported by the *Monroe News-Star*.

"Did you take an obligation as a Klansman not to reveal anything?"

"Yes, sir, I know I did."

"Do you decline to reveal the names of Klansmen because of your allegiance to the Klan?"

"Yes, sir."

"You take a Klannish attitude toward one another?"

"Yes, sir, we are not supposed to disclose things."[585]

Although the testimony is shorter, these few extremely important lines in which Harp declares his allegiance to the Klan more important than to the United States Constitution were mysteriously absent from the *Monroe News-Star* version.

"Did anyone speak to you this morning as to what your testimony might be?"

"Mr. Calhoun spoke to me," he said. [Laurie Calhoun is the sheriff's deputy sent to bring back McKoin and is an avowed Klansman.]

"What did he say?"

"I don't remember."[586]

---

[584]*Monroe News-Star*, 11 January 1923.

[585]*The New York Times*, 12 January 1923.

[586]Ibid.

The *Monroe News-Star* reported that after Harp was dismissed, W. R. Norseworthy, brother of J. T. Norseworthy, took his place on the witness stand.

"Have you seen Captain Skipwith lately?" Mr. Guion asked.

"No, not lately."

"When did you last talk with Captain Skipwith?"

"In September in his home in Vaughn, Louisiana."

"What caused you to call on Captain Skipwith?"

"I was on a business trip and when I arrived in Spencer, Louisiana, I was told by Carey Spencer that Laurie Calhoun said for me not to go home until you have seen him at his ranch. I went to Calhoun's ranch. John Spencer went with me. Calhoun told me that he had been in Bastrop and that he had heard that the Ku Klux were hunting me. He said that he found Dr. McKoin, John Keller and Roy Norris in Spencer looking for me with guns. They said that I was hired to kill 'Bunny' [Dr.] McKoin. I told Calhoun I wanted to speak with Skipwith. We came to Bastrop and told Sheriff Carpenter about what we had heard. He said he also heard that I attempted to kill Dr. McKoin. He told me where we could find Skipwith. We went to Vaughn and that's when I met Skipwith."[587]

Again we see a citizen attempt to seek help from Sheriff Carpenter only to realize that he was either unwilling or lacked the courage to challenge the Klan. The agony and frustration of those seeking shelter from the Klan can only be imagined. During the testimony of the witnesses, the state attempted to show that a "super government" had taken control of northeast Louisiana. The testimony will show conclusively that rather than a super government, Captain J. K. Skipwith had taken the reigns of government from the duly elected officials and had set himself up as dictator. Time and time again testimony reveals how all information was channeled to Skipwith, and how it was he who ultimately decided who stayed and who left, who was good or bad, and finally who lived or died in Morehouse Parish.

Norseworthy continued: "Skipwith said that it was lucky for me that I had two friends in this country. I asked him about the killing report. He said that he had a letter that said I had been hired by citizens of Mer Rouge to kill him and Dr. McKoin. Captain Skipwith said he had investigated and found out the report was true. The captain said he had six men in Arkansas spotting me."

---

[587]*Monroe News-Star*, 11 January 1923.

"How much did he say was reportedly paid you to take the job to kill Dr. McKoin by the citizens of Mer Rouge?"

"$1,500, Mr. Whipple heading the list with $500. The report said, he said, that I was paid $150 in advance."

"Did you discuss anything about the Klan?"

"Yes. We discussed about the disappearance of Daniel and Richards. He told me Daniel and Richards knew too much and had talked too much for their own good."

"Did he say the boys had killed themselves?"

"No."

"Are you a member of the Klan?"

"No, but Skipwith told me that I would make a good member."

"Did you ask for protection?"

"I did and he gave me his assurance that everything was all right."

"You planned to move to Texas?"

"Yes."

"Why?"

"Because conditions were so bad, that when a man left his home in the morning, he did not know if he would ever return. Things were mighty bad."

"When did you first hear about the kidnapping of Daniel and Richards?"

"The next day."

"When did you change your mind about going to Texas?"

"After I talked it over with Captain Skipwith and he had assured me of protection."

Dr. McKoin, who has had a place in the gallery since the beginning of the open hearings, listened intently to the testimony given by Norseworthy. It was noticed that the smile, which had graced his face at the beginning of the hearings, had been replaced by a permanent frown.

"Now, about Dr. McKoin being at Spencer, armed, looking for you, tell us about that."

"The two Spencer boys said Dr. McKoin was here with his gun pretending to be making insurance examinations. Roy Norris and John Keller were with him. They said that Dr. McKoin questioned them at length about me, about my character."[588]

Judge Odom called lunch recess. When court resumed, *The New York Times* reported that the next witness called was Leon Davenport. Mr.Guion of the attorney general's office began the questioning.

"Were you a member of committees to adjust differences in the community?"

"Yes, Mr. A. L. Smith asked me to see him in Mer Rouge, and I was told that my brother Hugo was the head and brains of the anti-Klan in Morehouse. He said he was just anxious to clear the Davenports. I told him I was going to call on him to go further and help us."

"Did Davenport deny the reports?"

"He did. Later there was a second conference and Smith suggested a committee to meet Dr. McKoin and Skipwith."

"Did they appoint a committee?"

"Yes. R. L. Dade, J. A. Davenport, Flood Madison, Dr. Palmer and Dr. Barham, to go to Monroe to confer with McKoin and Skipwith to determine authorship of letters attributed to Hugo Davenport."

"But you didn't attend that conference. Tell us about one that you did attend."

"Well, I was at another one at which Flood Madison was present. He's one of the best citizens in the state."

"How are conditions in Mer Rouge now?"

"Bad, mighty bad."

"What brought about this condition?"

"Threats from the Klan and the kidnapping of those two boys."

"Did you get some letters about this situation?"

"I did, from A. L. Smith, but the letters were destroyed."

"Did you get a letter from Smith that you showed around to the boys who had been threatened?"

"Yes."

"Where is that letter?"

"I destroyed it."

"Why did you destroy it?"

"Smith asked me to."

---

[588]Ibid.

"Was Smith a member of the Klan?"

"He was."

"Tell us what was in the letter?"

"Well, he told me about a conversation he'd had with Skipwith, that some of the boys hadn't lived up to their agreement."

"What was the agreement?"

"Smith said that Skipwith had told him of certain people who were going to be sent out of the community, and that he had vouched for A. C. Whipple's future conduct in order to prevent his banishment. Tom Milner was another man ordered out; also Walter Campbell."

"Did Milner leave?"

"Yes."

"Why?"

"Because Skipwith said to."[589]

The New York Times also recorded the testimony of seven witnesses on this date that could not be located in the *Monroe News-Star*. The testimony came from J. A. Davenport, John Barham, Carey Calhoun, George Sims, Conrad Duffy, Hugh Clark and J. C. Nettles. The testimony of Davenport is the first to be presented.

J. A. Davenport, brother of Leo Davenport, told of attending five of these peace conferences in the company of Dade, Madison, J. E. Johnson and Judge Odom, the very person sitting in the judgment seat in this hearing. As these revelations unfolded concerning Odom, it would appear to the average person that he may not be totally unbiased, and perhaps the attorney general should have asked Odom to remove himself because of a possible conflict of interest.

This witness testified that the purpose of these peace conferences was to mediate between the citizens of Bastrop and Mer Rouge. In actuality, the citizens were seeking some method of peaceful coexistence with the Klan. As testified by another witness, this witness also claimed that Judge Odom said that he could do nothing. Present at this conference in Monroe were Dade, John P. Parker of Monroe, A. L. Smith, Dr. McKoin, Captain Skipwith and Flood Madison.

---

[589] *The New York Times*, 12 January 1923.

"We were told by Captain Skipwith that Whipple, Campbell and Milner would have to get out."

"What do you mean by getting out?"

"Getting out of the country, quitting their homes and their friends and their business."

"Just what was said by Skipwith? Did he hold himself as a spokesman for the Klan?"

"I never held him in any other light."

"He was regarded as Klan spokesman?"

"Yes."

"How many Klansmen were present?"

"I understand that Skipwith, Parker and Dr. McKoin were members."

"Are you a Klansman?"

"No, and I have never been."

"Was there another conference?"

"Yes, Flood Madison, A. N. Williams, N. P. Clarke and J. A. Davenport were also present. Ten delegates were picked for a meeting to be held later, but that meeting never was held. We got a telegram that night saying if we would come over to Bastrop everything would be fixed. We went to Madison's office and met with Captain Skipwith. Skipwith made the statement that Whipple and Campbell would have to leave Mer Rouge. It was then I stood for Campbell. Will Pugh vouched for Campbell. By that I agreed that Whipple would be persuaded to stop his anti-Klan talk and Pugh did the same for his man. It was their anti-Klan talk that embittered Skipwith against the men. The conditions at the time were bordering on chaos. We did not think our courts were functioning properly and we discussed, because our children's lives were in danger, whether to request Governor Parker to declare martial law."

"What became of Milner?"

"He went away, and I don't think he ever came back."

"Captain Skipwith, then, held sovereignty over the community?"

"Well, testimony here makes it look something like that."

"Was this a peaceful, neighborly community before the Ku Klux Klan?"

"It certainly was."

"In your opinion, has there ever been any necessity for an invisible empire in this community at any time during the five years of your residence?"

"I have never seen any necessity for it."[590]

Davenport was dismissed and John Barham was called to the stand. He said that he had had a conversation with Marshall Mott of Oak Ridge, in which Mott told him of an encounter he had had with a traveling man (salesman). He said Mott told him that he had given a ride to the man, and, during the course of the ride, the man asked Mott, "What did you people do with the men you carried to the lake last night?"[591] This was all of the testimony recorded from this witness.

After Barham, Carey Calhoun was called. He said that he had heard allegations of misconduct against W. R. Norseworthy and of accompanying Norseworthy to Vaughn to visit Captain Skipwith.

"Had Norseworthy been spotted by the Klan?"

"Well, two men had been sent to look him up."[592] No other testimony was recorded from this witness.

After Calhoun, George Sims was called to the stand. He proudly testified that he was a Klansman.

"Are you willing to disclose any information about the Klan activities in which you have taken part?"

"I guess so."

"Were you approached regarding a plan to get Addie May Hamilton out of Mer Rouge?"

"I was."

"Were you asked to participate?"

"I was."

"Did you?"

"I did not."

"Did you ever take part in any Klan proceedings?"

"I've attended two meetings of the Klan: one between here and Monroe, the other near Mer Rouge."

"Did you ever have equipment or regalia of the Klan?"

---

[590]Ibid.
[591]Ibid.
[592]Ibid.

"I had a white regalia."

"Where were you on August 24?"

"At the ball game in Bastrop."

"Did you travel the Bastrop-Mer Rouge road on the way home?"

"Yes."

"Anything happen?"

"My car was stopped and I saw them get Daniel."

"You saw him on a truck?"

"Yes."

"How many men were on the truck?"

"I don't know. I knew Daniel. The other I was told was Richards. I saw the black-hooded men, but I didn't recognize them."[593]

After Sims came Conrad Duffy. He said that he attended the barbecue in Bastrop on August 24. He said he went to Monroe after the game and was returning home around 11 p.m. by way of the Bastrop-Monroe Road first and then transferred to the Rayville road, and eventually arrived home at about 1 a.m. While on the Rayville Road, he said he passed a Ford truck and another car not far from Mott's residence. He said they were headed toward Oak Ridge.

"Anyone in the rear of the truck?"

"I can't say."

"See any men in the car?"

"Four or five. I thought they were negroes, but Mott claimed they were white men with black masks. I wanted to turn back after them, just to prove they were negroes but we decided not to."

"How far from the Lake LaFourche ferry was it that you met them?"

"About two miles."[594]

Duffy was dismissed, and Hugh Clark was called to the stand. Clark told of taking a trip to Little Rock, Arkansas, where he met Addie May Hamilton, who was living with her sister in Little Rock. Ms. Hamilton was the young girl that had been driven out of Mer Rouge by Dr. McKoin and "Pink" Kirkpatrick. On this trip, Clark was accompanied by W. E. Hopkins. During the visit with Ms. Hamilton, Clark said she told them of her abduction and said on more than one occasion that

---

[593]Ibid.

she had positively recognized Dr. McKoin and "Pink" Kirkpatrick as part of the group that had kidnapped her.

"She wanted to return home and she asked me and Hopkins about it. I told her that I would try to make it possible for her to come back."

"When you got back to Mer Rouge, what arrangement did you make?"

"I talked with several I thought were Ku Kluxers to see if it was satisfactory for her return, and they seemed to think it was all right. Later I got a paper authorizing the return to her mother. The paper was signed by twelve Klansmen. I sent the paper on to her and went to see Captain Skipwith, who said it would be all right-he had no objections. I gave this word to her and she came home."

"To whom did you talk-that is, the men you thought were Klansmen?"

"I talked to Mr. L. T. Snider, Mr. G. M. Sims and Mr. W. P. 'Pink' Kirkpatrick. I talked to several others too."

"Did any of these or anyone else tell you how she had been sent away?"

"I didn't ask them. They didn't mention it."

"When did you join the Klan?"

"After I got back from Little Rock, where I saw her."

"After these people acquiesced in your proposal that the girl return, she was still fearful, wasn't she?"

"Yes, she wanted to be sure she wouldn't be harmed."

"To whom did you present the petition for her return?"

"There were six or seven I met."

"Who signed it-did Dr. McKoin sign it?"

"I think so. I can't remember all of the names. Sims, Kirkpatrick, Snider signed it."

"Whom did you find to be members?"

"I don't know. There was Sims. Doggone it, there is so many I can't remember them."

Clark told of having attended only two meetings of the Klan, but he claimed to be unable to recall any the identities of the persons who were in attendance. One of the meetings was held in the forest approximately four miles from Mer Rouge, and the second took place in an "oil mill" within the city limits of Bastrop.

---

[594]Ibid.

"Who presided?"

"I don't know. There were too many there for me to notice any in particular."

"Were they masked?"

"Some of them."

"Can't you give us some names of Klan members?"

"No."

"Is Mr. Kirkpatrick a member?"

"I think so."

"How about McKoin?"

"I think so. I believe I saw him at my first meeting."

"How many Klansmen were present at the first meeting?"

"I don't know, maybe three or four hundred-the woods were full of them."

"When you passed this petition around giving acquiescence for the return of Addie May Hamilton, you passed it only to Klansmen?"

"Yes."

"Then afterward you went to Captain Skipwith and showed him the petition of the citizens of Mer Rouge?"

"Yes."

"Why did you go to Captain Skipwith?"

"To make sure everything would be all right with the proper party. He was supposed to be the head of the Klansmen."

"You went to Captain Skipwith as a Klansman?"

"I am sure I had joined the Klan then."

"You signed the petition, didn't you?"

"Yes."

"As a Klansman?"

"Possibly. I'm not positive."

"Where were you on August 17, the day Richards was kidnapped by the Klan?"

"God knows-I heard about the kidnapping of Richards about 5 o'clock, maybe 4:30 that evening."

"Had you information that it was contemplated?"

"I had not."

"You heard about the attempted assassination of Dr. McKoin?"

"Yes. The same night, about a half hour after it happened."

"Where did you see McKoin?"

"At the home of Dr. Clark. It was between 10 and 12 o'clock Dr. Clark phoned me."

"Who did you find there?"

"Dr. Clark, Dr. McKoin and Kirkpatrick."

"How did McKoin describe it?"

"He said he was given a false call and was shot at after returning."

"Did you see the car?"

"Yes."

"Was it shot?"

"It was. There were marks showing there were several shots. One went through the car from the front. I first thought that someone had shot to scare him, but afterward I got a searchlight and examined the car. Then I saw there had been several shots. There was evidence of a charge of buckshot. Some of the shots struck the frame on top. The curtains showed the effects of the fire too. There was evidence that someone had fired after the car passed."

"What was McKoin's position?"

"He said he was leaning on the wheel: that was his explanation for the shot not striking him."

"Would the bullets that struck the back of the curtain and the back of the seat have struck the driver if he had been sitting upright?"

"Yes, I think so."

"Had you formed any suspicions?"

"Yes, against the bootleggers who had written him threatening letters."

"Had you ever heard him intimate that his suspicions were directed against any certain person?"

"No, I asked him and he said he didn't know who was responsible."

At the behest of Mr. Warren, Clark traced his travels on the date of August 24, the day that Daniel and Richards were kidnapped and murdered. He was able to place himself at specific locations, while he seemed unable or unwilling to at other times be more specific. He was, however, emphatic about fixing his attendance at a Masonic lodge meeting held on the night of the kidnappings and murders of Daniel and Richards.

"Did you have any fear of arrest?"

"No."

"Well, why did you want to know for sure where you were that night?"

"I just wanted to know. There were all sorts of rumors. Everyone in Mer Rouge was going to be arrested."

"But why should rumors that many were going to be arrested arouse you? You weren't afraid, were you?"

"No, but I wanted to know where I was."

"Someone told you were at the Masonic lodge that night, did he?"

"I don't remember."

"You have no positive recollection of anyone there that night?"

"No positive recollection."

"Were you in Bastrop on the night of August 24?"

"No."

"Did you make the statement in the streets of Bastrop that you could name six men responsible for the shooting of Dr. McKoin?"

"I may have."

"Why?"

"I think you are making it too strong. I don't remember saying that."

"Whom did you suspect?"

"I won't say. It was only a suspicion."

"Then your suspicion was based on your imagination?"

"I guess so."

"Were you on good terms with Daniel and Richards?"

"Yes, I never had any trouble with either."

"Did you make any move toward an investigation?"

"No, sir, we were kind of used to shooting and disturbances."

"Then it was a common thing?"

"Not exactly."

Clark categorically denied that he had ever participated in any raids by the Klan, but he did admit that he had seen black-hooded bands in action in and around Mer Rouge and Bastrop. He admitted that he did have two conversations with Captain Skipwith concerning the kidnappings of Daniel and Richards at committee meetings, as he said, "to straighten things out." He denied knowing any of the participants in either of the kidnapping episodes, but he did admit to being highly agitated concerning the alleged attempt on the life of Dr. McKoin, and he seemed to contradict his earlier statement by saying that he did not like Daniel or Richards. After the disappearance, he admitted he made the statement that the incidents had occurred due to "bad local conditions."

"Is Mer Rouge restless now?"

"The people are restless."

"You are in sympathy with the State in this hearing?"

"I am."[595]

The last of these witnesses unrecorded in the *Monroe News-Star* was J. C. Nettles, a fisherman at Lake LaFourche. He was the final witness for the day. He testified being among a group of motorists who were stopped by about 15 black-hooded men as he and the others were leaving the baseball game and barbecue at Bastrop on August 24. He was ordered out of his vehicle, and, while standing awaiting his release, he heard a member of the band say that the group had apprehended Watt and old man Daniel. Not long afterwards he was allowed to go on his way.[596]

Atlantic City Man Warned by Ku Klux[597]

Reports from Atlantic City, New Jersey indicated that the Ku Klux Klan had sent a warning to Christopher Carvis, manager of the Garden Inn Hotel, which had been raided as a disorderly house by the police. The letter warning read: "Please stop bootlegging and run a decent place. First and last notice." The letter was signed with the initials "K.K.K." The letterhead carried the words Imperial Palace, Invisible Empire, Knights of the Ku Klux Klan, Atlanta, Ga. The envelope was postmarked Atlantic City. Recently James Lightfoot, a black attorney, who had been active in fighting the proposed segregation of black students, received a warning letter from the Klan.

Would Arm Against Klan[598]

Abram B. Marcadell, former Commissioner of Taxation of Middletown, New York, issued a statement suggesting two means for protection of citizens against the

---

[595] Ibid.
[596] Ibid.
[597] Ibid.
[598] Ibid.

Ku Klux Klan. One would be apply to the county judge for the right to carry a gun. The other would be for each man to report any threats to the chief of police and that any body of men molesting him will do so at their own peril.

Harvard Negro Ban Declared Final: Associates of President Lowell Say There is No Reason for Reopening Subject.[599]

It is generally agreed in Harvard official circles today that a letter sent by President A. Lawrence Lowell to Roscoe Conkling Bruce in regard to the admission of his son to a Harvard freshman dormitory hit the nail on the head. Harvard does not wish negroes in those dormitories, as two or three negroes can attest, for they were told, after receiving certificates of admission, that a mistake had been made and that they would have to seek quarters elsewhere. Associates here today said Dr. Lowell had made the matter very clear and no other statement was necessary.

FRIDAY JANUARY 12, 1923

Klan Usurped Law in Reign of Terror, Mayor Testifies[600] [601]
Dr. M'Koin, Skipwith and Others Named by Bob Dade as Men Who Held Up and Disarmed Daniels[602]

The *Monroe News-Star* recorded that the first witness to be called this date as Mayor Dade of Mer Rouge. In preliminary questioning, Dade said that he was a barber by trade and that he assumed the office of mayor of Mer Rouge in May of 1922, from his predecessor, Dr. B. M. McKoin.

"Are you a member of the Klan?" asked Mr. Warren.

"I was."

"What made you join."

"Thought it was a good thing, but I objected to its methods and operations."

"Since its organization, hasn't there been a change among the people?"

"Yes, sir. It has caused bad blood. It has separated the people. Made enemies out of good friends."

"At this time, do you consider the parish at peace?"

"No, sir, I consider it in mighty poor condition."

"What is the condition in your home town today?"

"Mighty bad, it's in a critical condition."

"Do you remember the reported attempt to kill Dr. McKoin?"

---

[599]*The New York Times*, 12 January 1923.
[600]Ibid.
[601]*Monroe News-Star*, 12 January 1923.
[602]Ibid.

"Yes, sir, it caused quite a stir."

"What do your people believe?"

"The opinion of the people of the town is that they do not believe he was shot at."

"Then it is believed that he fired the shots himself?"

"Yes, sir."

"Did you examine the car?"

"Yes, sir."

"How did it look?"

"The prevailing opinion is that the shots were fired while nobody was behind the wheel."

"What kind of shots were they?"

"Buckshots."

"Do the people of Mer Rouge think Watt Daniel, T. F. Richards or W. C. Andrews had anything to do with the alleged attempt?"

"They do not."

"Did you ever hear of anybody being flogged by the Klan?"

"Yes, sir."

"Bootleggers?"

"Yes, sir. One white and two negroes were captured. They put the white in jail and they whipped the negroes."[603]

Dade said that he attended a meeting in Monroe which had been called for the expressed purpose of clearing the name of A. H. Davenport of Mer Rouge, whom Skipwith had labeled the "brains of the Anti-Klan element," and Skipwith had also laid the attempt to assassinate Dr. McKoin at the feet of Davenport. During questioning, Dade said that he was acquainted with both A. H. Davenport and A. L. Smith.

"In a conversation with Leon Davenport, did Smith state to him that A. H. Davenport was charged with being the brains of the Anti-Klan element in the parish, and responsible for the attempt to kill Dr. McKoin?"

"Yes, sir, he certainly did. He said that he had obtained this information from his son. Mr. Davenport came to me to try to clear the Davenport family."

---

[603] Ibid.

"Was there a meeting held?"

"Yes, we met at Monroe for the purpose of clearing up the Davenport matter. Floyd Madison, J. L. Smith, Dr. McKoin, Dr. Barham, John Parker, Captain Skipwith and myself."

There is an interesting side bar that will be reported a few days hence regarding John Parker. Parker was a former sheriff of Ouachita Parish. He was murdered less than 10 days after this testimony was given, by his cousin Cary Calhoun. This is the same Cary Calhoun whose testimony was given the previous day in the Daniel/Richards case. According to testimony given in the coroner's investigation, Calhoun killed Parker in a drunken fight at the cabin of Bessie Jones. It was rumored that Jones may have been Parker's black mistress. This would also have been a driving force to whitewash this incident, which did, in fact, happen not long after the coroner's inquest.

"Who was the spokesman?"

"Mr. Smith."

"What did Captain Skipwith say?"

"He said that he would see that the Davenports were protected, but that they would have to tell Mr. Whipple, Mr. Campbell and Milner to leave town. I told him I would deliver his message."

Assistant Attorney General Seth Guion took over questioning the witness as the topic changed to the Klan raid in Stampley when Watt Daniel, W. C. Andrews and Harry Neelis followed the Klan and were later questioned.

"Can you say whether J. D. Higgenbotham was with the band?"

"I am not positive as to whether he was there and can't say."

"What was the purpose of the trip?" continued Mr. Guion.

"We started up to investigate a report that a negro was running a gambling house in which white persons were permitted to gamble with negroes."

"Did you find that condition to exist?"

"No, the house was dark."[604]

Mr. Guion then moved the line of questioning to the holdup of Daniel, Andrews and Neelis by the Klan. He asked Dade what caused he and the other Klansmen to notice Neelis, Daniel and Andrews that night.

---

[604]Ibid.

"Neelis, Daniel and Andrews had stopped their automobile up the road and were sitting in the car. Some of the men approached and asked them who they were."

"Were they whipped?"

"No, there was no violence, but their guns were taken away from them."

"Was there anything else contemplated or suggested?"

"There was some talk of giving them a whipping, but I said, 'Fellows, that will not do. I have known those boys all the time and I cannot stand for that'"

"Who gave them a lecture?"

"Captain Skipwith."

"What kind of lecture?"

"A moral one, about drinking and gambling."

"Did Kelly Harp have anything to say?"

"He spoke his mind. He did say they were his friends and did not want to see them punished."

"How was the party organized to go on this gambling raid?"

"I ran into them in front of the bank in Mer Rouge. They asked me to go with them. They were in three automobiles."

"Where did you get your hood and gown?"

"Edward Ivy gave it to me. He used to live in Bastrop. He had an extra gown in his car. There were some men in the cars I did not know. Laurie Calhoun was there, I believe."

"Did they pick up anybody else in Mer Rouge?"

"Yes, sir. Dr. McKoin."

"He provided himself with a mask?"

"Yes, sir."

"All of you were masked?"

"Yes."

"What color were these masks?"

"Mine was a black one."

"Were there other black ones?"

"I believe I had the only one."

"You are certain of this?"

"Yes."

"Who else joined you?"

"Kelly Harp."

"What did they call themselves-the band as a whole?"

"Members of the K.K.K."

"Who was the leader?"

"Captain Skipwith."

"Who was it who took the pistol from Watt Daniel?"

"I don't know."

"You said Captain Skipwith talked with Daniel, Andrews and Neelis?"

"Yes, sir, he was the only one doing the talking."

"What was the name of the negro you were going to call on?"

"I don't know."

"What date was this?"

"In 1922."

"When did you join the Klan?"

"In March or April of 1922."

"Was that the first affair of the sort you had taken part in?"

"Yes, sir."

"Where did you get your Klan regalia, your white hood and white cloak?"

"My wife made it."

"Had you ever participated in any parades?"

"Once in Monroe."

"Repeat as near as you can what was said to Daniel, Andrews and Neelis about giving them a whipping."

"The best of my knowledge, they accused them of following them; someone said they should be given a thrashing. I said that would not do. They were my friends. I told Captain Skipwith that too."

"Who suggested the thrashing?"

"Ed Ivy."

"Did the three boys have anything to say?"

"Yes. Watt did some talking about making whiskey. He said he had quit and had not made any in a certain length of time."

"There was nothing of an altercation between the three boys and Klansmen?"

"No."

"Did you quit the Klan?"

"Yes, sir. I was only in it two months. My friends accused me of being an informant which resulted in raids on a negro grocer. Hooded men in daylight came into Mer Rouge and staged this raid. They told the negro to quit letting white men gamble in his store."

"How were they dressed?"

"In white."

"Was that before the attempt on Dr. McKoin's life?"

"Yes, sir."

"How soon after holding up Daniel, Neelis and Andrews was the attempt on Dr. McKoin's life?"

"Oh, several months."

"You received two letters after the kidnapping and final disappearance of Richards and Daniel?"

"Yes. They came through the mails."

At this point, two letters were delivered to the clerk of court for identification purposes, but were not yet entered into evidence. Because Mr. Dade did not bring his glasses with him to the hearing, Assistant Attorney General Warren read the letters.

Rayville, Sept. 7, or 8 (in pen and ink.)

To the mayor and good citizens of Mer Rouge
Mer Rouge, La.

You are wallowing in a cess pool of corruption and lawlessness that has become a menace to the entire parish and surrounding country. You are shielding within your gates men who live in open concubinage with negro women, who manufacture and sell whiskey, who formulate plots to assassinate good citizens in the night time and who are deluging the good, law-abiding citizens of your parish with written and oral threats against their lives. The condition of affairs must be rectified at once or we will sweep down upon your town and wipe out the organization that is responsible for these conditions and which are please to call themselves 'the anti-Ku Klux Klan.'

We know every one of the men who formulated and attempted to execute the plot to assassinate Dr. McKoin. Two of them have passed into obscurity and the balance will soon follow unless they read between these lines and leave your community while the leaving is good.

The Letter was signed "Regulators"[605]

The date on this letter is important because it is a full two weeks after the August 24th kidnappings and murders of Daniel and Richards. The passage of the letter which said, "two of them have passed into obscurity" was a direct reference to the murders of Daniel and Richards. This was another open indicator of the boldness and the belief maintained by Skipwith, McKoin and other Klan rank and file that they could act with impunity with regard to their foul and twisted deeds.

The other letter read as follows:

Hon. Mayor, Mer Rouge, La.
Dear Sir:
We are reliably informed that there is in your town a bunch of disreputable characters who call themselves Anti-K.K.K.s, who openly violate the laws by making whiskey, living in concubinage with negro women who are making a practice of writing some of the best citizens of your parish obscene, insulting and threatening letters and who actually attempted to assassinate one of your leading citizens and physicians recently, forcing him to leave the community.
This is to notify you as mayor of Mer Rouge that we will give you ample time to clean up this lawless condition of affairs and if you fail to do so, we will bring a thousand men down there and do the job for you right.
The names of the men who have sat at the roundtable and planned and submitted the planning of the assassination of Dr. McKoin are known to us. We have had able men to get all the data up so now we know what all have said and done, and we will attend to them in due time.

This letter was signed "100 percent Americans."[606]

After Mr. Warren had read the letters into the record, Mr. Guion continued with the questioning of Mayor Dade.

"When did you last see Ed Ivy?"

"Last Friday in Bastrop."

"The night they said they were going to give the boys a whipping, did they have their whipping strop along?"

"Yes, sir."[607]

---

[605]*Monroe News-Star*, 12 January 1923.
[606]Ibid.
[607]Ibid.

The New York Times reported Dade's testimony to be similar to that recorded by the *News-Star* with one important exception. It appears that the *News-Star* overlooked a portion of Dade's testimony in which he identified Deputy Sheriff Calhoun, an avowed Klan member and the same man who went to Baltimore and brought Dr. McKoin back to Louisiana, as part of the Klan raiding party that evening. Also, the final portion of Dade's testimony recorded by *The New York Times* is worth registering.

"Did you quit the Klan?"

"Yes."

"Why?"

"Well, there was a raid in Mer Rouge against a nigger grocery store where there was gambling and I was accused of reporting it. Then I saw the Klan was creating disorder all over the country and I wanted to get out."

"You were not on the raid at the nigger's place?"

"No."

"Were the raiders masked?"

"Yes."[608]

It should be noted that both *The New York Times* and the *Monroe News-Star* versions of Dade's letters were identical.

Exalted Cyclops of Morehouse Klan asks Attorney General to Confer on Kidnapping Atrocity[609]

It was reported this day in Bastrop that state's attorneys announced that Captain Skipwith had requested a conference with Attorney General Coco and his assistants in connection with Klan activities in Morehouse Parish. Skipwith was said to have requested the conference to establish that the operations of the black-hooded band was not under the supervision of the Klan.

---

[608]*The New York Times*, 12 January 1923.
[609]*Monroe News-Star*, 12 January 1923.

SATURDAY JANUARY 13, 1923

Klan Raid Victim Dragged From Home, Says Skipwith[610]

Difference of Opinion Exists: Asserts A. L. Smith, as to Whether Daniel and Richards were Killed by Klan or M'Koin Friends[611]
Skipwith Request Meets Approval of Officials of State[612]
Conference with Attorney General Agreed to for Presentation of Klan Side is Called Off[613]
Skipwith Declared Men Not in Sympathy With Morehouse Klan Would be Beaten, Says Stuckey[614]

The New York Times reported that today's high point in testimony came from Alonzo Braddock. Braddock described himself as a farmer who had lived all of his life in Morehouse Parish. His connection with the Ku Klux Klan had to do with a midnight raid made on his home by Klansmen. He said that he and his family were asleep one morning in November of 1922. At about 2 a.m., they were awakened by men yelling and loud banging at his door. Braddock went to the window, and he saw a group of men, some standing back from the house yelling, and others beating on his door telling him to come out. Braddock said he shouted to them to wait until he was dressed and he would come out.

Not wishing to wait that long, the mob broke down his door and dragged him out half-dressed. He said he recognized their leader as Captain Skipwith.

"We want you for making whiskey," said Skipwith, according to Braddock.

Mrs. Braddock attempted to intervene on her husband's behalf, but to no avail. Despite her tearful pleas, the Klansmen remained firm that they were taking her husband. Braddock, fearful for his own safety, pleaded with Skipwith to bring him to Sheriff Carpenter if they believed he had been making whiskey. He also implored Skipwith to promise his wife that he would be safe and that no harm would befall him. Skipwith did finally give them his word that he would not be beaten and that they would transport him to Sheriff Carpenter.

Braddock was taken to the home of Sheriff Carpenter, along with four black men the Klansmen had also abducted. Carpenter did not argue with the Klansmen. He locked up the four blacks and brought Braddock back to his home, where he spent the night.

---

[610]Ibid.

[611]*Monroe News-Star*, 13 January 1923.

[612]Ibid.

[613]Ibid.

Braddock said that he was released the following morning without having been charged. He said that Carpenter had simply let him go. Upon returning to his home, he said he discovered his wife to be seriously ill, and his children terrified. Braddock told of the state of terror that his family then lived. He said that his wife became terrified each time a car came close to their house. He said she had pleaded with him to sell the farm and move to another area.

"I am anxious to leave this parish for good. I no longer feel safe here. I am nervous at night, my wife is afraid, and my children are frightened," said Braddock. According to reports, Braddock appeared to have aged considerably due to his experience. "It's the Klan," said Braddock, in explaining how his physical condition had deteriorated. It was learned from sources on the attorney general's staff after the hearing had ended for the day that research was being conducted to determine if under Louisiana law the entering of Braddock's home under the described circumstances might have been an offense eligible for the death penalty.

Later that afternoon, Captain Skipwith made it known that he would not be meeting with Attorney General Coco as he had said the previous day. This information seemed to take Coco by surprise.

"I have not been informed either by Captain Skipwith or his attorney about this and I will say that the calling off of the arranged interview was not the result of any step taken by myself or any members of my staff," said Coco.[615]

The *Monroe News-Star* reported that an anonymous letter received today by the attorney general's staff has caused quite a stir. The unsigned letter claimed that five unnamed men were involved in the murders of Daniel and Richards and further made the assertion that none of the five were in Morehouse Parish. Although this letter had not been viewed by persons other than staff members of the attorney general, informed sources claimed that the much touted "torture device" did not exist. According to the author of the letter, the torture device was but "a simple windlass, through which passed a small steel [pipe/rod- this section is unreadable] ----was used in punishing the Mer Rouge victims." If the details in the letter were true, which is quite possible, then it is easy to understand why no trace of the machine was ever found.

---

[614]Ibid.

[615]*The New York Times*, 14 January 1923.

Commenting on the belief that Klansmen from Arkansas had participated in the kidnappings and murders of Daniel and Richards, Senator Stuckey told of a recent murder trial in Hamburg, Arkansas, where he defended F. S. Bullen, [Duncan?] Richardson and Ben Richardson, all anti-Klan, convicted of killing Ira Culp, a Klansman. All three were awaiting a Feb. 2 execution date in Little Rock following the loss of their appeal to the Arkansas Supreme Court. It was at this trial, claimed Stuckey, "that I saw hundreds of Klansmen from Louisiana, scores of them from Morehouse [Parish]. I can state positively that I saw at the trial of Bullen and the Richardsons, Morehouse Klansmen who were directly involved in the kidnapping of Daniel and Richards."[616]

It was also reported that Judge Odom, speaking on the condition and location of "Jeff" Burnett, said that he would not force the return of Burnett until such time as physicians in Shreveport indicate that he was well enough to return. Curiously enough, Judge Odom's position seems to fly in the face of another competent medical opinion. Dr. Charles Duvall, the same renowned medical school professor, pathologist, and member of the team that had performed the autopsies on Daniel and Richards after their mutilated bodies had been pulled from Lake LaFourche, who said unequivocally that Burnett was feigning illness. We can only speculate as to the motives and reasons that Judge Odom would have had to rebuff the opinion of this famous pathologist and accept the opinion of a local doctor, who almost certainly would have been influenced by the community, not to mention the fact that one of his colleagues and probably close friends was a principal in this double homicide.

Testimony began today with W. B. Stuckey, a lawyer and former state senator, being the first to be called to the witness stand. During the preliminary questioning, Stuckey related that he had had conversations with other Mer Rouge citizens with regard to the actions of the Ku Klux Klan.

"As a citizen of Mer Rouge, I am thoroughly familiar with the operations of the K.K.K. I am not a member of the Klan, but wherever I went in the parish, I found persons bitterly opposed to the criminal activities of the organization. Captain Skipwith, because I am and always have been an opponent of the Klan, has not spoken to me in more than a year.

---

[616]*Monroe News-Star*, 13 January 1923.

"On the day following the conference held in this building between members of the Klan and citizens, relative to the murders of Daniel and Richards and to restore peace in the parish, I heard Captain Skipwith remark to Smith Stevenson that every man in Morehouse parish who did not quit talking about the Klan would be whipped."[617]

"All of this happened after the disappearance of Daniel and Richards?" Mr. Warren asked.

"Yes."

"After an attempt had been made to kill Dr. McKoin?"

"It is not admitted that there was ever an attempt made to kill Dr. McKoin."

"Why do you say that?"

"Well, the theory is he shot up his own car in order to gain the support of members of the K.K.K."

"You wouldn't want to do anybody any injustice?"

"No, sir."

"You insist your theory is Dr. McKoin shot at his own car?"

"Yes, sir. My conclusions are from the information and ideas advanced by other people."

"Did Dr. McKoin have any enemies?"

"Yes, sir, many of them and long before the advent of the Ku Klux Klan because of his reform activities. This hatred gained after the advent of the Ku Klux Klan, because he then had an instrument to help him. When I first heard of the report of the attempted assassination of Dr. McKoin, I believed it. I accepted it as true, because I believe there were at least 50 people in the parish who had something against him. But after discussing it with people, together with the physical evidence, I changed my opinion. They were pistol shots and not buckshots. Department of Justice men agreed with me on this."

"How about the anonymous letter and the rounding up of people believed to be connected with the plot?"

"I have learned that Dr. McKoin wrote them himself. They were written on his typewriter."

"Who said the shots fired into Dr. McKoin's car were pistol shots?"

617Ibid.

355

"John Jones of Mer Rouge, he said he heard the report of a pistol."

"What kind of enemies did Dr. McKoin have?"

"Fighting enemies caused by his 'bull in the china shop' methods. His activities would not stop at the corporation limits."

"Could you name any of these enemies?"

"I don't believe I could. It was a general community feeling."

"How long did Dr. McKoin live in Mer Rouge?"

"About 10 or 12 years."

"How long was he mayor of Mer Rouge?"

"I believe two terms-of two years each."

"You said he was a bull in a china shop?"

"Yes, sir. A disturber of the peace."

"Do you know any of the enemies Watt Daniel and Richards may have had in the community?"

"I don't know Richards, but Daniel was a mighty good boy. I never saw him take a drink. I heard he drank during the last three years."

"You know Hugh Clark?"

"Yes."

"He is a Klansman?"

"I heard him admit on the witness stand that he was."

"Did you ever hear Mr. Clark say anything about the attempt to kill Dr. McKoin?"

"Yes, sir. I heard him say they he could name a half dozen men in Mer Rouge, out of whom two could be actually accused of shooting at Dr. McKoin."[618]

As usual, *The New York Times* version of Stuckey's testimony, although similar, was recorded differently. Also, the *Times* records the name of a local resident that the *News-Star* failed to list I Stuckey's testimony a follows:

"Have you ever heard Captain Skipwith say anything?"

"Yes, there was a conference that followed the kidnapping and the day after, while talking to John Freeland, I heard Smith Stevenson call out to Captain Skipwith, 'Captain, I heard you settled the Mer Rouge trouble.' 'Yes,' said Skipwith. 'On what basis?' Stevenson asked. 'I told them,' said Skipwith, 'that

---

[618]Ibid.

356

every man in Morehouse who didn't keep his mouth shut and quit talking about the Klan would get whipped until they couldn't sit down for some time.' " The name "J C. Freeland" appears on the original application for Morehouse Klan No. 34.[619]

Stuckey was dismissed and the president of the Ouachita Parish School Board, A. L. Smith, was called to testify. A striking man of 61 years sporting a full head of white hair and matching Vandyke beard, Smith said that his involvement in the Daniel/Richards case began when one of his friends, C. C. "Tot" Davenport, was kidnapped along with Daniel and Richards on August 24. He told of writing a letter to Davenport warning him of danger.

"A few days later, I heard a report of such startling nature that I decided to go to the rescue of my Morehouse Parish friends. I heard that a man named Norseworthy was out to kill Dr. McKoin. I had a conference with Leon and J. L. Davenport and my son to get all the information I could. I told Hugo Davenport there was a general opinion that there was a plot in Mer Rouge to assassinate Dr. McKoin and rumor was that he set up the plot.

"Afterward they called in Mr. Dade and he reported that Mr. Norseworthy was in town and they sent out after him. We decided to hold a conference the following day to be attended by McKoin and any one he wanted, the Davenport family and several others anxious for a peaceful solution of the situation. This conference was held in Monroe. I asked Flood Madison, John H. Parker and Dr. McKoin to take part. My statement was that the meeting was called to bring about peace in the Davenport family and to Dr. McKoin and his friends.

"At the conference Mr. Madison expressed a desire to bring about peace in the parish. Mr. Parker praised the Davenports and Dr. McKoin. Others expressed themselves along the same lines. Dr. McKoin stated that if we were seeking peace we had accomplished our purpose. He said that he left Mer Rouge for all time, and that he had left because he had no friends after the shooting. He said that after the shooting many of those whom he considered his friends turned out to be otherwise. He mentioned the names of Joe Davenport, Bob Dade and others. He felt, he said, that he was living in the wrong place, in a place where he had no friends and that this caused him to leave Mer Rouge.

---

[619]*The New York Times*, 14 January 1923.

"Everybody looked over at Skipwith. He said if he had known what he had just heard there would have been no trouble from the Klan, which he had the honor to represent. He said there would be no trouble for anyone, but three men, Milner, Campbell and Whipple [one word unreadable] he advised that these men would have to conduct themselves better or get out. He wanted them to quit talking about the Klan.

"After the conference for a while or so everything looked all right. Then things began to flare up. I first heard that the Government had sent [two words unreadable] into Morehouse Parish and I feared the conditions would be upset again. As a result I went to Mer Rouge and helped to organize conference No. 3. In that conference were Joe Davenport, Lee Davenport, Bob Dade, Hugh Clark, Mr. A. N. Williams and Flood Madison. I asked them for a plan to restore peace in Morehouse Parish without outside assistance, and I pointed to the possibility of martial law being established. I also tried to impress upon them the importance of getting themselves straight and calling the Governor off. We all felt that martial law would do great damage to the community and decided that it should be averted if possible.

"We decided to select a leading man from each ward, irrespective of whether he was a Klansman or not. The Klan was to be represented by Skipwith and ten of his selection and the peace problem would be settled. He would then inform the Governor that all was quiet and peaceful here. I saw Captain Skipwith and he said it was not necessary to hold a conference, that if the other gentlemen felt that way about it he would speak for the Klan. But we met and everyone was satisfied and contented. That was the end of conference No. 3, and it ended my connection with the matter."

"Why was the Klan considered as a necessary element to securing peace in Morehouse Parish?" asked by Mr. Guion.

"The people of Mer Rouge thought all of their troubles came out of the Klan, and they wanted to meet with the people who were making trouble."

"The Klan was composed of many leading men?"

"Yes, many good men."

"Are you a Klansman?"

"Yes, I'm a Klansman and I'm proud of it."

With this admission, the gallery of spectators filled with Klansmen began shouting their approval and wildly applauding Smith's statement. Judge Odom banged his gavel furiously in an attempt to restore order to the Klansmen who were shaking hands and patting each other on the back. Odom issued a warning against such outbursts but took no action against what may have been fellow Klansmen.

"I think the question is unfair, for when a man's membership in the Klan is known it hurts his usefulness as a member of the society."

"In several conferences following the kidnapping and murder of the two citizens of the parish, was there any effort or any steps taken to ferret out that particular crime?"

"No, sir, ours was a peace conference."

"What caused all the agitation and trouble?"

"The kidnapping of August 24."

"The conferences were not for the purpose of investigating the crime of August 24?"

"No, sir."

"It was common talk that the crime was committed by masked men?"

"Yes."

"Was it thought they were Klansmen or friends of the Klan?"

"No, sir, many thought it was friends of Dr. McKoin."[620]

This statement is, in itself, a contradiction. Smith stated clearly that during one of the conferences McKoin himself said that he left because he had no friends in Mer Rouge. Obviously, Smith, an admitted Klansman, is either speaking from his circle of Klansmen when he said the Klan was not involved, or he was committing outright perjury. From the testimony given so far and that which is to come, Smith, like all other Klansmen who came before him to testify, put the Klan oath before his loyalty to the United States and its system of justice by lying on the stand to protect his fellow Klan members and to shield the murderers of Daniel and Richards.

In his testimony, Smith continued by saying he was aware of some threatening letters that had been received by Dr. McKoin. He discounted the authenticity of these letters by saying it was commonly held by the citizens of the area, including Klan members, that McKoin had been the author of the letters. He further stated

---

[620]Ibid.

that the talk was that there was evidence that the letters had been typed on McKoin's own typewriter.

Smith was asked what Klan procedure was concerning testifying against another Klansman in a criminal trial. He responded by saying that he would not give any information to the court even if he had personal knowledge that the Klansman was guilty of a criminal act. In his own words he said, "You might get the information out of me, but you would have to drag it out, force me to tell." With this statement, Smith demonstrated openly the defiant and insurgent nature of the Klan. This *Klanishness* and secrecy demonstrates the danger represented by any secret organization whose oaths demand that loyalty to one's country takes second place to that of the organization and the actions, legal or illegal, of its membership.

The *Monroe News-Star* also recorded the testimony of A. L. Smith, a 66-year resident of Sterlington, a small town located between Monroe and Bastrop. Although similar, the testimony was far from being exact. Also missing from the *News-Star* version was the statement recorded by the *Times* in which Smith said that he would not give any information to the court of Klansmen guilty of a criminal act. Also the *News-Star* version of Smith's testimony indicated that Milner, Campbell and Whipple "would have to conduct themselves better or get out [of the parish]." The *Times*, on the other hand, recorded Smith as saying the three men would have to leave the parish. More of the many serious "oversights" in *News-Star* coverage.

Smith was told to step down, and A. N. Williams, a life-long resident of Morehouse Parish, was called to give testimony. Under the questioning of Assistant Attorney General Seth Guion, Williams revealed that the peace conferences conducted in both Bastrop and Mer Rouge "didn't seem to get anywhere." Williams explained that the situation was exacerbated when the Mayor Dade of Mer Rouge received the threatening letters. Instead of causing the citizens of Mer Rouge to cower in fear in their homes, the exact opposite occurred in that they actuated the citizens to form committees to seek peace.

"Were there any efforts made by the citizens of Mer Rouge to investigate the disappearance of Daniel and Richards?' asked Mr. Guion.

"No, we thought it a matter for the sheriff and other officials of the parish to investigate."[621]

The New York Times also recorded a brief visit of A. N. Williams to the witness stand. As usual, the testimony was similar to that of the *News-Star* but not exact.[622] The *Monroe News-Star* reported that the next witness to testify was Walter F. Campbell, marshal of Mer Rouge. Campbell was one of the three men that Skipwith had said repeatedly would have to leave the parish. During the preliminary questioning, Campbell said that he knew little about the attempt to assassinate Dr. McKoin.

"Did you know Watt Daniel and T. F. Richards?" asked Mr. Guion.

"Yes, sir. I knew both of them well."

"What are your duties as town marshal?"

"I am town marshal and superintendent of the light and water plant."

"You heard that these men had been kidnapped?"

"Yes."

"Did you ever assist in any search for them?"

"No, sir."

"Did anybody ever communicate to you that peace and harmony could never prevail until you got out of Mer Rouge?"

"Yes, sir. Mayor Dade told me that Captain Skipwith told him to deliver such a message to me."

"Do you know why they held charges against you?"

"No, in fact, I offered $1,000 to clear up these mysteries."

"What mysteries?"

"I was charged with sitting at a round table and aiding and plotting the death of Dr. McKoin; that I had been drunk on the streets and that I had been active against the Klan."

"So you were accused of being part of the 'brains' of the assassination plot?"

"Yes. Clyde Hopkins told me that a man by the name of Usury had told him that if they would take me out and give me a sound whipping they would find out all about it. I saw Usury and he denied this."

---

[621] *Monroe News-Star*, 13 January 1923.
[622] *The New York Times*, 14 January 1923.

"Do you know of any round table that exists in Mer Rouge?"

"No, but they were referring to the poker table at J. L. Daniel's home."

"Poker games were frequent at the Daniel home?"

"Yes."

"Did you ever participate?"

"No."

"Did you ever see the anonymous letter sent to Dr. McKoin?"

"Yes, he showed it to me. I went around and examined the typewriters of Watt Daniel, Mr. Doddy and others. Dr. McKoin told me later that it was written on his own machine."

"Do you know of others who received letters?"

"Only the one received by Mayor Dade and printed circulars thrown about the streets and tacked up at the post office. These letters threatened bootleggers and other law violators and were signed by the vigilance committee."

"Was there any such committee organized in Mer Rouge?"

"No."

"Did you ever see anyone in the regalia of the Ku Klux Klan in Mer Rouge?"

"Yes, sir. Two men dressed in white. This was the night automobiles stopped in Mer Rouge and departed in the direction of Stampley. On another occasion, which was on a Saturday afternoon, I saw a car of hooded men visit a negro restaurant in Mer Rouge. They warned, I am told, the proprietor of the restaurant to cut out letting white men gamble in his place."

"Do you know whether anybody ever vouched for you to allow you to remain in Mer Rouge?"

"Yes, after I had made a proposition to Captain Skipwith."

"What was the proposition?"

"I offered to put up $1,000 to prove that I was innocent of the charges preferred against me by the Klan. W. L. Pugh delivered this message to Skipwith. He came back and told me everything was all right."

"Did Richards tell you after he was kidnapped in Bastrop that he recognized two men wearing black hoods who held him prisoner?"

"Yes."

"Who did he name?"

"Jim Tisdale and A. D. Campbell."

362

"Is Campbell any relative to you?"

"Yes, my brother."

"Did you hear after the Stampley raid of anybody trying to sell some .45 calibre cartridges?"

"Yes."[623]

The New York Times also carried the testimony of Walter H. Campbell. The testimony recorded in the *Times* was more detailed than that of the *News-Star*, but it did not add much to what was recorded in the *News-Star*. Again, the versions were similar and no where near being exact.[624]

The *Monroe News-Star* reported the witness following Campbell was Alonzo Braddock. He was described as a "lifelong resident of Morehouse Parish, and an industrious, ambitious farmer and stock raiser." Braddock gave his account of a Klan raid on his home in the dead of night, led by Captain Skipwith.

"Did you have any visits from the Ku Klux Klan?" asked Guion.

"They woke me up one night yelling for me to come out."

"What time was it?"

"About 1 A.M."

"What time of the year?"

"About Nov. 24, 1922."

"What happened?"

"They came whooping and yelling for me to come out. My wife looked out and saw there was a crowd of men in the front. They began hammering and knocking and broke the lock off the door and came in."

"Was the lamp lit?"

"No, sir."

"House in darkness?"

"Yes, sir."

"Who came in?"

"Captain Skipwith, Marvin Pickett, his son Cud, and Ben Pratt, Sam Cox, Sam Hildridge, and there were about eight in the room. I'm trying to remember them all. There was a man named McIntoch, who runs the pressing shop."

---

[623]*Monroe News-Star*, 13 January 1923.

[624]*The New York Times*, 14 January 1923.

"You say these men came into your house and left others on the outside?"

"Yes, sir."

"How did you recognize them without a light?"

"By the light of the fireplace."

"What did they do?"

"They said they were after me for making whiskey. I spoke with Captain Skipwith and told him he was the oldest man there and that I trusted him and would go with him to the sheriff if he would see that I was not hurt in any way. He promised, and we started out in the car and drove to Mr. Carpenter's [the sheriff] house and woke him up."

"Anyone else with you as a prisoner?"

"Four negroes."

"Where did you sleep that night?"

"At the home of the sheriff."

"Do you know where and when they got the four negroes they arrested the same night?"

"I do not."

"Did the men you saw have guns?"

"Yes, I think they all had guns. One man had a shot gun, and another had a rifle."

"Did they use any force with you?"

"They hurried me along as I was dressing."

"How many cars were there in the party?"

"There was six I know, but my wife said she counted eight."

"Did they have a warrant for you?"

"They did not show one."

"Were you subsequently indicted?"

"We came up the next morning and fixed bond and went home but I never saw a warrant."

"Did you see Skipwith before you left Bastrop?"

"Yes, he told me to take things easy and be careful and that if anybody could handle Judge Odom it would be us." [meaning the Klan]

"Did your wife talk to the men?"

"Yes, she asked them what they were going to do with me. Captain Skipwith told her not to be uneasy, that they were going to take me over to the court, but that I'd be back the next morning."

"Have you had any threats, messages or heard any indicating it would be best for you to leave?"

"No, but I've been molested since that time."

As Attorney General Coco himself continued the questioning, Braddock declared that he was eager to leave Morehouse Parish and would do so immediately if he could sell his eighty-acre farm for half its current value.

"And yet you were born and raised here, your relatives and friends are here?"

"Yes, sir, but I'm anxious to leave this parish. I don't feel safe anymore. My wife is worried sick. Whenever she hears a motorcar she gets nervous. I do too, for that matter."[625]

As before, *The New York Times* carried Braddock's testimony similar to that which was recorded in the *News-Star*. No significant difference could be noted between the two versions, except to say that they were in no way identical.[626]

The *Monroe News-Star* recorded the final witness for the day as Fred Cobb. Cobb told of being kidnapped by a carload of black-hooded men as he walked along the road only 100 yards from his home near Bastrop on July 12, 1922.

"I was walking along the road, when a car containing five masked men came up. One of them, armed, came forward after the car stopped and asked me to get in. I began to laugh, but I decided to get in with them," said Cobb.

"What was done then?" Coco asked.

"One of the masked men got out on the running board and I was put in with the others. They moved out on the Bastrop road."

"Were they all masked?"

"They had either black or blue hoods on their heads but no robes. They wore hats over the hoods."

"Did you know any of them?"

"I knew one-Laurie Calhoun."

"How did you recognize Calhoun?" inquired Coco.

---

[625]*Monroe News-Star*, 13 January 1923.
[626]*The New York Times*, 14 January 1923.

"His mask was torn and I could see part of his face. Another thing, I'd seen him in the barber shop an hour and a half before and I had heard his voice. He did most of the talking when I met him with the masked men." Calhoun was the deputy sheriff sent by Sheriff Carpenter to bring back Dr. McKoin when he fled from Louisiana.

"You didn't recognize any of the others?"

"No, their masks concealed their faces."

"Why was it funny to you?"

"I don't believe I could explain it. It looked comical in a way, and yet was serious. I just couldn't help laughing. I'm from Texas, where it doesn't mean much to kill a man, but it's all on the level and above board."

"When were the shoes returned?" [The significance of the shoes will appear later.]

"The next day. They were left in Young's drug store."

"You were taken into the woods and accused of immoral conduct?"

"Yes, sir."

"Did they exhibit guns?"

"Yes, all of them."

"Where did you recognize Calhoun?"

"After we got out of the car I saw the torn hood and recognized him."

"You recognized Calhoun by his voice?"

"Yes, no one can forget that voice after hearing it once."[627]

The testimony attributed to Fred Cobb in *The New York Times* was similar but not exactly the same as the *News-Star* version. No significant differences could be located.[628]

Masked Men Flog Woman and Caller[629]

Goose Creek, Texas was reported in a state of excitement due to the flogging by masked men of Mrs. R. H. Harrison, 30, a widow, and R. A. Armand, a caller in her home. Harrison's 7-year-old daughter said she saw a mob of 15 or more men dressed "all in white," drag her mother from home, cut off her long hair and whip her.

---

[627] *Monroe News-Star*, 13 January 1923.

[628] *The New York Times*, 14 January 1923.

[629] Ibid.

"Two or three members of the party kept insisting that Mr. Armand and I be killed right there," Mrs. Harrison said. " 'Kill them both!' they cried, and 'throw their bodies in the bayou.' Upon my return, I found that my home had been completely ransacked. Every drawer, trunk and box in the house had been opened and the contents strewn about the floor." These pillars of the community were little more than common thieves.

Sheriff T. A. Binford, who was said to have the endorsement of the Ku Klux Klan at the election last Fall, denied that the Klan had anything to do with the flogging. "Similar cases previously had been reported in which residents of Goose Creek were taken from their homes and whipped, but few of those who returned covered with bruises are willing to talk."

Big Store Dynamited[630]

The indiscriminate use of dynamite in Louisiana was not a novel experience as a report from Baton Rouge indicated. The store of Bridges and West, at Norwood, was dynamited this day and $30,000 in liberty bonds were reported stolen from the safe, together with $1,000 in cash and some valuable paper. Recently the safe of the Roxey store had also been dynamited.

Flight of Helicopter Made at M'Cook Field[631]

A dispatch from Dayton, Ohio, told of a successful flight by a helicopter, described as "a machine which rises vertically and descends in the same manner," had been made at M'Cook Field. The flight at the experimental base of the United States Army Air Service lasted one minute and 40 seconds. The helicopter arose six feet from the ground. The machine was the invention of Dr. George de Bothezaat, a Russian inventor, who had been conducting experiments at M'Cook Field.

Bryan at Princeton Attracts Evolution[632]

An announcement from Princeton, New Jersey indicated that William Jennings Bryan had addressed a Princeton audience in the First Presbyterian Church this past evening and had attacked the theory of evolution as "an unsupported hypothesis."

"First of all," he said, "evolution is unproved: secondly; it is unsupported: thirdly, its logical tendency is to destroy belief in God by encouraging atheism or to impair faith in God by substituting the conception of a far away god for the God of

---

[630]*Monroe News-Star*, 13 January 1923.
[631]*The New York Times*, 14 January 1923.
[632]*The New York Times*, 14 January 1923.

the Bible."

MONDAY JANUARY 15, 1923

Morehouse Parish Sheriff Declares Captain Not Authorized to Act in any Official Capacity and no Warrant was[633]
Seventy Additional Witnesses to Testify in Probe of Hooded Mob Outrages in Morehouse[634]
M'Koin's Minister Friends in Monroe in Reply to Critic: Revs. Tripp and Evans not Opposing Hearing[635]
State has no Information to Show "Torture Machine" used on Victims Found, Says Guion[636]

The New York Times reported that today's testimony centered on providing Captain Skipwith with an alibi the evening of August 24, 1922. J. N. "Jap" Jones, a businessman from Bonita, and James F. Harp also from Bonita and both admitted Klansmen, were the agents of this obvious deception. It was their contention that Captain Skipwith was present in Bastrop shortly after the kidnapping and through till midnight on that date. They claimed they had constructed fortifications inside R. H. Thomas's Hardware Store located only a short distance from the steps of the Morehouse Parish Courthouse in Bastrop. When they learned of the kidnapping, they allegedly sent for Captain Skipwith, whom they conveniently located in his room a few blocks from the courthouse. They said they wanted to receive assurances from him that the kidnappings had not been the work of the Klan. Skipwith allegedly honored their summons and assured them that the kidnappings had not been the work of the Klan. They further testified that Skipwith was in and out of the hardware store until past midnight.

This was one of the first direct references to the actions of Skipwith since the beginning of the open hearing. Although he has not been in the courtroom, he was seen constantly circulating among groups of men outside of the courtroom and in the street, continually assuring his followers that there was nothing with which to be concerned. There was great reverence paid to him because he instantly became the center of attention as these groups would close around him, straining to hear his every word. That he was the undisputed leader was unquestioned.

---

[633]*Monroe News-Star*, 15 January 1923.
[634]Ibid.
[635]Ibid.
[636]Ibid.

Harp and Jones both told how the large stockpile of revolvers were loaded in the hardware store that night, and how the group that had assembled, Klansmen all, commenced loading them in anticipation of trouble because of the antagonistic atmosphere which existed between the townspeople of Bastrop and Mer Rouge. They said they were concerned that once the citizens of Mer Rouge learned of the kidnapping they would become outraged and attack Bastrop.

Each admitted their membership in the Ku Klux Klan. So different was the testimony given by "Jap" Jones, a white male of 46, that it took the barristers of the attorney general's office by complete surprise. Jones said he did not believe that the Klan was at all involved with the kidnappings and murders.

During the questioning, Mr. Guion asked, "Well, tell us just what you expected trouble from?"

"We weren't sure, but if any black-masked men had shown up we would have tried to arrest them. We would have protected ourselves."

"And you don't think those black-masked men who kidnapped Daniel and Richards were Klansmen?"

"No, I do not."

"You didn't think the Klan had anything to do with it?"

"I do not."

Mr. Guion asked Jones if any of the members of the Klan had attempted to investigate the kidnapping itself. He said he felt that such was the job of the grand jury, which was in session at the time.

Meanwhile, Captain Skipwith was on the lawn of Court House Square, just a short distance from the steps themselves. While Jones was on the stand, Skipwith was speaking with Klan members, assuring them that the investigation would amount to naught. Bolstered by the testimony of Klan members, Skipwith's alibi was weakened only by the testimony of F. C. Eason of Monroe, who said that Skipwith was in Bastrop on the day when the kidnappings occurred. Eason said that when he asked Skipwith about it later, the Exalted Cyclops told him that Daniel and Richards were "bad characters and needed attention."

The state paraded a total of 14 witnesses on this date, but aside from the testimony of Harp and Jones, what came forth from the stand was mostly a repeat of so many who had come before. Because some witnesses were not in court when the morning session began, a ten-minute recess was called which turned into an hour during which time Sheriff Carpenter's deputies combed the city for the no-shows.

While his deputies were searching for the witnesses, Carpenter himself was recalled to the stand to clarify testimony he had given on Saturday regarding the raid on the residence of Alonzo Braddock. Skipwith had informed on Braddock to the sheriff alleging Braddock was operating a whiskey still. Carpenter said that he deputized Skipwith and the men with him, Klansmen all, and directed them to bring him in. After realizing who Skipwith had arrested, Carpenter allowed Braddock to spend the night at his, Carpenter's, home instead of remaining overnight in a jail cell.

It was the contention of the state that the raid had been carried out and the arrest of Braddock made without a warrant. In his testimony, James T. Dalton, clerk of court for Morehouse Parish, asserted that no warrant existed at the time of the raid and arrest of Braddock.

The only testimony of note to come out of the morning session came from J. P. Inabet of Mer Rouge. It was he who said that A. L. Fleming, the local cobbler, had met with him about two weeks prior to the kidnappings. During the visit, the conversation came around to Daniel and Richards. Inabet said, "The boys seem to have put it over on the Klan." To this statement, Fleming answered, "Don't you believe it. In about two weeks from now you'll see a stunt put over that will surprise you."

The alleged attempt on the life of Dr. B. M. McKoin also arose in the day's testimony. John Jones, a farmer from Mer Rouge, said that he had heard shots while on Main Street in Mer Rouge on the night of the alleged attempt. He said that he heard the shot and moments later observed McKoin driving down the street. John McAdams, a clerk for the Missouri Pacific Railroad, testified that he was relaxing on his front porch when the shot rang out. He then observed McKoin drive up to the house across the street, which belonged to "Pink" Kirkpatrick. After hearing the banging on his door, Kirkpatrick emerged wearing only his underwear. McKoin and Kirkpatrick then surveyed the vehicle for an extended period of time.

Also giving testimony on this day was J. C. Hornbeck, a Mer Rouge merchant. He told of how Kirkpatrick tried to sell to him a large amount of cartridges not long after the night that Daniel and Neelis were accosted on the Gallion Road. Hugo Davenport, who had been dubbed by the pro-Klan faction as the "brains" of the anti-Klan group in Mer Rouge, gave testimony as did Guy Boyd, a Collinston storekeeper. Boyd told of selling gasoline to the black-hooded band who had kidnapped Daniel and Richards. He said that the drivers of the two cars, a Ford touring car and a Ford truck, all wore black masks, and he did not recognize any of them. He told of seeing two men in the rear of the truck, their faces being covered by white handkerchiefs. He said he could not positively say if these two men were Daniel and Richards. Boyd confirmed that he had been a member of the grand jury which was seated before and after the kidnapping. This was the same grand jury that made no attempt to investigate the kidnapping.[637]

The *Monroe News-Star* recorded that the proceedings in the open hearing began today with the calling of Fred Carpenter, sheriff of Morehouse Parish, to testify. Carpenter repudiated the assertion that he had either deputized or issued a special commission to Captain J. K. Skipwith with regard to the arrest of Alonzo Braddock. Braddock had testified on the previous Saturday that Skipwith and others, all unmasked, forced their way into his home, arrested him, transported him to Bastrop, and handed him over to Carpenter. Carpenter stated that no warrant had been issued for Braddock.

"Who brought Braddock to your house?" Mr. Guion.

"Captain Skipwith, Marvin Pickett, Benton Pratt, Mr. McIntoch, and Dave Cox."

"Was there a warrant used?"

"Not that I know of."

"Was there ever a warrant issued?"

"Not that I know of." ·

"Were these men deputized by you?"

"No sir."

"They were acting on their own authority?"

"Yes, except that Captain Skipwith said he had found some stills and asked me would I deputize him. I told him to go ahead and get the stills." This statement is contradictory in itself. While saying that he did not deputize Skipwith, in the same sentence he authorized him to "go ahead and get the stills." It would be easy to see how such a statement could be construed as authorization by Carpenter for

---

[637]*The New York Times*, 16 January 1923.

Skipwith and his Klansmen to carry out the raid.

"Was Captain Skipwith issued a commission by the court to act as your deputy or any member of his party?"

"He or they were not."[638]

Carpenter's testimony listed in *The New York Times* was similar to, but not the same as that carried by the *News-Star*. There were no significant differences.[639]

According to the *Monroe News-Star*, the next witness called was the clerk of Morehouse Parish District Court, J. T. Dalton. He was called to the stand next as a follow-up witness to Sheriff Carpenter's testimony. The attorney general's office wanted to set a time line as to when the search warrant had been issued for the premises of Alonzo Braddock, and if he was booked with illicit distilling and bonded out according to the papers delivered to him. When asked, Dalton said that the bond papers were delivered to him first and that the search warrant was received later.

Dalton was asked whether it appeared to him that the date on the warrant had been altered. He said that it seemed as though an attempt had been made to erase the original date and November 24 written over it. Dalton said that he had noticed the defect previously and that it was his belief that a deliberate attempt had been made to alter the document. He asserted that the warrant had been signed by "J. E. Lee."[640]

The New York Times also briefly recorded the testimony of James T. Dalton, the clerk of court for Morehouse Parish. Dalton testified that a search warrant had in fact been issued for the residence of Alonzo Braddock, but that the search warrant and the bond for Braddock's release were both done on the day following the arrest of Braddock.[641]

The *Monroe News-Star* recorded that the next witness called was McVey Young, a local druggist. He gave corroborating testimony to the assertions made by Fred Cobb, a previous witness, who told of being kidnapped by black-hooded men and taken into the woods where he was "lectured." Cobb claimed that a pair of shoes which had been taken from him and left in the woods were returned to him by Laurie Calhoun, the special deputy sent to Baltimore to bring back Dr. McKoin.

---

[638]*Monroe News-Star*, 15 January 1923.

[639]*The New York Times*, 16 January 1923.

[640]*Monroe News-Star*, 15 January 1923.

[641]*The New York Times*, 16 January 1923.

Calhoun, whom Cobb had recognized as one of his kidnappers that night because of a tear in his black mask, returned the shoes after Cobb sent a note to Calhoun's home requesting that he do so. The crux of Young's testimony was that Cobb's shoes were brought to his store, but he was unable, or more than likely too terrified, to identify the person who delivered the package.[642]

The New York Times also reported the testimony of McVey Young. This testimony was similar, but not exact as given in the *News-Star*. there were no significant differences.[643]

In support of the testimony of Cobb and Young, the *Monroe News-Star* reported that the state called Robert Anderson, a young man from Mer Rouge. He testified that he had brought the note given to him by Cobb to Mrs. Laurie Calhoun with regard to the shoes.[644] However, this was the extent of the testimony in the *News-Star*. On the other hand, *The New York Times* version was more explicit.

"Do you know Fred Cobb?" Guion inquired.

"Yes, sir."

"Do you remember when it was reported that he was taken out by a masked mob?"

"Yes, sir."

"Shortly after did he give you a note to be delivered?"

"Yes, a sealed letter to be delivered to Mr. Calhoun, the deputy Sheriff. I delivered the letter to his home. Mr. Calhoun was not at home, so I gave the letter to Mrs. Calhoun."

"Did you know the contents of the letter?"

"No, sir, it was sealed."[645] The relevance of this letter with regard to the incident involving Cobb was never revealed.

The New York Times recorded that the next witness to be called was J. H. Inabet.

"Do you know Fred Cobb?"

"Yes, sir."

---

[642]*Monroe News-Star*, 15 January 1923.

[643]*The New York Times*, 16 January 1923.

[644]*Monroe News-Star*, 15 January 1923.

[645]*The New York Times,* 16 January 1923.

"Do you remember the date of August 24, when Daniel and Richards were kidnapped?"

"Yes."

"Do you know A. L. Fleming?"

"Yes."

"What conversations have you had with him about the affair?"

"About two weeks before he was at my place, and I told him I believed the boys had the bluff on the Ku Klux Klan. He said, 'I don't believe it.' You wait two weeks and you will see the Klan pull off one of the biggest stunts pulled off that you ever heard of.' "

"And that was two weeks before the kidnapping of Daniel and Richards?"

"Yes, sir."

"Do you know Dr. McKoin?"

"Yes, sir."

"Cordial relations with him?"

"Well, I know him well."

"Did you have a conversation with him in Monroe shortly after the murder on August 24?"

"Yes, sir. I met him there by accident. He stopped and talked, and he asked me about the disturbance over Daniel and Richards. I told him that we thought the Klan was responsible. He said to me, 'You are doing too much talking up there, and unless there is less talking and more quiet a lot of good men are going to bite the dust.' "

"Did he ask you if Daniel and Richards had returned?"

"Yes, sir. He also mentioned Judge Whipple, and said he was a good man but was talking too much."[646]

The *Monroe News-Star* version of Inabet's testimony contained a detail not found in the *Times* version. This detail was that Fleming's statement had been made in the presence of Inabet's wife.

Although this witness's testimony is very brief, his testimony has far-reaching implications. If this witness is to be believed, then we must conclude that the plan to kidnap and murder Daniel and Richards was made at least two weeks in advance.

---

[646]*The New York Times*, 16 January 1923.

There is also the allusion that there was a network of "insiders," perhaps Klansmen all, who were privy to this advanced planning. As such, they were at least guilty of being accessories before the fact, if not outright conspirators in these hideous crimes.

The *Monroe News-Star* recorded the next called as J. B. Hornbeck, a hardware dealer from Mer Rouge.

"Do you deal in pistol shells and cartridges?" Mr. Guion asked.

"Yes."

"Did anybody try to sell you pistol shells after the Ku Klux Klan affair on the Gallion road?"

"Yes, it wasn't the day after the reported raid, but a man did ask me to handle a box of .45-caliber shells for him. I said that I would try to sell them for him."

"Who was that man?"

"W. P. (Pink) Kirkpatrick."[647] Kirkpatrick was said to have been a member of the mob that had held up Daniel and Neelis on Gallion Road the night of the raid on the black farmer's home.

The New York Times reported the testimony of D. C. Hornbeck [Probably the same person]. This testimony was similar, but not exactly the same as that of the *News-Star*.[648]

The New York Times recorded the next to take the witness stand as John McAdams, a clerk in the Mer Rouge station for the Missouri Pacific Railroad.

"Do you remember the date of the shooting at Dr. McKoin?" asked Mr. Warren.

"I think it was the first part of August."

"Where were you?"

"At Walter Camp's house about a block from the station."

"How soon did you hear that Dr. McKoin had been shot at?"

"Next morning."

"You heard no rumors that night?"

"No, but I saw McKoin drive up in front of Kirkpatrick's house and call Kirkpatrick out, and we could see them examining McKoin's car. That led me to believe that it was McKoin who had been shot at. They were examining the cover

---

[647] *Monroe News-Star,* 15 January 1923.

closely. Kirkpatrick, I think, was in his underwear."

"The next morning you heard for certain that Dr. McKoin had been fired on?"

"Yes, sir."

"Did you examine the bullet marks?"

"Yes, sir, the bullets appeared to have riddled the back seat."

"About how many marks?"

"I didn't count them, but it looked as though there were twenty of them."

"Did you see anyone else on the street?"

"Well, about an hour later we saw Daniel, Campbell and Andrews by the restaurant. We told them about the shots at Dr. McKoin and they were surprised."

"Did you see anyone else on the street?"

"Yes, some young boys."

"Did you see anything of Richards?"

"No, sir."[649] The *Monroe News-Star* also recorded the testimony of McAdams which appeared to be similar to that contained in the *Times*.

The New York Times described John Jones as a 47-year-old single farmer from Mer Rouge. His testimony began with inquiries about the alleged attempt on Dr. McKoin. He told of being in front of the store owned by Hugh Clark when he heard two shots fired.

"What did they sound like?" Mr. Guion asked.

"Like an automatic pistol."

"Did you hear of Dr. McKoin being shot at before you left town that night?"

"No. I did not hear of it until the second morning."

"Who told you that shots were fired at Dr. McKoin?"

"I believe it was Alex Williams."

"Who took you home?"

"Frank Bell."

"Where was he while you were waiting for him?"

"He said he was going to J. L. Daniel's to play poker. I asked him how late, and he said not long."

"Whom was he with?"

---

[648] *The New York Times*, 16 January 1923.

[649] *The New York Times,* 16 January 1923.

"It strikes me that he was with Watt Daniel and Richards."

"You are certain of that?"

"Well, I know they were together, talking about poker."

"Were you asked to play?"

"Yes," he said, "but they played too strong for me."

"Where did you wait?"

"Clark's store."

"How far from the depot?"

"About two blocks."

"Where were you when the shots were fired?"

"By the store."

"Did you see him stop?"

"No, sir."

"Did McKoin see you?"

"He told me afterward he didn't."

"What did McKoin say to you about it?"

"He said he had no idea who did it."

"It was ten minutes after the shots that Frank Bell came up?"

"Yes."

"What did you and Bell do?"

"Went home."

"Is Bell married?"

"He is a single man."

"Did he have a pistol that night?"

"I don't know."

"Are you and he friends?"

"Friends for years."

"Did he tell you how he came out in the poker game that night?"

"He said he lost $40."

During his testimony, Jones said that Bell had told him of a man named Hicks who was also involved in the poker game. Claiming himself to be a crayon portrait artist, Hicks had left the game a winner that evening.

"Where is Hicks now?"

"I think he left town. I think he got scared."

"Frank Bell stated he lost $40?"

"Yes, and he said none of the boys left the game while he was up there."

"You are certain that Watt Daniel and T. F. Richards were there and did not leave the game?"

"Yes, I asked about that, for I heard it rumored that they were going to be accused of the shooting. I learned that neither of them left the game."

"When did you hear of the shooting at Dr. McKoin?"

"The next morning in town."

"Are you afraid of Dr. McKoin?"

"Yes, sir."

"And he stated in conversation with you that he did not know who did the shooting?"

"Yes, sir."

"You knew that Bell had come directly from Daniel's house?"

"Yes."

"And he told you that Richards and Daniel had not left the poker game?"

"Yes, sir."

"Who else was in the game?"

"W. C. Andrews' name was mentioned there."

"What makes you say it was pistol shots you heard the night McKoin was shot at?"

"I judged it was a pistol by the rapidity of the shots."

"Have you examined the McKoin car since the shooting?"

"Yes."

"What were the shots?"

"Buckshot."[650]

The *Monroe News-Star* also recorded the testimony of John Jones. Although his testimony was similar, the *Times* version failed to contain one detail, the importance of which was never explored in this hearing. The testimony picks up with Guion asking Jones about going to play poker at J. L. Daniel's home.

"Were you invited?"

---

[650]*The New York Times,* 16 January 1923.

"Yes, but they played too heavy for me. I'm a penny ante boy. We were standing in Hugh Clark's place. Harper Donnan and myself was talking when the shots were fired. A little later we saw Dr. McKoin in his automobile with a bale of hay on the running board. Donnan said to me 'I wonder who is sick-there's Dr. McKoin.' I said, I don't know but I guess it must be a horse or a cow as he had a bale of hay. Bell came up later. I saw his car coming from the direction of 'J. L.'s' house. We went on home, Bell going to his home and I walked a mile to my home."[651] The significance of the bale of hay was never explained nor explored. The purpose of it on the running board of the vehicle perplexed the witness as well as this investigator.

The afternoon session began with the state calling Guy Boyd to the witness stand. *The New York Times* reported that Mr. Warren began questioning this married owner of a mercantile store.

"Where were you on August 24, 1922?"

"In Bastrop at a baseball game."

"When did you leave Bastrop?"

"After the game."

"On what road did you travel?"

"The Bastrop, Monroe Road."

"Who was with you?"

"My mother and three friends."

"What time did you reach Collinston?"

"About 6 P.M."

"Did you encounter any masked men on the road?"

"No, sir."

"When did you first hear about the holdup by masked men?"

"It must have been the next day or the following day."

"Did you see any masked men about Collinston?"

"Yes."

"About what time?"

"About 9 o'clock maybe later."

"State what you saw."

---

[651] *Monroe News-Star*, 15 January 1923.

"I heard an automobile horn and went out and saw a masked man, who told me to give him some gas. Then a Ford truck came on, and another masked man asked for gas. I think one man paid for both cars."

"What was the first car?"

"A Ford touring car."

"How many men were in it?"

"I only saw the man that got out."

"What kind of garb did they wear?"

"Just a black mask."

"Only one man got off the truck?"

"Yes, there were two sitting in the back, though, I think."

"The curtains were down?"

"Yes."

"Was the Ford truck a homemade body?"

"It looked like a Ford runabout with a body attached. It looked like a new car."

"How did you see the two men in the back?"

"When I gave the driver the hose to put in the gas."

"Were the two men in the back masked?"

"I think they had white handkerchiefs over their faces."

"Did you talk with them?"

"No."

"Did you know any of them?"

"I did not."

"None of them came into your store into the light?"

"No."

"When one of them paid you, could you tell his general size?"

"Yes, the one in the touring car was close to six feet."

"Did it seem to you that the two men sitting in the back of the truck were there voluntarily?"

"I had no idea."

"Did you know Watt Daniel?"

"Yes, sir."

"Did you know Richards?"

"No, sir."

This witness went on to say that "Tot" Davenport told him that they had taken him [Davenport] into custody in error, but later set him free. He also told the witness that the masked band had abducted Daniel and W. C. Andrews from their car.

"What time did you close your store?"

"I don't remember."

"Couldn't that crowd have been there before you closed the store?"

"Yes, sir."

"How was the mob dressed?"

"They wore black masks."

"Were you held up at the point of a gun?"

"No, they just whistled for me."

"Are you sure that no one went into your store that night with a black hood on?"

"I am sure of it."

"Did you feel any fear or apprehension when the masked men, armed with shotguns, called on you to give them gasoline?"

"I had no fear."

"It was rather unusual, wasn't it?"

"Well, I'd seen masked men before."

"Had you sold gas to masked men before?"

"No, but I'd seen them in Paradise [Louisiana]."

"Did Davenport, who came into your store ten minutes after the cars left, say that he recognized any of them?"

"He did not."

"How many cars did you see all told?"

"I think I saw three; a third car joined the other two."

"Weren't you aroused about this thing?"

"Well, I was interested."

"You made no effort to pursue them?"

"No, sir."

"Did you ever hear anyone say that they recognized anyone in that mob at your station that night?"

"No, sir."

"Did anyone ask if you recognized any one?"

"Yes, Ed Marsh and one or two others."

"Didn't 'Tot' Davenport tell you that Daniel and Richards were in the truck?"

"No, sir. He told me that the mob got them."

"Did you see J. L. Daniel?"

"No, sir."

"Who is Ed Marsh?"

"The depot agent."

"When did he ask?"

"A day or two ago."

"What was the conversation?"

"Well, he heard they were going to get me as a witness, and then he asked me if I recognized any of the mob. I told him that I recognized only two or three of them, but I was only joking."

"Did you ever have any of your cars in the vicinity of Cooper's Lake?"

"No, sir. I don't know where it is."

The witness stated that no records of his rental car business existed, so he could not tell who rented them. He did, however, admit that one of his cars could have been driven to Cooper's Lake without his knowledge or consent. Again, this seems an outright lie. This was not a thriving metropolis with strangers coming and going. His rentals were on a local basis, rented to local people. He knew only too well to whom he had rented the vehicle. Also, his testimony concerning the presence of black-hooded men in his store will be contradicted by other witnesses.

"Did you hear any rumors that any of the masked band went into any store in Collinston that night?"

"No, sir."

Mr. Warren began to question the witness.

"Who was in the store when 'Tot' Davenport came in?"

"Jerry Pettis, Robert Harkness and several others, I think."

"Did you ask any of them if they recognized the hooded men?"

"I think not."

" 'Tot' Davenport came in to hire a car, didn't he?"

"The Andrews boy asked for the car."

"Did Andrews tell you that he and old man Daniel had been released?"

"He told me that he and two others had been released."

"So you knew that three were released and that two were still held?"

"Yes."

"And the two, Watt Daniel and Richards, must have been in one of these first two cars?"

"I can't say. There were two men sitting in the back of the truck."

Mr. Walmsley then took over the questioning from Mr. Warren.

"Did you sell gasoline to Mr. Pipes just before these cars came in?"

"I don't remember."

"You saw these cars cross the railroad track?"

"Yes, I saw them, yes, sir."

"Wasn't it moonlight?"

"I don't remember."

"Do you remember a fourth car that picked up the two watchmen left there?"

"No, sir."

"You say you don't remember waiting on Mr. Pipes?"

"No, sir."

The questioning was then taken over by Mr. Paul A. Sompayrac, special assistant prosecutor, who began asking Boyd about the drinks he sold in his store. Boyd named several of them. It was clear that the purpose of this line of questioning escaped those in the gallery.

"What part of Illinois are you originally from?"

"Southern."

"Did you recognize any of the cars?"

"No, sir."

"Did you note any of the license plates?"

"No, sir. It was too dark."

"Of course, the cars threw no light on one another?"

"I don't know."

"Mr. Boyd, do you mean to tell us, as a member of the parish Grand Jury and as an automobile man, that you made no efforts to learn the identity of those men or the cars?"

"I do."

"You made no effort to recognize these men?"

383

"No."

"You could see the backs of their heads, and you made no attempt to recognize them?"

"No."

"And you, a member of the Grand Jury?"

"I made no effort to recognize them."

"After they went, did you make any effort to organize a posse to pursue them? Did you do anything as a member of the Grand Jury to investigate this unusual conduct?"

"No, I did not."

"You knew that those cars were going in the direction of Lake LaFourche?"

"I did, but I didn't know they were going to Lake LaFourche. They might have been going to Monroe."

"You knew there was a small swamp?"

"Yes, sir."

"Did black-masked men ever come around your place?"

"Yes, sir. They paraded once in the daylight through the town. The car license plates were covered up."

"How did you feel when you saw the masked men with guns?"

"Well, I knew they weren't after me."

"You didn't care what happened to the others?"

"Well, not exactly."

"Did you raise an alarm or anything?"

"No sir. There was nothing in a mask to get alarmed over. I'd seen lots of them."

"Then it was a common thing."

"Well, I don't know."[652]

The testimony of Guy Boyd contained in the *News-Star* was similar in most ways, but there were instances where the two versions clashed and in some areas the *News-Star* had greater detail. For example, in the *News-Star* version, Boyd was said to have seen black-hooded men in Collinston, and in the *Times* version the town he named was Paradise. Also, when asked to describe the man standing

---

[652]*The New York Times*, 16 January 1923.

outside of the vehicle, masked and armed with the gun, the *News-Star* version claimed that Boyd stated that the man was six feet tall and weighed 160 pounds. In the *Times* version, Boyd was supposed to have testified that the man was almost six feet tall and there was no mention of weight. [653] These are just the glaring examples of journalistic liberty taken with sworn testimony. It is impossible to tell which version is correct.

Just as there had been testimony taken from seven witnesses that had not recorded in the previous day's *Monroe News-Star*, there were five witnesses whose testimony appears in *The New York Times*, but not the *Monroe News-Star* for this date. This testimony comes from the following witnesses: F. C. Eason, Hugo Davenport, W. L. Pugh, James Harp and J. N. (Jap) Jones.

The New York Times next recorded the testimony of F. C. Eason. Eason told of being in Bastrop on August 24 to see the baseball game with his wife, John Huey and Joe Gold. After the game was over, he told of leaving for Monroe arriving there about 6:30 p.m. Mr. Warren asked if he had had any contact with Captain Skipwith since the kidnapping.

"In a restaurant here one day I had a casual conversation with him. Skipwith asked me if I knew anything about the Daniel-Richards case."

"Did he express an opinion about it?"

"He said something, what I don't remember."

"Didn't he say these three men were bad characters and needed attention?"

"I believe he did."

"Do you know anything about the kidnapping?"

"Nothing, I was only told about it."[654]

The New York Times recorded that the next witness to testify was Hugo Davenport, a 56-year resident of Mer Rouge.

"Do you know Dr. McKoin?" Warren asked.

"Yes."

"Have you received letters in the last several months from the Ku Klux Klan, vigilante committees or others attempting to regulate your conduct?"

"My brother Joe received such a letter about me."

---

[653] *Monroe News-Star,* 15 January 1923.
[654] Ibid.

"The notice was directed to you?"

"To him, but it said that if I didn't quit talking about the Klan I would get in trouble."

"That's the only written notice you had?"

"Yes."

"Were you and McKoin friendly?"

"Not friendly."

"Where were you when McKoin's automobile was shot at?"

"I was at home-all evening."

"How far is your residence from the place where he is said to have been shot at?"

"About two-thirds of a mile."

"Do you know who shot at the McKoin car?"

"I haven't any idea who did it."

"You discussed it with people?"

"I did. I talked about it with my family, my boys and others. It was a deep mystery."

"Did Dr. McKoin ever discuss the matter with you?"

"No, sir."

"Was it suggested in that note that your brother talk to you because you were talking too much about the Klan?"

"I don't think the Klan was mentioned. However, I'll get the letter and bring it to you."

"Do you know anything that will shed light upon the kidnapping of Daniel and Richards on August 24?"

"No, sir. I stayed at home that day. I heard that my son was in it. My son came and I asked him where he had been. He said, 'God only knows.' We took W. C. Andrews to the barber shop and washed the blood off him and sent him home." This was another in a litany of opportune areas for follow-up questioning that the attorney general's staff missed.

"Did your son tell you that he had been held up?"

"Yes."

"Did he know any of those who held him up?"

"He told me he didn't know any of them."

"When did you know that you were suspected of a part in the attempted killing of Dr. McKoin?"

"When A. L. Smith suggested the conference."

"That was after the kidnapping?"

"Yes."

"What were the general conditions around Mer Rouge before the kidnapping and subsequent to it?"

"Mer Rouge was a quiet, peaceful place until people of all kinds began to get notices telling them how they should conduct themselves."

"You were not a member of the Klan?"

"No, sir."

"About when did it become felt?"

"In January or February of 1922, I saw a parade of them in white robes."

"Do you recall the occasion of Addie May Hamilton being sent away?"

"Yes, sir."

"Did you see any other parades of masked men?"

"The next time they visited a negro restaurant in Mer Rouge. I was in the store and heard some one say, 'There goes the Ku Klux.' I was busy and did not get a good look at them as they turned the corner."

"How soon after the existence of the Ku Klux Klan became known did your citizens begin to get warnings?"

"About two months."

"These warnings continued right along?"

"Yes, sir, without interruption."[655]

Next to give witness was W. L. Pugh of Jones, Louisiana. He testified that he had lived in Jones for 26 years and that he was a farmer. His testimony was also missing from the *Monroe News-Star*.

"Did you know Watt Daniel?"

"Yes, fifteen or twenty years."

"Did you know T. F. Richards?"

"I met him once on the Mississippi River."

"Do you know W. C. Andrews?"

---

[655]Ibid.

"I know the family."

"Soon after the kidnapping on August 24, there were some committee meetings promoting peace in the parish, and you were called upon to vouch for the conduct of one of the three men of Mer Rouge who were deemed not good citizens. What did you do about it?"

"Campbell was once in my employ, and he told me he was in trouble and accused of shooting at Dr. McKoin, and asked me to come to his rescue and vouch for him at one of the conferences. I told him I was always willing to help anyone in an honorable way, and that I would do what I could. I told him I would come to Bastrop on the following day, which I did. On that day, a conference was held relative to the trouble in Mer Rouge. Citizens of Ouachita, Mer Rouge and Bastrop were present, and I spoke for Campbell."

"In other words, you vouched for Campbell. Now to whom?"

"I spoke to several."

"Who demanded that there should be any vouching for?"

"I really don't think anyone made a demand."

"Who made the complaint?"

"I don't know that he mentioned any names. There were several at the meeting: the Davenports, Mr. Smith, Mr. Dade, Captain Skipwith."

"Well, the Davenports or Smith or Dade didn't want Campbell vouched for?"

"No, but the idea came about, at a previous meeting at Monroe."

"Wasn't it the Ku Klux Klan of Morehouse demanding that Campbell be vouched for?"

"Well, I guess it was."

"Wasn't it your purpose to have at that conference leading men from all factions?"

"Yes, sir."

"Wasn't it Skipwith and the Klan that demanded that those men be vouched for?"

"I think so."

"Mr. Pugh, are you a member of the Klan?"

"I am."

"Mr. Pugh, the fact that you are a Klansman does not reflect upon you in my opinion. I am merely trying to get at the facts. You didn't hear any complaints against Whipple, Campbell and Milner, except with the Klan and Skipwith and the Klan, did you?"

"Yes, I heard some others complain; people whom I would consider the best in Mer Rouge."

"Who were some of these people?"

"I don't like to name people unless I have to."

The question was withdrawn.

"Were you in Bastrop on August 24, the day of the ball game?"

"Yes."

"Then where did you go?"

"After the game I started home."

"Did you go by the Mer Rouge Road?"

"No, I went north."

"Then you were not interrupted on the road?"

"No."

"When did you first hear of the kidnapping on the Bastrop-Mer Rouge Road?"

"The next day."

"Did you take any particular interest in the matter?"

"Not particular."

"Had you anticipated such a thing as happened to these men?"

"I had not."

"Had you heard of Daniel and Richards discussed as suspects in the attempted assassination of Dr. McKoin?"

"I heard that. I don't remember who discussed it."[656]

Following Pugh to the stand was James Harp. He stated that he lived on Iron Mountain Road just north of Mer Rouge. Harp's testimony was also missing from the *Monroe News-Star*.

"Were you acquainted with Watt Daniel?"

"Yes, sir: all of his life."

"Did you know T. F. Richards?"

"Slightly."

---

[656]Ibid.

During his testimony, the witness admitted that he had discussed the trouble brewing in Mer Rouge, but he was unable to recall with whom he had had that discussion.

"Did you hear any names mentioned as suspects in connection with the shooting at Dr. McKoin?"

"Yes, sir."

"Name them please."

"Watt Daniel, T. F. Richards, Campbell, Milner, Whipple, and Davenport."

"Did you come to the baseball game at Bastrop on August 24?"

"Yes, I came early in the morning."

"Who was with you?"

"My daughter, Bessie, Jack Jones and Mrs. Jones and others."

"After the baseball game, what did you do?"

"We started home but stopped at John Morris's, where we learned that the Ku Klux got some of the boys."

"Did you see any masked men passing through town?"

"No."

"When did you finally start back home?"

"About midnight."

"Where had you spent the evening in Bastrop?"

"At Thomas' store."

"Who came in during the evening, who was there all evening?"

"Captain Skipwith came in, and a lot came, and went. Nobody stayed long."

"They'd all heard about the kidnapping?"

"Oh, yes, everyone was talking about it."

"Were you out on the street any time that day?"

"No, there was a lot of wild talk, and I didn't want to get into trouble."

"Had you taken sides in any of the controversies?"

"Well, I had taken Dr. McKoin's side when he was shot at."

"You believed he was shot at?"

"I did."

"You believed that Daniel and Richards did the shooting?"

"I have heard that report, but I never believed that Watt did it. I didn't believe that Richards was in it either."

"You are a member of the Klan?"

"Yes."

"And most of the people around Thomas' store that night were Klansmen, weren't they?"

"Yes, sir."

"Smith Stevenson was there?"

"Yes."

"Who were some of the others?"

"There were some that I'd met, but I can't remember their names."

"You have heard of other incidents where men have been taken out by the Ku Klux Klan haven't you?"

"Yes. But none as serious as this."

"Men were taken out and told to improve their habits; that's about all, wasn't it?"

"Yes: in most cases the men were released after being warned. I heard of one Bastrop man getting whipped, a man named Osborne, that's all."

"Well, if these things were never so serious before, why did you and the other Klansmen wait up until midnight in Thomas' store to learn what had happened to Daniel and Richards and the others who were kidnapped?"

"There had been a lot of bad feeling in Mer Rouge and they were up in arms, and I wanted to see what was going to happen."

"Were you armed while in Thomas' store?"

"There were guns in the rack in Thomas' store."

"Were they loaded?"

"They were loaded after we got there."

"And men armed themselves?"

"Yes."

"Captain Skipwith, Jack Jones, John Morrison, yourself, all of you armed yourselves in the store and remained armed-is that correct?"

"Yes."

"What caused everyone to arm?"

"They were afraid the kidnapping would raise a storm in Mer Rouge and cause them to come over and start trouble."

"Do you remember seeing C. B. Pratt, Thomas Butler, Mr. Bolquarn, any of those that night?"

"No, sir."

"Who did you think did the kidnapping?"

"The Ku Klux, I thought."

"Why do you suppose they had done it?"

"I had to suppose that someone had done it."

"Did you suspect someone to make an attack on the Thomas' store?"

"No, but there was trouble in the air, and we wanted to be prepared. I wanted to be able to defend myself if something happened."

Mr. Guion then began to question the witness.

"You did not have a thing in the world against Daniel or Richards or any of those men, did you say?"

"No, sir."

"You saw Watt Daniel on August 24?"

"Yes, at the ball game. I talked to him."

"And that was the last time you ever talked to him?"

"Yes, the last time."[657]

The New York Times reported that the last witness to take the stand this day was a businessman from Bonita, J. N. (Jap) Jones. Jones said that he had gone to Bastrop on August 24 with Pugh, and further corroborated nearly all of the previous testimony given by Harp. Jones claimed he questioned Captain Skipwith about Klan involvement in the kidnappings, and Skipwith told him that the Klan was not associated with the incident. The testimony of this Klansman was also absent from the *Monroe News-Star*.

"You met with Stevenson at Thomas' store?"

"Yes."

"Did you send out for Captain Skipwith?"

"Yes, we didn't believe the Ku Klux could have done the kidnapping, and we sent out for the Captain to get some information."

"You had talked with Gus Calhoun about it?"

"Yes, and invited him over to Thomas' store."

---

[657] Ibid.

"Are you a Klansman?"

"Yes."

"Did you load the guns before Captain Skipwith arrived?"

"Yes, we felt it was a serious thing."

"What made you regard it as a serious thing?"

"Well, I knew that there had been shots between Mer Rouge people and a lot of trouble over people making whiskey."

"What did you ever hear against Richards?"

"Nothing except he was kind of wild and played poker and didn't work steady."

"Isn't it a fact that when you heard of the kidnapping, you knew it would be charged to the Ku Klux Klan, and you gathered at Thomas' store prepared to defend the Klan?"

"I didn't think the Klan did it, but I knew of the bad feeling and we wanted to be able to defend ourselves if something started."

"When have you attended a meeting of the Ku Klux Klan?"

"You mean prior to the kidnapping? I might have been at the August meeting."

"Do you know whether either Daniel or Richards were discussed at a Klan meeting?"

"I don't know. I remember it was once decided to let Mer Rouge go it alone and take care of herself."

"What did the Klan do about the attempted assassination of Dr. McKoin?"

"I think Dr. McKoin was advised to leave Mer Rouge."

"What did McKoin say?"

"I believe he accused Watt Daniel of writing him a couple of letters."

Jones was then questioned as to what attempts, if any, the Klan made to ascertain the details about the abduction of Daniel and Richards.

"The Klan couldn't have done anything. Anyway, it was the Grand Jury's business."

"You don't think the Klan had anything to do with the kidnapping?"

"I do not."

"You don't think it was the Klan's business to look into the kidnapping?"

"I'd think it was the Grand Jury's business."

"Concerning the armed Klansmen that had gathered in Thomas' store on the

393

evening of August 24. What was your plan? Your fears?"

"Well, we decided if any one came around there with black hoods on them, we'd arrest them or defend ourselves if attacked."

"You don't think the black-hooded men were Klansmen?"

"No, sir."

Mr. Guion then took over the questioning.

"You regret the death of Watt Daniel and Richards?"

"For a long time, I did not believe they were dead, but it looks now that they are and I regret it, of course."

Mr. Sompayrac assumed the questioning.

"Have you ever heard Captain Skipwith denounce the governor for bringing on this investigation?"

"I've seen something in the newspapers."

After continued questioning on that topic, Jones finally admitted that he had, in fact, heard Skipwith denounce the governor for calling the investigation.

"The Klan never called for an investigation of these crimes, did it?"

"No, of course."[658]

The *Monroe News-Star* reported that Attorney General A. V. Coco dismissed as "ridiculous, preposterous and not worthy of consideration" the rumor which was being circulated that Richards and Daniels were still alive. Coco asserted that the bodies recovered from Lake LaFourche the day of the dynamite explosion have been positively identified as those of Richards and Daniel. Because of these Klan-spawned rumors, Mrs. Anna Garretson, mother of Richards and a resident of West Monroe, authored the following letter which appeared in the paper that day:

> I wish to positively and emphatically deny the report that is being circulated in Morehouse that I have heard from my son, Thomas Richards, and that he is alive. I did not receive a letter from two months ago, as is being told. I have not heard one word from him since he was kidnapped on August 24, and I know positively that he is dead and that he was the victim of the hooded mob in Morehouse parish. The reports being circulated to the effect that my son is alive is simply for the purpose of obstructing the open hearing at Bastrop, which will prove conclusively that my son and Watt Daniel were tortured and murdered. No sensible person will believe or circulate such reports. The bodies were positively identified.[659]

---

[658] Ibid.

[659] *Monroe News-Star,* 15 January 1923.

Condemns Ku Klux Klan Resolution in Massachusetts House says it Threatens the Nation[660]

A bulletin from the Rules Committee of the state House of Representatives Boston announced an order declaring the Ku Klux Klan to be "an attempt to overthrow organized government." The resolution declared that the "House regards any such organization as the Klan as dangerous to American institutions and a threat to the freedom of thought and speech guaranteed to the American people."

Legion Endorses Anti-Klan Bill[661]

The Iowa Department of the American Legion announced this day that it will support a bill to be introduced in the state legislature prohibiting the wearing of masks in public.

Five Put to Death by Irish Free State[662]

From Dublin came the grim news that four men were executed at Roscrea and one at Carlow by the Free State Government this today. They were charged with possession of arms.

Three Men Drop Dead Drinking at Bar[663]

A dispatch from Jersey City, New Jersey, announced that bad liquor was believed to have killed three men who dropped dead, one after another, within a few minutes in a saloon at 458 Monmouth Street. They were seen by a man who entered the place just after they had been drinking to double up and slide to the floor without a word.

---

[660]*The New York Times*, 16 January 1923.
[661]Ibid.
[662]Ibid.
[663]Ibid.

Alibi For Skipwith is Offered by Klan: Two Members Testify Exalted Cyclops was in Bastrop on Night of Hooded Murders[664][665]

Bastrop Prepared for Raid on Night When Two Mer Rouge Men Were Kidnapped, Say Witnesses[666]
Davenport Relates Receipt of Letter Ordering Him Out[667]
Special Policeman is Quizzed as to Whether he was Member of Klan Party Reported Armed.[668]

The New York Times reported that an air of excitement permeated Court House Square early in the morning as the rumor spread that identification had been made of four of the black-hooded kidnappers of Daniel and Richards. It was said that E. N. Gray, a Klansman and reputed to have been one of those named, was to be the first called to the stand this morning to testify. Attorney General Coco, playing his cards close to his vest, refused to confirm or deny the rumors. The rumors purported that new evidence had surfaced in the case and that five men had been named as being definitely involved in the crimes. It was said that positive identification of members of the black-hooded band would be forthcoming. Part of this new evidence revolved around a statement taken from a self-admitted witness to the kidnapping, Barry Whetstone. In his statement, Whetstone told of being forced to be a "waterboy" for the Klan on the night and at the location where the Klan had kidnapped Daniel and Richards. It was alleged that Whetstone would be able to link these men to the crime.

Smith Stevenson was the first witness to take the stand in the morning. Through this witness, the state attempted to make three points. First was to prove that there were numerous Klansmen from Arkansas in Bastrop on August 24, the date of the kidnapping. Second, was tracking the location(s) of the truck owned by Stevenson on that date. Finally, the state was probing the depths of Stevenson's knowledge and involvement in the acquisition of the dynamite, and where any large caches of dynamite were stored in the vicinity of Bastrop.

The *Monroe News-Star* recorded the testimony of Smith Stevenson with Attorney General A. V. Coco delivering the questions. During the preliminary

---

[664]*The New York Times*, 16 January 1923.
[665]Ibid.
[666]*Monroe News-Star*, 16 January 1923.
[667]Ibid.
[668]Ibid.

questioning, Stevenson said that he was a special police officer in Bastrop on August 24, the day on which Daniel and Richards were kidnapped and murdered. He had been commissioned because of the baseball game and barbecue held in Bastrop that day. He maintained that he knew nothing of the kidnappings until he was informed by Andrews' mother that her son had been kidnapped by a black-hooded band.

"Was the town excited?"

"People were going in every direction, but I did not notice any particular excitement."

"Did you see any hooded men come through town?" inquired Mr. Coco.

"No," said the witness.

"If they did pass through Bastrop from the Mer Rouge-Bastrop road where the kidnapping occurred to the Monroe road, could they have done so without you seeing them?"

"Yes, they could have passed without me seeing them."

"Could they have gone from one road to the other by skirting the town?"

"Yes."

"The night of the kidnapping, did you make any effort to locate these parties and arrest the kidnappers?"

"No."

"Why?"

"I was just a special deputy, and it was nothing I could do right then."

"You heard that five men had been kidnapped?"

"Yes, Earl Andrews told me how many."

"Were you surprised at the kidnapping?"

"Yes."

"You had no intimation that there was going to be a kidnapping?"

"No."

"Did you know about any other cases of kidnapping?"

"Yes. I know about Richards and Harry Neelis."

"Did you know of any bitterness existing between Daniel and Richards?"

"No."

"You are a member of the Klan?"

"Yes."

"Did you know of any bitterness in the Klan against these men?"

"No. I don't think so."

"You know Mr. McKoin?"

"Yes."

"You know of any bitterness that might exist between him and these men?"

"No

Coco then changed the line of questioning to the night of the kidnapping. "Did you go into Thomas' store?"

"I passed by, but I didn't go in."

"You did not go into the rear of the store?"

"I believe I did."

"Did you see any guns?"

"Well, I think I did."

"Did you know whether they were loaded?"

"I don't think I did."

"Were you armed?"

"Yes, I had my gun as an officer of the law."

"What did you go to Captain Skipwith for?"

"I don't remember. I don't remember if I went or I sent for Captain Skipwith."

"You can't remember if you went or sent for Captain Skipwith?"

"I guess so-I have a faint recollection that something like that happened. Jap Jones said something about seeing Captain Skipwith."

"Do you know if Captain Skipwith came to Thomas' store?"

"I think he did."

"Where did you see Skipwith?"

"I saw him standing on the street near the restaurant."

"You didn't send [for] him at his home then; you sent for him while on the street?"

"Yes."

"If you had been with a bunch of armed men waiting for a riot, or the kidnappers, or the men, don't you think you could remember something?"

"I guess so."

"Well, can you remember going anywhere else?"

"Yes, I went to Turpin's store."

"Who did you see there?"

"I think I saw Jim Norseworthy and others."

"Who else?"

"I don't remember."

"What time did you go home?"

"I don't remember."

"Where else did you go?"

"Well, I went by the dance that night."

"Did you see Sidney White?"

"No."

"Did you see Fred Higgenbotham?"

"No."

"Did you go inside the dance hall?"

"No."

"Why did you go down there?"

"There was some talk of some whiskey coming to the dance for the boys."

"Did you have anybody under suspicion?"

"No, I didn't."

"Did you suspicion Watt Daniels [sic]?"

"No."

"Did you suspicion Richards?"

"No."

"Was Watt Daniels [sic] regarded as a bootlegger?"

"Yes."

"He had been under suspicion as having sold whiskey in Bastrop?"

"Yes."

"You were the day policeman?"

"Yes."

"You were at liberty to go home at any time at night?"

"Yes."

"How many stores were open that night?"

"I don't remember."

"You didn't have in mind any trouble that would arise from this kidnapping?"

"No, I don't think so."

"Nothing at all?"

"Well, I heard something on the street."

"Who was at 'Bub' Thomas' store besides Jap Jones?"

"I don't remember."

"Was Dr. Billington there?" The name "F. L. Billington" appears on the application for membership in Morehouse Klan No. 34.

"I don't remember."

"Was Thomas there himself?"

"I think so."

From here on, the print in the newspaper is of such poor quality that it either did not reproduce well enough to read, or it was simply not there to read at all.

"Was Mr. Laney (or Haney) there?"

"I don't remember."

"Was John Morris there?"

"I guess so-I don't remember."

"What time did you go there the last time?"

"I don't remember."

"Was the Klan discussed as being responsible for the kidnappings?"

"I don't think so."

"You own a truck?"

"Yes, I bought it from Harry Neelis."

"Was it a new truck?"

"No, it was second hand, I paid $30."

"Was it a regular stock car or was (unreadable---) home-made body?"

"It had a stock body."

"What was the (license) number?"

"I couldn't tell you."

"Where is the car now?"

"At my house."

"How long had you been using the (unreadable---)?"

"About thirty days before the [The word that follows looks like it may have been 'kidnapping')."

"Did you use the truck that day?" Although he did not specify which day, Stevenson obviously understood that he was asking about the August 24th kidnappings.

"(Unreadable----) haul water to the ballplayers at the ball game." The next two questions and answers are unreadable.

"Was it there the next morning?"

"I think so."

"Can't you be positive about it?"

"I think it was, but I don't remember exactly. Harry Neelis kept his car there, but I don't remember about it."

"You are positive that you saw Captain Skipwith that night?"

"Yes, I saw him on the street."

"Do you think it was as late as 8:30 o'clock?"

"I have no idea, but it wasn't as late as 9 o'clock."

"Were you deputized by the sheriff or the marshal?"

"The marshal and the mayor."

"Have you been deputized since that day by the mayor?"

"I don't think so."

"Was there any strained relationship between you and Watt Daniels [sic]?"

"I knew him, that's all."

"Who pointed out Richards to you?"

"J. D. Higgenbotham." This question was concerning the August 24th, 1922, baseball game in Bastrop.

"Was he intoxicated?"

"He was reeling in that way."

"Who was he with?"

"Kelly Harp."

"You are anxious to see this investigation successful?"

"Yes, sir."

"You are willing to give your aid to bring to light the murderers of Daniels [sic] and Richards?"

"Yes."

"You said that you assume that your car was at home that night?"

"Yes."

"Then if your car was seen on the roads out of Bastrop it was being driven without your permission?"

"Yes, sir."

"The 24th day of August is one date always to be impressed on the people of Bastrop?"

"Yes, sir."

"Watt Daniels [sic] and Richards haven't been seen since?"

"That's right."

"Did you see anybody point out Watt Daniels [sic] at the ball game?"

"No, sir."

"On your honor as a man your answer (unreadable--)?"

"Yes, sir."

"Did you see anybody point out Richards?"

"No, sir."

"Did you speak to Daniels [sic] on that date?"

"I believe I did." Here is an opportunity missed by the state. The next logical question would have been concerning the content of that conversation. This is one of the many opportunities that the state blindly passed by.

"Who are your brothers-in-law?"

"Jake Albright, Ira Morgan, Ned Chesser, John Edwin, and Oscar Naff."

"Do you know Will Chance?"

"Yes."

"Do you know H. E. Blankenship?"

"Yes, sir."

"How about Will Laney?"

"Yes, I know him."

"Didn't see him at the baseball game at Bastrop?"

"I don't remember."

"Did you see anybody from Arkansas at that game?"

"I don't remember. There was no special reason that I should. I spoke to so many people."

"Have you ever received a letter [from] or talked to Will Laney?"

"No, not that I can recall."

"Who told you that Watt Daniels [sic] was peddling liquor?"

"I don't recall."

"Do you know whether it was a bootlegger [who] told you that?"

"I don't recall.'

"Did you ever try to assist the officers of this parish to find out who spirited Watt Daniels [sic] and Richards away and later killed them?"

"No, sir."

"As a matter of fact, weren't a good many people in Bastrop and elsewhere blaming the K.K.K. for the kidnapping?"

"Yes."

"A crime had been committed?"

"That's what they tell me."

"It's a dead American lead pipe cinch Daniels [sic] and Richards have never come back, have they?"

"Yes, sir."

"You know by reason of the fact that they were hooded men, everybody was blaming the Klan?"

"Yes, I think so, although I am not sure."

"You just said that the Klan," Coco stopped in mid-sentence.

"Well, I don't know."

"Well, Jap Jones said on the stand yesterday that people were holding the Klan to blame. Don't you agree with him?"

"I don't know."

"You don't recall anything in Thomas' store?"

"I don't remember."

"Is it because you are unable to remember, to carry anything in your head of what occurred as far back as August?"

"Yes, that's it. I am unable to carry it in my head."

"Are you familiar with the use of dynamite?"

"Yes, although I never used it myself."

"Do you know whether anybody has a supply of dynamite on hand?"

"I do not."

"Have you been to Lake LaFourche since the discovery of the bodies?"

"I don't believe I have."

"Have you heard of any dynamite being stolen in this section?"

"I don't think so. No, I have no record of it."

"You are a blacksmith now?" It should be noted here that one of the witnesses identified one of the perpetrators of the August 24th kidnappings as "Blacksmith Smith."

"Yes."

"Did you miss any tools the night Lake LaFourche was dynamited?"

"I don't remember. The men working for me could tell you that."

"Who is he?"

"Floyd Van."

"When did Van start working for you?"

"Well, it was before Christmas."

"Has he ever said he missed a hacksaw?"

"I don't think so."

"Now lets go back to August 24. You recollect whether you saw Captain Skipwith on the street or at his home?"

"It was on the street."

"Where does Captain Skipwith live?"

"He lives in Vaughn."

"Oh, he doesn't live in Bastrop?"

"No, he lives on our place-the V. T. Stevenson estate."

"What are the names of Captain Skipwith's boys?"

"Oliver and William."

"Did you see William at the ball game?"

"I don't recollect."

"How about Oliver?"

"I don't remember."

"You said you did hear Jap Jones and Jim Harp testify?"

"That's right."

"Have you heard what they testified about?"

"Yes, on the streets."

"When was the first time you saw Captain Skipwith?"

"This morning."

"Did he tell you?"

"No, we just talked."

"Are you sure?"

"I am."

"You did not see him last night?"

"No."

"Do you know Jim Harp and Jap Jones said you were in Thomas' store all of that night?"

"Yes, I heard something about that."

"He told you?"

"Oh, I just heard it on the street."

"Where was your Klan regalia on the night of August 24?"

"I never owned one."

"Nobody ever loaned you one?"

"Yes, at the meetings."

"How many meetings did you attend?"

"Well, there was one down in the woods. We had a supper."

"Where did you attend?"

"Well, one between here and Monroe and in this courthouse."

"You wore the regalia?"

"Yes."

"Who was the presiding officer?"

"Some fellow. He had a robe on."

It is quite obvious that Stevenson appears to have been intentionally evasive in his testimony. Seeking to elicit more specific testimony from Stevenson, he was again called as a witness in the afternoon session, but to no avail. He continued his stonewall testimony.

The New York Times also recorded Smith Stevenson. As in the previous instances, the testimony was similar, but never exact. There were no significant departures from both versions except for the following section.

"Would you like to see the men who murdered Daniel and Richards brought to justice, regardless of whether they are Klansmen, Masons, Pythians or what not?"

Special note should be taken of this question. As has been demonstrated in previous testimony and the testimony to come, it was not uncommon for men to hold membership in a number of secret organizations. You may recall the Knights of Pythias band played at a Klan function reported by the *Monroe News-Star* in 1922. Indeed, it is safe to say that multiple membership in secret organizations was the norm rather than the exception.

"Yes, sir."

"Are you a Mason?"

"Yes, sir."

"There is nothing in Masonry to keep you from assisting the state in finding the men who committed these crimes. You know as a Mason that you can answer 'yes' to that question?" These passages that refer to Masons, Masonry and Pythians did not appear in the *Monroe News-Star* version.[669]

The New York Times reported the next to be summoned to testify was Robert Lee Harkness. Harkness, who had been on the stand yesterday, told of having sold gasoline to black-hooded men at his store in Collinston on the night of the kidnapping. Although he identified Daniel as being in the back of the truck, he claimed he was unable to identify any of the black-hooded band. It became clear that he feared for his safety and continued to stonewall attempts by the state to identify the kidnappers.

"What time did the masked men come up?"

"About 8 or 9 o'clock."

"What did they do?"

"Stopped and got gas."

"How many cars?"

"One was a Ford truck and one a touring car."

"How many men."

"Two in the truck, and maybe three, four or five in the touring car."

"You saw a man in the rear of the truck?"

"Yes, blindfolded and sitting there."

"Was anything said to indicate it was Watt Daniel?"

"No, sir."

"Did the masked men get out of the cars?"

"No, sir."

"What did you do for the men?"

"I got them a pail of water, and they all drank."

"Were you close to them when they drank?"

---

[669]*The New York Times*, 16 January 1923.

"No, sir."

"Did you know any of these masked men?"

"No, sir."

"Did you see a torn mask on one man?"

"Yes, he was the one that bought a bottle of beer."

Here was another prime opportunity that the state failed to capitalize upon. The question arises, How did the Klansman come to have this beer? Did someone bring it out to him? According to this witness, this Klansman "bought a bottle of beer." If the beer was not brought out to him, then he must have gone into the store to purchase it. If he did go inside, then Boyd was lying when he testified that Klansmen did not enter his store.

"Did you not recognize any voices?"

"No, sir. One man spoke to me and said they had been on the road all day and wanted some water."

"Were they there when 'Tot' Davenport came into the store?"

"I think so."

"You say one of the men on the truck was Watt Daniel?"

"Yes, sir."

"Your recollection is that there were four or five men in the touring car and one or two hooded men in the truck?"

"Yes, sir."

"Any of them armed?"

"A man on the truck had what looked to be a pistol."

"What road did they take?"

"The Monroe road."

"How far is that from Bastrop?"

"About five miles."

"If you knew any of these men would you tell us?"

"Yes, sir."

"Did anyone in that crowd resemble anyone you know?"

"Maybe, but I'm not sure."

"Did you have any suspicions that they may have been someone you knew?"

"I am not sure."

"But you did have an idea as to the identity of two or three?"

"I wouldn't swear to it."

"Will you tell the court?"

"I wouldn't like to."

"Why?"

"Because I am not certain who they were."

"But in your heart you are satisfied as to their identify?"

"I am not sure of that."

"Has anyone since then asked you if you identified anyone in the cars?"

"No one but a Government agent."

"You mentioned names to him?"

"I told him my own thoughts."

The government agent to whom Harkness was making reference was the assistant attorney general himself, Mr. Seth Guion. At this point, Mr. Guion took over the questioning in an effort to get Harkness to say the names in open court.

"You did give me the name of a person who you thought might have been one of the masked men. Now, if another witness should testify as to the name of the man, would you be willing to testify as to your belief in his identity?"

"No, sir. I wouldn't."

"Don't you remember making the statement in the butcher shop in Collinston that you recognized the man?"

"No, sir."

"Didn't you make that statement, and someone there told you to keep your mouth shut?"

"I don't remember making such a remark."

"Are you afraid to mention the name of the man you thought it was?"

"No, I don't think I ought to."

"Because you just think you know his name?"

"I don't think I know it now."

"When did you quit thinking that you knew the man?"

"About a month ago."

"You have reached the conclusion you were mistaken?"

"I don't think he was the man."

"Did somebody make you think you were wrong?"

"I just don't think he was the man."

"You want to see the murderers of Watt Daniel and T. F. Richards brought to justice?"

"I do."

"You intend to live here always?"

"No, sir, I don't."[670]

The *Monroe News-Star* version of Harkness' testimony was similar, but with one major exception. The *News-Star* version differed dramatically in that Harkness clearly stated that he saw one of the black-hooded men enter the store and make purchases.

"Did any masked man buy anything in the store?"

"Yes, a bottle of beer and cigarettes."

"Did one of them have his mask torn?"

"Yes, it was torn full in the face."[671]

As has occurred before, the testimony of the next three witnesses given this date did not appear in the *Monroe News-Star*, but did appear in *The New York Times*. After Harkness was dismissed, the *Times* reported that C. W. Walker was called to the stand. Walker, a member of the Fellowship Missionary Baptist Church, told of a visit made to the congregation by black-hooded Klansmen several months before the August kidnappings. Although they wore black hoods, the witness said he recognized two of them being Dr. B. M. McKoin and W. D. "Pink" Kirkpatrick, the latter packing two handguns.

"What was done?"

"Something was said about the third warning and what might happen next time."

"What was the warning about?"

"It was some trouble about public worship in church I thought they had reference to. They didn't mention any names."

"Did you recognize the other masked men?"

"No. They were near the door and I did not have time to see them."

"You did not recognize any masked men on the outside?"

"I saw only the four who came in."

---

[670]*The New York Times*, 16 January 1923.
[671]*Monroe News-Star*, 16 January 1923.

"Did Dr. McKoin or Kirkpatrick belong to your church?"

"No, sir."

"Was McKoin your family physician?"

"He was."

"Are you friends now?"

"We are. That is, there's no feeling but good between us, but if McKoin is implicated in things charged against him, that may make a difference."

"Was E. N. Gray in church the night of August 24?"

"He was not."[672]

Next called to testify about the Klan visit to the church was Jack Hayden. *The New York Times* reported that as he mounted the stand, he was grinning widely. He maintained this grin throughout his testimony. One can openly wonder what it was that gave him such amusement.

"How many men did you see?"

"Three."

"What color were their robes and hoods?"

"Black."

"What did they do?"

"One took out a paper and read for about fifteen minutes."

"What did he read about?"

"He read about a disturbance in the church."

"What was that?"

"A fight they had off from the church."

"Who read the warning in the church?"

"I took him to be Dr. McKoin."

"Who was the man with the guns?"

"Kirkpatrick, I think."[673]

The centerpiece of the day's testimony was made by the next witness, E. N. Gray, and it is strangely absent from the *Monroe News-Star*. Gray backed up the testimony of Hayden and Walker concerning the Klan visit to the church. However, he seemed to claim that he had, in fact, been present in the church on the night of the Klan visit. To this, he claimed he had been unable to recognize any of the

---

[672]Ibid.

Klansmen, but that he had heard other members of the congregation say that they believed that they might have been Dr. McKoin, "Pink" Kirkpatrick, Sam Walton, George Sims and others.

At this point, R. L. Todd, counsel for Burnett and McKoin, objected to the line of questioning due to the fact that Gray had been mentioned by the newspapers as one of those who would soon be charged in connection with the kidnappings and murders of Daniel and Richards. Judge Odom advised Todd that he lacked standing to object and ordered the questioning to continue.

"What time did you come to Bastrop that day (August 24)?"

"That morning."

"Who was with you?"

"My wife, her sister and Walter Butler and the Rev. L. M. Holmes."

"Did you attend the barbecue?"

"Yes."

"Where did you spend the afternoon?"

"Just about the time the game started my wife wanted to go home, so I went down to see the other folks, who were at the ball game and I carried them home and came back."

"Who did you carry home?"

"My wife and her sister, Mrs. Eubanks, and the Rev. L. M. Holmes."

"Which way did you go home?"

"Over the gravel road, east toward Mer Rouge."

"Then you did go on the Bastrop-Mer Rouge road?"

"Yes."

"Did you go immediately to your home?"

"Yes, sir."

"Who came back to Bastrop with you?"

"I came alone."

"What kind of car were you driving?"

"Overland."

"Well, what did you say to Willie Higgenbotham about going home with him?"

---

[673] Ibid.

"I said I would if I could get somebody else to take my car home, as I had people with me."

"Who did you have in your party?"

"Walter Butler, Addie May Eubanks and Emma Murdock."

"Were there other members of the Eubanks family in Bastrop?"

"Yes, Rufus Eubanks, my nephew."

"Why did Higgenbotham want you to go home with him?"

"He had received a threatening letter and was afraid."

"Did he fear trouble on the road?"

"There or at home."

"You went to Willie Higgenbotham's that night?"

"Yes."

"How far is his house from yours?"

"About three and a half miles."

"Who are some of his neighbors?"

"Dave Michie and J. B. Courtland."

"When did Higgenbotham tell you he had received a threatening letter?"

"That morning."

"What did he say were the contents of the letter?"

"He said he had gotten a very threatening letter, he had gotten two, but the first was not so severe."

"What was the nature of the threats?"

"He had been warned to leave; get out of the country; it read he might expect trouble soon."

"Jasper Jones is the only one that you know that Higgenbotham told about this letter?"

"Yes, sir."

"He really expected that if any trouble came it would come to him at his home, not on the road?"

"I think so."

"Did Higgenbotham indicate whom he suspected of writing the notes?"

"No, sir."

"Had he done anything to arouse the indignation of others?"

"Not that I know about."

"How large are his children?"

"The oldest daughter is about grown, I think. He has three other children."

As his testimony continued, Gray said Rufus Eubanks had driven his family home in his, Gray's, car. Gray said he accompanied them as far as the branch of the Cooper Lake Road, which leads to Mer Rouge. Gray said he then made his way to the home of Mr. Eldridge, where he encountered a Mr. Griffith, whom he described as an employee of the Bastrop Pulp Mill. When Tom Higgenbotham passed by Gray proceeded with him to Willie Higgenbotham's home. Gray said he did not go into Higgenbotham's home, not even for supper. He said Tom stayed there until around 11 or 12 midnight.

"Where did you stay?"

"Well, we parked the car under some pecan trees. Sometimes we sat in it and at other times we walked around."

"Did Tom Higgenbotham go into his house for a gun?"

"I think Tom had a gun, but I never did see. Willie Higgenbotham went into his house and got a gun and gave me one after I got there."

"What kind of gun did he give you?"

"A large pearl-handled six-shooter."

"Was there some traveling on the road-some disturbance?"

"There was some traveling but no disturbance."

"No one attempted to turn into the yard?"

"No, sir."

"Were those the only two men you saw that evening?"

"Well, we passed four or five cars on the road."

"Do you remember any of those you passed?"

"I took one of them for the Andrews. He was coming from Mer Rouge. It was Earl Andrews."

"Did you see any masked men?"

"Yes, I saw several of them."

"How many cars were there with masked men?"

"Three or four."

"Did you know any of the men?"

"No."

"Did any of them seem to be prisoners?"

"Yes, I saw two in a Ford truck; they were in the back. They were blindfolded with handkerchiefs."

"How many hooded men in the truck?"

"Two men in black masks were in the front seat. There were others in the back of the truck besides the blindfolded men."

"Did the truck lead the procession?"

"No, I think there was a car ahead of it."

"And cars behind it?"

Here again the witness verifies that there were more than two vehicles involved in the transportation of Daniel and Richards.

"Yes."

"What was said?"

"Higgenbotham asked me what it meant. We did not know what it meant."

"Did you know Watt Daniel?"

"I've seen him a few times. I could figure him out, I think."

"Haven't you seen Watt Daniel often in the last two years?"

"I don't think so. I recognized him when I saw him."

"Didn't you know T. F. Richards?"

"I did not."

"Didn't you recognize Watt as he passed on that truck?"

"No."

"You didn't recognize either of those blindfolded men?"

"No, sir."

"Are you a member of the Ku Klux Klan?"

"I am."

"Where were you initiated?"

"Here in the courthouse."

"Who was in the building at that time?"

"I don't believe I remember."

"Was Skipwith, Grand Cyclops, present?"

"Yes."

"Can't you remember other officers, the Secretary, or any of them?"

"No."

"What other meetings of the Klan have you attended?"

"Just one, the public parade in Monroe."

"Do you know who your fellow members are?"

"No, sir. I never attended any meetings and eventually I declared myself out."[674]

Massachusetts House Condemns Klan[675]

From Boston came the announcement that the House of Representatives, by unanimous vote, this day passed a resolution terming the Ku Klux Klan "dangerous to American rights." Also, an article from Fall River, Massachusetts, told how when Mayor Edmond P. Talbot opened his mail this day, he found the following letter mailed from Taunton and post-marked Sunday. "Mayor Talbot-Keep you eyes on your business, such as dance halls, and watch your step. KU KLUX KLAN." The mayor turned the letter over to Police Chief Feeney.

Texas Senate Commends Parker[676]

A dispatch from Austin, Texas, told of a resolution from the Texas Senate commending efforts at law enforcement by Governor Parker of Louisiana and approving his actions against "hooded mobs and masked political organizations."

Illinois House Get Anti-Klan Bill[677]

A news release from Springfield, Illinois, a told of an "Anti-Ku Klux Klan" bill among the principal measures introduced this day in the legislature.

WEDNESDAY JANUARY 17, 1923

Coco to Identify Mer Rouge Slayers
Attorney General Issues Statement That State Will Call Star Witness Soon[678]
Klansman Witness Denies He's Slayer[679]
Objection of Counsel for Grey is Overruled: Witness to Give Answers Without Involvement[680]
M'Koin Recognized as Participant of Unusual Gathering[681]

The New York Times reported an evening news conference called by Louisiana Attorney General Coco. He told reporters that the identities of the kidnappers/murderers of Daniel and Richards would soon be revealed in open

---

[674]Ibid.

[675]Ibid.

[676]Ibid.

[677]Ibid.

[678]Ibid.

[679]Ibid.

[680]Ibid.

court. He indicated that two key witnesses had finally been located and had said they were willing to testify as to their knowledge of the kidnapping and murders of Daniel and Richards. One was said to be a traveling salesman whose vehicle had broken down on the Monroe road just a short distance from Lake LaFourche. Coco said that this witness had seen the vehicles containing the bodies of Daniel and Richards pass his location en route to Lake LaFourche. The second witness was said to be a man who saw the Ford truck and the touring car and had given the license numbers of the vehicles to the government agents.

It was rumored that Barry Whetstone would be called to testify on the next day. Considered the state's star witness, Whetstone it was said told authorities that he had been walking pass the roadblock set up by the black-hooded Klansmen on the Bastrop-Mer Rouge road on the evening of August 24. As he was walking past, he was summoned by one of the Klansmen to fetch them water. He claimed that while he was on the scene, he personally observed the kidnapping of Daniel and Richards.

It was also announced on this date by Sheriff Carpenter that one of his former deputies, "Jeff" Burnett, who has already been charged with the murders of Daniel and Richards, would be returned to Bastrop on the coming Friday after having spent time convalescing in a Shreveport hospital from an alleged bout with pleurisy.

The New York Times reported that the first witness called this morning was Sheriff Carpenter. In his testimony, he revealed that although Alonzo Braddock had been arrested by Captain Skipwith and the Klansmen that had accompanied him to the Braddock residence. Carpenter said that Braddock stayed at his home the night of his arrest and that he released him later that morning. Carpenter also confirmed that it was not until Braddock had already been released that a warrant was issued for Braddock's arrest.[682]

The *Monroe News-Star* also recorded the testimony of Fred Carpenter, but in a bit more detail than did the *Times*. Yet, there were no significant differences between the two versions.[683]

The New York Times reported that after Carpenter followed Sam Conger. He told of seeing the black-hooded band on August 24, but told the court that he was

[681] Ibid.

[682] *The New York Times*, 18 January 1923.

[683] *Monroe News-Star*, 17 January 1923.

unable to recognize any of its members.[684] The names "A. B. Conger" and "W. E. Conger" also appear on the original application for Morehouse Klan No. 34. It is entirely possible that these were relatives of this witness. Therefore, there may have been good reason why he did not identify anyone on the stand. Also, Conger's testimony does not appear in the *Monroe News-Star*.

The New York Times reported that when E. N. Gray was called to the stand, W. C. Barnett, the lawyer representing Dr. McKoin, "Jeff" Burnett, and the interests of the Ku Klux Klan in general, made his objection to Gray's pending testimony. He said that Gray "was in a sense accused of being implicated in the Mer Rouge crime." He told the court that Gray had retained representation of which he, Barnett, was a part. He continued: "In his behalf, I say that he declines to give any further testimony on the ground that it might incriminate him. The constitution of this state provides that no man can give evidence against himself. As a representative of others in this matter, I want to say that we have permitted the state to go ahead in this hearing, but for the state to subject this witness or any other witness to cross examination or third degree is a violation of the constitution."[685]

Replying for the state Senator Warren said, "These matters have been submitted to the Grand Jury in this parish, to the District Attorney [Garrett], to other officials, and no one has been charged by them. The State has some evidence tending to show that some individuals have knowledge of the transactions which led to the deaths of two citizens of this parish. The sole purpose of this investigation is to get the true facts of the matter. The Attorney General of the State is not cross-examining; there is no third degree in this hearing. Every witness has been guaranteed protection and there has been no intimidation on either side, I think. The truth is all the State wants in these matters. The witness in this instance is free to refuse to testify. The court has told him so. The accusation against Mr. Gray, as published by an overzealous newspaper, is unfortunate. It was a wild story and the State had nothing to do with it." Mr. Guion then read case citations which showed that the State had standing in the hearings.

Barnett responded by citing that the constitution safeguarded a person against self-incrimination. Senator Warren replied by asking Barnett, "Will the gentlemen tell us the names of his prospective defendants?"

---

[684]*The New York Times*, 18 January 1923.

"We'll be here and let you know whenever they are called," answered Barnett.

With regard to the question, Judge Odom said "that had there been a charge lodged against Gray, he would not permit him to testify, but there is no complaint." Speaking directly to Gray he said, "I now reiterate to you, Mr. Gray, that you do not have to answer questions that may implicate or involve you in these alleged crimes. I now want to state a policy. I am not going to tolerate objections from attorneys. If an attorney wants to tell a witness of his rights under the Constitution, that will be all right, but I do not want objections. A witness here has the same right that he has before the Grand Jury. I am going to permit these witnesses to come here, and I shall require them to tell what they know so long as it does not incriminate them. That a witness might possibly say something that might incriminate him does not mean that he should not testify at all. I think now we understand each other." The *Monroe News-Star* also listed the incident involving E. N. Gray similarly as did the *Times*. There were no significant differences between the two.[686]

Judge Odom then allowed Barnett to consult with Gray in the ante-chamber. In the between time, the state called Tom Higgenbotham.[687] *The New York Times'* version of the testimony of Tom Higgenbotham was noticeably different than that recorded by the *Monroe News-Star*.

"Do you know E. N. Gray?"

"Yes, sir."

"Where is his home in relation to yours?"

"About three miles across the swamps."

"What road do you take?"

"Just a crossroad."

"Where were you on August 24."

"Baling hay with Mr. Montgomery on the bayou."

"Did you go to Bastrop the day before?"

"Yes, sir."

"Did you talk with anyone?"

---

[685]*The New York Times*, 18 January 1923.
[686]*Monroe News-Star*, 17 January 1923.
[687]Ibid.

"My cousin Will. He told me that he had received a threatening letter signed, 'Not Your Friend,' warning him to keep away from negroes and to quit making white lightning."

"Did you see the letter?"

"Yes."

"What else did he talk about?"

"Well, I told him that I'd better go back with him."

"Who else did you see?"

"J. D. and Fred Higgenbotham."

"Are you related to them?"

"Second cousins."

"Are you a member of the Klan?"

"Yes, sir."

"Do you know Watt Daniel?"

"Tolerably well."

"Did you know T. F. Richards?"

"Yes, sir, about a year, I think."

"Did you know J. L. Daniel, W. C. Andrews, and Tot Davenport?"

"Yes, sir."

"Did you hear rumors that they were in bad with the Klan?"

"No, sir."

"When you quit baling hay, where did you go?"

"Home."

"Did you come through Bastrop?"

"Yes, sir."

"Stop there?"

"No, sir."

"And you picked up Mr Gray at Washburn's place?"

"Yes, sir. I was glad to have him along."

"He was standing there alone?"

"Yes, sir; out in front of the gate."

"How many cars passed you?"

"Two or three."

"Any prisoners in them?"

"I didn't see any."

"You didn't halt when they passed?"

"No."

"How far was it from the point where you picked up Gray and where you met the masked men?"

"About a quarter of a mile."

"You had just about reached the Cooper Lake Road when you met the masked men?"

"Yes."

"Whom did you next meet?"

"Earl Andrews, I believe."

"You passed him?"

"Yes."

"Whom did you see next?"

"Nobody I recognized."

"You talked to no one you met by the road?"

"No, I was in a hurry to get home."

"After seeing the masked men?"

"Yes."

"You saw a car standing with people in it?"

"Yes."

"Did you know them?"

"No."

"How many men were standing outside the car?"

"Three, I think."

"In the car?"

"The car was crowded."

"You didn't know them to talk to them?"

"No."

"Were any of them masked?"

"No."

A prime opportunity was missed here. The witness clearly said that he was upset because of the masked men that he encountered. However, the state neglected to capitalize on this admission by obtaining the location and the circumstances under which Higgenbotham encountered these masked men. Obviously, there was some truth that went untold here.

"Then you proceeded on the Bastrop-Mer Rouge road for quite a way?"

"Yes."

"Pass anybody?"

"Yes, several cars, but I didn't know any of them."

"Did you pass any cars before you reached the fork in the road?"

"I passed all of them before I reached the swamp at Red Hill."

"After you passed the road where the large car was standing, did you pass other cars before you reached the fork?"

"Two or three, I think."

"Had you passed Gray's car, driven by Rufus Eubanks, you would have known it?"

"I think so."

"Or Tom Butler's car?"

"Yes, sir, I would have known it."

"What did you do when you got home?"

"Went in and had dinner."

"What did Gray do?"

"Waited outside with my cousin."

"What time did you leave there?"

"After midnight."

"Did you take Gray home?"

"Yes, sir."

"See anyone on the way?"

"No, sir."

"Did you see any of Mr. Gray's family when you got to his house?"

"No, sir."

"You went home?"

"I went to my cousin, Will Higgenbotham."

"Why did you and Gray think all the danger was over?"

"Well, it was midnight."

"Midnight would be a good hour for trouble, wouldn't it?"

"I don't think so."

"You have been Will Higgenbotham's only companion to stay with him?"

"Yes."

"How much have you stayed with him?"

"I've stayed there for a week at a time."

"You don't stay there now?"

"No."

"You decided the danger was over?"

"Yes."

"Had he any enemies?"

"None that I know of."

"Have you ever heard of anyone ever threatening him or Tom?"

"No."

"Had he been a good citizen?"

"Yes, sir."

"When you came in to get your dinner, did you see John Lang or Jeff Burnett?"

"No, sir."

"Do you know 'Jim' Vaughn or Dean Ashcraft?"

"No, sir."

"Did you see Captain Skipwith?"

"Yes, sir."

Here again the state was asleep at the wheel. This witness was not asked where and when he saw Captain Skipwith. In all likelihood, he saw Skipwith either with the masked men or somewhere on the road near the site of the kidnapping. This would have run contrary to the testimony given by witnesses who placed Skipwith in Bastrop in and out of the Thomas' store at about that same time. Unfortunately, this admission was never followed up, and we will never know what exactly the witness meant by that admission.

"Were you ever suspicious of anyone having fired upon Dr. McKoin?"

"No, sir; I didn't think he had an enemy."

"Was the community excited over it?"

"No, sir, it was very quiet."

"Do you mean to say that people were not interested in it?"

"It looked that way to me."

"When did you hear the news?"

"On the morning of the shooting."

"And you went to Mer Rouge and inquired?"

"Yes, sir."

"So far as you know there was mighty little effort to find out who did the shooting?"

"So far as I know."

"Did you see either Richards or Watt Daniel the day you came in from the Montgomery place?"

"I don't remember."

"Are you sure they did not pass in a car while you were sitting out under the pecan trees at Will Higgenbotham's?"

"I don't know; several cars passed." This response appears to be evasive.

"When did you first hear of the kidnapping of Daniel and Richards?"

"I met the mob that night."

"What did you think about the mob?"

"I felt they were after someone, and I hurried on at a good clip."

Once again the state missed a golden opportunity. Not only did the witness meet "the mob," but he also learned from them of the kidnapping of Daniel and Richards. How else would he have been able to answer this question, had he not talked with a member of the mob. Furthermore, had he talked with a member of the mob, it seems likely that he might have recognized the person with whom he talked. Instead of following up on these questions, the state asked about other threatening letters.

"Did anyone else get threatening letters that you know about?"

"Captain Skipwith got some."

"Did you see them?"

"No, but I heard about them."

"You are not sure Skipwith got them-you never read them?"

"No, sir."

"The night you picked up Gray, it was by accident?"

"Yes, sir."

"You didn't know which way he was going?"

"No, sir."

This too seems unlikely. Why would he have arbitrarily just stopped to pick up Gray if he did not already know that they were both going in the same direction.[688]

The *Monroe News-Star* version of the testimony of Tom Higgenbotham was not as detailed as that of the *Times*, and although there were glaring differences in which the testimony was recorded, these differences did not constitute offenses that would change the meaning of the testimony. As Higgenbotham finished his testimony, Judge Odom called the noon recess.[689]

The *New York Times* reported that Will Higgenbotham then followed his cousin Tom. He was asked to present the threatening letter to the court, which he did. The state's attorney then asked him to read the letter into the court record. The letter was as follows:

> Why don't you tend to your own business? It is no matter to you about our negro women or making whiskey. We intend to do as we please, and your bunch can't stop us. We know you and we are going to stop you. Take this for what it is worth and get close together. You can guess the rest. Not Your Friend.

It is clear by the text of the letter that it was not the type of threatening letter that Tom Higgenbotham had painted it out to be. There also exists the strong possibility that they all were validating each others' alibis

Senator Warren, realizing the inconsistency, continued by asking, "As I understood your cousin [Will Higgenbotham], the letter was a reprimand to you for immoral conduct and making whiskey. Instead of that, I find the letter reminds you it is none of your business if the writer is immoral and makes whiskey. Is that right?"

"Yes."

"Nobody was accusing you of immorality or making whiskey, but they objected to you interfering with their immoralities?"

"Yes."

"You didn't interfere in such ways with other peoples' business?"

"No."

On the witness stand, Higgenbotham, the quintessential agrarian, gave the appearance of a placid, reserved, elderly gentleman. The droll manner in which he responded to the questioning caused chuckles to emanate from the gallery and even

---

[688]*The New York Times*, 18 January 1923.
[689]*Monroe News-Star*, 17 January 1923.

Judge Odom on occasion.

"Whom did you show the letter to first?"

"To 'Jap' Jones when I met him at Bastrop. He advised me to get somebody to stay with me. Afterward I met 'Newt' Gray and asked him to stay with me all night or half the night."

"Did you have any idea who sent the letter?"

"No, sir, but I thought it might be some of them fellows at Mer Rouge selling whiskey."

"Who were they?"

"Well, I heard that Watt Daniel and Will Braddock were making and selling it."

"Did you hear that Jim Norseworthy had been making it but had quit?"

"Yes, sir."

"Had you and Watt ever talked about making whiskey?"

"No, sir."

"You and Braddock?"

"No, sir."

"Why did you think Braddock was making whiskey?"

"I heard it around."

"Did you suspect that anybody had cause to write that letter except those who made whiskey and sold it?"

"No, sir."

"When was the last time you saw Watt Daniel?"

"At Bastrop, the day of the ball game."

"Who was with him?"

"I don't know. There was someone with him, but I don't know the other man."

"You saw him no more?"

"No, I started home after that."

"Did you show that letter to your wife?"

"She read it before I got to the house."

"Did you ever hear that the Vigilance Committee was after Watt Daniel or anyone else?"

"No, sir."

"Had you heard of trouble between the Klan and the people of Mer Rouge?"

425

"I had heard there was some."

"Are you a member of the Klan?"

"I was a member, but I am too old to get out with them. I work all day and don't go out at night."

"Did you have the hood and regalia?"

"Yes, sir, a white one."

"Did you have a black one?"

"No, sir. I never tried to get one. I know the others had them, but I didn't feel I needed one. I don't just remember where I got the white one."

This piece of testimony is valuable because it continues to verify that Klan members possessed and used black hoods.

"You didn't have any idea of taking any part in night expeditions?"

"No, sir."

"And you didn't have any need for a black hood?"

"No."

"Did you see any men who had black hoods?"

"I saw them. I didn't know them. I did see Jim Norseworthy."

"Did he have a hood on?"

"No, he was standing in the road."

This was another prime opportunity missed by the state to ascertain where "in the road" Higgenbotham had seen Norseworthy, and how he was associated with a black hood at that time.

"When you told 'Jap' Jones about the letter, you addressed him as a Klansman and a lifelong friend?"

"Yes."

"You told him there was no reason for the letter?"

"Yes."

"How did you get Gray?"

"He came up to me in a car."

"He heard you were looking for him?"

"Yes."

"Did you talk to anyone else about the letter?"

"No."

"Did Tom know about it?"

"Yes, I told him at dinner."

"What did he say?"

"Said he would be back by dark."

"About what time did he get to Bastrop?"

"About 6:30 P.M., I guess."

"After dinner, now, Newt Gray came looking for you about this very thing?"

"I think Tom Higgenbotham told him."

"Gray made it clear to you that he had already been told about this letter?"

"Yes."

"He asked you if you had any way of getting him out to your house?"

"Yes."

"Did Gray tell you that he'd have to get somebody to drive his car home? To take his wife and party home?"

"No, he didn't. I just told him he could come out to my house with Tommy Higgenbotham."

"Did you think Gray was taking any chances on missing Tom as Tom came back from the ball field?"

"No, Gray said he'd catch him. I told him if he watched the street, he'd be sure to catch him."

"Did you bring any men up from Mer Rouge?"

"Yes, Jim Wemble."

"Did you go home by the Mer Rouge Road?"

"No, Grabball road. I wanted to get away from that crowd."

"You wanted to get home?"

"Yes, I wanted to get home before sundown."

"You were at home for more than an hour before the arrival of Gray and Tom?"

"Yes, sir."

"You left town with the main crowd?"

"Yes."

"When you got out on the road, the hooded men were there?"

"Yes, part of them."

"And they had stopped some cars and taken some prisoners?"

"Yes."

427

"Did you see two blindfolded men in the truck?"

"Yes."

"How many cars did you see?"

"About eight or ten."

"How did you pass?"

"A masked man indicated the right, and my girl drove the car to the right."

"What kind of hoods did you see?"

"Black."

"Where was the truck?"

"On the side of the road. There were hooded men all around it."

"About how many in hoods did you see?"

"About eighteen or twenty."

"You were not halted?"

"No, sir."

"No one overtook you?"

"No, sir, but I passed Frank Bell and John Jones coming this way."

"How far behind the hold up did you meet Frank Bell and John Jones?"

"About a half mile."

"Were they driving fast?"

"Yes."

"Did you meet anybody else?"

"No."

"Didn't overtake 'Newt' Gray or Tom Butler's car?"

"No, I did not."

"You drove fast?"

"Yes."

"Why couldn't you take Gray home in your car?"

"Well, I didn't want to crowd my wife and the girls."

"Have you ever heard that Tom Higgenbotham was a member of the Vigilance Committee?"

"No."

"Had he talked about things they were setting out to do?"

"Not to me."

"Did he want you to attend any meetings?"

"One in the woods."

"Do you remember anyone there?"

"Tom was there. Captain Skipwith and 'Pink' Kirkpatrick."

"Was Dr. McKoin there?"

"No."

"Do you know him?"

"Yes, sir."

"What did you hear at Mer Rouge about the shooting?"

"I heard that Dr. McKoin passed two men on the roadside and grew suspicious of them. Dr. McKoin told me this and said he didn't know how he escaped with his life."

"Did he say how far they were from the road?"

"They were in the ditch off the road."

"When he saw them, he squatted down in the car, and that is why he was not hit?"

"Yes."

"Did you ever hear any one say they suspected anyone of shooting at Dr. McKoin?"

"Leon Daniel said that he had heard Watt Daniel was planning to kill Dr. McKoin. Dr. McKoin also told me that weeks before the shooting."

"Did Leon Daniel say that or did someone say he said that?"

"Someone told me he said it."

"Do you know why Dr. McKoin carried a bale of hay on the side of his car the night he was shot at?"

"Didn't know he carried a bale of hay."

"You know whether Tom Higgenbotham ever went out on any Klan raids?"

"He never did."

"Has he a Klan regalia suit?"

"He's got a white one."

"Not a black one?"

"No, I know he don't have a black one."

"Now what did Gray do when he got out to your house that night?"

"He stayed outside and would not come in for supper because he said he didn't want to get the women folks worried. I brought him a gun and left him and Tom there. Gray went home about midnight."

"Did Gray take your gun with him?"

"Think he did. Suppose he did."

"Could they see anyone coming on the road?"

"Yes, sir."

"Did you see any cars pass?"

"No, sir."

"Tom went into the house and told you that Gray was there?"

"Yes."

"Did Gray enter the house?"

"No, sir; I took the pistol out to him."

"What conversation did you have with Gray?"

"I told him to watch and not to shoot until he found out who it was, that I didn't want him to shoot an innocent man."

"About how long did you stay out the first time?"

"About ten minutes."

"What then?"

"Tom and I went to supper."

"How long did you stay out after supper?"

"Till about 10:30 P.M."

"When was the letter opened-the threatening letter?"

"The day we got it, the day of the barbecue."

"Your wife opened the letter?"

"Yes, she read it and showed it to me."

"Did it scare you?"

"It bothered me. I was just mad, pardner. It would make anybody mad. If a man's going to shoot me, I want him to shoot me in the face, not in the back."

"And you don't want him to have a hood on, with eyeholes in it?"

"No, sir."

"Are you in favor of this investigation?"

"I am."

"Did you tell Judge Odom or Sheriff Carpenter?"

"I think I showed Carpenter the letter."

"Did your wife or girls see Gray that night?"

"No, sir."

"You went to Dr. McKoin when you heard he had been shot at?"

"I went right away."

"Is that when he told you that Watt's brother had said Watt had threatened to kill him?"

"Yes, he told me after the shooting and before the shooting, I think."

"Did you ever go to Watt Daniel's brother?"

"No, I didn't go to him."

"Did you go on to Bastrop?"

"Yes."

"Who did you see that you talked with about it?"

"J. D. and Will Higgenbotham."

"Can you identify any of those masked men that you say in the mob on that day [August 24]?"

"No, sir."

"Did you make any effort to find out who was responsible for the kidnapping?"

"Well, I asked several people about it."

"Did you go to Captain Skipwith?"

"Yes, sir."

"What Klansmen did you talk with?"

"I'll be honest with you, sir. I don't remember."

"Did you think the writer of that threatening letter intended to do you bodily harm on the night of August 24?"

"I didn't know, so I played it safe."

"Didn't you go to bed and leave your friend Gray standing guard with your nephew?"

"Well, sir, I was tired, worn out and miserable."

"You didn't know what took place outside the house."

"No, sir."

"Could it be possible that Daniel and Richards were taken here?"

"No, sir."

"Were you asleep in the house?"

"Yes, sir."

"Why did you think the danger was over?"

"I thought if anything came up, my nephew and friend would let me know."

"What time did they leave?"

"About 12:30, I think."

"Don't you know that if a man wanted to do you harm he would come in the early part of the morning, when people generally sleep and not before midnight?"

"Well, I was sitting up in the house with a gun until late."

There are a number of inconsistencies with this witness's testimony. First, he claimed that his wife did not know that Gray was outside. Considering the fact that it was late August and usually the hottest time of the year, surely the windows of the house would have been open. One would have to believe that Higgenbotham's wife did not look out of the windows, nor did she go outside for any reason, not even to use the outhouse. Second, if a person came to defend you and your family and refused to go inside to eat supper, would you not bring some out to him? Third, if you are in fear for your life and the lives of your family, is it logical to believe that a person could have the composure to go to sleep while two armed men waited for an attack? Fourth, he claimed he stayed up late with a gun by his side. Yet, in previous testimony he claimed he went to bed at about 10:30. This would hardly be considered late. Furthermore, could not his wife, who had already read the letter, not figure out something was afoot with him sitting up with a gun by his side? Finally, how could he have known what time Gray had left, if he was asleep at the time?

"Why did you say you feared Captain Skipwith?"

"I did not fear him, but he was a man not to be opposed."[690]

The *Monroe News-Star* version of William Higgenbotham was similar to that of the *Times* but for two significant differences. First, the *Times* version was much more extensive in that the testimony was over two times larger than that reported by the *News-Star*. Yet, there was one important portion of testimony in the *News-Star* that was not in the *Times* as indicated by the following:

"Did you recognize anyone wearing a black mask on August 24?" asked Warren.

---

[690]*The New York Times*, 18 January 1923.

"No, sir, the only person I saw was Jim Norseworthy standing there without a mask on with his hair standing right straight up."

The state missed the opportunity to capitalize on what the witness just said. Ordinarily, a person's hair does not just stand up straight. It will, however, take such a position if a garment is draped over the head and then taken off. Clearly, the *News-Star* slammed the *Times* on this one. By the same token, the *Times* version contained the letter sent to Higgenbotham, whereas the *News-Star* did not.

The New York Times, once again, recorded more witnesses this date than did the *Monroe News-Star*. The *Times* reported the testimony of Thomas W. Butler, and Frank L. Flewellyn, Bastrop's town barber.

Butler, who resided on the Collinston-Mer Rouge road, said that as he was returning from the ball game in Bastrop on August 24, he passed black hooded men in cars on the road near his home. This was the extent of his testimony. [691]

Flewellyn, in a bit of testimony that stretched tolerance and credibility to the limit, the barber said he "didn't remember" anything he had heard relative to discussions concerning the kidnapping and murder of Daniel and Richards. In reality, if there were any place in town where such conversation would have taken place, it would have been the barber shop.

Threat to Bomb Movies: Woonsocket Klan Threatens Ten Persons[692]

Reports of Ku Klux Klan activities in New England this day included the sending of threatening letters to 15 different persons. Ten letters, one to a priest, were received in Woonsocket, Rhode Island, and included threats to bomb three different moving picture houses. Five letters were received by persons in Lynn, Massachusetts. In Lawrence, the police were concerned over reported threats of Klavern 67 in that city to "completely annihilate" Council 67, Knights of Columbus. The Lawrence Klan for some time had been advising members of meeting nights and conveying other information through adroitly coded advertisements in the newspapers which had recently been deciphered.

Investigation Called[693]

A press release by Representative Thomas J. O'Grady of Chicago, announced a resolution calling for an investigation into the number of state house employees

---

[691] Ibid.

[692] *The New York Times*, 17 January 1923.

[693] Ibid.

who are members of the Ku Klux Klan.

Lansing, Michigan, was reported to be the site of an investigation of alleged activities of the Ku Klux Klan in Michigan under a resolution prepared for introduction into the legislature by Representative James A. Burns, of Detroit.[694]

THURSDAY JANUARY 18, 1922

State Begins its Presentation of Evidence to Identify the Hooded Mob of Morehouse[695]

"Newt Grey" Member of Masked Band That Held up Mer Rouge Victims August 24, Says Witness[696]

Sensational Charges Made by Fred Eubanks at Opening of Kidnapping Case Before Judge Odom at Bastrop This Morning[697]

The New York Times reported that today's testimony was highlighted by that given by Fred Eubanks, the brother-in-law of E. N. Gray. Eubanks told those present at the hearing that he positively recognized Gray as being one of those present at the roadblock set up by the Klan on the Bastrop-Mer Rouge Road on the evening of August 24.

During the questioning, he was asked, "These men wore black hoods?"

"They did," said he.

"And you recognized Gray as one of these men?"

"Yes."

Without a doubt, this calls into question the testimony given by both Tom and Will Higgenbotham who both have testified that Gray was present at Will Higgenbotham's home on the evening of August 24. This is the second witness to contradict the testimony given by the Higgenbothams as to the location of Gray on the evening of August 24.

It was said that the state was attempting to show that Gray's job was to point out the men who were to be kidnapped. According to information obtained by the investigators, Gray was the only Klan member present at the kidnapping site wearing an all-white Klan outfit. It was claimed that the remaining Klan members wore the black outfit worn by Klan gorillas, known in Klan jargon as "Terrors." It has already been established that a Klansman dressed all in white was the one who walked along the line of cars as they passed the roadblock and eventually pointed

---

[694] Ibid.

[695] *Monroe News-Star*, 18 January 1923.

[696] Ibid.

out Daniel, Richards, J. L. Daniel, W. C. Andrews and C. C. "Tot" Davenport. It was alleged that after he pointed the victims out, they were hogtied, blindfolded and thrown on the bed of the Ford truck. His acting as a spotter also lends credence to the assertion by some that Arkansas Klansmen had been present. Needless to say, a spotter would be necessary if these men did not know the intended victims beforehand.

An alibi was attempted for "Jeff" Burnett, accused of the murders of Daniel and Richards, by Dean Ashcraft, who identified himself as the field manager for the Southern Carbon Company at Spyker. An admitted Klansman, Ashcraft said that Burnett was working at the plant in Spyker on the evening of August 24 when Daniel and Richards were kidnapped and murdered. Ashcraft also testified that he was the last person to see Harold Teegerstrom, also employed at the Spyker plant as a timekeeper, before his mysterious disappearance only 24 hours after the investigation was opened into the Mer Rouge murders. It has been held that Teegerstrom had been abducted by an unknown group in cars after he told investigators that Burnett was not, in fact, working on the night of the murders. He had not been reported seen since that night, and his whereabouts at the time of the hearing were still unknown.

It was learned from Ashcraft that a substantial cashe of dynamite was kept at the carbon plant, to which he had access. It was a dynamite explosion that had brought the bodies of Daniel and Richards to the surface of Lake LaFourche just before Christmas. He was also asked about his knowledge of the use of dynamite and hacksaws. At the scene of the explosion and the recovery of the bodies at Lake LaFourche, a set of keys, said to be those to the dynamite shed at the carbon plant, and a hacksaw were found. It appeared as though the hacksaw had been used to free the skiff that had been chained to a tree by the lake. The state believed that the skiff was used to bring the bodies of Daniel and Richards to the point where they were dropped into the lake. He was also questioned about the wire used to secure the roofs of the meter houses to the frames. The state had established that the same type of wire had been used on the remains of Daniel and Richards.

The state also pointed out through the testimony of Ashcraft of the existence of a friendship between him and Henry Jones, a farmer who lived near Bastrop. It

---

[697] Ibid.

was Jones who told Sheriff Carpenter of the surprise visit paid to him by Harold Teegerstrom on the Sunday after Teegerstrom mysteriously disappeared from the carbon plant at Spyker. Jones told the court how Teegerstrom, nervous and scared, appeared at his door, switched clothes with Jones, borrowed $40 and left a set of keys and a wristwatch with his initials engraved in the back. He told Jones that he had to leave northeast Louisiana for a while, but did not explain why.

Ashcraft constructed for himself an alibi for the night of December 21, 1922, by claiming that he attended a wedding the night of the dynamite explosion at Lake LaFourche. He said that about three months prior a shipment of 20 cases containing 50 pounds each of dynamite had been received by the Southern Carbon Company at Spyker. He said that he personally attended to the storing of the dynamite in the dynamite house, and that only he and Superintendent Bennett, both Klansmen, possessed the keys to the house. During that period however, dynamite could be purchased without restriction or accounting for what had been sold or used.

A total of nine witnesses were called to testify on this date. First among them was Rufus Eubanks, the nephew of E. N. "Newt" Gray. He told how, on the night of the kidnappings, he dropped his uncle off on the Bastrop-Mer Rouge road very near the location of the site of the kidnappings. He also told the court that his uncle was acting suspiciously.

Leon Daniel, brother of Watt, testified as did Harley Rogers, an employee of the Southern Carbon Plant at Spyker. Rogers refuted the allegation that he had traveled to Mer Rouge with Burnett on the day of the kidnapping, and told the court that he had not left the plant. This ran contrary to the testimony given previously by Harry Neelis. Rogers told of his brief stint as a deputy sheriff in Morehouse Parish. This occurred when he accompanied Captain Skipwith, Charlie Cox and others. Allegedly, they were seeking to arrest a subject named Price, who was supposed to be manufacturing whiskey. This was the only time he served as a deputy. He testified that Burnett was working at the plant on August 24, the night of the kidnappings. Neelis stated that he had been stopped by black-hooded men on the Bastrop-Mer Rouge Road the day of the first kidnapping of Richards on August 17, 1922, and that he was able to recognize two of the band who were not wearing hoods at the time. He said they were "Jeff" Burnett and Harley Rogers.

First called to give testimony was Rufus Eubanks, nephew of E. N. "Newt" Gray. He told of attending the baseball game in Bastrop on August 24, and how he and Gray met. Gray told him to drive his car home after leaving it near the kidnap location on the Bastrop-Mer Rouge Road. Eubanks said that Gray told him that he was supposed to meet Tom Higgenbotham there.

"How far from the holdup spot did you leave Gray?"

"About 200 yards."

"On your way back to Mer Rouge that evening, did you meet any masked men?"

"Yes."

"How many were there?"

"There were several cars loaded with them."

"What did you do that night?"

"I went to the Fellowship Baptist Church."

"Is that the church attended by 'Newt' Gray?"

"Yes."

"Was Gray at church that night?"

"No."

"Did you see hooded men while you were taking Gray's car back toward Mer Rouge?"

"Yes."

"Did you take a peep after you started away from Gray?"

"Yes."

"What did you see?"

"I saw Gray standing in the road."

Following Rufus Eubanks, the state called Fred Eubanks, also a brother-in-law for "Newt" Gray. He told the court that he also was stopped on the Bastrop-Mer Rouge Road by black-hooded men on August 24.

"Did you recognize any of these men on the roadside?"

"Yes."

"Did they wear black hoods?"

"Yes."

"Did you recognize any of them?"

"I recognized one."

"Who was that?"

"Newt Gray."

Eubanks told of being stopped again farther down the road by three hooded men, but was unable to identify any of these men.

After Eubanks, Leon Daniel, the 40-year-old crippled brother of Watt Daniel, was called to the stand. He said that Watt had told him of the allegations against him and Richards of making whiskey and of shooting at Dr. McKoin. Leon said that Watt disapproved of the actions of the Ku Klux Klan and of the local Vigilance Committee, which were one and the same organization.

Next came Henry Pipes. He testified that he witnessed black-hooded men getting gasoline in Collinston on the evening of August 24 but that he was unable to recognize any of them. He did, however, say that he saw two men seated in the rear of the truck who appeared to be captives. Here was another "good citizen" who made no attempt to aid the captives, nor seek help from the authorities.

T. B. Pratt, a 21-year-old admitted Klansman, told the court that he knew nothing about the kidnappings or murders of Daniel and Richards and that he had no knowledge of anyone saying anything about it. Quoting the passage from *The New York Times* concerning this witness, "He was perfectly willing to qualify as a man who had lost his memory and would not admit that he ever had one." The names "T. B. Pratt" and "T. B. Pratt Jr." appear on the original application for membership of Morehouse Klan No. 34.

After Pratt, J. H. Jones was called. He told of a visit that he received from "Newt" Gray two days after the kidnapping of Daniel and Richards. Jones told of how Gray seemed to go out of his way to let him know what he was doing on the evening of August 24.

"Did Gray volunteer all this information?"

"Yes." The names "J. M. Jones", "J. Nelson Jones" and "J. N. Jones" appear on the original membership application for Morehouse Klan No. 34.

As the afternoon session began, Rufus Eubanks was again called to the stand. He was again questioned about taking Gray's car home and the names of the occupants at that time. The question of passing anyone on the road was again put to him.

"Did you meet anybody?" the state's attorney asked.

"Yes, Thomas Higgenbotham came by in a Ford Roadster."

"Who was in the car with Higgenbotham?"

"Nobody."

Higgenbotham and Gray have both given testimony in which each has attested to the assertion that Tom Higgenbotham picked up Gray and that both went to the home of Will Higgenbotham. All three, Tom and Will Higgenbotham and "Newt" Gray have admitted membership in the Klan. The names "J. D. Higgenbotham" and "F. L. Higgenbotham" both appear on the application for membership of Morehouse Klan No. 34.

Dean Ashcraft was then called. Prior to the hearing, he had told federal investigators that he had witnessed the kidnapping of Harold Teegerstrom from the Southern Carbon Plant at Spyker. In his testimony on the stand, Ashcraft attempted to establish an alibi for himself by saying that he had spent the night of August 24 at the home of "Jeff" Burnett and that he had gone there about 8:30 p.m. He testified that he was certain that Burnett was at work that evening because his work clothes were missing, and his black suit was in the bathroom. To listen to this witness, Burnett had only two sets of clothes, his work clothes and the black suit.

He did admit, however, to having seen Burnett at the ball game in Bastrop earlier in the day. By the line of questioning, it became clear that the state believed that the dynamite used at Lake LaFourche on December 21 had come from the carbon plant. When questioned about his whereabouts on that evening, Ashcraft said that he had gone to the wedding of an employee of the carbon plant, Jewell Harris. He said he returned to the home of "Jeff" Burnett about 10 p.m. after bidding the wedding party farewell in Collinston. He said that he did not go to the bunkhouse at the carbon plant, but he did say that Thomas Williams started sleeping in the bunkhouse for the first time that night. He also said that D. E. Wilson and Jim Williams had also been present at the bunkhouse. One can only wonder how he could have made these statements without having seen those men present in the bunkhouse at the time. The questioning continued into the area of the wire which was found bound around the bodies of Daniel and Richards and the suspicion that the wire had come from the carbon plant.

The version of this day's testimony in the *Monroe News-Star* was similar in some respects to that of the *Times*. The *Times* seemed to capture more of the testimony than did the *News-Star*, and the *Times* also captured more detail and, as usual, reported more witnesses than did the *News-Star*. For example, although the testimony of Fred Eubanks said that the kidnappers had on black hoods, this was not contained in the *News-Star*. Also, the testimony of Dean Ashcraft was not contained in the *News-Star*. Ashcraft could hardly be considered a throw-away witness.

'Minister From Georgia" Speaks at Freeport Meeting[698]

A bulletin from Freeport, Long Island, told of the appearance of a "Minister from Georgia" who refused to give his name and was introduced as "Mr. Brown." He appeared before 400 people in the Masonic Hall under the auspices of the J.O.U.A.N.[It is unknown what this stands for], to explain the principles of the Ku Klux Klan. Small white cards were distributed and the minister requested those present to write their names and addresses on one side and to write "yes" or "no" on the other side. He intimated that those writing "yes" would hear further from him but those who wrote "no" would not hear from him again

"The Klan believes in the preservation of the white race, which is now outnumbered by the colored races by about four to one. The biggest proposition of the Klan now is to combat the elements that are trying to make a Soviet Russia out of the United States," he said. Referring to the flaming cross, the speaker said "the uplifted cross stands for pure womanhood." The term "pure womanhood" had often been used by the Klan, but never explained. Evidently there was no concern for "pure manhood."

A dispatch from Daytona, Florida, told how Chief of Police Joseph Osborne was removed from office as a result of an altercation Tuesday night following a Ku Klux Klan parade when he shot former policeman Charles Pent after Pent and W. C. Perry had disrobed a trio of Klansmen.[699]

From Chicago came the news that by a vote of 56 to 2, the city council was on record today as being opposed to retaining members of the Ku Klux Klan on the city payroll. The vote was taken yesterday when the city council was asked to order the suspension of William H. Green, a city fireman and an alleged member of the Klan.[700]

---

[698]*The New York Times*, 19 January 1923.
[699]Ibid.
[700]Ibid.

FRIDAY JANUARY 19, 1923

Klansman Named as Kidnapper of 2 Mer Rouge Victims

Brother-in-Law Of Gray Says He Saw Him In Hooded Band On Murder Day[701]
Coco Undertakes to Disclose Identity of Men Who Participated in Mer Rouge Kidnapping Case[702]
State is Ready to Inaugurate Climax in Investigation[703]
Positive Identification of Prisoner Held at Direction of Attorney General at Shreveport Offered in Testimony at Bastrop[704]
Star Witness Whetstone to Identify Mob[705][706]

The *Monroe News-Star* reported that William A. McDonald, a 60-year-old resident of Mer Rouge and the brother-in-law of J. L. Daniel, father of Watt Daniel, to be the first witness called to testify this day. During the preliminary questioning, he said that Sam Daniel had told him of the alleged attempt to kill Dr. McKoin.

"Do you know 'Jap' Jones?'" inquired Assistant Attorney General Seth Guion.

"Yes."

"What did he say?"

"He said, 'we are going to clean out the whole damned Daniel family before this thing is settled.' He did not seem to realize that I was related to the Daniel family. I called his hand, and he told me that I needn't get so mad about it."

"What did you tell him?"

"I told him Dr. McKoin was never shot at."

"Do you know anything about the kidnapping?"

"Yes, sir. I knew it an hour before it happened. You see I was in Bonita at the time. You could hear all about it, except they didn't have all the right parties kidnapped."

"Let's have some more of what you heard?"

"Well, after the kidnapping Jim Harp and us got to talking in the butcher shop about the kidnapping, and he told me that they should have killed them the night they caught Daniel, Andrews and Neelis on the Gallion road, and they wouldn't have had any more trouble with them." [The Gallion road incident occurred August 17.]

---

[701] *The New York Times*, 20 January 1923.
[702] *Monroe News-Star*, 19 January 1923.
[703] Ibid.
[704] Ibid.
[705] Ibid.

"Jim Harp told you that?"

"Yes. I let it be known to him how much I approved of it, and I added a few other words to make it more binding."

After excusing McDonald from the witness stand, the state summoned T. B. Pratt, Sr., the owner of a sawmill near Bastrop. During the preliminary questioning, Mr. Guion quizzed Pratt on the operation of the sawmill, and in particular, about those whom he knew lived near the mill. Pratt also claimed he took part in the barbecue and baseball game in Bastrop on August 24, that he was, in fact, a Klansman, but that he had no knowledge of the kidnapping. He also declared that he had never heard anyone discussing the kidnapping, a claim that is next to impossible to believe in this small community and that he had not, at any time, tried to police the behavior of the citizens of Mer Rouge. Pratt, as well as other witnesses, had been questioned regarding the use and function of certain sawmill equipment, such as log loaders, carriages and the "dogs" used to hold logs on carriages when being sawed. Nothing more was said definitively concerning this equipment, and it was thought that the state was exploring the possible avenue of certain logging equipment being used to produce the damage inflicted on the bodies of Daniel and Richards.

R. A. Whetstone was the first witness to be called as the afternoon session of the open hearings began. During the preliminary questioning, he told of attending the festivities in Bastrop on August 24. After the baseball game and barbecue, he began walking toward Mer Rouge on the Bastrop-Mer Rouge Road with the hope that he could hitch a ride from a passing motorist. Not long outside of Bastrop, he encountered the hooded band.

"I started out and a black-hooder held me up. The fellow who told me to get the water said I was all right and that I was the 'water boy.' They told me to sit down on a log, and I sat there for about 30 minutes. I saw wires hanging down and looked up and saw the telephone wires had been cut. Pretty soon the crowd came from Bastrop and all of them got held up. Then about 20 minutes later someone told me that they had Watt Daniel, J. L. Daniel, W. C. Andrews and those other fellows. Then I got loose from them and caught a car and rode to Oak Ridge."

"Did you recognize any of the hooded men?"

---

[706]Ibid.

442

"Yes, T. J. Burnett."

"Are you positive?"

"Yes, he had his mask up."

"Do you know Burnett well?"

"Yes, all my life."

"Did he ever indicate afterwards that he knew you had recognized him?"

"Yes. every time I would see him he would smile at me just as if to say, 'Well, you know.' "

Henry Jones, who had been on the witness stand prior to the noon recess, was recalled to the stand, and Whetstone was excused. Mr. Guion asked Jones whether he had traveled to Monroe yesterday.

"Yes."

"Who did you go there with?"

"Captain Skipwith and a man named Camp."

Mr. Guion changed the line of questioning and began asking him about the disappearance of Harold Teegerstrom, timekeeper at the plant of the Southern Carbon Plant at Spyker, Louisiana. It was believed that Teegerstrom's disappearance was originally the result of another kidnapping by members of the Klan in order to prevent Teegerstrom from testifying at the open hearing. He not only would have been able to verify Burnett's alibi of being at work on August 24, but he was also charged with maintaining possession of a set of keys for the dynamite storage room, those being the keys found at the scene of the dynamite explosion at Lake LaFourche. Jones had testified that Teegerstrom had come to his residence two or three days after he escaped from his captors. Jones, who resided near Bastrop, was a former employee of the Southern Carbon Company at Spyker, and it was in this fashion that he came to know Teegerstrom and numerous other employees of the plant.

"Did you know Harold Teegerstrom?"

"Yes, he left the plant on a Friday night and came to my house on Sunday evening. That was the first time I knew he left the plant."

"What time on Sunday did he come to your home?"

"During the afternoon."

"Did you see in what direction he came from?"

"No, sir. I was on the back porch when I heard someone in the house. I found Teegerstrom in front."

"What did he say?"

"He said he had been bothered a great deal by U. S. detectives at the plant about the kidnapping. He said that on Friday night a man called him out of the office and told him he wanted to talk with him. The man took him to an automobile, which he said had several men inside, and he grew suspicious and broke and ran away. That is the reason he gave me for hiding out."

If Jones' statement is close to being accurate, then what Teegerstrom described to him sounded more like a group of Klansmen than government agents. Furthermore, what would he have "become suspicious of" that would have caused him to run away if, in fact, these were government agents? It appears as though he received one of the Klan's customary cowardly late night visits. Also, government agents did not travel en masse.

"How long did he stay at your house that Sunday?"

"He changed clothes, put on my hat, shoes and overcoat to change his identity and left in two hours. This was a week ago last Sunday after this hearing began." Logic seems to dictate that a great deal more would have been said, even if Teegerstrom had been there for only two hours, as the witness claimed.

"Have you any idea where he is now?"

"No."

"Have you received anything from him?"

"Yes, I got my watch which I loaned because his watch had his initial on it. It came in the mail. Before he left he gave me his watch to be sent to his brother and some keys to be sent to the carbon plant."

"It appeared to you that he was trying to make his getaway and was trying to shield his identity?"

"That's right."

"What is his brother's name?"

"Clarence Teegerstrom."

"Who did you deliver the keys to?"

"To S. I. Bennett, superintendent of the plant."

"What did the keys consist of?"

444

"Meter keys, warehouse keys, garage keys and office keys." Clearly Jones was very familiar with these keys to be capable of reciting them. Jones was asked if he was cognizant of Teegerstrom's present whereabouts. Jones said that he did not know, but that he believed that he was "all right." This conclusion he based on the return of the watch which he had loaned to him.

"Where was the watch mailed from?" Mr. Guion asked.

"Somewhere in the United States was written on the box above three two cent stamps," Jones responded. The state missed the opportunity to ask about the postmark, which must have been on the box.

"How long has it been since you received the watch?"

"It was about Monday."

"Did you lend him some money?"

"Yes, $40."

Jones said Teegerstrom left his clothes at his residence, but they later disappeared. Jones thought that Teegerstrom had returned for his clothes, while Jones and his wife were attending a movie in Bastrop. The state again was asleep at the wheel by not pursuing this aspect of the case. Judge Odom then called the noon recess.

The afternoon session began with Henry Jones again being called to the stand.

"When Teegerstrom came to your house, what was the condition of his mind?" asked Mr. Guion.

"He was worried-he was bothered so much, he said, about this trouble that he just couldn't work."

"What trouble?"

"Well, all of it seemed to be centered on the murders of Daniel and Richards."

"He went to you as a friend to aid him to get out of the country?"

"Yes."

"He said agents of the department of justice were questioning him?"

"Yes."

"Did he tell you where he had been Friday to Sunday?"

"No, sir, and I didn't ask."

In the remainder of his testimony, Jones said that he knew Daniel and Richards, and during the baseball game at Bastrop, he sat beside Richards.

Mrs. J. H. Inabet, a lifelong resident of Mer Rouge, was next called to testify after Jones had been excused. During the preliminary questioning, Mrs. Inabet told of being held up on the Bastrop-Mer Rouge Road on the evening of August 24.

"Two men waved us down. They threw their guns in our faces. They examined the car and found no men inside and let us go. Thelma Dade saw her grandfather [J. L. Daniel] and her uncle [Watt Daniel] and began to cry. We were stopped again, and the masked man near me had a torn place in his mask."

"Did you recognize him?"

"Yes. I don't feel I should come right out and say. They are friends of my family."

"Well, why not?"

"It was Mr. "Newt" Gray."

The New York Times version of the day's goings-on was not as complete as that of the *Monroe News-Star*. The *Times* did report the major highlights of today's testimony, and there were certain portions of the *Times* version not contained in the *News-Star* that will be mentioned here beginning with the killing of John P. Parker, Jr.

As though the present goings-on were not enough, yesterday Carey Calhoun, an anti-Klan witness, yet still a Klansman and a brother of Deputy Sheriff Calhoun and friend of Dr. McKoin and Exalted Cyclops Captain Skipwith, shot and fatally wounded John P. Parker, Jr., who had previously been the sheriff of Ouachita Parish. Ouachita and Morehouse are sister parishes. Calhoun also happened to be the brother of Gus Calhoun, who was a central figure in the investigation of the kidnappings and murders. In his testimony just a few days prior to this incident, Carey Calhoun displayed his hostility toward the Klan, although two of his brothers were Klansmen. He told of his going to Spencer to give a warning to William Norseworthy that friends of Dr. McKoin were seeking to kill him because they believed that he had been hired to assassinate McKoin.

John P. Parker, Jr. was the son of John P. Parker of Monroe. The senior Parker had been one of the Klansmen who had sat in on the peace conference between Klansmen and those opposed to the Klan from Bastrop and Mer Rouge.

According to the report given by the police, Calhoun, Parker Jr. and Wess Saunders had been drinking most of the day, and Parker and Saunders were attempting to persuade Calhoun to go to Parker's plantation, considered by many as one of the largest in the area. Upon reaching the outskirts of Monroe, they stopped at the residence of a black woman who was employed by Parker as a cook at the plantation.

Saunders claimed that he had fallen asleep while waiting for food to be cooked. Suddenly, he was awakened by the screams of the black woman. Upon investigating, he found Parker, Jr., in the next room laying on the floor with a .45-caliber bullet wound to the head. It has been suggested that Calhoun and Parker had gotten into an argument over the favors of the black cook and that Calhoun in a drunken rage shot Parker in the head. Awakened by this news, Attorney General Coco called his staff into conference. After learning the facts, they went back to bed feeling confident that this would have no bearing on the proceedings underway in Bastrop.

The *Times* recognized Whetstone as a graduate of Louisiana State University, and that he and Watt Daniel had been classmates there. And that after the testimony of Whetsone's and Inabet, who was described as "a handsome woman of about 35," great consternation was reported in the usually quiet lines of the Klan. Klansmen were scurrying hither and yon. The ever-present figure of the Exalted Cyclops Captain Skipwith was suddenly conspicuous by his absence from the grounds of the courthouse. He was later located down the street from the courthouse in the middle of a huddle of Klansmen, busily trying to calm their fears of exposure.

The testimony of Fred Redding, although brief, did not appear in the *News-Star*. He told of driving on the Bastrop-Mer Rouge Road headed for Mer Rouge on August 24, when he passed a vehicle driven by Tom Higgenbotham. Redding said that Higgenbotham was alone in the car. Both Gray and Higgenbotham have given previous testimony that Gray was in Higgenbotham's car.

The *News-Star* also did not record the following two hooded outrages that had occurred in the previous week. Judge Odom was told that, despite his orders to the contrary and the presence of the state military and federal investigators, black-hooded Klansmen of Morehouse Parish had perpetrated two acts of terrorism on area residents. At one site of a Klan gathering, all that remained as evidence for investigators were footprints in the mud near the Cooper Lake Road. A tense vigil was being kept by the remaining 40 members of the state militia cavalry, federal and state investigators and private citizens keeping their guns nearby.

The first manifestation of the hooded Klansmen occurred on the previous Monday, approximately six miles south of Bastrop on the Monroe-Bastrop Road near the gas fields. The young man, who asked not to be identified by the press, gave this account:

"I was driving toward Bastrop when my car was stopped by five or six men who suddenly came out into the road from behind some trees. The men all wore black hoods, and I could not recognize any of them. One had a flashlight and two others, standing close to me, had pistols in their hands. They looked into my face. 'That's not him,' one of them said. They whispered among themselves and turned to me. 'Now look here buddy,' the spokesman said, 'you keep on going, and if you know what's good for you, don't say anything about this.' Then they turned off into the side of the road, and I started up my car." This was not reported to the authorities until much later.

The second occurrence took place on Wednesday night when Sidney Rogers and his son, Charles, both farmers who lived on Cooper Lake Road approximately three miles northwest of Mer Rouge, were stopped by black-hooded Klansmen. The younger Rogers said that from the questions they were asked and the comments made by the Klansmen, he believed that they were searching for J. M. Knight, a local meat merchant from Mer Rouge, who was also a close friend of his father.

They said that they were driving their horse-drawn wagon home from Mer Rouge at about 8 p. m. As they were traveling down a sharp incline in a heavily wooded area, six black-hooded and armed Klansmen suddenly appeared from behind some trees. Their appearance was so sudden that it startled the horses, and they bolted down the road, ejecting the elder Rogers from the wagon and onto the ground. As he lay there on the ground temporarily stunned by the fall, the Klansmen approached him, and he heard one of them ask the others, "Is that Knight?" He said he managed to get up and began running down the road after the wagon. As he reached a turn in the road, he looked back and could see the Klansmen standing in the road, guns at the ready. At first, the elder Rogers was reluctant to allow his son to testify at the hearing because he feared for his safety. After learning of this Judge Odom dispatched Sheriff Carpenter to investigate the matter. We can expect that Sheriff Carpenter applied the same level of care in investigating these occurrences as he has in the past with regard to Klan-related activities.

According to Rogers, the Klan evidently learned that he had purchased some feed for his livestock from Knight earlier in the day and also that Knight had agreed to deliver it to Rogers that evening. He believed that the Klansmen thought that his son was Knight.

The younger Rogers described the leader of the Klansmen as tall and slender with a rough and strong voice. During his testimony, Knight told the court that he had gotten along with everyone in Mer Rouge save "Pink" Kirkpatrick. He and Kirkpatrick had had a disagreement concerning the rent for the store which was owned in partnership by Kirkpatrick and Dr. Clark of Mer Rouge.

Identification of the Klan leaders that terrorized the Rogers party on the Cooper Lake Road was to be made on the following day, said members of the attorney general's staff. It was also said by A. E. Farland, chief of the federal officers assisting the investigation of the Mer Rouge murders, that Rogers would identify "Pink" Kirkpatrick as one of the armed black-hooded Klansmen that terrorized them on the road.

Close watch was being kept on Rogers, the younger, as he was transported to Mer Rouge by Farland himself. While he was being questioned in Farland's office, Kirkpatrick was seen walking by, stopping to speak to a group of soldiers camped nearby. As Kirkpatrick was engaged in conversation with friends, Rogers and Farland approached to within earshot of Kirkpatrick as he told Farland, "That's the man." With regard to the younger Rogers saying that the leader of the band of Klansmen had a rough and strong voice, Farland said that Kirkpatrick was suffering from a bad cold at that time. It was believed that Rogers would be one of the first witnesses called on the following day, as would Knight.

Information was given to Sheriff Carpenter relative to an incident involving two cars alleged to have been filled with men who pulled up in front of the residence of William Higgenbotham on the previous evening, yelling for "Tommy" Higgenbotham. It was not known who these people were, if they wore black hoods, or what they wanted with Higgenbotham. Although William Higgenbotham refused to discuss the incident, Thomas Higgenbotham did say that the two cars stopped at the house around 9:30 p.m.

Tension was running high on this date as residents of both Bastrop and Mer Rouge braced for possible Klan action due to the departure of the machine gun company from New Orleans.[707]

Call Mass Meeting for Fight on Klan[708]

A press release from New York City announced that the American Unity League would begin its movement against the Ku Klux Klan the following Monday night at a public meeting at the Century Theatre. "The idea that the Ku Klux Klan can be destroyed by ridicule is entirely wrong," the chairman said. "It has a present membership of 1,400,000, and has set 2,500,000 as its membership goal for 1923. It seeks to obtain complete political control of the country."

Pharaoh's Robes Taken from Tomb[709]

A dispatch from Luxor, Egypt, told how Howard Carter had brought out from Tut's tomb ten additional egg-shaped boxes of meat, game, fowl and venison. After these boxes came a large oblong box, four feet long by two inches high and broad, containing more specimens of Tutankhamen's underwear. It was made of ebony, covered with white gilt and richly ornamented in gold.

SATURDAY JANUARY 20, 1923.

Says Skipwith's Son Guarded Victims on Murder Truck
Bastrop Witness Also Saw F. S. Smith, Vehicle's Owner, Among Kidnappers[710]
Burnett's Release On $5,000 Bond Ordered On His Arrival At Bastrop From Shreveport, Where He Has Been Confined In Hospital[711]
"Newt" Gray Held As Masker By Persons Giving Testimony[712]

The *Monroe News-Star* recorded H. E. Blankenship, 42, as the first witness to be called to the stand. During the preliminary questioning he declared that on August 17, the date of the kidnapping and release of Richards, that Captain Skipwith was one of those he saw who had Richards in custody. He recognized Skipwith because he was not wearing a mask. Blankenship said that he encountered Richards and his kidnappers on the Monroe-Bastrop Road approximately seven miles from Bastrop.

"Were you in Bastrop on August 24?" asked Coco.

"Yes."

---

[707]*The New York Times*, 20 January 1923.
[708]*The New York Times*, 20 January 1923.
[709]Ibid.
[710]Ibid.
[711]*Monroe News-Star*, 20 January 1923.
[712]Ibid.

"Do you know anything of a kidnapping that day?"

"Yes, sir, the cars passed my house that afternoon. When they drove past I noticed Watt Daniel with his hands tied behind and blindfolded, with other blindfolded men in the truck."

"Did you know the truck?"

"Yes, sir."

"Could you see the number?"

"No, sir."

"Did you look for it?"

"Yes, sir, and according to the various marks on it, I was able to recognize it."

"Did you take down the number that day?"

"Yes, sir."

"What is the number?"

Digging into his pants pocket, Blankenship produced a rumpled piece of paper from which he read, "74657, 1920 tag." Mr. Coco then introduced into evidence a letter from C. P. Bailey, officer in charge of the State Motor Vehicle at Baton Rouge. In this letter, it was said that the vehicle was registered to Smith Stevenson, of Bastrop.

"Did you recognize anyone in the cars when they passed?"

"Yes, sir. I am positive Oliver Skipwith and Smith Stevenson."

"He [Skipwith] is a son of Captain Skipwith?"

"Yes."

"How did you recognize young Skipwith?"

"By the clothes he had on. He was on the running board right close to me. Stevenson was driving the car. It was his car, and from his appearance I am sure it was him. In fact, I am as sure of these two men as if they were my brothers."

Stevenson, you recall, was on the stand previously. He testified that he had been specially deputized because of the activities being held in Bastrop on the 24th of August. He had admitted to ownership of the truck and that it had been used to haul water to the baseball game. He asserted, however, that the truck was at his residence on that night and that if the truck had been used that night it was without his permission or knowledge. During his testimony, Stevenson answered most of the questions with the response "I don't think so."

Harry Profit, of Monroe, was next to be called after Blankenship was excused. Profit said that he observed Captain Skipwith on the Bastrop-Mer Rouge Road where it forks towards Collinston on the evening of August 24th. He said he recognized him because he was unmasked, and he observed Skipwith speaking with a group of black-hooded men.

Profit was dismissed and Mrs. B. D. Carlist was summoned to take the witness stand. During the preliminary questioning, she told of being on the Bastrop-Mer Rouge Road on the evening of August 24th, and how she was held up by a group of black-hooded men.

"Two walked up to us and told us to drive our wagon to one side of the road. Our horses got tangled up in the cut telephone wires, and one of the black-hooded men untangled the wire."

"Who was that man?"

"I don't know."

"Do you now Jeff Burnett?"

"Yes, sir, I know him well."

"Did you recognize him?"

"Yes, I recognized him. He was the one who untangled the wire."

Assistant Attorney General Guion took over the questioning as he inquired about her having had a conversation with one of the black-hooded men she called, "Mr. Smith." The witness was making reference to Smith Stevenson.

"A lady I was with told me it was 'Blacksmith Smith.' "

"Do you know Newt Gray?"

"I do."

"Didn't you say you recognized Gray?"

"I thought I did but I don't know."

"What did Blacksmith Smith say?"

"He asked me if I recognized him on the road on August 24. I told him I did. He then offered me $1.50. I refused it and he gave it to my baby. He told me not to tell on him, and I said I wouldn't."

"You realize the responsibility of what you are saying?"

"Yes."[713]

---

[713]*Monroe News-Star*, 22 January 1923.

Mrs. Carlist was excused.

Next called to the stand was E. C. Osborne, a 20-year-old resident of Madison Parish. Madison Parish is located in the extreme northeast section of Louisiana. During the preliminary questioning, Osborne described receiving a letter telling him to leave Morehouse Parish in February 1922.

"I tried to make an investigation, but I was told to leave at once. The note was delivered to me by a masked man. I asked him to be allowed to stay here, but he flashed a light on his hood and rode away. I was up against it. I had to sell my property. I realized $160 for 60 acres of land. I went to the sheriff [Carpenter] and told him I had been accused of making whiskey and for him to go to my place and make a search. I then went to a lawyer, and he told me I was powerless, and he said the court was powerless. I was then advised to leave the parish.

"I stayed for about a day, and that night I was walking about three miles from Bastrop when I was surrounded by masked men. I made a break through the woods and got to Monroe." The witness claimed that his brother-in-law, Bud McCowin, had also received a warning, and it was this letter that was read into the record:

> This committee, after watching your mode of living and your utter disregard of the laws of our land against man and sale of liquor, the peaceable and unmolested possession of property have decided that your open violations of the law and your constant depredations upon the cattle, hogs, sheep, etc., of your neighbors makes you a most undesirable citizen.
> You will therefore accept this as a notice and warning to you to depart from the parish at the expiration of ten days from the time of receipt of same never to return again.
> If you fail to obey this order, you must stand the consequences.
> (signed) Vigilance Committee.[714]

Osborne was excused and "Bud" McCowin was called to the stand. He identified himself as a farmer in Morehouse Parish, and he too told of having received a letter from the Vigilance Committee.

"How did you get this notice?"

"Parties came to the house on horses. They were dressed in white masks and robes. They told me they had a little note for me. When I was handed the note, they spurred their horses and rode off."

"What had you done?"

---

[714]Ibid.

"I do not know of any reason why I should have received the note. I was working every day and had my wife to support. I broke my foot after leaving here and I appealed to the Vigilantes to allow me to come back. Mr. Lum Adams fixed it up for me to return."[715] Although the name Lum Adams does not appear on the original application for Morehouse Klan No. 34, he apparently had significant influence within the Klan because his name will surface in the testimony that follows.

McCowin was dismissed and Dewey Brown, the son-in-law of "Bud" McCowin, was called. Brown also told the court that he had received a letter from the Vigilance Committee.

"Went to the sheriff [Carpenter], and he told me he would do all he could." Brown said that he spoke to a number of other citizens, and he was told that he would hear from them the following day.

"Lum Adams the next morning told me that he had it all fixed. Then I met Fred Carpenter, the sheriff, and he told me everything was all right, that this was a 60-day notice and if I did not break any of the rules I would continue to stay. I told the sheriff I would continue to live just as I always have, and I haven't changed and I never will."[716] Brown said that he was of the opinion that the entire matter grew out of a debt that he owed Gus Calhoun. The name "A. B. Calhoun" appears on the original membership application of Morehouse Klan No. 34. It is uncertain if this is the same individual. This testimony directly links Sheriff Carpenter to the Klan in that he was an important instrument of the Klan.

H. C. Osborne, the brother of Ed Osborne, was the next to testify. When asked why he had left Bastrop, he told of a kidnapping and beating that he had received at the hands of the Klan.

"My brother had a notice to leave, and I was standing on a corner talking to Mr. Gus Calhoun. Four black-hooded men jumped out of an automobile, threw their guns in my face and told me to get into the car, and they carried me out on the Cooper Lake Road. They claimed I was doing some big talk. They told me I wasn't paying any attention to notices. They whipped me, but with my clothes on and while I was standing up. I got about 50 licks. They hurt, but I was still able to stand up. I begged for mercy and they quit.

---

[715]Ibid.

454

"They then told me to get out of Bastrop and get out quick, or they would break my neck. I left immediately and have not been back since until today, when I was summoned by the court."[717] Judge Odom adjourned at noon, not to reconvene until Monday evening.

The New York Times must have switched correspondents covering this story because the quality of the dispatches was not the same as those that were generated in the beginning. Although there were some areas where the Times excelled this day, the News-Star did a better job overall.

One area exclusive to the Times was an interview granted by Mrs. Carlisle the evening following her testimony. In the interview, she said that she had recognized other members of the Klan mob gathered that evening, but she refused to identify them. She said she was afraid that the Klan would kill her and her children should she name them. All totaled, she said there were about 20 Klansmen gathered at the roadblock. "I don't dare identify these men," she said. "What protection could the State afford me? Where would I and my children be after the Attorney General and his men and the State soldiers left Bastrop? I would fear from my life; I would fear that they would murder me and my children."

One area of the testimony that differed significantly from the News-Star was a portion given by Dewey Brown who had testified that he had received such a letter ordering him to leave. The difference between two version appears in the Times where he stated that he refused to leave, and that he assembled family and friends and fought off the efforts of the Klansmen to deport him. This defiant stand was not contained in the News-Star version.

After court adjourned for the day, Attorney General Coco departed to a scheduled meeting on Sunday with Governor Parker concerning the case in Bastrop. Jeff Burnett returned to Bastrop this date from the hospital in Shreveport, where he was sent because of a bogus case of pleurisy. He was allowed out on $5,000 bail by Judge Odom, the same amount Odom had released Dr. McKoin on during the week prior. This was done with the consent of the attorney general because it was said, "his health demanded his freedom." After his release, he proceeded immediately to Spyker, where he went into seclusion.

---

[716]Ibid.
[717]Ibid.

Captain Skipwith on this date made the statement that the release of Burnett was not to his liking. "I wanted him to stay in jail, so that we'd get the benefit of a preliminary trial." Speaking on the steps of the courthouse surrounded by fellow Klansmen, he said, "His family got him released without letting me know about it. I'm sorry of it." When this statement is examined, it suggests that, in some way, he believed that he should have had the final say with regard to the release of Burnett. Such arrogance tends to indicate that Skipwith truly believed that he was the monarch of Morehouse Parish.

In a related incident, it was learned that John P. Parker, Jr., the former sheriff of Ouachita Parish and son of a prominent plantation owner, had died of a gunshot would inflicted allegedly by his best friend, Carey Calhoun. Calhoun had been arrested and was being held in the Bastrop jail, this despite the knowledge that no charges had been made against him. Furthermore, the chief law officer of Ouachita Parish, Sheriff Grant, had made it plain that he would prefer no charges unless the Parker family decided to pursue it. In the between time, Besse Jones, the black woman who lived where Calhoun had killed Parker, wisely disappeared and, despite a parish-wide search, no trace of her could be found. It was believed that she might be able to give testimony as to the circumstances surrounding Parker's death. It was suggested that Jones' disappearance was not totally of her contrivance, but perhaps the doings of one or both of the families involved. The reason being that, although racism was and still is alive and well in northeast Louisiana, it was not at all uncommon for white men to have black concubines, and it would not have been beyond the realm of possibility that Calhoun shot Parker in a drunken dispute over the black woman. Clearly, neither family would have wanted Jones to make such statements from the stand.

During the coroner's inquest, Calhoun testified with tears streaming from his face, his lawyer, J. D. Theus, at his side. The following is his testimony:

"I loved Jack Parker like a brother, and Jack loved me. I met him and Wesley Saunders yesterday afternoon, and we were drinking together several hours. He decided to go to his home, about three miles from here, but on the way out we changed our minds and stopped at the home of Bessie Jones to have her cook some chicken for us. When we got in the house, Saunders went into another room and fell asleep. Neither Jack nor I had a gun, and if Saunders had one I do not know it. All of us were drunk. Jack and I sat in the hall, holding a conversation which turned to the Mer Rouge tragedies and the Klan. Jack declared that Jim Norseworthy had not acted right and when he said that an argument followed, for Jim is my friend.

"During the argument, Jack slapped me, and I slapped him back. Then he struck me, and I struck him. There was a big revolver in the next room on the dresser, and Jack rushed for it. We both tried to get the gun, and in the scuffle that followed the gun was discharged and Jack fell to the floor. Bessie Jones rushed in and asked what had happened. I said, 'I guess I killed Jack.'" Calhoun then began weeping uncontrollably, and it was reported that "dozens of men in the courtroom flocked to his side, and many of them, his friends for years, openly sympathized with him and offered their support, declaring they believed the killing to have been an accident." The scene is strangely reminiscent of how so many members of the community rushed to the defense of Dr. McKoin when he was charged with the murders of Daniel and Richards.

A physician who was called to the scene of the murder, Dr. C. H. Mosely of Monroe, said in a telephone interview with a *New York Times* reporter that when he arrived on the scene he was met at the door of Bessie Jones' residence by Saunders and Calhoun. Upon entering the house, he observed Parker laying on the floor, surrounded by a pool of blood. Parker's face was bruised, and near his body was a large pocket knife with an open blade. This was the only time any mention was ever made of a knife. There is no record of any testimony given at this inquest by Dr. Mosely. Imagine that!

Rose Jones, the daughter of Bessie Jones, testified that she had neither seen nor heard anything. She said when she entered the house her mother was not at home, and Parker's body was laying on the floor. She said that she immediately ran to her grandmother's house.

Wesley Saunders testified that he also did not see or hear anything until Bessie Jones awakened him with the news: "Get up Mr. Saunders, Mr. Carey shot Mr. Jack." He said he got up and observed the body of Parker on the floor, the gun on the floor in a room off the hall. Sam Jones, the 12-year-old son of Bessie Jones, identified the gun as being property of his mother.

With regard to the shooting itself, Chief Deputy Sheriff Cloverdale testified that "the bullet, after passing though Parker's head, struck the wall, rebounded and fell under a couch in the hall."

When all was said and done, it was really no surprise that the jury returned a verdict that Parker was killed during a scuffle for the gun with Calhoun with no recommendations. After speaking with the attorney for Saunders, Sheriff Grant decided to allow the matter to be decided by David I. Garrett, the local prosecutor who had already demonstrated his ability to cover up criminal behavior, particularly when the Klan is involved.

As for the story told by Calhoun, it seems all too convenient that a house full of people generated no witnesses to what obviously would have been a loud scuffle leading up to the shooting of Parker. In the final analysis, it would seem that the location of the incident dictated how the matter would be handled. Clearly, the emphasis was on allowing this incident to pass into oblivion with the least amount of fanfare as possible.

State Rests in Cases of Former Cyclops in Trial in De Ridder[718]

It was reported that the state had rested its case against Sheffield Bridgewater, a former Exalted Cyclops of Beauregard Klan No. 9, De Ridder, Louisiana. It was alleged that Bridgewater was among six Klansmen who visited the city prison and took John Mc Grady, a black man, to the woods, threatened him and put a rope around his neck. When Bridgewater was asked if he were a member of the Klan, he stated: "Yes, sir, I am a member and proud of it. I have my card, and it is paid up to 1924. Is there anything else you wish to know?"

Eleven More Irish Pay Death Penalty[719]

A dispatch from the Associated Press told of 11 executions that had been carried out in Ireland this day. Four persons were put to death at Tralee, five at Athlone and two at Limerick. These bring the total executions since last Nov. 17 to 45. Those at Athlone were executed for train wrecking, and those at Tralee and Limerick were executed for possessing arms and ammunition. Irregulars with explosives practically destroyed the railway viaduct spanning the sea at Malahide, near Dublin. Traffic of the Great Northern Railway was said to be greatly impeded.

Says Radio Cannot Rival Newspaper[720]

Chester S. Lord, editor, author and chancellor of the University of the State of New York predicted that the radio will not supplant the newspaper as a distributor

---

718 Ibid.
719 Ibid.
720 Ibid.

of news. Mr. Lord said that the radio requires its patrons to adapt themselves to its time, instead of adapting itself to their time, as the newspaper does.

MONDAY JANUARY 22, 1923

Mer Rouge Kidnapping Prompted by Alleged Attempt to Murder Dr. M'Koin, Hearing Discloses[721]
Coco Gives Notice of Important Step in Kidnapping Case: Twenty-five To Thirty Arrests To Be Made, Declares Attorney General[722][723]
Terrorists Face Trial on Dozens of Minor Counts[724]
Plot to Kidnap Whetstone, Anti-Klan Witness, Foiled[725]
Ku Klux Klan Built up Super Government[726]

The *Monroe News-Star* reported that due to a heavy rainfall over the weekend, many of the witnesses that were scheduled to appear on this date were not expected to appear because of the impassable condition of most of the roads in the parish. With only two witnesses present at the start of the morning session, the giving of testimony began with the calling of C. Wagsdale, of Wagster. During preliminary questioning, he said that he was at the home of J. L. Daniel engaged in playing poker on the night of the alleged assassination attempt upon Dr. McKoin. He claimed that Watt Daniel, J. L. Daniel, T. F. Richards, W. C. Andrews, Tom Bell and a man by the name of Hicks were also present.

"After I left the game, I went to a restaurant, after which I went to my home. On my way I heard two shots. I did not pay any attention to it. I was going away that night, and I left home and walked down to the restaurant again to wait for the train. I joined Watt Daniel, Richards, W. C. Andrews and others in the restaurant. I did not hear of any attempt to kill Dr. McKoin until I reached Bonita the next day."

Wagsdale was excused, and S. I. Bennett, 40, general manager of the Southern Carbon Company plant at Spyker, was next to take the witness stand.

"How long was Harold Teegerstrom in your employment?" asked Guion.

"About four years, both at Lampkin and at Spyker. He was employed as timekeeper."

"Do you remember some one reported to you that he had disappeared?"

---

[721]*Monroe News-Star*, 22 January 1923.
[722]Ibid.
[723]*Times-Picayune*, 22 January 1923.
[724]Ibid.
[725]Ibid.
[726]*Monroe News-Star,* 22 January 1923.

"Yes, the matter was reported to me by Dean Ashcraft after I made inquiry as to where 'Teeg' was. I was informed that 'someone had called him out last night.' I notified the sheriff at Bastrop. I also notified Teegerstrom's brother. The sheriff came to the plant and talked to Ashcraft."

"He was a trusted employee of yours?"

"Yes."

"He kept track of all other employees and had charge of shipping carbon black, etc.?"

"Yes."

"Did he read meters?"

"No, Ashcraft attended to that."

"How long was Ashcraft attending to this?"

"About five or six months."

"Who had access to the building where the meters were stored?"

"Ashcraft and myself."

"Do you remember a bunch of keys was handed to you after Teegerstrom's disappearance?"

"Yes. Ashcraft gave them to me. They are at my house now."

Bennett was shown a set of keys and asked whether any of the keys on that ring would open any of the meter houses. The witness held up one of the keys on the ring and identified it to be a master key which would open all of the meter boxes. Mr. Guion identified the keys as those found on the bank of Lake LaFourche by a fisherman, J. C. Nettles, the morning the dynamite explosion rocked the lake and caused the bodies of Daniel and Richards to bob to the surface. The keys, along with a hacksaw blade used to cut the chain which moored the ferry to a tree, were entered into evidence. The witness was then asked if he had any knowledge as to why Teegerstrom disappeared.

"Not a thing in the world. The boy was honest, and I can't believe he had gotten mixed up in anything. The last time I saw him he was in the best of spirits."

"Do you remember that agents of the justice department had questioned him?"

"Yes, he told me about that, but merely said it was all a lie."

Because of a lack of witnesses to testify, the morning session was recessed at 10 a.m. The first witness to be called in the afternoon session was J. L. Knight, of Mer Rouge. Knight's appearance to testify was in connection of the masked holdup of young Sidney Rogers on the previous Friday evening by black-hooded men who asked him if he was "Mr. Knight." During the preliminary questioning, Knight was asked if he had ever been "waited on." This term was commonly used to describe when Klan members would go to a person's residence and await his arrival. Knight said that on August 24th, the night of the Daniel and Richards kidnapping, "some white-robed men went to his home."

"My little boy said there were ladies in the front yard, but afterward I found out they were K.K.K."

"Did you know T. F. Richards?"

"Yes."

"Did he ever tell you that he was kidnapped?"

"Yes. He told me he was taken out in the woods and questioned regarding the attempt on Dr. McKoin's life, and they questioned him, he said, about me." This was the incident which occurred on August 17.

"Who did he say questioned him?"

"A man named Skipwith. I don't know him."

Prior to being excused, Knight was asked if he knew why anyone would have been waiting along the road for him last Friday night. He said that strangely enough he had intended to deliver a load of feed to the Rogers residence, but opted to do it the next day. Had he made the delivery that night, his route would have taken him directly past the spot where young Rogers was held up.

Next to take the stand after Knight was Victor S. Teegerstrom of Lampkin, the father of Harold.

"Do you know where Harold is?" asked Guion.

"No, sir, I do not."

"We want you to tell us what you know about Harold's disappearance."

"I don't know anything. My son, Clarence, received a letter from Harold on January 12th. The letter was dated 'Somewhere in the United States.'"

"Are you positive it was your son's handwriting?"

"Yes."

"Did it satisfy you that he was still alive?"

"Yes, it satisfied me."

"Have you any reason to believe what prompted him to leave Spyker?"

"None whatever. I have felt awfully uneasy."

461

"What was the contents of the letter received from your son?"

" 'Tell Daddy not to worry, I am safe. When the authorities want me to testify, I will come home.' We really expected him Saturday. We sat up and waited for him most of the night." At this point, the elder Teegerstrom began to cry openly, and Mr. Guion delayed until he regained his composure.

"Are you positive it was your boy's handwriting?"

"Yes."

"Don't you think that if it was possible he would have written you?"

"Yes, but I understand the government was intercepting my mail. However, I have learned different."

"Was there anything else in the letter?"

"No, sir. Pardon me, in the letter he said he was being bothered by newspapermen and government detectives that he decided to get away for a little while."

"I want to say to you that as far as the state of Louisiana is concerned, while you are on the witness stand, that we, the state, have nothing that would implicate your son in this crime." Teegerstrom again broke into tears and thanked Mr. Guion.

"You have a daughter?"

"Yes, sir, she is in school at Manchester."

"Has she heard from him?"

"No, but her letters to me indicate that she is frantic."

"Has anyone ever intimated to you where he might be?"

"No, sir."

The afternoon session continued as F. R. Surguine, of Monroe, was summoned to the stand. Although his testimony was brief, he told of being on the Bastrop-Mer Rouge Road on the evening of August 24th and being held up by a group of black-masked men. Although he said he did not recognize any of the hooded men, he did recognize Watt Daniel, whom he described as being blindfolded and in the rear of a truck. Surguine said that Daniel and his wife were related and that he was very familiar with him. Also called was Paul Melton, of Monroe. He testified to having been in the same vehicle as Surguine, and he supported Surguine's testimony.

The most important witness of the afternoon, Miss Lillian Weilmann, was next called to give testimony. During the preliminary questioning, Miss Weilmann said that she was employed as a telephone operator for the Bastrop exchange of the Cumberland Telephone Company.

"You have a telephone line from Bastrop to Mer Rouge?" asked Guion.

"Yes, sir."

"Do you remember whether you reported to your company someone had to be employed to repair telephone wires?"

"No, sir."

"Do you remember if any one came into your office and telling you not to send or receive any messages over your wire?"

"Yes, it was Captain Skipwith. He told me not to take or send any calls to Mer Rouge," declared the witness.

"Did he say anything further?"

"No, sir, that's all."

"Do you remember if this was on the day of the kidnapping?"

"I do not."

"It was a rather unusual request to make?"

"Yes, no one had ever asked me that before."

"Do you remember or not that the request was made when the connection with Mer Rouge was down?"

"I don't know."[727]

Because of the extraordinary events surrounding the kidnappings and murders of Watt Daniel and Thomas Richards, Miss Weilmann's credibility is stretched thin when she made the statement that she could not remember if Captain Skipwith's demand to communications be cut between Mer Rouge on a certain day. Surely, had that request been made on the date of the Daniel-Richards kidnapping, it would be difficult to forget. It should be noted that in order to place a call to any other person during that time, it was necessary for the caller to contact the operator first. The caller then informed the operator the party they wished to contact, and the operator would literally plug the jack into that party's line. Furthermore, the phone traffic immediately following the kidnapping must have been very heavy, and even for days afterwards it must have been the talk of the entire area. Under these circumstances, Miss Weilmann's story is next to impossible to believe.

---

[727] Ibid.

The *Times-Picayune* of New Orleans recorded the testimony of Miss Lillian Weilmann, who was described as a "pretty telephone operator" for the Cumberland Telephone Company which services the Bastrop-Mer Rouge area. She was described as having "a wealth of dark hair, blue eyes of the type sometimes described as dreamy, and wearing a dark brown coat with a fur collar well up around her chin." Clearly, she made a lasting impression on this particular correspondent. She was said to be all smiles when she began her testimony, but that her smiles soon faded away as the questioning became more intense. Isn't it ironic that the only person to defy Captain Skipwith, Exalted Cyclops and virtual dictator of Morehouse Parish, and live was a female telephone operator?

It was reported in the *Times-Picayune* that "state officials, however, have other information on the matter and are certain that the request was made by Captain Skipwith on the night of August 24, and that following the refusal of the operator to accede to his request, the wires between this town [Bastrop] and Mer Rouge were cut."

In a statement made to reporters, Coco said, "The state has proven that the Ku Klux Klan had established a super-government in Morehouse Parish, that J. K. Skipwith, Exalted Cyclops of the Klan, was an absolute czar who made the laws to suit himself, acted as judge over those accused of violating his edicts and passed sentence upon offenders.

"The evidence, part of which has not yet been presented, will warrant twenty-five to thirty arrests and from seventy-five to one hundred indictments. Against some of the hooded men who have been terrorizing the parish, there will be as high as six charges made.

"There will be probably thirty more witnesses examined before the close of the hearing, which we anticipate by Thursday. I am not at liberty to state what will be shown by this testimony, but it is expected to greatly strengthen our case.

"The state's case is solid. I believe all of the hooded outrages committed in Morehouse parish may be justly attributed to the Ku Klux Klan as an organization under the direction of Skipwith as leader."

"We have not yet taken that up," was Coco's response to a question regarding investigating the grand jury which was impaneled at that time in Morehouse Parish. "Whether we will ask the court to order a special grand jury drawn will be determined by developments."

The Ku Klux "Terrorists," as they were referred to by the *Times-Picayune*, stood to be charged with "murder; the kidnapping of J. L. Daniel, W. C. Andrews and C. C. 'Tot' Davenport, along with [Watt] Daniel and [Thomas] Richards the second time; the kidnapping of Addie May Hamilton and the assault and beating of her mother; breaking into Braddock's home at night; the holdup of hundreds of people on the highway; conspiracy; perjury; tampering with legal documents; unlawful assembly; writing threatening letters; misconduct of public officials by failing to perform their duties; cutting of telephone wires; moonshining and bootlegging; concubinage; falsification of records, and threats to drive people from places where they have a lawful right to be."

The reporter went on to point out: "Two of these crimes, murder and breaking and entering in the night time, are capital offenses and can be prosecuted only on indictments by a grand jury. All of the others, embracing penitentiary offenses and misdemeanors, can be prosecuted on bills of information filled by the district attorney or the attorney general."

Information was released of a plot to kidnap state witness Barry Whetstone. The plot was alleged to have originated in November 1922, when government agents first entered the case. Traveling through the parish interviewing potential witnesses, Klansmen kept watch on each and every person that the government agents called upon. One of these was Whetstone.

Whetstone told the agents that he could put T. J. "Jeff" Burnett on the scene of the kidnappings of J. L. Daniel, Watt Daniel, W. C. Andrews, C. C. "Tot" Davenport and Thomas Richards. He told them that he had seen Burnett's face clearly when he lifted his black hood to get a dipper of water which Whetstone had been forced to retrieve from a nearby farm. Because of the importance of this witness, the government agents decided to relocate him to New Orleans, where he had family. With this in mind, the possibility could exist that it was, in fact, government agents that had come to secret him away until the open hearing began on December 29, 1922, and he chose not to go with them.

This information reached the Klan, and they began to make plans to kidnap Whetstone and to murder the agents who were accompanying him. Here the story takes on the flavor of one which had been presented before.

The Klan learned that the government agents were to transport Whetstone by train to New Orleans. They learned which train they would be taking, and they made plans to intercept the train at Collinston, kidnap Whetstone and kill the government agents with him. Little doubt, Whetstone would have been murdered also to silence him.

Because the government had already planted undercover agents in the parish, they learned of the plot and took Whetstone out quietly on an earlier train. When the Klansmen intercepted the train at Collinston, they were surprised to find their quarry missing. This story sounds quite similar to one reported previously in which the Klansmen were supposed to be after information contained in a briefcase in the possession of federal agents investigating the disappearance of Daniel and Richards. The location and method of interception of that briefcase used the same plan as this, and it is entirely possible that the Whetstone kidnapping and murder plot was the rest of the story.

The state did not take any chances when Whetstone returned to Bastrop to testify in the Daniel-Richards case. The state intentionally leaked that Whetstone would be returning to Bastrop on Friday. Without notice, Whetstone was smuggled into Bastrop on Thursday, gave his testimony and was spirited out immediately by government agents.

In an effort to discredit Whetstone after learning his intention to expose Burnett as one of the Klansmen who kidnapped Daniel and Richards, the Klan began to circulate damaging rumors. Whetstone, a classmate of Daniel while they both attended Louisiana State University, they said, was a "dope fiend." The Klan had little success with this campaign because he and his family, like the Daniel family, had always enjoyed a good reputation, his father having served in the state legislature not to mention 14 years as president of the Morehouse Parish Police Jury.

In a related development, Captain Skipwith told reporters today that the death of John P. Parker, Jr. could be directly attributed to the open hearing being conducted in Bastrop, a quantum leap in logic.

"If there hadn't been an open hearing, John P. Parker, an excellent man, would still be alive." The inference made was that Carey Calhoun and John Parker, Jr. had gone to blows over a difference of opinion concerning the open hearing. This statement only serves to exemplify the level of hypocrisy maintained by Captain Skipwith and the Morehouse Klan in general.

In the testimony given before the coroner on the previous day, Carey Calhoun plainly stated that he and John Parker, Jr. had been drinking heavily all day and that they were totally drunk. According to Calhoun, they went to Bessie Jones' place to have her cook them some chicken, as though there were no restaurants around that would have been able to do this. As previously stated, it was entirely possible that instead of food, Parker and Calhoun went to Bessie Smith's home in search of a sexual encounter. That an argument erupted between the two drunk men seems quite possible, and that Calhoun killed Parker was a given.

Clearly, Calhoun admitted he and Parker had been drinking and were drunk. Considering Captain Skipwith and the Klan's stance on the manufacture, distribution, sale and consumption of alcohol, not to mention the keeping of a black female concubine, it would seem that it depended on who was involved as to whether Skipwith or the Klan would consider their actions to be a violation of the Klan's fluctuating violations of moral turpitude.[728]

Author of "Clansman" Condemns Modern Klan in Address in Gotham[729]

A report from New York City carried the news that Thomas Dickenson, author of *The Clansman*, had vigorously condemned the modern Ku Klux Klan declaring it had stolen the livery of the original order. The Klan's assault upon the foreigner is the acme of stupidity and inhumanity," he added. "We are all foreigners, except the few Indians we haven't killed."

Out of Boston came a dispatch from Fredrick W. Hamilton, supreme council deputy of the Masonic order for Massachusetts. He issued notice that no member of the Klan was entitled to membership in the order and "No Scottish Rite Free Mason can consistently be a Klansman."[730]

Reports from the police in Daytona, Florida, this day indicated that they had prevented a Klan rally in the Daytona baseball park. Dr. C. A. Ridley, Klansman and pastor of the Central Baptist Church at Atlanta, was scheduled to speak at the rally in "UnAmericanism." [731]

---

[728] *Times-Picayune*, 22 January 1923.
[729] *Monroe News-Star*, 23 January 1923.
[730] Ibid.
[731] *Times-Picayune*, 22 January 1923.

TUESDAY JANUARY 23, 1923

Brother of Missing Boy Tells Inquisitors That he is Unaware of Whereabouts of H. Teegerstrom

Letter With No Postmark Only Clue To Sudden Departure Of State Witness In Probe, Clarence Testifies At Bastrop Today[732]
Termination Of Open Hearing In Morehouse Slated For Next Wednesday[733]

The *Monroe News-Star* recorded the first called to testify this date as R. C. Carter. He identified himself as a night policeman for the town of Bonita. He said that early on the morning of August 25 he observed an automobile enter town. The car stopped, and "Jap" Jones and Jim Harp exited the car and went to their homes. The car then proceeded out of town. He said he did not recognize anyone else in the car

Clarence Teegerstrom, the brother of the missing Harold Teegerstrom, was next called to give testimony on this date. It is not known who was asking the questions.

"Do you know where your brother is?"

"I do not."

"When did you last hear from him?"

"I received a letter on January 10."

"Where is the letter?"

"I destroyed it."

Teegerstrom claimed that he received the letter from Dean Ashcraft. He said that Ashcraft told him that the letter had been found in the company mail box. The letter had a two cent stamp on it, but the stamp had not been canceled, and there was no postmark on it. In the letter, he said that his brother wrote that he was in a safe place, and that he would be returning around the 20th of January to "testify for Mr. Jeff," meaning Jeff Burnett.

"Did Burnett and others who lived at Spyker discuss what knowledge Harold might have in this case?"

"No, sir, no one."

"Whom did you read the letter to other than your father?"

"No one."

"What did Dean Ashcraft say to you when he handed you the letter?"

---

732 Ibid.
733 Ibid.

468

"He merely said here was a letter which Mr. Bennett found in the company's box that looked like Harold's writing."

"When did you destroy the letter?"

"I took it home, showed it to my wife and then burned it." This seems a bit contradictory since he previously said that his father was the only other person to know the contents of the letter. It seems more likely that he would be unwilling to show the letter to the court because of what it may have contained.

"Are you sure that his disappearance is voluntary and that he is not being sent or hidden away by anyone?"

"I am sure or at least feel certain it is voluntary."

"Do you know Jeff Burnett?"

"Yes, just casually though."

"You did not read the contents of the letter to any of Burnett's friends?"

"I did not."

"Did Harold ever say anything about Burnett since his arrest?"

"He said he was going to testify for Mr. Jeff."

"You have said that your brother is likely to turn up here at any time, but this hearing is likely to be over shortly. You cannot suggest a way in which he can be communicated with?"

"I do not. But if he does testify he will tell the truth regardless of who it hurts. He's that kind of boy. I am just as anxious to communicate with him as you gentlemen are, and I want to assure you that you will have my cooperation."

"Have you got any idea as to how the letter got into the company's box without having passed through the regular post office channels?"

"I do not. The stamp was uncanceled. I suppose he told whoever he is hiding out with where the company's box was located. It convinces me that he is in the vicinity."

"Did government agents call on you after you received the letter?"

"Yes, one came to see me and asked me had I heard from my brother. I told him no because I didn't think it was any of his business."

He was then ordered to give a sample of his handwriting, particularly numbers and fractions. This was taken into evidence.

"Are you a member of the Klan?"

"Yes."

469

"When did you join?"

"The first of this month." This would have been the first of January. Strangely enough, Harold Teegerstrom's disappearance occurred on December 30-31. This seems more than just a coincidence. Why would he choose to join the Klan when he was aware that it was highly likely that the Klan had kidnapped his brother, unless this was a form of blackmail forced upon him for the safe return of his brother.

Following Teegerstrom to the stand was Dr. L. N. Holmes, a Baptist preacher from Ouachita Parish. His testimony concerned "Newt" Gray, one of those already implicated in the kidnappings and deaths of Daniel and Richards. Holmes said that he had visited the Gray residence on the very night of the kidnappings and murders and that, to the best of his knowledge, "Newt" Gray did not return home that night. He said that he had accompanied both Mr. and Mrs. Gray to the house, but that "Newt" Gray had returned to Bastrop "to join some friends at the baseball game."

"Did Mr. Gray return home that night?" the minister was asked. He said that Gray had not returned home before he went to bed.

"When did he return?"

"I saw him the next morning-in the meantime I had attended church the night before and had heard of the kidnapping. When Mr. Gray made his appearance that morning, I joked with him about the kidnapping and expressed the hope that he wasn't a member of the band." He said that he did not see Gray at church services that evening.

"Did he make any reply?"

"No, he had no comment to make on the kidnapping, except that he was not held up on the road."

Gray testified that he was at the home of William Higgenbotham, acting as a guard because of a threatening letter that Higgenbotham had received. Gray said that he went home after midnight. Both William and Thomas Higgenbotham testified as to Gray's presence there. In effect, each providing the other with an alibi. Judge Odom called the noon recess.

After the noon recess, next on the stand was Huckett Mason, a resident of Gallion. With reference to the baseball game held in Bastrop on August 24, 1922 Mr. Guion asked the witness:

"Did you see Watt Daniels [sic], 'Tot' Davenport, T. F. Richards and W. C. Andrews?"

"Yes, I was with them at the baseball game, and afterwards we sat on the ground at the courthouse. I said to Watt Daniel and Richards that Captain Skipwith was walking around talking to the Ku Kluxers. He would walk up to a man and say something to him; then he would go to another man. I said to Richards, 'I guess they are up to something,' and Richards said to me, 'They don't want me; they had me last week.' Captain Skipwith, after approaching a man, would say a few words and then look at us."

Following Mason, Roy Broadnax of Gallion was called to the stand. He testified that he too had seen Watt Daniels [sic], T. F. Richards and "Tot" Davenport in Bastrop on August 24, 1922.

"I saw Daniels [sic] and Andrews sitting on the steps of the courthouse. Captain Skipwith was talking in a group of men near by, and I saw Captain Skipwith point out Daniels [sic] to the men. The men were strangers to me. I didn't think much of it at first, but after the kidnapping it looked mighty funny to me."[734]

As has been shown before, it was common practice for various Klans to join in with one another on certain projects. It was quite common for one Klan to bring in members of another Klan when there was something particularly sensitive to be done. Clearly, Skipwith had planned to murder both Daniel and Richards and had brought in the "strangers" to do his bidding. This was the reason he had to point out Daniel and Richards to them.

A staff member of the attorney general told reporters that it was expected that the open hearing would end on Wednesday, barring any unforeseen circumstances. The transcript of the testimony given during the open hearing would take a number of days before it would be ready. Once completed, it was to be taken to New Orleans, where preparations would be made for the formal presentation to a grand jury.

The *Times-Picayune* announced today that the keys found on the bank of Lake LaFourche the morning the bodies of Daniel and Richards were recovered fit the lock on the door of the meter house at the Southern Carbon Plant in Spyker. The meter house was where the company's store of dynamite was kept.

---

[734]Ibid.

The manager of the Southern Carbon Plant, S. I. Bennett, in his testimony said that the keys appeared to be the same as those which were reported lost by Sim Harris, a black man, who had been fired and who had been replaced by Dean Ashcraft. Ashcraft had testified earlier that this particular set of keys had been lost by Harris eight months prior during a flood. He said that Harris had been given a new set of keys and that these keys were returned upon his termination.

Bennett, although not asked while on the stand, admitted to the state's attorneys that he was a member of the Klan. This had not been reported in the *Monroe News-Star*, and his membership raises the specter of deeper involvement of the management and staff of the Southern Carbon Plant in the Daniel-Richards case. It was the belief of those investigating that the entire scheme to kidnap, murder and later dynamite Lake LaFourche had all been planned at the Southern Carbon Plant.

Because of the weather and the conditions of the roads, which were reported as impassable, witnesses were scarce, and the afternoon session did not begin until 3:30 p.m. with the calling of Sidney Rogers.

Rogers, a boy of 13 years, told how he had been held up on the previous Wednesday, during the height of this open hearing, by armed black-hooded Klansmen on the Cooper's Lake Road a few miles north of Mer Rouge. He said that they were eight in number, but he was unable or unwilling to identify any of them.

J. T. Ellis of Mer Rouge told of being in the line of cars that was held up after the baseball game on the Bastrop-Mer Rouge Road on August 24, 1922. Although he said that he was unable to identify any of the black-hooded men, he learned in a conversation with W. C. Andrews' brother, Hugo, that he did recognize a few of the members of the mob. This was all that was recorded of his testimony.

Mrs. Sallie Whetstone took the stand. The wife of Dexter Whetstone and sister-in-law of Barry Whetstone, Mrs. Whetstone told of a conversation in which her husband told her of an encounter he had with F. Smith Stevenson on the Bastrop-Mer Rouge Road on August 24, 1922. She claimed her husband told her that he hailed down Stevenson in his truck as Stevenson was driving out of Bastrop on the Bastrop-Mer Rouge Road headed toward Mer Rouge. She said her husband asked Stevenson for a ride, but that Stevenson declined, saying that he was only going a short distance. This would coincide with the roadblock which was set up just about a mile outside of Bastrop. This testimony would also run contrary to Stevenson's claim that he was in Bastrop serving as town marshal for that evening. Dexter Whetstone was never called to testify.

Convinced that Harold Teegerstrom was either being held against his will or was in hiding fearing for his own safety, government agents and the attorney general's staff drew up search warrants for the homes of Henry Jones and his father, Rufus, who lived just a short distance away. Their plan was doomed to failure in the same manner as was the raid on the Branch Davidian compound at Waco, Texas, because in both instances the element of surprise had been removed.

Surely by now the reader must have certain misgivings as to the loyalties of Judge Odom. Yet, it was Judge Odom who signed both of these warrants. This was the same Judge Odom who made certain that Jeff Burnett was sent to Shreveport on the very day that the open hearing began. The same Judge Odom who overlooked Dr. McKoin's outrageous behavior during the testimony of the father of the murdered Watt Daniel. The same Judge Odom who made big noises concerning what would happen to anyone intimidating any witnesses in this investigation, and yet, on the very next day following the signing of these warrants, would hear the testimony of W. H. Hearts, who said that he had heard Jim Harp say "that he would kill any man who swore to seeing him in a car at about 3:00 a.m. on the morning following the kidnapping of Daniel and Richards," and yet did nothing. [735]

If using Judge Odom was not bad enough, Sheriff Carpenter, a charter member and officeholder in Morehouse Klan No. 34, was also aware of the impending raids, because it was reported that he assigned two deputies to accompany Major E. P. Roy and 16 members of the cavalry troop and the state and government agents on the raid. Needless to say, both of these raids were fruitless. Clearly, whomever fostered this action must have been related to the lookout at Pearl Harbor.

---

[735] *Times-Picayune*, 24 January 1923.

WEDNESDAY JANUARY 24, 1923

Jones of Moselle Saw Hooded Mob in LaFourche Region
**Nation-Wide Search For Traveling Man Results In His Being Discovered[736]
State Prepares to Bring to Close Hooded Mob Investigations: Adjutant General
Toombs Goes Into War Zone With Drastic Instructions From Executive-Klan
Leaders Are Warned[737]
Teegerstrom's Book and Documents are Offered in Record: Mysterious Erasure
Indicates Tampering[738]**

The *Monroe News-Star* reported that the beginning of today's session was surrounded with an air of anticipation as the state made the announcement that they had located Leon L. Jones, a star witness, in a small town in Mississippi, and that he was scheduled to give testimony in the afternoon session. Jones, a traveling salesman, was said to have been traveling through Morehouse Parish on the afternoon of August 24, when his car broke down on the road a short distance from Lake LaFourche. Mr. Coco said that Jones claimed to have been waiting on the road for his car to be fixed when two vehicles passed him, his wife and child in the evening. One of the vehicles was said to have been a truck containing two blindfolded men in the company of black-hooded men. The vehicles were traveling in the direction of Lake LaFourche.

The military contingent has been steadily reduced to where now the forces have been cut down to 40 members of the Jennings Cavalry and four automatic riflemen from another troop. The hearing, which began in Bastrop on January 5th, was expected to close after the appearance of Jones.

Mr. Coco refrained from making any official pronouncements as to how the state would present its case to the grand jury. However, he did indicate that as soon as all of the evidence and testimony could be briefed, the state would call for a session of the grand jury. This was not expected to occur until after March 1, because the term of the grand jury in session at that time would not expire until then. Members of the grand jury were to be selected on February 1, a month before they are sworn in. The attorney general had the prerogative to draw up bills of information should the grand jury fail to return any indictments. Until the grand jury hears the evidence, the state would refrain from making any arrests, aside from those already made.

---

[736]*Monroe News-Star*, 24 January 1923.
[737]Ibid.

474

The open hearing began this date with the testimony of H. H. Riordan, the general manager of the Monroe district of the Southern Carbon Company. Riordan had brought to the hearing books and records, particularly Harold Teegerstrom's timekeeping book, from the plant in Spyker. After the books and records had been entered into evidence, Assistant Attorney General Guion continued the questioning.

"What is the last information you had from Teegerstrom?"

"Two days before he disappeared, I talked with him at Spyker."

"Who kept the time books at the Spyker plant?"

"Teegerstrom."

"Is this book the time book kept by Teegerstrom, the same one turned over to you after he disappeared?"

"Yes."

"From whose hands did you receive this book?"

"S. I. Bennett, superintendent at Spyker."

"When and where did you receive this book from Bennett, which is now marked state ex parte No. 3?"

"On January 2."

"Whose handwriting is in this book?"

"Harold Teegerstrom."

The witness then began a series of explanations about how the time was kept and the meanings of the entries in the time book. Under the date of August 24, the entry indicated that Jeff Burnett had worked as a watchman that night. There was, however, a discrepancy noticed.

"But there also appears a disturbance or an entire erasure on this line. [Mr. Guion said this as he pointed to the line where the Bennett entry was made.] "Can you explain how that occurred?" demanded Mr. Guion.

"I cannot," said the witness.

On page fifteen of the time book, T. J. Burnett's name had been entered, showing that he had worked a total of 142 hours during that period. However, his total hours worked for that period, according to the payroll book, was 160. This book was used for payroll purposes and spanned that period of time between August 16 and August 31, 1922. The book was entered into evidence.

---

[738] Ibid.

"Can you explain why there is a discrepancy between the time book and the payroll?"

"I cannot."

"Has there been any explanation of this discrepancy offered to you by Teegerstrom or Bennett?"

"There has not."

"There appears to be some erasures on this payroll opposite Burnett's name, don't you think?"

"It appears that it is."

"There are no erasures alongside the names of others on the roll?"

"No, sir. I don't see any."

"Has any explanation of this been made to you by Teegerstrom or Bennett?"

"No."

Burnett's canceled check was produced, and his pay for that period was $62.40. This was the correct pay according to the time book and not the payroll book. Both books and the check were placed in the custody of the court.

Tom Robinson, a Morehouse Parish farmer, followed Riordan to the stand.

"Have you been waited on by the K. K. K. or any hooded band?"

"Yes, by a band of hooded men."

"When did this happen?"

"On the 18th of June, 1922."

"Where were you when this happened?"

"I was at church, at Sunrise church, just before the congregation had begun to gather. I was there with my 15-year-old niece and one of my children. I was the song leader in the church and was expected to get there early.

"The little girl was playing the organ, and I was making preparations for the service. I heard a car coming. It turned out to be the Ku Klux. They stopped at the church. One fellow walked up to the church step, a gun in his right hand, and he motioned me to come to him. He motioned me to get into the car. They blindfolded me and drove off. They then took me off to administer punishment.

"How many were there?"

"Between 25 and 50."

"Well, after I got to the scene, I heard someone say, 'Where do you want him?' The reply was 'across that log.' They whipped me. They asked me if I could quit this lawless gang. I told them 'yes.' They whipped me again. Afterwards they led me to the road and told me if I didn't quit this lawless gang, dip my cattle, quit talking and be a man, they would come back and hang me. They turned my back to the cars, took off the blindfold and told me if I looked back they would shoot me. Of course, I did not look back. They left."

"What had you done?"

"Well, I got a note accusing me of blowing up dipping vats. This note was received about three days before I was whipped. I was told later they picked up Oscar Meek."

This was the victim that Jim Norseworthy, a professed Klansman, had admitted abducting and taking to the Arkansas line in his previous testimony. The morning session concluded shortly after Robertson's testimony.

At the beginning of the afternoon session, Attorney General A. V. Coco made the announcement that Leon Jones, the state's main witness who was to testify as having seen Daniel and Richards bound and blindfolded in the rear of a truck just a short distance from Lake LaFourche, was delayed because of automobile troubles, and he would not be available to give testimony until the following day. The state was expected to conclude the open hearing today with the testimony of Jones. Mr. Coco announced that the closure of the open hearings would be postponed until after the testimony of Jones on the following day.

The afternoon session was quite brief because B. J. Peterson was the only witness called. Peterson said that he was riding in the same vehicle with J. L. and Watt Daniel on the evening of August 24th when they were held up by a band of hooded men on the Bastrop-Mer Rouge Road just outside of Bastrop near the Collinston fork in the road. He said the men were all armed with shotguns, pistols and "Saturday night Harringtons."

"The man who came up to my car told me and Mr. Daniel to get out of the car three times. Then another came up, and they partially dragged old man Daniel out of the car. They told me to drive on."

"Did you recognize anyone?"

"No."

After Peterson, the hearing stood in recess until the following day.

Just as there had discrepancies between the testimony carried in the *Monroe News-Star* and *The New York Times*, so were there discrepancies in the testimony between the *Monroe News-Star* and *The Times-Picayune*. The *Picayune* version of today's testimony was similar to that of the *News-Star* but with a few important differences. For example, during the testimony of Riordan, Mr. Warren asked:

"Has Teegerstrom been dropped from the company employ of the Southern Carbon Company?"

"What do you mean?"

"I can hardly make it plainer. Is he still on the payroll of the company?"

"Why yes; an employee of the company is innocent until proven guilty." This question would seem to indicate that Teegerstrom was not only sill employed, but also that he was "still on the payroll of the company." That is a curious admission.

In the *Picayune* version, Senator Warren continued to hammer away at the discrepancies in the time sheet, particularly the erasures. It was revealed by Riordan that Harold Teegerstrom and Jeff Burnett were more than just acquaintances. They were also good friends. Prior to his disappearance, it was alleged by government agents that he had told them that Burnett was not at work on the night of August 24, 1922 and that this was the reason that he was kidnapped by Klansmen. The government was in possession of information that a single vehicle of Klansmen, and not several, carried Teegerstrom away from the bunkhouse that night and that he had been taken directly to Henry Jones' house. Teegerstrom remained hidden between the houses of Henry Jones and Rufus Jones, who lived just a short distance away from one another. On the night of the botched raids on the two Jones houses, Teegerstrom had been tipped off in advance and was in hiding at another.

Martial Law for Morehouse if State's Witnesses are in any way Threatened[739]

A dispatch from Baton Rouge announced that Governor Parker would declare martial law in Morehouse Parish if threats of any kind were made against the state's witnesses between adjournment of the Morehouse open hearing and trial of persons to be indicted for alleged participation in outrages by masked men in the parish.

Anti-Klan Measure Passed in Nebraska Lower House[740]

From Lincoln, Nebraska, came the news that in the face of strong opposition, the lower house of the Nebraska legislature had passed the Anti-Ku Klux Klan bill by a vote of 65 to 34. The bill prohibits non-law enforcing persons, single or collectively, from imposing or administering penalties for alleged infractions and

---

[739] *Monroe News-Star*, 24 January 1923.

placed a barrier on secret meetings for the purpose of carrying out threats or making investigations.

Lynched Wrong Man, Arkansans Think: Investigators Find Alibi for Victim of Harrison Mob, Accused of Bridge Burning[741]

Little Rock, Arkansas was the scene of a horrible tragedy. It was reported that evidence tending to prove that E. C. Gregor, a Harrison railroad man who had been hanged by a mob last week, could not have been implicated in the burning of bridges on the Missouri & North Arkansas Railroad. Gregor was a taking part in a strike when the murder occurred. The investigation developed evidence that at least two bridges on the road had been set afire recently by live coals which fell from fireboxes of engines.

Form 'Anti-Gimme League': Citizens of Cincinnati Organize Against Tipping and Petty Grafting[742]

An "Anti-Gimme League" has been formed in Cincinnati to eliminate all forms of petty grafting; to stop tipping in restaurants, hotels, Pullman cars, cabarets and other places; to establish a basis of agreement with wives so as to do away with continual and unreasonable demands upon husbands' incomes and earnings; to abolish street begging, and to prevent chronic borrowing of cigarettes, cigars, umbrellas, books, tools and household supplies by neighbors, fellow club members, office associates, etc.

Not the least important object of the new association is to prevent excessive demands of girls on young men for expenditures for theatre tickets, taxis, candies, perfumes and articles of personal adornment.

Hunt for Teegerstrom[743]

Counties in southern New York and those bordering in Pennsylvania are being searched, it was learned today, for a man believed to be Harold Teegerstrom, desired as a witness in the Mer Rouge, La., investigation of hooded bands.

---

[740]Ibid.

[741]*The New York Times*, 25 January 1923.

[742]Ibid.

[743]Ibid.

THURSDAY JANUARY 25, 1923
Skip Condone's Mob's Work
Klan Cyclops Insists Richards Still Is Alive[744]
Guion Brand's Skip's Tale That Richards Still Lives as "Rot": Klan Cyclops Believed To Be Nearing End Of "Reign"[745]
State Witnesses in Jeopardy, Says Mer Rouge Mayor: Vendetta Threatens To Follow Lull At Bastrop, Dade Hints[746]
Mississippian Who Was Last To Witness Kidnapping Offers His Testimony[747]

On the morning and final session of the open hearings, the *Monroe News-Star* reported that Attorney General A. V. Coco called Leon Jones of Moselle, Mississippi to the stand. Jones said he was traveling through Morehouse Parish with his wife and child and that he had chosen the route that brought them through the Lake LaFourche area because of road conditions.

"What happened to your car that day?"

"A mule and wagon met me on the road. The mule reared and turned across the road. I put on my emergency brake and stripped the hub. The car was out of commission. I was about three-quarters of a mile from the ferry at the lake [Lake LaFourche]. It was about noon."

Jones told of waiting all day for the part to be repaired, which had been taken to a nearby town to be welded by another passing tourist. He said that the vehicle had broken down in the center of the roadway and remained there until it was repaired two days later.

"When you were stopped there during the night, did you see any cars with masked men?"

"Yes, it was the first night. The mosquitoes were bad, and we couldn't sleep much. The cars, two of them, passed close by. They were two Fords, one a touring car and a roadster with a small truck body. The men wore black hoods. There seemed to be two men not masked. One was in the front seat of the truck, and there seemed to be two or three men in the body of the machine. One man in the touring car seemed to have something tied about his face. The cars were going toward Rayville, the touring car, I think, being in front." Rayville is almost due South of the ferry at Lake LaFourche.

---

[744]*Times-Picayune*, 25 January 1923.
[745]Ibid.
[746]Ibid.
[747]Ibid.

"How far did you watch them, and where did they appear to go?"

"They went toward the ferry and pretty soon appeared to be on one side of the ferry. I saw their lights shining against the trees. In a moment their lights went out. Pretty soon the lights came on again, one car came back, near us, turned out his lights, turned around and went back toward the lake. My wife and child and myself, who had been sleeping in the car, stepped out and went into a potato patch. We went into the patch when the car was approaching from the lake, stopped and put out its lights. We returned to our car, and later the two cars came back. They passed close by us. There didn't appear to be any with cloths tied about their faces."

Here again, the state missed an opportunity. It would seem logical to have asked Jones why he and his wife felt it necessary to conceal themselves in a potato patch. Although the answer would seem quite obvious, the expression of fear and trepidation with regard to the appearance of the black-hooded band would have counteracted the rather matter-of-fact attitude that other witnesses have displayed toward these black-masked cowards.

There were no other vehicles with masked men that passed them that night, Jones said. He did not leave the car all the next day, waiting for the repaired part, and spoke with passersby on horseback, but did not mention black-hooded men. Jones was dismissed, and Mr. Coco made the following statement to the court:

> May it please the court.
> The state has decided to discontinue these proceedings for the present at least and until such time as conditions may justify their resumption. The hope is expressed, however, that this may not become necessary.
> Before taking our leave of your honor and of this parish, I desire to express my gratification at the orderly and dignified manner in which these proceedings have been conducted and my pleasure in the assistance we have received from the officers in obtaining the prompt attendance of our witnesses and the preserving of order.
> On the other hand, it is my very painful and humiliating duty to refer to the deplorable conditions in this parish, as revealed by the evidence. The proof is convincing that since the advent of the K.K.K. in this parish there has gradually arisen a condition of disorder and lawlessness, which has ripened into a supercession of constituted authorities by the Ku Klux Klan and the establishment of a government of its own, from which a reign of terror and chaos has resulted, and the parish was on the brink of riot and bloodshed, when the government sent the militia here, and these proceedings were initiated.
> While it may be conceded that many Klansmen did not actually participate or encourage these many acts of lawlessness and crime, which finally culminated in the murder of Watt Daniel and T. F. Richards, they may, nevertheless, be deemed responsible therefore by reason of their silence and inaction. These offenses and

crimes were committed in the name of the order, under the protection of its regalia and in the use of its recognized methods and practices, and under the leadership of its officers, the principal of which has, for the last six months at least, brought about a condition in this parish which is a blot upon our civilization and brings into question the proud title of American citizen.

The flogging of citizens, their deportation and banishment and other kindred offenses were but pastimes and of such frequent occurrence that they were accepted as commonplace things, the protest against which was itself sufficient ground for deportation.

Without going into details, [I] beg to say that the conclusion we have reached is that many persons have been identified and connected with these many acts of violence and crime, leading to and including the kidnapping on August 24, 1922, and murder of Watt Daniel and T. F. Richards, and it is the purpose of the state to present this evidence to the grand jury for its consideration and action as soon as we can get a transcript of it.

Next to give a summation was Judge William C. Barnett, counsel for Dr. B. M. McKoin, T. J. Burnett, and E. N. "Newt" Gray. Judge Barnett's statement, the first formal comment for the defense, follows in part:

These proceedings have been held under section 1018 of the revised statutes of this state.

The statute does not provide that witnesses may be drawn before a court and grilled and cross-examined, but in order that their deposition be taken.

None of this has been done in this case; therefore, this whole proceeding, in my judgment, is annulled, and testimony adduced cannot be legally used in any proceedings whatsoever. It cannot even be used legally before a grand jury. It would be hearsay and any bill of indictment predicated upon this testimony would be quashed by the court.

The corpus delicti has not been established to a reasonable certainty, to say nothing of the rule that it must be established beyond a reasonable doubt. Two bodies were found in Lake LaFourche. The coroner of the parish, Dr. O. M. Patterson, a man of unquestionable integrity and standing, both as a citizen and as a physician, was not permitted to make an examination of them. He never got closer than 40 feet of the bodies while they were yet in the water, and he was told that he could not make further examination; while at the same time two pathologists seemed to have already been arranged with, even prior to the finding of the bodies, who were to come and made an examination which would disclose great brutality, etc., as to the manner in which the bodies found came to their death. And it might be said here that their testimony was not at all disappointing in this regard.

There is more than a doubt as to the identify of these bodies, which entertained the minds of the people generally. Those who heard the testimony without exception entertained such doubt, and after the pathologists had made their full report on the matter that there was a general unbelief left upon them in all fair-minded people.

Many witnesses were called to connect various and sundry persons with the mob that kidnapped and carried away Daniel and Richards, and the testimony produced showed every earmark of having been worked up by agents of the department of justice and was so conflicting that it destroyed itself. It was manifest from the very beginning that the real motive behind the prosecution was to convict the K.K.K. in the forum of public opinion, without regard to whether or not the perpetrators of the crime would be uncovered.

And many of those citizens have been subjected to the most brutal cross-examination, and the method of the cross-examination has been of such a nature as to amount to the administration of what is commonly known as 'third degree,' which is in direct violation of section 11 of the bill of rights of the constitution of the state of Louisiana.

This was an ex-parte hearing, where the defense was not permitted to speak in defense of the witnesses, and only in one instance where a client of my own was placed upon the stand, that I rose in his defense and stated the objection for him, which was promptly overruled by the judge, but he was never afterward called to the stand to testify further in the matter.

Without exception, there was no material or vital point against any individual established, except by the most partisan testimony and testimony which could not stand the fire of cross examination or the test [of] character necessary to give it verity.

The activities of the K.K.K. were gone into with great pains and, in my judgment, the evidence does not sustain the charge that they are responsible for this crime or had anything to do with it. There were other activities of major importance where immorality and lawlessness were being practiced, in which they did perhaps take some part, but in no case is a crime or misdemeanor disclosed where it is definitely shown that the K.K.K. took any part, and in no instance has any actually been shown except in furtherance of law enforcement and morality.

As a lawyer, having had a good many years of experience in the practice and years of experience as a district attorney and district judge, I am of the opinion that this proceeding, as it has been carried on, is an abuse of the law. I do not mean that in every instance and with every witness there was an abuse of the law or the machinery of the court, but in a number of instances during this proceeding methods were adopted which cannot be sanctioned by either the judicial or lay mind.

The state of Louisiana, and especially Morehouse parish, has been done incalculable harm by the publicity of sensational matters, ninety percent of which have been without any substantial foundation whatever; and from all of the evidence of the hearing and manner in which it was conducted, it impressed the reasonable mind that a great stage play was being given the public and with other motives behind it, rather than the desire on the part of the governor to really bring the guilty parties to trial.

I have another thing to say, and that is that the persons who have been named, as having been connected with the kidnapping affair, will prove their innocence when we have an opportunity of speaking before a court of justice.

It was now Judge Odom's turn, and it was clear that he took umbrage to the statement made by Judge Barnett.

I think the following allegation made in the statement of W. C. Barnett, chief counsel for the accused parties," said Judge Odom, "calls for a statement from me. It is not true that witnesses were put through the 'third degree.' It is true that some of them were put through rigid examination by counsel for the state, but at no time did the examination go beyond what should be permitted in a judicial proceeding.

With reference to that part of his statement which implies that witnesses were required to give evidence against themselves and that he made an objection on behalf of one of them that was 'promptly overruled by the judge ,' I have this to say:

When E. N. Gray was on the stand, W. H. Todd asked that he not be required to testify in as much as he could not be required to give evidence against himself. I at once informed Mr. Gray, the witness, that under no circumstances would he be required to make any statement or give any testimony which might in any way incriminate him. The witness said to the court that he had no objections to testifying and was at that time further examined.

On the following morning, Mr. Gray was recalled, at which time Mr. Barnett made the objection on behalf of the witness that he should not be called upon to testify. I again informed Mr. Gray, the witness, in open court, and in the presence of his attorneys of his constitutional right to refuse to give evidence against himself, and I then suggested to the witness that if there was any doubt in his mind as to whether he should testify further, he should consult with his attorneys, whereupon, I excused him from the witness stand, and he left the courtroom with his attorneys. He was not again called to the stand by the state. At that time, there was no charge pending against Mr. Gray or any other person who had been called to the witness stand and I stated in open court that I would not permit any person against whom any charge had been made to be called as a witness. I consider Judge Barnett's statement that witnesses were not treated fairly without foundation and uncalled for.

In a surprise announcement to the *Times-Picayune* today, Captain Skipwith said that Thomas Richards was not dead and that on the night of the kidnapping he had been put on a train out of town. He claimed that Watt Daniel and Thomas Richards were rowdy drunks who were a menace to the public, gamblers, kept the company of black women and lastly they were thieves.

With regard to the theft allegation, Skipwith said that one evening Daniel and Richards, in a drunken condition, burst into the home of an unnamed white woman and directed obscenities toward her. While in the home of this unnamed woman, Daniel was alleged to have called Richards a "yellow dog." Daniel was alleged to have said:

"Look at him, the yellow dog. We went out to shoot Dr. McKoin and he lost his nerve and I had to jerk the gun from his hands and shoot at McKoin."

Skipwith claimed that Richards was still alive and that he had been transported to Rayville where he was put on a train. He claimed that C. C. "Tot" Davenport had been kidnapped for the sole purpose of carrying the message to Mrs. Richards that her husband was alive, and that he had been run out of the parish.

484

"I think Masons and physicians killed Daniel," Skipwith said. "I just as good as know Richards is alive. He betrayed his friend Daniel to them." It would seem that the Captain became desperate to deflect the blame to someone else-anyone else.

Here we find Captain Skipwith, Exalted Cyclops of Morehouse Klan No. 34, making the assertion that Watt Daniel was dead. In doing so, Skipwith confirms that the body taken from Lake LaFourche was, in fact, that of Watt Daniel, thereby debunking the stories being written in Klan publications that both Daniel and Richards were alive and would be produced at the proper time.

Skipwith either did not or would not identify who the woman was that allegedly witnessed the statement of Watt Daniel. The allegation of theft was not substantiated either. With regard to his statement about "Masons and physicians" being involved in the kidnappings and murders, it should be pointed out again that it was quite common then for Masons to hold membership in the Klan. Skipwith then delivered his version of the kidnappings.

> I know McKoin did not know anything about the kidnapping. His friends did it. All this stuff that's been said on the stand is all lies. Can't you see that they will do anything to bring the name of 'Old Skip' in?
>
> My theory is that Richards, when he was first kidnapped, told the band that Watt Daniel shot at McKoin. My information is that they told him they would give him money, see that he was protected and take him to any country in the world if he'd deliver Watt to them.
>
> He delivered Watt after the barbecue at the kidnapping grounds. That boy, 'Tot' Davenport, who was kidnapped too and never touched, he knows all about it; well, they took Richards to Rayville to put him on the train. To get to Rayville, they had to pass Lake LaFourche, see what I mean?
>
> This Watt was a dangerous man, a holy terror. He was always armed to the teeth. Everybody was *askeered* of him. Even I was afraid. Richards hated him but was afraid.
>
> Richards got his orders to deliver Daniel, and he was planning to do it. He stuck right to him. Then he told 'Tot' Davenport and Sam White to deliver Watt. I don't believe Sam knew what he was doing.
>
> Then when they got to the kidnapping grounds, they took the whole bunch. You remember in the testimony it showed that Tot did not even have his hands tied. Can you tell me he would keep the bandage over his eyes all that time without his hands tied? He knows more than he ever told.
>
> They killed Watt for shooting at McKoin. McKoin had recognized Daniel and Richards right after the shooting, driving slowly about Dr. Clark's home, his partner, where he went after he was shot at. They all plotted to kill McKoin. They all sat around a round table, him, Richards, Hugh Davenport, the black sheep of a good family, old man Whipple and Campbell. I told them they would have trouble if they didn't get rid of those boys over there.

Old Skip appeared to be making this up as he went along, and from the looks of it, he did not do a good job of it. He claims that what has been said on the witness stand during the open hearing was "all lies." Naturally, this would include all of the lies that his fellow Klansmen had constructed to give him an alibi. He claimed to have knowledge that Richards was alive, and that Richards had set Daniel up. He claimed that Dr. McKoin named Daniel and Richards as those who attempted to kill him the night he claimed to have been fired upon on the streets of Mer Rouge. McKoin had stated repeatedly that he did not know the identities of his assailants.

As in the interview granted to Rogers of the *St. Louis Post-Dispatch*, Captain Skipwith's big mouth becaamce his own undoing. This statement again implicates him and the Klan in the kidnappings and murders of Daniel and Richards.

Skipwith admitted that it was friends of McKoin who killed Daniel, but just who were these friends? It has been established that McKoin had to leave Mer Rouge because the town was hostile toward him. It seems the only friends that McKoin had were Klansmen. That being the case, it would follow that the Klan perpetrated the actions.

Skipwith said, "My information is that . . . Richards had revealed at his first kidnapping that Watt Daniel had shot at McKoin." From the testimony of Mrs. Richards, it was learned that Richards had identified Captain Skipwith as being present at and being the one to ask the questions at the first kidnapping.

This same correspondent gave a vivid description of Skipwith's appearance, which bears listing. "In his room tonight, sharply silhouetted against the fading light that streamed through the one window, the old man seemed dejected, broken, spiritless. Gone was the military manner, the sharp replies, the court orders that made him feared in Morehouse parish, where peaceful men's homes have been violated; where innocent men have been tied and lashed; where others have been driven from their homes into neighboring states, and where two men were murdered by a cowardly band that masked their operations under the cover of night and behind black hoods."

From information gathered from present-day area residents, it has been learned that C. C. "Tot" Davenport had been kidnapped on August 24, 1922, along with Watt Daniel, J. L. Daniel, W. C. Andrews and Thomas Richards, by mistake. Conventional wisdom has it that the Klansmen were really searching for Hugh

Davenport, and they took "Tot" by mistake. It is for this reason that "Tot" was not beaten or killed.[748]

The testimony of Lawrence Jones, the traveling man who had broken down with his wife and child on the road a short distance from Lake LaFourche, told the same story, but with one interesting twist. He claimed that he could not tell whether the two blindfolded men were dead or alive. Sources interviewed by this writer indicated that it was said that Watt Daniel had been present at the beating of his father and that he had recognized some of the principals involved. It was alleged that he called these Klansmen by name and told them that he would kill them.

Watt Daniel was no small man, and it was generally believed that he had the disposition and intent to carry out the threat. This being the case, the Klansmen felt that they had no other alternative but to kill Daniel and, since Richards was such a good friend of Daniel and had also heard the names Daniel had called out, he too had to die. Some believe that Watt Daniel and Thomas Richards were shot in the head and killed before they reached Lake LaFourche. If this were the case, this should have happened before the caravan of cars filled with Klansmen and carrying Daniel and Richards reached Collinston. It would be hard to conceive, but not be totally out of the question, for the Klansmen to stop for gas with these obvious dead bodies in the back of the truck.[749]

New information surfaced on this date concerning Harold Teegerstrom, the witness who disappeared from the Southern Carbon Plant in Spyker on December 29, 1922. Investigators had information that Teegerstrom had been kidnapped by the Klan and that he was held in custody until a "treaty of peace" could be negotiated with the Teegerstrom family. This would seem to fit with Clarence Teegerstrom's joining of the Klan, which occurred shortly after the kidnapping of his brother Harold. It was believed that the joining of the Klan by Clarence was a good faith gesture on the part of the Teegerstrom family that they would cooperate, and in doing so they received assurance from the Klan that no harm would befall Harold.

---

[748]Personal interview with confidential witness. The date, time and location was promised to be kept confidential.
[749]Ibid.

Adjutant General Toombs Brings Message to People of Morehouse From Governor Parker, Urging Protection of Witnesses

Bastrop, Jan. 25--Adjutant General L. A. Toombs, in a formal statement early today announced that he brought to Bastrop a message from Governor John M. Parker to the people of Morehouse parish expressing his intention to protect witnesses who have testified at the open hearings here and declared that should there be a recurrence of disorders and should the civil authorities fail to maintain order martial law would be proclaimed.

The adjutant general also announced that troops on duty at Mer Rouge and Bastrop would be relieved today. The statement follows:

"I have been instructed by Governor Parker to trust my judgment as to the retention of troops in Morehouse parish after completion of the open hearing. I have carefully inquired into the situation and am thoroughly convinced that the presence of troops would not be necessary to maintain law and order. The decision is concurred in by the court. All troops will be relieved of duty today at noon.

"The governor has further directed me to say to the people of Morehouse parish that he is confident that law and order will prevail without the presence of troops, but should there be a recurrence of disorder in the parish, and the civil authorities fail to maintain order, that he will have troops returned, and he will declared martial law; that he is determined that the court shall be allowed to proceed in a peaceful and judicial manner, and that no intimidation of any witnesses in the case shall be permitted.

"Sheriff Fred Carpenter has informed me that he is determined to put a stop to any further disorders, and I believe that he will do it."

After General Toombs had read the statement of Governor Parker, he read his own prepared statement:

"In accordance with the instructions from Governor Parker, I have just had a conference in Bastrop at which there were present H. Flood Madison, Sheriff Fred Carpenter and Captain Skipwith. They were informed that the governor has determined that there would be law and order in Morehouse parish, and all witnesses that had appeared at the open hearing would be protected; that the sheriff would be expected to do his duty and that any recurrence of disorder in the parish, if not controlled by the sheriff, would be the cause for the immediate return of troops to the parish and the promotion of martial law.

"Sheriff Carpenter stated that he proposed from now on to see that order would prevail and that at the first outbreak he was determined to jail the offenders.

"Captain Skipwith stated that he understood the situation thoroughly and that so far as he was concerned, he would do nothing to encourage disorder.

"This afternoon, I expect to visit Mer Rouge and there inform a committee of the governor's police and give them the same warning that I have given to the citizens of Bastrop. I am firmly of the opinion that the law-abiding citizens of the parish will by their influence mold public opinion to such an·extent that there will be no recurrence of disorder. My advise has been to all concerned that now, since the open hearing has ended, that there be no further discussion of the merits or demerits of the situation and that the legal machinery of the parish be allowed to decide the question in accordance with the laws of the state.

"The state of Louisiana need have no fear that any witness will be intimidated or mistreated in any way after the withdrawal of soldiers from Morehouse parish," was the comment from Sheriff Fred Carpenter. "I will do everything possible," Carpenter continued, "to maintain law and order, and my deputies will assist me in doing this. A great many people have expressed the opinion that there would be a renewal of lawlessness with the departure of troops, but I want to say it is my personal opinion that there will not be any trouble of any kind. The witnesses are not going to be molested. They may remain right where they are in the parish, and they will not be intimidated in any way."[750] [751]

[750]Ibid.
[751]*Monroe News-Star*, 25 January 1923.

CHAPTER SIX

THE AFTERMATH OF THE OPEN HEARING

FRIDAY, JANUARY 26, 1923

State Witnesses to be Protected and Outbreak in Morehouse, Improbable, Says Sheriff

Open Hearing at Bastrop Brought to Close by State's Order Yesterday[752]

Military goes with State's Att'y Gen'l[753]

Coco Aide Boils with Rage Over Skipwith 'Yarn': Morehouse Cyclops to get Chance to Tell Court What He Knows[754]

Unlike the previous three weeks, dawn broke over the town of Bastrop on this date without the sight of Louisiana National Guardsmen manning their machine-gun nests around the Morehouse Parish courthouse. As the day continued on, there was absent the excitement, noise and suspense which had accompanied each day of the open hearings. The usual hordes of out-of-state newspapermen, photographers and the ever-present cadre of Klansmen and Klan sympathizers were all absent. The Jennings Cavalry Troop had already entrained and had left along with most of the staff of the attorney general. Government agents on the scene were being relieved by replacements, whose job it would be now to continue the investigation and persist in searching for Harold Teegerstrom, the timekeeper and vital witness as to the whereabouts of Jeff Burnett on the night of August 24th, whose disappearance from the carbon plant at Spyker on December 29th still remained a mystery.

Of the many days of testimony given by numerous witnesses during the open hearing concerning acts of lawlessness, floggings, deportations, kidnappings and murder, it can be safely said that the following was established:

> 1) T. "Jeff" Burnett, E. N. "Newt" Gray, Smith Stevenson and Oliver Skipwith had been positively identified by witnesses as having been members of the group of black-hooded men who kidnapped Daniel and Richards on August 24.
>
> 2) Captain J. K. Skipwith, Exalted Cyclops of the Morehouse Parish Ku Klux Klan, was directly connected with the Daniel-Richards kidnappings and murders by Harry Profitt of Monroe, who testified that he saw Captain Skipwith at the location of the kidnapping having a conversation with a black-hooded Klansman. Skipwith was also seen in Bastrop by a number of witnesses talking to others, thought to be Klansmen, and pointing out Daniel and Richards to them.

---

[752] Ibid.

[753] Ibid.

[754] *Times-Picayune*, 26 January 1923.

3) Dr. B. M. McKoin, former mayor of Mer Rouge, and W. P. Kirkpatrick had also been identified as part of the hooded gang who had deported Addie May Hamilton, a 17-year-old girl, to Little Rock, Arkansas a year previous. Further, these two were also identified as members of the group who burst in on services in a church near Thompson.

4) Captain Skipwith, along with six other men, were identified by witnesses as having taken part in the armed midnight raid of the home of Leon Braddock, and that he was kidnapped from his home and taken to the sheriff who held him without charges or warrant.

5) Laurie Calhoun, who had been a deputy sheriff and used by Sheriff Carpenter to travel to Baltimore to bring Dr. McKoin back to Louisiana during the extradition proceedings in Baltimore, was also identified as one of the hooded band who seized Fred Cobb in Bastrop and later allowed him to go on his way, further lecturing him.

6) Captain Skipwith, R. L. Dade, mayor of Mer Rouge, Dr. McKoin, Kelly Harp and others were identified as being part of the hooded group who held up Watt Daniel, W. C. Andrews and Harry J. Neelis during a Klan raid on the black farmstead near Stampley.

7) Captain Skipwith was identified as having taken part in the August 17 kidnapping of Richards in Bastrop.

8) It was also alleged that Sheriff Carpenter was standing on the steps of the courthouse 100 feet away when the August 17, 1922 kidnapping of Richards took place during that afternoon, and he did nothing, as usual, to stop it.

In addition to the violations cited above, testimony was given which indicated that Skipwith ordered the flogging and deportation of numerous others and that notice had been served by him personally that four Mer Rouge citizens would have to leave, "unless they quit talking about the Klan."

The business community at Bastrop had been in a state of turmoil during the time the open hearings were being conducted. They contended that they were suffering an economic depression because of the revelations concerning the lawless nature of the area and vowed that they must exert all effort to renew trade in the community. A mass meeting of businessmen was scheduled for the following week to attempt to control the damage caused to the area by the Morehouse Klansmen.

Sheriff Carpenter continued to repeat his earlier message of reassurance that the parish would remain free from violence. "We shall remain at normal despite the departure of the soldiers," said Carpenter. One can only wonder just what Carpenter considered "normal" in light of the manner in which he discharged, or better put, failed to discharge his duties as sheriff.

The *Times-Picayune* reported that the interview given by Captain Skipwith on the previous day drew a quick response from T. Semmes Walmsley of the attorney general's staff. Skipwith's contention that Richards had been put on a train and sent out of the state after he had betrayed Watt Daniel brought this response from Mr. Walmsley:

> The time will come for Skipwith to explain this interview. Until then we are not even inclined to comment on anything so utterly ridiculous and absurd. Skipwith's alleged statement is purely fabricated. It is a clumsy attempt to shield the guilty and a damnably outrageous effort to discolor the facts which is ridiculous in the face of it.

Walmsley pointed out that Skipwith had called for and Attorney General Coco had agreed to a conference to be held between the two of them during which Skipwith was to place all of the information that the Klan had at Coco's disposal. Walmsley pointed out that it was Skipwith who crawfished out at the last moment.

Imperial Wizard Declares Mer Rouge Investigation Frame-Up Against Klan by Gov. Parker[755]

While in Chicago, Hiram Evans, Imperial Wizard of the Invisible Empire, Knights of the Ku Klux Klan, declared that the investigation of the killings at Mer Rouge, Louisiana, was a "frame-up on the K.K.K." He said that it had been staged by enemies of the Klan "represented by Governor Parker" and that it had "signally failed."

Police Seize 8 as Ku Klux Plotters[756]

Eight men, said to be members of Ku Klux Klonklave 2 of Brooklyn, were booked by police following their arrest in an automobile at Clermont and DeKalb Avenues, Brooklyn, New York. When officers searched the automobile they found a bottle of Scotch whisky, two blackjacks, records of the Brooklyn Klan and a white robe with eyelets cut out in the head, the kind used by Klansmen.

Eleven Prominent Citizens to be on Trial in Oklahoma[757]

[Ardmore, Oklahoma] Eleven prominent citizens of Carter county were to face trial today in district court here on charges of murder growing out of the slaying of three men near Wilson, during the operations of a masked band on the night of December 15, 1921.

The Ku Klux Klan was definitely brought into the case by the state when it questioned witnesses at the preliminary hearing as to the existence of the organization in the county and a meeting which was said to have been held here a few nights prior to the killings. The hearing was brought to an abrupt close after one witness refused to answer a number of categorical questions concerning the Klan.

---

[755] Ibid.

[756] *The New York Times*, 25 January 1923.

[757] *Monroe News-Star*, 26 January 1923.

The story of the affair, as related by the then County Attorney James Mathers, in what he termed an outline of evidence, was that on the night of December 15, a band of more than 50 men, led by C. G. Sims, local police detective, left here in automobiles to "get Joe Carroll for alleged dealings in illicit whiskey." They took with them "buckets of tar and pillows of feathers."

After traversing the oil field districts to a point a few miles outside of Wilson, where Carroll lives, the band halted in a field and a committee of a dozen or more men was assigned to bring Carroll before the gathering.

They summoned Carroll to the door of his hut and shot him down when they discovered he was armed. A hail of bullets was poured down on the masked men by members of his family, and after the marauders had taken to their automobiles Carroll's lifeless body was picked up a few paces from his doorstep.

Sees in Japanese Menace to Hawaii[758]

A report made public this day in Washington, D.C. sounded the alarm concerning Japanese domination of the Hawaiian Islands almost 20 years in advance of the Japanese attack on Pearl Harbor. "The menace from a military standpoint can be fully verified by referring to the records of related Federal departments. The question of national defense submerges all others in significance."[759]

SATURDAY JANUARY 27, 1923

M'Koin Going Back to Baltimore: Will Resume His Studies
Leading Figure in Morehouse Investigation Secures Permission From Coco[760]
Monroe Soldiers are Commended by State's Governor[761]
Story in Ku Klux Journal Arouses Mer Rouge People: Citizens Depicted as Moral Lepers and Vigilants Reported Active[762]

The *Times-Picayune* reported that Dr. McKoin announced this day that he would be returning to Johns Hopkins University to continue his graduate studies, from which he was originally taken. Still free under his original $5,000 bond, McKoin said that he had been in contact with Attorney General Coco, who advised him that the state would raise no objection to his temporary relocation to Baltimore.

Governor Parker took this opportunity to issue letters of commendation to two soldiers who served during the Louisiana National Guard's occupation of Morehouse Parish during the just-finished open hearings. First to be commended are Privates First Class Fred O. Andrews and Leroy M. Thomas, who were both

---

[758]*The New York Times*, 25 January 1923.
[759]Ibid.
[760]Ibid.
[761]Ibid.
[762]*Times-Picayune*, 27 January 1923.

attached as members of Company G, 156th Infantry. While under the command of Captain W. W. Cooper, Commander of Company G, Governor Parker's letter commended them for their bravery while assigned to guard Lake LaFourche during the night of December 22, 1922. It was during this assignment that they were fired upon by a person or persons unknown and that they ran to Mer Rouge to bring back reinforcements for the besieged troops.

The governor's letter read as follows:

> State of Louisiana.
> Executive Department.
> Baton Rouge.
> Jan. 24, 1923.
>
> Private Fred O. Andrews,
> Ouachita National Bank,
> Monroe, La.
> Dear Sir:
> This office is advised that on December 22, 1922, between 1 and 2 a.m. at a time when it was felt re-enforcements were necessary, you made a trip of more than six miles, on foot, through unfamiliar and seemingly hostile country for that purpose.
> It is a source of great satisfaction to know that members of the Louisiana National Guard have not only performed their duty, but unhesitatingly and with unflinching courage have complied with instructions and assisted in maintaining law and order, and I write to officially commend your appreciated action.
>
> Yours very truly
> John M. Parker
> Governor.[763]

Citizens of Mer Rouge were outraged over an article printed in the *Fellowship Forum*, a Ku Klux Klan newspaper published at Washington, D. C. The journal depicted the people of this town as moral lepers and attacked the prosecution in the open hearing at Bastrop. The article, which is printed in the form of a letter, dated Bastrop, January 17, concludes with the following significant paragraph: "In the meantime, the vigilance committee is as vigilant as ever and will maintain its watch over the welfare and morals of the community."

---

[763] Ibid.

SUNDAY JANUARY 28, 1923

Skipwith Warns Cohorts Against Law Violations[764]
Questionnaires Sent to Candidates on Ku Klux Issue: Office Seekers' Attitude To Be Placed Under Spotlight[765]

It was reported today in the *Times-Picayune* that *The Progressive*, a newspaper of the town of DeQuincy, located in Calcasieu Parish, had assembled and mailed to all political candidates in their area a questionnaire concerning that candidate's stand on the Ku Klux Klan. A copy of the form follows:

> As you have announced yourself as a candidate for public office in Calcasieu parish, it is fair that the people whom you expect to vote for you are apprized as to how you stand upon a question that a gentleman in robe and hood journeyed all the way from the city of New Orleans to Lake Charles last November to announce was the paramount issue to be settled at the polls. The issue was the Ku Klux Klan. The Progressive as a public journal therefore is offering you the medium through which you can make your position known. It does so in all sincerity and with profound respect for those to whom it addresses this questionnaire.
>
> These questionnaires are mailed out from time to time and that fact will be published, as will be your exact reply verbatim. If you do not reply, that fact will also be published, and the public can form their own conclusions.
>
> Kindly return the enclosed questionnaire, which is being registered at your earliest convenience if reply is to be made at all.
>
> 1. Are you, or have you ever been naturalized as a citizen of the invisible empire, commonly known as the Ku Klux Klan?
>
> 2. Which do you consider the most sacred oaths: the oath you take when qualifying for office or that of any secret organization under the sun?
>
> 3. Do you believe in the right to worship God according to the dictates of your own conscience, the absolute separation of church and state, and that all religious denominations should be protected so long as they comply with the written laws of the land and do not make themselves obnoxious to society?
>
> 4. If elected, will you abstain from affiliating with any and all secret organizations who conceal the membership by permitting perjury and concealing the identity behind white or black masks?

Obviously, the Ku Klux Klan issue was a hot item in state-wide and local elections due to the goings-on at Mer Rouge. A hotly contested race for the governor's chair in Louisiana was already in progress with Klan and anti-Klan candidates.

Unable to resist the limelight of publicity, Captain Skipwith once again gave a demonstration of the power he wielded as Exalted Cyclops of Morehouse Klan No. 34, when he made the following press release:

---

[764] Ibid.

[765] Ibid.

496

"I have given my promise to Attorney General Coco as a Southern Gentleman that I would do all that I could to keep down any trouble in Morehouse parish until the grand jury is convened on the first Monday in March," said Skipwith. "I thought this would be sufficient, but there have been signs that some persons thought I was joking, and I believe it necessary for me to repeat that, so far as I am concerned, I do not want any monkey business."

Skipwith was asked about a claim he had made to another reporter that Richards was alive. "I am not giving out any interviews any more. But I will say that I have always believed that Richards is alive. I am sincere in this belief. I believe that it can be proved that Richards was sent out of the country after he had told all that he knew about Daniel. Richards was afraid of Daniel and he wanted to go."

When asked about a possible upcoming appearance before the grand jury, Skipwith said, "I have never held back. I have always been willing to tell all I know when the proper time comes, but not before." Captain Skipwith clearly was a man impressed with his own importance, and he relished the notoriety and attention that his position gave him.

Letter Reveals Ku Klux Klan to Rule Louisiana: Political Dictatorship Is called Aim Of Hooded Organization.[766]

[Baton Rouge, Louisiana] Evidence that a political klan has been organized inside the Ku Klux Klan in Louisiana and other states is disclosed in a secret statement by E. Y. Clarke, former acting imperial wizard of the klan, sent to a selected few from Atlanta headquarters. A copy of the document was obtained through a Louisianan who quit the hooded order when he discovered the existence of the political klan in this state.

The authenticity of the statement is confirmed by Norman Hapgood in an article by him on "The New Threat of the Ku Klux Klan," published in the February issue of Hearst's International Magazine, a portion of it being quoted by Mr. Hapgood. Clarke's statement, which is dated July 11, 1922, reveals the purpose of the political klan or imperial klan, as it is known officially at klan headquarters. Its object is to take in congressmen, senators, governors, judges and others of political prominence, who are to form an inner circle. Clarke's statement in part follows:

"We are face to face with the opportunity of bringing into the organization men of large type, but men whose identity we want to conceal from even their local klan. For instance, congressmen, senators, governors, judges and others whom we can line up as klansmen, but it would be best for them and for us for their identity to be concealed.

"These men can be passed upon in the imperial klan and put upon the roster of the imperial klan and given the imperial passport to enter their local klan at any time it is thought best to disclose their identity as klansmen. I believe this feature of the imperial klan's possibilities justifies its establishment.

---

[766]*Times-Picayune,* 28 January 1923.

"It will not be long before klans in all parts of the nation will begin to send in petitions of various kinds to be discussed by the imperial klan, problems of local character. Problems of national character will come before this body to be discussed by the heads of the operating forces of the organization, and the action taken will be passed down in full detail to all of the klans throughout the nation. I think we have made a forward step."

The closing paragraph of the Clarke statement shows that the group composing the imperial klan is to dictate political policy of the masked organization and that the local members are expected to obey orders without question.

MONDAY JANUARY 29, 1923

Surprise Witness Will be Heard in Hooded Mob Case
Texan Located Who can Identify all of Post Murder Band[767]

Assistant Attorney General Walmsley told reporters on this date that the state had found a witness who was capable of identifying about 24 of those involved in the kidnappings and murders of Daniel and Richards. The name of this mystery witness was not released, and it is not known whether he really ever existed for he was never heard from nor mentioned again. Possibly the Klan learned who he was, or perhaps this was a ploy on the part of the attorney general to cause the snakes to start biting one another.

It was also mentioned today that it was known that Morehouse Klan No. 34 had a meeting on the day after Daniel and Richards were kidnapped and murdered. The purpose of this meeting was not known. However, speculation had it that they returned to the scene of the crime to a) be certain that no evidence remained, or b) to dig up the bodies of Daniel and Richards which had been buried and pitch them into Lake LaFourche.

TUESDAY JANUARY 30, 1923

Teegerstrom Takes Old Job After His Journey to Spyker
Sheriff Carpenter Orders His Arrest and Release on Bond as Case Witness[768]
Vanishing Witness in Mob Case Boasts of Visit to Capital: Evader is Hailed as Hero in Bastrop[769]

The *Monroe News-Star* reported that just as mysteriously as he disappeared on December 29, 1922, Harold Teegerstrom, timekeeper at the Southern Carbon Plant at Spyker and long-sought witness during the open hearings, re-emerged this day at the Spyker plant and was given back his old job. Not long after his arrival, he was

---

[767] Ibid.

[768] *Monroe News-Star*, 30 January 1923.

[769] *Times-Picayune*, 30 January 1923.

arrested by federal agents and brought to the Morehouse Parish jail for booking.

Teegerstrom told friends that during his sojourn, he visited El Dorado, Arkansas, Alexandria, Baton Rouge and various other locations in Louisiana which he refused to identify. He said that he had not been kidnapped, but departed Morehouse Parish, "because I felt I was doing the right thing. I did it for my friends." This statement seems to suggest that he was protecting wrongdoing.

He explained his absence by saying that at about 11 p.m. on the night of December 29 he was visited by a "number of persons." "They said they would give me all the time I wanted to get my clothes and go with them," explained Teegerstrom. "I did not go with the men, but was wandering around in the woods all night. I do not know what became of the party. I was not interested in them after I made my getaway."

He said he caught a train out of the Monroe gas fields and fled to El Dorado, Arkansas on the following morning. This contradicts the testimony given by "Jap" Jones, who told of Teegerstrom's visit to his home on Sunday, two days after Teegerstrom was visited the previous Friday night.

Teegerstrom claimed that he even visited Bastrop while the open hearings were in progress and that he was recognized by a number of his acquaintances. He did not remain long in the parish, he said, because he feared being arrested.[770]

The *Times-Picayune* also recorded the return of Harold Teegerstrom. The account of his travels in the *Picayune* was similar to that in the *News-Star*, except for a portion describing his being in Baton Rouge and his debate with himself whether or not to speak directly to Governor Parker.

"I could have talked with Governor Parker if I had wanted to," Teegerstrom said, "as I saw him daily. I was tempted to go up to the executive mansion at times and tell him who I was, lay all my cards on the table and ask him what I had better do. I did not want to injure any of my friends, however.

"I thought it was best to let Mr. Jeff testify. I did not want to **injure him** or **anybody else**, but I want to do the right thing. I was not frightened away. I was not kidnapped, but I left because I felt I was doing the right thing to go not because I wanted to **injure** any of the state's chances to get at the bottom of this thing. I thought it best to let Jeff Burnett's case come up before I do anything or say

---

[770]Ibid.

anything." teegerstrom repeated that he did not want to injure his friends. Why would his testimony injure his friends unless what he had to say would not support their claims of innocence? We are left to ponder just what Teegerstrom meant by this statement.

Rising Patriotism Sweeps Germany to Verge of War[771]

[Berlin]Germany tonight is engulfed in a wave of nationalism which is likely to plunge her into a war for which she is entirely unprepared and which she is totally unable to wage.

The continued fall of the mark, resulting in high prices, has almost erased the workers, who are willing to do almost anything rather than tolerate the present situation and who see war or revolution as the best method of action.

The only question is whether the government will be able to check the young enthusiasts, and if not, whether after all the Allied control commission may not have overlooked sufficient munitions to make war possible.

WEDNESDAY JANUARY 31, 1923
Klux Will Deny Daniel, Richards Were Murdered
Officials Prepare To Cast Doubt on Identity of Bodies Recovered[772]
Mer Rouge Mayor Gets Death Threat: Anonymous Writer in Arkansas Orders Him to Leave Town Since He Opposes Klan[773]
Jackson Parish Educator Forced to Leave as Result of Klan Warning[774]

From Baton Rouge, came a report of a letter from T. H. Harris, superintendent of education, to George A. Odom, superintendent and member of the Jackson Parish School Board. The letter stated that interference by the Ku Klux Klan in school affairs in Louisiana would not be tolerated. The letter was the result of the closing of the Eros High School at Eros, Louisiana, because the principal of the school fled the state after receiving a threatening letter from Eros Ku Klux Klan, No. 65. The letter bore the seal of the Klan. The letter in part from State Superintendent Harris follows:

The order to this teacher represents an effort on the part of an organization, or an individual parading under the name of an organization, to disregard the constitutional and legislative methods provided for by government of the public schools and to administer the affairs of the school outside of the plans prescribed by the laws of this state. The writer of the letter does not bring to the attention of the constituted school authorities the alleged rumors concerning the misconduct of two teachers with the request that the authorities make the necessary investigation and take such action as the facts may warrant. Nothing of that kind was done.

---

[771]*Times-Picayune*, 30 January 1923.

[772]*Times-Picayune*, 31 January 1923.

[773]Ibid.

[774]*Monroe News-Star*, 31 January 1923.

To the contrary, the writer of the letter places himself, or themselves, entirely above the constituted school authorities and announces to one of the teachers concerned that the rumors of misconduct are afloat and orders him out of the community.

If the Eros Ku Klux Klan, No. 65 authorized the writing of the letter, to which I called your attention, as was apparently the case, that organization should be told very pointedly that its assistance and cooperation will be welcomed, if it wishes to call attention to any wrongs that may exist in any public school and to support methods of relief, but it won't be permitted to usurp the authority of the Jackson parish school board and administer the affairs of the schools of that parish as it may see fit. If an individual, parading under the name of the Klan wrote the letter, his identity should be ascertained, if possible, in order that he may be held up to public scorn, which he merits.

The Times-Picayune reported this day that Mayor Robert L. Dade was threatened with death unless he left town in 10 days. The warning came in an anonymous letter, bearing a Hot Springs, Ark., post mark. The letter written on stationary of the National Park Hotel, at Hot Springs, follows:

Dear Sir: You are hereby notified to pack up and get out of town within ten days of receipt of this notice. You have never been any good as a man or as a citizen. Use your own judgment and either leave or become a corpse.

LAW ABIDING.

In view of the threat to clear out Mer Rouge made by Bastrop Klansmen, Friends of the mayor were said to be very anxious and many brought out their guns. Many believed that Governor Parker would proclaim martial law in Morehouse Parish.

Meanwhile, unnamed officials of the Louisiana Ku Klux Klan announced today that they were busily preparing a defense for those Klansmen that will be accused of the murders and kidnappings of Watt Daniel and Thomas Richards. This unnamed official gave the following points of contention:

1. An attempt to show that black hoods, which the state has so convincingly connected with the murder band that spirited Daniel and Richards away, are part of the regalia of other organizations.

2. An effort to prove that the bodies of the two men, taken from Lake LaFourche and identified at the Bastrop hearing as those of Daniel and Richards, are, in reality, not the bodies of the two men.

3. That the bodies identified as Richards and Daniel were never in Lake LaFourche any great length of time, but were thrown in as part of a "frame-up" and fished out after the charge of dynamite had been touched off to lend plausibility to the story of their having been weighted down and sunk in the lake the night of the murders, more than five months ago.

"We will have our say when the time comes, but that will not be until the state has picked the men it is going to charge for the Morehouse parish crimes and has placed those men on trial," said the unnamed Klan official. "We will prove a few things there.

In support of his allegations of other organizations employing the black hood, the unnamed official displayed to reporters what he claimed was a copy of a ritual of the Knights of Columbus. Some of these pictures showed men in black hoods.

"We will prove that the klan is not responsible for those outrages in Morehouse," he said. "In other words, we'll show that this whole business, so far as the effort to blame it on the klan are concerned is a frame-up."

"If these were not the bodies of Richards and Daniel, where are Richards and Daniel now?" one of the reporters asked.

"We don't know," he responded. "We only know that the state did not find the bodies of those two men."

The statement of this unknown Klan official is very important because for the first time the allegation arises that the bodies of Daniel and Richards had only been in the waters of Lake LaFourche for a short period of time. This assertion will later be verified by the attorney general, but not until November 1923, some nine months after this date. How did he know this since it was not made public either by those who performed the autopsies or the attorney general's office? The logical answer is that he was privy to some firsthand knowledge from other Klansmen who were aware of that fact, because of their personal participation in the disposition of the bodies.

He also continually makes reference to the claim that the bodies recovered were not those of Daniel and Richards. There seems to be the unsaid assertion that "those are not the bodies because we know where the true bodies are located."

The assertion that Daniel and Richards were alive and that those were not the bodies of Daniel and Richards runs contrary to the claims made by Captain Skipwith, Exalted Cyclops of Morehouse Parish Klan No. 34, when he said earlier that he believed that Daniel was dead, but that Richards was still alive. Clearly, the Klan was having a difficult time getting their act together because of Captain Skipwith's proclivity to allow his alligator mouth to overload his hummingbird ass.

Finally, the assertion that somehow the Knights of Columbus perpetrated these crimes displays the desperation of those involved. We have seen time and again how just being Catholic was enough to be given an imperial edict from Captain Skipwith to leave Morehouse Parish. The idea that an unknown group of Knights

502

of Columbus were running rampant through the countryside of Morehouse Parish is ridiculous when you consider the treatment dispensed by the Klan on unsuspecting Catholics, in general. In New Orleans, John X. Wegmann, past deputy and head officer of the Knights of Columbus in Louisiana, commented on these assertions.

> The Knights of Columbus have no books containing the ritualistic ceremonies of the order in which there appear pictures of any officers in robes. If the party referred to has in his possession that which he says is a copy of the Knights of Columbus ritual, it is not authentic, but more than likely a copy of a book published by an Eastern concern purporting to be an expose of the Knights of Columbus ceremonies.
> Neither officers nor members of the Knights of Columbus wear hoods which cover the head or any part of their degree work. As with other organizations who conduct degree work, the officers of the Knights of Columbus wear robed regalia which distinguish them. The statements made by this party with reference to the regalia of the Knights of Columbus are preposterous and absurd.

FRIDAY FEBRUARY 2, 1923
No Official Steps to Investigate in Mer Rouge Threat
Attorney General Coco States that Author of Mayor Dade Letter not Known[775] Dr. M'Koin Leaves to Resume Studies at Johns Hopkins[776]

Despite all of his loud noises, no official action would be taken by Attorney General Coco regarding a threatening letter received by Mayor Dade of Mer Rouge. Coco said the identity (of) the writer was unknown to him and that his department could take no action unless an attempt was made to put the threat into execution.

It was also learned this day that Dr. McKoin had left this morning for Baltimore, where he will resume his studies at Johns Hopkins University. McKoin was accompanied by Dr. Jesse L. Adams, a Monroe physician.

TUESDAY FEBRUARY 13, 1923
Selecting Morehouse Kidnap Grand Jury
Jury Includes Some of Best Citizens of Parish, Assert Commissioners; Will Convene on March 5[777]

It was announced in the *Monroe News-Star* this date that the Morehouse Parish Jury Commission consisting of Clerk of Court James Dalton, of Bastrop, ex-officio chairman of the jury commission; A. P. Broadnax, of Gallion; W. E. Hopkins, of Mer Rouge; and Eugene Wolff, W. E. McMean and C. C. Tisdale, all of Bastrop,

---

[775] *Monroe News-Star*, 2 February 1923.
[776] Ibid.
[777] *Monroe News-Star*, 13 February 1923.

had selected the initial 20 citizens of Morehouse Parish from which the 12 members of the grand jury will be selected. Those selected were:

Ward 1-George Hayden, farmer.
Ward 2-P. A. Little, of Bookman, farmer.
Ward 2-S. H. Stevenson, farmer.*
Ward 4-A. G. McBride, of Bastrop, building contractor.
Ward 4-S. B. Shell, of Bastrop, merchant.
Ward 4-B. U. Hood, of Bastrop, oil field worker.*
Ward 5-J. C. Evans, of Oak Ridge, farmer.
Ward 5-D. B. Williamson, Oak Ridge, farmer.
Ward 5-J. F. Files, of Oak Ridge, clerk.
Ward 6-M. Dunnam, of Mer Rouge, sawmill man.
Ward 6-C. R. Hullshare[?], of Mer Rouge, farmer. [Copy was very poor.]
Ward 6-E. M. White, of Mer Rouge, farmer.
Ward 7-Joe McClain, of Gallion, box factory employee.
Ward 7-T. J. White, R. F. D. 1. Bastrop, farmer.
Ward 8-J. B. Jordan, of Collinston, merchant.
Ward 8-R. E. Bramlett, of Collinston, farmer.
Ward 9-F. M. Jones, of Tilou(?), farmer.* [Copy was very poor.]
Ward 10-A. S. Riddick, of Bonita, farmer.
Ward 10-G. A. Allen, of Bonita, merchant.
Ward 10-F. E. Hope, of Bonita, farmer.
Those names with the asterisk [*] were either known Klansmen, or they had the same surname as known Klansmen.

According to the jury commissioners, those persons chosen for jury duty were not either directly or indirectly connected to the kidnappings of J. L Daniel, W. C. Andrews, C. C. "Tot" Davenport, Watt Daniel and Thomas Richards, and the subsequent murders of Watt Daniel and Richards "as far as they knew." Also they claimed that it included no one who was even mentioned in the investigation.

"We used the greatest of care in the selection," said some unnamed members of the commission. "We have gotten some of the best citizens of Morehouse parish in whom we have every confidence to do their duty in any matter that may come before them."

We have seen the phrase "some of the best citizens" used over and again by the Klan in an attempt to sanctify and validate their actions. As has been demonstrated, the overwhelming majority of these "best citizens" were either Klansmen or Klan sympathizers. Since we only have access to the membership list that was printed in the *Times-Picayune* when they put a photocopy of the original application executed to form Morehouse Klan No. 34, and since Captain Skipwith boasted and it was generally accepted that the Morehouse Klan numbered about 500, there was obviously a great multitude of Klansmen who went unnamed. As it stands, the name "B. U. Hood" appeared on the original application to form Morehouse Klan No. 34, as did the name "John T. Hood," who was the Kluud or Chaplain. B. U. Hood was also selected to serve on this grand jury. So much for their diligent work!

Also on the application form there appears a considerable number of persons with the same surname. It is, therefore, logical to assume that many others were drawn into the Klan by their relatives and friends, thereby giving rise to the suspicion that at the very least anyone with a surname that appears on that original application form could either be a Klansman or a Klan sympathizer. All of this taken into consideration, it is easy to see how the grand jury could have easily been stacked with Klansmen.

Although the jury pool had been chosen by the commission, it was incumbent upon Judge Fred Odom to select a jury foreman and the 11 others who would serve on the jury. In all fairness to Judge Odom, if the jury pool was contaminated with Klansmen, he may not have had much of a choice, especially if he were unaware that they were Klansmen. It would have, however, been in his power to dismiss this grand jury if he believed it to be improperly formed. The grand jury was set to convene on March 5, 1923 to deal with the atrocities perpetrated by the Ku Klux Klan in Morehouse Parish.

The following 3 by 4 inch ad appeared in the lower right portion of the front page in the *Monroe News-Star* this date. It is reproduced as nearly as possible.

---

[778] Ibid.

MONDAY, FEBRUARY 19, 1923
Will Find Out How Jury Stands as to Klan Proposition
Fifteen Reported to be Members of K. K. K[779]

The *Monroe News-Star* reported that that 15 of the 20 men drawn for the grand jury to investigate the kidnapping and murders of Daniel and Richards and other alleged outrages in Morehouse Parish were members of the Ku Klux Klan. Attorney General Coco left Shreveport at an early hour this morning for Morehouse Parish. While enroute he made this statement:

> When I left home, I was stopped by a newspaperman, and he told me that five of the men drawn for the grand jury are known Klansmen, five of them are known anti-Klansmen and the other ten are suspected of being Klansmen. I am going to Bastrop to investigate what the conditions exactly are and see if anyone on the jury is related to any of the suspects. I'll try to get a line on all of them. I would like to have it so there will be no Klansmen on it at all: that all the jurors are free from bias and prejudice, but whether I can arrange it that way, I don't know yet. Neither do I know yet what steps are to be taken, but, of course, I have an idea.

SATURDAY FEBRUARY 24, 1923
Ready to Give Klan Chance to Vindicate Itself, Asserts Coco[780]

Having long since left the front pages of all of the newspapers, this article appeared buried in the *Monroe News-Star* between a cartoon and some lumber advertisements. According to Coco, all was well in Morehouse Parish. Still suffering from the delusion that he could get the Klan to convict its own members, he made the following statement to the media:

> I am pleased to say that the conditions have greatly improved in the parish of Morehouse since the close of the open hearing conducted in that parish by the state. The [elected] officers appear to have taken charge and are in the saddle, and I have every assurance that there shall be no reoccurrence of the disorders and lawlessness which existed in said parish previous to the hearing, as far as they will be able to prevent it.
>
> A careful investigation of the manner in which the panel of the grand jury was drawn for the March term has satisfied me that the jury commissioners acted fairly and with the view of obtaining the best representative citizens as grand jurors who are to conduct the investigations in that parish at the opening of the criminal term of court on March 5, and in drawing the grand jury the commissioners acted without reference to Klan affiliation or opposition, but solely with regard to their qualification as jurors.
>
> Of course it was impossible, under the law, to exclude citizens by reason of their affiliation with the Klan, or opposition to the order, and the commissioners

---

[779] *Monroe News-Star*, 19 February 1923.

[780] *Monroe News-Star*, 24 February 1923.

pursued the only course left to them, that is, of selecting jurors with reference purely to their personal qualifications.

From the best available information I believe the men selected as jurors are all good men and true, who are of good social standing and occupy different avenues of life, have considerable property interests in the parish, who have, as a rule, been life-long citizens in the parish and reared large families, who have also settled there and are otherwise identified with every public interest. They have the reputation of being law-abiding citizens and are for the maintenance of social equilibrium. The general belief is that they will do their duty irrespective of Klan affiliation or influence, unless, as has been suggested to me, those who are Klansmen should be bound by stronger ties to the order and their fellow members than they are to their oath as jurors and their duty to the government.

It has further been suggested that the present occasion will afford the Ku Klux Klan the opportunity of vindicating themselves from the charge that they are bound to their order by stronger ties than to their government and I welcome the opportunity afforded them for this self-vindication, and will, under the circumstances, submit the state's case to them and await their verdict, in a case involving the majesty of the law on the one hand and mob violence on the other, with the hope and expectation of the vindication of the former.

Judging from the content of Coco's statement, one would think that he had been living on another planet and had just fallen to Earth filled with high ideals and a naiveté rivaling that of Candide in his search for El Dorado. Having been present during the open hearing in Bastrop and having experienced the manner in which the Klan had blocked every effort to uncover the perpetrators of all the hooded activity in northeast Louisiana, surely he had to be aware that this Klan-filled grand jury would have to protect those involved in these activities, if for no other reason than to protect themselves.

WEDNESDAY FEBRUARY 28, 1923

M'Koin Returns to Johns Hopkins for Work's Resumption
Faculty Does Not Wish To Handicap Defendant In Morehouse Charges[781]

Judging by the support that McKoin had received from Johns Hopkins, there should have been little doubt that permission would be granted for him to return and continue his post-graduate work. A statement issued said that to refuse re-admission to McKoin "would undoubtedly prove a serious handicap" to him and also "might prove to be a great injustice." "It therefore, has been decided to allow Dr. McKoin to continue with his work until it shall become apparent that in the interest of the university and hospital other action is indicated."

---

[781] *Monroe News-Star*, 28 February 1923.

FRIDAY MARCH 2, 1923
'Imperial Giant' of Klan Indicted Under Mann Act
Alleged Offense Involves Trip to New Orleans Feb. 11, 1921[782]

From Houston, Texas came an indictment from a federal grand jury charging a violation of the White Slave Act against Edward Young Clarke of Atlanta, former Imperial Wizard of the Ku Klux Klan. The specific charge was that Clarke transported a woman from Houston to New Orleans, February 11, 1921, for immoral purposes. Knowing how the Klan loves to make up the rules as they go along, it was surprising to see them fail to rise to Clark's defense. Perhaps they found themselves fighting on too many fronts.

MONDAY MARCH 5, 1923
No Good Citizen is in Accord With Mob Violence of Parish: Must do Full duty, Says Odom
Hooded Outrages Likely to Destroy Government, Putting End to Civil and Criminal Laws and Resulting in Chaos, Declares Judge[783]

The Morehouse Parish grand jury convened today, and on the top of the agenda was the kidnappings and murders of Watt Daniel and Thomas Richards. Of the original pool of 20 potential grand jurors, Judge Odom selected the following:

1. J. E. Evans, Oak Ridge, farmer, and foreman of the grand jury.
2. C. R. Tillman, Mer Rouge, farmer.
3. S. H. Stevenson, farmer.
4. G. A. Allen. Bonita, merchant.
5. D. B. Williamson, Oak Ridge, farmer.
6. J. H. Jordan, Collinston, merchant.
7. George Hayden, Bastrop, farm superintendent.
8. E. M. White, Mer Rouge, farmer.
9. R. E. Bramlet, Collinston, merchant.
10. F. M. George, Gallion, farmer. [Not in the orignial 20 on p. 504]
11. Frank Hope, Bonita, farmer.
12. U. B. Hood, Bastrop, oil well worker.

As mentioned on the listing of the original pool of grand jurors the name U. B. Hood appeared on the original charter application for Morehouse Klan No. 34. Already we know that this grand jury has at least one Klansman and, in all likelihood, many more. Also, this list appears to differ slightly from the previous list.

---

[782]*Times-Picayune*, 2 March 1923.
[783]Ibid.

Attorney General Coco, along with Assistant Attorney General Seth Guion, arrived on March 4 in anticipation of the commencement of the proceedings, which will be conducted by District Attorney David I. Garrett. It has already alleged that Garrett was also a Klansman. If this was true, then this grand jury was doomed before it heard its first witness. The operation of a grand jury, unlike that of the open hearing, is totally secret. The district attorney, who in this case was Mr. Garrett, has full sway over whom and what is presented before them. He could have excluded evidence, which has always been, and still is, common practice when the district attorney is either seeking to indict or not to indict.

The grand jury was seated by 10 a.m. Evidently feeling that the occasion called for more than just simply speaking to the grand jury from the bench, Judge Odom had a written charge for the grand jury from which he read:

> I desire to call to your special attention to certain violations of the law which have been more or less frequent in Morehouse parish during the last year or more. I refer especially to the activities of bands of hooded or masked men who have on different occasions kidnapped, beaten and deported citizens of the parish, and more especially the incident on the Bastrop and Mer Rouge public road on August 24th, 1922, when scores of citizens on their way home from Bastrop were held up, five of them kidnapped and carried several miles away, where two of them were beaten and turned loose, one turned loose without punishment, the other two not having been since seen alive. The incidents to which I refer are matters of common knowledge and need no further special mention by me. The details were fully gone into at the public hearing held here some time ago, and I feel sure that those who represent the state will see that all available facts in connection with each separate case will be presented to you in the course of your deliberations.
>
> I call your special attention to and urge your most careful, thorough and vigorous investigation to these violations of law because, aside from the fact that no violations of law should be tolerated, there are in these principles which are of more than ordinary concern to us all; because in them there is shown a tendency on the part of certain individuals which if unchecked will result ultimately in the destruction of organized society or organized government.
>
> Under the guise and pretext of assisting in the enforcement of the laws and within the avowed purpose of bettering conditions of the parish morally, certain individuals and groups have taken upon themselves the regulation of the morals and the conduct of their fellow citizens through methods devised by themselves. At various times letters have been sent to individuals censuring their conduct and admonishing them to mend their ways. Some of these letters were signed "Vigilance Committee" and "Ku Klux Klan": some of them were typewritten, some written with pen and ink or pencil; some sent through the mails and others left at the front door or gate of the individuals for whom they were intended. These letters usually contained a veiled or open threat of violence if the offender did not amend his conduct.
>
> At other times citizens have formed themselves into groups, regaled themselves in black robes and masks, boldly seized individuals who in the opinion of the

masked group or band had offended the law of decency and carried them to secluded spots and there, in some instances administering admonition and in others severe beatings. In some instances the offending individual was ordered to leave the parish and not to return; and, finally, a large group, estimated by some at fifteen and others by forty, all wearing black masks held up large crowds on the Bastrop-Mer Rouge public road on August 24th and actually kidnapped and carried away five of them as before recited.

Thus far I have heard no good citizen who condones the conduct of the mob on the occasion of August 24th. But there are those and among them some of our best citizens, who are or were at one time apparently in accord and sympathy with those who were engaged in these activities generally, and who attempt to justify the conduct of the mob on the ground that the members of it were actuated by the desire and purpose of suppressing lawlessness, crime and indecency in the community; that the individuals punished or deported as the case might be were invariably undesirable citizens whose conduct either had not been, or could not be reached through courts, and that after all these hooded or masked bands were doing real service to the state.

Now gentlemen, insofar as any citizen is possessed of the desire and purpose to be of assistance in upholding and enforcing its law; insofar as he felt it is his duty to suppress crime and curb indecency; and insofar he is willing to devote his time and energies to the task of upbuilding moral standards and making the community and the state a better place in which to live (the next few lines are located at the bottom corner of the page, and were torn off.). . . who are engaged in the activities, about which I am speaking, I must be conceded they have fallen into the stupendous fatal error of becoming law-breakers themselves.

They ordered certain individuals to live within the law; and in order to enforce their edicts, they themselves have broken the law. In doing so they have pursued a course which if persisted in and put into general practice would utterly destroy our government; would put an end to the laws of this state, both civil and criminal; would act at naught with the will of the majority, the rule of law and substitute therefore the will of a few who take it upon themselves to regulate the conduct of their neighbors and administer punishment according to their own ideas.

The natural inescapable result of such conduct is to set aside all law, all legal authority. If men are to form themselves into groups and decide who shall be punished and what punishment shall be inflicted, there is no need of the courts; there is no need of any kind of organized government.

In all these various activities, there is no case so far, as I have been informed, where the offender went first to the court for correction and punishment; but in each case, these parties have constituted themselves the accusers, the jury and the executioners. It cannot be said on behalf of these parties that they have acted only after the court had failed; they have not given the court a chance. Instead of these citizens rendering assistance to the court in ferreting out and punishing crime, they usurped the functions of the court altogether.

If these parties have the right to tell you what you must and must not do and then punish you because you disobey, they have a right to go to your barn and appropriate to themselves, without compensation, your corn and your hay, or if they do not desire it for themselves to dispense it to others as they see fit. And with equal show of right, they could say that you must give to them a portion of your lands. If men can kidnap you and take you from your home and thereby deprive you of your liberty because they are stronger physically than you are, or because they have, for the moment, the advantage of you, why may they not, by the same process, take from you your earthly possessions and thereby deprive you and your families of the fruits of your labor? If your neighbor, who is possessed of a strong arm and no conscience should go into your field or your home, order you out, take possession, you would feel terribly outraged; and in order to protect your rights you would have to resort either to the shotgun or the courts, I need not ask what you would do under such circumstances, for you are law-abiding citizens. But suppose there was no law, no authority, no court to which you night appeal? You would have to resort to violence, and if he happened to be more violent and a better gunman than you are, the result would be that you would lose both your property and your life.

The very thought that such a condition strikes us with horror; and yet if men may set aside criminal statutes and substitute their own will for that of the law maker and usurp the functions of the courts by accusing, trying and punishing their neighbors, they may as easily set aside the Civil Law and regulate property rights.

When you are disturbed in the possession of your home and other properties, which you have acquired through toil, you at once, appeal to the constituted authorities; you have your goods restored through orderly, legal process. If your neighbor claims to own a portion of your land, you go to the public records, which the law provides shall be made and kept in order to settle the dispute. You don't protect your title by might, by physical strength; you do not resort to the shotgun; you invoke the arm of the law for protection. Now, gentlemen, the same authority, the law, to which you appeal to protect you in your property rights, protects your person from the assaults and outrages of the bully, the mob. The same authority, the law, prescribes rules and regulations governing of conduct of the individual, and it prescribes penalties for the infractions of such rules and establishes the method which must be followed in order to establish the guilt or innocence of one accused of such violations. All such rules and regulations are established by us through officers whom we have selected to represent us, and as citizens are therefore bound by them.

The citizen must obey them, and the officers of the law, including you as grand jurors, for you are now as much an officer of the court as I am, must see that these laws governing society, regulating the conduct of the citizen, are enforced. If the citizens refuse to obey and the officers, the constituted authorities will not or cannot force obedience to the laws, then there is an end to organized government; the machinery of the state has broken down. And as concerns us, if we have reached that state or condition of society where men may organize into bands or groups and condemn and punish citizens when and as they see fit without regard to the laws of the land and the established rules of judicial procedure, then gentlemen, the day of our doom is upon us. We have seen the end of civilized, organized society. The laws of civilized governments must be enforced; otherwise civilization cannot survive.

The persons who kidnapped and otherwise did violence to citizens of this parish violated the law, and they must be punished if evidence of their guilt can be secured.

As grand jurors you are officers of the court. You have registered a most solemn oath that you will do your duty as such. You are bound not only by the ties of the state as good patriotic American citizens, but also by your oath as officers to support and enforce the laws of the state. The state expects and requires that of you. You cannot be true to yourselves and not be true to the state.

511

But, gentlemen, as grand jurors you are not expected, you are not permitted to allow your personal feelings to enter into your deliberations.

You must rise above sentiment and excitement. You must not present or indict anyone merely because any man or set of men demand it; nor must you leave anyone unprecedented because any man, set or group of men would applaud such a course. If you have ever entertained any bias or prejudice in connection with the matters to be brought before you, by assuming the oath that you have, by becoming officers of the court, you are placed in a position where you cannot permit your feelings to sway you in the slightest.

When a man becomes an officer of the law or of the court, he forfeits, absolutely, the right and privilege of favoring a friend or antagonizing an enemy. The violations of the law to which I have called your special attention have been laid at the door of the Ku Klux Klan. Whether that organization is responsible for these outrages or not is a matter which does not concern you in the slightest. You are not here to unmask the Klansmen or to disrupt the Ku Klux Klan as an organization. You are to present and indict criminals without regard for their affiliations. Before the law, all men, whether they be member of the Ku Klux Klan, the Masonic fraternity, the Knights of Columbus, the B'nai B'rith or Methodist church, stand precisely upon the same place; with men, not with organizations, societies or fraternities.

If in your deliberations you should become convinced that a certain citizen has violated the law, it would never occur to you that you should then inquire whether he was of the Christian or Hebrew faith or whether he was a Mason or a Woodman of the World and if such should be suggested to you, you would feel insulted. Why then should you be concerned over the question of whether these crimes were committed through the Klan as an organization or by Klansmen as individuals.

I make these suggestions, gentlemen, in the hope that I may impress upon you the fact that it is your sworn duty to help enforce the laws of the state, regardless of sentiment and regardless of the affiliations or creed of the individual who violates them.[784]

After delivering his address to the grand jury, which lasted until about 11 p.m., Judge Odom recessed the jury until 9 a.m. the following morning.

Although there were daily press reports concerning the persons called before the Morehouse Parish grand jury, it was simply a rehash of the parade of witnesses as during the open hearing. There was, however, no way for the journalists to know the testimony being given because of the cloak of secrecy of the grand jury. During this period, the Ku Klux Klan was still quite active, and there were still some associated goings-on in Morehouse Parish, and these will be listed.

K.K.K. Exercises[785]

A report from Alexandria, Louisiana told how 12 robed members of the Alexandria Ku Klux Klan knelt in silent prayer and laid a wreath of red roses in the

---

[784] Ibid.

shape of a cross on the grave of Sterling S. Boatner, 45, a prominent citizen of Jonesville.

THURSDAY MARCH 8, 1923

Tractor is Used in Efforts to Conceal Murders of Mer Rouge
Bodies Were Broken into Bits by Hooded Men With use of Great Tractor[786]
Grand Jurors hear many Witnesses in Morehouse "Probe": Majority Testified at January Hearing[787]
Klansmen Place Wreath of Flowers on Bier of Tally[788]
Capt. Skipwith gets Flattering Offer to Become a Movie Actor[789]

It was revealed today that the office of the attorney general has received a number of anonymous letters from persons claiming to know what type device had been used to generate the crushing injuries that had been inflicted on the bodies of Watt Daniel and Thomas Richards. It had been said on numerous occasions that some special type of "torture devices" had been constructed, but the state was not able to find, much less postulate, what kind of device it may have been.

According to the persons who wrote the letters, they claimed it was a piece of equipment used for road-grading. The correspondent recorded it this way:

> About three miles from Bastrop on the Bastrop-Collinston-Monroe highway is a huge tractor, used to pull a road scraper, a typical machine of its kind, propelled by a heavy gasoline motor. The iron wheels are seven or eight feet in diameter while their rims have a width of approximately three feet. Riveted to the rims to prevent the wheels from slipping in the soft earth are steel cleats, the width of the wheels and about fifteen inches apart.
> The bodies apparently had been stretched full length when they were mutilated with the arms above their heads. Fractures of the forearms were on a level with the heads, and those who assert the bodies must have been broken with a tractor believe they were stretched on the ground, and the machine run or pushed over them. Such a machine as the one near here, it is contended, would inflict such injuries, the heavy cleats on the wide wheels fracturing the arm and leg bones, crushing the heads and chests and severing completely the hands and feet at the wrists and just above the ankles, where little flesh protects the bones.

It would seem on the surface that this could well have been the instrumentality that had been used to produce the injuries on Daniel and Richards. As a matter of fact, it may have been that the road grader in question may have had cleats three and one-half inches apart, or perhaps the bodies had been laid out on the ground, and

---

[785] Ibid.
[786] Ibid.
[787] Ibid.
[788] *Monroe News-Star*, 8 March 1923.
[789] Ibid.

the grader moved back and forth over them. Federal and state agents had already inspected all of the machinery used in all of the sawmills in the area and had conducted experiments with this that they felt might be suspect, but to no avail.

Some new names appeared this day on the witness stand that had not been called to testify at the open hearing in January. They were Louis Felton, D. J. Peterson and J. M. Keen. Although we will never know to what they testified in that closed session, Louis Felton was named by John Rogers, the correspondent from the *St. Louis Post Dispatch*, as a person who was most helpful to him.

Just when we think we've seen the last of Rev. Frank Tripp, he pops up in the news again. This time he had just finished preaching the funeral service of J. A. Tally 10 robed Klansmen drove up to the house at 1812 Jackson St. in Monroe, alighting from two closed cars, and marched in single file into the room where the coffin lay. After placing "a beautiful and expensive" wreath of flowers on the coffin, they bowed for a minute in silent prayer, and silently marched out again and drove away. Imagine that, the Klan showing up with Rev. Tripp. What a coincidence.

Captain Skipwith was reported to have received an offer to enter "movies" or undertake a lecture tour on behalf of the Klan. The exact nature of the offer, or the company making it, was unknown, but it was reported that the sum mentioned was close to $75,000.

FRIDAY MARCH 9, 1923
Teegerstrom Gives Testimony Before Morehouse Probers
Timekeeper for Southern Carbon Company is Bastrop Witness Today[790][791]

Testimony continued being taken from witnesses today. Most notable among the list of today's witnesses was Harold Teegerstrom, the long-sought witness during the January open hearing. According to the *Monroe News-Star* this date it stated that Teegerstrom had been "recalled today to resume his testimony. . . " Obviously he was before the grand jury on the previous day, but it was not recorded in that day's dispatches. We are left to wonder as to the content of his testimony. Other names on the witness list who were not called to testify before in the January open hearing were Fred Clemmons and Ernest Vaughn.

---

[790]Ibid.
[791]*Times-Picayune*, 9 March 1923.

The *Times-Picayune* reported that rumors once again surfaced that the bodies recovered were not those of Daniel and Richards. Captain Skipwith, who has in the past been very vocal on this point, was asked this day concerning the rumor, and his claim was that the Klan knew where Daniel and Richards were and would produce them at the proper time. Skipwith responded by telling the correspondent that he had ever said any such thing.

Jim Norseworthy was one of the witnesses scheduled to testify this day. He had testified that the black hoods were worn by the Klan when they went on raids and that the white outfits were for formal occasions. Norseworthy had also said that Captain Skipwith told him "six men had been marked and that the klan already had gotten two of them [Daniel and Richards] and would get the other four."

SATURDAY MARCH 10, 1923
Morehouse Quiz to End[792]

Along with the usual reports of witnesses appearing before the grand jury came an adjoining article which demonstrated how certain Morehouse Parish residents were preparing should the grand jury return indictment on certain persons. The *Monroe News-Star* reported it this way:

"Ten or twelve residents of Morehouse parish have left there within the past few days for Laferia (La Feria), Tex., on the Mexican border, it is reported at Monroe. At the office of Sheriff Fred Carpenter at Bastrop today, it was stated that quite a number of persons recently emigrated to the border. Investments were said to have been made in the area by Carey and Laurie Calhoun, John Freeland, J. B. Rawlinson, Charles Fisher and others.

"Before their departure for Texas, some of the members of the Morehouse contingent said they expected to make their future home along the border. 'People of Morehouse parish are getting wild about that country,' said a citizen of Bastrop today, 'and I expect there will be others who will go.'" It would appear that the rats were leaving the sinking ship.

A check of the map revealed that La Feria is located on U.S. Highway 83 between the towns of Weslaco and Harlingen and about three miles north of the border between the United States and Mexico, with a current population of about 4,300. What better place to be than minutes from an international border should you

---

[792]*Monroe News-Star*, 10 March 1923.

be indicted for a criminal charge by a grand jury, especially when that grand jury would be over a 1,000 miles away during the 1920s. Clearly, the idea was to simply cross the border into Mexico if any indictment was handed down and to remain there until it could be handled.

WEDNESDAY MARCH 14, 1923

Morehouse Probe at its Close: All Testimony Secured
Practically Every Witness Who Testified at Open Hearing Before Jury[793]
Parker Refused to Name Klan Candidates for Appeals Court[794]

At long last, the Morehouse Parish grand jury investigating the depredations of the Ku Klux Klan and the kidnappings and murders of Watt Daniel and Thomas Richards ended. According to parish Clerk of Court James Dalton, the grand jury will be in deliberations at least for the remainder of this date. He said he felt that the jury would probably complete its work and submit its findings to Judge Fred Odom on the following day.

Meanwhile, Governor Parker was busily fighting the Klan on another front, by eliminating two candidates for the court of appeals of the state of Louisiana because they were members of the Klan. They were Robert Roberts, of Minden, and J. E. Reynolds, of Arcadia. Although large delegations had appeared before Parker to push for these candidates, Governor Parker stood fast.

"A lawyer knows the majesty of the law," said the governor, "and a judge on the bench must enforce the law. I will certainly not name a man who has taken the Klan oath as judge to enforce the laws of the state." Parker was said to have produced a list of Klansmen, and on that list was Roberts' name. It was reported that Reynolds had admitted to Parker verbally that he was a Klansman.

THURSDAY MARCH 15, 1923

Inquisitors' Work is Completed at Bastrop[795]

As the Morehouse grand jury continued its deliberations today, it was generally believed that it would finish its work on this day, and submit its findings to Judge Fred Odom before 4 p.m. Rumors of numerous bills of indictment were rampant with little credence placed on any.

---

[793]*Monroe News-Star*, 14 March 1923.
[794]Ibid.
[795]*Monroe News-Star*, 15 March 1923.

On this afternoon, Attorney General Coco, Assistant Attorney General Guion and Senator Warren were making preparations to leave Morehouse Parish, their work being done. They made it clear that they would not await the report of the grand jury.

FRIDAY MARCH 16, 1923

Insufficient Evidence to Bring in True Bills of Indictment, Reports Morehouse Grand Jury

Brief Report of Inquisitors takes no Cognizance of Floggings in Parish[796]
Conference Monday or later to Decide State's Mer Rouge Plan[797]
Grand Jury Failure Supports Klan Rule Charge of Governor: Investigators Ignore Two Murders by Hooded Mob in Morehouse[798]

To the amazement of citizens across the United States, but not the residents of Morehouse Parish, the grand jury investigating the kidnappings and deaths of Watt Daniel and Thomas Richards and other outrages committed by the Ku Klux Klan failed to return any bills of indictment regarding any of the testimony given in these matters. After hearing the testimony of over 125 witnesses concerning these events, the grand jury made the following statement:

> As to the deplorable crime of August 24, 1922, when five men were kidnapped on the highway of Morehouse parish, we have carefully considered all the evidence brought before this grand jury as to the activities of masked, hooded men. The majority of this body are of the opinion that the evidence furnished was not sufficient to warrant the finding of true bills against any particular party. As to the reports published in certain newspapers that friction has developed between the grand jury and the attorney general and his assistants, we wish to brand same as absolutely false and unfounded. The relations between individual members of this grand jury and the attorney general and his staff have at all times been pleasant and harmonious.
>
> Some 125 witnesses have been examined during the session, and we have inquired into all matters reported to us, having returned seven true bills on matters aside from the mob cases. We find little law violations except in the case of the prohibition law, and in several of these the district attorney has already filed bills of information."

Judge Odom dismissed the jury without comment.

Captain Skipwith was quick to register his pleasure with the impotent members of the grand jury. "The state has done its duty," said Skipwith, "and I hope it is satisfied and will let the matter rest." It is clear to see why he would be relieved, as having been the prime mover in the Klan goings-on in Morehouse Parish and the

---

[796]*Monroe News-Star*, 16 March 1923.
[797]Ibid.

party behind the kidnappings and murders of Watt Daniel and Thomas Richards. It was also Skipwith who predicted on the day he saw the list of names picked for the grand jury that "there will be no indictments." He had obviously recognized the names of Klansmen he knew he could count on.

A sigh of relief must have gone up in La Feria, Texas, that could be audible in Bastrop, as those who were waiting to make a run for the Mexican border on receipt of the news of their indictment now felt free to return to Morehouse Parish.

Although Attorney General Coco could not be reached for comment, Assistant Attorney General Walmsley was outspoken of his displeasure.

"I am very much surprised at the news," said Walmsley. "The state had counted on indictments, at least for the lesser offenses, but to learn that none at all were returned in the face of the mass of evidence is amazing to me. The public can feel assured that Attorney General Coco will take prompt action on the matter."

The reactions of one unidentified citizen in Bastrop expressed the sentiments of the residents. "Bastrop was not surprised at the results of the investigation." This grand jury session was not, however, to be a total loss. They find the courage to indict seven men, all of whom just happened to be black.

The reader should be aware that there is a world of difference between a grand jury believing there is sufficient evidence to indict or charge a person with a crime and a jury at a trial finding a defendant guilty of a crime. If we conceded that the grand jury would have, at least, heard the same testimony as that delivered at the open hearing in January, it is then inconceivable that absolutely no indictments flowed from all of these witnesses.

Through testimony, it was established that Jeff Burnett took part in the kidnapping of Watt Daniel, J. L. Daniel, W. C. Andrews, C. C. "Tot" Davenport and Thomas Richards. At least two eye witnesses placed him on the scene. Again through testimony we know that Dr. B. M. McKoin and "Pink" Kirkpatrick took part in the kidnapping of Addie Mae Hamilton and that Dr. McKoin committed a battery upon Mrs. Hamilton. At the very least, these true bills should have been handed down by the grand jury.

In the vast majority of the cases where people were named as having participated in one criminal act or another, the only way they could have escaped

---

[798]*Times-Picayune*, 16 March 1923.

indictment was for the grand jury to have been stacked with Klansmen. This was, indeed, a dark day as the mutilated bodies of Watt Daniel and Thomas Richards lay silently side by side on the tranquil and serene banks of Bayou Bonne Idee, awaiting the justice for the atrocities committed against them that would never come. How magnified must have been the anguish of the family and friends of the slain and abused, who by now must have realized that not only would there not be justice for the outrages already committed, but that the future was also bleak as it was clear that the Klan still dominated the power structure in Morehouse Parish.

How should we class these craven cowards who took a solemn oath before God to uphold the law? Should their actions be considered as treasonous? Clearly, the Klan was always openly critical of Catholics saying that they owed their allegiance to a Papal dictator. These spineless worms used the Constitution of the United States as toilet tissue as they displayed their loyalty and allegiance to some pillowcase fraternity who delighted in murder, kidnapping, beatings, deportations, theft and lying on their fellow citizens all the while hiding their identity and wrapping themselves in the American flag and "100% Americanism."

If ever there deserved to be a monument erected to the cruel injustice delivered first by the Ku Klux Klan and secondly by the gutless wonders on both of the Morehouse grand juries which held hearings on these incidents, this surely is it. Many of those whose relatives participated in these horrible crimes still live in northeast Louisiana. However, instead of acknowledging the past, they try to hide their shame some 70 years afterward through fear and intimidation.

While I was working on my Masters degree at the Northeast Louisiana University (NLU), I became familiar with some of the faculty who remembered an incident involving a history professor employed at NLU in the late 1960s named Alton E. Ingram. As the story goes, Ingram had received his Masters degree from Louisiana State University in Baton Rouge, his thesis being entitled, *The Twentieth Century Ku Klux Klan In Morehouse Parish, Louisiana* (1961). He was also a member of the History Department at NLU.

Around 1970, Ingram was asked to deliver a paper to the Louisiana Historical Society in which he did little more than tell the story of the Klan in Louisiana and included an abbreviated version of the Morehouse incident in 1922. In his presentation, he included the names of some of those involved. Unknown to him, present in the audience were numerous relatives of those mentioned.

Evidently, the descendants of those dead Klansmen, now affluent members of society and, in all likelihood, heavy contributors to the university, contacted the president of NLU to express their outrage. The next day it was said that Ingram was summoned to the office of the president of the university to explain his actions. It was decided that Ingram would issue an apology, and it was hoped that over a period of time the issue would die down. This, however, was not to be.

Ingram received threatening notes from the Ku Klux Klan in his mailbox at the university and it was said that these now pillars of the community eventually forced Ingram to leave NLU because of this incident, but this could not be confirmed. This author contacted Mr. Alton E. Ingram during the summer of 1994 to request an interview. Is it any wonder that Mr. Ingram refused to be interviewed?

Agents Hunt Down Vanished Ku Klux Leader[799]

The nationwide search by federal officers for Edward Young Clarke, former Imperial Wizard of the Ku Klux Klan. He was wanted for a violation of the Mann Act. This developed here today when Sidney Smith, Atlanta attorney, appeared in federal court to ask for a continuance. Mrs. Smith said Clarke had left Atlanta this day, and his whereabouts were unknown.

SATURDAY MARCH 17, 1923

Morehouse Klan Fears New Move on Part of Coco
Transfer of Possible Cases to Union Parish also Causes Worry[800]

The euphoria being experienced by Morehouse Parish Klansmen was cut short today when the *Times-Picayune* reported that Attorney General Coco was preparing to move the trials on the soon-to-be-filed bills of information against certain Klansmen to Union Parish. Union Parish was known not to be a stronghold of the Klan. Actually, it was believed that Union Parish had fewer Klansmen than any other parish in the state. It was also said that political differences between Morehouse and its sister parish to the west had created considerable friction between the two before the advent of the Klan.

"These fellows in Union parish would hang us on any kind of a charge," said an unnamed prominent Klansman. "We will fight any move to try us there to the very limit if bills of information are filed by the attorney general."

---

[799]*Times-Picayune*, 16 March 1923.
[800]*Times-Picayune*, 17 March 1923.

Residents of the parish let a Klan organizer know in no uncertain terms that they did not want the Klan in their parish, and it was said that they "waited on him." Of the few that did join the Klan, they were served notice by the resident that "the first time any masked bands were seen on the public roads they could expect to be fired on first and their identities fixed afterwards."

This being the day after the Morehouse Parish grand jury presented its disgusting lack of action to Judge Fred Odom, the correspondent writing the story gave this impression of the city of Bastrop.

> Dismissal of the murders of Watt Daniel and T. F. Richards without any reference to them in the grand jury report is a reflection of the klan sentiment here. Klan leaders and their sympathizers have displayed absolute indifference to the two murders from the first and have left nothing undone to discredit all evidence brought out to show that two murders were committed.

Driving home the control the Klan exerted on the entire parish, the correspondent repeated the words of Captain Skipwith on the day the second grand jury was called into session. After he had scanned the list, Captain Skipwith declared, "This is the last you will hear of it. There will be no indictments."

TUESDAY OCTOBER 30, 1923
Bodies of Morehouse Victims Tied to Wheels of Cart and Rolled Into Lake, Says Klan Prober
Imperial Palace Pays Monroe and Shreveport Attorneys, says Witness[801]

For a number of months, an internal struggle had been in progress for the leadership of the Ku Klux Klan between Dr. Hiram Evans and William Simmons. This struggle forced the Klan into receivership, and depositions were being taken from Klan officers in Atlanta, Georgia. Eventually, Evans would win, forcing Simmons out, but not without Simmons receiving $145,500 for this interest in the Klan.[802]

This day a Klan operative named S. N. Littlejohn was being deposed in the Klan receivership case when he revealed some startling information concerning the murders of Watt Daniel and Thomas Richards in Morehouse Parish. Littlejohn said that he had been employed by the Klan as an investigator and dispatched to Bastrop along with eight other Klan investigators on or about January 12, 1923. This would have been at the height of the open hearing being held in Bastrop. Littlejohn said

---

[801] *Monroe News-Star*, 30 October 1923.

[802] *Times-Picayune*, 13 February 1924.

that when he and the other Klan investigators arrived in Bastrop they met the lead Klan investigator, J. J. Bracewell, who was to give them "advice and instructions."

Operating under the alias of George K. Lawrence, Littlejohn said that he and the other investigators were advised upon their arrival that they need not go to Mer Rouge. According to Littlejohn, he was told "that the two bodies found in the lake had been tied or 'spread eagled' on logging cart wheels and rolled down the hill and that that was what crushed the heads off the two bodies."

Littlejohn said that he was instructed by the Klan Imperial Palace in Atlanta to do the bidding of Captain Skipwith. Furthermore, he was given instructions by Skipwith "to work with the end view that there might be no indictments."

Littlejohn said that Klan officials in Atlanta were worried about Captain Skipwith's propensity to run his mouth with the reporters. In that regard his instructions were to "keep Captain Skipwith quiet, and not to crowd the issue." Clearly, they feared that Skipwith would talk too much.

According to Littlejohn, the lawyers who represented the Klansmen in Morehouse Parish were paid with funds from Klan headquarters in Atlanta. He named these lawyers as Todd, Newton, Sandel and Judge Barnett of Shreveport. He said that Todd, Newton and Sandel all received an initial payment of $820 and a final payment of $250. Judge Barnett, however, received a whopping $5,000 for his efforts on behalf of the Klan. Littlejohn said that he received a $50-a-week salary and that he had a $75-a-week expense account, a substantial sum for that era.

Speaking of the other Klan investigators, Littlejohn listed them as "M. Hamilton, of Houston, Texas; J. A. Bracewell, Lloyd Ingel, H. L. Talisfere and C. C. McIlwain, all from Atlanta; M. Murray, of Shreveport, and O. D. Jackson and W. Mann of New Orleans. Littlejohn also said that a "strong arm" or "wrecking crew" had been selected to work in the Morehouse Parish area. The purpose of the strong arm and wrecking crew was to crush or neutralize by use of force whatever Klan opposition may exist. He said that special care had been taken to be certain that the members of these groups were brought in from other areas so that they would not be recognized as Klansmen.

In March 1923, Littlejohn said he was recalled to Klan headquarters in Atlanta by T. J. McKinnon, a Klan official of unknown title or position, for a conference on the Mer Rouge case. During this conference held at the Klan Imperial Palace in Atlanta, McKinnon was made aware of the presence of C. R. Upchurch and Harry

Terrell who "were at Mer Rouge at that time securing affidavits in connection with the said Mer Rouge case which was not known to this deponent at that time, but that the said McKinnon did then and there speak to this deponent: 'You have got your machine down there, use it and get them out of the way.' This deponent understood this language that the strong arm squad or wrecking crew was to pump up Upchurch and Terrell." It was also reported that Littlejohn said "that H. W. Evans gave him specific instructions to 'beat up' Harry Terrell and to charge whatever the fine was to his expense account."

Of Dr. B. M. McKoin, the deacon of the church who lied continuously by denying his membership in the Klan, Littlejohn told a different story. He said that when McKoin was arrested in Baltimore in connection with the murders of Daniel and Richards "J. A. Bracewell was sent to Baltimore to handle Dr. McKoin's fight against extradition from Baltimore." He said that, "Bracewell, using the alias of Baker, went to the offices of Attorney Ecke and Mack and said to them 'we have a man in jail here and I have $10,000 and want to get him out.'" Littlejohn said that Bracewell did not handle the situation properly in Baltimore and that he had to be sent to Baltimore to close the deal with the attorneys for Dr. McKoin. Finally, we have definitive proof from the lips of Klan operatives that not only was Dr. McKoin lying about his membership in the Klan, but also that McKoin must have been very important to the Klan for them to treat him in this manner.

WEDNESDAY OCTOBER 31, 1923
Pathologist Gives Views Regarding Mer Rouge Case
Information Brought out in Klan Receivership Case in Atlanta[803]

Grabbing today's headlines was the statement made by Dr. Charles Duval, one of the pathologists who performed the autopsies on the bodies of Watt Daniel and Thomas Richards. He told reporters in New Orleans that the bodies of Daniel and Richards could not have been in the waters of Lake LaFourche any more than 48 hours. Needless to say, this information created quite a stir. This statement was verified by Dr. Landford, the other attending physician and teacher of medicine at the Tulane School of Medicine in New Orleans. Both pathologists did, however, maintain the assertion that the bodies recovered were those of Watt Daniel and Thomas Richards.

---

[803] *Monroe News-Star*, 31 October 1923.

This information played into the hands of the Klan as it had maintained all along that the bodies taken from Lake LaFourche on that December morning were not those of Daniel and Richards. We are still left to wonder how they could be so sure unless of course they had hidden them in some other place.

With regard to the information given by Mr. Littlejohn in Atlanta concerning the bodies of Daniel and Richards being tied to a log cart and then rolled down a hill, causing the damage to the bodies found under autopsy, Dr. Duval discounted that assertion. He said that although some of the injuries to the bodies could have been caused by such treatment, there were others that would not. He referred directly to the bones in both bodies that had been broken at three-and-one-half-inch intervals. Another condition which Dr. Duval neglected to mention was the surgical castration of Watt Daniel. Surely this could not have been the result of the log cart.

Reporters asked why this information had been excluded from the autopsy reports on both men. Dr. Duval responded by saying that it had not been excluded, but rather it had not been included. It appears as though the doctor was playing with semantics.

Governor Parker denied any knowledge that the bodies had not been in Lake LaFourche the entire time. "I know nothing about the report of Drs. Duval and Landford, the pathologists. I never saw the report. It was made to the attorney general's office, and I know nothing about it at the time, except what was published."

When asked about the report, Attorney General A. V. Coco also dismissed the failure to include such information as inconsequential. Coco said that he thought it would be entirely possible for the bodies to have been held at another location until the night of the dynamite explosion at Lake LaFourche. He believed that the bodies may have been brought there that evening, thrown in the lake, and the dynamite set off to cover over the bodies.

THURSDAY NOVEMBER 1, 1923

Mer Rouge Calm, Expecting Clash With Hooded Men
Mayor Asserts Klan Plans to "Wipe Out" Town after Trial[804]

The *Times-Picayune* reported today that, as the time moved toward the date of trial of a score of Klansmen on misdemeanor charges, the Klan was hard at work

---

[804] *Times-Picayune*, 1 November 1923.

attempting to frighten and intimidate those who would testify against them. Word was circulated that those who did not quit talking about the Klan and the Daniel-Richards case "would meet the same fate as Watt Daniel and T. F. Richards."

Residents of the area were concerned because a major portion of the black population, although not involved with the depredations of the Klan before the courts, had either fled the area or had been driven off the plantations. Farmers feared that without the necessary black labor force to harvest crops, they would be ruined. Businessmen were also crying the blues because they claimed that their incomes had suffered dramatically since the advent of the Daniel-Richards incident.

Residents of Mer Rouge, including Mayor Dade, were saying openly that they feared what will happen once the trials are over, and the attention of the state was no longer focused on Morehouse Parish. Klan threats had been received by community leaders, and many were told to leave town or face the consequences. For the most part, the residents of Mer Rouge had become defiant of the Klan. Most of the residents were of the old stock who had many generations buried in these grounds, and they had no intention of abandoning their roots. One resident said that they would not "let an organization controlled by an alien upstart who didn't know where his next meal was coming from until he was made exalted cyclops. . ." force them to leave their homes.

Mayor Dade said that he had information "from a reliable source" that the Klan would "wipe out" Mer Rouge when the trials were over, and the interest in these cases died down. Dade said that they would "die fighting rather than let another be taken to suffer as Daniel and Richards did."

"We are not going to start any trouble," said some other citizens, "but let a hooded man set foot in the town of Mer Rouge, and he's going to be shot at. And when that shot is fired, then will the question as to whether the klan shall rule Morehouse parish be settled."

On the local political front, it was rumored that the anti-Klan faction of Mer Rouge was going to support S. R. Ingram of Mer Rouge as its candidate for the office of sheriff of Morehouse Parish. It was understood that the pro-Klan faction in Bastrop was going to support its candidate and fellow Klansman, the incumbent, Sheriff Fred Carpenter. This information brought this response from unnamed persons in Mer Rouge:

"Carpenter is the klan candidate, but Ingram is not the candidate of Mer Rouge nor of the anti-klan faction, and we doubt if he will poll more than three votes at the Mer Rouge box. George Williamson is our candidate, and every anti-klan vote in the parish is pledged to him.

"Some time ago we held a conference in Mer Rouge to plan for the defeat at the polls of the klan in Morehouse parish and we agreed Williamson was our candidate for sheriff, and we believe he will win in the first primary by a majority of at least 300. Ingram came in at the last minute to qualify and declare himself as the Mer Rouge and anti-klan candidate, which was just an effort to muddy the water and split the vote between himself and Williamson, thereby allowing Carpenter to win. However, he has failed in his attempt to deceive us for we know he is a klansman, and we will vote accordingly."

It was confirmed that S. R. Ingram was the grandfather of Alton E. Ingram, the history professor at Northeast Louisiana University. The same Alton Ingram who suffered considerable social castigation by the now influential survivors of the 1922-23 Morehouse Klansmen.

SUNDAY NOVEMBER 4, 1923
Trial at Bastrop Likely to Prove Slayer's Identity
Minor Charges Growing out of Kidnapping Case up Monday[805]

It was reported today that the trials of misdemeanor cases to be held the following day in Bastrop could well be pivotal in identifying those responsible for the kidnappings and murders of Watt Daniel and Thomas Richards. Although the Daniel-Richards kidnappings and murders will not be addressed directly, there are a number of other offenses allegedly perpetrated by the Klan that will be placed before the court which could directly or indirectly implicate the Klan and those on trial for these misdemeanors. Those especially sensitive to this would be Captain Skipwith, T. J. Burnett and E. N. "Newt" Gray, all of whom have been placed on the scene of the August 24, 1922 kidnapping scene on the Bastrop-Mer Rouge Road.

It was also reported today that Attorney General Coco and his first assistant, Seth Guion, arrived in Bastrop this date in preparation for the trial of the upcoming misdemeanor cases. For the first time it was reported that Captain Skipwith was charged with two counts of "conspiring to murder," one count in the death of Watt

---

[805]*Times-Picayune*, 4 November 1923.

Daniel and the second count for Thomas Richards. This was the first and only reference found to such a charge. No disposition could be located.

MONDAY NOVEMBER 5, 1923

Sixth District Judge Faces Task of Trying Friends, Neighbors Involved in Mer Rouge Case

Charge against M'Intosh is First on Docket[806]
Misdemeanors Before Judge Fred M. Odom in Sixth District Court[807]

The first of the trials emanating from the depredations of the black-hooded Klansmen of Morehouse Parish began this date in the chambers of Judge Fred Odom of the Sixth Judicial District. Those cases being brought before the bar of justice this day were:

> 1) Captain J. K. Skipwith, W. G. McIntosh, Marvin Pickett, Benton Prat "Cud" Pickett, Sam Ethridge and Sam Cox. These were charged with "carrying firearms on the premises of another."
>
> 2) Laurie Calhoun, T. J. "Jeff" Burnett and Harley Rogers were charged with "assault with a dangerous weapon."
>
> 3) Captain J. K. Skipwith, T. J. Burnett and Fred Higgenbotham charged with "conspiring to compel a person to leave his place of business."
>
> 4) Captain J. K. Skipwith, Marvin Pickett, Cud Picket, Sam Cox, Benton Pratt, Sam Ethridge and G. G. McIntosh charged with "conspiring to compel a person to leave Bastrop."

Cases that were set to be tried after these in the days following were:

> 1) W. H. Kirkpatrick and Dr. B. M. McKoin charged with "assault with a dangerous weapon."
>
> 2) W. H. Kirkpatrick and Dr. B. M. McKoin charged with "conspiring to compel a person to leave the parish."
>
> 3) Captain J. K. Skipwith, T. J. Burnett, E. N. Gray, Oliver Skipwith and Smith Stevenson charged with "conspiracy to compel a person to leave an automobile." This was the only charge which grew out of the testimony given concerning the kidnappings of Watt Daniel, J. L. Daniel, C. C. "Tot" Davenport, W. C. Andrews and Thomas Richards on August 24, 1922, at the roadblock set up on the Bastrop-Mer Rouge Road by black-hooded Klansmen.

Unlike the open hearing held in January, the various tabloids did not carry much in the way of verbatim testimony of witnesses and defendants.

First to be called to testify today was Alonzo Braddock. He told how the mob broke down his door, and how armed men entered his home. Under the questioning of Senator Warren, Braddock first said that there were men with shotguns and pistols and that he was unable to say who was carrying what type of

---

[806] *Monroe News-Star*, 5 November 1923.
[807] Ibid.

weapon. Pressed by Warren, Braddock said that Benton Pratt was carrying a shotgun. With regard to "Cud" Pickett, Braddock said that he was mistaken in his identification of him. All told, Braddock said that there were about 30 or 40 in the raiding party. When cross examined by Klan defense lawyer Judge J. W. Barnett of Shreveport, Braddock said that he had also seen Marvin Pickett with a shotgun and that Benton Pratt had been the first one that he had seen with a shotgun. While it is understandable why Barnett would want to question the identification of Pratt, it would seem that the testimony that Marvin Pickett possessed a shotgun was brought out by Barnett and not the state. This does not speak very highly of Barnett.

In the afternoon, testimony was taken from Mrs. Alonzo Braddock concerning the midnight raid on her home by Captain J. K. Skipwith, W. G. McIntosh, Marvin Pickett, Benton Pratt, "Cud" Pickett, Sam Ethridge and Sam Cox, when they kidnapped her husband. During the testimony, Mrs. Braddock said that she recognized Captain Skipwith as one of the band who invaded her home and had kidnapped her husband that night, and that Captain Skipwith was armed with a "pistol." This immediately drew protests from the defense, as Judge Odom had already ruled that the only weapon which could be made reference to in the trail was a "shotgun." After some discussion, Judge Odom allowed the bills of information to be amended, and the term "pistol" was accepted.

Harkness was called to the stand after Mrs. Braddock, and he told of hearing Marvin Pickett boast that he had participated in the raid on the Braddock farm and that he had been the first to burst into the house. This he said he heard Pickett say the day following the raid. The state then rested, and the defense began.

Sam Ethridge was called by the defense. He said that he was not present at the raid on the Braddock farm and made the claim that he had attended a dance on that evening. He said that it was three months after the raid that he learned that he had been implicated in the affair. Ethridge said he remembered immediately where he was at the time, as did the family with whom he boarded. It was not said whether this "family" was called to testify. Presumably, they could only have testified that he was not in the house at that time and that he was out, unless they had attended the dance also. No more information was forthcoming this date.

Ku Klux Editor Kills Attorney for Ex-Wizard[808]

A bulletin from Atlanta, told of a Klan-on-Klan murder that occurred in the halls of the Imperial Palace. Phillip Fox, public affairs officer for the Ku Klux Klan, shot and killed W. C. Coburn, an Atlanta attorney and counsel for the faction that was fighting Imperial Wizard H. W. Evans and other officials of the order Coburn was shot five times as he sat in his office.

When taken into custody Fox was quoted as having said: "I am sorry to have had to do it, but I am glad he is dead. He was planning to ruin me, and I had just as soon be hung as hurt."

TUESDAY NOVEMBER 6, 1923

Exalted Cyclops is Found Guilty at Bastrop Trial
Three Others Supposed Members Held for Carrying Guns[809]
Morehouse Citizens are Tried for Raiding House of Alonzo Braddock[810]
Bastrop is Tense as Guilt is Fixed on Klan Leader[811]

Of the seven who were tried for the raid on the home of Alonzo Braddock on the previous day, four were found guilty and three not guilty, reported the *Monroe News-Star*. Those found guilty of carrying firearms on the premises of another were Captain J. K. Skipwith, Benton Pratt, Marvin Pickett and W. G. McIntosh. Those acquitted were Sam Ethridge, Sam Cox and "Cud" Pickett. We are left to wonder if the conviction of Marvin Pickett was due to the skillful cross-examination the previous day by Klan attorney Judge Barnett.

This conviction drew immediate cries from the defense for a new trial and the assertion that Judge Odom was biased in the case. Arguing the merits of the convictions with Klan defense counsel Judge Barnett was co-Klan defense counsel Percy Sandel, the very man for whom the Sandel Memorial Library was named on the campus of Northeast Louisiana University. Sandel attempted to argue the point concerning the "shotgun-pistol" issue, which had already been put to rest on the previous day by Judge Odom. Sandel's argument fell on deaf ears, as Judge Odom refused to reconsider.

Although no details of the trial were carried by any of the newspapers, Laurie Calhoun was found not guilty of the charge of assault with a dangerous weapon

---

[808]*Times-Picayune*, 5 November 1923.

[809]*Times-Picayune*, 5 November 1923.

[810]*Monroe News-Star*, 6 November 1923.

[811]*Times-Picayune*, 6 November 1923.

and conspiring to compel a person to leave the town of Bastrop by Judge Odom. This case grew out of the Fred Cobb kidnapping and threats when he was taken at gunpoint off the streets of Bastrop by a black-hooded group, one of which he identified as Calhoun. Calhoun, it was later reported, said that he was playing cards at the home of a friend, and he produced witnesses to support his contention.

The *Times-Picayune* offered little new information. It did, however, mention that Captain Skipwith "took it for granted that it [Sheriff Carpenter's sending him out to get Braddock] was equivalent to a commission as a deputy sheriff. . ." On this issue and this issue alone, I find myself in agreement with Captain Skipwith. If, as Sheriff Carpenter testified, he was approached beforehand by Captain Skipwith and told of the alleged illegal operation, and Sheriff Carpenter did tell Skipwith to bring Braddock in, it is difficult to understand how Judge Odom could have rendered the verdict that he did in this case. In the Laurie Calhoun case, the person in whose home he claimed to have been playing cards was Ernest Baker.

As to the tenor of the town of Bastrop itself, there was some indication of friction between the attorney general and his staff and the general public gathered around the courthouse, most of whom were either Klansmen or Klan sympathizers. For the most part, however, these groups gathered around the courthouse were described as "good natured." Despite the dire predictions of an all-out war between the towns of Mer Rouge and Bastrop should there be any convictions, these prognostications did not materialize.

WEDNESDAY NOVEMBER 7, 1923
"Old Skip" Weeps at Tribute Paid Him by Attorney
Fight for Self-Control Lost by Aged Ruler of Parish Klan[812]
Former Deputy Sheriff not Frank with Court, View of Judge, Who Says He "Does Not Blame Him"[813]
Morehouse Counsel for Defendants to Apply for Recusal of District Judge:
Appeal to Supreme Court May be Made to get Judge Odom out of the Way[814]

In a move that must have surely shook Klansmen in Morehouse Parish, the *Monroe News-Star* reported that Judge Fred Odom handed down a verdict of guilty on the charge of assault with a dangerous weapon against T. J. Burnett. This charge growing out of the holdup of Harry Neelis on August 17, 1922, when it

---

[812]*Times-Picayune*, 7 November 1923.
[813]*Monroe News-Star*, 7 November 1923.
[814]Ibid.

was alleged that Burnett, along with Harley Rogers both wearing black hoods, held up Neelis and his black helper on the Bastrop-Mer Rouge Road. This occurred on the day prior to the first kidnapping of Richards, which occurred in the garage at Bastrop. Judge Odom advised that he was taking the case of Harley Rogers "under consideration." The maximum fine for Burnett would be $100.

During the trial, Burnett paraded a number of witnesses, all of whom were employees of the Southern Carbon Plant at Spyker. Each of these witnesses claimed that on August 17, 1922, Burnett was at work at the Southern Carbon Plant in Spyker. Obviously, for one reason or another, Judge Odom did not believe them. This was the same defense that Burnett planned to use should his cases come to trial concerning the Daniel-Richards case. Clearly, they must have been severely shaken because if Odom did not believe his witnesses in this case, chances were he would not go along with the same defense in the Daniel-Richards cases. Especially in light of the fact that considerable doubt had been cast on the time book kept by Harold Teegerstrom, which clearly showed an erasure in the space where Burnett's name was listed for that date.

The first character witness to take the stand was J. Scoggins, the former sheriff of Morehouse Parish. Scoggins testified that he had been familiar with Burnett since childhood, and that he knew him to have a good reputation. Following Scoggins came W. T. Smith, parish president and admitted Klansman; J. T. Dalton, the clerk of court; and Sheriff Fred Carpenter, a Klan official in Morehouse Klan No. 34 and a man of despicable reputation. All three praised the character and reputation of Burnett. I mean, go figure!

Last, but certainly not least, to mount the stand to testify to the cherubic nature of Burnett was David I. Garrett, district attorney for Morehouse Parish, alleged Klansman, and the leader of the impotent Morehouse grand juries investigating the outrages of the Ku Klux Klan. As expected, he spoke of the sterling nature of Burnett's character. It can only be wondered why, after such an impressive entourage of reputable citizens and Klansmen, that Judge Odom rendered the verdict of guilty on Burnett.

In rendering the verdict of guilt to Burnett, Judge Odom delivered what was termed "a remarkable address from the bench." The address follows:

> Mr. Burnett could not come here and confess to complicity in that affair. The court knows the stress under which he is laboring. He has been connected with a serious tragedy, which occurred in this parish shortly after that time. He was

even arrested on a charge of murder. He was under guard while in a sanatorium in Shreveport, and later he was at liberty under $5,000 bond.

Mr. Burnett is named in other charges on this docket, all of these leading to the final disappearance of Watt Daniel and T. F. Richards, the conditions which set in motion the tragic ending of the two. I do not mean to say Mr. Burnett is guilty of the various cases here charged against him. Nor do I mean to infer that he had anything to do with the Daniel-Richards tragedies.

The court does not expect Mr. Burnett to be candid and, it does make allowance for this and for all others involved in these cases. Had I been in Mr. Burnett's place, I would have done as he has done.

This speech of Judge Odom could be taken in two different ways, depending on his vocal inflections while delivering same. It could have either been sarcastic or sympathetic. It is difficult to tell because the correspondent failed to include any reference to this, and this speech was carried only by the *Monroe News-Star,* making it impossible to check against another source.

This second conviction of Klansmen, the first being Captain Skipwith and others who were convicted the previous day of the assault on the home of Alonzo Braddock, sent the Klan attorneys Barnett, Newton and Sandel into a conference. That same afternoon, they filed a motion for Judge Odom to remove himself from the remainder of the misdemeanor cases on the ground of his being prejudiced against the defendants.

The Klan defense attorneys also filed a motion for a new trial for Skipwith and the others convicted of the assault on the Braddock home. Klan attorney Barnett said:

"The penalty for this offense is the lightest of any provided by the state statutes. In the case of Captain Skipwith, there is a man known for his integrity; a man who has stood for white supremacy since the Civil War; a man 75 years old, who is teetering on the edge of the grave. Does the court believe he would perjure himself for the sake of getting out of payment of a trivial fine?"

After further discussion, this motion, along with the motion that Judge Odom remove himself from the remainder of the misdemeanor trials was not granted, and the trials of Burnett and Rogers continued at about 3 p.m. as the defense put on a parade of character witnesses on behalf of Burnett.

Appearing this date in the *Times-Picayune* was an article which might have been more at home in the *Monroe News-Star*. This article described how Captain J. K. Skipwith, Exalted Cyclops of the Ku Klux Klan, lost control and began crying during the trial proceedings. The correspondent described the occasion as follows:

> It was during the argument of Judge W. C. Barnett, chief counsel for the defense,
> for a new trial in the cases where "guilty" was the verdict that the aged ruler of
> the parish klan could no longer control himself. A great effort at control was
> noticed, but tears started trickling down his cheeks. Judge Barnett had reviewed
> the evidence and testimony as presented and was arguing as to the credibility of
> such. He said all the defendants were strangers to him, with the exception of
> Captain Skipwith, and said although I differ in opinion in some instances with
> Captain Skipwith, there is one thing that impresses me about him, and that is
> his undeniable integrity.
>
> It was at this point that 'Old Skip' lost his fight with self-control. It was only
> for a minute, though, for he soon recovered his poise and, while Judge Odom
> was explaining his view of the case and a subsequent refusal of a new trial, he
> assumed a belligerent expression and leaned forward in his chair as if challenging
> the jurist to refuse the request and in the end acquittal.

This article seem to have been written in the same reverent manner as other articles written concerning Captain Skipwith and the Klan in general by the staff of the *Monroe News-Star*.

Also surfacing this date was a strong dislike for Judge Odom by Klansmen and Klan sympathizers in Bastrop. It was said that Judge Odom had committed political suicide by handing down these convictions in this stronghold of the Ku Klux Klan. Indeed, it must have taken a great deal of intestinal fortitude to hand down these convictions, knowing full well that he and his family would continue to live in Morehouse Parish.

Ridley's Case Put Off: Illness Prevents Answering Drunk Charges[815]

More bad news emanating from Atlanta this day. Charges of driving while intoxicated were brought by police against Rev. Caled A. Ridley, chaplain of the Ku Klux Klan. Mr. Ridley was formerly pastor of an Atlanta church but resigned when other Baptist churches started to withdraw fellowship. W. S. Coburn, who was killed yesterday afternoon by Phillip Fox, had been Ridley's attorney. Were it not for his bad luck, he would have had none at all!

From Lancaster, Pennsylvania, came the news of Ku Klux Klan involvement in local elections. Early in the morning, posters were distributed throughout Lancaster, bearing a skull and crossbones. During the day automobiles containing robed Klansmen visited every polling place, some passing slowly, others making brief stops.[816]

---

[815]*Times-Picayune*, 7 November 1923.

[816]*The New York Times*, 7 November 1923.

THURSDAY NOVEMBER 8, 1923

Delay in Hooded Band Cases Won by Defense Move
Appeal to Supreme Court is Hinted if Judge Fails to Recuse Self[817]

Trials were temporarily postponed and witnesses sent home today as Judge Odom took under advisement motions filed for his recusal from the remainder of the Klan cases left on his docket, and for a new trial for those Klansmen convicted yesterday for the attack on the home of Alonzo Braddock, and for the conviction of T. J. Burnett. Judge Odom said that he would rule on the motions the following day. Meanwhile, it was said that if Judge Odom did not grant these motions, such could be appealed to the state supreme court.

Klan Parade a Mile Long: Men And Women Take Part In Bay Shore Demonstration[818]

From Bay Shore, Long Island, came the news that 500 men and 200 women marched in a Ku Klux Klan parade touted to be a mile long. Major E. D. Smith mounted on a horse, led the parade. Behind him came 15 riders, one of whom carried an American flag, while another carried a six-foot cross lit with red light bulbs supplied by a storage battery on the saddle. One band in Klan uniforms and four others were in the parade. About 200 men wore robes and masks. Three hundred automobiles followed the procession, and there were 5,000 automobiles containing spectators lined up in the streets.

Klan Loses in Pittsburgh: Democrat Polls Record Vote As Result Of Ku Klux Opposition[819]

A press release from Pittsburgh, Pennsylvania declared that the Ku Klux Klan had thrust itself into a political campaign for the first time in overwhelmingly Republican and Protestant Allegheny County. County Commissioner James Houlshen, democratic candidate for re-election as the third or minority Commissioner, drew the fire of the Klan because he happened to be a Catholic and was opposed by W. T. McCullough, Klan candidate, and nominee of the Prohibition Party.

---

[817] *Times-Picayune*, 8 November 1923.
[818] Ibid.
[819] Ibid.

FRIDAY NOVEMBER 9, 1923
Judge Overrules Recusal Motion, Fines Klan Head
Skipwith and Three Others must Pay for Armed Invasion[820]

Judge Odom denied the motions set forth by Klan defense counsel for new trials for Captain Skipwith and the others convicted of the raid on the farm of Alonzo Braddock and the conviction of T. J. Burnett. Judge Odom also denied the motion by defense attorneys that he recuse himself from the remainder of the upcoming trials of those Klansmen named in the bills of information filed by Attorney General Coco. With regard to all those convicted, which include Captain Skipwith, Marvin Pickett, Benton Pratt, W. G. McIntosh and T. J. Burnett, all were given "Fines of $10 and costs or five days in jail. . . " This is the manner in which justice was dispensed bu Judge Odom in Klan-dominated Morehouse Parish!

Klan is Defeated at Memphis Polls[821]

A bulletin from Memphis announced the victory of Mayor Rowlett Paine and his entire administration, running on an anti-Klan platform. Clifford Davis, running on the Klan ticket, was elected to the office of City Judge.

Klan Calls 100,000 to Youngstown[822]

The news from Youngstown, Ohio, told of a gathering there of Klansmen numbering "more than 100,000," from Ohio, Pennsylvania and West Virginia. The Klonclave was to celebrate "the biggest victory won by the Klan north of the Mason and Dixon line," said Colonel E. A. Watkins, a spokesman of the Klan. The victory was the election of Charles Scheible, the Klan candidate for Mayor.

FRIDAY NOVEMBER 23, 1923
Skipwith Must Face Judge Odom for Conspiracy[823]

The Louisiana State Supreme Court denied an order for Judge Odom to recuse himself or call another judge to hear evidence on the charges for which his recusation was asked by "Old Skip" and three others. No reasons were given by the high court for the refusal except that Judge Odom was correct in refusing to call in another judge to act on the request.

---

[820]*Times-Picayune*, 9 November 1923.

[821]*The New York Times*, 9 November 1923.

[822]Ibid.

[823]*Times-Picayune*, 23 November 1923.

Skipwith, T. Jeff Burnett, Alfred Higgenbotham and Harley Rogers of Morehouse Parish all were charged with conspiracy to deport Thomas Richards from the parish and in the deaths of Richards and Watt Daniel August 24, 1922. These charges did not emanate from any Morehouse Parish Grand Jury, nor did they come from the office of District Attorney Garrett. Instead the conspiracy charges were filed by Attorney General Coco when the Morehouse Parish Grand Juries and district attorney failed to act in connection with the murders of Daniel and Richards.

SATURDAY JANUARY 12, 1924

Simmons, Clarke Ousted by Evans Faction of Klan
Giant says Move to "Clean Up" Order Forced Action[824]

Because of the heat generated by the Klan outrages in Morehouse Parish, associated allegations of misappropriation of Klan funds by Ku Klux Klan Imperial Giant Edward Young Clarke, Clarke's federal indictment with the Mann Act because of his transportation of a woman from Houston to New Orleans "for immoral purposes," the driving while intoxicated arrest of the Ku Klux Klan Chaplin, the Reverend Caled A. Ridley, and the forced receivership of the Klan, Hiram W. Evans, a dentist from Texas, was able to force Simmons and Clarke from the organization. This came in the form of a banishment signed into effect in Washington, D. C. on January 9, 1924, when all of the grand dragons from all 48 states met and signed the charges against the two men. Both men were charged with "activity attempting to disrupt the organization" and "allying himself with enemies of the order and bringing it into disrepute."

Legion, Kluxers Fight at Dedication: Klan Wreath Termed Desecration Of Heroes' Monument[825]

A dispatch from Ceaderhurst, New York, told of a fight between members of the American Legion and the Ku Klux Klan that marred the dedication of a monument to nine youths who lost their lives in World War I. The Klansmen attempted to place a wreath on the monument, but a "gold star" mother protested. The Legion men forced the Klansmen to withdraw and finally tore their memento to shreds.

---

[824]*Times-Picayune*, 12 January 1924.
[825]*Times-Picayune,* 30 November 1923.

WEDNESDAY FEBRUARY 6, 1924
Carpenter Plans No Fight Against Removal Order
Worry Over Shortage In Accounts Makes Sheriff Ill[826]

Sheriff Fred Carpenter of Morehouse Parish, was reported to be seriously ill at his home in Bastrop as a result of the strain and worry over the shortage in his accounts as ex-officio tax collector. These shortages, yes, there was more than one, were reported by W. N McFarland, State Supervisor of Public Accounts at Baton Rouge.

The sheriff issued a statement this day reiterating that he intended to relinquish the Democratic nomination for sheriff he had won on January 15. He also said that he did not intend to make any fight against Governor Parker's removal order. "I am doing this," he was quoted as saying, "to be fair to the people of Morehouse Parish and for no other reason." What a novel concept for the top cop of the parish!

The Morehouse Parish citizens who had secured the sheriff's bond and who were liable for the additional $3,494 shortage reported by McFarland, were notified by telegrams. They were told that they would be held liable for the existing deficit, if it was not made good by Carpenter at once. A previous shortage of $18,953 in the sheriff's account was handled by friends of Carpenter. The reader may recall that J. L. Daniel, the father of the murdered Watt Daniel, had been one of the bondsmen for Sheriff Carpenter. It is unknown if Daniel became responsible for Carpenter's fiscal irresponsibility.

Carpenter's successor as sheriff since his removal by Governor Parker had been a matter of conjecture. Dr. O. M. Paterson, Morehouse Parish Coroner, was to automatically succeed him, unless Governor Parker appointed a successor.

WEDNESDAY FEBRUARY 13, 1924
Simmons Sells Interest in Klan for $145,500
Insurgent Founder Reported Forming New 'Knights' Order[827]

In an communication that surely did nothing to help the flattering image of the Klan, and official announcement was made from the Imperial Palace of the Knights of the Ku Klux Klan in Atlanta that William Joseph Simmons, emperor and founder of the Klan, had resigned from the Klan and that he had disposed of his interests in the Klan for the sum of $145,500. At the same time, Simmons announced that he

---

[826] *Times-Picayune*, 6 February 1924.

[827] *Times-Picayune*, 13 February 1924.

had placed himself at the head of a new organization, known as the "Knights of the Flaming Sword." It would certainly appear that Simmons' interest in the Klan had nothing to do with "pure womanhood" or Klanishness and everything to do with power and money.

In the final analysis, Governor Parker, Attorney General Coco and his staff did their best to obtain murder indictments against "Old Skip" and his fellow Klansmen. However, two grand juries in Bastrop refused to return indictments on murder. Undaunted, they still did not give up. In November of 1923, Coco was finally successful in bringing J. K. Skipwith, The Exalted Cyclops of the Morehouse Ku Klux Klan, Dr. McKoin, and eighteen other Morehouse Parish Klansmen to trial. The charges, however, were nothing more than minor misdemeanors consisting of assault with a dangerous weapon, carrying firearms on the property of another, and ancillary violations. "Old Skip" and two others were eventually found guilty of the firearms violations, and each was fined a total of $10. The remainder of the charges were dismissed against "Old Skip" and the others. After being convicted, "Old Skip," who still maintained that he was justified in all of his actions, was heard to say, "What is this world coming to?"[828] It can be truly said that "Old Skip" and his Klan associates did, in fact, get away with murder most foul. The publicity of the Daniel-Richards murders eventually caused resentment to escalate toward the Klan in Louisiana.[829] No information could be located on McKoin.

From the Cajun parishes in south Louisiana came the most vehement response to the Morehouse Parish Klan's outrage. The few Klans that were in existence in those parishes voted to disband. Feelings ran so high that in New Iberia the names of men believed to be members of the Klan were posted on the door of the parish courthouse with a letter accompanying commanding them to take up residence in Morehouse Parish. Sentiment ran so deep in Lafayette that the Catholic Bishop, Jules Jeanmard, pleaded with the predominantly Catholic populous for coolness toward Klansmen and the residing Protestant minority because "they are entirely at our mercy."[830]

---

[828]Hair, 1991, 52.
[829]Ibid., 44.
[830]Ibid., 45.

Although north Louisiana continued to be the Klan stronghold, it would never hold the power that it once did. Churches that were once patronized by Klan contributions made it known that the perpetual trick or treaters were no longer welcome. Feelings were at such a peak that in the Tullos Baptist Church in LaSalle Parish a discussion on this topic "resulted in the out break of fist fights among members of the congregation."[831]

I attempted to learn more about the fate of Captain Skipwith, but he seemed to have faded into obscurity. While attempting to locate the cemetery where Daniel and Richards were buried, I located some independent writings of local residents in the Morehouse Parish Library, which is also located across the street from the courthouse where the open hearings took place. There I located writings entitled, "Louisiana Tombstone Inscriptions, Volume 2, Morehouse Parish, Louisiana, compiled by the Louisiana Society of the Daughters of the American Revolution." In it I located burial records that indicated that J. Skipwith Company I 3rd Louisiana Cavalry of the Confederate States of America is buried in the Old Bastrop Cemetery located in Bastrop on Washington Street. The same applies to his son, Oliver Gayle Skipwith La. Corp. 167 AIR. Sq., who died October 31, 1929.[832] One wonders whether it is a coincidence that his demise just happened to coincide with Halloween.

These same burial records also showed that a headstone for Watt Daniel existed in the Daniel-Harp Cemetery located four miles north of the Mer Rouge-Oak Grove highway on a gravel road on the banks of Bayou Bonne Idee. Recorded in 1954, the tombstone read:

> Filmore Watt Daniel
> Louisiana Sgt.
> 334 B. N. Tank Corps
> Died Aug. 24, 1922[833]

Although it is recorded that Daniel and Richards were buried in the same place at the same time, no tombstone exists for Richards when the record was made in 1954. A search of current maps indicated the location of Bayou Bonn Idee, but the

---

[831]Ibid., 46.

[832]McDuffie, Queenie. *Louisiana Tombstone Inscriptions, Volume 2 Morehouse Parish, Louisiana.* (Louisiana Society of the Daughters of the American Revolution, 1954), 48.(No place of printing given. Typed on old manual typewriter in Morehouse Parish Library collection.)

[833]Ibid., 144.

only cemetery that could be located in the general vicinity was not the one I was looking for. This necessitated a trip to the Registrar of Deeds Office for Morehouse Parish. The ladies there were very courteous and helpful, and with their assistance, the cemetery was located. While I was there, I asked for their assistance in locating the Southern Carbon Plant in Spyker. When they pointed to the location on the map, the notation on the map indicated that the property that was once the Southern Carbon Plant is now the property of Northeast Louisiana University. WOW!! This could explain a great deal with regard to the plight of Alton Ingram as well as the problems that I was soon to encounter.

We drove to the Daniel-Harp cemetery, which is located on the banks of Bayou Bonne Idee. Just as it was described in the article which told of the funeral scene, the cemetery is on a winding gravel road that you are guaranteed to miss if you do not know where it is. Looking into the cemetery from the gravel road, the weathered, toppled and fractured tombstones are framed on a beautiful canvas of moss-covered cypress trees standing in the bayou. We located the tombstone of Watt Daniel and directly next to the tomb of Watt Daniel there is clearly another burial, but this grave is unmarked. This is, undoubtedly, the grave of Thomas Richards, because this is the location described as the site of his burial. It is, indeed, a peaceful resting place for two innocent men so brutally murdered.

A search of birth and marriage records indicated a large number of McKoin and Daniel entries indicating that these families heavily populated the Morehouse Parish area. There seems little doubt that the descendants of these families still inhabit the area.

The final entry in the whatever-happened-to-them department concerns Percy Sandel, one of the lead lawyers for the Klan at the open hearing, and the man in whose honor the Northeast Louisiana University Library was named. On November 25, 1932, Judge Percy Sandel died of an unmentioned protracted illness. Whatever the illness was, toward the end of his life it caused the amputation of his left leg. Sandel was born on July 7, 1873, six miles south of Monroe on his father's plantation. His father, Dr. William Sandel, was a prominent physician in the area.

Sandel attended Washington and Lee University where he studied law graduating at the early age of 20. He returned to Monroe where, at the age of 31, he became the district attorney of Ouachita and Morehouse Parishes. This was the position held by D. I. Garrett during the investigation and open hearings. Sandel held this office from 1904 to 1908.

Perhaps most interesting in the biographical sketch in the obituary of Sandel made by the *Monroe News-Star* was the fact that in 1924, Sandel was elected as judge in the Fourth Judicial District, for which he ran unopposed. As you may recall, this was the seat held by none other than Judge Odom. Odom had been elected to the Louisiana State Court of Appeals. I wonder how that happened?

Sandel was eulogized as a tireless civic leader. He was past worshipful master of the Western Star Masonic Lodge, a charter member of the Knights Templar and a Shriner. One can only wonder if there was not one other secret fraternal organization in which the judge held membership. Other accolades came from his law partner, W. B. Clarke, and from D. I. Garrett who, by the way, was still identified as the district attorney of Ouachita and Morehouse Parishes. Clarke said that Sandel was a man of "the highest ideals." Garrett called him "one of the most able and brilliant as well as conscientious judges that can be found anywhere."[834] Imagine that!

Activities of Ku Klux Klan Organizations in the United States Part 3
Hearings Before the Committee on Un-American Activities House of Representatives Eighty-Ninth Congress January 4-7, 11-14, 18 and 28, 1966[835]

Although many may have thought that the Klan ceased to exist in northeast Louisiana, the above captioned Congressional hearings were to display proof that the Klan was alive and well in the Bible Belt of Louisiana. A number of persons from northeast Louisiana were subpoenaed to give testimony before the House Committee on Un-American Activities. Perhaps most notable of these was one Murray H. Martin who, on the 27th day of October, received his subpoena at 2303 Rowland Street, Winnsboro, Louisiana. Winnsboro is located about 30 miles east southeast from Bastrop. The subpoena also required that Martin produce the following:

---

[834] *Monroe News-Star*, 26 November 1932.
[835] *Activities of Ku Klux Klan Organizations in the United States Part 3: Hearings Before the Committee on Un-American Activities House of Representatives Eighty-Ninth Congress January 4-7, 11-14, 18 and 28, 1966.* (Washington, D.C.: U.S. Government Printing Office, 1966).

> All books, records, documents, correspondence, and memoranda relating to the organization of and the conduct of business and affairs of the National Knights of the Ku Klux Klan, Original Knights of the Ku Klux Klan, and affiliated organizations, namely, Christian Constitutional Crusaders, in your possession, custody or control, or maintained by you or available to you as Grand Dragon and/or member of the Original Knights of the Ku Klux Klan of America, and/or National Knights of the Ku Klux Klan.[836]

Martin's response was the following:

> Mr. Chairman, I respectfully decline to produce these books, documents, and records on the constitutional grounds of the fourth and fifth amendment, the Constitution guaranteeing the freedom of unreasonable search and seizure.[837]

When asked by the chairman of the committee if he was invoking his constitutional right against self-incrimination, Martin responded that he was. The questions by committee members to Martin that followed all received this same response: "I must decline to answer on the grounds that it may incriminate me under the first, fourth, and fifth amendment to the Constitution."[838]

Despite his attempts to shield the nefarious operations of the Klan behind the Constitution, the documents presented and previous statements made by Martin and one James R. Venable, Imperial Wizard of the Ku Klux Klan and counsel to Martin, revealed the manner in which the Klan attempted to hide its activities and certain operations of the Klan heretofore not known.

Before he took cover behind the Constitution, Martin said that he was a building contractor in Winnsboro. He not only claimed membership in the Original Knights of the Ku Klux Klan, but that he was also the Grand Dragon of the organization. He described this level of leadership "the same as the Chairman of the Board of Directors."[839] These things he admitted while in his talkative mode. However, that changed when congressional investigators displayed documents indicating that the Klan had systematically hidden its membership under the names of innocent sounding sporting organizations. The documentation used to make the connections between these organizations and the Klan were signature cards, checking accounts and checks drawing on the Central Savings Bank & Trust Co. of Monroe, Louisiana and the Winnsboro State Bank and Trust Company in

---

[836]Ibid., 2362.

[837]Ibid.

[838]Ibid., 2363.

[839]Ibid., 2384.

Winnsboro, Louisiana, that passed between members and the organizations.

Louisiana organizations cited by the committee as using "cover names for the Klavern rather than the unit designation given to it by the Klan"[840] according to deposit slips and other bank records contained in the Winnsboro State Bank and Trust Company[841] were as follows:

Christian Constitutional Crusaders	Ouachita Parish Fishing and Hunting Club
Stirlington Hunting and Fishing Club	Concordia Sportsman Club
Clinton Hunting and Fishing Club	Deere Creek Sportsman's Club
Jena Hunting and Fishing Club	Northeast Gun Club
Tensas Sportsman Club	Black River Lake Sporting Club
Arcadia Sportsman Club	West Carroll Rifleman Club
Watson Hunting Club	Delta Sportsman Club
Baker Hunting and Fishing Club	Delhi Sportsman Club
Okalossa Hunting and Fishing Club	Many Hunting and Fishing Club
Catahoola Sportsman Club	Deville Hunting and Fishing Club
Folsom Hunting and Fishing Club	Turkey Creek Rod and Gun Club
Hineston Hunting and Fishing Club	Madison Parish Rifle Club
Bouef River Hunting Club	Varnado Sportsman Club
Vadalia Sportsman's Club	New River Rifle Club
Homer Hunting and Fishing Club	Roseland Hunting Club
Pride Sportsman League, E. Baton Rouge	Swartz Hunting and Fishing Club
Choudrant Rod and Gun Club	Valley Hunting Club
Covington Hunting and Fishing Club	Pine Grove Hunting and Fishing Club
Big River Sportsman's Club[842]	

As to whether or not any of these clubs still survive today is not known.

It was interesting to note the continued involvement of the religious community with the Klan in that the Reverend Louis Warren was listed as the treasurer of the Monroe Hunting and Fishing Club in 1963. Another familiar name appeared as the Vice President of the Monroe Hunting and Fishing Club in 1964, that of one F. T. Odom.[843] It could not be ascertained whether or not this individual was the same as Judge Fred Odom who presided over the open hearings in Bastrop in January of 1923 or some relative.

Two other interesting aspects of the Klan were revealed in the pages of these hearings. First, that the application of any individual "naturalized" or accepted into the Klan was immediately destroyed and from that time on they were known only by a number. Second, that the Klan did have standing "wrecking crews" and what

---

[840]Ibid., 2372.

[841]Ibid.

[842]Ibid.

the duties of these members entailed. From The Original Ku Klux Klan Konstitution, one of the committee members read into the record the following:

> Any Klansman who is known to violate our rules, especially those that give information to any aliens [That means anyone who is not a Klansman], shall be expelled immediately, then is to be watched and visited by the Wrecking Crew if necessary.[844]
> Each unit will set up at least one team of six men to be used for wrecking crew. These men should be appointed by the Kloklan in secrecy.[845]

One of the committee members asked Martin, "Is this not for the purpose of intimidating members of the Klan, if they ever get out and speak against it, that physical harm will come to them?"[846] Martin's response to this question was the same as he had responded all along. He took refuge behind the Constitution.

The congressman continued his questioning on the operations of the "wrecking crew" by asking:

> Mr. Appell. Was there discussion as to what you might do, that is the Klan groups affiliated in the National Knights, with people who could not be controlled and whom the groups wished to be quieted?
> Mr. Martin. Sir, I must respectfully decline to answer that question on the constitutional grounds previously stated.
> Mr. Appell. Was there discussed the subject of castration?[847]

Aside from confirming that the Klan was alive and well in northern Louisiana in 1966, these hearings also confirmed a few points made concerning the Daniel-Richards case. First, that the Klan did attempt to control by threats and intimidation not only present and past members, but also other "people who could not be controlled," and who "the groups wished to be quieted."[848] Second, that there did exist "wrecking crews" and that each Klavern was required to have at least one. Finally, one of the methods discussed to control and quiet those who presented a problem for the Klan was castration. Clearly, these were the same techniques that were employed by the Klan in 1922 against Daniel and Richards and the general population as well.

---

[843] Ibid., 2371.
[844] Ibid., 2376.
[845] Ibid., 2377.
[846] Ibid.
[847] Ibid., 2379.
[848] Ibid.

CHAPTER SEVEN
THE PRESENT-DAY KLAN IN LOUISIANA

Two More Admit Burning Crosses in Junction City Unrest[849]

In June of 1996, two men pleaded guilty to burning crosses to intimidate blacks in Junction City near Monroe, Louisiana. Prosecutors said that 11 whites from the Junction City area burned two gasoline-soaked crosses, one in front of an apartment building and one in a black neighborhood, on March 24, 1994. Three men were indicted and eight cited in bills of information. Some were accused of firing guns into the air from a rooftop after one of the crosses were lighted. A young black man who would not give his name said he is afraid to walk in Junction City at night because of racial tension. Clearly, the Klan is still alive and well in northeast Louisiana.

As I mentioned at the beginning of this work, I stumbled across this story quite by accident, never thinking that it would ever develop into a book. There have, however, been a number of interesting encounters that I have made during the time I have been gathering the data for this book. Foremost among these occurrences is my encounter with Dr. Glenn Jordan, archivist at the Sandel Memorial Library on the campus of Northeast Louisiana University.

While working on my master's degree, I was employed in a student security position at the library. I came to know most of the employees in the library, and I spoke freely about the research that I was conducting. I was directed to speak to Dr. Jordan as he might aid my search for information.

I spoke with Dr. Jordan on a number of occasions concerning the kidnapping and murders of Daniel and Richards of which he admitted he was familiar. In fact, he was the person who related the incident involving Alton Ingram, the history professor that was pressured to leave Northeast Louisiana University after making a presentation to the North Louisiana Historical Society on the murders of Daniel and Richards. He confirmed that it was not at all uncommon to find that the rolls of churches, Masonic organizations, chambers of commerce, and alike civic organizations were identical to those of Klan rolls. "Back then," he said, "it was

---

[849] *Baton Rouge Morning, Advocate*, 2 June 1996.

considered the civic thing to do."[850]

Most intriguing, however, was the conversation we had on February 2, 1992 in his office. It was then that he told me of the existence of a donation that had been made to the collection of Sandel Memorial Library which allegedly contained information concerning these murders. What intrigued me was the fact that this was donated on the stipulation that the contents of the donation would be kept secret until the year 2009. He would not reveal the contents of the donation, except to say that, in his opinion, it was not all that important.

As I was assembling this work, I wished to confirm our conversation, and, on June 17, 1994, I wrote a letter to Dr. Jordan requesting confirmation that the donation existed in the holdings of the library. I also requested that he supply whatever meager information that he could. Having not received a reply, on October 3, 1994, I sent a registered letter to Dr. Jordan making the same request. This letter went unanswered.

As I was nearing the end of this work, I attempted to once more obtain verification that the donation existed in the Sandel Memorial Library. On April 9, 1997, I sent another request by Express Mail, this time to the director of the library, Dr. Don Smith. Enclosed in this letter were copies of the two previous letters that I had sent to Dr. Jordan, requesting his assistance in confirming the existence of the donation mentioned by Dr. Jordan. When this request went unanswered, I sent Dr. Smith a copy of the last few pages of this book to show how this incident would be portrayed. This brought an immediate response.

I received a fax from Dr. Smith indicating that a letter had already been sent by Dr. Jordan concerning this matter. I received no such letter and, considering the totality of the circumstances surrounding attempt to access this collection, I am not at all convinced that this letter existed before my second letter to Dr. Smith. In any event, I shall allow the reader to draw whatever conclusion s/he may from the lead paragraph of the letter from Dr. Jordan which is as follows:

> Upon examination of the restrictions relating to the collection in which you have expressed an interest, I discovered that I had provided incorrect information to you. Both Mrs. Sibley and myself were convinced that the restrictions applied until 2010, but, in actuality, those restrictions were only for ten (10) years. Moreover, those restrictions were not applicable after 1989.[851]

---

[850]Conversation with Dr. Glenn Jordan, archivist, Sandel Memorial Library. 6 February 1992.

[851]Excerpt from a letter from Dr. H. Glenn Jordan, Curator of Special Collections, dated 11 April

The letter went on to say that the collection was open to the public and that he would be happy to make arrangements for me to view the collection if I could not come during regular library hours. The only reference made by Dr. Jordan to all of the problems I encountered in obtaining a response was contained in the final line of his letter. "I apologize for any inconvenience that you may have faced and am ready to assist you in any way possible."[852]

It should also be noted that in the Masters thesis by Alton Ingram was the fact that the entire transcript of the open hearings held in the Morehouse Parish Courthouse in January of 1923 regarding the depredations of the Klan was missing from the office of the Clerk of Court of Morehouse Parish. In an attempt to verify this, on July 28, 1994, I sent a letter to the Clerk of Court for Morehouse Parish requesting information concerning the open hearing. On May 3, 1997, I sent another request by registered mail to Jamie Patrick, Morehouse Parish Clerk of Criminal Court. After explaining the case in which I was interested, I said, "My request is to gain access to the transcript of this open hearing. Please advise its location, and how I may go about gaining access to it." I made it clear that what I was interested in was the "open hearing."

I did receive a reply from Mr. Patrick's office postmarked May 10, 1997. Typed on the bottom of the letter I sent Mr. Patrick was the following:

May 9, 1997

Mr. Ruiz:

Enclosed please find copies of the Bills of Information you requested. Unfortunately, this was the only information I could find on the individuals you requested.

Thank you,

Joyce Goleman

The Bills of Information were filed as follows:

1) April 8, 1923, "J. K. Skipwith, T. J [Jeff] Burnett, E. N Gray, Oliver Skipwith and Smith Stevenson . . . on the 24th of August 1922 . . . did unlawfully conspire with various persons unknown, to compel by violence and threats of violence, one W. C. Andrews to leave an automobile where he the said W. C. Andrews, at the time lawfully was."

1997
[852]Ibid.

2) April 18, 1923, "W. D. McIntosh . . . on the 24th of November 1923 . . . unlawfully did carry a firearm, to wit a shotgun, on the premises owned by one Alonzo Bradock, being at that time and now a citizen of the United States, and a resident of the State of Louisiana, Parish of Morehouse, and said firearm, having been carried on said premises without the consent of said Alonzo Bradock, and the said W. D. McIntosh at the time not in lawful discharge of civil or military order." [Clearly, this is a faulty bill. The date of the offense should have been 1922 and not 1923.]

3) April 18, 1923, "One Marvin Pickett . . . on the 24th of November, 1923 . . . unlawfully did carry a firearm to wit, a shotgun, on the premises owned by one Alonzo Bradock, he the said Alonzo Bradock being at that time and now a citizen of the United States, and a resident of the State of Louisiana and Parish of Morehouse, and said firearm having been carried on said premises without the consent of said Alonzo Bradock, and the Said Marvin Pickett at the time not in the lawful discharge of civil or military order." [Another faulty bill.]

4) April 18, 1923. "One J. K. Skipwith . . . on the 24th of November 1922 . . . unlawfully did carry a firearm to wit, a shotgun, on the premises owned by one Alonzo Bradock, he the said Alonzo Bradock being at that time and now a citizen of the United States, and a resident of the State of Louisiana and Parish of Morehouse, and said firearm having been carried on said premises without the consent of said Alonzo Bradock, and the Said Marvin Pickett at the time not in the lawful discharge of civil or military order." [The date of offense is correct on this one.]

5) April 8, 1923, "One Jeff Burnett . . . on the 24th of August 1922 . . . did wilfully (sic) and feloniously and of his malice aforethought, armed with a dangerous weapon, to wit, a shotgun, lie in wait, with intent wilfully (sic), feloniously and of his malice aforethought to kill and murder one T. F. Richards and F. W. Daniels (sic)."

6) April 8, 1923, "One B. M. McKoin . . . on the 2nd of January, 1922 . . . did wilfully (sic) and unlawfully with a dangerous weapon, to wit, a shotgun, make an assault upon one Addie May (sic) Hamilton, in the peace of the state then and there being, contrary to the form of the statute of the State of Louisiana in such case made an provided, in contempt of the authority of the said State, and against the peace and dignity of same.

"And your appearer further given this court to understand and be informed that said crime was never brought to knowledge of any officer of the State of Louisiana, qualified and authorized to direct a prosecution, until the first day of January, 1923."

7) October 10, 1923, "Harley Rogers and others unknown . . . on the 17th of August 1922 . . . did wilfully (sic) and unlawfully conspire with other persons to compel by violence and threats of violence, one T. F. Richards to leave his place of business in the town of Bastrop, Parish of Morehouse, where he, the said T. F. Richards, at the time lawfully was, which offense was not made known to a public officer having the power to direct a public prosecution until within one year next proceeding the filing of this information."

What does this rather brief letter and these Bills of Information tell us? First, as would be expected, the request for information on the open hearing was totally ignored. This was not a surprise. This was what I expected. Second, although the response was brief, he did say, "Unfortunately, this was the only information I could find on the individuals you requested." This sentence is highly significant. This confirms that a) the transcript of the open hearing is missing, and b) that the records of the convictions and fines of Skipwith and others are also missing. Third, that the Bill of Information filed on Dr. McKoin was done AFTER he had returned to Johns Hopkins. Yet, there is no information as to how this was resolved. Finally, all of the records concerning the arrests of Jeff Burnett and Dr. McKoin, including McKoin's extradition fight and any record of the bail that he and later Burnett posted, has also mysteriously vanished. Imagine that!

As unbelievable as it may sound in this day and age, there appears to be a conspiracy of silence on the matter of the murders of Daniel and Richards. It is as though all of those from whom I have asked information on the matter of Daniel and Richards believe that if they do not respond, I will go away. Or, at the very least, avoidance of my request shields them from the wrath of those who so skillfully dispatched Alton Ingram. Clearly, there now currently exists a level of control over the populace by the powers at be to the same level as it was back during the reign of the Klan in the 1920s. Perhaps, it is even worse now!

I should also mention that on January 20, 1992, I wrote to the Knights of Pythias, located at 125 1/2 St. John Street, Monroe, Louisiana, because I intended to use the Klan initiation article that appeared in an August edition of the *Monroe News-Star* in which they were mentioned as the organization that provided the music for the event. In the letter I said, "Rather than make assumptions as to the position of the Knights of Pythias on the Ku Klux Klan, I thought I would give you the opportunity to respond and state your position." To date, I have received no response.

This type of reaction to inquiries for information regarding the activities of the Ku Klux Klan in northeast Louisiana during the 1920s is quite common. On the faces of the residents of the area, there appears a pall of fear and trepidation whenever the topic is brought up. When one considers the fate of Alton Ingram, whose innocent presentation brought he and his family untold heartache and grief, it is understandable why anyone would avoid the topic, particularly if they enjoyed their job. Considering what happened to him, it is completely understandable why Alton Ingram or anyone else would refuse to speak with me on this topic.

While gathering data for this book, I made several discreet inquiries around the campus of Northeast Louisiana University as to whether anyone knew of a local resident that I could speak with who might have some personal knowledge of this incident. I received a call one day from a friend who told me that contact had been made with one such person, and the phone number was given to me. When I contacted this person, I was told that we could meet, but that our meeting would have to be totally confidential. A date and location was agreed, and as I drove there the thought suddenly came into my mind, "What if this is a set up?" It was quite clear that the same influential people in Morehouse and Ouachita Parishes who squashed Alton Ingram like a bug might just be planning to do the same thing to me. Nevertheless, I continued on.

Our meeting was cordial, but my contact insisted that we not stay in one place and that we not be seen in public. So for nearly three hours, we drove the backroads of Morehouse Parish, and I don't mind saying that there were times when I had no idea where we were. I was totally at the mercy of my contact. Most of the information I received was not new. However, there was one tidbit that was passed on that made the trip worth while.

I was told that a "Death Watch" was instituted for all of the Klansmen that had been involved in the kidnapping and murders of Watt Daniel and Thomas F. Richards. When any Klansman who had been involved in the Daniel-Richards affair was near death, a "Death Watch" commenced. The "Death Watch" consisted of a Klansman remaining by the death bed around the clock to make sure that there would be no dying declaration that could cause problems for any individual Klansman or any of the surviving families.

It should be noted that no information could be gathered from the *Bastrop Enterprise*, the local Bastrop newspaper. In a conversation with editor, Mr. Bill Warner, on May 21, 1997, he said that he had heard of the incident some time ago from a resident, and that he went to the *Bastrop Enterprise* newspaper morgue to see what had been written on the Daniel-Richards case. He said that ALL of the copies of the *Bastrop Enterprise* from that period were missing. It should be noted that Mr. Warner is not a native of Morehouse Parish, and, in fact, that he had been hired from out-of-state a year prior to our conversation.

Finally, just when you think you've heard the last of David Duke, he demonstrates his resilience and ability to appeal to the electorate. His latest coup was to be named Chairman of the St. Tammany Parish Republican Party. He did this by taking a page right out of the Christian Coalition political play book. Just as they have maneuvered their supporters into orphic and many times non-contentious elections to nondescript positions, so did he with regard to positions on the St. Tammany Parish GOP Executive Committee. Once he had his people in position, they promptly named Duke as their Chairman. Imagine that![853]

Tensions Run High in Ville Platte: KKK, NAACP Face off in St. Landry Parish[854]

The above headlines were blazoned across the front page of the April 27, 1997 editions of the *Acadiana Sunday* section of the *Sunday Advertiser* in Lafayette. Regrettably, one vestige of the Klan still exists in southern Louisiana, and it reared its ugly head on, of all places, the local open cable channel in Lafayette, Louisiana. What is even more unusual was that the self-anointed Klan leader was not a native of the state, and had been a resident of Louisiana for only a few years.

The leader of these sheeted hobgoblins was one Darrell Flinn. He and his linen-draped followers had a weekly hour-long television show on the public access channel in Lafayette, Louisiana. The organization gave the following address:

Knights of the White Kamelia
Ku Klux Klan
P.O. Box 80942
Lafayette, Louisiana 705948-0942
www. Acadian.net/-Sandman
Hauptman@Hotmail.com

Just as William Simmons, the man who almost single-handedly can be credited with the second coming of the Ku Klux Klan, Darrell Flinn attempted to do the same with the Klan in Lafayette. Dressed in his royal purple satin sheet with the accompanying Kone-head hat, he professed to be a self-anointed reverend but refuses to divulge the origin of his degree in divinity. He had also graciously granted himself the title Imperial Wizard. His wife served as the Kligrapp, or secretary. The "Nighthawk" or "Enforcer" for the Kamelia Klan, who went by the alias of "T-Lollie," also makes occasional appearances dressed in a foreboding black satin bed sheet.

---

[853] *The Times of Acadiana*, 1 October, 1997.
[854] *The Sunday Advertiser*, 27 April 1997.

Once weekly, actually twice because it was replayed the following day on tape, he and his ilk made a spectacle of themselves by appearing in full dress garb. During this rather crudely manufactured production, Flinn and those around him lay out the tenets of the Klan, which had not changed one iota. They hate everything that is not white. They attack Jews, blacks, Catholics, homosexuals and anything else that does not subscribe to the bilge that they spewed weekly. There also had been segments that they have aired in which they touted the "Weapon of the Week." On the June 17, 1996 show, he displayed an M-16 while singing its praises. On this same show, he also announced that he had discovered the cause of the rash of black church fires occurring across the country. He proclaimed that it was the oil used in the "Gerrycurl" preparation that caused spontaneous combustion.

Flinn, who relished his position like some preschool potentate, played to the ignorance and hatred of the uneducated and uninformed, but occasionally, he did have something of note to impart. On the show aired May 19, 1996, he made the statement that "The Klan 'disciplined' more white people than it did black people." Perhaps that was supposed to make his audience believe that the violence dispensed by the Klan was even-handed. This statement not only reinforces all that has been revealed about the activities of the Klan in Morehouse Parish, but it also speaks to what would happen in the present if such ignorance would be allowed to run rampant.

If this were not entertainment enough, they took live phone calls from the public. Whenever they are challenged intellectually with regard to their creed or tenets, they retreat behind the "Kone of Silence," ridicule the caller or simply refuse to answer the question. When blacks call to challenge them, they refuse to engage them in dialog. They simply hung up on them. Perhaps the most frightening portion of this production are the comments made by their mentally-challenged supporters. Wow! To listen to their comments, it would be a safe bet to say that the majority completed, at least, the sixth grade.

In a series of articles that appeared in the *Lafayette Daily Advertiser* in December of 1996, facts that had been previously unknown about the Reverend Imperial Wizard were revealed. Flinn is a native of McCurtain, Oklahoma, and a well-known character in that county, according to Sheriff William Fiedler. Commenting on an incident involving Flinn, his wife and child and a shotgun, Fiedler described how Flinn "blew a hole in the front door of his house, with the woman and little girl inside."[855]

Also, according to the June 19, 1997 edition of *The Daily Advertiser*, Flinn owed more than $11,000 in back child support. Debbie Brown, Flinn's former wife, claimed that he had not paid the $300 a month 1992 Oklahoma court ordered support for his six-year old daughter.[856] Had the Reverend Imperial Wizard of the Knights of the White Kamelia engaged in this type of moral neglect of his family in 1922, he would have been kidnapped by black-hooded Klansmen, chained to a tree and beaten with a whip. My, how the Klan has changed!

There was also one other revelation made in this series of articles that surely must have shaken the foundations of some of Flinn's loyal sheet-frocked followers. It seems as though the Reverend Imperial Wizard of the Knights of the White Kamelia lived with a black woman in 1994, one year after "The Klan in Akadiana" began on the Acadian Open Channel. Confirmation of this fact was given by the black woman, who did not want her identity disclosed, and by bank checks which indicated that they had a joint account. It was reported that Roger Harris, a local Klan leader of the Bayou Knights of Choudrant said, "If there is anything to this, then Darrell Flinn is a joke."[857] I guess the Klan might list the Reverend Imperial Wizard of the Knights of the White Kamelia's association with a black woman in their Klan glossary of terms as a "Konflict" of interest.

The latest information on Reverend Imperial Wizard Flinn is that he has fled Lafayette, Louisiana and now hangs his sheet in Vidor, Texas. The web site for his new Vidor Klan is quite impressive and can be found at the following site: "http://member.aol.com/realmoftex/index.html".

Needless to say, the black community was up in arms over the Klan television program, and they did all in their power to see the "The Klan in Akadiana" removed from the airways. Having seen some of the black programming on the Acadian Open Channel, I must say that I found some of it to be just about as racist as the Klan show. That not withstanding, I believe it would be a mistake to remove either the Klan program or the black programming from the Open Channel.

I believe that we should make certain that such freedom of speech is protected, particularly in programs such as "The Klan in Akadiana." We should never allow

---

[855]*The Daily Advertiser*, 17 December 1996.

[856]*The Daily Advertiser*, 19 June 1997.

[857]*The Daily Advertiser*, 20 December 1996.

ourselves for one moment to forget the violence, hatred, hypocrisy and bigotry that is the Klan and made manifest by its emissaries. Rather, we should take notice of Flinn and his cohort the same as we would a pebble in our collective shoe or the buzzing of a gnat, for he and his ilk are a continuing reminder of the danger that lurks just beneath the surface of our society.

A Klan Lexicon

Ayak	(The Challenge) "Are you a Klansman?"
Akia	(The Password) "A Klansman I am."
Imperial Wizard	Chief of the Invisible Empire
Grand Dragon	Head of a realm, usually a state
Titan	Head of a province, usually a Congressional District
Cyclops	Head of Klavern
Klaliff	Vice President of a Klavern
Kligrapp	Secretary
Klabee	Treasurer
Kludd	Chaplin
Klokard	Lecturer
Kleagle	Organizer
Klonsel	Supreme legal counsel
Klexter	An official
Klarogo	An official
Klokan	An official
Kloran	The Klan Bible
Klavern	Klan den or chapter
Klankraft	Practices and beliefs of the Klan
Klonvocation	The Imperial Legislature
Kloncilium	The Klonvocation's advisory group
Klonkave	Monthly meeting
Klorero	State meeting
Klectoken	Initiation fee
Invisible Empire	The universal geographical jurisdiction of the Klan
Knock-off Squads	A Klan action group, also known as "Wrecking Crews." They bomb, flog, tar and feather, abduct, raid and murder.
Night-Hawk	Chief Investigator: most Klans now have a KBI-Klan Bureau of Investigation made of Klansmen who spy on "the enemy."

Austin, Moses, 6
Austin, Stephen, 6
Austin, TX, 415
Avoylles Parish, LA, 170, 215

Bailey, C. P., 451
Bailey, Jordan [See Baley, Jurden], 295
Baker, Ernest, 258, 530
Baker Hunting and Fishing Club, 543
Baldonido, Dominick [See Coco], 219
Baldounel Airdome, 107
Baldwin, Al, 107
Baley, Jurden [See Bailey, Jordan], 292
Baltimore, MD, 58, 89, 96, 168, 184, 186,
    196, 197, 202, 203, 205, 214, 220,
    235, 240, 254, 270, 284, 492, 494,
    523
B'Nai B'Rith, 6, 135, 512
Baptist Church at Monroe, 55
Barham, Dr. B. E., 255, 334, 346
Barham, John, 320, 335, 337
Barham, R. E., 258
Barham, T. E., 258
Barnes, 'Bill', 307
Barnes, Clarence H., 179
Barnett, Judge W. C., 214, 234, 248, 417,
    418, 482, 483, 484, 522, 528, 529,
    532, 533
Baron de Bastrop, 5, 6, 7
Baron de Carondelet, 5
Barr, Rev. Dan C. [D. D.], 90, 91, 505
Barrett, William H., 148
Bastrop-Collinston-Monroe Road, 513
Bastrop's First Baptist Church, 41
Bastrop, Louisiana, 1, 2, 5, 7, 39, 50,
    55, 57, 61, 62, 64, 66, 67, 68, 77,
    113, 114, 122, 129, 130, 150, 151,
    155, 156, 163, 164, 166, 167, 169,
    170, 172, 173, 174, 180, 181, 183,
    189, 190, 197, 199, 200, 208, 209,
    210, 214, 215, 216, 218, 220, 221,
    222, 226, 233, 234, 236, 237, 240,
    242, 243, 245, 247, 253, 254, 256,
    258, 259, 261, 266, 268, 269, 278,
    283, 285, 286, 290, 292, 293, 294,
    297, 298, 307, 310, 311, 312, 313,
    314, 314, 318, 321, 323, 326, 332.
    335, 336, 338, 339, 342, 343, 347,
    350, 351, 360, 362, 364, 365, 368,
    369, 371, 379, 385, 388, 389, 390,
    392, 394, 396, 399, 402, 403, 407,

411, 412, 416, 418, 419, 422, 425,
    427, 433, 434, 435, 436, 441, 442,
    445, 446, 447, 448, 449, 450, 453,
    454, 455, 456, 462, 464, 466, 468,
    473, 474, 480, 488, 491, 492, 495,
    498, 503, 504, 507, 508, 509, 513,
    518, 521, 525, 526, 527, 530, 531,
    537, 541, 550
Bastrop-Mer Rouge Road, 321, 327, 338,
    379, 389, 397, 411, 416, 421, 436,
    437, 442, 446, 447, 452, 462, 471,
    472, 477, 501, 526, 527, 531
Bastrop Pulp Mill, 413
Bastrop Supply Company, 317
Baton Rouge Klan No. 3, Knights
    of the Ku Klux Klan, 48, 60, 130
Baton Rouge, Louisiana, 44, 104, 112,
    121, 123, 130, 131, 149, 156, 232,
    367, 451, 478, 495, 497, 499, 500,
    537
Battle of Shiloh, 15
Bay Shore, L.I., 534
Bayou Bartholomew, 7
Bayou Bonn Idee, 176, 177, 298, 319, 519,
    539
Bayou LaFourche, 78
Bayou Knights of Choudrant, 553
Baxter, Gov. Percival P., 101
Bearas, Hiram L., 149
Beaumont, TX, 79, 226
Beauregard Klan No. 9,
    DeRidder, LA, 458
Belfast, Northern Ireland, 66
Bell, Alexander Graham, 50
Bell, C. C., 71
Bell, Frank, 376, 377, 378, 379, 428
Bell, Tom, 459
Belleville, NJ, 179
Bennett, Rev. Mr., 132
Bennett, S. I., 436, 444, 459, 460, 469,
    472, 475, 476
Bennett, S. T., 221, 222
Benton, LA, 72
Berlin, Germany, 500
Bernhardt, Sara, 185
Bessemer, AL, 213
Bethel Church, 10
Betts, George W., 93
Bible, 48, 90, 110, 147, 368
Bible Belt, 2
Big River Sportsman's Club, 543

558

Great Depression, 31
Green, William H., 440
Gregor, E. C., 479
Griffin, "Ice man", 171, 172
Griffin, G. A. , 50
Griffith, David Ward, 25, 28, 86, 258
Griffith, Mr., 413
Groves, Mrs., 320
Guatemala, 147
Guerre, Col. Louis F., 51, 53, 163, 169, 184
Guildge, W. L., 258
Guion, Seth, 247, 249, 250, 266, 277, 279, 298, 302, 316, 330, 332, 334, 346, 358, 360, 361, 363, 368, 369, 371, 373, 375, 376, 378, 392, 394, 408, 417, 441, 442, 443, 445, 452, 459, 460, 461, 462, 463, 470, 475, 509, 517, 526

Halloween, 37
Hamburg, AR, 47, 354
Hamilton, Addie Mae, 187, 188, 284, 285, 287, 291, 292, 296, 298, 300, 301, 302, 304, 305, 330, 337, 338, 340, 387, 465, 492, 518, 548
Hamilton, Fredrick W., 467
Hamilton, M., 522
Hamilton, Mrs., 320
Hapgood, Norman, 497
Harding Girls Club, 121
Harding, Pres. Warren, 103, 104, 105, 107, 109, 111, 121, 160, 168, 201, 329
Hardwick, Thomas W., 93
Harkness, Robert, 382, 406, 408, 528
Harlingen, TX, 515
Harp. G. C., 258
Harp, James F., 258, 368, 441, 442, 468, 473
Harp, Kelly, 320, 330, 331, 347, 348, 369, 385, 389, 391, 401, 404, 405, 492
Harper, D. N., 258
Harris, Jewell, 439
Harris, Mr. [?], 315
Harris, Sim, 472
Harris, T. H., 500
Harrison, Mrs. R. H., 366, 367
Harris, Roger, 553
Hart Boys, The, 317
Hart, Albert R., 101
Hart, Chief W. C., 179

Hatch, General, 23
Hartford, CT, 178, 286
Hattiesburg, MS, 237
Harvard University, 110, 344
Hawaiian Islands, 494
Hawker, Fed. Agent, 93
Hawkins, Dr. J. G., 168, 214
Hayden, George, 504, 508
Hayden, Jack, 410
Hayes, Prohibition Commissioner, 141
Haynes, G. B, 71
Haynesville, LA, 131
Hayward, Rev. E. W., 176, 177
Haywood, Rev. Oscar, 108, 125, 126, 133, 138
Hearts, W. E., 473
Hell's Half Acre, 145
Hemphill, TX, 79
Hendry, Ruby, 138
Henrietta, OK, 101
Herrin, IL, 45, 47
Hetsler, E. L., 258
Hewes, Thomas H. , 215, 216
Hicks, [?], 377, 459
Higgenbotham, F. L., 258, 315, 319, 320, 321, 325, 328, 399, 419, 439, 527, 536
Higgenbotham, J. D., 257, 258, 292, 307, 317, 326, 346, 401, 419, 431, 439
Higgenbotham, Tom, 413, 418, 424, 427, 428, 429, 438, 439, 447, 449, 470
Higgenbotham, Willie, 411, 412, 413, 421, 422, 424, 431, 432, 434, 439, 449, 470
Higgenbotham, Zoo, 284
Highland Baptist Church, 67, 73
Highland Park, MI, 67
Hildridge, Sam, 363
Hineston Hunting and Fishing Club, 543
Hippocratic Oath, 187
Hitchcock, Alfred, 278
Holcombe, Mayor Oscar F., 216
Holland, 6
Hollingsworth, William, 85
Holloway, M. F., 284, 289
Holmes, Rev. L. M., 411, 470
Holmes, Oliver W., 36
Holston, Dep. Sheriff, 237
Homer Hunting and Fishing Club, 543
[Homer, LA] Klan No. 63,
        Knights of the Ku Klux Klan, 131

564

568

Methodist Episcopal Church
[Midvale, NJ], 142
Mexican, 6, 293
Mexico, 293, 515, 516
Miami, FL, 54
Michie, Dave, 412
Michie, J. H., 258
Middletown, NY, 125, 343
Midnight jury, 65
Midvale, NJ, 142
Milan, Italy, 143
Milner, Thomas [Miller], 225, 293, 296,
335, 336, 346, 358, 389, 390
Millier, Floyd, 128
Milligan, Tom, 307
Milliken, T. M., 257, 258
Minden, LA, 516
Minot, ND, 3
Mineola, L.I., 98
Minot State University, 1
Miranda v. Arizona, 155
Mississippi, 30, 107, 141, 151, 181, 192,
219, 474
Mississippi Burning, 33
Mississippi River, 131, 238, 387
Missouri & North Arkansas Railroad, 479
Missouri Pacific Railroad, 182, 183, 370,
375
Molly Maguires, 6
Monarchs of Monroe, 10
Monroe-Bastrop Road, 448, 450
Monroe Gas Company, 221
Monroe Horror, 8
Monroe Hunting and Fishing Club, 543
Monroe Klan No. 4 Knights of
the Ku Klux Klan, 47, 48, 64, 73, 74,
75, 76, 90, 94, 165, 204, 258, 400,
417, 454, 485, 505
Monroe, LA, 2, 3, 38, 43, 56, 67, 74, 82,
83, 86, 95, 104, 116, 117, 128, 149,
150, 178, 180, 182, 184, 187, 193,
197, 198, 203, 207, 213, 220, 225,
226, 233, 234, 245, 246, 253, 254,
255, 277, 281, 283, 286, 290, 334,
335, 338, 345, 346, 348, 357, 360,
369, 374, 384, 385, 396, 405, 407,
415, 416, 446, 447, 452, 453, 457,
462, 475, 491, 495, 499, 503, 514,
515, 540, 545, 549
Monroe, Sheriff [Woodland, CA], 260
Montclair, NJ, 179

Montreal University, 134
Montgomery, J. W., 258, 418
Montgomery Place [residence], 423
Moodie, R. H., 257
Moore County, NC, 54
Morris, John, 390
Morhouse, 6
Morehouse Clarion, 40
Morehouse, Col. Abraham, 5, 6, 7, 226
Morehouse Klan No, 34 Knights of
The Ku Klux Klan, 44, 45, 71, 72,
113, 115, 189, 198, 317, 327, 357,
438, 473, 496, 498, 502, 504, 508,
531
Morehouse Parish, 2, 4, 7, 36, 40, 41, 43,
46, 50, 52, 58, 61, 61, 62, 65, 66,
68, 70, 77, 77, 78, 79, 80, 81, 82,
83, 84, 87, 88, 104, 112, 113, 117,
120, 122, 123, 124, 129, 130, 160,
161, 163, 166, 168, 169, 171, 172,
173, 175, 180, 181, 182, 184, 188,
189, 192, 194, 195, 196, 198, 199,
207, 209, 211, 212, 220, 223, 224,
229, 231, 233, 235, 236, 237, 239,
240, 245, 246, 247, 248, 251, 252,
255, 257, 258, 272, 280, 283, 294,
300, 301, 302, 307, 318, 319, 320,
329, 332, 351, 352, 353, 355, 357,
358, 360, 363, 365, 370, 371, 394,
436, 439, 446, 447, 453, 456. 464,
466, 474, 476, 478, 480, 482, 486,
488, 491, 494, 497, 499, 501, 502,
503, 504, 505, 506, 508, 509, 512,
515, 516, 517, 519, 520, 521, 522,
525, 527, 530, 531, 535, 536, 537,
538, 539, 540, 541, 550, 552
Morehouse Parish Clerk of Court, 361,
371, 547
Morehouse Parish Courthouse, 368, 547
Morgan, J. P., 110
Morris, L. L., 258
Morris, Mrs., 320
Morris, S. R., 258
Morrison, John, 391
Morrison, Gov., 54
Moscow, Russia, 99, 132
Moselle, MS, 480
Mosely, Dr. C. H., 457
Mosher, M. B., 53
Mosher, Walter, 53
Moss, Spanish, 12

569